Exploring **LANGUAGE**

Exploring **LANGUAGE**

TENTH EDITION

Gary Goshgarian

NORTHEASTERN UNIVERSITY

PEARSON
Longman

New York • San Francisco • Boston
London • Toronto • Sydney • Tokyo • Singapore • Madrid
Mexico City • Munich • Paris • Cape Town • Hong Kong • Montreal

Senior Vice President and Publisher: Joe Opiela
Senior Acquisitions Editor: Lynn M. Huddon
Marketing Manager: Ann Stypuloski
Senior Supplements Editor: Donna Campion
Media Supplements Editor: Nancy García
Production Manager: Charles Annis
Project Coordination, Text Design, and Electronic Page Makeup: Nesbitt Graphics, Inc.
Cover Design Manager: John Callahan
Cover Designer: Joan O'Connor
Cover Illustration: Courtesy of Getty Images, Inc.
Photo Researcher: PhotoSearch, Inc.
Manufacturing Manager: Lucy Hebard
Printer and Binder: R. R. Donnelley and Sons Co.
Cover Printer: Lehigh Press, Inc.

For permission to use copyrighted material, gratedful acknowledgement is made to the copyright holders on pp. 601–607, which are hereby made part of this copyright page.

Library of Congress Cataloging-in-Publication Data

Exploring language / edited by Gary Goshgarian.—10th ed.
    p. cm.
  Includes index.
  ISBN 0-321-12221-6 (pbk.)
    1. Language and languages. 2. English language—United States. I. Goshgarian, Gary.
P107.E93 2004
808'.0427—dc21   2003047660

Please visit our Website at http://www.ablongman.com/goshgarian

ISBN 0-321-12221-6

2 3 4 5 6 7 8 9 10—DOC—06 05 04

This book is dedicated to my sons,
Nathan and David

Contents

day long . . . that is the situation of the quarter of a million or more deaf people in North America."

Homemade Education   61
Malcolm X

"In the street, I had been the most articulate hustler out there. . . . But now, trying to write simple English, I not only wasn't articulate, I wasn't even functional."

A Word for Everything   65
Helen Keller

"The beautiful truth burst upon my mind—I felt that there were invisible lines stretched between my spirit and the spirits of others."

The Language of Silence   72
Maxine Hong Kingston

"When I went to kindergarten and had to speak English for the first time, I became silent. A dumbness—a shame—still cracks my voice in two. . . . "

The Jellyfish   77
Susan Kinsolving

"A jellyfish was in my eyes! . . . "It bleeded and singed!" In a poem, Susan Kinsolving describes the innocence and discovery of her three-year-old daughter Caroline's journey into language.

Spanish Lessons   79
Christine Marín

"I learned the power of both the English and Spanish language on that [school] band trip."

Seneca Falls Declaration   86
Elizabeth Cady Stanton

"The history of mankind is a history of repeated injuries and usurpations on the part of man toward women, having in direct object the establishment of an absolute tyranny over her."

"Letter from Birmingham Jail"   90
Martin Luther King, Jr.

"I submit that an individual who breaks a law that conscience tells him is unjust, and who willingly accepts the penalty of imprisonment in order to arouse the con-

science of the community over its injustice, is in reality expressing the highest respect for the law."

Aren't I a Woman? 100
Sojourner Truth

"[T]hat little man in black there, he says women can't have as much rights as man,
'cause Christ wasn't a woman. Where did your Christ come from?"

The Struggle for Human Rights 102
Eleanor Roosevelt

"We must not be confused about what freedom is. Basic human rights are simple
and easily understood."

2 Writers Writing: Words in Contexts 113

■ THE WRITING PROCESS 115

Writing for an Audience 115
Linda Flower

"The goal of the writer is to create a momentary common ground between the
reader and the writer."

The Maker's Eye: Revising Your Own Manuscripts 119
Donald M. Murray

"When students complete a first draft, they consider the job of writing done—and
their teachers too often agree. When professional writers complete a first draft,
they usually feel that they are at the start of the writing process."

Getting Started 123
Anne Lamott

"The very first thing I tell my new students on the first day of a workshop is that
good writing is about telling the truth."

What My Students Have Taught Me About Writing 128
Pamela Childers

"I'm a writer, but I am a better writer than I was when I started writing because of
my students."

How I Write 134
Evan Miller

"The first sentence is usually the toughest for me, because I know that it will shape
the second, will shape the third . . . I try to experiment with different openers . . .

but in some papers, [my first sentences] miss the purpose of the paper entirely and are, in the vernacular, crap."

3 Politically Speaking   154

4 The Art of Conversation   238

**EXPLORING THE LANGUAGE OF VISUALS: *HUCKLEBERRY FINN*
BANNED!** 457

Author's Afterword from *Fahrenheit 451*   460
Ray Bradbury

"For it is a mad world and it will get madder if we allow the minorities, be they dwarf or giant, orangutan or dolphin, nuclear-head or water-conservationalist, pro-computerologist or Neo-Luddite, simpleton or sage, to interfere with aesthetics."

■ CASE STUDY: CENSORSHIP AND FREE SPEECH ON CAMPUS   464

The Betrayal of Liberty on America's Campuses   464
Alan C. Kors

"It is . . . almost inconceivable that anyone . . . could live on a college campus unaware of the repression, legal inequality, intrusions into private conscience, and malignant double standards that hold sway there."

Regulating Racist Speech on Campus   471
Charles R. Lawrence III

Defending racist language in the name of liberty of free speech "has placed the bigot on the moral high ground and fanned the rising flames of racism."

There's No Such Thing as Free Speech, and It's a Good Thing, Too   475
Stanley Fish

"Free speech . . . is not an independent value but a political prize, and if that prize has been captured by a politics opposed to yours, it can no longer be invoked in ways that further your purposes, for it is now an obstacle to those purposes."

Muzzling Free Speech   487
Harvey A. Silverglate

The speech-zone movement presents a major threat to the ideals of free thought and free inquiry to which colleges and universities should be devoted.

SPEECH CODES AT HARVARD LAW SCHOOL?   490

Difficult Conversations   490
Dorothy Rabinowitz

"At Harvard Law today, skill in hard combative argument is no longer prized, nor even considered quite respectable."

Censor This?   492
Austin Bramwell

"Like many, I am concerned that a speech code [at Harvard Law School] would chill valuable speech on campus."

Preface

I think that those instructors who have used earlier editions of *Exploring Language* will agree with me that this is, by far, the best edition to date. The tenth edition provides a wide and diverse range of engaging and informative readings connected to language issues. It also aims to embrace changes in how we approach critical reading and writing in modern college classrooms.

More than 60 percent of the readings are replacements, and many were written since the last edition. There are eight new subthemes in this edition. Additionally, a large component of visual selections have been integrated with the written selections—drawings, cartoons, posters, print ads, photographs, newspaper headline collages, and so forth—to illustrate nonverbal communication.

Why the large revision? Because new and fascinating language issues constantly emerge in our culture, whereas others become dated and lose a sense of urgency or relevance. In just three years, dramatic language changes have taken place in America—evolutions and innovations that reveal something about us, our world, our values, our recent history.

No recent event has had greater impact on America as a nation than the terrorist attacks of September 11, 2001. Almost immediately, old terms took on new meanings, and new and exotic ones pushed their way into the general lexicon. Perhaps the most painfully familiar term coming out of that terrible event was "Ground Zero," the epicenter of World Trade Center disaster where 3,000 people lost their lives. In the wake of that event and the subsequent "war on terrorism" (itself a recent expression), the media began to crackle with frightening, esoteric, and strange new terms: *bioterrorism, jihad, Al-Quaeda, bourqa, warlords, anthrax, suicide bomber, weapons of mass destruction,* and *homeland security.* Reflecting "post-9/11" America, we have included a new case study, "Terrorism and the War of Words."

While the most significant historical events of the last three years, terrorism and America's war against it were not the only forces of change on language. A new president was elected, and with George W. Bush came a different style than his predecessors and a new shape to presidential rhetoric—as well as some curious "Bushisms." While critics poked fun at Bush's odd twists of the tongue ("misunderestimate," "suiciders," "ooching"), usage of the Internet continued to soar, and with it a reshaping of communication and identity.

More than ever, movies and television have come under fire for celebrating dumb and crude use of language; the news media, for reporting news in slanted prose; nighttime television, for increased use of profanity; daytime talk shows, for rendering complex human issues in a sensational mixture of crude discourse and the latest psychobabble. Advertisers continue making bloated claims. Politicians are blasted for reducing intricate social issues to sound bites. Higher education is still locked in First Amendment debates over what to do about hate speech—racist, sexist, and other forms of offensive discourse—on American campuses. The growing multiculturalism in American society has spawned verbal battles over "political correctness." Crying cultural imperialism and racism, proponents of bilingual education go head-to-head with English-only advocates, who are fighting to make English the official tongue of the nation. While all this was happening, thousands of new terms have entered our vocabulary. Since the last edition of this book in 2001, wordsmiths have provided us with such items as *cryonize, overnet, nico-teen, transtheism, Enroned, twenty-four/seven, listeria, Euro,* and *bandwidth,* which may or may not be with us by the next edition.

In spite of the many revisions to the tenth edition, the original character and objective of *Exploring Language* remains the same: to bring together exciting and readable pieces that explore the various ways language and American society are interconnected. Once again, the aim is to lead students to a keener understanding of how language works: how it reconstructs the real world for us and how it can be used to lead, mislead, and manipulate us. Organized around nine major language areas, these selections demonstrate the subtle complexities and richness of English. They also invite students to debate current social and cultural issues that are inseparable from language. And they serve as models for composition, representing a diversity of expository techniques—narration, illustration, definition, process analysis, argumentation, persuasion, comparison, and contrast—and a diversity of genres—editorial essays, personal narratives, opinion columns, position papers, letters, memoirs, autobiographical musings, personal diaries, academic articles, humorous satires, play script excerpts, jokes, interviews, and poetry.

New to the Tenth Edition

A glance at the nine chapters' themes—five of which are new to this edition—will give you a good idea of the breadth of coverage (**boldface** highlights the chapter topics that are new):

1. Breaking Silences
2. Writers Writing: Words in Contexts
3. **Politically Speaking**
4. **The Art of Conversation**
5. The Language of Humor
6. The Language of Television and Advertising
7. **Censorship and Free Speech**

8. **Political Correctness and Hate Speech**
9. **Language in the USA**

I chose these themes because they seemed to best reflect the wide spectrum of language issues affecting us and because they help define our contemporary culture. Many new topics were added to the already broad spectrum covered—essays that treat English in its present relation to race and ethnic identity, debates about "politically correct" bias-free language, political propaganda, bureaucratic doublespeak, advertising, journalism, e-mail, celebrity influence, censorship on the Internet, sports mascots, graffiti, insult humor, ethnic prejudice, slang, body language, and other matters that suggest the endless potential of the language to be used and abused.

More Variety and More Genres in the Readings

In addition to updating 60 percent of the readings, this edition is infused with more variety and more genres than in any other edition of *Exploring Language*. Reflecting the wide range of expository modes and genres students are exposed to, this current text includes examples of personal narratives, objective reportage, newspaper opinion columns, position papers, various political arguments, editorials, op-ed essays, letters to the editor, memoirs, autobiographical musings, personal diaries, descriptive narratives, academic articles, pointed arguments, humorous satires, and more. Interviews, an excerpted play script, and several poems are also included.

Paired Essays and Debates

A key feature of *Exploring Language* since its first edition is the debate format. Each of the nine chapters contains essays on emotional or controversial topics paired with others presenting opposing views. Some might be juxtaposed on a common obsession. For instance, in the Chapter 1 subtheme "Personal Recollections: Coming to Language," two people from diverse backgrounds—Malcolm X and Helen Keller—give inspiring accounts of their discovery of words. Some juxtaposed pieces might be indirect debates, such as advertising guru Charles O'Neill's defense of his craft, "The Language of Advertising," and William Lutz's condemnation of the weasel language of advertisers, "With These Words I Can Sell You Anything." Or the debates might run head-on, such as Gabriella Kuntz's essay, "My Spanish Standoff," and Lourdes Rovira's "Let's Not Say Adios to Bilingual Education." Or Michiko Kakutani, whose "The Word Police" directly attacks the efforts of Rosalie Maggio, author of "Bias-Free Language." Or Charles R. Lawrence III, who goes head-to-head with Alan C. Kors over free speech versus censorship on college campuses.

New Rhetorical Features

While my hope is that the selections here are stimulating and fun, we cannot lose sight of the fact that the greater objective is to help students become better readers and writers. Therefore, the readings are accompanied by innovative exercises and activities on some aspects of language to spur thoughtful response and reflection and to help students develop their writing skills.

Updated Introduction to Critical Inquiry and Critical Reading

The premise of *Exploring Language* is that good writing grows out of good thinking, and good thinking grows out of good reading. Therefore, the text begins with a new specially tabbed introduction "Thinking and Reading Critically," which discusses what critical thinking and critical reading are, how to do each with step-by-step guidelines, and how each helps readers become better writers. The introduction illustrates the process in a detailed sample analysis of an essay on the language—both verbal and visual—of advertising, "The Selling of Rebellion" by *U.S. News & World Report* columnist John Leo. The sample not only illustrates a language issue that should appeal to students, but the analysis prepares them for the vast array of other language-based readings that follow and the writing they will generate.

Updated "Making Connections" Exercises

Each chapter subtheme is followed by several special writing and research exercises, "Making Connections." These exercises ask students to connect essays within the subtheme or chapter (and sometimes to other parts of the book) and research issues in greater depth.

Revised Apparatus

All of the remaining apparatus in the book has been improved and updated with great effort to create penetrating and stimulating assignments. Each selection is preceded by a headnote containing useful thematic and biographical information, as well as clues to writing strategies. Each essay is followed by a series of review questions, "Thinking Critically," covering both thematic and rhetorical strategies as well as engaging writing assignments and other exercises. Specifically, we added more library and Internet research questions to the critical thinking exercises following each essay in the book.

New Case Studies

This edition features nine new Case Studies that focus on particular language issues, such as speeches that inspired change in Chapter 1, language and the presidency and the language of war in Chapter 3, and a study of conversation in action in Chapter 4. In these clusters, several selections take differing slants on a particular aspect of language, thus broadening the reader's understanding of the issue. Following *each* Case Study is a group of "Making Connections" exercises that ask students to explore some language themes and issues that interconnect the various selections in that unit, others in the text, and their own experience.

Visuals

Recognizing the importance of visual communication, this tenth edition of *Exploring Language* has integrated the text with a large number of different kinds of graphics for students to analyze and discuss. In addition to the nine photographic chapter openers, we have included cartoons, print ads, comic strips, posters, e-mail messages, signs, Web pages, a book cover, and more. Following each are Critically Thinking questions directing students to analyze the "language" of the images—the messages and commentary projected from the designs and layouts. Our hope is to foster stimulating responses in class and in papers. But more than that, we hope to encourage students to better integrate visual images into their own writing.

More than ever before, students are making use of visual presentations in their writing, including their English essays. And the task is made easier because of the computer. With all the sophisticated software and printers, students are designing their own graphics and incorporating scanned illustrations, charts, graphs, and photos. Likewise, the Internet provides them opportunities to create their own Web pages and disseminate their work globally.

Companion Website

The Companion Website to accompany *Exploring Language,* 10/e (http://www .ablongman.com/goshgarian) offers a wealth of resources for both students and instructors. Students can access detailed chapter summaries, Web exercises, online readings, case studies, Web resources, and list of Web sites to help students explore the language of visuals. Instructors will find Web resources, and the *Instructor's Manual* available for download.

Instructor's Manual

The *Instructor's Manual,* which is available to adopters, includes suggested responses to all the questions in the text.

Acknowledgments

Many people behind the scenes are, at the very least, deserving of thanks and acknowledgment for their help with this tenth edition. It is impossible to thank all of them, but there are some for whose help I am particularly grateful. I would like, first, to thank those instructors who answered lengthy questionnaires on the effectiveness of the essays and supplied many helpful comments and suggestions: David Bowie, Brigham Young University; Karen L. Hollis, Villanova University; Jeffrey Michels, Rock Valley College; David Sprunger, Concordia College; Nancy Strow Sheley, California State University, Long Beach; and Nancy A. Taylor, California State University, Northridge.

A special thanks to William C. Snyder of Saint Vincent College for his astute and helpful suggestions for improving the logical fallacies section of the introductory material. My gratitude to Daisy Pignetti for her help with the *Instructor's Manual*. And a very special thanks to Kathryn Goodfellow for her invaluable assistance in the selection of material, the writing of the apparatus, and the preparation of the manuscript. This could not have been done without you. Thanks also to Darren Beals for his help with the permissions requests.

To all the instructors and students who have used *Exploring Language* over the past nine editions, I am enormously grateful. Finally to the people of Longman Publishers, especially my editor Lynn Huddon, her assistant Esther Hollander, Donna Campion, Supplements Editor, and Cyndy Taylor, thank you for your continuing support and enthusiasm.

Gary Goshgarian

Introduction:
Thinking and Reading Critically

What Is Critical Thinking?

Whenever you read a magazine article, newspaper editorial, or a piece of advertising and find yourself questioning the claims of the authors, you are exercising the basics of critical thinking. Instead of taking what you read at face value, you look beneath the surface of words and think about their meaning and significance. And, subconsciously, you ask the authors questions such as:

- What did you mean by that?
- Can you back up that statement?
- How do you define that term?
- How did you draw that conclusion?
- Do all the experts agree?
- Is this evidence dated?
- So what?
- What is your point?
- Why do we need to know this?

You make statements such as:

- That's not true.
- You're contradicting yourself.
- I see your point, but I don't agree.
- That's not a good choice of words.
- You're jumping to conclusions.
- Good point. I never thought of that.
- That was nicely stated.
- This is an extreme view.

Whether conscious or unconscious, such responses indicate that you are thinking *critically* about what you read. You weigh claims, ask for definitions, evaluate information, look for proof, question assumptions, and make judgments. In short, you process another person's words, not just take them in.

Why Read Critically?

When you read critically, you think critically. And that means instead of blindly accepting what's written on a page, you separate yourself from the text and decide for yourself what is or is not important or logical or right. And you do so because you bring to your reading your own perspective, experience, education, and personal values, as well as your powers of comprehension and analysis.

Critical reading is an active process of discovery. You discover an author's view on a subject; you enter a dialogue with the author; you discover the strengths and weaknesses of the author's thesis or argument; and you decide if you agree or disagree with the author's views. The end result is that you have a better understanding of the issue and the author. By asking the author questions and analyzing where the author stands with respect to other experiences or views of the issue—including your own—you actively enter a dialogue or a debate. You seek out the truth on your own instead of accepting at face value what somebody else says.

In reality, that is how truth and meaning are achieved—through interplay. Experience teaches us that knowledge and truth are not static entities, but are the by-products of struggle and dialogue—of asking tough questions. We witness this phenomenon all the time, re-created in the media through dialogue and conflict. We've recognized it over the years as a force of social change. Consider, for example, how our culture has changed its attitudes with regard to race, its concepts of success, kinship, social groups, and class since the 1950s. Perhaps the most obvious example regards gender: were it not for people questioning old rigid conventions, most women would still be bound to the laundry and the kitchen stove.

The point is that critical reading is an active and reactive process—one that sharpens your focus on a subject and your ability to absorb information and ideas while encouraging you to question accepted norms, views, and myths. And that is both healthy and laudable, for it is the basis of social evolution.

Critical reading also helps you become a better writer, because critical reading is the first step to critical writing. Good writers look at another's writing the way a carpenter looks at a house: they study the fine details and how those details connect and create the whole. Likewise, they consider the particular slants and strategies of appeal. Good writers always have a clear sense of their audience—their readers' racial makeup, gender, and educational background; their political and/or religious persuasions; their values, prejudices, and assumptions about life; and so forth. Knowing one's audience helps writers determine nearly every aspect of the writing process: the kind of language to use; the writing style (casual or formal, humorous or serious, technical or philosophical); the particular slant to take (appealing to the readers' reason, emotions, or ethics, or a combination of these); what emphasis to give the essay; the type of evidence to offer; and the kinds of authorities to cite.

It's the same with critical reading. The better you become at analyzing and reacting to another's written work, the better you will analyze and react to your own. You will ask yourself: Is it logical? Do my points come across clearly? Are my examples solid enough? Is this the best wording? Is my conclusion persuasive? Do I have a clear sense of my audience? What appeal strategy did I take—to logic, emotions, or ethics? In short, critical reading will help you to evaluate your own writing, thereby making you both a better reader and a better writer.

While you may already employ many strategies of critical reading, here are some techniques to make you an even better critical reader.

How to Read Critically

To help you read critically, use these six proven basic steps:

- Keep a journal on what you read.
- Annotate what you read.
- Outline what you read.
- Summarize what you read.
- Question what you read.
- Analyze what you read.

To demonstrate just how these techniques work, let's apply them to a sample essay. Reprinted below is the essay, "The Selling of Rebellion," by John Leo taken from his column in *U.S. News & World Report,* first published in the October 12, 1998 issue. I chose this piece because, like all selections in this book, it addresses an interesting contemporary language issue, because it is accessible, and because the author raises some serious questions about the attitudes and values of perhaps the most ubiquitous form of language persuasion—advertising.

1   Most TV viewers turn off their brains when the commercials come on. But they're worth paying attention to. Some of the worst cultural propaganda is jammed into those 60-second and 30-second spots.

2   Consider the recent ad for the Isuzu Rodeo. A grotesque giant in a business suit stomps into a beautiful field, startling a deer and jamming skyscrapers, factories, and signs into the ground. (I get it: Nature is good; civilization and business are bad.) One of the giant's signs says, "Obey," but the narrator says, "The world has boundaries. Ignore them." Trying to trample the Rodeo, the hapless giant trips over his own fence. The Isuzu zips past him and topples a huge sign that says "Rules."

3   Presumably we are meant to react to this ad with a wink and a nudge, because the message is unusually flat-footed and self-satirical. After all, Isuzus are not manufactured in serene fields by adorable lower mammals. The maddened giant makes them in his factories. He also hires hip ad writers and stuffs them in his skyscrapers, forcing them to write drivel all day, when they really should be working on novels and frolicking with deer.

4   But the central message here is very serious and strongly antisocial: We should all rebel against authority, social order, propriety, and rules of any kind. "Obey" and "Rules" are bad. Breaking rules, with or without your Isuzu, is good. Auto makers have been pushing this idea in various ways since "The Dodge Rebellion" of the mid-1960s. Isuzu has worked the theme especially hard, including a TV ad

showing a bald and repressive grade-school teacher barking at kids to "stay within the lines" while coloring pictures, because "the lines are our friends."

5   **Away with standards.** A great many advertisers now routinely appeal to the so-called postmodern sensibility, which is heavy on irony (wink, nudge) and attuned to the message that rules. Boundaries, standards, and authorities are either gone or should be gone. Foster Grant sunglasses has used the "no limits" refrain. So have Prince Matchabelli perfume ("Life without limits"), Showtime TV (its "No Limits" campaign) and AT&T's Olympics ads in 1996 ("Imagine a world without limits"). No Limits is an outdoor-adventure company, and No Limit is the name of a successful rap record label. Even the U.S. Army used the theme in a TV recruitment ad. "When I'm in this uniform I know no limits," says a soldier—a scary thought if you remember Lt. William Calley in Vietnam or the Serbian Army today.

6   Among the ads that have used "no boundaries" almost as a mantra are Ralph Lauren's Safari cologne, Johnnie Walker Scotch ("It's not trespassing when you cross your own boundaries"), Merrill Lynch ("Know no boundaries"), and the movie *The English Patient* ("In love, there are no boundaries").

7   Some "no boundaries" ads are legitimate—the Internet and financial markets, after all, aim at crossing or erasing old boundaries. The antisocial message is clearer in most of the "no rules" and "antirules" ads, starting with Burger King's "Sometimes, you gotta break the rules." These include Outback steakhouses ("No rules. Just right."), Don Q rum ("Break all the rules"), the theatrical troupe De La Guarda ("No rules"), Neiman Marcus ("No rules here"), Columbia House Music Club ("We broke the rules"), Comedy Central ("See comedy that breaks rules"), Red Kamel cigarettes ("This baby don't play by the rules"), and even Woolite (wool used to be associated with decorum, but now "All the rules have changed," an ad says under a photo of a young woman groping or being groped by two guys). "No rules" also turns up as the name of a book and a CD and a tag line for an NFL video game ("no refs, no rules, no mercy"). The message is everywhere—"The rules are for breaking," says a Spice Girls lyric.

8   What is this all about? Why is the ad industry working so hard to use rule-breaking as a way of selling cars, steaks, and Woolite? In his book *The Conquest of Cool,* Thomas Frank points to the Sixties counterculture. He says it has become "a more or less permanent part of the American scene, a symbolic and musical language for the endless cycles of rebellion and transgression that make up so much of our mass culture . . . rebellion is both the high- and mass-cultural motif of the age; order is its great bogeyman."

9   The pollster-analysts at Yankelovich Partners Inc. have a different view. In their book *Rocking the Ages: The Yankelovich Report on Generational Marketing,* J. Walker Smith and Ann Clurman say rule-breaking is simply a hallmark of the baby boom generation: "Boomers always have broken the rules. . . . The drugs, sex, and rock 'n roll of the '60s and '70s only foreshadowed the really radical rule-breaking to come in the consumer marketplace of the '80s and '90s."

10   This may pass—Smith says the post-boomers of generation X are much more likely to embrace traditional standards than boomers were at the same age. On the other hand, maybe it won't. Pop culture is dominated by in-your-face transgres-

sions now and the damage is severe. The peculiar thing is that so much of the rule-breaking propaganda is largely funded by businessmen who say they hate it, but can't resist promoting it in ads as a way of pushing their products. Isuzu, please come to your senses.

Keep a Journal on What You Read

Unlike writing an essay or a paper, keeping a journal is a personal exploration in which you develop your own ideas without set rules. It is a process of recording impressions and exploring feelings and ideas. It is an opportunity to write without restrictions and without judgment. You don't have to worry about breaking the rules—because in a journal, anything goes.

Reserve a special notebook just for your journal—not one that you use for class notes or homework. Also, date your entries and include the titles of the articles to which you are responding. Eventually, by the end of the semester, you should have a substantial number of pages to review so you can see how your ideas and writing style have developed over time.

What do you include in your journal? Although it may serve as a means to understanding an essay you're assigned, you are not required to write only about the essay itself. Perhaps the piece reminds you of something in your personal experience. Maybe it triggered an opinion you didn't know you had. Or perhaps it prompted you to explore a particular phrase or idea presented by the author.

Some students may find keeping a journal difficult because it is so personal. They may feel as if they're exposing their feelings too much. Or they may feel uncomfortable thinking that someone else—a teacher or another student—may read their writing. But such apprehensions shouldn't prevent you from exploring your impressions and feelings. Just don't record anything that you wouldn't want your teacher or classmates to read; or if you do, don't show anybody your journal. You may even consider keeping two journals—one for class and one for personal use.

Reprinted below is one student's journal entry on our sample essay, "The Selling of Rebellion," by John Leo, *U.S. News & World Report*, October 12, 1998:

> John Leo seems to think that breaking rules is a bad thing—
> something that's promoted by advertising and the media and that
> should be stopped. While some rules are good and we should follow
> them, others are bad and should be broken, regardless of whether
> the media encourages us to do so or not. If women didn't break the
> "rules," they may never have gotten the vote. If African
> Americans hadn't broken the "rules" they could still be riding at
> the back of the bus and drinking from separate water fountains.
> My point is that Leo should consider that breaking the rules is not

necessarily a negative attitude. The media is just tapping into our spirit to challenge the status quo—and personally, I think that is a good thing.

Annotate What You Read

It's a good idea to underline (or highlight) key passages and make marginal notes when reading an essay. (If you don't own the publication in which the essay appears, or choose not to mark it up, it's a good idea to make a photocopy of the piece and annotate that.) I recommend annotating on the second or third reading, once you've gotten a handle on the essay's general ideas.

There are no specific guidelines for annotation. Use whatever technique suits you best, but keep in mind that in annotating a piece of writing, you are engaging in a dialogue with the author. As in any meaningful dialogue, you may hear things you may not have known, things that may be interesting and exciting to you, things that you may agree or disagree with, or things that give you cause to ponder. The other side of the dialogue, of course, is your response. In annotating a piece of writing, that response takes the form of underlining (or highlighting) key passages and jotting down comments in the margin. Such comments can take the form of full sentences or some shorthand codes. Sometimes "Why?" or "True" or "NO!" will be enough to help you respond to a writer's position or claim. If you come across a word or reference that is unfamiliar to you, underline or circle it. Once you've located the main thesis statement or claim, highlight or underline it and jot down "Claim" or "Thesis" in the margin.

Below is the Leo essay reproduced in its entirety with sample annotations.

Most TV viewers turn off their brains when the commercials come on. But they're worth paying attention to. Some of the worst cultural propaganda is jammed into those 60- second and 30-second spots.   1   *opinion*

Consider the recent ad for the Isuzu Rodeo. A (grotesque) giant in a business suit stomps into a beautiful field, startling a deer and jamming sky- scrapers, factories, and signs into the ground. (I get it: Nature is good; civilization and business are bad.) One of the giant's signs says "Obey," but the narrator says "The world has boundaries. Ignore them." Trying to trample the Rodeo, the hapless giant trips over his own fence. The Isuzu zips past him and topples a huge sign that says "Rules."   2   *is that what it means?*

Presumably we are meant to react to this ad with a wink and a nudge, because the message is unusually flat-footed and self-satirical. After all, Isuzus are not   3

manufactured in serene fields by adorable lower
mammals. The maddened giant makes them in his
factories. He also hires hip ad writers and stuffs
them in his skyscrapers, forcing them to write drivel
all day, when they really should be working on novels
and frolicking with deer.

ironic?

author's sarcasm

But the central message here is very serious and
strongly antisocial: We should all rebel against
authority, social order, propriety, and rules of any
kind. "Obey" and "Rules" are bad. Breaking rules,
with or without your Isuzu, is good. Auto makers
have been pushing this idea in various ways since
"The Dodge Rebellion" of the mid-1960's. Isuzu has
worked the theme especially hard, including a
TV ad showing a bald and repressive grade-school
teacher barking at kids to "stay within the lines"
while coloring pictures, because "the lines are our
friends."

4

– is this the message of the commercial?

look up history

Away with standards. A great many advertisers
now routinely appeal to the so-called postmodern
sensibility, which is heavy on irony (wink, nudge)
and attuned to the message that rules, boundaries,
standards, and authorities are either gone or should
be gone. Foster Grant sunglasses has used the "no
limits" refrain. So have Prince Matchabelli perfume
("Life without limits"), Showtime TV (its "No
Limits" campaign) and AT&T's Olympics ads in
1996 ("Imagine a world without limits"). No Limits
is an outdoor-adventure company, and No Limit is the
name of a successful rap record label. Even the U.S.
Army used the theme in a TV recruitment ad. "When
I'm in this uniform I know no limits," says a soldier –
a scary thought if you remember Lt. William Calley
in Vietnam or the Serbian Army today.

5

what does this mean?

limits = rules?

who is Lt. W. Calley?

Among the ads that have used "no boundaries"
almost as a mantra are Ralph Lauren's Safari cologne,
Johnnie Walker Scotch ("It's not trespassing when you
cross your own boundaries"), Merrill Lynch ("Know
no boundaries"), and the movie *The English Patient*
("In love, there are no boundaries").

6

I don't think this is the same thing as the message of the Isuzu ad!

Some "no boundaries" ads are legitimate–the
Internet and financial markets, after all, aim at
crossing or erasing old boundaries. The antisocial
message is clearer in most of the "no rules" and
"antirules" ads, starting with Burger King's

7

how are these messages antisocial?

"Sometimes, you gotta break the rules." These include Outback steak houses ("No rules. Just right"), Don Q rum ("Break all the rules"), the theatrical troupe De La Guarda ("No rules"), Neiman Marcus ("No rules here"), Columbia House Music Club ("We broke the rules"), Comedy Central ("See comedy that breaks rules"), Red Kamel cigarettes ("This baby don't play by the rules"), and even Woolite (wool used to be associated with decorum, but now "All the rules have changed," as the ad says under a photo of a young woman groping or being groped by two guys). "No rules" also turns up as the name of a book and a CD and a tag line for an NFL video game ("no refs, no rules, no mercy"). The message is everywhere "the rules are for breaking," says a Spice Girls lyric.

see context of ad.

not related to advertising...

8

What is this all about? Why is the ad industry working so hard to use rule-breaking as a way of selling cars, steaks, and Woolite? In his book *The Conquest of Cool,* Thomas Frank points to the Sixties counterculture. He says it has become "a more or less permanent part of the American scene, a symbolic and musical language for the endless cycles of rebellion and transgression that make up so much of our mass culture… rebellion is both the high- and mass-cultural motif of the age; order is its great bogeyman."

aren't we glad they broke music "rules"?

is our culture really like this?

9

The pollster-analysts at Yankelovich Partners Inc. have a different view. In their book *Rocking the Ages: The Yankelovich Report on Generational Marketing,* J. Walker Smith and Ann Clurman say rule-breaking is simply a hallmark of the baby boom generation: "Boomers always have broken the rules…. The drugs, sex, and rock 'n roll of the '60's and '70's only foreshadowed the really radical rule-breaking to come in the consumer marketplace of the '80's and '90's.

explain this!

10

This may pass–Smith says the post-boomers of generation X are much more likely to embrace traditional standards than boomers were at the same age. On the other hand, maybe it won't. Pop culture is dominated by in-your-face transgression now and the damage is severe. The peculiar thing is that so much of the rule-breaking propaganda is largely funded by businessmen who say they hate it, but can't resist promoting it in ads as a way of pushing their products. Isuzu, please come to your senses.

how?!

why?

Outline What You Read

Briefly outlining an essay is a good way to see how writers structure their ideas. When you physically diagram the thesis statement, claims, and the supporting evidence, you can better assess the quality of the writing and decide how convincing it is. You may already be familiar with detailed, formal essay outlines in which structure is broken down into main ideas and subsections. However, for our purposes, I suggest a brief and concise breakdown of an essay's components. Simply jotting down a one-sentence summary of each paragraph does this. Sometimes brief paragraphs elaborating the same point can be lumped together:

- Point 1
- Point 2
- Point 3
- Point 4
- Point 5
- Point 6, etc.

Even though such outlines may seem rather primitive, they demonstrate at a glance how the various parts of an essay are connected—that is, the organization and sequence of ideas.

Below is a sentence outline of "The Selling of Rebellion":

Point 1: Commercials are promoting cultural propaganda.

Point 2: An example is the commercial for the Isuzu Rodeo, which depicts an evil corporation giant stomping through a field trying to enforce a message of conformity only to be foiled by the SUV making its "escape."

Point 3: Leo points out the irony in the commercial commenting that obviously a large corporation manufactures Isuzu.

Point 4: Leo analyzes the commercial, and others like it, to mean that advertisers are promoting a campaign in which "rule-breaking" is considered admirable and good.

Point 5: He supports this assertion with other examples of "rule-breaking" advertising campaigns, including Prince Matchabelli, Foster Grant, No Limits outdoor gear, Burger King, Neiman Marcus, and even Woolite.

Point 6: Leo cites Thomas Frank's book that identifies the Sixties' counterculture as the source of this culture of rebellion.

Point 7: Leo continues to explore the reason behind this advertising trend conjecturing that rule-breaking is a legacy of the baby-boomer generation.

Point 8: Leo concludes that this trend of rebellion is having a detrimental effect on our culture and should stop.

At this point you should have a fairly good grasp of the author's stand on the issue. Now let's analyze the essay in its parts and as a whole.

Summarize What You Read

Summarizing is perhaps the most important technique to develop for understanding and evaluating what you read. This means boiling the essay down to its main points. In your journal or notebook, try to write a brief (about 100 words) synopsis of the reading in your own words. Note the claim or thesis of the discussion (or argument) and the chief supporting points. It is important to write these points down, rather than to highlight them passively with a pen or pencil, because the act of jotting down a summary helps you absorb the argument.

Now let's return to our sample essay. In the brief paragraph below, I offer a summary of Leo's essay, mindful of using my own words rather than those of the author to avoid plagiarism. At times, it may be impossible to avoid using the author's own words in a summary, but if you do, remember to use quotation marks.

In his article "The Selling of Rebellion," John Leo explores the advertising trend promoting "rule-breaking" behavior. The message advertisers present to their viewers is that rebellion and breaking boundaries is a positive and desirable trait—a message Leo questions. Companies such as Isuzu, Prince Matchabelli, Ralph Lauren, Johnnie Walker, Merrill Lynch, Burger King, and Columbia House Music all have advertising campaigns featuring the theme of rule-breaking. Leo conjectures that this trend began with the Sixties generation in which baby boomers reacted against conventional boundaries and established their own culture of rebellion. He concludes that such advertising is ultimately socially damaging and could have detrimental effects on our culture.

Although this paragraph seems to do a fairly good job of summarizing Leo's essay, it took me a few tries to get it down to under a hundred words. So, don't be too discouraged when trying to summarize a reading on your own.

Question What You Read

Although we break down critical reading into discrete steps, these steps will naturally overlap in the actual process. While reading this essay you were simultaneously summarizing and evaluating Leo's points in your head, perhaps adding your own ideas or even arguing with him. If something strikes you as particularly interesting or insightful, make a mental note. Likewise, if something rubs you the wrong way, argue back. For beginning writers, a good strategy is to convert that automatic mental response into actual note taking.

In your journal (or, as suggested below, in the margins of the text), question and challenge the writer. Jot down any points in the essay that do not measure up to your expectations or personal views. Note anything you are skeptical about. Write down any questions you have about the claims, views, or evidence. If some point or conclusion seems forced or unfounded, record it and briefly explain why. The more skeptical and questioning you are, the better reader you are. Likewise, note what features of the essay impressed you—outstanding points, interesting wording, clever or amusing phrases or allusions, particular references, the general structure of the piece. Record what you learn from the reading and what aspects of the issue you would like to explore.

Of course, you may not feel qualified to pass judgment on an author's views, especially if that author is a professional writer or an expert on a particular subject. Sometimes the issue discussed might be too technical, or you may not feel informed enough to make critical evaluations. Sometimes a personal narrative may focus on experiences completely alien to you. Nonetheless, you are an intelligent person with an instinct to determine if the writing impresses you or if an argument is sound, logical, and convincing. What you can do in such instances—and another good habit to get into—is think of other views on the issue. If you've read or heard of experiences different from the author's or arguments with opposing views, jot them down. Even if you haven't, the essay should contain some inference or reference to alternate experiences or opposing views (if it's an argument) from which you could draw a counterposition.

Let's return to Leo's essay, which, technically, is an argument. Although it's theoretically possible to question or comment on every sentence in the piece, let's select a couple of key points that may have struck you as presumptuous, overstated, or inconsistent with your own experience.

Paragraph 1: "Some of the worst cultural propaganda is jammed into . . ."—this is the author's opinion. Some people may not find it negative or "propagandistic."

Paragraph 2: Comments in parentheses present the author's sarcastic attitude toward the advertisers and their message.

Paragraph 3: Leo seems to read a great deal more into the commercial ("maddened giant", "enslaved ad writers") than what was actually shown on TV. He is trying to make the commercial seem even worse. Also, note Leo's use of descriptive words.

Paragraph 4: Leo determines what the message of the commercial is, but in a skewed way. He thinks that breaking rules is a bad thing—but is it really?

Paragraphs 5–7: Leo interprets "no limits" and "no boundaries" to mean "no rules." Do they really mean the same thing? Some people may interpret "no limits" to mean endless possibilities and "no boundaries" to mean that they have more freedom (a positive American trait). He fails to consider the possible alternative meanings of these expressions.

Paragraph 8: Citing the sixties' counterculture of rebellion (such as in their music) may not be the best example to support his negative attitude toward the "no rules" advertising campaigns. Many people think that the revolution of the sixties was a good thing (especially in music).

Paragraph 9: Leo sweepingly identifies baby boomers as a generation of sex, drugs, and rock and roll. Is this fair?

Paragraph 10: Leo fails to explain how these advertising campaigns are "damaging" to our culture.

Analyze What You Read

To analyze something means breaking it down into its components, examining those components closely and evaluating their significance, and determining how they relate as a whole. In part, you already did this by briefly outlining the essay. But there is more, because analyzing what you read involves interpreting and evaluating the points of a discussion or argument as well as its presentation—that is, its language and structure. Ultimately, analyzing an essay after establishing its gist will help you understand what may not be evident at first. A closer examination of the author's words takes you beneath the surface and sharpens your understanding of the issue at hand.

Although there is no set procedure for analyzing a piece of prose, here are some specific questions you should raise when reading an essay, especially one that is trying to sway you to its view.

- What kind of audience is the author addressing?
- What are the author's assumptions?
- What are the author's purposes and intentions?
- How well does the author accomplish those purposes?
- How convincing is the evidence presented? Is it sufficient and specific? Relevant? Reliable? Not dated? Slanted?
- How good are the sources of the evidence used? Were they based on personal experience, scientific data, or outside authorities?
- Did the author address opposing views on the issue?
- Is the author persuasive in his or her perspective?

What Kind of Audience Is Being Addressed?

Before the first word is written, a good writer considers his or her audience—that is, the age group, gender, ethnic and racial makeup, educational background, and socioeconomic status. Also considered are the values, prejudices, and assumptions of the readers, as well as their political and religious persuasions. Some writers, including several in this book, write for a "target" audience—readers who share the same interests, opinions, and prejudices. For example, some of the essays in Chapter 3, "Politically Speaking," were written for people familiar with current events and issues. Other writers write for a "general" audience. Although general audiences consist of very different people with diversified backgrounds, expectations, and standards, think of them as the people who read *Time, Newsweek,* and your local newspaper. That is, people whose average age is 35, whose educational level is high school plus two years of college, who make up the vast middle class of America, who politically stand in the middle of the road, and whose racial and ethnic origins span the world. You can assume they are generally informed about what is going on in the country, that they have a good comprehension of language and a sense of humor, and that they are willing to listen to new ideas.

Because John Leo's essay appeared in his column in *U.S. News & World Report,* he is clearly writing for a "general" audience. A closer look tells us more:

- The language level suggests a general audience with at least a high school education.
- The tone suggests an older audience—one able to identify with his comments about baby boomers and the Sixties' countercultural revolution.
- The books cited by Thomas Frank, J. Walker Smith, and Ann Clurman imply that the audience is likely to be college educated and familiar with using such references to support a point.
- The overall message that "rule-breaking" advertising is culturally damaging suggests a conservative audience likely to agree with the author.

What Are the Author's Assumptions?

Having a sense of one's audience leads writers to certain assumptions. If a writer is writing to a general audience, as is Leo, then he or she can assume a certain level of awareness about language and current events, certain values about education and morality, and certain nuances of an argument. After going through Leo's essay, one might draw the following conclusions about the author:

- The examples supporting the thesis assume an audience that watches television and is familiar with the products advertised—including more "sophisticated" companies such as Merrill Lynch and Neiman Marcus.
- The reference to the "Dodge Rebellion" advertising campaign of the 1960s assumes that readers will be old enough to remember and recall this campaign.
- The sarcastic comments ("I get it: Nature is good, civilization and business are bad.") assumes an audience familiar with irony, social convention, and cultural trends.

What Are the Author's Purpose and Intentions?

A writer writes for a purpose beyond wanting to show up in print. Sometimes it is simply expressing how the writer feels about something; sometimes the intention is to convince others to see things in a different light; sometimes the purpose is to persuade readers to change their views or behavior. Of the Leo essay, it might be said that the author had the following intentions:

- To convince people that a "rebellious" theme in advertising is permeating our culture.
- To raise awareness of how pervasive this advertising trend really is.
- To impress upon readers the socially damaging nature of these campaigns.
- To urge businesses to stop promoting messages of rebellion and rule breaking.

How Well Does the Author Accomplish Those Purposes?

Determining how well an author accomplishes such purposes may seem subjective, but in reality it comes down to how well the case is presented. Is the thesis clear? Is it well-laid out or argued? Are the examples sharp and convincing? Is the author's conclusion a logical result of what came before? Back to Leo's essay:

- He provides many examples of the rebellious and rule-breaking advertising campaigns from a highly diverse group of companies.
- He keeps to his point for most of his essay.
- He supports his assertions well.
- He fails to present evidence of the damaging effects of this advertising.

How Convincing Is the Evidence Presented? Is It Sufficient and Specific? Relevant? Reliable? Not Dated? Slanted?

Convincing writing depends on convincing evidence—that is, sufficient and relevant facts along with proper interpretations of facts. Facts are pieces of information that can be verified—such as statistics, examples, personal experience, expert testimony, and historical details. Proper interpretations of such facts must be logical and supported by relevant data. For instance, it is a fact that the SAT verbal scores in America went up in 2000. One interpretation might be that students are spending more time reading and less time watching TV than in the past. But without hard statistics documenting the viewing habits of a sample of students, that interpretation is shaky, the result of a writer jumping to conclusions.

Is the Evidence Sufficient and Specific? Writers use evidence on a routine basis, but sometimes it may not be sufficient. Sometimes the conclusions reached have too little evidence to be justified. Sometimes writers make hasty generalizations based solely on personal experience as evidence. How much evidence is enough? It's hard to say, but the more specific the details, the more convincing the argument. Instead of generalizations, good writers cite figures, dates, and facts; instead of paraphrases, they quote experts verbatim.

Is the Evidence Relevant? Good writers select evidence based on how well it supports the point being argued, not on how interesting, novel, or humorous it is. For instance, if you were arguing that Mark McGwire is the greatest living baseball player, you wouldn't mention that he was born in Pomona, California, and has a brother Dan who played quarterback for the Seattle Seahawks. Those are facts, but they have nothing to do with McGwire's athletic abilities. Irrelevant evidence distracts readers and weakens an argument.

Is the Evidence Reliable? Not Dated? Evidence should not be so vague or dated that it fails to support one's claim. For instance, it wouldn't be accurate to say that Candidate Jones fails to support the American worker because 15 years ago she purchased a foreign car. It's her current actions that are more important. Readers expect writers to be specific enough with data for them to verify. A writer supporting animal rights may cite cases of rabbits blinded in drug research, but such tests have been outlawed in the United States for many years. Another may point to medical research that appears to abuse human subjects, but not name the researchers, the place, or the year of such testing. Because readers may have no way of verifying evidence, suspicious claims will weaken an argument.

Is the Evidence Slanted? Sometimes writers select evidence that supports their case while ignoring evidence that doesn't. Often referred to as "stacking the deck," this practice is unfair and potentially self-defeating for a writer. Although some evidence may have merit, an argument will be dismissed if readers discover that evidence was slanted or suppressed. For example, suppose you heard a classmate claim that he would never take a course with Professor Sanchez because she gives surprise quizzes, assigns 50 pages of reading a night, and doesn't grade on a curve. Even if these reasons are true, that may not be the whole truth. You might discover that Professor Sanchez is a dynamic and talented teacher whose classes are stimulating. Withholding that information may make an argument suspect. A better strategy is to acknowledge counterevidence and to confront it—that is, to strive for a balanced presentation by raising views and evidence that may not be supportive of your own.

How Good Are the Sources of the Evidence Used? Were They Based on Personal Experience, Scientific Data, or Outside Authorities?

Writers enlist four basic kinds of evidence to support their views or arguments: personal experience (theirs and others'), outside authorities, factual references and examples, and statistics. In your own writing, you'll be encouraged to use combinations of these.

Personal testimony should not be underestimated. Think of the books you've read or movies you've seen based on word-of-mouth recommendations. (Maybe even the school you're attending!) Personal testimony provides eyewitness accounts not available to you or readers—and sometimes they are the most persuasive kind of evidence. Suppose you are writing about the rising alcohol abuse on college campuses. In addition to statistics and hard facts, quoting the experience of a first-year student who nearly died one night from alcohol poisoning would add dramatic impact. Although personal observations are useful and valuable, writers must not draw hasty conclusions from them. Because you and a couple of friends are in favor of replacing letter grades with a pass–fail system does not support the claim that the student body at your school is in favor of the conversion.

Outside authorities are people recognized as experts in a given field. The appeal to such authorities is a powerful tool in writing, especially for writers wanting to persuade readers of their views. We hear it all the time: "Scientists have found . . . ," "Scholars inform us that . . . ," "According to his biographer, Abraham Lincoln. . . ." Although experts try to be objective and fair-minded, sometimes their testimony is biased. You wouldn't turn to scientists working for tobacco companies for unbiased opinions on lung cancer.

Factual references and examples do as much to inform as to persuade. If somebody wants to sell you something, they'll pour on the details. Think of the television commercials that show sport utility vehicles climbing rocky mountain roads while a narrator lists all the great standard features—permanent four-wheel drive, alloy wheels, second-generation airbags, power brakes, cruise control, etc.—or, the cereal "infomercials" in which manufacturers explain how their new Yumm-Os now have 15 percent more fiber to help prevent cancer. Although readers may not have the expertise to determine which data are useful, they are often convinced by the sheer weight of the evidence—like courtroom juries judging a case.

Statistics impress people. Saying that 77 percent of your school's student body approves of women in military combat roles is much more persuasive than saying "a lot of people" do. Why? Because statistics have a no-nonsense authority. Batting averages, polling results, economic indicators, medical and FBI statistics, demographic percentages—they're all reported in numbers. If accurate, they are hard to argue with, though they can be used to mislead. If somebody claims that 139 people on campus protested the appearance of a certain controversial speaker, it would be a distortion of the truth not to mention that another 1,500 attended the talk and gave the speaker a standing ovation. Likewise, the manufacturer who claims that its potato chips are 100 percent cholesterol free misleads the public, because no potato chips cooked in vegetable oil contain cholesterol—which is found only in animal fats. That is known as the "bandwagon" use of statistics—in other words, appealing to crowd-pleasing, healthy eating awareness.

Now let's examine briefly Leo's sources of evidence:

- Leo presents many examples of advertising campaigns that feature the theme of the "selling of rebellion." These examples come from actual advertisements on television, radio, and in magazines.

- Leo may skew some of his evidence in that he connects rule-breaking with other words, such as "limits" and "boundaries." He assumes that the phrases in these advertising campaigns are synonymous.

- Leo supports his points with several authoritative references; however, these references do not consider alternative points of view.

Did the Author Address Opposing Views on the Issue?

Many of the essays in this book will, in varying degrees, try to persuade you to agree with the author's position or argument. But, of course, any slant on a topic can have multiple points of view. In developing their ideas, good writers will anticipate different and opposing views. They will cite contrary opinions, maybe even evidence unsupportive of their own position. Not to do so leaves their own stand open to counterattack, as well as to claims of naiveté and ignorance. This is particularly damaging when arguing some controversial issue. Returning to the Leo essay:

- Leo does not introduce alternative points of view into his editorial. It is, after all, an editorial article and thus, based on his opinion as he can best support it.

Is the Author's Perspective Persuasive?

Style and content make for persuasive writing. Important points are how well a paper is composed—the organization, the logic, the quality of thought, the presentation of evidence, the use of language, the tone of discussion—and the details and evidence. Turning to Leo's essay, we might make the following observation:

- Leo is very persuasive in convincing his audience that the "rebellious" theme is pervading American advertising. He does not, however, effectively persuade his readers that this trend is damaging to American culture.

Logical Fallacies—What They Are and How to Avoid Them

Sometimes writers make errors in logic. In fact, we've already pointed out a few of them above. Such errors are called *logical fallacies,* a term derived from the Latin *fallere,* meaning, "to deceive." Used unintentionally, these fallacies deceive writers into feeling that what they're saying is more persuasive than it really is. Even though an argument may be well developed and contain evidence, a fallacy creates a flaw in logic, thereby weakening the structure and persuasiveness.

Not all logical fallacies are unintentional. Sometimes a fallacy is deliberately employed—for example when the writer's goal has more to do with persuading than arriving at the truth. Every day we are confronted with fallacies in commercials and advertisements. Likewise, every election year the airwaves are full of candidates' bloated claims and pronouncements rife with logical fallacies of all sorts.

Recognizing logical fallacies when they occur in a reading is an important step in critical thinking—assessing the effectiveness of the writer's argument. Following are some of the most common logical fallacies to look for.

LOGICAL FALLACIES

Ad Hominem Argument:

Attacks the opponent rather than the opponent's views.

Of course she supports bilingual education. She's a bleeding-heart liberal.

PROBLEM: Name-calling makes us question the writer's real motives or credibility.

Ad Misericordium Argument (or so-called *pity appeal*):

Appeals to reader's emotions rather than reason.

It makes no difference if he was guilty of Nazi war crimes. This man is eighty years old and in frail health, so he should not be made to stand trial.

PROBLEM: Pity appeal feels like manipulation and distraction from the real issue.

The Bandwagon Appeal:

Plays on our fears of being left out or different.

Everybody knows he's the best candidate for the office.

PROBLEM: We're asked to "get with it" without weighing the evidence.

Begging the Question:	Assumes that something is a fact when it really has yet to be proven.

That judge will probably go easy on that defendant because they are both women.

PROBLEM: Assumes that because the judge is female she will be more compassionate to another female which in itself assumes that women are more compassionate than men.

Circular Reasoning:	Where the conclusion of an argument is hidden in the argument's premise.

Steroids are dangerous because they ruin your health.

PROBLEM: Steroids are dangerous because they're dangerous. Repetition of key terms or ideas is not evidence.

False Analogy:	An analogy is a comparison. False analogies compare two things that seem alike but really are not.

The attack on the World Trade Center was the Pearl Harbor of the 21st Century.

PROBLEM: Although the two have similarities, they are also very different events. For example, the attack on Pearl Harbor was a military attack on a naval base while the attack on the World Trade Center was committed by terrorists on a civilian target.

False Dilemma:	A claim or solution that presents only two extremes, when a possible or practical middle ground exists.

I stumbled on my way up the aisle. My wedding was a disaster.

PROBLEM: A single incident doesn't necessary ruin the entire event. The rest of the wedding could have been quite satisfactory and enjoyable.

Hasty Generalization:	A conclusion that is based on too little evidence, or reached when the evidence itself is too broad, not factual, or not substantiated.

Television has caused a significant increase in violence and sexual promiscuity in America's youth.

PROBLEM: This oversimplifies the relationship between television and violence and promiscuity in youth, and discounts other factors that may be connected to the issue.

| Non Sequitur: | Draws a conclusion that does not follow logically from the premise or previous statement leading to an error in deduction. |

Mrs. Marshall is a fabulous tennis player and knows how to dress with style. She comes from money.

PROBLEM: The ability to play tennis or dress well has nothing to do with one's financial background.

| Faulty Cause-and-Effect Reasoning: | (Also known as *post hoc, ergo propter hoc* reasoning, from the Latin "after this, therefore because of this.") Establishes a questionable cause-and-effect relationship between chronological events. It assumes that because one event happened before another, the first influenced the second. |

Every time Bill goes with me to Jacobs Field, the Cleveland Indians lose.

PROBLEM: Although the Indians lose whenever Bill joins you at Jacobs Field, his presence does not cause the team to lose. It's just coincidence.

| Slippery Slope: | Presumes one event will inevitably lead to a chain of other events that ends in a catastrophe—as one slip on a mountain will cause a climber to tumble down and bring with him or her all those in tow. |

Censorship of obscene material will spell the end of freedom of speech and freedom of the press.

PROBLEM: This domino-effect reasoning is fallacious because it depends more on presumption than on hard evidence.

| Stacking the Deck: | Offers only the evidence that supports the premise while disregarding or withholding contrary evidence. |

"Our Wonder Wieners all-beef hot dogs now contain 10 percent less fat."

PROBLEM: Sounds like good news, but what the ad doesn't tell us is that Wonder Wieners still contain 30 percent fat.

| Red Herring: | A fact that is thrown into an argument in order to distract the reader from the real issue. |

Jennifer isn't the sort of girl who shoplifts; she is on the girl's lacrosse team, the honor society, and she volunteers at the retirement home twice a month.

PROBLEM: Simply because Jennifer is athletic, a good student, and a volunteer doesn't mean she isn't capable of shoplifting.

Exploring the Language of Visuals

We have all heard the old saying, "a picture is worth a thousand words." In addition to many insightful and interesting articles on language, this edition of *Exploring Language* features selected visuals to help illustrate the nonverbal ways we use and process language. We constantly react to nonverbal cues in our daily lives. Symbols, images, gestures, and graphics all communicate instant information that we process as language.

To better understand how such "visual language" works, we have interspersed throughout this text various cartoons, posters, and photographs that highlight the different ways we communicate without using words. For example, a cartoon, featured in little boxes with drawn characters, communicates a certain set of expectations before a reader even begins to examine it. We know instantly that it is a cartoon, and that, as such, it is supposed to convey some form of humor. In well-known cartoons, we may even instantly recall the personalities of the characters depicted and expect certain reactions or attitudes from them. In advertisements, cultural cues of imagery, symbolism, the use of light and dark, and the product's purpose are all used by advertisers to tap into our presumed set of expectations. Sometimes it is the symbolic representation of an action—such as the portrait of a gagged Margaret Sanger in Chapter 1—that instantly conveys meaning. Sanger's gag immediately tells us that she is being silenced against her will, and our common sense of the sanctity of freedom of speech reacts to her predicament in the photo.

As you review the various visual presentations throughout the text, consider the ways symbolism, brand recognition, stereotyping, and cultural expectations contribute to how such illustrations communicate their ideas. Try to think abstractly, taking into account the many different levels of consciousness that visuals use to communicate. Consider also the way shading, lighting, and subject placement in the photos all converge to make a point. "Read" them as you would any text, as part of the overall purpose of this book to "explore language."

In the chapters that follow, you will discover more than one hundred different selections—both written and visual—that range widely across contemporary language matters that we hope you will find exciting and thought provoking. Arranged thematically into nine chapters, the writings represent widely diverse language topics—from the evolution of English from tribal dialects to cybernetic slang; from the dangers of political gobbledygook to the pleasures of language that make us laugh; from the way TV influences our general discourse to gender differences in language; from arguments against the use of Indian names and mascots by sports teams to arguments for and against campus speech codes. Some of the topics will be familiar; others will be first-time exposure. Regardless of how these language issues touch your experience, critical thinking, critical reading, and critical writing will open you up to a deeper understanding of our language, our culture, and of yourself as a vital member of that language community.

SOME USEFUL URLS ON WRITING AND LANGUAGE

Search Engines

- Alta Vista: <http://altavista.com>
- Google: <http://google.com>
- Lycos: <http://lycos.cs.cmu.edu/>
- WebCrawler: <http://webcrawler.com/>
- Yahoo: <http://www.yahoo.com/>

Online Writing Resources

- The Modern Language Association (MLA) Guide to Style
  <http://www.wilpaterson.edu/wpcpages/library/mla.htm>
- The American Psychological Association (APA) Guide to Style
  <http://www.wilpaterson.edu/wpcpages/library/apa.htm>
- Roget's Thesaurus <www.thesaurus.com>
- Merriam-Webster Dictionary <www.m-w.com>
- Merriam Webster Slang Dictionary
  <www.m-w.com/lighter/flap.htm>
- Quotations <http://www.starlingtech.com/quotes/ >
- Bartletts Familiar Quotations
  <www.bartlettquotations.com>
- The Internet Public Library's Online Literary Criticism Collection contains more than one thousand critical and biographical Web sites about authors and works that can be referenced by author, title, or literary period.
  <www.ipl.org/ref/litcrit/>

- Project Gutenberg provides a huge library of electronically sorted books that can be downloaded for free and viewed offline. <www.promo.net/pg / >

- The University of California, Santa Barbara, maintains a Web site on general English literature resources, as well as categories for time period and genre. <www.ucsb.edu/shuttle/english.html>

- The Academy of American Poet's Web site features an online poet database and critical essays on writing about poetry. <www.poets.org>

- The Write Way contains one of the best lists of Web site links for students of writing on the Internet. Included here are links to dictionaries, style guides, professional writers associations, leading newspapers, encyclopedias, movie reviews, and so forth. <http://www.mailbag.com/users/lrjohnson/Writing.html>

Breaking Silences

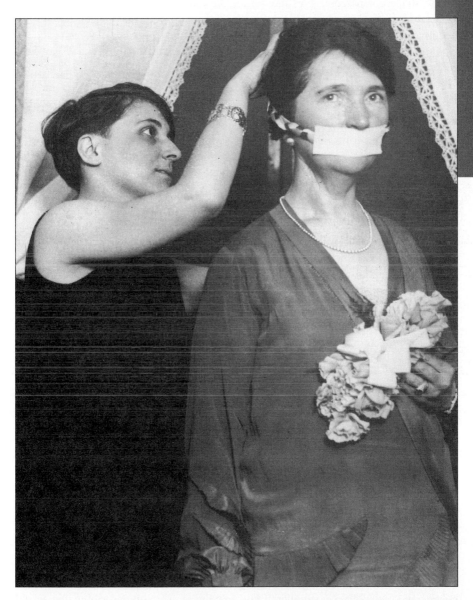

■ Social change doesn't happen through silence and inaction. Throughout history, some voices rose above the pack to speak out against discrimination and oppression. One such voice belonged to Margaret Sanger (1879–1966) who championed women's rights. This image from 1929 shows Sanger satirizing how she was silenced by lawmakers for speaking out about birth control.

Language is such an intricate part of culture that we often lose sight of its power: how language leads and misleads us; how it is used to distort reality, to hurt others, and to shape our perception of the world. We may also take for granted how language empowers us, and how it can forge understanding, break silences, and inspire action. In this chapter we will explore the ways language "breaks silences"—that is, how the power of language moves us as individuals, as social beings, and as leaders.

Beginnings: Moving from Silence into Language

We begin this chapter with a look at some fundamental aspects of language that may open your eyes to truths about it and about yourself. The book begins with an essay by linguist Susanne K. Langer who examines the uniquely human phenomenon of language symbolism. "Language and Thought" explores the relationship between word and thought and the difference between symbols and signs—differences that separate humans from the rest of the animal kingdom. In "A Brief History of English," Paul Roberts discusses the evolution of our native language beginning with the tongue of obscure Germanic tribes that invaded England in the sixth century to the contemporary English spoken by over 350 million people around the world. But as C. M. Millward explains in "The Story of Writing," civilization still depends on the written word. This aspect of the power of written language is examined by Margalit Fox in "Another Language for the Deaf," in which she takes a closer look at a new type of pictographic writing that crosses the boundaries of language itself. The section is capped with some examples of this remarkable form of communication.

Personal Recollections: Coming into Language

As individuals, we come to language in different ways, yet we share in the magic that opens the world to us and us to it. The next four essays explore how people from diverse backgrounds discovered the power of the word in shaping the world and the self within it. In "Homemade Education," Malcolm X explains how as a young man he was possessed by words. He did not discover the power of words in a school library or the cozy confines of a bedroom, but in a prison cell, where the influential black leader taught himself how to read and write, liberating his mind while his body was behind bars. "A Word for Everything" describes how the blind and deaf Helen Keller literally broke her silence when she discovered "the key to all language" and connected the concept of words to the things around her. Next, Maxine Hong Kingston, the daughter of Chinese immigrants, describes her traumatizing introduction to the English language. The way young children come into language, and their simple yet incredibly perceptive way of describing the world around them is explored by Susan Kinsolving in her poem, "The Jellyfish." The section ends with Christine Marín's equally dramatic account of her discovery of the power of language to shape one's identity in "Spanish Lessons."

Leadership: Speeches That Challenged the Status Quo

The final section in this chapter takes a look at how some people used language to challenge social convention and assumption. Many of these speakers took personal risk in using their voices to confront issues connected to racism, personal liberty, and inequality. Often speaking for a powerless or silenced segment of society, these speakers incited social change through a powerful use of language. First, Elizabeth Cady Stanton's "Seneca Falls Declaration" on women's suffrage demands equal political representation for women. Sojourner Truth lends her voice to this issue as both a woman, and a former slave in "Aren't I a Woman?" The matter of civil rights is addressed by Martin Luther King, Jr. in "A Letter from Birmingham Jail," in which he argues compellingly that nonviolent protest can end hatred and bigotry. Finally, Eleanor Roosevelt addresses basic human rights and freedoms for people of all nations in a speech presented to the United Nations in "The Struggle for Human Rights." As you read the articles and inspect the visuals in this section, consider how the words and actions of these individuals challenged us to think, and changed our world by breaking silences.

■ BEGINNINGS: MOVING FROM SILENCE INTO LANGUAGE

Language and Thought
Susanne K. Langer

Language is the highest intellectual activity we practice. It is the way we define ourselves—who we are as a species, as a society, as a culture, and as individuals. It is the basis of thought because it contains the symbols of thought. How are thought and language connected? How do signs, which even some animals respond to, differ from the symbols that constitute language? The following essay by Susanne Langer answers these and many other questions about language and thought.

Susanne Langer was one of the twentieth century's most influential philosophers. A graduate of Radcliffe and Harvard, she is the author of *Philosophy in a New Key: A Study in the Symbolism of Reason, Rite and Art* (1942) and *Language and Myth* (1946). She died in 1985, a few years after completing the culmination of her life's work, the three-volume *Mind: An Essay on Human Feeling* (1982).

1 A symbol is not the same thing as a sign; that is a fact that psychologists and philosophers often overlook. All intelligent animals use signs; so do we. To them as well as to us sounds and smells and motions are signs of food, danger, the presence of other beings, or of rain or storm. Furthermore, some animals not only attend to

signs but produce them for the benefit of others. Dogs bark at the door to be let in; rabbits thump to call each other; the cooing of doves and the growl of a wolf defending his kill are unequivocal signs of feelings and intentions to be reckoned with by other creatures.

2   We use signs just as animals do, though with considerably more elaboration. We stop at red lights and go on green; we answer calls and bells, watch the sky for coming storms, read trouble or promise or anger in each other's eyes. That is animal intelligence raised to the human level. Those of us who are dog lovers can probably all tell wonderful stories of how high our dogs have sometimes risen in the scale of clever sign interpretation and sign using.

3   A sign is anything that announces the existence or the imminence of some event, the presence of a thing or a person, or a change in the state of affairs. There are signs of the weather, signs of danger, signs of future good or evil, signs of what the past has been. In every case a sign is closely bound up with something to be noted or expected in experience. It is always a part of the situation to which it refers, though the reference may be remote in space and time. Insofar as we are led to note or expect the signified event we are making correct use of a sign. This is the essence of rational behavior, which animals show in varying degrees. It is entirely realistic, being closely bound up with the actual objective course of history—learned by experience, and cashed in or voided by further experience.

4   If man had kept to the straight and narrow path of sign using, he would be like the other animals, though perhaps a little brighter. He would not talk, but grunt and gesticulate the point. He would make his wishes known, give warnings, perhaps develop a social system like that of bees and ants, with such a wonderful efficiency of communal enterprise that all men would have plenty to eat, warm apartments—all exactly alike and perfectly convenient—to live in, and everybody could and would sit in the sun or by the fire, as the climate demanded, not talking but just basking, with every want satisfied, most of his life. The young would romp and make love, the old would sleep, the middle-aged would do the routine work almost unconsciously and eat a great deal. But that would be the life of a social, superintelligent, purely sign-using animal.

5   To us who are human, it does not sound very glorious. We want to go places and do things, own all sorts of gadgets that we do not absolutely need, and when we sit down to take it easy we want to talk. Rights and property, social position, special talents and virtues, and above all our ideas, are what we live for. We have gone off on a tangent that takes us far away from the mere biological cycle that animal generations accomplish; and that is because we can use not only signs but symbols.

6   A symbol differs from a sign in that it does not announce the presence of the object, the being, condition, or whatnot, which is its meaning, but merely *brings this thing to mind*. It is not a mere "substitute sign" to which we react as though it were the object itself. The fact is that our reaction to hearing a person's name is quite different from our reaction to the person himself. There are certain rare cases where a symbol stands directly for its meaning: in religious experience, for instance, the Host is not only a symbol but a Presence. But symbols in the ordinary sense are not mystic. They are the same sort of thing that ordinary signs are; only

they do not call our attention to something necessarily present or to be physically dealt with—they call up merely a conception of the thing they "mean."

7   The difference between a sign and a symbol is, in brief, that a sign causes us to think or act *in the face* of the thing signified, whereas a symbol causes us to think *about* the thing symbolized. Therein lies the great importance of symbolism for human life, its power to make this life so different from any other animal biography that generations of men have found it incredible to suppose that they were of purely zoological origin. A sign is always embedded in reality, in a present that emerges from the actual past and stretches to the future; but a symbol may be divorced from reality altogether. It may refer to what is not the case, to a mere idea, a figment, a dream. It serves, therefore, to liberate thought from the immediate stimuli of a physically present world; and that liberation marks the essential difference between human and nonhuman mentality. Animals think, but they think *of* and *at* things; men think primarily *about* things. Words, pictures, and memory images are symbols that may be combined and varied in a thousand ways. The result is a symbolic structure whose meaning is a complex of all their respective meanings, and this kaleidoscope of *ideas* is the typical product of the human brain that we call the "stream of thought."

8   The process of transforming all direct experience into imagery or into that supreme mode of symbolic expression, language, has so completely taken possession of the human mind that it is not only a special talent but a dominant, organic need. All our sense impressions leave their traces in our memory not only as signs disposing our practical reactions in the future but also as symbols, images representing our *ideas* of things; and the tendency to manipulate ideas, to combine and abstract, mix and extend them by playing with symbols, is man's outstanding characteristic. It seems to be what his brain most naturally and spontaneously does. Therefore his primitive mental function is not judging reality, but *dreaming his desires.*

9   Dreaming is apparently a basic function of human brains, for it is free and unexhausting like our metabolism, heartbeat, and breath. It is easier to dream than not to dream, as it is easier to breathe than to refrain from breathing. The symbolic character of dreams is fairly well established. Symbol mongering, on this ineffectual, uncritical level, seems to be instinctive, the fulfillment of an elementary need rather than the purposeful exercise of a high and difficult talent.

10   The special power of man's mind rests on the evolution of this special activity, not on any transcendently high development of animal intelligence. We are not immeasurably higher than other animals; we are different. We have a biological need and with it a biological gift that they do not share.

11   Because man has not only the ability but the constant need of *conceiving* what has happened to him, what surrounds him, what is demanded of him—in short, of symbolizing nature, himself, and his hopes and fears—he has a constant and crying need of *expression.* What he cannot express, he cannot conceive; what he cannot conceive is chaos, and fills him with terror.

12   If we bear in mind this all-important craving for expression, we get a new picture of man's behavior; for from this trait spring his powers and his weaknesses. The process of symbolic transformation that all our experiences undergo is nothing

more nor less than the process of *conception,* underlying the human faculties of abstraction and imagination.

13   When we are faced with a strange or difficult situation, we cannot react directly, as other creatures do, with flight, aggression, or any such simple instinctive pattern. Our whole reaction depends on how we manage to conceive the situation—whether we cast it in a definite dramatic form, whether we see it as a disaster, a challenge, a fulfillment of doom, or a fiat of the Divine Will. In words or dreamlike images, in artistic or religious or even in cynical form, we must *construe* the events of life. There is great virtue in the figure of speech, "I can *make* nothing of it," to express a failure to understand something. Thought and memory are processes of *making* the thought content and the memory image; the pattern of our ideas is given by the symbols through which we express them. And in the course of manipulating those symbols we inevitably distort the original experience, as we abstract certain features of it, embroider and reinforce those features with other ideas, until the conception we project on the screen of memory is quite different from anything in our real history.

14   Conception is a necessary and elementary process; what we do with our conceptions is another story. That is the entire history of human culture—of intelligence and morality, folly and superstition, ritual, language, and the arts—all the phenomena that set man apart from, and above, the rest of the animal kingdom. As the religious mind has to make all human history a drama of sin and salvation in order to define its own moral attitudes, so a scientist wrestles with the mere presentation of "the facts" before he can reason about them. The process of *envisaging* facts, values, hopes, and fears underlies our whole behavior pattern; and this process is reflected in the evolution of an extraordinary phenomenon found always, and only, in human societies—the phenomenon of language.

15   Language is the highest and most amazing achievement of the symbolistic human mind. The power it bestows is almost inestimable, for without it anything properly called "thought" is impossible. The birth of language is the dawn of humanity. The line between man and beast—between the highest ape and the lowest savage—is the language line. Whether the primitive Neanderthal man was anthropoid or human depends less on his cranial capacity, his upright posture, or even his use of tools and fire, than on one issue we shall probably never be able to settle—whether or not he spoke.

16   In all physical traits and practical responses, such as skills and visual judgments, we can find a certain continuity between animal and human mentality. Sign using is an ever evolving, ever improving function throughout the whole animal kingdom, from the lowly worm that shrinks into his hole at the sound of an approaching foot, to the dog obeying his master's command, and even to the learned scientist who watches the movements of an index needle.

17   This continuity of the sign-using talent has led psychologists to the belief that language is evolved from the vocal expressions, grunts and coos and cries, whereby animals vent their feelings or signal their fellows; that man has elaborated this sort of communion to the point where it makes a perfect exchange of ideas possible.

18   I do not believe that this doctrine of the origin of language is correct. The essence of language is symbolic, not signific; we use it first and most vitally to formulate and hold ideas in our own minds. Conception, not social control, is its first and foremost benefit.

19   Watch a young child that is just learning to speak play with a toy; he says the name of the object, e.g.: "Horsey! horsey! horsey!" over and over again, looks at the object, moves it, always saying the name to himself or to the world at large. It's quite a time before he talks to anyone in particular; he talks first of all to himself. This is his way of forming and fixing the *conception* of the object in his mind, and around this conception all his knowledge of it grows. *Names* are the essence of language; for the *name* is what abstracts the conception of the horse from the horse itself, and lets the mere idea recur at the speaking of the name. This permits the conception gathered from one horse experience to be exemplified again by another instance of a horse, so that the notion embodied in the name is a general notion.

20   To this end, the baby uses a word long before he *asks* for the object; when he wants his horsey he is likely to cry and fret, because he is reacting to an actual environment, not forming ideas. He uses the animal language of *signs* for his wants; talking is still a purely symbolic process—its practical value has not really impressed him yet.

21   Language need not be vocal; it may be purely visual, like written language, or even tactual, like the deaf-mute system of speech; but it *must be denotative*. The sounds, intended or unintended, whereby animals communicate do not constitute a language because they are signs, not names. They never fall into an organic pattern, a meaningful syntax of even the most rudimentary sort, as all language seems to do with a sort of driving necessity. That is because signs refer to actual situations, in which things have obvious relations to each other that require only to be noted; but symbols refer to ideas, which are not physically there for inspection, so their connections and features have to be represented. This gives all true language a natural tendency toward growth and development, which seems almost like a life of its own. Languages are not invented; they grow with our need for expression.

22   In contrast, animal "speech" never has a structure. It is merely an emotional response. Apes may greet their ration of yams with a shout of "Nga!" But they do not say "Nga" between meals. If they could *talk about* their yams instead of just saluting them, they would be the most primitive men instead of the most anthropoid of beasts. They would have ideas, and tell each other things true or false, rational or irrational; they would make plans and invent laws and sing their own praises, as men do.

THINKING CRITICALLY

1. Langer's opening statement is "A symbol is not the same thing as a sign." In your own words, what is the difference between signs and symbols? Give some examples from your own experience.

2. What would human beings be like if they used only signs? What would be the state of human communications?

3. According to Langer, how did language develop?

4. Langer says that symbols cause us to think about the thing symbolized. What do the following symbols make us think about, or what messages are communicated by them: clothes with the Tommy Hilfiger trademark on them; a dorm windowsill stacked with beer cans; an American flag pin; a peace sign window decal; a Harley-Davidson motorcycle; a swastika; a happy face button?

5. In the opening paragraphs, Langer uses comparison to clarify the differences between signs and symbols. What comparisons does she specifically use? How effective are they in helping the reader understand her points?

6. In paragraph 2, Langer gives some examples of signs, yet she waits until paragraph 3 to define *sign.* Why do you think she uses this strategy? Is it effective for her purpose?

WRITING ASSIGNMENTS

1. Write a paper entitled "A Sign of the Times" in which you choose and discuss an appropriate sign of the state of today's world.

2. Write an essay describing all the different symbols and signs to which you responded on your way to class today.

3. What are some of the signs and symbols of the Internet? Write an essay in which you describe how Internet symbols have changed our world.

4. The very clothes we wear convey symbolic messages of some sort—socioeconomic status, awareness, worldliness, sometimes even political statements. Describe some of the messages you like to project through your choice of clothing, boots, shoes, jewelry, and so on.

A Brief History of English
Paul Roberts

While nobody knows exactly how languages began, Paul Roberts explains in this famous essay that language development is best understood if we examine its historical transformations. With engaging storytelling flair, Roberts makes accessible the long and complicated evolution of the English language. Tracing over 1,400 turbulent years from its Anglo-Saxon roots to the contemporary utterances of over 600 million people around the world, Roberts's brief history makes clear that language is in a constant state of change. Every day the English language adds new words to its lexicon, redefines old ones, and grows in dialectical diversity.

Paul Roberts was a well-known linguist and author of several books on English history and grammar including *Patterns of English* (1956) and *Understanding English* (1958), from which this essay was adopted.

1 No understanding of the English language can be very satisfactory without a notion of the history of the language. But we shall have to make do with just a notion. The history of English is long and complicated, and we can only hit the high spots.

2 The history of our language begins a little after A.D. 600. Everything before that is pre-history, which means that we can guess at it but can't prove much. For a thousand years or so before the birth of Christ our linguistic ancestors were savages wandering through the forests of northern Europe. Their language was a part of the Germanic branch of the Indo-European family.

3 At the time of the Roman Empire—say, from the beginning of the Christian Era to around A.D. 400—the speakers of what was to become English were scattered along the northern coast of Europe. They spoke a dialect of Low German. More exactly, they spoke several different dialects, since they were several different tribes. The names given to the tribes who got to English are *Angles, Saxons,* and *Jutes.* For convenience, we can refer to them all as Anglo-Saxons.

4 Their first contact with civilization was a rather thin acquaintance with the Roman Empire on whose borders they lived. Probably some of the Anglo-Saxons wandered into the Empire occasionally, and certainly Roman merchants and traders traveled among the tribes. At any rate, this period saw the first of our many borrowings from Latin. Such words as *kettle, wine, cheese, butter, cheap, plum, gem, bishop, church* were borrowed at this time. They show something of the relationship of the Anglo-Saxons with the Romans. The Anglo-Saxons were learning, getting their first taste of civilization.

5 They still had a long way to go, however, and their first step was to help smash the civilization they were learning from. In the fourth century the Roman power weakened badly. While the Goths were pounding away at the Romans in the Mediterranean countries, their relatives, the Anglo-Saxons, began to attack Britain.

6 The Romans had been the ruling power in Britain since A.D. 43. They had subjugated the Celts whom they found living there and had succeeded in setting up a Roman administration. The Roman influence did not extend to the outlying parts of the British Isles. In Scotland, Wales, and Ireland the Celts remained free and wild, and they made periodic forays against the Romans in England. Among other defense measures, the Romans built the famous Roman Wall to ward off the tribes in the north.

7 Even in England the Roman power was thin. Latin did not become the language of the country as it did in Gaul and Spain. The mass of people continued to speak Celtic, with Latin and the Roman civilization it contained in use as a top dressing.

8 In the fourth century, troubles multiplied for the Romans in Britain. Not only did the untamed tribes of Scotland and Wales grow more and more restive, but the Anglo-Saxons began to make pirate raids on the eastern coast. Furthermore, there was growing difficulty everywhere in the Empire, and the legions in Britain were siphoned off to fight elsewhere. Finally, in A.D. 410, the last Roman ruler in England, bent on becoming emperor, left the islands and took the last of the legions with him. The Celts were left in possession of Britain but almost defenseless against the impending Anglo-Saxon attack.

9   Not much is surely known about the arrival of the Anglo-Saxons in England. According to the best early source, the eighth-century historian Bede, the Jutes came in 449 in response to a plea from the Celtic king, Vortigern, who wanted their help against the Picts attacking from the north. The Jutes subdued the Picts but then quarreled and fought with Vortigern, and, with reinforcements from the Continent, settled permanently in Kent. Somewhat later the Angles established themselves in eastern England and the Saxons in the south and west. Bede's account is plausible enough, and these were probably the main lines of the invasion.

10   We do know, however, that the Angles, Saxons, and Jutes were a long time securing themselves in England. Fighting went on for as long as a hundred years before the Celts in England were all killed, driven into Wales, or reduced to slavery. This is the period of King Arthur, who was not entirely mythological. He was a Romanized Celt, a general, though probably not a king. He had some success against the Anglo-Saxons, but it was only temporary. By 550 or so the Anglo-Saxons were finally established. English was in England.

11   All this is pre-history, so far as the language is concerned. We have no record of the English language until after 600, when the Anglo-Saxons were converted to Christianity and learned the Latin alphabet. The conversion began, to be precise, in the year 597 and was accomplished within thirty or forty years. The conversion was a great advance for the Anglo-Saxons, not only because of the spiritual benefits but because it reestablished contact with what remained of Roman civilization. This civilization didn't amount to much in the year 600, but it was certainly superior to anything in England up to that time.

12   It is customary to divide the history of the English language into three periods: Old English, Middle English, and Modern English. Old English runs from the earliest records—i.e., seventh century—to about 1100; Middle English from 1100 to 1450 or 1500; Modern English from 1500 to the present day. Sometimes Modern English is further divided into Early Modern, 1500–1700, and Late Modern, 1700 to the present.

13   When England came into history, it was divided into several more or less autonomous kingdoms, some of which at times exercised a certain amount of control over the others. In the century after the conversion the most advanced kingdom was Northumbria, the area between the Humber River and the Scottish border. By A.D. 700 the Northumbrians had developed a respectable civilization, the finest in Europe. It is sometimes called the Northumbrian Renaissance, and it was the first of the several renaissances through which Europe struggled upward out of the ruins of the Roman Empire. It was in this period that the best of the Old English literature was written, including the epic poem *Beowulf.*

14   In the eighth century, Northumbrian power declined, and the center of influence moved southward to Mercia, the kingdom of the Midlands. A century later the center shifted again, and Wessex, the country of the West Saxons, became the leading power. The most famous king of the West Saxons was Alfred the Great, who reigned in the second half of the ninth century, dying in 901. He was famous not only as a military man and administrator but also as a champion of learning. He

founded and supported schools and translated or caused to be translated many books from Latin into English. At this time also much of the Northumbrian literature of two centuries earlier was copied in West Saxon. Indeed, the great bulk of Old English writing which has come down to us is in the West Saxon dialect of 900 or later.

15   In the military sphere, Alfred's great accomplishment was his successful opposition to the Viking invasions. In the ninth and tenth centuries, the Norsemen emerged in their ships from their homelands in Denmark and the Scandinavian peninsula. They traveled far and attacked and plundered at will and almost with impunity. They ravaged Italy and Greece, settled in France, Russia, and Ireland, colonized Iceland and Greenland, and discovered America several centuries before Columbus. Nor did they overlook England.

16   After many years of hit-and-run raids, the Norsemen landed an army on the east coast of England in the year 866. There was nothing much to oppose them except the Wessex power led by Alfred. The long struggle ended in 877 with a treaty by which a line was drawn roughly from the northwest of England to the southeast. On the eastern side of the line Norse rule was to prevail. This was called the Danelaw. The western side was to be governed by Wessex.

17   The linguistic result of all this was a considerable injection of Norse into the English language. Norse was at this time not so different from English as Norwegian or Danish is now. Probably speakers of English could understand, more or less, the language of the newcomers who had moved into eastern England. At any rate, there was considerable interchange and word borrowing. Examples of Norse words in the English language are *sky, give, law, egg, outlaw, leg, ugly, scant, sly, crawl, scowl, take, thrust.* There are hundreds more. We have even borrowed some pronouns from Norse *they, their,* and *them.* These words were borrowed first by the eastern and northern dialects and then in the course of hundreds of years made their way into English generally.

18   It is supposed also—indeed, it must be true—that the Norsemen influenced the sound structure and the grammar of English. But this is hard to demonstrate in detail.

19   We may now have an example of Old English. The favorite illustration is the Lord's Prayer, since it needs no translation. This has come to us in several different versions. Here is one:

> Fæder ure [thorn]u[eth]e eart on heofonum si [thorn]in nama gehalgod. Tobecume [thorn]in rice. Gewur[eth]e [thorn]in willa on eor[eth]an swa swa on heofonum. Urne gedæghwamlican hlaf syle us to dæg. And forgyf us ure gyltas swa swa we forgyfa[thorn] urum glytendum. And ne gelæd [thorn]u us on costnunge ac alys us of yfele. So[eth]lice.

20   Some of the differences between this and Modern English are merely differences in orthography. For instance, the sign *æ* is what Old English writers used for a vowel sound like that in modern *hat* or *and.* The *th* sounds of modern *thin* or *then* are represented in Old English by [thorn] or [eth]. But of course there are many differences in sound too. *Ure* is the ancestor of modern *our,* but the first vowel was

like that in *too* or *ooze. Hlaf* is modern *loaf;* we have dropped the *h* sound and changed the vowel, which in *hlaf* was pronounced something like the vowel in *father.* Old English had some sounds which we do not have. The sound represented by *y* does not occur in Modern English. If you pronounce the vowel in *bit* with your lips rounded, you may approach it.

21   In grammar, Old English was much more highly inflected than Modern English is. That is, there were more case endings for nouns, more person and number endings for verbs, a more complicated pronoun system, various endings for adjectives, and so on. Old English nouns had four cases—nominative, genitive, dative, accusative. Adjectives had five—all these and an instrumental case besides. Present-day English has only two cases for nouns—common case and possessive case. Adjectives now have no case system at all. On the other hand, we now use a more rigid word order and more structure words (prepositions, auxiliaries, and the like) to express relationships than Old English did.

22   Some of this grammar we can see in the Lord's Prayer. *Heofonum,* for instance, is a dative plural; the nominative singular was *heofon. Urne* is an accusative singular; the nominative is *ure.* In *urum gyltendum* both words are dative plural. *Forgyfap* is the third person plural form of the verb. Word order is different: "urne gedæghwamlican hlaf syle us" in place of "Give us our daily bread." And so on.

23   In vocabulary Old English is quite different from Modern English. Most of the Old English words are what we may call native English: that is, words which have not been borrowed from other languages but which have been a part of English ever since English was a part of Indo-European. Old English did certainly contain borrowed words. We have seen that many borrowings were coming in from Norse. Rather large numbers had been borrowed from Latin, too. Some of these were taken while the Anglo-Saxons were still on the continent (*cheese, butter, bishop, kettle,* etc.); a large number came into English after Conversion (*angel, candle, priest, martyr, radish, oyster, purple, school, spend,* etc.). But the great majority of Old English words were native English.

24   Now, on the contrary, the majority of words in English are borrowed, taken mostly from Latin and French. Of the words in *The American College Dictionary* only about 14 percent are native. Most of these, to be sure, are common, high-frequency words—*the, of, I, and, because, man, mother, road,* etc.; of the thousand most common words in English, some 62 percent are native English. Even so, the modern vocabulary is very much Latinized and Frenchified. The Old English vocabulary was not.

25   Sometime between the year 1000 and 1200 various important changes took place in the structure of English, and Old English became Middle English. The political event which facilitated these changes was the Norman Conquest. The Normans, as the name shows, came originally from Scandinavia. In the early tenth century they established themselves in northern France, adopted the French language, and developed a vigorous kingdom and a very passable civilization. In the year 1066, led by Duke William, they crossed the Channel and made themselves masters

of England. For the next several hundred years, England was ruled by kings whose first language was French.

26 One might wonder why, after the Norman Conquest, French did not become the national language, replacing English entirely. The reason is that the Conquest was not a national migration, as the earlier Anglo-Saxon invasion had been. Great numbers of Normans came to England, but they came as rulers and landlords. French became the language of the court, the language of the nobility, the language of polite society, the language of literature. But it did not replace English as the language of the people. There must always have been hundreds of towns and villages in which French was never heard except when visitors of high station passed through.

27 But English, though it survived as the national language, was profoundly changed after the Norman Conquest. Some of the changes—in sound structure and grammar—would no doubt have taken place whether there had been a Conquest or not. Even before 1066 the case system of English nouns and adjectives was becoming simplified; people came to rely more on word order and prepositions than on inflectional endings to communicate their meanings. The process was speeded up by sound changes which caused many of the endings to sound alike. But no doubt the Conquest facilitated the change. German, which didn't experience a Norman Conquest, is today rather highly inflected compared to its cousin English.

28 But it is in vocabulary that the effects of the Conquest are most obvious. French ceased, after a hundred years or so, to be the native language of very many people in England, but it continued—and continues still—to be a zealously cultivated second language, the mirror of elegance and civilization. When one spoke English, one introduced not only French ideas and French things but also their French names. This was not only easy but socially useful. To pepper one's conversation with French expressions was to show that one was well-bred, elegant, *au courant*. The last sentence shows that the process is not yet dead. By using *au courant* instead of, say, *abreast of things*, the writer indicates that he is no dull clod who knows only English but an elegant person aware of how things are done in *le haut monde*.

29 Thus French words came into English, all sorts of them. There were words to do with government: *parliament, majesty, treaty, alliance, tax, government;* church words: *parson, sermon, baptism, incense, crucifix, religion;* words for foods: *veal, beef, mutton, bacon, jelly, peach, lemon, cream, biscuit;* colors: *blue, scarlet, vermilion;* household words: *curtain, chair, lamp, towel, blanket, parlor;* play words: *dance, chess, music, leisure, conversation;* literary words: *story, romance, poet, literary;* learned words: *study, logic, grammar, noun, surgeon, anatomy, stomach;* just ordinary words of all sorts: *nice, second, very, age, bucket, gentle, final, fault, flower, cry, count, sure, move, surprise, plain.*

30 All these and thousands more poured into the English vocabulary between 1100 and 1500, until at the end of that time many people must have had more French words than English at their command. This is not to say that English be-

came French. English remained English in sound structure and in grammar, though these also felt the ripples of French influence. The very heart of the vocabulary, too, remained English. Most of the high-frequency words—the pronouns, the prepositions, the conjunctions, the auxiliaries, as well as a great many ordinary nouns and verbs and adjectives—were not replaced by borrowings.

31   Middle English, then, was still a Germanic language, but it differed from Old English in many ways. The sound system and the grammar changed a good deal. Speakers made less use of case systems and other inflectional devices and relied more on word order and structure words to express their meanings. This is often said to be a simplification, but it isn't really. Languages don't become simpler; they merely exchange one kind of complexity for another. Modern English is not a simple language, as any foreign speaker who tries to learn it will hasten to tell you.

32   For us Middle English is simpler than Old English just because it is closer to Modern English. It takes three or four months at least to learn to read Old English prose and more than that for poetry. But a week of good study should put one in touch with the Middle English poet Chaucer. Indeed, you may be able to make some sense of Chaucer straight off, though you would need instruction in pronunciation to make it sound like poetry. Here is a famous passage from the *General Prologue to the Canterbury Tales,* fourteenth century:

> Ther was also a nonne, a Prioresse.
> That of hir smyling was ful symple and coy,
> Hir gretteste oath was but by Seinte Loy,
> And she was cleped Madam Eglentyne.
> Ful wel she song the service dyvyne,
> Entuned in hir nose ful semely.
> And Frenshe she spak ful faire and fetisly,
> After the scole of Stratford-atte-Bowe,
> For Frenshe of Parys was to hir unknowe.

33   Sometime between 1400 and 1600 English underwent a couple of sound changes which made the language of Shakespeare quite different from that of Chaucer. Incidentally, these changes contributed much to the chaos in which English spelling now finds itself.

34   One change was the elimination of a vowel sound in certain unstressed positions at the end of words. For instance, the words *name, stone, wine, dance* were pronounced as two syllables by Chaucer but as just one by Shakespeare. The *e* in these words became, as we say, "silent." But it wasn't silent for Chaucer; it represented a vowel sound. So also the words *laughed, seemed, stored* would have been pronounced by Chaucer as two-syllable words. The change was an important one because it affected thousands of words and gave a different aspect to the whole language.

35   The other change is what is called the Great Vowel Shift. This was a systematic shifting of half a dozen vowels and diphthongs in stressed syllables. For in-

stance, the word *name* had in Middle English a vowel something like that in the modern word *father; wine* had the vowel of modern *mean; he* was pronounced something like modern *hey; mouse* sounded like *moose; moon* had the vowel of *moan.* Again the shift was thoroughgoing and affected all the words in which these vowel sounds occurred. Since we still keep the Middle English system of spelling these words, the differences between Modern English and Middle English are often more real than apparent.

36   The vowel shift has meant also that we have come to use an entirely different set of symbols for representing vowel sounds than is used by writers of such languages as French, Italian, or Spanish, in which no such vowel shift occurred. If you come across a strange word—say, *bine*—in an English book, you will pronounce it according to the English system, with the vowel of *wine* or *dine.* But if you read *bine* in a French, Italian, or Spanish book, you will pronounce it with the vowel of *mean* or *seen.*

37   These two changes, then, produced the basic differences between Middle English and Modern English. But there were several other developments that had an effect upon the language. One was the invention of printing, an invention introduced into England by William Caxton in the year 1475. Where before books had been rare and costly, they suddenly became cheap and common. More and more people learned to read and write. This was the first of many advances in communication which have worked to unify languages and to arrest the development of dialect differences, though of course printing affects writing principally rather than speech. Among other things it hastened the standardization of spelling.

38   The period of Early Modern English—that is, the sixteenth and seventeenth centuries—was also the period of the English Renaissance, when people developed, on the one hand, a keen interest in the past and, on the other, a more daring and imaginative view of the future. New ideas multiplied, and new ideas meant new language. Englishmen had grown accustomed to borrowing words from French as a result of the Norman Conquest; now they borrowed from Latin and Greek. As we have seen, English had been raiding Latin from Old English times and before, but now the floodgates really opened, and thousands of words from the classical languages poured in. *Pedestrian, bonus, anatomy, contradict, climax, dictionary, benefit, multiply, exist, paragraph, initiate, scene, inspire* are random examples. Probably the average educated American today has more words from French in his vocabulary than from native English sources, and more from Latin than from French.

39   The greatest writer of the Early Modern English period is of course Shakespeare, and the best-known book is the King James Version of the Bible, published in 1611. The Bible (if not Shakespeare) has made many features of Early Modern English perfectly familiar to many people down to present times, even though we do not use these features in present-day speech and writing. For instance, the old pronouns *thou* and *thee* have dropped out of use now, together with their verb forms, but they are still familiar to us in prayer and in Biblical quotation: "Whither thou goest, I will go." Such forms as *hath* and *doth* have been replaced by *has* and

does; "Goes he hence tonight?" would now be "Is he going away tonight?"; Shakespeare's "Fie on't, sirrah" would be "Nuts to that, Mac." Still, all these expressions linger with us because of the power of the works in which they occur.

40   It is not always realized, however, that considerable sound changes have taken place between Early Modern English and the English of the present day. Shakespearean actors putting on a play speak the words, properly enough, in their modern pronunciation. But it is very doubtful that this pronunciation would be understood at all by Shakespeare. In Shakespeare's time, the word *reason* was pronounced like modern *raisin; face* had the sound of modern *glass;* the *l* in *would, should, palm* was pronounced. In these points and a great many others the English language has moved a long way from what it was in 1600.

41   The history of English since 1700 is filled with many movements and countermovements, of which we can notice only a couple. One of these is the vigorous attempt made in the eighteenth century, and the rather halfhearted attempts made since, to regulate and control the English language. Many people of the eighteenth century, not understanding very well the forces which govern language, proposed to polish and prune and restrict English, which they felt was proliferating too wildly. There was much talk of an academy which would rule on what people could and could not say and write. The academy never came into being, but the eighteenth century did succeed in establishing certain attitudes which, though they haven't had much effect on the development of the language itself, have certainly changed the native speaker's feeling about the language.

42   In part a product of the wish to fix and establish the language was the development of the dictionary. The first English dictionary was published in 1603; it was a list of 2500 words briefly defined. Many others were published with gradual improvements until Samuel Johnson published his *English Dictionary* in 1755. This, steadily revised, dominated the field in England for nearly a hundred years. Meanwhile in America, Noah Webster published his dictionary in 1828, and before long dictionary publishing was a big business in this country. The last century has seen the publication of one great dictionary: the twelve-volume *Oxford English Dictionary,* compiled in the course of seventy-five years through the labors of many scholars. We have also, of course, numerous commercial dictionaries which are as good as the public wants them to be if not, indeed, rather better.

43   Another product of the eighteenth century was the invention of "English grammar." As English came to replace Latin as the language of scholarship it was felt that one should also be able to control and dissect it, parse and analyze it, as one could Latin. What happened in practice was that the grammatical description that applied to Latin was removed and superimposed on English. This was silly, because English is an entirely different kind of language, with its own forms and signals and ways of producing meaning. Nevertheless, English grammars on the Latin model were worked out and taught in the schools. In many schools they are still being taught. This activity is not often popular with school children, but it is sometimes an interesting and instructive exercise in logic. The principal harm in it is that it has tended to keep people from being interested in English and has obscured the real features of English structure.

44   But probably the most important force in the development of English in the modern period has been the tremendous expansion of English-speaking peoples. In 1500 English was a minor language, spoken by a few people on a small island. Now it is perhaps the greatest language of the world, spoken natively by over a quarter of a billion people and as a second language by many millions more. When we speak of English now, we must specify whether we mean American English, British English, Australian English, Indian English, or what, since the differences are considerable. The American cannot go to England or the English-man to America confident that he will always understand and be understood. The Alabaman in Iowa or the Iowan in Alabama shows himself a foreigner every time he speaks. It is only because communication has become fast and easy that English in this period of its expansion has not broken into a dozen mutually unintelligible languages.

THINKING CRITICALLY

1. Roberts states in the opening of his essay that there can be no real understanding of the English language without an understanding of its history. Discuss some of the ways, as outlined by Roberts, in which history has had a bearing on the development of the English language since the time of the Roman Empire.

2. In paragraph 4, Roberts lists English words borrowed from Latin, noting that in their nature these words "show something of the relationship of the Anglo-Saxons with the Romans." What kind of relationship do you suppose these two peoples had, based on the list of words given by Roberts?

3. In terms of grammar, Roberts says that Old English was much more highly inflected than Modern English (paragraph 21). What does he mean by this statement?

4. What political event facilitated the change from Old to Middle English? How did this change occur? Do you think that political events still play a part in language development? Explain your answer.

5. What was the position of the French language after the Norman Conquest? What remnants of this class-split society are still reflected in our language today? Can you think of any contemporary societies where there is a class split along language lines—that is, with one language spoken by "polite society" and another by "the people"? How does this language split affect those countries?

6. How does Roberts organize the material in his essay? Is his organizational method effective in terms of the content of the piece? Why or why not?

7. Characterize the style and tone of this essay. To what audience do you suppose Roberts is aiming this piece?

8. Is Roberts successful in demonstrating the connection between history and language development? Locate one or two passages in which you find that connection to be especially strong.

WRITING ASSIGNMENTS

1. Roberts' piece is based on the idea that English has been affected by historical events. Choose a recent event—White House politics, the terrorist attacks of September 11, 2001, the violence in Israel, or the American war with Iraq—and write a paper exploring how English has been influenced by it.

2. Choose a short passage of modern prose. Using a dictionary, look up a dozen of the words in the passage, paying special attention to the origins of the words. Write a paragraph in which you detail your findings, noting whether or not they reflect Roberts' claims about the historical development of the English language.

3. Write a paper on how the Internet and computers in general have influenced our current language. What words have been "invented" or reappropriated by our use of this medium? How do Internet-influenced words cross the boundaries between computers and our common tongue?

The Story of Writing
C. M. Millward

As we have learned from the preceding articles, spoken and written language serve very different purposes. How much does our current language depend on the written word? How does the written word force our language to change, and how does it help it stay the same? The next excerpt by C. M. Millward examines why writing was invented and how writing systems grow and evolve.

A highly regarded language scholar and educator, Millward probes the relationship between speech and the written word and the importance of writing to the study of speech. The following essay is from her book, *The Biography of the English Language* (1996).

To be a well-favoured man is the gift of fortune: but to write and read comes by nature.

William Shakespeare

1 Speech is of course primary to language. People were speaking for hundreds of thousands—perhaps millions—of years before writing was invented. Human beings speak before they learn to read and write; even today, many people never learn to read and write, and there are still languages with no writing systems. People learn how to speak without formal training, but most have to be taught how to read and write. Further, all forms of writing are ultimately based on spoken language. In other words, writing is a derivative of speech; it is a secondary form of language. Speech is, quite properly, the focus of most linguistic study.

2 Nonetheless, we should not underestimate the importance of writing. Civilization as we know it depends on the written word. We study speech by means of writ-

ing and we use writing to represent the phonetics of speech. Most of our information about language, and certainly all of our information about the history of languages, is in writing.

3   Writing has become so important that, for the educated person, it can become almost totally independent of speech. Most of us know many words that we can read, understand, and even write but that we would hesitate to try to pronounce. For example, I think of the word *gneiss*. I know that it is a kind of rock, that it is usually metamorphic in origin, and that (to my untrained eye) it looks somewhat like granite. Yet I do not normally speak this word and I have to refer to a dictionary—another written source—to discover that *gneiss* is pronounced /nɑis/ and not /nis/ or /gnɑis/ or /nɪs/. We also use words and grammatical constructions in writing that we rarely if ever spontaneously produce in speech. Who uses the subordinating conjunction *lest* in a casual conversation? What does a paragraph sound like? Many people read and sometimes even write fluently in languages that they cannot speak. Skilled readers take in and mentally process written texts at a rate so rapid that the words cannot possibly have been silently articulated and "listened to"; clearly, for such readers, writing has become a form of language virtually independent of speech. Finally, there is even physiological evidence that writing is more than simply a secondary form of speech: Some brain-damaged people are competent in reading and writing but are unable to speak or understand speech.

The Effects of Writing on Speech

4   Writing has numerous effects on the spoken language, and the more literate a culture is, the greater these effects are. Because of the prestige, the conservatism, and the permanency of writing, it tends to act as a brake on changes in the spoken language. Conversely, writing tends to spread changes from one area or group of speakers to another; this is especially true of vocabulary items. Most of us can recall new words that we first encountered in a written text and only later—or perhaps never—heard spoken. Writing also preserves archaisms that have been lost in the spoken language and sometimes even revives words that have become obsolete in the spoken language. For example, Edmond Spenser probably introduced *rampant* in the meaning of "fierce" through his writings; the OED's last citation in this meaning prior to Spenser is nearly two hundred years earlier.

5   Writing and literacy give rise to spelling pronunciations, that is, the pronunciation of words as they are spelled. These may take the form of the reinsertion of lost sounds or the insertion of unhistorical sounds. Many people today pronounce the word *often* as [oftən], even though the [t] dropped out of the spoken language centuries ago, and even though they do not pronounce a [t] in such parallel words as *soften* or *listen*. Similarly, because English readers associate the letter sequence <th>* with the sounds [θ] and [ð], words spelled with that sequence that historically

---

*When it is necessary to distinguish graphemic forms phonological representations, angle brackets (< >) are used for the graphemes.

were pronounced with [t] have come to be pronounced with [θ]. Examples include the given names *Katherine* and *Arthur* (compare the short forms *Art* and *Kate* that retain the [t]. The river *Thames* is pronounced [tɛmz] in Britain, but [θemz] in Connecticut because the influence of the spelling proved stronger than earlier oral tradition.

6   Conventional spellings for vocal gestures involving noises outside the English phonemic system may also lead to a literal pronunciation. Examples include the vocal gesture for disapproval or commiseration, an alveolar click. Because this sound is written *tsk-tsk,* it is occasionally pronounced [tɪsk tɪsk]. Even more familiar are the pronunciations [bər:] for <brrr>, a spelling originally intended to represent a voiced bilabial trill, and [i:k] for *eek,* a spelling intended to represent a high-pitched scream.

7   Literacy and our alphabet so permeate our culture that even our vocabulary is affected. The widespread use of acronyms presupposes speakers who are familiar with the letters with which words begin. We even use letter shapes as analogies to describe objects: The words *T square, U-turn, ell* (as a wing of a building), *S-curve,* and *V-neck* are all derived from the names of alphabetic characters.

8   In sum, writing has been such an integral part of English for the past thirteen hundred years or so that it is impossible to image what the spoken language would be like today if English had never been committed to writing. Indeed, without writing, English probably would have split up into numerous mutually unintelligible dialects long ago.

Why Was Writing Invented?

9 Efficient as speech is, it is severely limited in both time and space. Once an utterance has been made, it is gone forever, and the preservation of its contents is dependent on human memory. Writing is as permanent as the materials used in producing it; readers can return to a written record as often as or after as long a period of time as they like. Further, speech is much more limited in space than is writing. Until the recent developments of electronic media—all of which require supplementary apparatus in the form of transmitters and receivers—speech was spatially limited to the range of the unamplified human voice. Writing can be done on portable materials and carried wherever people can go.

10   Although it would perhaps be esthetically comforting to think that the first writing systems were created to preserve literary works, all the evidence indicates that the first true writing was used for far more mundane purposes. Although "creative" literature arose long before the invention of writing, it was orally transmitted, with devices such as alliteration, repetition, and regular meter being used as aids to memory. Writing was invented for the same practical purpose to which, in terms of sheer bulk, most writing today is dedicated, commercial recordkeeping—the number of lambs born in a season, the number of pots of oil shipped to a customer, the wages paid to laborers. A second important early use of writing was to preserve the exact wording of sacred texts that would otherwise be corrupted by imperfect mem-

A POOR DEVIL

Slips of the tongue and pen have always been a part of natural language, but perhaps only medieval monks would invent a patron demon for them. Titivillus, as he was named, collected fragments of mispronounced, mumbled, or skipped words in the divine services. He put them all into a sack and carried them to his master in hell, where they were registered against the offender.

Later, Titivillus's jurisdiction was extended to orthographic and printing errors. He never lacked for material to put in his sack. For instance, when Pope Sixtus V (1585–1590) authorized the printing of a new edition of the Vulgate Bible, he decided to insure against printing errors by automatically excommunicating ahead of time any printer who altered the text in any way. Furthermore, he himself proofread every page as it came off the press. Nonetheless, the final text was so full of errors that the Pope finally had to recall every copy for destruction.

Titivillus was well enough known, both in England and on the Continent, to appear as a character in medieval mystery plays and other literature. Hence, his introduction in *Myroure of Oure Ladye,* an anonymous fifteenth-century devotional treatise.

I am a poure dyuel and my name ys Tytyuyllus ... I muste eche day ... brynge my master a thousande pokes full of faylynges, and of neglygences in syllables and wordes. (Myroure of Oure Ladye 1.xx.54)

ories and changes in the spoken language. For most of the history of writing, literacy has been restricted to a small elite of bookkeepers and priests; often, the two occupations were combined in one scribe. To the illiterate, writing would have seemed a form of magic, an impression that was not discouraged by those who understood its mysteries.

Types of Writing Systems

11   If we can judge by the delight a child takes in its own footprints or scribbles made with any implement on any surface, human beings have always been fascinated by drawing. The urge to create pictures is revealed by the primitive drawings—early forms of graffiti—found in caves and on rocks all over the world. But pictures as such are not writing, although it is not always easy to distinguish pictures from writing. If we define writing as human communication by means of a system of conventional visible marks,* then, in many cases, we do not know whether the marks are systematic because we do not have a large enough sample. Nor do we know if the marks were intended to communicate a message. For example, Figure 1 is an American Indian **petroglyph** (a drawing or carving on rock) from Cottonwood Canyon, Utah. Conceivably, the dotted lines, wavy lines, spiral, and semicircle had some conventional meaning that could be interpreted by a viewer familiar

---

*The definition is adapted from I. J. Gelb, *A Study of Writing,* rev. ed. (Chicago: University of Chicago Press, 1963), p. 12.

Figure 1. American Indian Petroglyph

with the conventions. If so, the petroglyph might be called prewriting, but not actual writing.*

Pictographs and Ideograms

12 More clearly related to writing are the picture stories of American Indians. Like the modern cartoon strip without words, these **pictographs** communicate a message. Further, they often include conventional symbols. Figure 2 is from a birch-bark record made by Shahâsh'king (b), the leader of a group of Mîlle Lacs Ojibwas (a) who undertook a military expedition against Shákopi (e). Shákopi's camp of Sioux (c) was on the St. Peter's river (d). The Ojibwas under Shahâsh'king lost one man (f) at the St. Peter's River, and they got only one arm of an Indian (g).†

13   Although such pictographs do communicate a message, they are not a direct sequential representation of speech. They may include **ideographic** symbols, symbols that represent ideas or concepts but do not stand for specific sounds, syllables, or words. In Figure 2, the drawing at (f) means that the Ojibwas lost one man, but it does not represent a unique series of sounds or words. It could be translated as "We

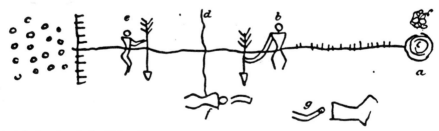

Figure 2. American Indian Picture Story

---

*Drawing adapted from Roland Siegrist, ed., *Prehistoric Petroglyphs and Pictographs in Utah* (Salt Lake City: Utah State Historical Society, 1972), p. 62. Reproduced with permission of the Utah State Historical Society.
†Adapted from Garrick Mallery, "Picture-Writing of the American Indians." in *Tenth Annual Report of the Bureau of Ethnology* (Washington, D.C.: Government Printing Office, 1893), pp. 559–60.

lost one man" or "The Sioux killed a warrior" or "Little Fox died on this expedition" or "One man fell by the river." To take a more familiar example, the picture ☞ is an **ideogram;** it does not represent a sequence of sounds, but rather a concept that can be expressed in English in various ways: "go that way" or "in this direction" or "over there" or, combined with words or other ideographs, such notions as "the stairs are to the right" or "pick up your luggage at that place." Ideograms are not necessarily pictures of objects; the arithmetic "minus sign" is an ideogram that depicts not an object, but a concept that can be translated as "minus" or "subtract the following from the preceding" or "negative."

Logograms

14 Ideograms are not writing, but they are the ancestors of writing. If a particular ideogram is always translated by the same spoken word, it can come to stand for that word and that word alone. At this point, **logograms,** or symbols representing a single word, have been invented, and true writing has begun. Indeed, an entire writing system may be based on the logographic principle. This is the case with Chinese, in which each character stands for a word or part of a compound word. In their purest forms, logographic symbols have no relationship to individual sounds, but only to entire words. For example, the Chinese character 吊 stands for a verb meaning "to hang, to suspend"; it is pronounced roughly as [diɑu] in Standard Chinese, but no particular part of the character represents [d] or [i] or [ɑ] or [u]. By itself, the top part of the character, 口, is pronounced [kou], and the bottom part, 巾, is pronounced [jin]. The character 钓 is pronounced in exactly the same way as 吊, but 钓 means "to fish with a hook and line." Like all writing systems actually used for natural languages, Chinese is less than totally pure; many characters contain both ideograhic and phonetic components. Still, the Chinese system is basically logographic in that each character stands for an entire word or morpheme, and one cannot determine the pronunciation of an unfamiliar character from its components.

15 The distinction between ideograms and logograms is somewhat arbitrary. If, within a given language, a symbol is always interpreted as representing one word and one word alone, it is a logogram for that language. However, if it has the same meaning but is represented by different words in other languages, it is, strictly speaking, an ideogram. An example would be the symbol &, which stands only for the word *and* in English, but for *agus* in Irish, *et* in French, *och* in Swedish, *u* in Russian, *na* in Swahili, and so forth. It is a logogram within a given language, but an ideogram across languages.

Syllabaries

16 Logographic systems are inefficient for most languages because, if every single word in the language is to be represented by a different symbol, an astronomical number of complex symbols is required. Therefore, while the writing is still at the ideographic-logographic stage, scribes may begin to use symbols to represent

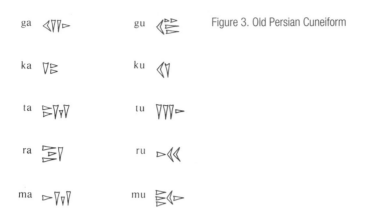

Figure 3. Old Persian Cuneiform

sounds instead of concepts. They probably begin by punning on existing logo-grams. For example, assume that English used the logogram 👁 to stand for the word *eye*. Noting that, in speech, the word *eye* sounds like the word *I,* a clever scribe might decide to use 👁 to mean *I* in writing too. If the logogram for *scream* were 😮 then *ice cream* could be written 👁 😮. Symbols would now represent sound sequences or syllables instead of entire words.

17   When this kind of punning becomes widely used, the writing system is turning into a **syllabary,** or a system in which each symbol stands for a syllable. Over time, the sound values of symbols become predominant and their picture values less im-portant. As scribes simplify the symbols to save time and space, the original pic-tures often become unrecognizable. To use our hypothetical example from English again, the logogram for *eye* might change from 👁 to ◍ to ◌ to ▷ as a syl-labic writing system evolved.

18   Old Persian cuneiform provides an example of a syllabic writing system that lost its pictorial qualities completely. The symbols in Figure 3 are not alphabetic because one cannot separate the consonant portions from the vowel portions. That is, there is no particular part of 𒋫 [ta] that represents either [t] or [a]; the sign stands only for the syllable as a whole.*

19   The first syllabaries were developed among the Semites of the Middle East, perhaps as long ago as seven or eight thousand years, and the concept of the syl-labary rapidly spread over the entire area. Although, strictly speaking, a syllabary represents vowel differences as well as consonant differences among syllables, most of the Semitic syllabaries indicated only consonants. That is, while [ba], [ma], and [ka] were represented by distinct symbols, [ba], [be], and [bi] were all written the same way.

---

*Although the signs illustrated in Figure 3 are purely syllabic, the Old Persian system also retained four logograms and even included alphabetic features. Real writing systems are never as tidy as theoretical ones.

20   For languages with very simple syllable structures, such as Japanese or Chinese, a syllabary provides an efficient writing system because relatively few symbols are needed to represent every possible syllable in the language. Modern Japanese has two syllabaries, the *katakana* and the *hiragana.* The simpler of these, the *katakana,* consists of only 47 basic signs, plus a few diacritical marks. Although the syllabaries are completely adequate for writing anything in Japanese, the prestige of Chinese logograms is so great that contemporary Japanese continues to use a mixture of Chinese characters and *kana* syllabic signs—illustrating how cultural factors may outweigh logic and efficiency in determining the written form of a language.

Alphabets

21 The final step in the phonemicization of writing is the **alphabet,** in which each symbol represents a separate phoneme, not an entire syllable. So far as we know, the alphabet has been invented only once. The Greeks borrowed the Semitic syllabary and, probably over a fairly long period of time, began using unneeded characters to represent vowels separately from consonants. Once there were separate characters for vowels, the originally syllabic characters could always be used for consonants alone, and the alphabet had been invented.

22   The precise form of the Greek letters, or **graphemes,** changed somewhat over time, and the Romans introduced still further changes when they borrowed the Greek alphabet to write Latin, partly because the sound system of Latin differed in a number of important ways from that of Greek. The Romans did not adopt the Greek letters Θ Ξ Φ Ψ or Ω at all. They modified the most common forms or orientations of Greek Γ Δ Λ Σ to *C, D, L,* and *S,* respectively, and then added a tail to *C* to form *G.* The archaic Greek letter *F* had represented [w], but the Romans used it for [f] instead. In Greek, *H* is a vowel symbol, but it became a consonant in Latin. The grapheme *P* represents [r] in Greek, but, because the Romans used *P* for [p], they had to modify it to *R* to represent [r]. The Romans adopted the obsolete Greek character *Q* to represent [k] before [w], as in Latin *quo.* Because Latin used three symbols, *C, Q,* and *K* (though *K* was rarely used) to represent [k], the Latin alphabet almost from the beginning violated the principle of an ideal alphabet, a one-to-one correspondence between phoneme and grapheme.

23   Primarily through the spread of Christianity from Rome, the Latin version of the alphabet was eventually adopted in all of Western Europe. Because Russia was Christianized by the Eastern Church, whose official language was Greek, its alphabet (the Cyrillic alphabet) was borrowed independently from Greek; in many ways it is closer to the classical Greek alphabet than the Latin alphabet is. For example, its forms Γ Д Л Н П Р Ф Х for [g d l n p r f x], respectively, are similar to their Greek originals. However, the Cyrillic alphabet uses *B* for [V], and Б, a modified form of *B,* for [b]. *C* represents [s], and y represents [u]. З , a modified form of Greek *Z,* is used for [z]. Because Russian is much richer in fricatives and affricates than Greek, new symbols were devised to represent them: Ж, Ц, Ч, Ш, Щ stand for [ž, ts, č, š, šč,], respectively. The Cyrillic characters И, Ы, Э, Ю, Я repre-

---

WORDS FROM MISTAKES

New words can originate in many different ways. One entertaining kind of origin is simple misreading due to confusion of similar letter forms. For example, the English word *gravy* comes from Old French *grave,* but the original French form was probably *grane;* the letters *n* and *v (u)* looked much alike in medieval handwriting. The word *sneeze* is apparently the result of misreading an *f* for an *s;* its Old English ancestor was *fneosan* (*f* and *s* were formed in much the same way in Old English times). In some instances, both the correct and the erroneous form have survived, with differentiation of meaning. Hence we have both the original Greek form *acme* and the misread form *acne.*

---

sent the vowels or diphthongs [i y ε ju ja], respectively. Finally, Russian also uses two graphemes as diacritics; they represent no sound of their own, but indicate that a preceding consonant is palatalized (Ь) or not palatalized (Ъ).

24   English has had two different alphabets. Prior to the Christianization of England, the little writing that was done in English was in an alphabet called the **futhorc** or **runic alphabet.** The futhorc was originally developed by Germanic tribes on the Continent and probably was based on Etruscan or early Italic versions of the Greek alphabet. Its association with magic is suggested by its name, the runic alphabet, and the term used to designate a character or letter, **rune.** In Old English, the word *rūn* meant not only "runic character," but also "mystery, secret." The related verb, *rūnian,* meant "to whisper, talk secrets, conspire." . . .

25   As a by-product of the Christianization of England in the sixth and seventh centuries, the English received the Latin alphabet. Although it has been modified somewhat over the centuries, the alphabet we use today is essentially the one adopted in the late sixth century. However, its fit to the sound system is much less accurate than at the time of its adoption because many phonological changes have not been reflected in the writing system.

26   An ideal alphabet contains one symbol for each phoneme, and represents each phoneme by one and only one symbol. In practice, few alphabets are perfect. Even if they are a good match to the sound system when they are first adopted (not always the case), subsequent sound changes destroy the fit. Writing is always much more conservative than speech, and, as the years go by, the fit between phoneme and grapheme becomes worse and worse unless there is regular spelling and even alphabet reform. Such reform has taken place in a number of countries; regular reform is even required by law in Finland. Major reform in the Soviet Union occurred after the 1917 revolution. In 1928, Turkey under Kemal Atatürk switched from the Arabic writing system to the Latin alphabet. However, as the history of Russian and Turkish suggests, resistance to reform is usually so strong that it takes a cataclysmic event like a revolution to achieve it. In general, reform is easier in small countries that do not use a language of worldwide distribution and prestige. Even under these circumstances, resistance to reform will be fierce if the country has a long tradition of literacy and literature. Icelandic, for instance, is spoken by fewer

than a quarter of a million people, a large proportion of whom are bilingual or trilingual in other European languages. However, pride in their long native literary traditions has to date prevented any significant spelling reform. A person reasonably skilled in Old Norse (c. A.D. 900–c. A.D. 1350) can read modern Icelandic without much difficulty even though the spoken language has undergone vast changes since Old Norse times and even though the present match between grapheme and phoneme is poor indeed. Clearly, people become as emotionally entangled with their writing systems as with their spoken languages.

THINKING CRITICALLY

1. Why, according to Millward, was writing invented? Has its primary function changed from its early origins? Explain.

2. What does Millward mean when she says that writing is "mysterious"? How might writing have seemed mystical to ancient civilizations? What makes writing more secretive and powerful than the spoken word?

3. Millward says that an alphabet was invented only once. What makes it a true alphabet? Who invented this alphabet? What challenge does the alphabet face when transcribing human speech, and why?

4. Explain what Millward means when she says, "Writing has become so important that, for the educated person, it can become almost totally independent of speech" (paragraph 3). What problems do people face when their knowledge of the written word exceeds their knowledge of verbal communication?

5. What is the difference between logographic systems of writing and true alphabets? Why are logographic systems inefficient for recording and writing in most languages?

6. In her closing paragraph, Millward comments, "few alphabets are perfect. Even if they are a good match to the sound system when they are first adopted . . . , subsequent sound changes destroy the fit." Identify some sound changes in our modern spoken language that no longer match their written equivalents.

7. Discuss the structure and organization of this essay. Is Millward's organization effective and predictable? How important is organization to the overall effectiveness of this essay?

8. To present her points, Millward depends a great deal on pictures and symbols. How do these visuals help present her ideas? How does Millward herself use early styles of communication to support her essay?

9. Millward presents her readers with many linguistic terms and symbols throughout her essay. How accessible does she make these terms to her readers? Does she explain them effectively? Do the many terms detract from her essay or support it?

WRITING ASSIGNMENTS

1. An exciting development in computers today involves speech recognition technology, in which computers either recognize the spoken word and transcribe it or convert written text to

speech. The Center for Spoken Language Understanding at the Oregon Graduate Institute of Science and Technology studies and teaches the innovative ways computers and speech are linked. Access their Web site at <cslu.cse.ogi.edu> and write an essay discussing the future of speech as it is connected to this type of emerging technology. How might this technology influence speech in the future?

2. Millward states that the ideal alphabet contains one symbol for each phoneme. Draft a sample alphabet based on the dialect of English spoken in your area. Create symbols for your phonemes. Then, working from your alphabet key, write a few sentences based on your alphabet. Explain the logic behind your phonemes.

3. From the time you rise in the morning to the time you go to bed at night, write down all the pictographic and ideographic writings you encounter. Write an essay in which you discuss your data. What conclusions do you think archeologists would draw from our current pictographic and ideographic writings?

Another Language for the Deaf
Margalit Fox

While sign language opened the doors of language to the deaf, the thousands of people who use it still must learn two languages to communicate in their world—the language of signing and the alphabet of general population. For years, the primary language of the deaf—signing—could not be written down. SignWriting hopes to change this situation. In the next piece, Margalit Fox explains how SignWriting, a system of graphic symbols based on dance notation, aims to capture the world's signed languages in written form. But as Fox explains, the concept faces many challenges.

Margalit Fox is a reporter for the *New York Times* and an editor for that paper's *Book Review*. This article first appeared in the April 2002 edition of the *New York Times*.

1 Imagine a language that can't be written. Hundreds of thousands of people speak it, but they have no way to read a newspaper or study a schoolbook in the language they use all day long.

2 That is the situation of the quarter-million or more deaf people in North America whose primary language is American Sign Language. Although they form a vast linguistic minority, their language, as complex as any spoken one, has by its very nature defied most attempts to write it down. In recent years, however, a system of graphic symbols based on dance notation has allowed the world's signed languages to be captured on paper. What's more, the system's advocates say, it may

---

furnish deaf children with a long-sought bridge to literacy in English and other spoken languages, often a great struggle for signers.

3   But despite its utility, the system, called SignWriting, has yet to be widely adopted by deaf people: for many, the issue of whether signed languages need to be written at all remains an open question. "The written form is used by a small number of educated people," Valerie Sutton, the creator of SignWriting, said in a telephone interview from her office in La Jolla, Calif.

4   Little by little, though, SignWriting is gaining footholds in individual homes and classrooms in America and abroad. Disseminated by Ms. Sutton's nonprofit organization <www.signwriting.org>, it can now be found in 27 countries, including Italy, South Africa, Nicaragua, Japan and Saudi Arabia.

5   American Sign Language is not English. Spoken in the United States and parts of Canada, it uses word orders and grammatical constructs not found in English (in certain respects it resembles Navajo).

6   For a deaf child whose first language is A.S.L., English—that is, written English—must be learned as a foreign language, just as a hearing person might study Sanskrit. But there is a catch: "The letters of the alphabet are based on sounds they can't hear," Ms. Sutton explained. For this reason, many deaf students never become fully literate in English, a perennial concern of educators. According to a long-term study by the Gallaudet Research Institute in Washington, deaf high school seniors score, on average, just below the fourth-grade level on standardized reading tests.

7   Dawn McReynolds of Clinton Township, Mich., ran into the problem three years ago, when she discovered her 12-year-old did not know what "bread" meant. Born deaf, and fluent in A.S.L., Nicole McReynolds, then a sixth-grader in public school, was clearly bright. But standardized tests put her academic skills at a first- to second-grade level. As her stunned mother discovered after she pulled Nicole from the classroom and began home schooling, though Nicole had learned by rote to spell simple English words—"bread," "map," "yell"—she had little idea what they actually meant.

8   "Anything I could draw a picture for, she was O.K. with," Mrs. McReynolds said. "But things like 'what,' 'where,' 'when,' 'who'—she had no idea. It was horrible. It was as if she'd never been educated."

9   Advocates of SignWriting hope the system can help bridge the literacy gap. Though no formal studies have been published, anecdotal evidence from parents and teachers suggests its potential. "It's made English come alive for her," said Mrs. McReynolds, who introduced Nicole to SignWriting two and a half years ago, after seeing it on local television.

10   Where spoken languages operate acoustically, signed languages work spatially. Each sign is a compact bundle of data, conveying linguistic information by three primary means at once: the shape of the signer's hands, the location of the hands in space and the direction in which the hands move. (Facial expression also matters.)

11   Devising a writing system that can capture this blizzard of data for each of A.S.L.'s thousands of signs is no simple task. "When you write English, we're using two-dimensional paper to represent a one-dimensional language, because English is just a series of sounds in a sequence, and we write down the sounds in the order we say them," said Karen van Hoek, a linguist who helped develop SignWriting. "But with sign language, it's the reverse: we're trying to get a three-dimensional language compressed down onto two-dimensional, flat paper."

12   Other writing systems have been created for A.S.L. during its century-and-a-half-long history. Some, used by linguists, are too abstract for everyday communication. Another, developed recently at the University of Arizona, is meant to help teach written English but not to handle literary traffic, like novel-writing, entirely in A.S.L.

13   SignWriting, which grew out of a system for transcribing movement that Ms. Sutton developed in the 1970s to notate choreography, can be handwritten, or typed using special software. Written vertically, it uses simple geometric forms to collapse a sign's three basic parameters—hand shape, location and movement—into a streamlined icon, topped by a stylized face.

14   Few embraced the system at first. Many signers, mindful of a long paternalistic history of hearing people tampering with A.S.L., questioned Ms. Sutton's motives. Educators feared it would deter the deaf from learning English.

15   Though hostility has subsided, SignWriting is used today by only a small fraction of the deaf population, between 5,000 and 8,000 people worldwide, Ms. Sutton estimates. As Jane Fernandes, the provost of Gallaudet University, the prestigious school for the hearing impaired, said in an e-mail interview: "There are many deaf adults who were raised with Sign Language in their homes and schools and who have learned to read and write English quite fluently. They were able to navigate between Sign Language and English, without a system for writing their signs down."

16   While acknowledging SignWriting's potential usefulness in teaching English, Dr. Fernandes, who is deaf, expressed doubt about the larger need for written A.S.L. "English is the language of society," she wrote. "It works well for us and I believe English will remain the language in which we write in America."

17   Nicole McReynolds mastered SignWriting fairly easily, and the English words that eluded her began gradually to fall into place. Now 15 and a ninth-grader, she is back in public school, maintaining a B average in a program for hearing-impaired students conducted in English.

18   Before SignWriting, Mrs. McReynolds said, "I didn't think she would be able to live an independent life." These days, Nicole talks of college. "We believe that SignWriting is going to accompany her through her life," her mother said. "There is so much more hope for the future for her because she has this ability now."

THINKING CRITICALLY

1. How is sign language different from "spoken" languages? What challenges does sign language face in order to transition into written form? Explain.

2. In what ways is learning written English for a deaf child much like learning a foreign language? What literacy obstacles must deaf children address when trying to learn written English?

3. Why does SignWriting hold promise over other forms of ASL writing systems? Explain.

4. Sign languages are true languages, with vocabularies of thousands of words and complex and sophisticated grammars. Attend a speech or watch a program that has an ASL interpreter present and focus your attention on the interpreter. If you could not hear, could you understand the context of the speech based on the signing? How does the interpreter augment his/her signing to complement the meaning of the speech? Explain.

5. Fox explains that when Sutton first developed SignWriting, it was met with suspicion by many members of the deaf world "mindful of a long paternalistic history of hearing people tampering with ASL." What does Fox mean? Why would deaf people question Sutton's motives?

6. In what ways did SignWriting represent a "coming into language" for Nicole McReynolds? Explain.

WRITING ASSIGNMENTS

1. Visit the Web site for SignWriting maintained by Sutton at <www.signwriting.org> and review how the system works. Prepare an analysis of the written system explaining its basic premise, how to read it, and its ease of use.

2. Interview at least one deaf person on campus and discuss his/her knowledge and opinions of SignWriting. Ask them to explain, if possible, Fox's statement that when SignWriting was first introduced, the deaf community first viewed it with suspicion. Based on your interview, develop an essay on some of the social implications of SignWriting.

3. Explore the challenges of conveying a gestured language, such as ASL, into a written form. Try to tell a simple story, such as "The Three Little Pigs" or "Goldilocks and the Three Bears" without using a phonetic alphabet (heard sounds), but with pictograms (visual depictions) instead. Describe your experience and how it connects to your understanding of language and communication in general in an exploratory essay.

Exploring the Language of V I S U A L S

SignWriting

To hearing individuals, the disconnect between written English and American Sign Language (ASL) is hard to understand. But imagine trying to learn a language that you cannot hear. How would you know what "sh," "oo," or "ch" or any phonetic sound actually meant? In the preceding piece, Margalit Fox describes how SignWriting, developed by Valerie Sutton, is attempting to bridge the literacy gap between ASL and written English.

SignWriting is a visually designed set of symbols that records sign language. It aims to capture the visual subtleties of sign language by recording body movement. Because it records sign language rather than spoken languages such as English or Spanish, SignWriting can be used internationally to communicate.

Valerie Sutton is the inventor of Sutton Movement Writing, a visual alphabet for writing the movements of the human body. Her system includes DanceWriting, used to record dance choreography, and SignWriting—which she developed in 1974—used to communicate sign languages used by the deaf. She is the author of several books on dance choreography, including *DanceWriting Shorthand for Modern and Jazz Dance* (1982), and *The Bournonville School* (1975,1976). The article that follows, "SignWriting: A Deaf Perspective" employs Sutton's SignWriting alphabet. The article is written by born-deaf, native American Sign Language instructor Lucinda O'Grady Batch, who wrote her thoughts directly in ASL in SignWriting. The English translation of the ASL was done after the ASL article was written. SignWriting gives the Deaf the opportunity to write directly in their own language.

1. Visit Sutton's Web site and read the section "What is SignWriting?" at <www.signwriting .org/>. Then review some of the lessons on SignWriting featured on the Web site. Does the system seem easy to follow and understand? In your opinion, could the system forge stronger language connections between the hearing and nonhearing people? Explain.

2. After reviewing the SignWriting alphabet featured at the SignWriting Web site <www .signwriting.org/>, write a short message using the SignWriting system. Exchange your message with a classmate, and try to translate. How easy or difficult did you find the system to use? Explain.

3. In your opinion, is SignWriting a language or merely a system of symbols? What constitutes "language"? What is an alphabet? Explain.

4. Sutton states on her Web site that SignWriting can be used to read, write, and learn sign language. Explore how SignWriting and sign language are connected. Using two or three examples, compare the movements of ASL for certain words to their SignWriting counterparts.

SignWriting®

A Deaf Perspective...

by Lucinda O'Grady Batch

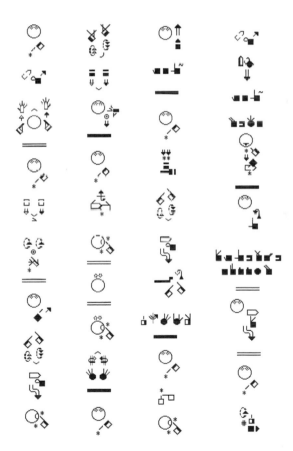

I am writing to tell you how strongly I feel about SignWriting and how much it can benefit Deaf people.

I was born Deaf to a Deaf family and I am a native American Sign Language (ASL) user. I have been working with SignWriting since 1982. I was the first Deaf person to write articles in ASL, in SignWriting, for the SignWriter Newspaper. Later, Valerie Sutton and I established....

VISUALS
continued ➤

the Deaf Action Committee For SignWriting (the DAC) in 1988.

I think it is very important to spread the word about SignWriting. ASL is a language in its own right, yet until the development of SignWriting, it was a language without a written form. When I found out about Sign Writing I was thrilled to think that at last we would have a way to write our language.

Deaf Americans are one of the very few linguistic minorities that are unable to get books teaching English in

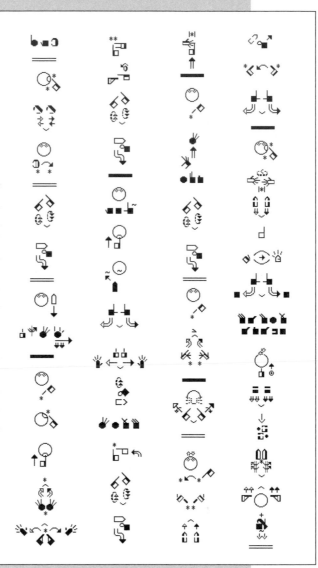

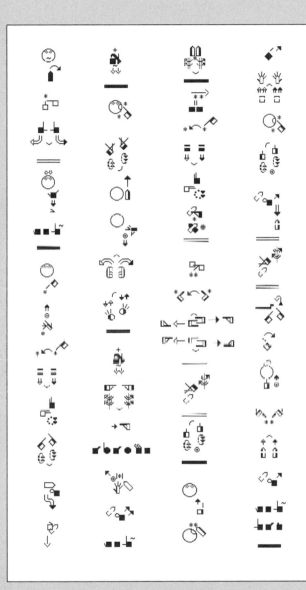

their native language. I feel that we can use SignWriting in order to learn English. Deaf people will benefit greatly from books explaining English grammar and idioms in written ASL.

We can also use it to write down and preserve our stories, poetry and plays. As you know, there are many Deaf playwrights and poets, and up until now, they have not had a way to write the ASL in their literature.

No matter what the project, SignWriting encourages us to read and write and I feel that is important.

All of us hope that you will enjoy learning SignWriting. Your interest and support is a great help to our Deaf community.

Lucinda
O'Grady
Batch

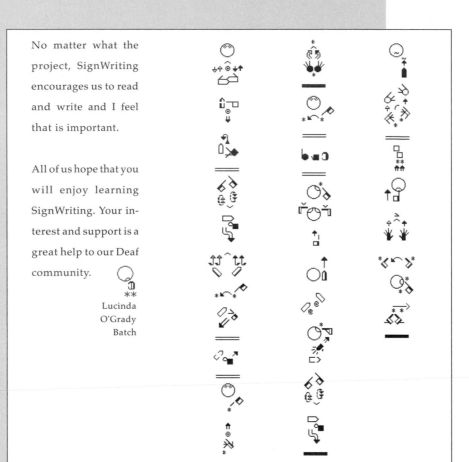

■ MAKING CONNECTIONS

1. Which do we depend on more, signs or symbols? Which are we most apt to misconstrue? Can you think of any words that function as both signs and symbols?

2. Consider the ways we communicate without actually using words. Make a detailed report of a morning's activities in which information is relayed to and by you without speaking. Does a friend gesture for you to approach? Do you see a sign or even a color that warns you to stop? What other nonverbal cues communicate meaning to you? Connect your record to the points made by the authors in this section.

3. Write a hypothetical study of the language development of a child (or possibly two) raised in isolation from spoken language. Describe the different variables and elements of your study and its possible outcome. Support your conclusions with evidence from the essays by Langer, Roberts, and Millward.

4. Sony's Computer Science Laboratory in Paris is conducting a language origins experiment called the "Talking Heads Experiment," investigating how humans apply meaning to sounds. Access their Web site at <talking-heads.csl.sony.fr/Experiments/index.html> and read about the study. Write an essay evaluating the concept of this experiment and linking it to some of the ideas expressed by the authors in this section.

5. Working in groups of four or five, select a short news report from your local newspaper and try to convey its meaning without using any words. Try to avoid "charade" tactics, such as shouting out guesses or using "sounds like" hints. After you complete the exercise, write about your feelings about the experience and what obstacles, if any, you encountered.

■ PERSONAL RECOLLECTIONS: COMING INTO LANGUAGE

Homemade Education
Malcolm X

It was said that he was the only man in America who could start a race riot—or stop one. A one-time street hustler, Malcolm X was born Malcolm Little in 1925. He rose to become one of the most articulate, fiery, and powerful leaders of black America during the 1960s. His writings and lectures taught African-Americans that by taking action, they could take control over their own destiny. In 1946, Malcolm X was arrested for robbery. While in prison, Malcolm became a follower of Elijah Muhammad, the leader of the Nation of Islam (which was sometimes called the Black Muslim Movement). He rescinded his "slave name," Little, and was assigned the new name "X." It was during this time that he discovered the world of language and became obsessed with the written word and books, which he called "intellectual vitamins." After his release, he quickly rose through the ranks of the Nation of Islam and became one of its top administrators. In 1964, Malcolm X left the Nation of Islam to form his own organization, the Muslim Mosque, that articulated a more secular black nationalism. After a trip to Mecca, however, he began to change his views towards whites, considering the possibility that some whites could contribute to the struggle for racial equality. A year later, on February 21, 1965, Malcolm X was assassinated in the Audubon Ballroom while addressing a full house.

The following article is Malcolm X's account of coming to language—an inspiring glimpse of one man's struggle to find self-expression and the power of words. This excerpt comes from *The Autobiography of Malcolm X* (1965), an absorbing personal narrative written with the assistance of *Roots* author Alex Haley.

1   I've never been one for inaction. Everything I've ever felt strongly about, I've done something about. I guess that's why, unable to do anything else, I soon began writing to people I had known in the hustling world, such as Sammy the Pimp, John Hughes, the gambling house owner, the thief Jumpsteady, and several dope peddlers. I wrote them all about Allah and Islam and Mr. Elijah Muhammad. I had no idea where most of them lived. I addressed their letters in care of the Harlem or Roxbury bars and clubs where I'd known them.

2   I never got a single reply. The average hustler and criminal was too uneducated to write a letter. I have known many slick sharp-looking hustlers, who would have you think they had an interest in Wall Street; privately, they would get someone else to read a letter if they received one. Besides, neither would I have replied to anyone writing me something as wild as "the white man is the devil."

3   What certainly went on the Harlem and Roxbury wires was that Detroit Red was going crazy in stir, or else he was trying some hype to shake up the warden's office.

4   During the years that I stayed in the Norfolk Prison Colony, never did any official directly say anything to me about those letters, although, of course, they all passed through the prison censorship. I'm sure, however, they monitored what I wrote to add to the files which every state and federal prison keeps on the conversation of Negro inmates by the teachings of Mr. Elijah Muhammad.

5   But at that time, I felt that the real reason was that the white man knew that he was the devil.

6   Later on, I even wrote to the Mayor of Boston, to the Governor of Massachusetts, and to Harry S. Truman. They never answered; they probably never even saw my letters. I handscratched to them how the white man's society was responsible for the black man's condition in this wilderness of North America.

7   It was because of my letters that I happened to stumble upon starting to acquire some kind of a homemade education.

8   I became increasingly frustrated at not being able to express what I wanted to convey in letters that I wrote, especially those to Mr. Elijah Muhammad. In the street, I had been the most articulate hustler out there—I had commanded attention

when I said something. But now, trying to write simple English, I not only wasn't articulate, I wasn't even functional. How would I sound writing in slang, the way I would *say* it, something such as, "Look, daddy, let me pull your coat about a cat. Elijah Muhammad—"

9   Many who today hear me somewhere in person, or on television, or those who read something I've said, will think I went to school far beyond the eighth grade. This impression is due entirely to my prison studies.

10   It had really begun back in the Charlestown Prison, when Bimbi first made me feel envy of his stock of knowledge. Bimbi had always taken charge of any conversation he was in, and I had tried to emulate him. But every book I picked up had few sentences which didn't contain anywhere from one to nearly all of the words that might as well have been in Chinese. When I just skipped those words, of course, I really ended up with little idea of what the book said. So I had come to the Norfolk Prison Colony still going through only book-reading motions. Pretty soon, I would have quit even these motions, unless I had received the motivation that I did.

11   I saw that the best thing I could do was get hold of a dictionary—to study, to learn some words. I was lucky enough to reason also that I should try to improve my penmanship. It was sad. I couldn't even write in a straight line. It was both ideas together that moved me to request a dictionary along with some tablets and pencils from the Norfolk Prison Colony school.

12   I spent two days just riffling uncertainly through the dictionary's pages. I'd never realized so many words existed! I didn't know *which* words I needed to learn. Finally, just to start some kind of action, I began copying.

13   In my slow, painstaking, ragged handwriting, I copied into my tablet everything printed on that first page, down to the punctuation marks.

14   I believe it took me a day. Then, aloud, I read back, to myself, everything I'd written on the tablet. Over and over, aloud, to myself, I read my own handwriting.

15   I woke up the next morning, thinking about those words—immensely proud to realize that not only had I written so much at one time, but I'd written words that I never knew were in the world. Moreover, with a little effort, I also could remember what many of these words meant. I reviewed the words whose meanings I didn't remember. Funny thing, from the dictionary's first page right now, that "aardvark" springs to my mind. The dictionary had a picture of it, a long-tailed, long-eared, burrowing African mammal, which lives off termites caught by sticking out its tongue as an anteater does for ants.

16   I was so fascinated that I went on—I copied the dictionary's next page. And the same experience came when I studied that. With every succeeding page, I also learned of people and places and events from history. Actually the dictionary is like a miniature encyclopedia. Finally the dictionary's A section had filled a whole tablet—and I went on into the B's. That was the way I started copying what eventually became the entire dictionary. It went a lot faster after so much practice helped me pick up handwriting speed. Between what I wrote in my tablet, and writing letters, during the rest of my time in prison I would guess I wrote a million words.

17   I suppose it was inevitable that as my word-base broadened, I could for the first time pick up a book and read and now begin to understand what the book was saying. Anyone who has read a great deal can imagine the new world that opened. Let me tell you something: from then until I left that prison, in every free moment I had, if I was not reading in the library, I was reading on my bunk. You couldn't have gotten me out of books with a wedge. Between Mr. Muhammad's teachings, my correspondence, my visitors . . . and my reading of books, months passed without my even thinking about being imprisoned. In fact, up to then, I never had been so truly free in my life.

THINKING CRITICALLY

1. What exactly motivates Malcolm X to "get a hold of a dictionary—to study, to learn some words"?

2. Explain how Malcolm X could be the "most articulate hustler" on the street yet be unable to write simple English that was articulate and functional.

3. In your own words, summarize what Malcolm X means when he says, "In fact, up to then, I never had been so truly free in my life." Can you in any way relate to his sense of freedom here? Have you ever had a similarly intense learning experience? If so, what was it like?

4. Would this essay be likely to inspire an illiterate person to learn to read? Why or why not?

5. Having read this essay, do you feel that studying a dictionary is or is not an effective way to improve language skills?

6. Consider the introductory paragraph. What would you say is its function? Does it establish the thesis and controlling idea of the essay? Did it capture your attention and make you want to read on? Explain.

WRITING ASSIGNMENTS

1. Think of a situation in which you lacked the language skills you needed to communicate effectively. It may have been in a college interview, writing a letter to a friend, or expressing your ideas in class. Write an essay explaining the circumstances—how it made you feel and how you solved or coped with the problem. The tone of the piece may be serious, dramatic, or even humorous.

2. Do a little research to find out what kinds of services your community offers to adults who want to learn to read. You might start by contacting town hall, the department of education, and reading clinics. After gathering information, write an essay outlining what is available and whether or not you feel these services are adequate.

3. Access the CMG Web site on Malcolm X at <www.cmgww.com/historic/malcolm/index .html>. Write an essay connecting his background to the excerpt from his autobiography. How did his determination to read lead to his success as a great orator? Would Malcolm X have been as successful if he had not had this experience in jail?

A Word for Everything
Helen Keller

Most of us take for granted the ability to acquire language and communication skills. We develop these skills from infancy. As young children, we are constantly bombarded with visual and verbal stimuli, from which we begin to acquire language. But for Helen Keller (1880–1968), deaf and blind from the age of 19 months, a silent and dark world was her reality. She was unable to effectively communicate her needs and desires and to connect with the people around her.

When Helen was almost seven years old, her parents sought the help of Anne Mansfield Sullivan, a teacher familiar with communicating with the blind and deaf. Anne Sullivan changed Helen's world forever. The following excerpt is from Helen Keller's autobiography, *The Story of My Life*. In this essay, Keller remembers the arrival of her teacher and how Sullivan introduced her to the wonders of language. Specifically, Keller recalls the exact moment when she realized that everything had a name, and her joyous realization that she was connected to the world and the people around her.

1 The most important day I remember in all my life is the one on which my teacher, Anne Mansfield Sullivan, came to me. I am filled with wonder when I consider the immeasurable contrasts between the two lives which it connects. It was the third of March, 1887, three months before I was seven years old.

2 On the afternoon of that eventful day, I stood on the porch, dumb, expectant. I guessed vaguely from my mother's signs and from the hurrying to and fro in the house that something unusual was about to happen, so I went to the door and waited on the steps. The afternoon sun penetrated the mass of honeysuckle that covered the porch, and fell on my upturned face. My fingers lingered almost unconsciously on the familiar leaves and blossoms which had just come forth to greet the sweet southern spring. I did not know what the future held of marvel or surprise for me. Anger and bitterness had preyed upon me continually for weeks and a deep languor had succeeded this passionate struggle.

3 Have you ever been at sea in a dense fog, when it seemed as if a tangible white darkness shut you in, and the great ship, tense and anxious, groped her way toward the shore with plummet and sounding-line, and you waited with beating heart for something to happen? I was like that ship before my education began, only I was without compass or sounding-line, and had no way of knowing how near the harbour was. "Light! Give me light!" was the wordless cry of my soul, and the light of love shone on me in that very hour.

4 I felt approaching footsteps. I stretched out my hand as I supposed to my mother. Some one took it, and I was caught up and held close in the arms of her who had come to reveal all things to me, and, more than all things else, to love me.

5 The morning after my teacher came she led me into her room and gave me a doll. The little blind children at the Perkins Institution had sent it and Laura

Bridgman had dressed it; but I did not know this until afterward. When I had played with it a little while, Miss Sullivan slowly spelled into my hand the word "d-o-l-l." I was at once interested in this finger play and tried to imitate it. When I finally succeeded in making the letters correctly I was flushed with childish pleasure and pride. Running downstairs to my mother I held up my hand and made the letters for doll. I did not know that I was spelling a word or even that words existed; I was simply making my fingers go in monkey-like imitation. In the days that followed I learned to spell in this uncomprehending way a great many words, among them *pin, hat, cup* and a few verbs like *sit, stand* and *walk.* But my teacher had been with me several weeks before I understood that everything has a name.

6   One day, while I was playing with my new doll, Miss Sullivan put my big rag doll into my lap also, spelled "d-o-l-l" and tried to make me understand that "d-o-l-l" applied to both. Earlier in the day we had had a tussle over the words "m-u-g" and "w-a-t-e-r." Miss Sullivan had tried to impress it upon me that "m-u-g" is *mug* and that "w-a-t-e-r" is *water,* but I persisted in confounding the two. In despair she had dropped the subject for the time, only to renew it at the first opportunity. I became impatient at her repeated attempts and, seizing the new doll, I dashed it upon the floor. I was keenly delighted when I felt the fragments of the broken doll at my feet. Neither sorrow nor regret followed my passionate outburst. I had not loved the doll. In the still, dark world in which I lived there was no strong sentiment or tenderness. I felt my teacher sweep the fragments to one side of the hearth, and I had a sense of satisfaction that the cause of my discomfort was removed. She brought me my hat, and I knew I was going out into the warm sunshine. This thought, if a wordless sensation may be called a thought, made me hop and skip with pleasure.

7   We walked down the path to the well-house, attracted by the fragrance of the honeysuckle with which it was covered. Some one was drawing water and my teacher placed my hand under the spout. As the cool stream gushed over one hand she spelled into the other the word *water,* first slowly, then rapidly. I stood still, my whole attention fixed upon the motions of her fingers. Suddenly I felt a misty consciousness as of something forgotten—a thrill of returning thought; and somehow the mystery of language was revealed to me. I knew then that "w-a-t-e-r" meant the wonderful cool something that was flowing over my hand. That living word awakened my soul, gave it light, home, joy, set it free! There were barriers still, it is true, but barriers that could in time be swept away.

8   I left the well-house eager to learn. Everything had a name and each name gave birth to a new thought. As we returned to the house every object which I touched seemed to quiver with life. That was because I saw everything with the strange, new sight that had come to me. On entering the door I remembered the doll I had broken. I felt my way to the hearth and picked up the pieces. I tried vainly to put them together. Then my eyes filled with tears; for I realized what I had done, and for the first time I felt repentance and sorrow.

9   I learned a great many new words that day. I do not remember what they all were; but I do know that *mother, father, sister, teacher* were among them—words that were to make the world blossom for me, "like Aaron's rod, with flowers." It

would have been difficult to find a happier child than I was as I lay in my crib at the close of that eventful day and lived over the joys it had brought me, and for the first time longed for a new day to come.

10   I had now the key to all language, and I was eager to learn to use it. Children who hear acquire language without any particular effort; the words that fall from others' lips they catch on the wing, as it were, delightedly, while the little deaf child must trap them by a slow and often painful process. But whatever the process, the result is wonderful. Gradually, from naming an object we advance step by step until we have traversed the vast distance between our first stammered syllable and the sweep of thought in a line of Shakespeare.

11   At first, when my teacher told me about a new thing I asked very few questions. My ideas were vague, and my vocabulary was inadequate; but as my knowledge of things grew, and I learned more and more words, my field of inquiry broadened, and I would return again and again to the same subject, eager for further information. Sometimes a new word revived an image that some earlier experience had engraved on my brain.

12   I remember the morning that I first asked the meaning of the word "love." This was before I knew many words. I had found a few early violets in the garden and brought them to my teacher. She tried to kiss me; but at that time I did not like to have any one kiss me except my mother. Miss Sullivan put her arm gently round me and spelled into my hand, "I love Helen."

13   "What is love?" I asked.

14   She drew me closer to her and said, "It is here," pointing to my heart, whose beats I was conscious of for the first time. Her words puzzled me very much because I did not then understand anything unless I touched it.

15   I smelt the violets in her hand and asked, half in words, half in signs, a question which meant, "Is love the sweetness of flowers?"

16   "No," said my teacher.

17   Again I thought. The warm sun was shining on us.

18   "Is this not love?" I asked, pointing in the direction from which the heat came, "Is this not love?"

19   It seemed to me that there could be nothing more beautiful than the sun, whose warmth makes all things grow. But Miss Sullivan shook her head, and I was greatly puzzled and disappointed. I thought it strange that my teacher could not show me love.

20   A day or two afterward I was stringing beads of different sizes in symmetrical groups—two large beads, three small ones, and so on. I had made many mistakes, and Miss Sullivan had pointed them out again and again with gentle patience. Finally I noticed a very obvious error in the sequence and for an instant I concentrated my attention on the lesson and tried to think how I should have arranged the beads. Miss Sullivan touched my forehead and spelled with decided emphasis, "Think."

21   In a flash I knew that the word was the name of the process that was going on in my head. This was my first conscious perception of an abstract idea.

22   For a long time I was still—I was not thinking of the beads in my lap, but trying to find a meaning for "love" in the light of this new idea. The sun had been under a cloud all day, and there had been brief showers; but suddenly the sun broke forth in all its southern splendour.

23   Again I asked my teacher, "Is this not love?"

24   "Love is something like the clouds that were in the sky before the sun came out," she replied. Then in simpler words than these, which at that time I could not have understood, she explained: "You cannot touch the clouds, you know; but you feel the rain and know how glad the flowers and the thirsty earth are to have it after a hot day. You cannot touch either; but you feel the sweetness that it pours into everything. Without love you would not be happy or want to play."

25   The beautiful truth burst upon my mind—I felt that there were invisible lines stretched between my spirit and the spirits of others.

26   From the beginning of my education Miss Sullivan made it a practice to speak to me as she would speak to any hearing child; the only difference was that she spelled the sentences into my hand instead of speaking them. If I did not know the words and idioms necessary to express my thoughts she supplied them, even suggesting conversation when I was unable to keep up my end of the dialogue.

27   This process was continued for several years; for the deaf child does not learn in a month, or even in two or three years, the numberless idioms and expressions used in the simplest daily intercourse. The little hearing child learns these from constant repetition and imitation. The conversation he hears in his home stimulates his mind and suggests topics and calls forth the spontaneous expression of his own thoughts. This natural exchange of ideas is denied to the deaf child. My teacher, realizing this, determined to supply the kinds of stimulus I lacked. This she did by repeating to me as far as possible, verbatim, what she heard, and by showing me how I could take part in the conversation. But it was a long time before I ventured to take the initiative, and still longer before I could find something appropriate to say at the right time.

28   The deaf and the blind find it very difficult to acquire the amenities of conversation. How much more this difficulty must be augmented in the case of those who are both deaf and blind! They cannot distinguish the tone of the voice or, without assistance, go up and down the gamut of tones that give significance to words; nor can they watch the expression of the speaker's face, and a look is often the very soul of what one says.

THINKING CRITICALLY

1. Helen Keller was almost seven years old before her teacher Anne Sullivan began to teach her language. Would her experience have been different if she had been younger or older? Explain.

2. How do young children understand words such as think, know, or feel that have no physical or visual representation? How does Helen Keller begin to understand these terms?

3. Why doesn't the young Helen feel sorry for breaking her new doll? What accounts for her later remorse? What made the difference in Helen's emotional perspective? How are emotions connected to language?

4. What are the "amenities of conversation" that Keller alludes to in her final paragraph? Why are they important to communication? How can a look be "the very soul of what one says"?

5. How does Keller describe things that she has never seen nor heard? How do her descriptions help her connect to her audience?

6. Evaluate Keller's tone in this essay. How does her tone help her audience relate to her essay? Who do you think her audience is, and what is she hoping to convey to them?

7. How does Keller use simile and metaphor in her writing? Why do you think she employs this literary convention?

WRITING ASSIGNMENTS

1. How would you describe sound and sight to a person who could experience neither? Describe some everyday events such as a sunset or an ocean wave to a person who has never had sight or hearing. What descriptive alternatives would you use? After writing, explain the rationale behind your description.

2. Sit down with a friend and try to communicate using the Anne Sullivan and Helen Keller method of tracing letters into the palm of the hand. You may wish to use blindfolds for this exercise; do not speak throughout the exercise. Write an essay about your experience. Did it make you view your own method of communication differently?

3. Keller describes the moment when she first made the connection between Sullivan's palm tracings and the object described. She identifies this moment as the moment her soul was awakened and given "light, hope, [and] joy." Write about an experience of your own in which you had a moment of awakening that forever changed the way you understood your world. Following Keller's format, relate the events leading up to this moment. How did it change your life?

4. Read more about the life of Helen Keller. For a brief biographical sketch, try the Great Women Hall of Fame at <www.greatwomen.org> or read the autobiography from which this essay was taken. The American Foundation for the Blind's archives features more information about Keller, her teacher Anne Sullivan, and Keller's early experiences with language acquisition at <www.afb.org/default.asp>. Write a paper on how this remarkable woman became one of the most well-known and respected women in America. What role did language play in her fame?

Exploring the Language of **V I S U A L S**

Sign Language

Many of us take for granted the ability to verbally communicate—to shout a greeting across a court-yard, to hear a warning of imminent danger, to cluck baby talk to a giggling infant, or to whisper a secret in a friend's ear. However, many Americans who are hearing impaired must find alternative ways to communicate to others. Although sign language is one way of addressing this obstacle, it presents its own challenges as well. Few hearing people know sign language well enough to use it to communicate effectively. Moreover, it requires face-to-face contact between signers. As you study the photograph and answer the questions that follow, consider the ways you communicate verbally with others around you. What would happen if you could not verbally express yourself and, instead, had to rely on sign language to be understood?

THINKING CRITICALLY

1. What is happening in this photograph? Do you know what the teacher is signing to the students? Can you make any assumptions based on what is presented in this picture? For example, where are the subject's eyes focused? What do you think the banner in the background means? Explain.

2. American Sign Language (ASL) is taught in many colleges and universities to hearing students. Contrary to popular assumption, ASL is not a signed form of English, but a language in its own right that developed gradually and still evolves, as many languages do. Find out if your school offers courses in ASL. If so, ask permission to attend a class and write about the experience. Try to apply some of the things you have learned about language in this class to your assessment of ASL.

3. If you have a hearing or speech impairment, discuss how this challenge affects your daily life and your communication with others. If you do not have any unique hearing or speech difficulties, discuss how you communicate with people who do. What issues do you confront, and how do you deal with them? Explain.

4. Sign languages are true languages, with vocabularies of thousands of words and complex and sophisticated grammars. Attend a speech or watch a program that has an ASL interpreter present. Focus your attention on the interpreter. If you could not hear, could you understand the context of the speech based on the interpreter's signing? How does the interpreter augment his/her signing to complement the meaning of the speech? Explain.

5. Visit the Web site for the National Association for the Deaf and read about legislation that was passed relating to Janet DeVinney's experience in a Maine hospital at <www.nad.org/infocenter/newsroom/nadnews/TransformingDeVinney.html>. Discuss her experience and the circumstances that led to it. Does reading about her situation give you any insights into the communication challenges faced by the hearing impaired? Explain.

6. Although many people do not know American Sign Language (ASL), they do rely on some form of sign language to express themselves, such as by nodding or shaking their heads or through waving and other hand gestures. Discuss the ways you use sign language to convey meaning.

The Language of Silence
Maxine Hong Kingston

Maxine Hong Kingston, born in 1940, was raised in a Chinese immigrant community in Stockton, California. As a first-generation American, she found herself having to adjust to two distinctly contrasting cultures. For a young girl, this was confusing and difficult, as she recalls in this selection from her highly praised and popular autobiography, *The Woman Warrior: Memoirs of a Girlhood Among Ghosts* (1976). To the Chinese immigrant, white Americans are "ghosts"—pale, threatening, and at times, comical specters who speak an incomprehensible tongue. For Kingston, becoming American meant adopting new values, defining a new self, and finding a new voice.

Before the publication of her award-winning autobiography, Kingston taught in several high schools and business schools. Since then, she has published *China Men* (1980) a novel, *The Tripmaster Monkey: His Fake Book* (1989), and reflections on writing, *To Be the Poet* (2002). She currently teaches English at the University of California, Berkeley.

1 Long ago in China, knot-makers tied string into buttons and frogs, and rope into bell pulls. There was one knot so complicated that it blinded the knot-maker. Finally an emperor outlawed this cruel knot, and the nobles could not order it anymore. If I had lived in China, I would have been an outlaw knot-maker.

2 Maybe that's why my mother cut my tongue. She pushed my tongue up and sliced the frenum. Or maybe she snipped it with a pair of nail scissors. I don't remember her doing it, only her telling me about it, but all during childhood I felt sorry for the baby whose mother waited with scissors or knife in hand for it to cry—and then, when its mouth was wide open like a baby bird's, cut. The Chinese say "a ready tongue is an evil."

3 I used to curl up my tongue in front of the mirror and tauten my frenum into a white line, itself as thin as a razor blade. I saw no scars in my mouth. I thought perhaps I had had two frena, and she had cut one. I made other children open their mouths so I could compare theirs to mine. I saw perfect pink membranes stretching into precise edges that looked easy enough to cut. Sometimes I felt very proud that my mother committed such a powerful act upon me. At other times I was terrified—the first thing my mother did when she saw me was to cut my tongue.

4 "Why did you do that to me, Mother?"

5 "I told you."

6 "Tell me again."

7 "I cut it so that you would not be tongue-tied. Your tongue would be able to move in any language. You'll be able to speak languages that are completely different from one another. You'll be able to pronounce anything. Your frenum looked too tight to do those things, so I cut it."

8 "But isn't 'a ready tongue an evil'?"

9 "Things are different in this ghost country."

10   "Did it hurt me? Did I cry and bleed?"

11   "I don't remember. Probably."

12   She didn't cut the other children's. When I asked cousins and other Chinese children whether their mothers had cut their tongues loose, they said "What?"

13   "Why didn't you cut my brothers' and sisters' tongues?"

14   "They didn't need it."

15   "Why not? Were theirs longer than mine?"

16   "Why don't you quit blabbering and get to work?"

17   If my mother was not lying she should have cut more, scraped away the rest of the frenum skin, because I have a terrible time talking. Or she should not have cut at all, tampering with my speech. When I went to kindergarten and had to speak English for the first time, I became silent. A dumbness—a shame—still cracks my voice in two, even when I want to say "hello" casually, or ask an easy question in front of the check-out counter, or ask directions of a bus driver. I stand frozen, or I hold up the line with the complete, grammatical sentence that comes squeaking out at impossible length. "What did you say?" says the cab driver, or "Speak up," so I have to perform again, only weaker the second time. A telephone call makes my throat bleed and takes up that day's courage. It spoils my day with self-disgust when I hear my broken voice come skittering out into the open. It makes people wince to hear it. I'm getting better, though. Recently I asked the postman for special-issue stamps; I've waited since childhood for postmen to give me some of their own accord. I am making progress, a little every day.

18   My silence was thickest—total—during the three years that I covered my school paintings with black paint. I painted layers of black over houses and flowers and suns, and when I drew on the background, I put a layer of chalk on top. I was making a stage curtain, and it was the moment before the curtain parted or rose. The teachers called my parents to school, and I saw they had been saving my pictures, curling and cracking, all alike and black. The teachers pointed to the pictures and looked serious, talked seriously too, but my parents did not understand English. ("The parents and teachers of criminals were executed," said my father.) My parents took the pictures home. I spread them out (so black and full of possibilities) and pretended the curtains were swinging open, flying up, one after another, sunlight underneath, mighty operas.

19   During the first silent year I spoke to no one at school, did not ask before going to the lavatory, and flunked kindergarten. My sister also said nothing for three years, silent in the playground and silent at lunch. There were other quiet Chinese girls not of our family, but most of them got over it sooner than we did. I enjoyed the silence. At first it did not occur to me I was supposed to talk or to pass kindergarten. I talked at home and to one or two of the Chinese kids in class. I made motions and even made some jokes. I drank out of a toy saucer when the water spilled out of the cup, and everybody laughed, pointing at me, so I did it some more. I didn't know that Americans don't drink out of saucers.

20   I liked the Negro students (Black Ghosts) best because they laughed the loudest and talked to me as if I were a daring talker too. One of the Negro girls had her

mother coil braids over her ears Shanghai-style like mine; we were Shanghai twins except that she was covered with black like my paintings. Two Negro kids enrolled in Chinese school, and the teachers gave them Chinese names. Some Negro kids walked me to school and home, protecting me from the Japanese kids, who hit me and chased me and stuck gum in my ears. The Japanese kids were noisy and tough. They appeared one day in kindergarten, released from concentration camp,* which was a tic-tac-toe mark, like barbed wire, on the map.

21 It was when I found out I had to talk that school became a misery, that the silence became a misery. I did not speak and felt bad each time that I did not speak. I read aloud in first grade, though, and heard the barest whisper with little squeaks come out of my throat. "Louder," said the teacher, who scared the voice away again. The other Chinese girls did not talk either, so I knew the silence had to do with being a Chinese girl.

22 Reading out loud was easier than speaking because we did not have to make up what to say, but I stopped often, and the teacher would think I'd gone quiet again. I could not understand "I." The Chinese "I" has seven strokes, intricacies. How could the American "I," assuredly wearing a hat like the Chinese, have only three strokes, the middle so straight? Was it out of politeness that this writer left off strokes the way a Chinese has to write her own name small and crooked? No, it was not politeness; "I" is a capital and "you" is a lower-case. I stared at that middle line and waited so long for its black center to resolve into tight strokes and dots that I forgot to pronounce it. The other troublesome word was "here," no strong consonant to hang on to, and so flat, when "here" is two mountainous ideographs.† The teacher, who had already told me every day how to read "I" and "here," put me in the low corner under the stairs again, where the noisy boys usually sat.

23 When my second grade class did a play, the whole class went to the auditorium except the Chinese girls. The teacher, lovely and Hawaiian, should have understood about us, but instead left us behind in the classroom. Our voices were too soft or nonexistent, and our parents never signed the permission slips anyway. They never signed anything unnecessary. We opened the door a crack and peeked out, but closed it again quickly. One of us (not me) won every spelling bee, though.

24 I remember telling the Hawaiian teacher, "We Chinese can't sing 'Land where our fathers died.'" She argued with me about politics, while I meant because of curses. But how can I have that memory when I couldn't talk? My mother says that we, like ghosts, have no memories.

25 After American school, we picked up our cigar boxes, in which we had arranged books, brushes, and an inkbox neatly, and went to Chinese school, from 5:00 to 7:30 P.M. There we chanted together, voices rising and falling, loud and soft, some boys shouting, everybody reading together, reciting together and not alone with one voice. When we had a memorization test, the teacher let each of us come to his desk and say the lesson to him privately, while the rest of the class

---

Concentration camp: refers to one of the U.S. camps where Japanese Americans were imprisoned during World War II.
†Ideographs: composite characters in Chinese writing made by combining two or more other characters.

practiced copying or tracing. Most of the teachers were men. The boys who were so well behaved in the American school played tricks on them and talked back to them. The girls were not mute. They screamed and yelled during recess, when there were no rules; they had fistfights. Nobody was afraid of children hurting themselves or of children hurting school property. The glass doors to the red and green balconies with the gold joy symbols were left wide open so that we could run out and climb the fire escapes. We played capture-the-flag in the auditorium, where Sun Yat-sen and Chiang Kai-shek's pictures hung at the back of the stage, the Chinese flag on their left and the American flag on their right. We climbed the teak ceremonial chairs and made flying leaps off the stage. One flag headquarters was behind the glass door and the other on stage right. Our feet drummed on the hollow stage. During recess the teachers locked themselves up in their office with the shelves of books, copybooks, inks from China. They drank tea and warmed their hands at a stove. There was no play supervision. At recess we had the school to ourselves, and also we could roam as far as we could to—downtown, Chinatown stores, home—as long as we returned before the bell rang.

26   At exactly 7:30 the teacher again picked up the brass bell that sat on his desk and swung it over our heads, while we charged down the stairs, our cheering magnified in the stairwell. Nobody had to line up.

27   Not all of the children who were silent at American school found voice at Chinese school. One new teacher said each of us had to get up and recite in front of the class, who was to listen. My sister and I had memorized the lesson perfectly. We said it to each other at home, one chanting, one listening. The teacher called on my sister to recite first. It was the first time a teacher had called on the second-born to go first. My sister was scared. She glanced at me and looked away; I looked down at my desk. I hoped that she could do it because if she could, then I would have to. She opened her mouth and a voice came out that wasn't a whisper, but it wasn't a proper voice either. I hoped that she would not cry, fear breaking up her voice like twigs underfoot. She sounded as if she were trying to sing through weeping and strangling. She did not pause or stop to end the embarrassment. She kept going until she said the last word, and then she sat down. When it was my turn, the same voice came out, a crippled animal running on broken legs. You could hear splinters in my voice, bones rubbing jagged against one another. I was loud, though. I was glad I didn't whisper. There was one little girl who whispered. . . .

28   How strange that the emigrant villagers are shouters, hollering face to face. My father asks, "Why is it I can hear Chinese from blocks away? Is it that I understand the language? Or is it they talk loud?" They turn the radio up full blast to hear the operas, which do not seem to hurt their ears. And they yell over the singers that wail over the drums, everybody talking at once, big arm gestures, spit flying. You can see the disgust on American faces looking at women like that. It isn't just the loudness. It is the way Chinese sounds, ching-chong ugly, to American ears, not beautiful like Japanese sayonara words with the consonants and vowels as regular as Italian. We make guttural peasant noise and have Ton Duc Thang names you can't remember. And the Chinese can't hear Americans at all; the language is too soft and western music unhearable. I've watched a Chinese audience laugh, visit,

talk-story, and holler during a piano recital, as if the musician could not hear them. A Chinese-American, somebody's son, was playing Chopin, which has no punctuation, no cymbals, no gongs. Chinese piano music is five black keys. Normal Chinese women's voices are strong and bossy. We American-Chinese girls had to whisper to make ourselves American-feminine. Apparently we whispered even more softly than the Americans. Once a year the teachers referred my sister and me to speech therapy, but our voices would straighten out, unpredictably normal, for the therapists. Some of us gave up, shook our heads, and said nothing, not one word. Some of us could not even shake our heads. At times shaking my head no is more self-assertion than I can manage. Most of us eventually found some voice, however faltering. We invented an American-feminine speaking personality. . . .

THINKING CRITICALLY

1. Kingston employed silence rather than language in the early grades. What accounts for the difference in attitude between kindergarten, where she "employed the silence," and first grade, where "silence became a misery"?

2. Kingston's teacher punished her for failing to read "I" and "here." How does this episode demonstrate the clash between Chinese and American cultures? Are there other episodes in the essay that also demonstrate this struggle?

3. How did Kingston's Chinese school differ from the American one? What impact did the former have on her language development?

4. What do you make of Kingston's paintings? What was Kingston's personal view of her work? How do they relate to her "language of silence"?

5. Examine the conclusion of the essay. Would you say this is a moment of triumph or defeat for Kingston? Explain.

6. At what point in the essay do you know Kingston's focus? What are the cues to her purpose? Does this lead capture your attention? Explain.

7. Kingston writes this essay using the first person. How is this ironic in light of what she writes in the piece? Would this essay be as effective if it were told from a third-person point of view? Explain.

WRITING ASSIGNMENTS

1. Assume that you are a teacher with Kingston as a pupil. How would you handle her? What different tactics would it take to get her to come out of herself? Write a paper in which you describe your role.

2. Did you have difficulties "coming to language" as a child? Do you remember resorting to protective silence because of your accent, a different primary language, or a different cultural identity? Did you feel fear and/or embarrassment because of your difference, and did you carry the results of your experience into your adult life? If so, in what way? In a personal narrative, describe your experience.

3. Kingston admits that even as an adult, she has "a terrible time talking." She says that she still freezes with shame, that she can hardly be heard, that her voice is broken and squeaky. What about her writing style? Do you see any reflection of her vocal difficulties—any signs of hesitation or uncertainty? In a paper, consider these questions as you try to describe her style as it relates to her experiences as a young girl.

4. Bilingual education is a controversial form of education designed to instill educational confidence in school children, allowing them to learn using the language spoken in their homes. See the National Clearinghouse for Bilingual Education's Web site maintained by George Washington University for more information on this form of education at <www .ncbe.gwu.edu>. Kingston relates that she had to go to a separate Chinese school after her regular school day. Do you think Kingston's educational experience would have been different had she been taught in a bilingual classroom?

The Jellyfish
Susan Kinsolving

Very young children come into language through an amazing process of repetition and original generalizations. They begin with simple words and sentences, and then begin fledgling attempts at conjugating verbs and grammatical constructions. MIT language expert Steven Pinker observes that sometime between the second and third year, children all begin to add -*ed* to irregular verbs, such as "I breaked it" or "he taked it," as they begin to grapple with the complex structures of adult language. While linguists continue to wrestle with the peculiarities of how children acquire and process language, parents marvel over the purity of their expressions and the poetic simplicity of their words. In the poem that follows, Susan Kinsolving captures her daughter's words at this unique moment in language development.

Poet and lyricist Susan Kinsolving is a critically acclaimed writer and a finalist for the Walt Whitman Award. She has taught at the California Institute of the Arts, and the University of Connecticut. Kinsolving has published many poems in magazines and journals, including *The Paris Review, The New Republic,* and *The Nation.* She is the author of two books of poetry, *Among Flowers* (1993) and *Dailies and Rushes* (2000), which was nominated for the National Book Critics Circle Award.

Moving its translucent mass through the watery
shadows of the dock and then, past the dock (something so real which now is not), the jellyfish
swam in its slow float while we (I and my daughter,
then just three) ran back and forth predicting that limp
pink gleam and each embodiment it would seem.
"A jello umbrello!" she began and turned
to me expectantly. Censoring (an after-
birth, broken veins, or Medusa's myth, the monstrous

queen made mortal and mother), I stood in silence
until it ended with a shout: the jelly-
fish glided out. Now months have passed, but surprise!
"The jellyfish was in my eyes!" Caroline calls
while caught between depth and surface of a dream.
"It bleeded and it singed!" Her conjugations
soon will exact simple irregularities
and tensing will be not verbs, but time's tentacles
untangling her parachute, waving at me.
——SUSAN KINSOLVING, "THE JELLYFISH," 1999

THINKING CRITICALLY

1. What grammatical errors does Caroline make? Why do you think she makes them? What is noteworthy about her use of language? Explain.

2. Do you recall struggling with language as a young child? Were there any particular words or conjugations that baffled you? Describe your own experience with language.

3. What is happening in this poem? How does the poem connect back to this chapter's sub-theme of "coming into language"?

4. Evaluate this poem for its artistic and linguistic merits. Do you like the poem? Why or why not? Explain.

5. What are your impressions of the people in the poem? How do the words of the poem characterize the people in it?

6. What message about language does Kinsolving make in this poem? Explain.

7. Examine in greater detail the words used by Kinsolving to describe the jellyfish and her daughter Caroline. What is the effect of these words? Are the adult's words more effective than the child's? Why or why not?

WRITING ASSIGNMENTS

1. Listen to the speech of some young children between the ages of two and four. How do they conjugate verbs, form possessives, and use different tenses? Describe your observations, and any conclusions you can draw from them, in a short essay on children's language development.

2. Read the short essay on children's language acquisition at <www.facstaff.bucknell.edu/rbeard/acquisition.html>. Why is the period between the ages of two and seven so critical to learning how to use language? Building upon the information from this Web site and outside research, write a paper exploring this period of life as it relates to language acquisition and cognition.

3. Ask a young child (three or four) to describe a simple object, such as a toy, or a person (a concealed tape recorder may be helpful in this experiment). Then, ask an older child (around six or seven) to describe the same object (make sure the children do not hear each other's responses). What differences do you observe in both the language they use and their control of syntax? Explain.

Spanish Lessons
Christine Marín

Christine Marín was born to bilingual Mexican American parents in Globe, Arizona. Remembering the discrimination they encountered during their own childhoods, the elder Maríns determined that their children would speak English in their home. Her parents recognized the power of language—they told their children to "speak better English than the gringo, so that he could not ridicule [them] the way they had been ridiculed in school and work." In this environment, Christine Marín began to encounter some mixed messages. On the one hand, she was encouraged to be proud of her heritage and cultural background; on the other, she was discouraged from speaking Spanish. It was not until high school that she began to recognize the power of the Spanish tongue. The essay that follows describes Marín's gradual awakening to the power of her cultural language, her emerging respect for this language, and how it ultimately shaped her identity.

Christine Marín is the curator for the Chicano Research Collection at the University of Arizona, where she also teaches in the Women's Studies program. She is the author of *Latinos in Museums: Heritage Reclaimed* (1990).

1 The reality of being a Mexican American whose mother tongue was English and who did not speak Spanish came in the form of a 1958 high school band trip and the song "La Bamba" by Ritchie Valens (I didn't even know he was Mexican-American!), which was quite popular. I wasn't any different from the other high school kids who learned the words of popular songs we heard on the radio. Anglo and Mexican-American kids would sit together in the back of the bus and sing loudly and attempt to drown out the singing of those kids who sat toward the front of the bus. The game was to see who could sing the best and the loudest, and consequently drown out the singing of those in front.

2 On one band trip we sang "La Bamba." I didn't realize we were singing so loudly and in Spanish! My "voice" came out in the form of Spanish lyrics, although I was unaware of it. My Mexican-American identity shone through. I remember how proud I was for singing in Spanish, even though I didn't understand all the words of the song. I didn't know what a *bamba* was or what a *marinero* was. I hadn't heard those words before, and I wondered if my Mexican-American girlfriends knew the meaning of the song. I stumbled over the words, mispronouncing many of them. Suddenly, one popular Anglo girl sitting toward the front of the bus stood up in the middle of the aisle and shouted out loud so that everyone could hear: "Hey, you Mexicans! This is America! Stop singing in Spanish!" She proceeded to loudly sing "God Bless America" and "My Country 'Tis of Thee." To my surprise, her Anglo friends joined her in singing those patriotic songs. Well, our group of Mexican-American girls was not to be outdone. We sang the words to "La Bamba" even louder, and this infuriated her even more! Eventually, our band director jumped up

from his seat and demanded that we all shut up. That stopped the singing. I could see that our band director was agitated, but I wasn't sure if it was because of that stupid, racist remark from that little twerp or because of all the noise throughout the bus.

3   It didn't take me long to figure out what had happened. I realized that the girl and her friends did not resent being outsung but resented the fact that we were singing in Spanish, using words that weren't even a part of my everyday vocabulary! All I was doing was singing a song. I felt like getting up out of my seat and beating up that insensitive, stupid girl—and good! But I didn't. I learned the power of both the English and Spanish languages on that band trip. And what a lesson it was! The Spanish language posed a threat to that girl, and it made me feel proud of being a Mexican American despite the fact that I didn't speak Spanish. I felt superior to her because I knew two languages and I could understand both English and Spanish, while she could only understand English.

4   In high school, I was an above-average student but certainly not one who made straight A's. I excelled in English and writing assignments, and my work was noticed by my English teachers, especially Mrs. Ethel Jaenicke. She hoped I would attend college after high school, something I hadn't thought was possible. She spent extra time with me and encouraged me to continue my writing. Unfortunately, my father's pay didn't stretch far enough to pay for a college education. My parents, however, knew the value and importance of a good education and wanted their children to continue on to college. They made great sacrifices to help all of us begin our college education and were encouraging, nurturing, and understanding about our struggles to stay in school. It was ultimately up to us to somehow find the money to stay in school and continue our education.

5   After graduation from Globe High School in 1961, I moved to Phoenix, where I lived with my older brother and his wife. A friend of his helped me get a job as a salesgirl at Jay's Credit Clothing, a Jewish-owned clothing store in downtown Phoenix. Customers bought their goods on credit. The clothing lines were fashionable, stylish, and overpriced. Most of the customers were African Americans, Mexicans, Mexican Americans, and some Anglos. Mexican-American saleswomen were paid a small weekly salary but earned most of their money through sales commissions. Making those sales was very competitive, and I didn't do so well. I couldn't speak Spanish well enough to assist Spanish-speaking customers who came into the store, which left me frustrated and embarrassed. One of the senior Mexican-American saleswomen felt sorry for me; she noticed how desperately I struggled with the language. She often gave me her own sales after she had assisted Spanish-speaking customers by putting my name on her sales tickets. She knew I would be attending Arizona State University in August and needed to save money for school. She took me under her wing and spoke to me of her childhood wishes of going to college, though her family couldn't afford to send her. This woman worked in that clothing store for many years. She taught me another lesson about the power of language: bilingualism paid well—monetarily well! I decided to recapture my lost na-

tive tongue and consciously worked on speaking more Spanish so that I could earn more money.

6   At ASU, I enrolled in liberal arts courses and had many interests. I took classes in psychology, sociology, history, and English, to name but a few. One college adviser even suggested that I major in Spanish because "Mexicans make good Spanish teachers and you could always find a job teaching it." If he only knew how badly I spoke the language! I didn't want to major in Spanish. Chalk up two more lessons learned about the power of language. First, someone assumed I spoke Spanish simply because of my surname and brown-colored skin. Second, by knowing the Spanish language, I would always be guaranteed a teaching job. However, I didn't want to be a teacher. . . .

7   During my freshman year, an English professor insulted my character and intelligence when she accused me of taking credit for a writing assignment she believed was written by someone else. According to her, the essay was extremely well written, but I couldn't have written it because "Mexicans don't write that well." "You people don't even speak the language correctly." Another hard lesson to learn about the power of language! This time the lesson was that my skin color and Spanish surname—not my language proficiency and ability in English—served as criteria to discriminate against me. My English ability was questioned and discredited. The academy had silenced my English voice. No matter how hard I tried, I couldn't convince her I had written that essay and that I had not paid someone to write it for me, as she presumed. This incident angered me. I had done what my parents said—be better than the gringo through language. But since this gringa professor had power and status, she felt she could accuse me of cheating. Needless to say, I dropped the class and never spoke to her again. I didn't care whether she believed me or not. . . .

8   In 1970 I applied for and was hired for a bibliographer position, where I learned all aspects of verifying English-language bibliographic entries and citations for monographs, serials, periodicals, and government documents, among others. I learned the intricacies of checking and verifying library holdings and how to use bibliographic tools and sources. I grew intellectually in my work. Because of my knowledge of library-related information, I became the "expert" and "voice" for my classmates and their friends who either were unfamiliar with the library system or found learning how to use book or serial catalogs confusing. I taught them how to use the library's catalogs and reference tools and encouraged them to enjoy the library setting. My job empowered me. I had learned a new code—the library code.

9   The year 1970 was an important one for Mexican-American students at ASU in other ways. My friends were beginning to call themselves "Chicanos" as a term of self-identification and tossed aside the term "Mexican Americans." For them, the term "Chicano" meant empowerment, and they found a new identity as Chicanos. But it was not a new word to me. I had heard it used by my parents and their friends when I was growing up in Globe. My father called himself a Chicano, and so did his friends from his military service days in World War II. For them the word "Chicano" was used in friendship—as a term of endearment, as a term of identity.

10   Now my college friends were using the word "Chicano" differently and in a defiant manner, with the word "power" after it: "Chicano Power!" For them and for me, it became a term of self-identity. The word was an assertion of ethnic and cultural pride, a term heard in a new form of social protests and associated with student activism and civil rights militancy. Chicanos throughout the Southwest were caught up in the Chicano Movement, a civil rights movement. They made new demands—that they become visible rather than invisible on their college and university campuses—and wanted a voice. They demanded courses that described the history, culture, and experiences of Chicanos in the Southwest. They wanted Chicano counselors and professors to teach bilingual-bicultural education courses and courses in social work on their campuses. Arizona State University was going to be at the forefront in making these changes. Two scholars, Dr. Manuel Patricio Servín and Dr. H. William Axford, played in integral role in this demand for change. Hayden Library was to be the setting that allowed students to legitimize history, culture, art, language, and literature by acknowledging the presence of Mexican Americans, Chicanos, and Mexicans. . . .

11   Servín and Axford quickly became my friends; the scholar and the librarian took me under their wings. They anticipated what Chicano students were going to do: demand that their library have books *by* and *about* them. They were right, and they gave students their voice. This is where I came in. Not long after his arrival, Dr. Axford came to the bibliography department and asked if anyone was familiar with Chicano materials. Being the only Chicana in the department, I was the one who spoke up.

12   In 1969 my friends had organized the Mexican American Students Organization (MASO) on the ASU campus, and I attended the meetings. MASO students came from various Arizona places, including mining towns, cities, and rural towns. The majority spoke English, so meetings were conducted in English; the MASO newsletter was written in English, with a few slogans in Spanish thrown in for effect, such as *¡Basta Ya!, ¡Viva La Raza!, Con Safos,* and *¡Viva La Huelga!* By 1970, I had attended Chicano Movement–related meetings, had participated in United Farmworker rallies in Phoenix, and had leafleted pro-union literature urging the boycott of lettuce sold at Safeway stores. I became well acquainted with Chicano Movement ideologies and with the events of the times.

13   I met with Drs. Axford and Servín and listened to a new idea that they proposed to me. Dr. Axford suggested that I become the bibliographer for the Chicano Studies Collection, with my first task being to conduct an inventory of the library's holdings of Chicano-related materials. Dr. Servín provided me with various bibliographies listing the Chicano Studies' holdings of university libraries in California. I kept a record of the library's strengths and weaknesses in Chicano Studies by searching publishers' catalogs, listing the titles we didn't have, and marking them as available for purchasing. In that meeting with Drs. Axford and Servín, I learned that it was their intent to build a Chicano Studies Collection that would support Servín's teaching and research needs in Chicano Studies and the needs of those students who would enroll in the American Studies program. Dr. Axford wanted to

strengthen the library's holding in Chicano Studies so that he would be prepared to justify those holdings to Chicano students when they demanded that the library have them. I agreed to become the bibliographer for the Chicano Studies Collection. I was the staff of one. In essence, Axford and Servín empowered me to take over the Chicano Studies Collection. I became the expert, the liaison for scholars, students, and researchers. The Chicano Studies Collection became another means by which my voice was heard. I now had the opportunity to tell others of my culture, of which I was proud. . . .

14   Dr. Axford was open to the idea of meeting with MASO. I agreed to work with MASO representatives in selecting books for the Chicano Studies Collection. It was a positive relationship, reflective of Dr. Axford's philosophy of open access to library materials and sources. Chicano students began to utilize the library, and brown faces were now appearing in greater numbers in the study areas in and around the collection. Soon I was collecting and saving MASO newsletters, leaflets, minutes from meetings, membership lists, and other Chicano movement materials for my own interest. Dr. Servín encouraged me to collect these materials for the library and planted the seed in my mind to someday build a Chicano Studies archives. What a great idea! He also encouraged me to return to school and enroll in his courses to familiarize myself with the historical literature of the Southwest. It was my fate and destiny to encounter Drs. Servín and Axford and to find a new direction that would satisfy my intellectual growth and development. I learned more about Chicano history from Dr. Servín's classes, where I was exposed to the writings, research, and thought of Chicano scholars and writers. He also gave me the opportunity to do research and helped me publish my first article about the Chicano Movement in a scholarly journal that he edited. In 1974 my scholarly voice came through.

15   Outside the classroom, I continued to be exposed to Chicano Movement ideas and activities, and I easily made friends and contacts who would lead me to those elusive materials that are archival prizes in academic libraries today. I was challenged to improve my Spanish language skills by those individuals who were community activists. They spoke in both English and Spanish, and I learned what the term "codeswitching" meant. As a reflection of the times, MASO students changed their name in 1971 to MECHA, which stands for Movimiento Estudiantil Chicano de Aztlán.

16   I've continued working at Hayden Library, where I am now the curator/archivist for the Chicano Research Collection. I have built the Chicano Studies Collection into an important archival repository. During the last ten years, I've been an adjunct faculty associate in the Women's Studies program, where I have taught the courses "La Chicana" and "Women in the Southwest." I have assigned my students to write about the history of Chicanas in their families, to become curious about their family histories, and to incorporate oral history into their research. Through this assignment, they give voice to their own family histories, and they acquire their own voices in the discovery of their identities. Their manuscripts, as well as those of others, are in the Chicano Research Collection. These

materials provide information about the past. Students, researchers, and scholars from all over the world have access to records, documents, oral histories, photographs, diaries, correspondence, videos, pamphlets, leaflets, and posters about the history, culture, and heritage of Chicanos, Chicanas, and Mexican Americans in the United States. I am proud and honored to preserve these records for future Chicana and Chicano scholars. It is these materials that transmit the voices of *nuestra raza* vis-à-vis the printed page.

17   As I conclude my journey and the sharing of my story of growing up in an Arizona mining town, I have come to discover the many voices and modes of communication I had available to me and how they have contributed to the formation of self and identity. These voices have empowered me, educated me, sensitized me. Empowerment came through my work as an archivist and MASO/MECHA student, my scholarship, and my work in academe. My English voices as a young child, in school, and throughout ring clear: the discrimination in academe that I encountered in my English class and also my knowledge of the intricacies of library language. My Spanish voices are also evident: in the back of the band bus in high school; when, for economic survival, I was a salesclerk; and when, through activism, I worked for change in the Chicano community. My empowerment coming full circle is evident through the sharing of my voice in my scholarship and my roles as teacher, lecturer, and historian. From the back of the bus to the ivory tower, I have learned the power of language.

THINKING CRITICALLY

1. What is the catalyst for Christine Marín's awareness of the power of Spanish in her life? How does she react to this event? How does it connect to her identity and her growing consciousness of the power of language?

2. How does Marín's physical appearance conflict with the expectations of the "Anglos" around her? Cite some examples in which her ethnic appearance causes cultural confusion and how she deals with this.

3. How does Marín learn to appreciate her heritage? Having been raised in an English-only household as an American, how does her ancestry begin to blend with her identity? Review the changes described by Marín to the term Chicano. What did the word mean to her when she was a child in a Mexican American household? How did the word change in the early 1970s while she was in college? What do you think accounts for this transition?

4. Until college, Marín says that she did not really feel that her Mexican heritage made her any different from her peers. What event does Marín experience as a freshman that changes her perspective? How does she react to it?

5. How does the Chicano Studies Collection at the University of Arizona become a means by which Marín's voice can be heard? What is this voice? How does it empower her?

6. What do you think is the meaning of the author's last sentence? Does it connect to her essay as a whole? Explain.

WRITING ASSIGNMENTS

1. Marín details some of the experiences that contributed to her awareness of the power of her ancestral language and its connection to her identity. Can you recall any events in your life that made you realize the connections between your language and your sense of self? Write about your experience.

2. When Marín was a freshman, she encountered a teacher who refused to believe that she was capable of writing well because of her physical appearance. Have you ever experienced a similar situation in which someone judged you by your looks and not by your verbal or intellectual skills? Alternatively, have you ever assumed the limits of another person's abilities based on what they looked like? Explain.

3. Is the way you personally use language something that you take for granted? Write an essay in which you explore the power of your own language. As you write, consider how language contributes to your identity and how you fit into your culture. How does your language empower you?

■ MAKING CONNECTIONS

1. Most students probably take literacy for granted. Imagine that you were illiterate—that is, you could not read or write. Brainstorm and make a list of all the things you could not do. Select one or two of the items on your list and write in your journal about what it might be like to be illiterate. You might try adopting the point of view of an illiterate young parent or a successful salesperson who has kept his or her illiteracy a secret.

2. Recall any communication difficulties you had as a child. Perhaps you are bilingual or had difficulty pronouncing certain words, or maybe an older sibling prevented you from expressing yourself. Explain how your experience made you feel, recalling, if possible, any particularly telling experiences. Can you identify with any of the authors in this section? If so, which ones and why?

3. Did your parents or grandparents come to America from another country? If not, are you acquainted with anyone who did? Conduct an interview with this person about his or her language choices. What is his or her view of the importance of language? What happened to his or her language after they moved to America? Provide a brief biographical sketch of the person you interviewed and present your research to the class.

4. Helen Keller writes that the acquisition of language "set her free." Malcolm X expresses similar views on the freeing power of language. In your journal, record your own feelings about the different ways that language provides freedom. In addition to drawing from some of the essays in this section, you may wish to add an experience of your own.

5. Each of the authors in this section recollects a moment in which they realized the power of language. For Malcolm X, it was when he realized how language could set him free. For Helen Keller, it was when she first connected words to abstract concepts. For Christine Marín, it was when she connected ethnic pride to the language of her ancestors. Write about a defining moment in your life when you felt the power of language.

6. Research the origins and development of American Sign Language. How does this system of communication qualify as "a language"? How has this language changed the lives of non-hearing people? Explain.

■ SPEAKING OUT: LANGUAGE THAT INSPIRED CHANGE

Seneca Falls Declaration
Elizabeth Cady Stanton

Elizabeth Cady Stanton (1815–1902) was one of the first activists for women's rights in America. Born in Johnstown, New York, she was educated at Johnstown Academy, an all-male school to which she was admitted under special arrangement. After a few years of study at the Troy Female Seminary, she turned to law, but was denied admission to the New York Bar because of her gender. Following her marriage to abolitionist Henry B. Stanton, she was denied recognition as a delegate at London's World Anti-Slavery Convention in 1840 because she was a woman. Incensed by such prejudice, Stanton dedicated the rest of her life to the abolition of laws that restricted the freedom and denied the civil rights of women.

In 1848, Stanton helped organize the Seneca Falls Convention, which inaugurated the movement for women's suffrage. In 1869, she was elected the first president of the National Woman's Suffrage Association, a post she held until 1890. Her writings include the three-volume *History of Woman's Suffrage* (1896), *A Woman's Bible* (1895), and her autobiographical *Eighty Years and More* (1898). The following speech, enumerating women's grievances and demanding equal rights, is modeled after Thomas Jefferson's Declaration of Independence. Stanton delivered this speech at the 1848 Seneca Falls Convention.

1 When in the course of human events, it becomes necessary for one portion of the family of man to assume among the people of the earth a position different from that which they have hitherto occupied, but one to which the laws of nature and of nature's God entitle them, a decent respect to the opinions of mankind requires that they should declare the causes that impel them to such a course.

2   We hold these truths to be self-evident: that all men and women are created equal; that they are endowed by their Creator with certain inalienable rights; that among these are life, liberty, and the pursuit of happiness; that to secure these rights governments are instituted, deriving their just powers from the consent of the governed. Whenever any form of government becomes destructive of these ends, it is the right of those who suffer from it to refuse allegiance to it, and to insist upon the

institution of a new government, laying its foundation on such principles, and organizing its powers in such form, as to them shall seem most likely to effect their safety and happiness. Prudence, indeed, will dictate that governments long established should not be changed for light and transient causes; and accordingly all experience hath shown that mankind are more disposed to suffer, while evils are sufferable, then to right themselves by abolishing the forms to which they were accustomed. But when a long train of abuses and usurpations, pursuing invariably the same object evinces a design to reduce them under absolute despotism, it is their duty to throw off such government, and to provide new guards for their future security. Such has been the patient sufferance of the women under this government, and such is now the necessity which constrains them to demand the equal station to which they are entitled.

3   The history of mankind is a history of repeated injuries and usurpations on the part of man toward woman, having in direct object the establishment of an absolute tyranny over her. To prove this, let facts be submitted to a candid world.

4   He has never permitted her to exercise her inalienable right to the elective franchise.

5   He has compelled her to submit to laws, in the formation of which she had no voice.

6   He has withheld from her rights which are given to the most ignorant and degraded men—both natives and foreigners.

7   Having deprived her of this first right of a citizen, the elective franchise, thereby leaving her without representation in the halls of legislation, he has oppressed her on all sides.

8   He has made her, if married, in the eye of the law, civilly dead.

9   He has taken from her all right in property, even to the wages she earns.

10   He has made her, morally, an irresponsible being, as she can commit many crimes with impunity, provided they be done in the presence of her husband. In the covenant of marriage she is compelled to promise obedience to her husband, he becoming, to all intents and purposes, her master—the law giving him power to deprive her of her liberty, and to administer chastisement.

11   He has so framed the laws of divorce, as to what shall be the proper causes, and in case of separation, to whom the guardianship of the children shall be given, as to be wholly regardless of the happiness of women—the law, in all cases, going upon a false supposition of the supremacy of man, and giving all power into his hands.

12   After depriving her of all rights as a married woman, if single, and the owner of property, he has taxed her to support a government which recognizes her only when her property can be made profitable to it.

13   He has monopolized nearly all the profitable employments, and from those she is permitted to follow, she receives but a scanty remuneration. He closes against her all the avenues to wealth and distinction which he considers most honorable to himself. As a teacher of theology, medicine, or law, she is not known.

14   He has denied her the facilities for obtaining a thorough education, all colleges being closed against her.

15   He allows her in Church, as well as State, but a subordinate position, claiming Apostolic authority for her exclusion from the ministry, and, with some exceptions, from any public participation in the affairs of the Church.

16   He has created a false public sentiment by giving to the world a different code of morals for men and women, by which moral delinquencies which exclude women from society, are not only tolerated, but deemed of little account in man.

17   He has usurped the prerogative of Jehovah himself, claiming it as his right to assign for her a sphere of action, when that belongs to her conscience and to her God.

18   He has endeavored, in every way that he could, to destroy her confidence in her own powers, to lessen her self-respect, and to make her willing to lead a dependent and abject life.

19   Now, in view of this entire disfranchisement of one-half the people of this country, their social and religious degradation—in view of the unjust laws above mentioned, and because women do feel themselves aggrieved, oppressed, and fraudulently deprived of their most sacred rights, we insist that they have immediate admission to all the rights and privileges which belong to them as citizens of the United States.

20   In entering upon the great work before us, we anticipate no small amount of misconception, misrepresentation, and ridicule; but we shall use every instrumentality without our power to effect our object. We shall employ agents, circulate tracts, petition the State and National legislatures, and endeavor to enlist the pulpit and the press on our behalf. We hope this Convention will be followed by a series of Conventions embracing every part of the country.

Resolutions

21 Whereas, The great precept of nature is conceded to be, that "man shall pursue his own true and substantial happiness." Blackstone in his Commentaries remarks, that this law of Nature being coeval with mankind, and dictated by God himself, is of course superior in obligation to any other. It is binding over all the globe, in all countries and at all times; no human laws are of any validity if contrary to this, and such of them as are valid, derive all their force, and all their validity, and all their authority, mediately and immediately, from this original; therefore,

22   *Resolved,* That such laws as conflict, in any way, with the true and substantial happiness of woman, are contrary to the great precept of nature and of no validity, for this is "superior in obligation to any other."

23   *Resolved,* That all laws which prevent woman from occupying such a station in society as her conscience shall dictate, or which place her in a position inferior to that of man, are contrary to the great precept of nature, and therefore of no force or authority.

24   *Resolved,* That woman is man's equal—was intended to be so by the Creator, and the highest good of the race demands that she should be recognized as such.

25 *Resolved,* That the women of this country ought to be enlightened in regard to the laws under which they live, that they may no longer publish their degradation by declaring themselves satisfied with their present position, nor their ignorance, by asserting that they have all the rights they want.

26 *Resolved,* That inasmuch as man, while claiming for himself intellectual superiority, does accord to woman moral superiority, it is preeminently his duty to encourage her to speak and teach, as she has an opportunity, in all religious assemblies.

27 *Resolved,* That the same amount of virtue, delicacy, and refinement of behavior that is required of woman in the social state, should also be required of man, and the same transgressions should be visited with equal severity on both man and woman.

28 *Resolved,* That the objection of indelicacy and impropriety, which is so often brought against woman when she addresses a public audience, comes with a very ill-grace from those who encourage, by their attendance, her appearance on the stage, in the concert, or in feats of the circus.

29 *Resolved,* That woman has too long rested satisfied in the circumscribed limits which corrupt customs and a perverted application of the Scriptures have marked out for her, and that it is time she should move in the enlarged sphere which her great Creator has assigned her.

30 *Resolved,* That it is the duty of the women of this country to secure to themselves their sacred right to the elective franchise.

31 *Resolved,* That the equality of human rights results necessarily from the fact of the identity of the race in capabilities and responsibilities.

32 *Resolved, therefore,* That, being invested by the Creator with the same capabilities, and the same consciousness of responsibility for their exercise, it is demonstrably the right and duty of woman, equally with man, to promote every righteous cause by every righteous means; and especially in regard to the great subjects of morals and religion, it is self-evidently her right to participate with her brother in teaching them, both in private and in public, by writing and by speaking, by any instrumentalities proper to be used, and in any assemblies proper to be held; and this being a self-evident truth growing out of the divinely implanted principles of human nature, any custom or authority adverse to it, whether modern or wearing the hoary sanction of antiquity, is to be regarded as a self-evident falsehood, and at war with mankind.

[At the last session Lucretia Mott offered and spoke to the following resolution:]

33 *Resolved,* That the speedy success of our cause depends upon the zealous and untiring efforts of both men and women, for the overthrow of the monopoly of the pulpit, and for the securing to women an equal participation with men in the various trades, professions, and commerce.

THINKING CRITICALLY

1. Why did Elizabeth Cady Stanton model her "Declaration of Sentiments and Resolutions" after the United States' Declaration of Independence? Do you think her strategy was effective? Why or why not? What statements does she make concerning the equality of men and women?

2. Which of the "repeated injuries and usurpation on the part of man toward woman" are still going on today?

3. What is the "great precept of nature" that Stanton refers to in paragraph 21? How does Stanton use this argument to provide a foundation for her resolutions? Where in the resolutions does she qualify her evidence from a higher authority when she refers to "a perverted application of the Scriptures"?

4. What do you think Stanton means when she urges women to be as responsible as men in promoting "every righteous cause by every righteous means" (paragraph 32)?

5. List the ways in which Stanton attempts to break down the social limitations placed upon women of her time. How does she attack these boundaries?

WRITING ASSIGNMENTS

1. Review the Seneca Falls Declaration and rewrite the resolutions that you feel have not yet been achieved. Use the same form employed by Stanton, but you may update the diction.

2. You are a newspaper reporter covering the Seneca Falls Convention in New York in 1848, for a front-page story. Write a newspaper article addressing the social and political implications of the rally. Be sure to include a title for your article.

3. Access the Library of Congress's photo archive of the Women's Suffrage Movement at <www.memory.loc.gov/ammem/today/jan11.html>. Drawing from the information gathered from this site and its many useful links, write a letter inviting one of the political activists from this era such as Alice Paul, Lucy Burns, Susan B. Anthony, Julia Ward Howe, Lucy Stone, or Carrie Chapman Catt to a twenty-first-century discussion on women's rights. Include some things about women's rights today that might provoke their interest.

"Letter from Birmingham Jail"
Martin Luther King, Jr.

In 1963, Martin Luther King, Jr. was arrested at a sit-in demonstration in Birmingham, Alabama. Written from a jail cell, the famous letter reprinted here was addressed to King's fellow clergy, who were critical of his activities in the name of social justice. The letter, however, has a second audience in mind—the collective conscience of the American people. As such, the letter functions much like one of King's speeches, in which he applies both emotion and logic to strategically make his point.

Martin Luther King, Jr. was one of the most prominent and charismatic leaders for black civil rights in America. An ordained minister with a doctorate in theology, King organized the Southern Christian Leadership Conference in 1957 to promote justice and equality for African Americans. Under King's leadership, the civil rights movement eventually eliminated racist laws that prohibited blacks from using restaurants, public swimming pools, and seats in the front sections of buses. For his efforts, King was awarded the Nobel Peace Prize in 1964. Four years later, while supporting striking sanitation workers in Memphis, Tennessee, King was assassinated.

"When your first name becomes "nigger," your middle name becomes "boy" (however old you are) and your last name becomes "John," and your wife and mother are never given the respected title "Mrs."; . . . when you are forever fighting a degenerating sense of "nobodiness"—then you will understand why we find it difficult to wait."

(Excerpt from Martin Luther King, Jr.'s "Letter From Birmingham Jail")

My Dear Fellow Clergymen:

1   While confined here in the Birmingham city jail, I came across your recent statement calling my present activities "unwise and untimely." Seldom do I pause to answer criticism of my work and ideas. If I sought to answer all the criticisms that cross my desk, my secretaries would have little time for anything other than such correspondence in the course of the day, and I would have no time for constructive work. But since I feel that you are men of genuine good will and that your criticisms are sincerely set forth, I want to try to answer your statement in what I hope will be patient and reasonable terms.

2   I think I should indicate why I am here in Birmingham, since you have been influenced by the view which argues against "outsiders coming in." I have the honor of serving as president of the Southern Christian Leadership Conference, an organization operating in every southern state, with headquarters in Atlanta, Georgia. We have some eighty-five affiliated organizations across the South, and one of them is the Alabama Christian Movement for Human Rights. Frequently we share staff, educational and financial resources with our affiliates. Several months ago the affiliate here in Birmingham asked us to be on call to engage in a nonviolent direct-action program if such were deemed necessary. We readily consented, and when the hour came we lived up to our promise. So I, along with several members of my

staff, am here because I was invited here, I am here because I have organizational ties here.

3   But more basically, I am in Birmingham because injustice is here. Just as the prophets of the eighth century B.C. left their villages and carried their "thus saith the Lord" far beyond the boundaries of their home towns, and just as the Apostle Paul left his village of Tarsus and carried the gospel of Jesus Christ to the far corners of the Greco-Roman world, so am I compelled to carry the gospel of freedom beyond my own home town. Like Paul, I must constantly respond to the Macedonian call for aid.

4   Moreover, I am cognizant of the interrelatedness of all communities and states. I cannot sit idly by in Atlanta and not be concerned about what happens in Birmingham. Injustice anywhere is a threat to justice everywhere. We are caught in an inescapable network of mutuality, tied in a single garment of destiny. Whatever affects one directly, affects all indirectly. Never again can we afford to live with the narrow, provincial "outside agitator" idea. Anyone who lives inside the United States can never be considered an outsider anywhere within its bounds.

5   You deplore the demonstrations taking place in Birmingham. But your statement, I am sorry to say, fails to express a similar concern for the conditions that brought about the demonstrations. I am sure that none of you would want to rest content with the superficial kind of social analysis that deals merely with effects and does not grapple with underlying causes. It is unfortunate that demonstrations are taking place in Birmingham, but it is even more unfortunate that the city's white power structure left the Negro community with no alternative.

6   In any nonviolent campaign there are four basic steps: collection of the facts to determine whether injustices exist; negotiation; self-purification; and direct action. We have gone through all these steps in Birmingham. There can be no gainsaying the fact that racial injustice engulfs this community. Birmingham is probably the most thoroughly segregated city in the United States. Its ugly record of brutality is widely known. Negroes have experienced grossly unjust treatment in the courts. There have been more unsolved bombings of Negro homes and churches in Birmingham than in any other city in the nation. These are the hard, brutal facts of the case. On the basis of these conditions, Negro leaders sought to negotiate with the city fathers. But the latter consistently refused to engage in good-faith negotiation.

7   Then, last September, came the opportunity to talk with leaders of Birmingham's economic community. In the course of the negotiations, certain promises were made by the merchants—for example, to remove the stores' humiliating racial signs. On the basis of these promises, the Reverend Fred Shuttlesworth and the leaders of the Alabama Christian Movement for Human Rights agreed to a moratorium on all demonstrations. As the weeks and months went by, we realized that we were the victims of a broken promise. A few signs, briefly removed, returned; the others remained.

8   As in so many past experiences, our hopes had been blasted, and the shadow of deep disappointment settled upon us. We had no alternative except to prepare for direct action, whereby we would present our very bodies as a means of laying our case before the conscience of the local and the national community. Mindful of the

difficulties involved, we decided to undertake a process of self-purification. We began a series of workshops on nonviolence, and we repeatedly asked ourselves: "Are you able to accept blows without retaliating?" "Are you able to endure the ordeal of jail?" We decided to schedule our direct-action program for the Easter season, realizing that except for Christmas, this is the main shopping period of the year. Knowing that a strong economic-withdrawal program would be the by-product of direct action, we felt that this would be the best time to bring pressure to bear on the merchants for the needed change.

9   Then it occurred to us that Birmingham's mayoralty election was coming up in March, and we speedily decided to postpone action until after election day. When we discovered that the Commissioner of Public Safety, Eugene "Bull" Connor, had piled up enough votes to be in the run-off, we decided again to postpone action until the day after the run-off so that the demonstrations could not be used to cloud the issues. Like many others, we waited to see Mr. Connor defeated, and to this end we endured postponement after postponement. Having aided in this community need, we felt that our direct-action program could be delayed no longer.

10   You may well ask: "Why direct action? Why sit-ins, marches and so forth? Isn't negotiation a better path?" You are quite right in calling for negotiation. Indeed, this is the very purpose of direct action. Nonviolent direct action seeks to create such a crisis and foster such a tension that a community which has constantly refused to negotiate is forced to confront the issue. It seeks so to dramatize the issue that it can no longer be ignored. My citing the creation of tension as part of the work of the nonviolent-resister may sound rather shocking. But I must confess that I am not afraid of the word "tension." I have earnestly opposed violent tension, but there is a type of constructive, nonviolent tension which is necessary for growth. Just as Socrates felt that it was necessary to create a tension in the mind so that individuals could rise from the bondage of myths and half-truths to the unfettered realm of creative analysis and objective appraisal, so must we see the need for nonviolent gadflies to create the kind of tension in society that will help men rise from the dark depths of prejudice and racism to the majestic heights of understanding and brotherhood.

11   The purpose of our direct-action program is to create a situation so crisis-packed that it will inevitably open the door to negotiation. I therefore concur with you in your call for negotiation. Too long has our beloved Southland been bogged down in a tragic effort to live in monologue rather than dialogue.

12   One of the basic points in your statement is that the action that I and my associates have taken in Birmingham is untimely. Some have asked: "Why didn't you give the new city administration time to act?" The only answer that I can give to this query is that the new Birmingham administration must be prodded about as much as the outgoing one, before it will act. We are sadly mistaken if we feel that the election of Albert Boutwell as mayor will bring the millennium to Birmingham. While Mr. Boutwell is a much more gentle person than Mr. Connor, they are both segregationists, dedicated to maintenance of the status quo. I have hope that Mr. Boutwell will be reasonable enough to see the futility of massive resistance to desegregation. But he will not see this without pressure from devotees of civil rights.

My friends, I must say to you that we have not made a single gain in civil rights without determined legal and nonviolent pressure. Lamentably, it is an historical fact that privileged groups seldom give up their privileges voluntarily. Individuals may see the moral light and voluntarily give up their unjust posture; but, as Reinhold Niebuhr has reminded us, groups tend to be more immoral than individuals.

13   We know through painful experience that freedom is never voluntarily given by the oppressor; it must be demanded by the oppressed. Frankly, I have yet to engage in a direct-action campaign that was "well timed" in the view of those who have not suffered unduly from the disease of segregation. For years now I have heard the word "Wait!" It rings in the ear of every Negro with piercing familiarity. This "Wait" has almost always meant "Never." We must come to see, with one of our distinguished jurists, that "justice too long delayed is justice denied."

14   We have waited for more than 340 years for our constitutional and God-given rights. The nations of Asia and Africa are moving with jet-like speed toward gaining political independence, but we still creep at horse-and-buggy pace toward gaining a cup of coffee at a lunch counter. Perhaps it is easy for those who have never felt the stinging darts of segregation to say, "Wait." But when you have seen vicious mobs lynch your mothers and fathers at will and drown your sisters and brothers at whim; when you have seen hate-filled policemen curse, kick, and even kill your black brothers and sisters; when you see the vast majority of your twenty million Negro brothers smothering in an airtight cage of poverty in the midst of an affluent society; when you suddenly find your tongue twisted and your speech stammering as you seek to explain to your six-year-old daughter why she can't go to the public amusement that has just been advertised on television, and see tears welling up in her eyes when she is told that Funtown is closed to colored children, and see ominous clouds of inferiority beginning to form in her little mental sky, and see her beginning to distort her personality by developing an unconscious bitterness toward white people; when you have to concoct an answer for a five-year-old son who is asking: "Daddy, why do white people treat colored people so mean?"; when you take a cross-country drive and find it necessary to sleep night after night in the uncomfortable corners of your automobile because no motel will accept you; when you are humiliated day in and day out by nagging signs reading "white" and "colored"; when your first name becomes "nigger," your middle name becomes "boy" (however old you are) and your last name becomes "John," and your wife and mother are never given the respected title "Mrs."; when you are harried by day and haunted by night by the fact that you are Negro, living constantly at tiptoe stance, never quite knowing what to expect next, and are plagued with inner fears and outer resentments; when you are forever fighting a degenerating sense of "nobodiness"— then you will understand why we find it difficult to wait. There comes a time when the cup of endurance runs over, and men are no longer willing to be plunged into the abyss of despair. I hope, sirs, you can understand our legitimate and unavoidable impatience.

15   You express a great deal of anxiety over our willingness to break laws. This is certainly a legitimate concern. Since we so diligently urge people to obey the Supreme Court's decision of 1954 outlawing segregation in the public schools, at

first glance it may seem rather paradoxical for us consciously to break laws. One may well ask: "How can you advocate breaking some laws and obeying others?" The answer lies in the fact that there are two types of laws: just and unjust. I would be the first to advocate obeying just laws. One has not only a legal but a moral responsibility to obey just laws. Conversely, one has a moral responsibility to disobey unjust laws. I would agree with St. Augustine that "an unjust law is no law at all."

16   Now, what is the difference between the two? How does one determine whether a law is just or unjust? A just law is a man-made code that squares with the moral law or the law of God. An unjust law is a code that is out of harmony with the moral law. To put it in the terms of St. Thomas Aquinas: An unjust law is a human law that is not rooted in eternal law and natural law. Any law that uplifts human personality is just. Any law that degrades human personality is unjust. All segregation statutes are unjust because segregation distorts the soul and damages the personality. It gives the segregator a false sense of superiority and the segregated a false sense of inferiority. Segregation, to use the terminology of the Jewish philosopher Martin Buber, substitutes an "I-it" relationship for an "I-thou" relationship and ends up relegating persons to the status of things. Hence segregation is not only politically, economically and sociologically unsound, it is morally wrong and sinful. Paul Tillich has said that sin is separation. Is not segregation an existential expression of man's tragic separation, his awful estrangement, his terrible sinfulness? Thus it is that I can urge men to obey the 1954 decision of the Supreme Court, for it is morally right; and I can urge them to disobey segregation ordinances, for they are morally wrong.

17   Let us consider a more concrete example of just and unjust laws. An unjust law is a code that a numerical or power majority group compels a minority group to obey but does not make binding on itself. This is *difference* made legal. By the same token, a just law is a code that a majority compels a minority to follow and that it is willing to follow itself. This is *sameness* made legal.

18   Let me give another explanation. A law is unjust if it is inflicted on a minority that, as a result of being denied the right to vote, had no part in enacting or devising the law. Who can say that the legislature of Alabama which set up that state's segregation laws was democratically elected? Throughout Alabama all sorts of devious methods are used to prevent Negroes from becoming registered voters, and there are some counties in which, even though Negroes constitute a majority of the population, not a single Negro is registered. Can any law enacted under such circumstances be considered democratically structured?

19   Sometimes a law is just on its face and unjust in its application. For instance, I have been arrested on a charge of parading without a permit. Now, there is nothing wrong in having an ordinance which requires a permit for a parade. But such an ordinance becomes unjust when it is used to maintain segregation and to deny citizens the First-Amendment privilege of peaceful assembly and protest.

20   I hope you are able to see the distinction I am trying to point out. In no sense do I advocate evading or defying the law, as would the rabid segregationist. That would lead to anarchy. One who breaks an unjust law must do so openly, lovingly,

and with a willingness to accept the penalty. I submit that an individual who breaks a law that conscience tells him is unjust, and who willingly accepts the penalty of imprisonment in order to arouse the conscience of the community over its injustice, is in reality expressing the highest respect for law.

21   Of course, there is nothing new about this kind of civil disobedience. It was evidenced sublimely in the refusal of Shadrach, Meshach and Abednego to obey the laws of Nebuchadnezzar, on the ground that a higher moral law was at stake. It was practiced superbly by the early Christians, who were willing to face hungry lions and the excruciating pain of chopping blocks rather than submit to certain unjust laws of the Roman Empire. To a degree, academic freedom is a reality today because Socrates practiced civil disobedience. In our own nation, the Boston Tea Party represented a massive act of civil disobedience.

22   We should never forget that everything Adolf Hitler did in Germany was "legal" and everything the Hungarian freedom fighters did in Hungary was "illegal." It was "illegal" to aid and comfort a Jew in Hitler's Germany. Even so, I am sure that, had I lived in Germany at the time, I would have aided and comforted my Jewish brothers. If today I lived in a Communist country where certain principles dear to the Christian faith are suppressed, I would openly advocate disobeying that country's antireligious laws.

23   I must make two honest confessions to you, my Christian and Jewish brothers. First, I must confess that over the past few years I have been gravely disappointed with the white moderate. I have almost reached the regrettable conclusion that the Negro's great stumbling block in his stride toward freedom is not the White Citizen's Counciler or the Ku Klux Klanner, but the white moderate, who is more devoted to "order" than to justice; who prefers a negative peace which is the absence of tension to a positive peace which is the presence of justice; who constantly says: "I agree with you in the goal you seek, but I cannot agree with your methods of direct action"; who paternalistically believes he can set the timetable for another man's freedom; who lives by a mythical concept of time and who constantly advises the Negro to wait for a "more convenient season." Shallow misunderstanding from people of good will is more frustrating than absolute misunderstanding from people of ill will. Lukewarm acceptance is much more bewildering than outright rejection.

24   I had hoped that the white moderate would understand that law and order exist for the purpose of establishing justice and that when they fail in this purpose they become the dangerously structured dams that block the flow of social progress. I had hoped that the white moderate would understand that the present tension in the South is a necessary phase of the transition from an obnoxious negative peace, in which the Negro passively accepted his unjust plight, to a substantive and positive peace, in which all men will respect the dignity and worth of human personality. Actually, we who engage in nonviolent direct action are not the creators of tension. We merely bring to the surface the hidden tension that is already alive. We bring it out in the open, where it can be seen and dealt with. Like a boil that can never be cured so long as it is covered up but must be opened with all its ugliness to the natural medicines of air and light, injustice must be exposed, with all the tension its

exposure creates, to the light of human conscience and the air of national opinion before it can be cured.

25   In your statement you assert that our actions, even though peaceful, must be condemned because they precipitate violence. But is this a logical assertion? Isn't this like condemning a robbed man because his possession of money precipitated the evil act of robbery? Isn't this like condemning Socrates because his unswerving commitment to truth and his philosophical inquiries precipitated the act by the misguided populace in which they made him drink hemlock? Isn't this like condemning Jesus because his unique God-consciousness and never-ceasing devotion to God's will precipitated the evil act of crucifixion? We must come to see that, as the federal courts have consistently affirmed, it is wrong to urge an individual to cease his efforts to gain his basic constitutional rights because the quest may precipitate violence. Society must protect the robbed and punish the robber.

26   I had also hoped that the white moderate would reject the myth concerning time in relation to the struggle for freedom. I have just received a letter from a white brother in Texas. He writes: "All Christians know that the colored people will receive equal rights eventually, but it is possible that you are in too great a religious hurry. It has taken Christianity almost two thousand years to accomplish what it has. The teachings of Christ take time to come to earth." Such an attitude stems from a tragic misconception of time, from the strangely irrational notion that there is something in the very flow of time that will inevitably cure all ills. Actually, time itself is neutral; it can be used either destructively or constructively. More and more I feel that the people of ill will have used time much more effectively than have the people of good will. We will have to repent in this generation not merely for the hateful words and actions of the bad people but for the appalling silence of the good people. Human progress never rolls in on wheels of inevitability; it comes through the tireless efforts of men willing to be co-workers with God, and without this hard work, time itself becomes an ally of the forces of social stagnation. We must use time creatively, in the knowledge that the time is always ripe to do right. Now is the time to make real the promise of democracy and transform our pending national elegy into a creative psalm of brotherhood. Now is the time to lift our national policy from the quicksand of racial injustice to the solid rock of human dignity.

27   You speak of our activity in Birmingham as extreme. At first I was rather disappointed that fellow clergymen would see my nonviolent efforts as those of an extremist. I began thinking about the fact that I stand in the middle of two opposing forces in the Negro Community. One is a force of complacency, made up in part of Negroes who, as a result of long years of oppression, are so drained of self-respect and a sense of "somebodiness" that they have adjusted to segregation; and in part of a few middle-class Negroes who, because of a degree of academic and economic security and because in some ways they profit by segregation, have become insensitive to the problems of the masses. The other force is one of bitterness and hatred, and it comes perilously close to advocating violence. It is expressed in the various black nationalist groups that are springing up across the nation, the largest and best known being Elijah Muhammad's Muslim movement. Nourished by the Negro's

frustration over the continued existence of racial discrimination, this movement is made up of people who have lost faith in America, who have absolutely repudiated Christianity, and who have concluded that the white man is an incorrigible "devil."

28   I have tried to stand between these two forces, saying that we need emulate neither the "do-nothingism" of the complacent nor the hatred and despair of the black nationalist. For there is the more excellent way of love and nonviolent protest. I am grateful to God that, through the influence of the Negro church, the way of nonviolence became an integral part of our struggle.

29   If this philosophy had not emerged, by now many streets of the South would, I am convinced, be flowing with blood. And I am further convinced that if our white brothers dismiss as "rabble-rousers" and "outside agitators" those of us who employ nonviolent direct action, and if they refuse to support our nonviolent efforts, millions of Negroes will, out of frustration and despair, seek solace and security in black-nationalist ideologies—a development that would inevitably lead to a frightening racial nightmare.

30   Oppressed people cannot remain oppressed forever. The yearning for freedom eventually manifests itself, and that is what has happened to the American Negro. Something within has reminded him of his birthright of freedom, and something without has reminded him that it can be gained. Consciously or unconsciously, he has been caught up by the *Zeitgeist,* and with his black brothers of Africa and his brown and yellow brothers of Asia, South America and the Caribbean, the United States Negro is moving with a sense of great urgency toward the promised land of racial justice. If one recognizes this vital urge that has engulfed the Negro community, one should readily understand why public demonstrations are taking place. The Negro has many pent-up resentments and latent frustrations, and he must release them. So let him march; let him make prayer pilgrimages to the city hall; let him go on freedom rides—and try to understand why he must do so. If his repressed emotions are not released in nonviolent ways, they will seek expression through violence; this is not a threat but a fact of history. So I have not said to my people: "Get rid of your discontent." Rather, I have tried to say that this normal and healthy discontent can be channeled into the creative outlet of nonviolent direction action. And now this approach is being termed extremist.

31   But though I was initially disappointed at being categorized as an extremist, as I continue to think about the matter I gradually gained a measure of satisfaction from the label. Was not Jesus an extremist for love: "Love your enemies, bless them that curse you, do good to them that hate you, and pray for them which despitefully use you, and persecute you." Was not Amos an extremist for justice: "Let justice roll down like waters and righteousness like an everflowing stream." Was not Paul an extremist for the Christian gospel: "I bear in my body the marks of the Lord Jesus." Was not Martin Luther an extremist: "Here I stand; I cannot do otherwise, so help me God." And John Bunyan: "I will stay in jail to the end of my days before I make a butchery of my conscience." And Abraham Lincoln: "This nation cannot survive half slave and half free." And Thomas Jefferson: "We hold these truths to be self-evident, that all men are created equal. . . ." So the question is not

whether we will be extremists, but what kind of extremists we will be. Will we be extremists for hate or for love? Will we be extremists for the preservation of injustice or for the existence of justice? In that dramatic scene on Calvary's hill three men were crucified. We must never forget that all three were crucified for the same crime—the crime of extremism. Two were extremists for immorality, and thus fell below their environment. The other, Jesus Christ, was an extremist for love, truth and goodness, and thereby rose above his environment. Perhaps the South, the nation and the world are in dire need of creative extremists. . . .

32   If I have said anything in this letter that overstates the truth and indicates an unreasonable impatience, I beg you to forgive me. If I have said anything that understates the truth and indicates my having a patience that allows me to settle for anything less than brotherhood, I beg God to forgive me.

33   I hope this letter finds you strong in the faith. I also hope that circumstances will soon make it possible for me to meet each of you, not as an integrationist or a civil-rights leader but as a fellow clergyman and a Christian brother. Let us all hope that the dark clouds of racial prejudice will soon pass away and the deep fog of misunderstanding will be lifted from our fear-drenched communities, and in some not too distant tomorrow the radiant stars of love and brotherhood will shine over our great nation with all their scintillating beauty.

Yours for the cause of Peace and Brotherhood,
Martin Luther King, Jr.

THINKING CRITICALLY

1. King states in paragraph 26, "We will have to repent in this generation not merely for the hateful words and actions of the bad people but for the appalling silence of the good people." What does this statement mean to you? Do you agree? In what situations might silence be appalling?

2. Describe the voice and tone King uses in this letter. What does his voice reveal about his personality, and how does it affect his argument? How does he establish credibility, authority, and personality in his letter? Explain.

3. In paragraph 12, King states that the Birmingham officials at the time were "dedicated to maintenance of the status quo." What was the status quo in the Birmingham of 1963? What is the status quo today?

4. In paragraph 14, King provides a "catalogue" of reasons why the civil rights movement cannot wait any longer. Analyze this technique in terms of King's argument. What effect does this cataloguing have on the reader?

5. Martin Luther King, Jr. was first and foremost a preacher. How does the language in his letter reveal his profession? Would this letter be as effective as a speech? Would it be better? How does the medium (letter or speech) affect the choice of language used?

6. In paragraphs 15 through 20 King provides "proof" regarding the differences between just and unjust laws. Examine the language in this section and decide whether his logic is effective. Explain your conclusions.

WRITING ASSIGNMENTS

1. Some critics have commented that King was considered a great leader by the white status quo because he preached a program of nonviolence and used a rhetoric that reflected "acceptable American values." Explore this idea further by researching some additional speeches made by King. Then, write an essay addressing this issue expressing your opinion, and drawing on information from your research.

2. Using the language techniques employed by King in his letter, write your own letter directed toward people you respect protesting an injustice that you feel they may not entirely understand. Consider the concerns of your audience as you explain the nature of the injustice, the history/sociology behind it, and why you feel your argument is valid and should be accepted by your readers.

3. In his letter, King justifies civil disobedience by arguing that the established laws are unjust. Are there any current laws that seem unjust to you? Would you demonstrate to protest a current unjust law or practice? Why or why not?

Aren't I a Woman?
Sojourner Truth

Sojourner Truth was born into slavery with the name Isabella Baumfree around 1797. In 1826, she escaped to freedom with her infant daughter Sophia. In 1843, she changed her name to Sojourner Truth, which some biographers attribute to her intention to travel the country "telling the truth." Other historians report that her name change was connected to a religious experience. During her lifetime she spoke for women's rights and prison reform and even addressed the Michigan Legislature speaking against capital punishment. She was highly respected among abolitionists and met Abraham Lincoln in 1864 at the White House. She also met Elizabeth Cady Stanton in 1867, while traveling through the South. After a long life fighting for human rights, Sojourner Truth died at her home in Battle Creek, Michigan, in 1883.

In May of 1851, Sojourner Truth attended a women's rights convention held in Akron, Ohio. The only black woman in attendance, on the second day of the convention, Truth rose from her seat and approached the podium. Nearly six-feet tall, with a deep clear voice, Truth systematically refuted the claims of some of the male speakers that day. What follows is a transcription of that speech as recorded by Frances D. Gage, who presided at the convention.

1   Well, children, where there is so much racket there must be something out o' kilter. I think that 'twixt the Negroes of the South and the women of the North all a-talking about rights, the white man will be in a fix pretty soon.

2   But what's all this here talking about? That man over there says that women need to be helped into carriages, and lifted over ditches, and to have the best place

everywhere. Nobody ever helps me into carriages, or over mud puddles or gives me any best place *(and raising herself to her full height and her voice to a pitch like rolling thunder, she asked),* and aren't I a woman? Look at me! Look at my arm! *(And she bared her right arm to the shoulder, showing her tremendous muscular power.)* I have plowed, and planted, and gathered into barns, and no man could head me—and aren't I a woman? I could work as much and eat as much as a man (when I could get it), and bear the lash as well—and aren't I a woman? I have borne thirteen children and seen them almost all sold off into slavery, and when I cried out with a mother's grief, none but Jesus heard—and aren't I a woman? Then they talk about this thing in the head—what's this they call it? *("Intellect," whispered someone near.)* That's it honey. What's that got to do with woman's rights or Negroes' rights? If my cup won't hold but a pint and yours holds a quart, wouldn't you be mean not to let me have my little half-measure full? *(And she pointed her significant finger and sent a keen glance at the minister who had made the argument. The cheering was long and loud.)*

3   Then that little man in black there, he says women can't have as much rights as man, 'cause Christ wasn't a woman. Where did your Christ come from? *(Rolling thunder could not have stilled that crowd as did those deep, wonderful tones, as she stood there with outstretched arms and eye of fire Raising her voice still louder, she repeated,)* Where did your Christ come from? From God and a woman. Man had nothing to do with him. *(Oh! what a rebuke she gave the little man.)*

4   *(Turning again to another objector, she took up the defense of mother Eve. I cannot follower [sic] her through it all. It was pointed, and witty, and solemn, eliciting at almost every sentence deafening applause; and she ended [sic] by asserting that)* If the first woman God ever made was strong enough to turn the world upside down, all alone, these together *(and she glanced her eye over us),* ought to be able to turn it back and get it right side up again; and now they are asking to do it, the men better let them. *(Long-continued cheering.)*

5   'Bliged to you for hearing on me, and now old Sojourner hasn't got anything more to say.

THINKING CRITICALLY

1. How does Truth prefix each of her "answers" to the male dissenters? Can you figure out what the men said from Truth's words? Explain.

2. What is the biblical argument against the equality of women? How does Truth address this argument?

3. According to historians, the women at the Akron convention asked Frances Gage to prevent Truth from speaking, fearing that it would "mix and confuse" causes. What do you think was the basis of their fear? How do you think they felt about Truth after she spoke?

4. What kind of courage did it take for Truth to speak at this convention, both as a woman and as an ex-slave? How does she use her background to assert her convictions? Is she effective in making her point? Explain.

WRITING ASSIGNMENTS

1. Visit the Sojourner Truth Institute at <www.sojournertruth.org> and read more about this remarkable woman. Write an essay on how her achievements as a woman and as a former slave left their mark on our history. How do you think Truth would react to our society today?

2. Both Stanton and Truth address the "biblical" argument made against women's rights. Stanton calls this argument "perverted," and Truth likewise challenges it. To what argument are they referring? Evaluate this "biblical argument" against women's rights. Then write an essay in which you address this issue. How does the biblical argument factor into our modern ideology?

3. Compare the general status of American women with that of women in other countries in order to demonstrate the wide range of women's rights and roles. Using library research and, if possible, personal testimony from people from other countries, develop your findings in a paper. A good Web site on international women's rights is at <www.wld.org/org.html>, which provides links to other Internet Web sites addressing women's rights.

The Struggle for Human Rights
Eleanor Roosevelt

Anna Eleanor Roosevelt was the wife of Franklin D. Roosevelt, the thirty-second president of the United States. As First Lady during her husband's presidency from 1933 to 1945, Roosevelt served as her husband's political right arm. She expanded the role of the president's wife into a position involving political action and public service. Their marriage is considered one of the "greatest political partnerships in history." After her husband's death while still in office in 1945, Roosevelt remained active in international politics. In 1946, she was elected head of the United Nation's Human Rights Division, and she played a central role in the adoption of the Declaration of Human Rights by the United Nations in 1948. She remained a member of the UN delegation until 1953, but continued to participate in international human rights issues until her death in 1962.

Roosevelt delivered the following speech on September 28, 1948, at the Sorbonne during a meeting of the United Nation's General Assembly in Paris. Several months later, on December 10, 1948, the Human Rights Declaration was passed by the UN.

1 I have come this evening to talk with you on one of the greatest issues of our time—that is the preservation of human freedom. I have chosen to discuss it here in France, at the Sorbonne, because here in this soil the roots of human freedom have long ago struck deep and here they have been richly nourished. It was here the Declaration of the Rights of Man was proclaimed, and the great slogans of the French Revolution—liberty, equality, fraternity—fired the imagination of men. I have cho-

sen to discuss this issue in Europe because this has been the scene of the greatest historic battles between freedom and tyranny. I have chosen to discuss it in the early days of the General Assembly because the issue of human liberty is decisive for the settlement of outstanding political differences and for the future of the United Nations.

2   The decisive importance of this issue was fully recognized by the founders of the United Nations at San Francisco. Concern for the preservation and promotion of human rights and fundamental freedoms stands at the heart of the United Nations. Its Charter is distinguished by its preoccupation with the rights and welfare of individual men and women. The United Nations has made it clear that it intends to uphold human rights and to protect the dignity of the human personality. In the preamble to the Charter the keynote is set when it declares: "We the people of the United Nations determined . . . to reaffirm faith in fundamental human rights, in the dignity and worth of the human person, in the equal rights of men and women and of nations large and small, and . . . to promote social progress and better standards of life in larger freedom." This reflects the basic premise of the Charter that the peace and security of mankind are dependent on mutual respect for the rights and freedoms of all.

3   One of the purposes of the United Nations is declared in article 1 to be: "to achieve international cooperation in solving international problems of an economic, social, cultural, or humanitarian character, and in promoting and encouraging respect for human rights and for fundamental freedoms for all without distinction as to race, sex, language, or religion."

4   This thought is repeated at several points and notably in articles 55 and 56 the Members pledge themselves to take joint and separate action in cooperation with the United Nations for the promotion of "universal respect for, and observance of, human rights and fundamental freedoms for all without distinction as to race, sex, language, or religion."

5   The Human Rights Commission was given as its first and most important task the preparation of an International Bill of Rights. The General Assembly, which opened its third session here in Paris a few days ago, will have before it the first fruit of the Commission's labors in this task, that is the International Declaration of Human Rights.

6   The Declaration was finally completed after much work during the last session of the Human Rights Commission in New York in the spring of 1948. The Economic and Social Council has sent it without recommendation to the General Assembly, together with other documents transmitted by the Human Rights Commission.

7   It was decided in our Commission that a Bill of Rights should contain two parts:

8   1. A Declaration which could be approved through action of the Member States of the United Nations in the General Assembly. This declaration would have great moral force, and would say to the peoples of the world "this is what we hope human rights may mean to all people in the years to come." We have put down here the rights that we consider basic for individual human beings the world over to

have. Without them, we feel that the full development of individual personality is impossible.

9   2. The second part of the bill, which the Human Rights Commission has not yet completed because of the lack of time, is a covenant which would be in the form of a treaty to be presented to the nations of the world. Each nation, as it is prepared to do so, would ratify this covenant and the covenant would then become binding on the nations which adhere to it. Each nation ratifying would then be obligated to change its laws wherever they did not conform to the points contained in the covenant.

10   This covenant, of course, would have to be a simpler document. It could not state aspirations, which we feel to be permissible in the Declaration. It could only state rights which could be assured by law and it must contain methods of implementation, and no state ratifying the covenant could be allowed to disregard it. The methods of implementation have not yet been agreed upon, nor have they been given adequate consideration by the Commission at any of its meetings. There certainly should be discussion on the entire question of this world Bill of Human Rights and there may be acceptance by this Assembly of the Declaration if they come to agreement on it. The acceptance of the Declaration, I think, should encourage every nation in the coming months to discuss its meaning with its people so that they will be better prepared to accept the covenant with a deeper understanding of the problems involved when that is presented, we hope, a year from now and, we hope, accepted.

11   The Declaration has come from the Human Rights Commission with unanimous acceptance except for four abstentions—the U.S.S.R., Yugoslavia, Ukraine, and Byelorussia. The reason for this is a fundamental difference in the conception of human rights as they exist in these states and in certain other Member States in the United Nations.

12   In the discussion before the Assembly, I think it should be made crystal clear what these differences are and tonight I want to spend a little time making them clear to you. It seems to me there is a valid reason for taking the time today to think carefully and clearly on the subject of human rights, because in the acceptance and observance of these rights lies the root, I believe, of our chance of peace in the future, and for the strengthening of the United Nations organization to the point where it can maintain peace in the future.

13   We must not be confused about what freedom is. Basic human rights are simple and easily understood: freedom of speech and a free press; freedom of religion and worship; freedom of assembly and the right of petition; the right of men to be secure in their homes and free from unreasonable search and seizure and from arbitrary arrest and punishment.

14   We must not be deluded by the efforts of the forces of reaction to prostitute the great words of our free tradition and thereby to confuse the struggle. Democracy, freedom, human rights have come to have a definite meaning to the people of the world which we must not allow any nation to so change that they are made synonymous with suppression and dictatorship.

15   There are basic differences that show up even in the use of words between a democratic and a totalitarian country. For instance "democracy" means one thing to the U.S.S.R. and another to the U.S.A. and, I know, in France. I have served since the first meeting of the nuclear commission on the Human Rights Commission, and I think this point stands out clearly.

16   The U.S.S.R. Representatives assert that they already have achieved many things which we, in what they call the "bourgeois democracies" cannot achieve because their government controls the accomplishment of these things. Our government seems powerless to them because, in the last analysis, it is controlled by the people. They would not put it that way—they would say that the people in the U.S.S.R. control their government by allowing their government to have certain absolute rights. We, on the other hand, feel that certain rights can never be granted to the government, but must be kept in the hands of the people.

17   For instance, the U.S.S.R. will assert that their press is free because the state makes it free by providing the machinery, the paper, and even the money for salaries for the people who work on the paper. They state that there is no control over what is printed in the various papers that they subsidize in this manner, such, for instance, as a trade-union paper. But what would happen if a paper were to print ideas which were critical of the basic policies and beliefs of the Communist government? I am sure some good reason would be found for abolishing the paper.

18   It is true that there have been many cases where newspapers in the U.S.S.R. have criticized officials and their actions and have been responsible for the removal of those officials, but in doing so they did not criticize anything which was fundamental to Communist beliefs. They simply criticized methods of doing things, so one must differentiate between things which are permissible, such as criticism of any individual or of the manner of doing things, and the criticism of a belief which would be considered vital to the acceptance of Communism.

19   What are the differences, for instance, between trade-unions in the totalitarian states and in the democracies? In the totalitarian state a trade-union is an instrument used by the government to enforce duties, not to assert rights. Propaganda material which the government desires the workers to have is furnished by the trade-unions to be circulated to their members.

20   Our trade-unions, on the other hand, are solely the instrument of the workers themselves. They represent the workers in their relations with the government and with management and they are free to develop their own opinions without government help or interference. The concepts of our trade-unions and those in totalitarian countries are drastically different. There is little mutual understanding.

21   I think the best example one can give of this basic difference of the use of terms is "the right to work." The Soviet Union insists that this is a basic right which it alone can guarantee because it alone provides full employment by the government. But the right to work in the Soviet Union means the assignment of workers to do whatever task is given to them by the government without an opportunity for the people to participate in the decision that the government should do this. A society in which everyone works is not necessarily a free society and may indeed be a slave

society; on the other hand, a society in which there is widespread economic insecurity can turn freedom into a barren and vapid right for millions of people.

22   We in the United States have come to realize it means freedom to choose one's job, to work or not to work as one desires. We, in the United States, have come to realize, however, that people have a right to demand that their government will not allow them to starve because as individuals they cannot find work of the kind they are accustomed to doing and this is a decision brought about by public opinion which came as a result of the Great Depression in which many people were out of work, but we would not consider in the United States that we had gained any freedom if we were compelled to follow a dictatorial assignment to work where and when we were told. The right of choice would seem to us an important, fundamental freedom.

23   I have great sympathy with the Russian people. They love their country and have always defended it valiantly against invaders. They have been through a period of revolution, as a result of which they were for a time cut off from outside contact. They have not lost their resulting suspicion of other countries and the great difficulty is today that their government encourages this suspicion and seems to believe that force alone will bring them respect.

24   We, in the democracies, believe in a kind of international respect and action which is reciprocal. We do not think others should treat us differently from the way they wish to be treated. It is interference in other countries that especially stirs up antagonism against the Soviet Government. If it wishes to feel secure in developing its economic and political theories within its territory, then it should grant to others that same security. We believe in the freedom of people to make their own mistakes. We do not interfere with them and they should not interfere with others.

25   The basic problem confronting the world today, as I said in the beginning, is the preservation of human freedom for the individual and consequently for the society of which he is a part. We are fighting this battle again today as it was fought at the time of the French Revolution and at the time of the American Revolution. The issue of human liberty is as decisive now as it was then. I want to give you my conception of what is meant in my country by freedom of the individual.

26   Long ago in London during a discussion with Mr. Vyshinsky, he told me there was no such thing as freedom for the individual in the world. All freedom of the individual was conditioned by the rights of other individuals. That of course, I granted. I said: "We approach the question from a different point of view/we here in the United Nations are trying to develop ideals which will be broader in outlook, which will consider first the rights of man, which will consider what makes man more free; not governments, but man."

27   The totalitarian state typically places the will of the people second to decrees promulgated by a few men at the top.

28   Naturally there must always be consideration of the rights of others; but in a democracy this is not a restriction. Indeed, in our democracies we make our freedoms secure because each of us is expected to respect the rights of others and we are free to make our own laws. Freedom for our peoples is not only a right, but also

a tool. Freedom of speech, freedom of the press, freedom of information, freedom of assembly—these are not just abstract ideals to us; they are tools with which we create a way of life, a way of life in which we can enjoy freedom.

29   Sometimes the processes of democracy are slow, and I have known some of our leaders to say that a benevolent dictatorship would accomplish the ends desired in a much shorter time than it takes to go through the democratic processes of discussion and the slow formation of public opinion. But there is no way of insuring that a dictatorship will remain benevolent or that power once in the hands of a few will be returned to the people without struggle or revolution. This we have learned by experience and we accept the slow processes of democracy because we know that shortcuts compromise principles on which no compromise is possible.

30   The final expression of the opinion of the people with us is through free and honest elections, with valid choices on basic issues and candidates. The secret ballot is an essential to free elections but you must have a choice before you. I have heard my husband say many times that a people need never lose their freedom if they kept their right to a secret ballot and if they used that secret ballot to the full. Basic decisions of our society are made through the expressed will of the people. That is why when we see these liberties threatened, instead of falling apart, our nation becomes unified and our democracies come together as a unified group in spite of our varied backgrounds and many racial strains.

31   In the United States we have a capitalistic economy. That is because public opinion favors that type of economy under the conditions in which we live. But we have imposed certain restraints; for instance, we have antitrust laws. These are the legal evidence of the determination of the American people to maintain an economy of free competition and not to allow monopolies to take away the people's freedom.

32   Our trade-unions grow stronger because the people come to believe that this is the proper way to guarantee the rights of the workers and that the right to organize and to bargain collectively keeps the balance between the actual producer and the investor of money and the manager in industry who watches over the man who works with his hands and who produces the materials which are our tangible wealth.

33   In the United States we are old enough not to claim perfection. We recognize that we have some problems of discrimination but we find steady progress being made in the solution of these problems. Through normal democratic processes we are coming to understand our needs and how we can attain full equality for all our people. Free discussion on the subject is permitted. Our Supreme Court has recently rendered decisions to clarify a number of our laws to guarantee the rights of all.

34   The U.S.S.R. claims it has reached a point where all races within her borders are officially considered equal and have equal rights and they insist that they have no discrimination where minorities are concerned.

35   This is a laudable objective but there are other aspects of the development of freedom for the individual which are essential before the mere absence of discrimination is worth much, and these are lacking in the Soviet Union. Unless they are being denied freedoms which they want and which they see other people have, people do

not usually complain of discrimination. It is these other freedoms—the basic freedoms of speech, of the press, of religion and conscience, of assembly, of fair trial and freedom from arbitrary arrest and punishment, which a totalitarian government cannot safely give its people and which give meaning to freedom from discrimination.

36 It is my belief, and I am sure it is also yours, that the struggle for democracy and freedom is a critical struggle, for their preservation is essential to the great objective of the United Nations to maintain international peace and security. Among free men the end cannot justify the means. We know the patterns of totalitarianism—the single political party, the control of schools, press, radio, the arts, the sciences, and the church to support autocratic authority; these are the age-old patterns against which men have struggled for three thousand years. These are the signs of reaction, retreat, and retrogression.

37 The United Nations must hold fast to the heritage of freedom won by the struggle of its people; it must help us to pass it on to generations to come.

38 The development of the ideal of freedom and its translation into the everyday life of the people in great areas of the earth is the product of the efforts of many peoples. It is the fruit of a long tradition of vigorous thinking and courageous action. No one race or one people can claim to have done all the work to achieve greater dignity for human beings and greater freedom to develop human personality. In each generation and in each country there must be a continuation of the struggle and new steps forward must be taken since this is preeminently a field in which to stand still is to retreat.

39 The field of human rights is not one in which compromises on fundamental principles are possible. The work of the Commission on Human Rights is illustrative. The Declaration of Human Rights provides: "Everyone has the right to leave any country, including his own." The Soviet Representative said he would agree to this right if a single phrase was added to it—"in accordance with the procedure laid down in the laws of that country." It is obvious that to accept this would be not only to compromise but to nullify the right stated. This case forcefully illustrates the importance of the proposition that we must ever be alert not to compromise fundamental human rights merely for the sake of reaching unanimity and thus lose them.

40 As I see it, it is not going to be easy to attain unanimity with respect to our different concepts of government and human rights. The struggle is bound to be difficult and one in which we must be firm but patient. If we adhere faithfully to our principles I think it is possible for us to maintain freedom and to do so peacefully and without recourse to force.

41 The future must see the broadening of human rights throughout the world. People who have glimpsed freedom will never be content until they have secured it for themselves. In a truest sense, human rights are a fundamental object of law and government in a just society. Human rights exist to the degree that they are respected by people in relations with each other and by governments in relations with their citizens.

42 The world at large is aware of the tragic consequences for human beings ruled by totalitarian systems. If we examine Hitler's rise to power, we see how the chains are forged which keep the individual a slave and we can see many similarities in the

way things are accomplished in other countries. Politically men must be free to discuss and to arrive at as many facts as possible and there must be at least a two-party system in a country because when there is only one political party, too many things can be subordinated to the interests of that one party and it becomes a tyrant and not an instrument of democratic government.

43   The propaganda we have witnessed in the recent past, like that we perceive in these days, seeks to impugn, to undermine, and to destroy the liberty and independence of peoples. Such propaganda poses to all peoples the issue whether to doubt their heritage of rights and therefore to compromise the principles by which they live, or try to accept the challenge, redouble their vigilance, and stand steadfast in the struggle to maintain and enlarge human freedoms.

44   People who continue to be denied the respect to which they are entitled as human beings will not acquiesce forever in such denial.

45   The Charter of the United Nations is a guiding beacon along the way to the achievement of human rights and fundamental freedoms throughout the world. The immediate test is not only to the extent to which human rights and freedoms have already been achieved, but the direction in which the world is moving. Is there a faithful compliance with the objectives of the Charter if some countries continue to curtail human rights and freedoms instead of to promote the universal respect for an observance of human rights and freedoms for all as called for by the Charter?

46   The place to discuss the issue of human rights is in the forum of the United Nations. The United Nations has been set up as the common meeting ground for nations, where we can consider together our mutual problems and take advantage of our differences in experience. It is inherent in our firm attachment to democracy and freedom that we stand always ready to use the fundamental democratic procedures of honest discussion and negotiation. It is now as always our hope that despite the wide differences in approach we face in the world today, we can with mutual good faith in the principles of the United Nations Charter, arrive at a common basis of understanding.

47   We are here to join the meetings of this great international Assembly which meets in your beautiful capital of Paris. Freedom for the individual is an inseparable part of the cherished traditions of France. As one of the Delegates from the United States I pray Almighty God that we may win another victory here for the rights and freedoms of all men.

THINKING CRITICALLY

1. How does Roosevelt connect to her audience at the beginning of her speech? Who is her audience? Would her speech be as effective without her introductory remarks? Identify other areas in her speech where she reaches out to her audience in a distinctly personal way.

2. What countries abstained from ratifying the International Declaration of Human Rights? What reasons does Roosevelt give for this abstention? How does she feel about their abstention?

3. Evaluate the overall strengths and weaknesses of this speech. Identify specific parts of her oration, and explain why you think they are effective or ineffective.

4. What, according to Roosevelt, is the definition of freedom? Do you agree with her definition? Is there anything you would add or change? Explain.

5. In paragraph 17, Roosevelt discusses the word "free" as it applies to the idea of freedom of the press. How is the word "free" interpreted by the U.S.S.R.? How does their interpretation differ from that of the U.S.? In what ways can different interpretations of the same word cause political dissent? Explain.

6. In paragraph 21, Roosevelt notes that a vital human right is the "Right of Choice." Yet she does not include this right in her definition of freedom at the beginning of her speech. Was this an oversight, or a deliberate omission? Is there a difference between freedom and human rights? Explain.

7. Roosevelt ends her speech with a plea to God. Why does she make this appeal? How does it contribute to her speeches? What thoughts and ideas does it leave with her audience? Explain.

8. Evaluate Roosevelt's use of the word "our" in paragraph 10, and "we" in paragraph 24. How does she use these words? How does her rhetorical use of language make what she has to say more powerful and compelling? Explain.

WRITING ASSIGNMENTS

1. Research the Declaration of the Rights of Man (France) Roosevelt mentions in her opening remarks. How does this document compare to the Declaration of Independence (U.S.)? Why do you think Roosevelt references one document and not the other? Evaluate and discuss the two documents considering the language used in each.

2. Eleanor Roosevelt was a highly respected woman, but was still participating in a distinctly male-dominated political arena. Does gender play a role in her speech and her mission? Explore the way gender does, or does not affect her speech, her audience's reception of her words, and her subject matter.

3. Write an essay in which you create your own declaration of inalienable human rights. If you wish, you may compare your version to that ratified by the United Nations in 1948, at <www.un.org/overview/rights.html> and discuss how your version is similar and/or different, and why.

Exploring the Language of **V I S U A L S**

Margaret Sanger

Through the ages, women and other minority groups have broken silence to protest discrimination. One such woman was Margaret Sanger (1879–1966) who championed women's rights, especially the right to use birth control. The image from 1929 featured on the title page of this chapter shows Sanger satirizing measures to ban her from speaking out about birth control. Although Sanger wasn't allowed to speak out (she was arrested for doing so in 1914 and again after opening a birth control clinic in 1916), consider how this photograph does, in fact, serve as an expression of speech.

TOPICAL CONSIDERATIONS

1. How does the photograph make you feel, and why? Explore the implications of the photograph and the ways it is designed to elicit a response from the viewer.

2. Freedom of speech is a fundamental right that many Americans hold dear. Does it surprise you that as recently as 1929 you could be arrested for speaking out on something such as birth control? Does such control exist today? Explore this issue and then discuss the results of your research in class.

3. Research the career of Margaret Sanger at <www.nyu.edu/projects/sanger/index.htm>. In what ways did Sanger "break a silence" by challenging the status quo? What was she fighting for? What did her fight represent? Explain.

■ MAKING CONNECTIONS

1. Write a letter to the editor expressing your opinion about one of the "speeches" included in this section as if it had been recently delivered. Write your letter as if you were living in the historical period of the selection. For example, you could be a man from 1848 commenting on the Seneca Falls Convention or a woman expressing her opinion of Eleanor Roosevelt's speech to the United Nations.

2. In paragraph 26 in his "Letter from Birmingham Jail," Martin Luther King, Jr. states, "We will have to repent in this generation not merely for the hateful words and actions of the bad people but for the appalling silence of the good people." Compare the implications of his statement to a speech given on April 22, 1999, by Nobel Peace Prize winner, Elie Weisel, *The Perils of Indifference* <http://www.historyplace.com/speeches/weisel.htm>, given as part of the White House Millennium lecture series. Write an essay exploring the ideas expressed by each man, as well as your own perspective on "indifference" and "silence."

3. Select a current (within the last two years) photo, essay, or article that you think represents an example of someone challenging the status quo. Explain why you think your selection fits within the overall theme of this section. How does your photo or article compare/contrast with the selections featured in this section? What do you think will be the long-term implications of your example of broken silence?

4. Martin Luther King, Jr.'s most famous speech, "I Have a Dream," was delivered on the steps of the Lincoln Memorial in Washington, D.C., in 1963. Review the text of his speech at <http://www.americanrhetoric.com/speeches/ihaveadream.htm>. How is this speech an example of "language that inspired change"? Consider the symbolism of his choice of venue. How does the location of his speech connect to the speech itself? Would a different location have served his purpose as well? Why or why not? Write an essay in which you address how this speech changed (or did not change) the way people thought about civil rights.

5. Compare the use of repetition in Martin Luther King, Jr.'s "I Have a Dream" speech to that of Sojourner Truth's "Aren't I a Woman?". In what ways do they employ similar linguistic devices? How do you think each would respond to the other's oratory style? Subject matter? Explain.

Writers Writing:
Words in Contexts

■ All writers put their personal stamp on their work. Think about how the words you chose—and how you express them—influence your audience's opinion of your message.

Each of the essays in this text explores how language constructs reality for us: how it can be used to communicate, inform, lead, mislead, and even manipulate us. Although many pieces celebrate the joys of language, others lament its woes—that politicians and bureaucrats talk gobbledygook, that advertisers torture language to sell their goods, and that the ability of students to write clearly is deteriorating. In short, you hear a lot about bad writing.

This chapter offers insights and advice about good writing. From a practical point of view, the essays in this chapter are intended to help prepare you for the writing projects featured in this book and in your academic studies. The readings in this chapter also aim to provide the foundations of basic rhetorical principles and strategies so that you can participate with confidence in lively and informed debates about language.

Most college writing is an exercise in persuasion—an attempt to influence readers' attitudes toward the subject matter. This is true whether you're discussing tragic irony in *Oedipus Rex,* analyzing the causes of World War I, writing a lab report on the solubility of salt, protesting next year's tuition increase, or explaining the joys of bungee jumping. How successful you are at persuading your readers will have a lot to do with the words you choose.

The Writing Process

Our opening piece, "Writing for an Audience" by Linda Flower offers some key points of advice on establishing common ground with one's readers. The key to good writing is rewriting. And that fact is the thrust of the final essay in this set, "The Maker's Eye: Revising Your Own Manuscript." As Donald Murray explains, many student writers look upon a paper's first draft as the final product. But to most professional writers, the first draft is just the beginning of the writing process; and he gives some useful tips on how to do it.

The next two articles are by writers who are also writing instructors. Anne Lamott explains how she helps her students find their muse in "Getting Started." Pamela Childers shares her classroom and writing center insights in "What My Students Have Taught Me About Writing." The section closes with a personal narrative, "How I Write," written by one of Childers' former students, Evan Miller.

Finding the Right Words

The second section features essays providing advice and suggestions on how to choose the right words to effectively express your message, and how to formulate that message so that your reader will be receptive and open to your ideas. Beginning writers often opt for cluttered expressions, empty jargon, and convoluted constructions to make what they say sound "smarter." However, all they achieve with this approach is poor writing. Richard Lederer explains in the section's first essay,

"The Case for Short Words," that often the best way to say something is with short, clear, pure words that are rich with meaning. And nobody could agree more than popular novelist, Kurt Vonnegut, who gives eight friendly tips on writing with style. Patricia T. O'Conner builds on his tips by adding thirteen more of her own in "Saying Is Believing" in which she explains that the best writers are the ones who are easily understood—ones you can read, "without breaking a sweat." Next, James Isaacs illustrates how *not* to communicate in his parody of what nearly every high school and college graduate must endure—the commencement speech in "Clichés, Anyone?" The section closes with an amusing insert featured in the business newspaper *The Wall Street Journal,* "The Financial Media's 25 Worst Clichés," which pokes fun at phrases used often by financial journalists.

■ THE WRITING PROCESS

Writing for an Audience
Linda Flower

One of the most important things an educated person does is manage information. And writing is an important part of managing information. We write to keep track of things (lists, inventories, databases), to organize materials (outlines, tables of contents, indexes), and to develop ideas too complex to manage in our heads. We also write to tell people what we know, what conclusions we've drawn about a situation, and how we'd like them to proceed. In the following essay, Linda Flower tells us that to be successful managers of information we need to know how our audience will see the information we present, so that we can choose and shape information to help them understand our perspective.

Linda Flower is a professor of English at Carnegie-Mellon University and is, through her many books and articles, a prominent voice in the field of composition and rhetoric. She is the author of several textbooks, including *Problem Solving Strategies for Writing in College and the Community,* 1985, and *The Construction of Negotiated Meaning: A Social Cognitive Theory of Writing,* 1994. Her suggestions on creating common ground with your audience should be useful in writing situations you encounter in your college and professional career.

1   The goal of the writer is to create a momentary common ground between the reader and the writer. You want the reader to share your knowledge and your attitude toward that knowledge. Even if the reader eventually disagrees, you want him or her to be able for the moment to *see things as you see them.* A good piece of writing closes the gap between you and the reader.

Analyze Your Audience

2 The first step in closing that gap is to gauge the distance between the two of you. Imagine, for example, that you are a student writing your parents, who have always lived in New York City, about a wilderness survival expedition you want to go on over spring break. Sometimes obvious differences such as age or background will be important, but the critical differences for writers usually fall into three areas: the reader's *knowledge* about the topic; his or her *attitude* toward it, and his or her personal or professional *needs*. Because these differences often exist, good writers do more than simply express their meaning; they pinpoint the critical differences between themselves and their reader and design their writing to reduce those differences. Let us look at these three areas in more detail.

Knowledge

3 This is usually the easiest difference to handle. What does your reader need to know? What are the main ideas you hope to teach? Does your reader have enough background knowledge to really understand you? If not, what would he or she have to learn?

Attitudes

4 When we say a person has knowledge, we usually refer to his conscious awareness of explicit facts and clearly defined concepts. This kind of knowledge can be easily written down or told to someone else. However, much of what we "know" is not held in this formal, explicit way. Instead it is held as an attitude or image—as a loose cluster of associations. For instance, my image of lakes includes associations many people would have, including fishing, water skiing, stalled outboards, and lots of kids catching night crawlers with flashlights. However, the most salient or powerful parts of my image, which strongly color my whole attitude toward lakes, are thoughts of cloudy skies, long rainy days, and feeling generally cold and damp. By contrast, one of my best friends has a very different cluster of associations: to him a lake means sun, swimming, sailing, and happily sitting on the end of a dock. Needless to say, our differing images cause us to react quite differently to a proposal that we visit a lake. Likewise, one reason people often find it difficult to discuss religion and politics is that terms such as "capitalism" conjure up radically different images.

5 As you can see, a reader's image of a subject is often the source of attitudes and feelings that are unexpected and, at times, impervious to mere facts. A simple statement that seems quite persuasive to you, such as "Lake Wampago would be a great place to locate the new music camp," could have little impact on your reader if he or she simply doesn't visualize a lake as a "great place." In fact, many people accept uncritically any statement that fits in with their own attitudes—and reject, just as uncritically, anything that does not.

6   Whether your purpose is to persuade or simply to present your perspective, it helps to know the image and attitudes that your reader already holds. The more these differ from your own, the more you will have to do to make him or her *see* what you mean.

Needs

7 When writers discover a large gap between their own knowledge and attitudes and those of the reader, they usually try to change the reader in some way. Needs, however, are different. When you analyze a reader's needs, it is so that you, the writer, can adapt to him. If you ask a friend majoring in biology how to keep your fish tank from clouding, you don't want to hear a textbook recitation on the life processes of algae. You expect the friend to adapt his or her knowledge and tell you exactly how to solve your problem.

8   The ability to adapt your knowledge to the needs of the reader is often crucial to your success as a writer. This is especially true in writing done on a job. For example, as producer of a public affairs program for a television station, 80 percent of your time may be taken up planning the details of new shows, contacting guests, and scheduling the taping sessions. But when you write a program proposal to the station director, your job is to show how the program will fit into the cost guidelines, the FCC requirements for relevance, and the overall programming plan for the station. When you write that report your role in the organization changes from producer to proposal writer. Why? Because your reader needs that information in order to make a decision. He may be *interested* in your scheduling problems and the specific content of the shows, but he *reads* your report because of his own needs as station director of that organization. He has to act.

9   In college, where the reader is also a teacher, the reader's needs are a little less concrete but just as important. Most papers are assigned as a way to teach something. So the real purpose of a paper may be for you to make connections between two historical periods, to discover for yourself the principle behind a laboratory experiment, or to develop and support your own interpretation of a novel. A good college paper doesn't just rehash the facts; it demonstrates what your reader, as a teacher, needs to know—that you are learning the thinking skills his or her course is trying to teach.

10   Effective writers are not simply expressing what they know, like a student madly filling up an examination bluebook. Instead they are *using* their knowledge: reorganizing, maybe even rethinking their ideas to meet the demands of an assignment or the needs of their reader.

THINKING CRITICALLY

1. Who does Flower assume to be her audience for this essay on audience? What evidence can you point to in the text that supports this answer?

2. Flower speaks of three areas of difference between a writer and her/his audience. List these three areas and, for each area, find two places in the text where Flower's writing seems designed to reduce those differences, or to close the gap.

3. What is Flower's position on persuasiveness in writing? How is this attitude important to her point overall?

4. Do you find her discussion persuasive? Has she effectively closed the gaps between you, as audience, and herself, as writer? Discuss places in this text where she has been successful. Can you find places where she has not been successful? Or where you think she might have done a better job? Write out any suggestions you have where you think she might have done a better job.

5. Make a list of different writing situations you have recently encountered or might expect to encounter in your work or profession. Identify a specific audience, then think very specifically about the knowledge, attitude, and needs of that audience and brainstorm a list of adjustments you'll have to make in order to bridge any gaps between you and your audience. Be ready to compare your answers with those of other students in the class.

6. Flower does not directly address what happens when an audience is comprised of different kinds of people. Can you think of instances where this has happened or might happen? What kinds of choices might an author make in order to meet the needs of many different kinds of people at one time? What happens when the writer fails to establish common ground with some part of her/his audience?

WRITING ASSIGNMENTS

1. Flower is an expert in writing. Think of something you know really well and write an essay in which you explain it (or some element of it) to an audience that does not have your expertise.

2. Find samples of text (in the broadest sense of the word) on the same topic, but which are focused on different audiences. For your samples, you might look at an encyclopedia, news article, biography, textbook, expert opinion/testimonial, video clip, photograph or drawing, instruction manual, and so on. Consider differences in age, gender, culture, and educational backgrounds. Once you've gathered a range of materials, choose three that offer the most variety. Write an essay in which you describe the audience intended by the author(s) or creator(s) of each text; also discuss the strategies each author employed to bridge the presumed gaps in knowledge, attitude, and needs. Finally, draw conclusions about the relevance of these differences. Your focus should be on choices made with regard to language; organization; visual elements, including layouts; visual aids; and rhetorical elements such as narrative, exemplification, definition, comparison/contrast, exposition, and anything else that seems important.

3. Find a piece of text that is intended for an audience other than yourself. Perhaps find a journal from your major area that is targeted at professors/scholars; or find a discussion on a subject matter in which you have little or no background. Discuss the places where you have trouble and/or the different kinds of trouble you have. Explain what the author has done to meet the needs of her/his presumed audience. Then, talk about different strategies that might be employed in a revised version of the text aimed at you rather than at the intended audience. Ap-

pend a one-page rewrite of this text (or some portion of it) to illustrate how the rewrite could be accomplished.

The Maker's Eye: Revising Your Own Manuscripts

Donald M. Murray

The secret of good writing is rewriting. Every line of copy in this book has undergone the process—a process that many people underestimate. Because they see only the finished product, they aren't aware of the amount of culling, rewording, reorganizing, and rewriting that goes into a piece to make it sound smooth and effortless. It is that process of revision— and the importance of it—that Donald Murray talks about in the next essay. The basic message in Murray's essay is that revision is a continuous process.

Donald M. Murray has made the art of writing well his business for decades. In 1954, he won the Pulitzer Prize for his editorials in the *Boston Globe*. He has also been an editor of *Time* magazine. Although he has published novels, short stories, and poetry, he is perhaps best known for his compositions on writing. His book, *Write to Learn,* is a popular college composition text. His most recent book is a personal memoir, *My Twice-Lived Life: A Memoir* (2001). This essay, perhaps appropriately, is a rewrite of the original, which first appeared in *The Writer* magazine.

1   When students complete a first draft, they consider the job of writing done—and their teachers too often agree. When professional writers complete a first draft, they usually feel that they are at the start of the writing process. When a draft is completed, the job of writing can begin.

2   That difference in attitude is the difference between amateur and professional, inexperience and experience, journeyman and craftsman. Peter F. Drucker, the prolific business writer, calls his first draft "the zero draft"—after that he can start counting. Most writers share the feeling that the first draft, and all of those which follow, are opportunities to discover what they have to say and how best they can say it.

3   To produce a progression of drafts, each of which says more and says it more clearly, the writer has to develop a special kind of reading skill. In school we are taught to decode what appears on the page as finished writing. Writers, however, face a different category of possibility and responsibility when they read their own drafts. To them the words on the page are never finished. Each can be changed and rearranged, can set off a chain reaction of confusion or clarified meaning. This is a different kind of reading which is possibly more difficult and certainly more exciting.

4   Writers must learn to be their own best enemy. They must accept the criticism of others and be suspicious of it; they must accept the praise of others and be even more suspicious of it. Writers cannot depend on others. They must detach themselves from their own pages so that they can apply both their caring and their craft to their own work.

5   Such detachment is not easy. Science fiction writer Ray Bradbury supposedly puts each manuscript away for a year to the day and then rereads it as a stranger. Not many writers have the discipline or the time to do this. We must read when our judgment may be at its worst, when we are close to the euphoric moment of creation.

6   Then the writer, counsels novelist Nancy Hale, "should be critical of everything that seems to him most delightful in his style. He should excise what he most admires, because he wouldn't thus admire it if he weren't . . . in a sense protecting it from criticism." John Ciardi, the poet, adds, "The last act of the writing must be to become one's own reader. It is, I suppose, a schizophrenic process, to begin passionately and to end critically, to begin hot and to end cold; and, more important, to be passion-hot and critic-cold at the same time."

7   Most people think that the principal problem is that writers are too proud of what they have written. Actually, a greater problem for most professional writers is one shared by the majority of students. They are overly critical, think everything is dreadful, tear up page after page, never complete a draft, see the task as hopeless.

8   The writer must learn to read critically but constructively, to cut what is bad, to reveal what is good. Eleanor Estes, the children's book author, explains: "The writer must survey his work critically, coolly, as though he were a stranger to it. He must be willing to prune, expertly and hard-heartedly. At the end of each revision, a manuscript may look . . . worked over, torn apart, pinned together, added to, deleted from, words changed and words changed back. Yet the book must maintain its original freshness and spontaneity."

9   Most readers underestimate the amount of rewriting it usually takes to produce spontaneous reading. This is a great disadvantage to the student writer, who sees only a finished product and never watches the craftsman who takes the necessary step back, studies the work carefully, returns to the task, steps back, returns, steps back, again and again. Anthony Burgess, one of the most prolific writers in the English-speaking world, admits, "I might revise a page twenty times." Roald Dahl, the popular children's writer, states, "By the time I'm nearing the end of a story, the first part will have been reread and altered and corrected at least 150 times. . . . Good writing is essentially rewriting. I am positive of this."

10   Rewriting isn't virtuous. It isn't something that ought to be done. It is simply something that most writers find they have to do to discover what they have to say and how to say it. It is a condition of the writer's life.

11   There are, however, a few writers who do little formal rewriting, primarily because they have the capacity and experience to create and review a large number of invisible drafts in their minds before they approach the page. And some writers slowly produce finished pages, performing all the tasks of revision simultaneously,

page by page, rather than draft by draft. But it is still possible to see the sequence followed by most writers most of the time in rereading their own work.

12   Most writers scan their drafts first, reading as quickly as possible to catch the larger problems of subject and form, then move in closer and closer as they read and write, reread and rewrite.

13   The first thing writers look for in their drafts is *information.* They know that a good piece of writing is built from specific, accurate, and interesting information. The writer must have an abundance of information from which to construct a readable piece of writing.

14   Next, writers look for *meaning* in the information. The specifics must build to a pattern of significance. Each piece of specific information must carry the reader toward meaning.

15   Writers reading their own drafts are aware of *audience.* They put themselves in the reader's situation and make sure that they deliver information which a reader wants to know or needs to know in a manner which is easily digested. Writers try to be sure that they anticipate and answer the questions a critical reader will ask when reading the piece of writing.

16   Writers make sure that the *form* is appropriate to the subject and the audience. Form, or genre, is the vehicle which carries meaning to the reader, but form cannot be selected until the writer has adequate information to discover its significance and an audience which needs or wants that meaning.

17   Once writers are sure the form is appropriate, they must then look at the *structure,* the order of what they have written. Good writing is built on a solid framework of logic, argument, narrative, or motivation which runs through the entire piece of writing and holds it together. This is the time when many writers find it most effective to outline as a way of visualizing the hidden spine on which the piece of writing is supported.

18   The element on which writers may spend a majority of their time is *development.* Each section of a piece of writing must be adequately developed. It must give readers enough information so that they are satisfied. How much information is enough? That's as difficult as asking how much garlic belongs in a salad. It must be done to taste, but most beginning writers underdevelop, underestimating the reader's hunger for information.

19   As writers solve development problems, they often have to consider questions of *dimension.* There must be a pleasing and effective proportion among all the parts of the piece of writing. There is a continual process of subtracting and adding to keep the piece of writing in balance.

20   Finally, writers have to listen to their own voices. *Voice* is the force which drives a piece of writing forward. It is an expression of the writer's authority and concern. It is what is between the words on the page, what glues the piece of writing together. A good piece of writing is always marked by a consistent, individual voice.

21   As writers read and reread, write and rewrite, they move closer and closer to the page until they are doing line-by-line editing. Writers read their own pages with

infinite care. Each sentence, each line, each clause, each phrase, each word, each mark of punctuation, each section of white space between the type has to contribute to the clarification of meaning.

22   Slowly the writer moves from word to word, looking through language to see the subject. As a word is changed, cut, or added, as a construction is rearranged, all the words used before that moment and all those that follow that moment must be considered and reconsidered.

23   Writers often read aloud at this stage of the editing process muttering or whispering to themselves, calling on the ear's experience with language. Does this sound right—or that? Writers edit, shifting back and forth from eye to page to ear to page. I find I must do this careful editing in short runs, no more than fifteen or twenty minutes at a stretch, or I become too kind with myself. I begin to see what I hope is on the page, not what actually is on the page.

24   This sounds tedious if you haven't done it, but actually it is fun. Making something right is immensely satisfying, for writers begin to learn what they are writing about by writing. Language leads them to meaning, and there is the joy of discovery, of understanding, of making meaning clear as the writer employs the technical skills of language.

25   Words have double meanings, even triple and quadruple meanings. Each word has its own potential for connotation and denotation. And when writers rub one word against the other, they are often rewarded with a sudden insight, an unexpected clarification.

26   The maker's eye moves back and forth from word to phrase to sentence to paragraph to sentence to phrase to word. The maker's eye sees the need for variety and balance, for a firmer structure, for a more appropriate form. It peers into the interior of the paragraph, looking for coherence, unity, and emphasis, which make meaning clear.

27   I learned something about this process when my first bifocals were prescribed. I had ordered a larger section of the reading portion of the glass because of my work, but even so, I could not contain my eyes within this new limit of vision. And I still find myself taking off my glasses and bending my nose towards the page, for my eyes unconsciously flick back and forth across the page, back to another page, forward to still another, as I try to see each evolving line in relation to every other line.

28   When does this process end? Most writers agree with the great Russian writer Tolstoy, who said, "I scarcely ever reread my published writing. If by chance I come across a page, it always strikes me: all this must be rewritten; this is how I should have written it."

29   The maker's eye is never satisfied, for each word has the potential to ignite new meaning. This article has been twice written all the way through the writing process, and it was published four years ago. Now it is to be republished in a book. The editors made a few small suggestions, and then I read it with my maker's eye. Now it has been re-edited, revised, re-read, re-re-edited, for each piece of writing is to the writer full of potential and alternatives.

30   A piece of writing is never finished. It is delivered to a deadline, torn out of the typewriter on demand, sent off with a sense of accomplishment and shame and pride and frustration. If only there were a couple more days, time for just another run at it, perhaps then. . . .

THINKING CRITICALLY

1. In what ways do amateur writers differ from professional writers according to Murray?

2. How must writers "learn to be their own best enemy"?

3. In paragraph 12, Murray says that most professional writers go over the drafts of their writing looking for the "larger problems of subject and form" before closing in on the rewrites. Does it surprise you that so many professional writers go through so much revision of their work? Do you follow such procedures when you write? If not, do you think you can?

4. Murray names eight things that writers must consider in the process of revising their own manuscripts. What are they?

5. What does Murray mean by the statement, "A piece of writing is never finished"?

6. In paragraph 9, Murray quotes Roald Dahl: "Good writing is essentially rewriting." How well does Murray illustrate this fundamental thesis in his essay?

7. How does Murray use his own essay to illustrate the statement, "A piece of writing is never finished"?

WRITING ASSIGNMENTS

1. Write an essay in which you describe the process you go through in writing a paper. Consider what difficulties you have in coming up with an idea or slant or opening. Do you make the same eight considerations Murray lists when revising? Is it ever fun? Do you ever feel "immensely satisfied" when you think you've got it right?

2. Using Murray's list of eight considerations for revising, rework an essay recently returned to you by your instructor in this or another course you are taking. After you have completed your revisions, write a short evaluation on how the revised piece compares to the original. Turn in both papers to your instructor for his or her feedback on your revision effort.

Getting Started
Anne Lamott

For many students, the biggest writing challenge they face is simply getting started. In the next essay, writer and creative writing instructor Anne Lamott gives advice on how to get the ball rolling. The task of getting started, and feeling comfortable with what you write, is a challenge to students and published writers alike.

Anne Lamott is the author of several novels and memoirs, including *Hard Laughter* (1980), *All New People* (1989), *Operating Instructions* (1993), and *Crooked Little Heart* (1997). A past recipient of a Guggenheim, she has been a book review columnist for *Mademoiselle* magazine, and a restaurant critic for *California* magazine. She teaches writing at the University of California, Davis, and is a featured instructor at writing seminars throughout the state. The following piece is an excerpt from her 1995 book on writing, *Bird by Bird: Some Instructions on Writing and Life*.

1   The very first thing I tell my new students on the first day of a workshop is that good writing is about telling the truth. We are a species that needs and wants to understand who we are. Sheep lice do not seem to share this longing, which is one reason they write so very little. But we do. We have so much we want to say and figure out. Year after year my students are bursting with stories to tell, and they start writing projects with excitement and maybe even joy—finally their voices will be heard, and they are going to get to devote themselves to this one thing they've longed to do since childhood. But after a few days at the desk, telling the truth in an interesting way turns out to be about as easy and pleasurable as bathing a cat. Some lose faith. Their sense of self and story shatters and crumbles to the ground. Historically they show up for the first day of the workshop looking like bright goofy ducklings who will follow me anywhere, but by the time the second class rolls around, they look at me as if the engagement is definitely off.

2   "I don't even know where to start," one will wail.

3   Start with your childhood, I tell them. Plug your nose and jump in, and write down all your memories as truthfully as you can. Flannery O'Connor said that anyone who survived childhood has enough material to write for the rest of his or her life. Maybe your childhood was grim and horrible, but grim and horrible is okay if it is well done. Don't worry about doing it well yet, though. Just start getting it down.

4   Now, the amount of material may be so overwhelming that it can make your brain freeze. When I had been writing food reviews for a number of years, there were so many restaurants and individual dishes in my brainpan that when people asked for a recommendation, I couldn't think of a single restaurant where I'd ever actually eaten. But if the person could narrow it down to, say, Indian, I might remember one lavish Indian palace, where my date had asked the waiter for the Rudyard Kipling sampler and later for the holy-cow tartare. Then a number of memories would come to mind, of other dates and other Indian restaurants.

5   So you might start by writing down every single thing you can remember from your first few years in school. Start with kindergarten. Try to get the words and memories down as they occur to you. Don't worry if what you write is no good, because no one is going to see it. Move on to first grade, to second, to third. Who were your teachers, your classmates? What did you wear? Who and what were you jealous of? Now branch out a little. Did your family take vacations during those

years? Get these down on paper. Do you remember how much more presentable everybody else's family looked? Do you remember how when you'd be floating around in an inner tube on a river, your own family would have lost the little cap that screws over the airflow valve, so every time you got in and out of the inner tube, you'd scratch new welts in your thighs? And how other families never lost the caps?

6   If this doesn't pan out, or if it does but you finish mining this particular vein, see if focusing on holidays and big events helps you recollect your life as it was. Write down everything you can remember about every birthday or Christmas or Seder or Easter or whatever, every relative who was there. Write down all the stuff you swore you'd never tell another soul. What can you recall about your birthday parties—the disasters, the days of grace, your relatives' faces lit up by birthday candles? Scratch around for details: what people ate, listened to, wore—those terrible petaled swim caps, the men's awful trunks, the cocktail dress your voluptuous aunt wore that was so slinky she practically needed the Jaws of Life to get out of it. Write about the women's curlers with the bristles inside, the garters your father and uncles used to hold up their dress socks, your grandfathers' hats, your cousins' perfect Brownie uniforms, and how your own looked like it had just been hatched. Describe the trench coats and stoles and car coats, what they revealed and what they covered up. See if you can remember what you were given that Christmas when you were ten, and how it made you feel inside. Write down what the grown-ups said and did after they'd had a couple of dozen drinks, especially that one Fourth of July when your father made Fish House punch and the adults practically had to crawl from room to room.

7   Remember that you own what happened to you. If your childhood was less than ideal, you may have been raised thinking that if you told the truth about what really went on in your family, a long bony white finger would emerge from a cloud and point at you, while a chilling voice thundered, "We *told* you not to tell." But that was then. Just put down on paper everything you can remember now about your parents and siblings and relatives and neighbors, and we will deal with libel later on.

8   "But how?" my students ask. "How do you actually do it?"

9   You sit down, I say. You try to sit down at approximately the same time every day. This is how you train your unconscious to kick in for you creatively. So you sit down at, say, nine every morning, or ten every night. You put a piece of paper in the typewriter, or you turn on your computer and bring up the right file, and then you stare at it for an hour or so. You begin rocking, just a little at first, and then like a huge autistic child. You look at the ceiling, and over at the clock, yawn, and stare at the paper again. Then, with your fingers poised on the keyboard, you squint at an image that is forming in your mind—a scene, a locale, a character, whatever—and you try to quiet your mind so you can hear what that landscape or character has to say above the other voices in your mind. The other voices are banshees and drunken monkeys. They are the voices of anxiety, judgment, doom, guilt. Also, severe hypochondria. There may be a Nurse Ratched–like listing of things that must

be done right this moment: foods that must come out of the freezer, appointments that must be canceled or made, hairs that must be tweezed. But you hold an imaginary gun to your head and make yourself stay at the desk. There is a vague pain at the base of your neck. It crosses your mind that you have meningitis. Then the phone rings and you look up at the ceiling with fury, summon every ounce of noblesse oblige, and answer the call politely, with maybe just the merest hint of irritation. The caller asks if you're working, and you say yeah, because you are.

10 Yet somehow in the face of all this, you clear a space for the writing voice, hacking away at the others with machetes, and you begin to compose sentences. You begin to string words together like beads to tell a story. You are desperate to communicate, to edify or entertain, to preserve moments of grace or joy or transcendence, to make real or imagined events come alive. But you cannot will this to happen. It is a matter of persistence and faith and hard work. So you might as well just go ahead and get started.

11 I wish I had a secret I could let you in on (. . .) some code word that has enabled me to sit at my desk and land flights of creative inspiration like an air-traffic controller. But I don't. All I know is that the process is pretty much the same for almost everyone I know. The good news is that some days it feels like you just have to keep getting out of your own way so that whatever it is that wants to be written can use you to write it. It is a little like when you have something difficult to discuss with someone, and as you go to do it, you hope and pray that the right words will come if only you show up and make a stab at it. And often the right words do come, and you—well—"write" for a while; you put a lot of thoughts down on paper. But the bad news is that if you're at all like me, you'll probably read over what you've written and spend the rest of the day obsessing, and praying that you do not die before you can completely rewrite or destroy what you have written, lest the eagerly waiting world learn how bad your first drafts are.

12 The obsessing may keep you awake, *or* the self-loathing may cause you to fall into a narcoleptic coma before dinner. But let's just say that you do fall asleep at a normal hour. Then the odds are that you will wake up at four in the morning, having dreamed that you have died. Death turns out to feel much more frantic than you had imagined. Typically you'll try to comfort yourself by thinking about the day's work—the day's excrementitious work. You may experience a jittery form of existential dread, considering the absolute meaninglessness of life and the fact that no one has ever really loved you; you may find yourself consumed with a free-floating shame, and a hopelessness about your work, and the realization that you will have to throw out everything you've done so far and start from scratch. But you will not be able to do so. Because you suddenly understand that you are completely riddled with cancer.

13 And then the miracle happens. The sun comes up again. So you get up and do your morning things, and one thing leads to another, and eventually, at nine, you find yourself back at the desk, staring blankly at the pages you filled yesterday.

And there on page four is a paragraph with all sorts of life in it, smells and sounds and voices and colors and even a moment of dialogue that makes you say to yourself, very, very softly, "Hmmm." You look up and stare out the window again, but this time you are drumming your fingers on the desk, and you don't care about those first three pages; those you will throw out, those you needed to write to get to that fourth page, to get to that one long paragraph that was what you had in mind when you started, only you didn't know that, couldn't know that, until you got to it. And the story begins to materialize, and another thing is happening, which is that you are learning what you *aren't* writing, and this is helping you to find out what you *are* writing. Think of a fine painter attempting to capture an inner vision, beginning with one corner of the canvas, painting what he thinks should be there, not quite pulling it off, covering it over with white paint, and trying again, each time finding out what his painting isn't, until finally he finds out what it is.

14   And when you do find out what one corner of your vision is, you're off and running. And it really is like running. It always reminds me of the last lines of *Rabbit, Run:* "his heels hitting heavily on the pavement at first but with an effortless gathering out of a kind of sweet panic growing lighter and quicker and quieter, he runs. Ah: runs. Runs."

15   I wish I felt that kind of inspiration more often. I almost never do. All I know is that if I sit there long enough, something will happen.

THINKING CRITICALLY

1. What does Lamott mean when she says, ". . . writing is about the truth"? Although she describes a creative writing workshop, how do you think this principle of truth could apply to other types of writing? Explain.

2. Who is "Nurse Ratched" and how can "she" interfere with your writing? What recommendations does Lamott give for stilling the voice of Nurse Ratched and other anxieties that may interfere with your writing?

3. Evaluate Lamott's style and tone in this essay. Does her writing reflect the lessons she teaches in this piece? How does her style connect with her audience? Do you think you would like to have her as a writing instructor? Why or why not?

4. Lamott observes that her class begins eager to begin writing, but soon grows frustrated with the actual mechanics of the process. Think about your own writing process. How do you write? Why do you write? Have you experienced frustrations similar to the students in Lamott's class? Explain.

5. What audience do you think Lamott is writing for? Support your answer by citing examples from her essay.

6. Lamott comments that one challenge many writers—including herself—face is dealing with a sense of "self-loathing" toward what they have written. Can you relate to this feeling? Why or why not?

WRITING ASSIGNMENTS

1. Follow Lamott's advice to her class on getting started. Recall an incident from your childhood and write about it each day for a week. Focus on recalling memories, feelings, and impressions of the event. Return each day to add to and rework what you have written. At the end of the week, describe the experience of writing this way. Turn in both the creative writing piece you wrote and your analysis of the exercise to your instructor.

2. Have you ever had writer's block? How did you overcome it? What suggestions could you add to Lamott's advice for "getting started"?

3. The next time you have an essay assigned, keep a log or diary in which you can write about your own writing process. Include comments about how you approach and think about the assignment, how you prepare and actually write the piece, and how you revise and edit your essay. Be sure to include commentary on your feelings and impressions of the process as well as the actual mechanics of writing.

What My Students Have Taught Me About Writing
Pamela Childers

In the preceding essay, Anne Lamott described the advice she gave her creative writing students. In the next piece, another writing instructor, Pamela Childers, discusses what her students have taught *her* about writing. As the director of a high school writing center, Childers is often reminded that writing is a constantly evolving process of discovery. Through freewriting and collaborative writing exercises, students develop and polish their skills. But collaboration, as Childers explains, can be as illuminating for the instructor as it is for the student writer.

Pamela Childers is director of the McCallie Writing Center at the McCallie School in Chattanooga, Tennessee. She is the author of many articles on writing and the teaching of writing. She would like to thank her students, Tripp Grant, Wesley Bell, Matt Lockaby, Evan Miller, and Chad Littleton for their advice and assistance in preparing this essay.

1   I'm a writer, but I am a better writer than I was when I started teaching because of my students. They have taught me how to improve my own writing by writing with them, getting feedback on my writing from them and listening to their questions about writing. Evan Miller took an independent study course with me his senior year, and I asked him to describe his writing process as I have with many students. Although an experienced writer who probably had not reflected upon his own writing process before, Evan has clearly practiced writing for years. Other students are not necessarily as motivated as Evan, but over the years they teach us, their teachers, many lessons about writing. Here are a few:

2 Lesson #1—You Need to Be Able to Write for a Variety of Purposes and Audiences

The purpose of an essay for class is to demonstrate knowledge of information in a formal, well-written format, and the audience is usually the teacher who will grade the paper. The purpose of other writing may be to gain acceptance to college, to learn information, to inform, to discover or to entertain. Linda Flower reminds us to know who the audience is for our writing, and often it may just be ourselves.

3   Listen to the voice of Tripp in a freewrite assignment to describe his writing process:

4   Writing to me is an expression. My earliest memories of writing are when I was very young. I used to write stories of my friends and I going on fictional adventures that were fun to write. Then it was a pleasure. Now it is a burden. Now my days are filled with papers of cell division, the life of John Donne, and the typical existentialist. The fond memories of fictional stories and eighth grade journal writing are rapidly being taken over by the typical school research project.

5   The reason that I don't like the typical paper is because I never mastered the language. When it comes to gramer and vocabulary I am on the level of an eighth grader. I cannot write from the heart on what I feel and I feel very restricted. Pleasure writing comes from the heart it is very relieving to be able to write about anything.

6   The process I use is pretty simple. I write what I think will get me the best grade and not what comes from what I feel for a lot of projects. I don't plan out some fancy outline. I usually just come up with a good opening paragraph and then support it with crummy paragraphs and then bring it all together at the end. It is what every teacher tells you to do. I am just not good at it because of the language. I don't know how to express my thoughts in a persuasive form.

7   Tripp's experiences in secondary school probably continued through college as well. With some luck, he might have encountered some real-life writing experiences and some that allowed him to write about what "comes from the heart." Tripp has learned to write for his audience—what most of us do for publication because the "grade" is acceptance of our article, chapter or book, for instance. It is sheer joy when what we care about can be presented in a form that is acceptable for the particular audience that will publish the piece of writing.

8   In Tripp's case, his audiences so far have been teachers of science, history and English, and he has learned the "formula" for those papers. However, is Tripp not writing from the heart in this freewrite? Is he not persuasive? Again and again college writing teachers who have read Tripp's piece say, "I want him in my class because he clearly has his own voice." Notice that they do not say, "That student really has a problem with mechanics; he does have trouble with language."

⁹ Lesson #2—Keep That Editor Inside Your Head Until the Last Possible Moment

Donald Murray talks about all the revisions one must make, but he focuses on information, form, structure, development, dimension, and voice. There are revision processes before the final edit for grammar, spelling and punctuation. He is focusing on the content of a piece of writing that is never done. If Murray looked at Tripp's paper, he wouldn't talk about the spelling, run-on sentences, or incorrect pronoun usage. The writing was clearly written for Tripp alone (or possibly to share with me); but Murray would encourage Tripp's strong voice and use of detail. What made Tripp think he was not good with language?

¹⁰   This year I have been working with John, an honors student who needs some guidance in writing timed essays. Since I read Advanced Placement Language and Composition essays, I thought I might be able to work with John on improving his writing to respond to a prompt not previously seen. We discovered in talking about his writing process that John was trying to write precisely the perfect sentence for each and every line of his written response. It was taking him forever, and he never had time left to look at what he had written before the paper had to be submitted. We decided to try some practice freewrites on the computer with the monitor turned off. John loved the freedom to just let ideas flow through his hands on the keyboard without looking at them on the monitor. Now we both know that John had been allowing the editor in his head to critique each sentence as he wrote it. We will continue to do freewrites, some by hand and some on the computer, keeping the editor in the back of his head until he is ready to read through the final draft of the whole paper. I find myself doing this exercise, too, just to help me focus more on ideas and less on format on timed writings, which essentially are organized, timed early drafts.

¹¹ Lesson #3—Write About What You Know

Writer and educator Stephen Tchudi says, "To write well, one must know something well." It becomes obvious to readers who knows what they are talking about and who does not. It is easier to have the dilemma of knowing too much about something than not knowing enough to write about it intelligently. For the former, the problem is explaining one's knowledge clearly to the audience who does not know what you know; for the latter, the problem is finding anything specific to say. As in battle, when you are preparing, you want all the reinforcements you can gather. In writing those reinforcements are specific details or primary and secondary sources in research to back up your knowledge.

¹²   During the semester that I taught Tripp, he began to work with an eighth-grade physics class on their portfolios. He had to read about writing, about portfolios, about evaluating writing, and actually work with students on creating an assessment tool for their portfolios. Students wrote letters to him and the other seniors in his class, explaining a physics concept to them. Tripp had to evaluate the students'

understanding of the concept as part of his evaluation of their portfolios. In the process, he learned a great deal about his own writing.

13 Lesson #4—Collaboration and a Real Audience Make a Difference

Tripp and two of his classmates had conducted the sessions with the eighth graders and gathered documentation from their experiences. A friend was editing a collection on assessment for *The Clearing House,* a national educational journal; so I suggested that he consider an article written by these three students. Tripp was scared; he felt confident that he could not write well. When the three of them each wrote a first draft, they were amazed at how much they could add to each other's writing with details. Through many drafts, they helped each other develop the article. During this process, I would ask them questions to help get them closer to a finished product. After they sent it to the editor, he phoned and each of them had a chance to take notes on the feedback he gave them. That was a real audience who would determine whether their article would be published! Tripp wrote a note at the end of the year in which he said, "I now think I might be a writer who has his own voice for the first time." Now for the first time Tripp realized he had a writing style of his own! The three students were college freshmen at Samford, Wake Forest, and Madison when they received their copies of the publication. I wish I could have been there for their reaction to seeing their article published in a national professional journal.

14   Collaboration on a publication helps students gain confidence in their ability to write and also helps them discover new ways of thinking from a trusted colleague. Throughout the years, I have written numerous articles and chapters with students, teachers of other subjects and colleagues at other institutions. Each collaboration makes me work harder on my own writing, reevaluate my thinking in drafts, and appreciate the writing and thinking of others. It creates a supportive and critical en vironment, one with respected peers.

15 Lesson #5—If You Are Comfortable with Your Writing, You Will Take Risks to Write Better

Wes has always been an A student; however, when it came time to work on his college application essays, he had writer's block. In fact, his writing about himself became stilted, formal, without humor. Having known Wes for several years, I had heard his corny jokes and puns quite often. After four or five drafts of his essays, I would ask him what he might do to demonstrate who he really was that did not appear on the application form. We took a phrase or sentence from one of the other drafts and started again. Granted, these were still not the real voice of Wes, but the final drafts he submitted gave the picture of a humanistic, well-rounded individual who was academically and physically talented. However, when Wes had to write scholarship essays, he started taking some big risks, using irony, satire, and allusions to literature, history, current events, and science. I asked him why his voice had changed in these papers and he responded, "I know that I have been accepted into the school; now I can truly be myself without the danger of not being able to go to the college of my choice." The difference in style was amazing, and he was pleased with the results.

16   As we become more comfortable with writing for a particular audience, whether known or unknown, we may become more willing to experiment with writing. A few years back a senior came to me saying, "Doc, I know the formula for getting a good grade on essays, but I want to learn how to write well." After I recovered, I asked him, "Are you willing to take some risks with your thinking and writing?" For an entire semester we played with language, including the writing of his college application essay for early decision. On Christmas Eve, I received a phone call from this student saying he had been accepted to the college of his choice. The success of his writing involved his commitment to improving and his willingness to experiment with his own writing.

17 ## Lesson #6—You Need to Allow Time to Write More Than One Draft

When I first started teaching, it was common practice for most students to turn in something they had written the night before. In the 1980s real writers began talking about drafts, pre-writing, peer response and feedback, more pre-writing, drafts, revision, and editing; they called it the writing process. As much as English language arts teachers tried to encourage a real process for their students' writing, students resisted. Teachers were still putting red marks on their papers and making the corrections for the students on the graded papers. For the most part, that has changed; students now have class activities that help them prepare for the writing of a paper, and they have a chance to get feedback from classmates before they write and submit a final draft. However, the students who do well with their writing have started early, allowed time to distance themselves from their own writing, and actually "revisioned" their own papers. A dozen years ago students would come to the writing center, type in and print one draft to submit to their teachers. Now, they start earlier, bounce ideas off others, allow themselves time to rethink, and reread materials before they start writing a final draft.

18 ## Lesson #7—Don't Take Yourself Too Seriously; Be Open to Criticism

I have directed two secondary school writing centers at public and private institutions and found that the atmosphere of mutual respect and humor in a low-risk environment makes a big difference in long-term writing improvement. I listen to the soft laughter, sometimes uproars, that emerge from various corners of the room and know that learning is occurring. Students are reading their papers aloud, and others are listening intently and jotting notes or questions. The reader will say something and realize how absurd it is with a word missing or an illogical conclusion, and the two of them will laugh.

19   Matt had been a regular in the writing center; however, it wasn't until he started working on college application essays that he felt comfortable coming to ask

for some feedback. When a student writes well enough to get good grades in high school, he seldom sees the need for any input from someone else. This was Matt, my friend who came to talk with me quite regularly but not someone who "needed help" at least not until he had to write application essays. The help that Matt needed focused on continuity and consistency in the use of metaphors or the precise tone he wished to convey to his audience—the people who would determine his academic future. Through a series of 15 drafts for one essay and multiple drafts of other ones, Matt and I spent many hours laughing. Sometimes other students would look at us as if we could not possibly be doing serious work, but what they did not know was that we were talking about expanding his metaphor of cooking pasta for assimilation in America or his use of irony in defining freedom. It was delightful to be part of Matt's experience with important assignments that allowed him to enjoy the process because he did not take himself too seriously.

20   When I have to write something to be sent to their parents, I hand it to a group of students and laughter invariably results. They know the intended audience much better than I do, so they set me straight on phrases that would make no sense to their parents. If I am proposing a new course, I run the proposal by the current seniors who tell me that no one would sign up for this course the way I have described it. "Help me out here," I say, and they do! Last year, one student wrote on our writing center flyer: "We poke fun at your papers in a supportive way." Not really, but the message indicates the humorous environment we create to allow someone to say that.

21   Each day as I leave the writing center or the classroom, I think about the lessons I have learned from my students. Some come from students who are now returning as alumni, many reminding me of specific lessons we have learned together. When I had lunch with Matt, I asked if he was doing okay meeting deadlines in college. He began telling me about a research project that he loved because it was creative, required much more research than he would normally have done and took the form of a proposal for a real course. I asked him if he would read my essay for college students and critique it for me; once again, he was teaching me about his writing process, but this time we were collaborating on *my* paper.

THINKING CRITICALLY

1. Childers uses many examples of her own students' writing to support her essay. Is this an effective technique? Did you find the examples helpful? Explain.

2. When Childers first introduces Tripp, we learn that while he writes for his audience, he doesn't seem to enjoy writing. Why? What advice do you think Anne Lamott would give him? What would you suggest, and why?

3. What have Childers's students taught her about writing? Explain.

4. Has fear, like the fears Wes faces when writing his college entrance essays, ever affected or restricted your own writing? Explain.

5. Why is it important for students to find their own voice and style and be comfortable with writing?

WRITING ASSIGNMENTS

1. Childers describes how a collaborative writing effort helped Tripp and two other classmates find their own voice and prepare a paper for publication. Repeat this exercise with two other students in your writing class. Prepare a short essay together, and then edit the piece as individuals, asking questions to draw out each other's points, voice, and style. How does the final piece compare to essays you have written without the benefit of collaboration? Explain.

2. Freewriting has helped many of Childers's students find their own voice. Conduct a freewriting assignment in which you explore and discuss your own writer's voice. What is your voice? How do you know it is yours? What makes it different or unique? Is voice important to your writing? Why or why not?

3. Write about a personal experience in which you realized how important effective communication skills really were. It could be from a college application process, a job or school experience, or a miscommunication between family members or friends. In your answer, be sure to address how using language effectively helped solve the problem.

4. If your school has one, interview instructors at your school's writing lab or writing resource center and ask them for their own observations on effective writing and if they have learned anything about writing from the students who come to the lab/center. Share the results of your interview with the rest of the class for group discussion on effective writing practices.

How I Write
Evan Miller

> Evan Miller is currently a student at Williams College, and a former student of Pamela Childers (see the preceding essay). In this piece, Miller explains his own writing technique and how he approaches the art of writing.

1 Here's how I write:

2   The first sentence is usually the toughest for me, because I know that the first sentence will shape the second will shape the third, et cetera et cetera et cetera. I get the feeling that the two or three basic sentences that I'm wrestling with as opener-contenders each could result in a profoundly different paper—and significantly different grades in some cases. The opener sets the tone, the modus operandi and levels of irony and deepness and playfulness and straightforwardness all at once. I like to experiment with different openers, and it usually results in a nifty variety of papers, but some of those papers miss the purpose of the paper entirely or are, in the vernacular, crap.

3   But refined crap. I write obsessively—I meticulously think through the upcoming structure of sentences a few times, then actually put it to the computer screen

(oh, the commitment), then change a few words, rearrange others, scratch-cut-and-paste until it sounds, well, perfect. Sometimes I just know what the perfect word is in a particular context, but I can't quite remember it, but I can tell you other words that sound like it or have similar meanings (or both). Other times I know just the right word for a sentence, even though I don't know the meaning of the word and I'm not sure where I heard it, but I use it anyway then look it up in the dictionary and it's usually right. I don't know why my mind works like this when it comes to diction; it's weird, but it works.

4   And sometimes I pull some eye-catching literary devices that I learned in Latin class, like chiasmus and synecdoche and tricolon crescens. I've started integrating other rules into my basic sentence formulation, like not starting all my sentences with the same noun (unlike this free-write—excuse the mess) and avoiding linking verbs and aiming for conciseness and clarity rather than decoration and decadence (eek alliteration).

5   And so that's how the paper grows—sentence by careful sentence, building arguments (or whatever elements I'm dealing with) as I imagine and integrate them, getting up frequently to walk and think about where I've come and where I'm going, sitting back down and editing a little then crafting more. The writing gets me thinking—hard—so I tend to write slowly, deliberately. Sometimes I'll have to cover a few holes in the paper with convincing transitions, and sometimes those papers turn out rather rotten.

6   Then I finish up. The paper sounds good, if I've spent sufficient time on it. If I realize that it's pretty devoid of meat, or that the style really doesn't fit the task, I'll try to redo the paper, with the newfound understanding of my task, telling myself that the experience was worthwhile. The rewritten papers are usually the best ones, but I've produced some winning first-drafts in my time (they take the longest, though).

7   Oh yeah, about style. From the outset, I'll pick a tone and voice that I think fits the assignment, or just something I want to try out. I wax blunt/dramatic for debate cases or flowery/analytical for an English paper now and then or simple/emotional for those types of essays or witty/incisive for a good tirade. Some work better than others—my faves (and most successful) have been the flowery/analytical and witty/incisive voices probably because they both had genuine argumentative purpose and do the job with style. Plus, I enjoy writing them the most. And maybe it's because if I think of a witty connection or clever phraseology I have a tough time resisting the temptation to throw it in.

8   That's all I have to say.

THINKING CRITICALLY

1. How does the process Miller describes compare to the advice given by other writers and instructors of writing in this section, such as Anne Lamott and Linda Flower? How do you think they would respond to his essay?

2. What are the "Latin class" literary devices Miller uses to jazz up his writing? How could these devices improve his essays? Explain.

3. What elements of writing pose the greatest challenge for Miller? How does he address these challenges? Explain.

4. At the end of his essay, Miller writes that when it comes to choosing a style, he picks "a tone and voice that he thinks fits the assignment." What is Miller's tone and style in this essay? How does his tone affect the content of his essay? Explain.

WRITING ASSIGNMENTS

1. In this essay, Evan Miller described his personal approach to writing. Using the same title as Miller's essay, write your own narrative on how you write.

2. Miller prepared this piece as a freewriting assignment. Unstructured and informal, freewriting allows you to consider a question or topic and let the ideas simply flow. Try this technique yourself. Freewrite for 10 to 20 minutes using one of these phrases as a lead in: "The toughest thing about writing is . . .," "What I love about writing is . . .," or "Writing skills are important [or unimportant] because . . .". Remember that freewriting allows for spelling errors and does not require revisions. Turn in the unedited piece to your writing instructor for comments and feedback.

■ MAKING CONNECTIONS

1. The authors in this chapter all describe different aspects of the writing process—from audience identification, to finding your inspiration, to editing the final product. During your next essay assignment, keep a journal of your impressions of each step of the writing process as you compose your essay. In your journal, consider your approach to the writing process during each step and the feedback you received from teachers and peers.

2. Many writing instructors encourage freewriting exercises that promote the unencumbered flow of ideas as a way to develop writing skills. Try to write about a topic—for example, teenage use of alcohol or a particular type of controversial music—for two different audiences. Keep your audience in mind as you write, but remain mindful of simply allowing your ideas to flow freely. After you complete this writing exercise, consider how freewriting compares to more structured methods of writing.

3. After reading the work of the authors featured in this section, do you have a better sense of the writing process? Explain why or why not.

4. In your own opinion, which stage of the writing process is the most important? Support your answer by drawing from material provided in this section as well as from your personal writing experiences.

5. What common advice and/or suggestions do the authors in this section make? Identify similarities and differences in their essays.

■ FINDING THE RIGHT WORDS

The Case for Short Words
Richard Lederer

> Sometimes students pull out the dictionary or thesaurus in an effort to find words that seem more "academic." We seem to think that the longer or more difficult the word is to pronounce, the more intelligent the writer must be. But this isn't necessarily the case. In many situations, short words do the job better than long or complicated ones. In the next essay, writer and former high-school teacher Richard Lederer explains why small, short words can be the most powerful words of all.
>
> Richard Lederer is the author of several best-selling books on words and language, including *Get Thee to a Punnery* (1988), *Crazy English* (1989), and *Fractured English* (1996). Lederer, who holds a Ph.D. in linguistics, is a regular contributor to *Writer's Digest*, and a language commentator on National Public Radio (NPR). The following essay was published in the August 1999 issue of the San Diego *Writers Monthly*, and was featured in Lederer's 1991 book, *The Miracle of Language*.

1 When you speak and write, there is no law that says you have to use big words. Short words are as good as long ones, and short, old words—like sun and grass and home—are best of all. A lot of small words, more than you might think, can meet your needs with a strength, grace, and charm that large words do not have.

2 Big words can make the way dark for those who read what you write and hear what you say. Small words cast their clear light on big things—night and day, love and hate, war and peace, and life and death. Big words at times seem strange to the eye and the ear and the mind and the heart. Small words are the ones we seem to have known from the time we were born, like the hearth fire that warms the home.

3 Short words are bright like sparks that glow in the night, prompt like the dawn that greets the day, sharp like the blade of a knife, hot like salt tears that scald the cheek, quick like moths that flit from flame to flame, and terse like the dart and sting of a bee.

4 Here is a sound rule: Use small, old words where you can. If a long word says just what you want to say, do not fear to use it. But know that our tongue is rich in crisp, brisk, swift, short words. Make them the spine and the heart of what you speak and write. Short words are like fast friends. They will not let you down.

5 The title of this essay and the four paragraphs that you have just read are wrought entirely of words of one syllable. In setting myself this task, I did not feel especially cabined, cribbed, or confined. In fact, the structure helped me to focus on the power of the message I was trying to put across.

6 One study shows that twenty words account for twenty-five percent of all spoken English words, and all twenty are monosyllabic. In order of frequency they are: *I, you, the, a, to, is, it, that, of, and, in, what, he, this, have, do, she, not, on,* and

they. Other studies indicate that the fifty most common words in written English are each made of a single syllable.

7   For centuries our finest poets and orators have recognized and employed the power of small words to make a straight point between two minds. A great many of our proverbs punch home their points with pithy monosyllables: "Where there's a will, there's a way," "A stitch in time saves nine," "Spare the rod and spoil the child," "A bird in the hand is worth two in the bush."

8   Nobody used the short word more skillfully than William Shakespeare, whose dying King Lear laments:

9   And my poor fool is hang'd! No, no, no life!
10   Why should a dog, a horse, a rat have life,
11   And thou no breath at all? . . .
12   Do you see this? Look on her, look, her lips.
13   Look there, look there!

14   Shakespeare's contemporaries made the King James Bible a centerpiece of short words—"And God said, Let there be light: and there was light. And God saw the light, that it was good." The descendants of such mighty lines live on in the twentieth century. When asked to explain his policy to parliament, Winston Churchill responded with these ringing monosyllables: "I will say: it is to wage war, by sea, land, and air, with all our might and with all the strength that God can give us." In his "Death of the Hired Man" Robert Frost observes that "Home is the place where, when you have to go there,/They have to take you in." And William H. Johnson uses ten two-letter words to explain his secret of success: "If it is to be,/It is up to me."

15   You don't have to be a great author, statesman, or philosopher to tap the energy and eloquence of small words. Each winter I asked my ninth graders at St. Paul's School to write a composition composed entirely of one-syllable words. My students greeted my request with obligatory moans and groans, but, when they returned to class with their essays, most felt that, with the pressure to produce high-sounding polysyllables relieved, they had created some of their most powerful and luminous prose. Here are submissions from two of my ninth graders:

16   What can you say to a boy who has left home? You can say that he has done wrong, but he does not care. In spite of the breeze that made the vines sway, we all wished we could hide from the glare in a cool, white house. But, as there was no one to help dock the boat, we had to stand and wait.

17   At last the head of the crew leaped from the side and strode to a large house on the right. He shoved the door wide, poked his head through the gloom, and roared with a fierce voice. Five or six men came out, and soon the port was loud with the clank of chains and creak of planks as the men caught ropes thrown by the crew; pulled them taut, and tied them to posts. Then they set up a rough plank so we could cross from the deck to the shore. We all made for the large house while the crew watched, glad to be rid of us.

THINKING CRITICALLY

1. What, according to Lederer, are the "big things" that small words describe? Can you think of additional small words that describe "big things"?

2. In paragraph 7, Lederer points out several proverbs that use small words. Identify at least three or four more and test his observation. Do short words predominate? If so, what explains the high proportion of small words in proverbs?

3. Review the examples of student writing Lederer cites in his essay. What seems special about their writing? Does it seem constrained by the requirements of his assignment? Why or why not?

4. Why do so many students feel pressured to use long or complicated words instead of smaller ones? Do teachers reinforce the idea that big words are better? Do you think your grades would suffer if you opted for smaller words in your essays and homework assignments? Explain.

5. Evaluate Lederer's introductory paragraphs (1–4), which only use one-syllable words. Did you realize that he was using only short words when you first read these paragraphs? What impression did you have of his writing in these first four paragraphs? Explain.

WRITING ASSIGNMENTS

1. Duplicate Lederer's assignment to his class. Write a full paragraph describing an every day event, idea, or scene (getting up in the morning, viewing a sunrise, looking up at a night sky, a visit with your parents, how you feel about a significant other, etc.). After writing your paragraph and checking that it is indeed written using only one-syllable words, describe the challenges you faced and impressions you had of the composition processes.

2. Find a paragraph or two from an essay or free writing assignment that you think is a good representation of your academic voice. Try re-writing the paragraph(s) using only short words. In addition to comparing the two from your own perspective, give the two pieces to a friend or family member and ask them to evaluate each. Ask your reviewer to explain what makes the piece they prefer better in their opinion. Describe the results in a short essay, drawing your own conclusions from your experiment.

Saying Is Believing

Patricia T. O'Conner

In the preceding piece, Richard Lederer made his case for short words. In the next essay, grammarian and writer Patricia T. O'Conner explains how to avoid some pitfalls facing many college writers by embracing the principles of "plain English." Too often, complexity, confusion, wordiness, and redundancy sidetrack writers. Her solution is a list of thirteen points that will improve your writing, and guide you through the writing blunders many students make.

A former editor of the *New York Times Book Review*, Patricia T. O'Conner is the author of three books on writing and has published articles on grammar and writing in many newspapers and journals including the *New York Times* and *Newsweek*. She is the author of *Words Fail Me: What Everyone Who Writes Should Know About Writing* (2000) and of *You Send Me* (2002) written with husband Stewart Kellerman. This essay was first published in her grammar guidebook, *Woe Is I: The Grammarphobe's Guide to Better English in Plain English* (1996).

1 A good writer is one you can read without breaking a sweat. If you want a workout, you don't lift a book—you lift weights. Yet we're brainwashed to believe that the more brilliant the writer, the tougher the going.

2 The truth is that the reader is always right. Chances are, if something you're reading doesn't make sense, it's not your fault—it's the writer's. And if something you write doesn't get your point across, it's probably not the reader's fault—it's yours. Too many readers are intimidated and humbled by what they can't understand, and in some cases that's precisely the effect the writer is after. But confusion is not complexity; it's just confusion. A venerable tradition, dating back to the ancient Greek orators, teaches that if you don't know what you're talking about, just ratchet up the level of difficulty and no one will ever know.

3 Don't confuse simplicity, though, with simplemindedness. A good writer can express an extremely complicated idea clearly and make the job look effortless. But such simplicity is a difficult thing to achieve, because to be clear in your writing you have to be clear in your thinking. This is why the simplest and clearest writing has the greatest power to delight, surprise, inform, and move the reader. You can't have this kind of shared understanding if writer and reader are in an adversary relationship.

4 Now, let's assume you know what you want to say, and the idea in your head is as clear as a mountain stream. (I'm allowed a cliché once in a while.) How can you avoid muddying it up when you put it into words?

5 There are no rules for graceful writing, at least not in the sense that there are rules for grammar and punctuation. Some writing manuals will tell you to write short sentences, or to cut out adjectives and adverbs. I disagree. The object isn't to simulate an android. When a sentence sounds nice, reads well, and is easy to follow, its length is just right. But when a sentence is lousy, you can take steps to make it more presentable. These are general principles, and you won't want to follow all of them all of the time (though it's not a bad idea).

6 **1.** *Say what you have to say.*

Unless you're standing at a lectern addressing an audience, there's no need to clear your throat. Your listeners aren't finding their seats, putting down their forks, wrapping up a conversation, or whatever. Your audience—the reader—is ready. So get to it.

7 These are the kinds of throat-clearing phrases you can usually ditch:

8 *At this juncture I thought you might be interested in knowing . . .*

9 *Perhaps it would be valuable as we arrive at this point in time to recall. . .*

10   *I can assure you that I'm sincere when I say . . .*

11   *In light of recent developments the possibility exists that . . .*

12   (Of course, some messages could do with a bit of cushioning: *We at the bank feel that under the circumstances you would want us to bring to your attention as soon as possible the fact that . . . your account is overdrawn.*)

13   **2.** *Stop when you've said it.*

Sometimes, especially when you're on a roll and coming up with your best stuff, it's hard to let go of a sentence (this one, for example), so when you get to the logical end you just keep going, and even though you know the reader's eyes are glazing over, you stretch one sentence thinner and thinner—with a semicolon here, a *however* or *nevertheless* there—and you end up stringing together a whole paragraph's worth of ideas before you finally realize it's all over and you're getting writer's cramp and you have to break down and use a period.

14   When it's time to start another sentence, start another sentence.

15   How do you know when it's time? Well, try breathing along with your sentences. Allow yourself one nice inhalation and exhalation per sentence as you silently read along. If you start to turn blue before getting to the end, either you're reading too slowly (don't move your lips) or the sentence is too long.

16   **3.** *Don't belabor the obvious.*

Some writers can't make a point without poking you in the ribs with it. A voice isn't just pleasing; it's pleasing *to the ear.* You don't just give something away; you give it away *for free.* The reader will get the point without the unnecessary prepositional phrases (phrases that start with words like *by, for, in, of,* and *to*): pretty *in appearance,* tall *of stature,* blue *in color,* small *in size,* stocky *in build,* plan *in advance,* drive *by car,* assemble *in a group.* You get the picture.

17   **4.** *Don't tie yourself in knots to avoid repeating a word.*

It's better to repeat a word that fits than to stick in a clumsy substitute that doesn't. Just because you've called something a spider once doesn't mean that the next time you have to call it an arachnid or a predaceous eight-legged creepy-crawly.

18   Editors sometimes call this attempt at elegant variation the Slender Yellow Fruit Syndrome. It is best explained by example: *Freddie was offered an apple and a banana, and he chose the slender yellow fruit.*

19   **5.** *Be direct.*

Too many writers back into what they have to say. A straightforward statement like *He didn't intend to ruin your flower bed* comes out *His intention was not to ruin your flower bed.*

20   Don't mince words. If what you mean is, *Mom reorganized my closet brilliantly,* don't water it down by saying, *Mom's reorganization of my closet was brilliant.*

21   Here are a couple of other examples:

22   *Their house was destroyed in 1993.* Not: *The destruction of their house oc-
      curred in 1993.*

23   *We concluded that Roger's an idiot.* Not: *Our conclusion was that Roger's an
      idiot.*

24   If you have something to say, be direct about it. As in geometry, the shortest
distance between two points is a straight line.

25   **6.** *Don't make yourself the center of the universe.*

      Of course we want to know what happened to you. Of course we care what you
think and feel and do and say. But you can tell us without making every other word
I or *me* or *my.* (Letter writers, who are fast becoming an endangered species, are often guilty of this. Next time you write a letter or memo, look it over and see how
many sentences start with *I.*)

26   You can prune phrases like *I think that,* or *in my opinion,* or *let me emphasize
that* out of your writing (and your talking, for that matter) without losing anything.
Anecdotes can be told, advice given, opinions opined, all with a lot fewer first-per-
son pronouns than you think.

27   This doesn't mean we don't love you.

28   **7.** *Put descriptions close to what they describe.*

      A television journalist in the Farm Belt once said this about a suspected out-
break of hoof-and-mouth disease: *The pasture contained several cows seen by news
reporters that were dead, diseased, or dying.*

29   Do you see what's wrong? The words *dead, diseased, or dying* are supposed to
describe the cows, but they're so far from home that they seem to describe the reporters. What the journalist should have said was: *Reporters saw a pasture containing several cows that were dead, diseased, or dying.*

30   When a description strays too far, the sentence becomes awkward and hard to
read. Here's an adjective (*bare*) that has strayed too far from the noun (*cupboard*) it
describes: *Ms. Hubbard found her **cupboard,** although she'd gone shopping only a
few hours before, **bare.*** Here's one way to rewrite it: *Although she'd gone shopping
only a few hours before, Ms. Hubbard found her **cupboard bare.***

31   And here's an adverb (*definitely*) that's strayed too far from its verb (*is suing*):
*She **definitely,** if you can believe what all the papers are reporting and what everyone is saying, **is suing.*** Put them closer together: *She **definitely is suing,** if you can
believe what all the papers are reporting and what everyone is saying.*

32   The reader shouldn't need a map to follow a sentence.

33   **8.** *Put the doer closer to what's being done.*

      Nobody's saying that sentences can't be complex and interesting; they can, as
long as they're easy to follow. But we shouldn't have to read a sentence twice to get
it. Here's an example that takes us from Omaha to Sioux City by way of Pittsburgh:

34   *The **twins,** after stubbornly going to the same high school despite the advice of
their parents and teachers, chose different colleges.*

35 Find a way to say it that puts the doer (the subject, *twins*) closer to what's being done (the verb, *chose*): *The **twins chose** different colleges, after stubbornly going to the same high school despite the advice of their parents and teachers.*

36 If you need a compass to navigate a sentence, take another whack at the writing.

37 **9.** *Watch out for pronounitis.*

A sentence with too many pronouns (*he, him, she, her, it, they, them,* and other words that substitute for nouns) can give your reader hives: *Fleur thinks that Judy told **her** boyfriend about **their** stupid little adventure and that **she** will come to regret it.*

38 Whose boyfriend? Whose stupid little adventure? Who'll regret what?

39 When you write things like this, of course, you know the cast of characters. It won't be so clear to somebody else. Don't make the reader guess.

40 **10.** *Make sure there's a time and place for everything.*

While the merger specialist was vacationing in Aspen she said she secretly put the squeeze on Mr. Buyout by threatening to go public with candid photos of him in one of those foil helmets, getting his hair streaked at Frederic Fekkai.

41 Did the merger specialist tell this story when she was vacationing in Aspen, or is that where she put the squeeze on Mr. Buyout? Were the photos taken earlier? And where is Frederic Fekkai? This calls for two sentences:

42 *While vacationing in Aspen, the merger specialist faxed us her secret. She had put the squeeze on Mr. Buyout in New York the week before by threatening to go public with candid photos of him in one of those foil helmets, getting his hair streaked at Frederic Fekkai.*

43 Where are we? What's going on? What time is it? These are questions the reader shouldn't have to ask.

44 **11.** *Imagine what you're writing.*

Picture in your mind any images you've created.

Are they unintentionally funny, like this one? *The bereaved family covered the mirrors as a reflection of its grief.* If you don't see what's wrong, reflect on it for a moment.

45 Are there too many of them, as in this sentence? *The remaining bone of contention is a thorn in his side and an albatross around his neck:* Give the poor guy a break. One image at a time, please.

46 **12.** *Put your ideas in order.*

Don't make the reader rearrange your messy sentences to figure out what's going on. The parts should follow logically. This doesn't mean they should be rattled off in chronological order, but the sequence of ideas should make sense. Here's how Gracie Allen might have talked about a soufflé recipe, for instance:

47 *It is possible to make this soufflé with four eggs instead of eight. But it will collapse and possibly even catch fire in the oven, leaving you with a flat, burned*

soufflé. Now, you wouldn't want that, would you? So if you have only four eggs, re-duce all the other ingredients in the recipe by half.

48   Rearrange the ideas:

49   *This soufflé recipe calls for eight eggs. If you want to use fewer, reduce the other ingredients accordingly. If the proportions aren't maintained, the soufflé could flatten or burn.*

50   **13.** *Read with a felonious mind.*

     Forget the details for a minute. Now step back and take a look at what you've written. Have you said what you wanted to say? After all, leaving the wrong impression is much worse than making a couple of grammatical boo-boos. Get some perspective.

51   Assuming you've made your point, ask yourself whether you could make it more smoothly. Somebody once said that in good writing, the sentences hold hands. See if you can give yours a helping hand. It may be that by adding or subtracting a word here or there, you could be even clearer. Or you could switch two sentences around, or begin one of them differently.

52   There's no easy way to raise your writing from competence to artistry. It helps, though, to read with a felonious mind. If you see a letter or memo or report that you admire, read it again. Why do you like it, and what makes it so effective? When you find a technique that works, steal it. Someday, others may be stealing from you.

THINKING CRITICALLY

1. O'Conner comments in her first sentence, "A good writer is one you can read without breaking a sweat." Do you agree with this observation? Why or why not? What makes a writer "good"?

2. Evaluate O'Conner's tips as they compare to your own writing challenges. Which ones seem to be particularly helpful, and why? If none of them seem relevant, explain why you hold this point of view.

3. O'Conner observes that many people are "brainwashed into believing that the more brilliant the writer, the tougher the going." What does she mean by this statement? Do you agree? Explain.

4. Which items in O'Conner's list endorse the use of "active voice"? What are the merits of active voice? How can using the active voice help writers and readers?

5. In paragraph 3, O'Conner warns, "don't confuse simplicity . . . with simplemindedness." Clear writing is the result of clear thinking. Think about your own writing process. How do you perceive the connection between your own thought process and your writing? Explain.

WRITING ASSIGNMENTS

1. In her introduction, O'Conner comments that readers are "brainwashed" into thinking that brilliant writers are difficult to understand. Select two or three writers who you consider to be "brilliant," and evaluate how difficult their writing is to understand by analyzing a few pages of their writing. Based on your analysis, write an essay in which you agree or disagree with O'Conner's viewpoint.

2. Write with a "felonious mind." Pick two or three writers whose prose you admire and analyze their writing styles. Pick one writer to imitate, and, using that writer's particular style, write three or four paragraphs of your own. How does it "feel" to write like another writer? Did it make your writing stronger? Was it strange to write in another writer's voice? Explain.

3. Using an essay you have recently written, compare your writing to the thirteen points O'Conner outlines in her article. Identify areas where you meet her recommendations, and where you fall into some of the writing pitfalls she describes.

How to Write With Style
Kurt Vonnegut

Kurt Vonnegut is one of America's most popular contemporary humorists and novelists. He is the author of such favorites and critically acclaimed novels as *Sirens of Titan* (1959), *Cat's Cradle* (1963), *Slaughterhouse Five* (1969), *Breakfast of Champions* (1973), *Hocus Pocus* (1990), and *Timequake* (1993). Vonnegut has also written short stories for many magazines and journals, and has occasionally made cameo appearances in popular films. The enormous success of his writing can be attributed to his imagination, his satiric voice, and his writing style. In the next piece, Vonnegut gives his own practical advice on writing well, and how to approach writing with style and a sense of self.

1 Newspaper reporters and technical writers are trained to reveal almost nothing about themselves in their writings. This makes them freaks in the world of writers, since almost all of the other ink-stained wretches in that world reveal a lot about themselves to readers. We call these revelations, accidental and intentional, elements of style.

2 These revelations tell us as readers what sort of person it is with whom we are spending time. Does the writer sound ignorant or informed, stupid or bright, crooked or honest, humorless or playful—? And on and on.

3 Why should you examine your writing style with the idea of improving it? Do so as a mark of respect for your readers, whatever you're writing. If you scribble your thoughts any which way, your readers will surely feel that you care nothing about them. They will mark you down as an egomaniac or a chowderhead—or worse, they will stop reading you.

4 The most damning revelation you can make about yourself is that you do not know what is interesting and what is not. Don't you yourself like or dislike writers mainly for what they choose to show you or make you think about? Did you ever admire an empty-headed writer for his or her mastery of the language? No.

5 So your own winning style must begin with ideas in your head.

1. Find a Subject You Care About

6 Find a subject you care about and which you in your heart feel others should care about. It is this genuine caring, and not your games with language, which will be the most compelling and seductive element in your style.

7   I am not urging you to write a novel, by the way—although I would not be sorry if you wrote one, provided you genuinely cared about something. A petition to the mayor about a pothole in front of your house or a love letter to the girl next door will do.

2. Do Not Ramble, Though

8 I won't ramble on about that.

3. Keep It Simple

9 As for your use of language: Remember that two great masters of language, William Shakespeare and James Joyce, wrote sentences which were almost child-like when their subjects were most profound. "To be or not to be?" asks Shakespeare's Hamlet. The longest word is three letters long. Joyce, when he was frisky, could put together a sentence as intricate and as glittering as a necklace for Cleopatra, but my favorite sentence in his short story "Eveline" is this one: "She was tired." At that point in the story, no other words could break the heart of a reader as those three words do.

10   Simplicity of language is not only reputable, but perhaps even sacred. The *Bible* opens with a sentence well within the writing skills of a lively fourteen-year-old: "In the beginning God created the heaven and the earth."

4. Have the Guts to Cut

11 It may be that you, too, are capable of making necklaces for Cleopatra, so to speak. But your eloquence should be the servant of the ideas in your head. Your rule might be this: If a sentence, no matter how excellent, does not illuminate your subject in some new and useful way, scratch it out.

5. Sound Like Yourself

12 The writing style which is most natural for you is bound to echo the speech you heard when a child. English was the novelist Joseph Conrad's third language, and much that seems piquant in his use of English was no doubt colored by his first language, which was Polish. And lucky indeed is the writer who has grown up in Ireland, for the English spoken there is so amusing and musical. I myself grew up in Indianapolis, where common speech sounds like a band saw cutting galvanized tin, and employs a vocabulary as unornamental as a monkey wrench.

13   In some of the more remote hollows of Appalachia, children still grow up hearing songs and locutions of Elizabethan times. Yes, and many Americans grow up hearing a language other than English, or an English dialect a majority of Americans cannot understand.

14   All these varieties of speech are beautiful, just as the varieties of butterflies are beautiful. No matter what your first language, you should treasure it all your life. If it happens not to be standard English, and if it shows itself when you write standard English, the result is usually delightful, like a very pretty girl with one eye that is green and one that is blue.

15   I myself find that I trust my own writing most, and others seem to trust it most, too, when I sound most like a person from Indianapolis, which is what I am. What alternatives do I have? The one most vehemently recommended by teachers has no doubt been pressed on you, as well: to write like cultivated Englishmen of a century or more ago.

6. Say What You Mean to Say

16 I used to be exasperated by such teachers, but am no more. I understand now that all those antique essays and stories with which I was to compare my own work were not magnificent for their datedness or foreignness, but for saying precisely what their authors meant them to say. My teachers wished me to write accurately, always selecting the most effective words, and relating the words to one another unambiguously, rigidly, like parts of a machine. The teachers did not want to turn me into an Englishman after all. They hoped that I would become understandable— and therefore understood. And there went my dream of doing with words what Pablo Picasso did with paint or what any number of jazz idols did with music. If I broke all the rules of punctuation, had words mean whatever I wanted them to mean, and strung them together higgledy-piggledy, I would simply not be understood. So you, too, had better avoid Picasso-style or jazz-style writing, if you have something worth saying and wish to be understood.

17   Readers want our pages to look very much like pages they have seen before. Why? This is because they themselves have a tough job to do, and they need all the help they can get from us.

7. Pity the Readers

18 They have to identify thousands of little marks on paper, and make sense of them immediately. They have to *read,* an art so difficult that most people don't really master it even after having studied it all through grade school and high school— twelve long years.

19   So this discussion must finally acknowledge that our stylistic options as writers are neither numerous nor glamorous, since our readers are bound to be such imperfect artists. Our audience requires us to be sympathetic and patient teachers, even willing to simplify and clarify—whereas we would rather soar high above the crowd, singing like nightingales.

20   That is the bad news. The good news is that we Americans are governed under a unique Constitution, which allows us to write whatever we please without fear of punishment. So the most meaningful aspect of our styles, which is what we choose to write about, is utterly unlimited.

8. For Really Detailed Advice

21 For a discussion of literary style in a narrower sense, in a more technical sense, I commend to your attention *The Elements of Style,* by William Strunk, Jr., and E. B. White (Allyn & Bacon, 2000). E. B. White is, of course, one of the most admirable literary stylists this country has so far produced.

22   You should realize, too, that no one would care how well or badly Mr. White expressed himself, if he did not have perfectly enchanting things to say.

THINKING CRITICALLY

1. Examine one of your essays that was recently corrected by your English instructor. On the basis of the corrections, do you think your instructor agrees or disagrees with Vonnegut's advice?

2. According to Vonnegut, what is the advantage of reading "all those antique essays and stories" (paragraph 16)?

3. This article was originally published as an advertisement sponsored by the International Paper Company. Do you feel the average reader would enjoy and profit from the essay?

4. Why do you think Vonnegut chose Shakespeare and Joyce from the hundreds of great writers of the past to demonstrate the value of simplicity?

5. A key piece of advice Vonnegut gives is, "Sound like yourself." Do you think he follows his own advice? Give examples to support your answer.

6. Occasionally Vonnegut uses a simile or metaphor to make a point. Cite some examples from the essay. How do they contribute to the piece?

WRITING ASSIGNMENTS

1. Select an essay you have studied in this book—one that is considerably more formal than Vonnegut's. Rewrite a paragraph the way you think Vonnegut would have written it. Which style do you prefer, and why?

2. Write an essay showing how Vonnegut's essay embodies his own advice.

3. If you have read any of Vonnegut's novels, write a paper in which you try to demonstrate how Vonnegut the essayist sounds like Vonnegut the novelist.

4. Compose a letter to Kurt Vonnegut, providing your personal observations about one or more of his works of fiction. In your letter, employ the writing advice he gives in this essay.

Clichés, Anyone?

James Isaacs

Clichés are trite or overused expressions, and most writing books will tell you to avoid them. The problem with clichés is that they fail to have real substance—they are weakened by overuse. And because they are phrases on tap, users don't bother to come up with their own ideas or fresh wording. In the next essay, James Isaacs presents a commencement speech, which tend to serve as venues of packaged oratory. As you read this parody, try to identify the clichés and their intended meanings. You might even hear echoes of your own high school commencement!

James Isaacs is a writer, musician, and music critic for Microsoft's Sidewalk Boston Web site. He was nominated for a Grammy in 1986 for co-producing the reissue of Frank Sinatra's work. For the past fifteen years, Isaacs has hosted and produced jazz, soul, and pop-music programs for National Public Radio. This piece first appeared in the *Boston Globe* on May 8, 1998.

1   *Commencement fast approaches. On college campuses and in high school auditoriums and gymnasiums across the land, a parade of orators will loft the traditional airballs of homespun homilies, peppy locker room bromides, and windbuggery under many sails.*

2   *In recent years I have picked up extra income writing graduation addresses for a few locally based notables, including a second-string television news anchor, several lieutenants of industry, and a minor pol or two.*

3   *The only instruction I received was that I should write in their voices, and this I think I did. However, as this spring finds me happily and inordinately busy at work on a made-for-community-access-TV musical "The Alchemy of Opie and Anthony," I hereby offer the following to any and all commencement speakers:*

4   Good morning (afternoon, evening), members of the Class of 1998 at (name of institution of learning) and your families and friends.

5   At this point in time, as we near the dawn of the new millennium and each of us seeks some sort of defining moment, it has never been more important to send a message, big time. Two words: "Work ethic." Or "speed bump." Or "role model." Whatever, as you young folks put it so succinctly.

6   That we're all on the same page and bring something to the table is the postmodern buzz that's on the cutting edge, you know what I'm saying? And in order to deconstruct the spin control, to be some kind of player—an icon, if you will—you will at some time in your life have to draw a line in the sand, even if your agenda is granularly challenged. So, do the math. Right there in the sand, go figure! It ain't rocket science.

7   It is then, and only then, once you step up to the plate, no matter how much you may have on your plate, that you'll get over it and start turning your life around by

taking it to the next level. I know because I've been there, done that, while on my watch. And a fine Swiss watch it was until an 800-pound gorilla with in-your-face attitude hurled it almost over-the-top of Fenway Park's famous Green Monster.

8   So much for quality time.

9   And as you know, it ain't over till it's over. Or until the fat lady sings. But that's a story for another day.

10   To the young women among this year's graduates: Going out into the world can be a no-brainer, no problem, provided, of course, you have all your ducks in a row and they're in a full attack mode feeding frenzy, ready to push the envelope and deliver an awesome slam dunk that's in the zone.

11   It's also imperative that you keep this in mind: In order to distance yourself from every victim, enabler, and co-dependent on your radar screen, you might have to go right off the charts to reinvent yourself. And when it's time to move on, well, you go, girl! Hey, even if it's on my dime, never forget that it's your call as to who will carry your water, no matter what he said or, for that matter, she said.

12   As for you young men, I recall that many years ago when I first expressed interest in a career in photojournalism, my father said, "Read my lips: Get a 'Life.'"

13   "Dad," I replied, "you just don't get it." Which certainly was true at the time, since we subscribed to "Collier's." But when I also mentioned that I wanted to move to New York, his advice was equally blunt: "Don't go there." To which I answered: "Dad, even though you da man, you don't have a clue. But thanks for sharing."

14   So at the end of the day, life is face time. But it's also about show-me-the-money. And that's a good thing. First and foremost, however, I cannot stress strongly enough the notion that if you don't ask, don't tell, you will begin the healing process, get over it, and come to closure. It doesn't get any better than this.

15   End of story. To coin a phrase.

THINKING CRITICALLY

1. Give your own definition of a cliché. How often do you use clichés in your own speech? How does Isaacs tap into our common knowledge of clichés in this commencement speech spoof?

2. Would this article be funny to a non-American audience? For example, would German- or Chinese-speaking people understand its humor? What about an English or Irish audience? Explain.

3. Although Isaacs pokes fun at the overuse of clichés during commencement speeches, clichés do enable speakers to connect to their audience. Identify some situations where clichés would be useful linguistic devices.

4. What is Isaacs's message in this article? What point is he trying to convey? Explain.

5. Recall your own commencement speech. Do you remember what was said? How does the memory of your commencement speech compare to your classmates' memories of it? As a group, how do the speeches compare in style and content?

6. What is Isaacs saying about the basic substance of the commencement speech? Do you agree with his perspective? Why or why not?

WRITING ASSIGNMENTS

1. Write your own commencement speech. What would you say to connect to your audience? Would you use common linguistic conventions? Would you use clichés?

2. Write a letter to a friend using as many clichés as you can as long as they are appropriate to your message. Evaluate what you have written. Was this exercise easy or difficult? Explain.

3. Evaluate a political speech made by a politician. You may find it useful to record the speech or obtain a transcript of it. Did the official use any clichés? If so, identify and analyze them. Are some expressions more noticeable than others? Did any escape your notice the first time you heard the speech? Explain.

The Financial Media's 25 Worst Clichés
Jonathan Clements

This item appeared in the *Wall Street Journal* on March 10, 2002.

1   Cigarettes come with health warnings. Maybe financial journalists should, too.

2   In recent years, I have done a handful of columns where I took phrases frequently heard on Wall Street and then offered my translation for what those comments really mean. Along the way, I have poked fun at brokers, market strategists, money managers and ordinary investors.

3   But why stop there? Often, financial journalists also fail to say what they really mean. Examples? Consider the 25 comments below, variations of which often appear in the media. The list was put together with help from investment experts William Bernstein, Kevin Bernzott, Meir Statman and Alan Weiss.

4   • *"The banking community is divided"*: We called two sources and got different opinions.

5   • *"A spokesman for the state securities commission declined to comment, citing its ongoing investigation"*: Which got started when we called the agency and asked whether investigators were looking at the issue.

6   • *"Ms. Smith, who isn't involved in the lawsuit, says the late-day announcement is good news for the plaintiff"*: We were on deadline, and nobody was picking up the phone, so we called Ms. Smith instead.

7   • *"A company spokeswoman declined to comment"*: But off the record, we got an earful from the executive vice president.

8   • *"Experts are still trying to untangle the legal issues involved"*: We talked to three lawyers, and we still don't understand what's going on.

9 • *"The euro set new lows for the session on signs of a U.S. economic rebound"*: We haven't the slightest inkling what the connection is between the euro and the U.S. economy. But there has to be some explanation for the currency's tumble.

10 • *"Stocks are expected to open lower on Monday"*: Sure, we're right only half the time. But Sammy Sosa would kill for that sort of batting average.

11 • *"Considered one of Wall Street's most iconoclastic strategists, Mr. Wharton predicts the Dow Jones Industrial Average will plunge below 5000"*: Sure, the guy is off his rocker. But he makes great copy.

12 • *"Bond prices fell in anticipation of higher interest rates"*: Or maybe interest rates rose in anticipation of lower bond prices. How could we possibly know? We majored in English.

13 • *"Many investors fear there's more stock-market carnage to come"*: Everybody in the newsroom is totally freaked out.

14 • *"Want to become a millionaire? Try our five-step program"*: With enough time, a high savings rate and outsize investment returns, we can assume our way to anything.

15 • *"Looking for big gains in the year ahead? Here are seven stocks that are set to sizzle"*: Reader amnesia is our best friend.

16 • *"While many small investors have suffered big losses recently, few can rival the dismal record of Mr. Warren, who owns just three stocks—Kmart, Enron and Global Crossing"*: Can you believe this guy agreed to speak to us? It's amazing what people will tell the press.

17 • *"Jim and Betty Hancock, shown in the accompanying photograph, began diligently saving for college soon after their first child was born"*: Actually, the Hancocks seem to spend most of their spare time at the local mall. But they sure photograph well.

18 • *"Like thousands of other investors, Wendy Evans was badly burned by last month's partnership debacle"*: You wouldn't believe how many calls we had to make and how many Internet bulletin boards we had to scour before we found this woman.

19 • *"Here are our 10 funds to buy now"*: One will be a great performer, seven will be mediocre and two will be total dogs. But which is which? You will have to figure that out on your own.

20 • *"See our list of last year's top-performing mutual funds"*: Which may be useful if you are the kind of person who drives using only the rearview mirror.

21 • *"Many investors ignore costs when picking mutual funds. But that can be a big mistake"*: First, we make an unsubstantiated claim about investor behavior. Then, we argue that these folks are foolish. Ah, sometimes there's no sweeter scent than a straw man burning.

22 • *"Indeed, if you had blindly bought into the prior year's hottest sector, you wouldn't have made any money over the past decade, once you figure in inflation, taxes and trading costs"*: We tortured the data base until it confessed.

23 • *"The fund's risk-adjusted performance is among the best in the growth-and-income category"*: Its raw performance stinks.

24 • *"Despite the fund's dazzling record, analysts say it should account for only a small portion of your portfolio"*: If you stick any money in this fund, don't blame us.

25 • *"The fund's recent performance reads like a chapter out of a Stephen King novel"*: When we were kids, we used to pull the legs off spiders.

26 • *"Last quarter's top-performing fund manager thinks further gains lie ahead"*: Remember what we said about ignoring short-term performance? Scratch that.

27 • *"The fund's manager avoids swinging for the fences, instead aiming to hit singles and doubles"*: Maybe the sports page has some openings.

28 • *"Today's boardroom Sturm und Drang left many observers with a sense of déjà vu"*: And if the foreign editor asks, tell her our Italian is also pretty good.

■ MAKING CONNECTIONS

1. Select an essay you have already written and apply some of the principles of writing described by Lederer and Vonnegut in their articles. Identify the parts of your essay that you change and how the altered sections employ the techniques described in the two essays. How does your revised essay compare to its first version? Explain.

2. Find two magazines or newspapers covering the same event or person — maybe a movie star or political figure or athlete. How do they differ? How do they use the facts? How do they change and use language?

3. Which of the authors in this section provided you with the most useful information for improving your own writing and why? Use examples from the article to support your response.

4. Several of the writers in this section provided lists of advice designed to improve your personal writing style. Create a list of your own in which you provide advice to less experienced writers, such as students just beginning junior high school. You may draw from the advice of the writers in this chapter, your own experience, and points made during class discussion. Remember to "write to your audience" when composing your list.

3 Politically Speaking

GOVERNOR BUS

Our governmen
a surplus, an
nation has a

■ Often ambiguous, political language carries tremendous power to influence national policy, laws, and social mores. What are our expectations of political language? How do we filter the fluff from the substance?

Political language can be the language of power. It influences government policy and action, identifies the dominant values of the moment, and wins votes. Likewise, it is language that is capable of making war, establishing peace, and electing presidents. However, political language also reflects the political needs of its users at a particular time. Thus, it has a reputation for being flexible and ambiguous, or worse, evasive and irresponsible as politicians shift the language to achieve their personal agendas. It is this "shifty" nature of political language that has contributed to the traditional American distrust of politicians and their promises. The essays in this chapter explore the various ways in which political language persuades the masses, manipulates words and meanings, promotes or supports certain value systems, and influences public opinion.

Political Word Play

The first section examines how political language persuades the public by tapping into its common beliefs, fears, anxieties, hopes, and expectations. This political word play comes in many forms, some more damaging than others. If the fundamental objective is to bend minds, its misuse may have dangerous implications. That misuse of language is the subject of the first selection, "How to Detect Propaganda," composed in 1937 by members of the former Institute for Propaganda Analysis—a group that monitored the various kinds of political propaganda circulating before and during World War II. This famous, timeless piece examines the particular rhetorical devices that constitute propaganda and serves as a tool to understanding the language of political manipulation, a concept further explored by George Orwell in the next article, "Politics and the English Language." In this classic attack on politicians, Orwell reminds us that those who control language—the double-talk, pious platitudes, and hollow words—hold the power to twist the native tongue to political advantage. Hugh Rank describes how to understand these common patterns of persuasion in political language in "Pep Talk." And rounding out the chapter, professional word watcher William Lutz defines the different kinds of "doublespeak" used by government bureaucrats in "Doubts About Doublespeak."

Language and the Presidency

The next section takes a close look at the relationship between the presidency and language. What are the linguistic responsibilities of the president? How is the public's perception of the president connected to his command of language? How is a presidential speech written, and how much does the president have to do with the finished product? Political communications analysts Robert E. Denton, Jr. and Dan F. Hahn explore the ways the president serves as the mouthpiece of the nation in "The Rhetorical Presidency." From their general observations the next authors focus more specifically on the language of George W. Bush. First, Ian Frazier describes early perceptions of the president's speech in "Dubya and Me: We've Got

No Idea." Then, D.T. Max describes the etymology of the speech that "changed a presidency," given on September 20, 2001, in response to the attacks on the World Trade Center and the Pentagon. The section ends with the actual speech described by Max, "Address to a Joint Session of Congress and the American People."

Case Study: Terrorism and the War of Words

The last section in this chapter considers the relationship between language and terrorism, especially as it is connected to September 11, and the political situation in the Middle East. Amir Taheri and Jim Guirard express their views on the language used to justify terrorist acts in editorials that discuss the disparity between what Islam proclaims and what much of the Islamic world is willing to permit. Jon Hooten discusses the language of war in "Fighting Words: The War Over Language." In "A Lot to Learn," David Brudnoy asserts that politically correct language reveals that America is so steeped in "political politeness" that we are afraid to offend even terrorists. The next piece is a poem by songwriter and singer Ani DiFranco. Her poem "Self Evident," written in response to her feelings about September 11, describes people who are "90% metaphor," where the political status quo makes people mere "pawns" in a struggle for power. The section closes with a piece by language maven William Safire who wonders what the final "name" of September 11, 2001, will be. Will we ever be able to find the words?

■ POLITICAL WORD PLAY

How to Detect Propaganda
Institute for Propaganda Analysis

During the late 1930s, like today, political propaganda was rife, both in the United States and abroad. In 1937, Clyde R. Miller of Columbia University founded the Institute for Propaganda Analysis to expose propaganda circulating at the time. With the backing of several prominent businesspeople, the Institute continued its mission for nearly five years, publishing various pamphlets and monthly bulletins to reveal its findings. The following essay is a chapter from one of its pamphlets. It presents a specific definition of propaganda, with an analysis of seven common devices necessary to bend the truth—and minds—to political causes.

1 If American citizens are to have clear understanding of present-day conditions and what to do about them, they must be able to recognize propaganda, to analyze it, and to appraise it.

2 But what is propaganda?

3   As generally understood, *propaganda is expression of opinion or action by individuals or groups deliberately designed to influence opinions or actions of other individuals or groups with reference to predetermined ends.* Thus propaganda differs from scientific analysis. The propagandist is trying to "put something across," good or bad, whereas the scientist is trying to discover truth and fact. Often the propagandist does not want careful scrutiny and criticism; he wants to bring about a specific action. Because the action may be socially beneficial or socially harmful to millions of people, it is necessary to focus upon the propagandist and his activities the searchlight of scientific scrutiny. Socially desirable propaganda will not suffer from such examination, but the opposite type will be detected and revealed for what it is.

4   We are fooled by propaganda chiefly because we don't recognize it when we see it. It may be fun to be fooled but, as the cigarette ads used to say, it is more fun to know. We can more easily recognize propaganda when we see it if we are familiar with the seven common propaganda devices. These are:

1. The Name Calling Device
2. The Glittering Generalities Device
3. The Transfer Device
4. The Testimonial Device
5. The Plain Folks Device
6. The Card Stacking Device
7. The Band Wagon Device

5   Why are we fooled by these devices? Because they appeal to our emotions rather than to our reason. They make us believe and do something we would not believe or do if we thought about it calmly, dispassionately. In examining these devices, note that they work most effectively at those times when we are too lazy to think for ourselves; also, they tie into emotions which sway us to be "for" or "against" nations, races, religions, ideals, economic and political policies and practices, and so on through automobiles, cigarettes, radios, toothpastes, presidents, and wars. With our emotions stirred, it may be fun to be fooled by these propaganda devices, but it is more fun and infinitely more to our own interests to know how they work.

6   Lincoln must have had in mind citizens who could balance their emotions with intelligence when he made this remark ". . . but you can't fool all of the people all of the time."

Name Calling

7   "Name Calling" is a device to make us form a judgment without examining the evidence on which it should be based. Here the propagandist appeals to our hate and fear. He does this by giving "bad names" to those individuals, groups, nations, races, policies, practices, beliefs, and ideals which he would have us condemn and reject. For centuries the name "heretic" was bad. Thousands were oppressed, tor-

tured, or put to death as heretics. Anybody who dissented from popular or group belief or practice was in danger of being called a heretic. In the light of today's knowledge, some heresies were bad and some were good. Many of the pioneers of modern science were called heretics; witness the cases of Copernicus, Galileo, Bruno. Today's bad names include: Facist, demagogue, dictator, Red, financial oligarchy, Communist, muckraker, alien, outside agitator, economic royalist, Utopian, rabble-rouser, trouble-maker, Tory, Constitution-wrecker.

8   "Al" Smith called Roosevelt a Communist by implication when he said in his Liberty League speech, "There can be only one capital, Washington or Moscow." When "Al" Smith was running for the presidency many called him a tool of the Pope, saying in effect, "We must choose between Washington and Rome." That implied that Mr. Smith, if elected President, would take his orders from the Pope. Likewise Mr. Justice Hugo Black has been associated with a bad name, Ku Klux Klan. In these cases some propagandists have tried to make us form judgments without examining essential evidence and implications. "Al Smith is a Catholic. He must never be President." "Roosevelt is a Red. Defeat his program." "Hugo Black is or was a Klansman. Take him out of the Supreme Court."

9   Use of "bad names" without presentation of their essential meaning, without all their pertinent implications, comprises perhaps the most common of all propaganda devices. Those who want to *maintain the status quo* apply bad names to those who would change it. . . . Those who want to *change the status quo* apply bad names to those who would maintain it. For example, the *Daily Worker* and the *American Guardian* apply bad names to conservative Republicans and Democrats.

Glittering Generalities

10 "Glittering Generalities" is a device by which the propagandist identifies his program with virtue by use of "virtue words." Here he appeals to our emotions of love, generosity, and brotherhood. He uses words like truth, freedom, honor, liberty, social justice, public service, the right to work, loyalty, progress, democracy, the American way, Constitution-defender. These words suggest shining ideals. All persons of good will believe in these ideals. Hence the propagandist, by identifying his individual group, nation, race, policy, practice, or belief with such ideals, seeks to win us to his cause. As Name Calling is a device to make us form a judgment to *reject and condemn* without examining the evidence, Glittering Generalities is a device to make us *accept and approve* without examining the evidence.

11   For example, use of the phrases, "the right to work" and "social justice," may be a device to make us accept programs for meeting labor-capital problems which, if we examined them critically, we would not accept at all.

12   In the Name Calling and Glittering Generalities devices, words are used to stir up our emotions and to befog our thinking. In one device "bad words" are used to make us mad; in the other "good words" are used to make us glad.

13   The propagandist is most effective in the use of these devices when his words make us create devils to fight or gods to adore. By his use of the "bad words," we

personify as a "devil" some nation, race, group, individual, policy, practice, or ideal; we are made fighting mad to destroy it. By use of "good words," we personify as a godlike idol some nation, race, group, etc. Words which are "bad" to some are "good" to others, or may be made so. Thus, to some the New Deal is "a prophecy of social salvation" while to others it is "an omen of social disaster."

14   From consideration of names, "bad" and "good," we pass to institutions and symbols, also "bad" and "good." We see these in the next device.

Transfer

15 "Transfer" is a device by which the propagandist carries over the authority, sanction, and prestige of something we respect and revere to something he would have us accept. For example, most of us respect and revere our church and our nation. If the propagandist succeeds in getting church or nation to approve a campaign in behalf of some program, he thereby transfers its authority, sanction, and prestige to that program. Thus we may accept something which otherwise we might reject.

16   In the Transfer device, symbols are constantly used. The cross represents the Christian Church. The flag represents the nation. Cartoons like Uncle Sam represent a consensus of public opinion. Those symbols stir emotions. At their very sight, with the speed of light, is aroused the whole complex of feelings we have with respect to church or nation. A cartoonist by having Uncle Sam disapprove a budget for unemployment relief would have us feel that the whole United States disapproves relief costs. By drawing an Uncle Sam who approves the same budget, the cartoonist would have us feel that the American people approve it. Thus the Transfer device is used both for and against causes and ideas.

Testimonial

17 The "Testimonial" is a device to make us accept anything from a patent medicine or a cigarette to a program of national policy. In this device the propagandist makes use of testimonials. "When I feel tired, I smoke a Camel and get the grandest 'lift.'" "We believe the John L. Lewis plan of labor organization is splendid; C.I.O. should be supported." This device works in reverse also; counter-testimonials may be employed. Seldom are these used against commercial products like patent medicines and cigarettes, but they are constantly employed in social, economic, and political issues. "We believe that the John L. Lewis plan of labor organization is bad; C.I.O. should not be supported."

Plain Folks

18 "Plain Folks" is a device used by politicians, labor leaders, businessmen, and even by ministers and educators to win our confidence by appearing to be people like ourselves—"just plain folks among the neighbors." In election years especially do

candidates show their devotion to little children and the common, homey things of life. They have front porch campaigns. For the newspaper men they raid the kitchen cupboard, finding there some of the good wife's apple pie. They go to country picnics; they attend service at the old frame church, they pitch hay and go fishing; they show their belief in home and mother. In short, they would win our votes by showing that they're just as common as the rest of us—"just plain folks"—and, therefore, wise and good. Businessmen often are "plain folks" with the factory hands. Even distillers use the device. "It's our family's whiskey, neighbor; and neighbor, it's your price."

Card Stacking

19 "Card Stacking" is a device in which the propagandist employs all the arts of deception to win our support for himself, his group, nation, race, policy, practice, belief, or ideal. He stacks the cards against the truth. He uses under-emphasis and over-emphasis to dodge issues and evade facts. He resorts to lies, censorship, and distortion. He omits facts. He offers false testimony. He creates a smoke screen of clamor by raising a new issue when he wants an embarrassing matter forgotten. He draws a red herring across the trail to confuse and divert those in quest of facts he does not want revealed. He makes the unreal appear real and the real appear unreal. He lets half-truth masquerade as truth. By the Card Stacking device, a mediocre candidate, through the "build-up," is made to appear an intellectual titan; an ordinary prize fighter, a probable world champion; a worthless patent medicine, a beneficent cure. By means of this device propagandists would convince us that a ruthless war of aggression is a crusade for righteousness. Some member nations of the Non-Intervention Committee send their troops to intervene in Spain. Card Stacking employs sham, hypocrisy, effrontery.

The Band Wagon

20 The "Band Wagon" is a device to make us follow the crowd, to accept the propagandist's program en masse. Here his theme is: "Everybody's doing it." His techniques range from those of medicine show to dramatic spectacle. He hires a hall, fills a great stadium, marches a million men in parade. He employs symbols, colors, music, movement, all the dramatic arts. He appeals to the desire, common to most of us, to "follow the crowd." Because he wants us to "follow the crowd" in masses, he directs his appeal to groups held together by common ties of nationality, religion, race, environment, sex, vocation. Thus propagandists campaigning for or against a program will appeal to us as Catholics, Protestants, or Jews; as members of the Nordic race or as Negroes; as farmers or as school teachers; as housewives or as miners. All the artifices of flattery are used to harness the fears and hatreds, prejudices, and biases, convictions and ideals common to the group; thus emotion is

made to push and pull the group on to the Band Wagon. In newspaper articles and in the spoken word this device is also found. "Don't throw your vote away. Vote for our candidate. He's sure to win." Nearly every candidate wins in every election—before the votes are in.

Propaganda and Emotion

21 Observe that in all these devices our emotion is the stuff with which propagandists work. Without it they are helpless; with it, harnessing it to their purposes, they can make us glow with pride or burn with hatred, they can make us zealots in behalf of the program they espouse. As we said at the beginning, propaganda as generally understood is expression of opinion or action by individuals or groups with reference to predetermined ends. Without the appeal to our emotion—to our fears and to our courage, to our selfishness and unselfishness, to our loves and to our hates—propagandists would influence few opinions and few actions.

22 To say this is not to condemn emotion, an essential part of life, or to assert that all predetermined ends of propagandists are "bad." What we mean is that the intelligent citizen does not want propagandists to utilize his emotions, even to the attainment of "good" ends, without knowing what is going on. He does not want to be "used" in the attainment of ends he may later consider "bad." He does not want to be gullible. He does not want to be fooled. He does not want to be duped, even in a "good" cause. He wants to know the facts and among these is included the fact of the utilization [of] his emotions.

23 Keeping in mind the seven common propaganda devices, turn to today's newspapers and almost immediately you can spot examples of them all. At election time or during any campaign, Plain Folks and Band Wagon are common. Card Stacking is hardest to detect because it is adroitly executed or because we lack the information necessary to nail the lie. A little practice with the daily newspapers in detecting these propaganda devices soon enables us to detect them elsewhere—in radio, newsreel, books, magazines, and in expression[s] of labor unions, business groups, churches, schools, and political parties.

THINKING CRITICALLY

1. Look at the definition of the word *propaganda* in paragraph 3. How many sets of people are involved—how many parties does it take to make propaganda? What are the roles or functions of each set of people?

2. Supply an example of the way emotion overrides reason for each of the seven common propaganda devices the authors identify.

3. Can you supply "bad names" from your own experience as a student? Some examples to get you started might include "geek," "nerd," and "teacher's pet" to refer to students; you can

probably think of some generic terms for teachers as well. Compare these terms to the definition for propaganda. Do you think these terms qualify as propaganda?

4. How are name calling and glittering generalities similar devices? How are they different? What do the authors of the document say? What additional features can you find?

5. How do transfer, testimonial, and plain folks devices all make use of power or prestige to influence our thinking? Can you think of something or someone you respect that could be used as a propaganda device—for example, a major sporting event, such as the Super Bowl, or a football hero?

6. Give examples of times in your life when you have used the card stacking or band wagon devices to try to get something you wanted—such as permission from a parent, or an excused absence from a teacher.

7. What is the difference between "the propagandist" and "the scientist" in paragraph 3? What is their relationship to "truth and fact"? What is their relationship to each other? What is their relationship to the language they use?

8. What is "socially desirable propaganda"? Can you give examples from your own experience? Do you think that socially desirable propaganda uses the same devices that the authors of this article identify? Consider the "safe-sex" campaigns you've been exposed to.

9. What is the difference between a "bad name," as the authors describe it in the section "Name Calling," and a racial, ethnic, gender-based, or other kind of slur?

10. Who do you think the audience for this pamphlet was? What kinds of people was it written for—scientists? propagandists? professors? What did the authors assume about readers' lifestyles, reading skills, and values?

WRITING ASSIGNMENTS

1. Based on your understanding of the whole article, and on class discussion, develop your own definition of propaganda. Make sure you define each key term that you use.

2. Following the suggestions set down in the final paragraph of this essay, collect examples of propaganda from at least five different sources. Examine them, then describe in a paper what devices they use. How do the creators of each kind of propaganda show that they are aware of their audience's emotions? What emotions do they appeal to? How much "truth and fact" do they seem to rely on?

3. Research and collect newspaper articles on an election—a race for student government on your campus, a recent town or state proposition, or even a national election. Be sure to collect a handful of articles from at least two major candidates, or from two sides of the issue. What propaganda devices did each side use? Which side won? How much of a role do you think propaganda played in deciding the outcome?

4. Do you think the authors of this article would advocate getting rid of all propaganda? Why, or why not? Be sure to include a discussion of what propaganda is, and what function or role it serves.

Politics and the English Language
George Orwell

In the next essay, George Orwell explains how the language of politics, especially what is known as "political rhetoric," is designed to cloud the public's perception of political issues. Like the propaganda examined in the previous essay, political rhetoric disguises real issues behind a mask of political mottos, character assassinations, and catchphrases, all designed to confuse the public. There are many reasons to use such evasive tactics to garner support, to get votes, to dodge political responsibility, and to discredit political opponents. As in his novel *1984*, in this essay Orwell confronts the social forces that endanger free thought and truth. Political rhetoric, he explains, is the enemy of truth and the cause of linguistic degeneration.

George Orwell was a novelist, an essayist, and one of the most important social critics of the twentieth century. In 1945, he wrote the acclaimed political satire, *Animal Farm* and in 1949, his famous nightmare vision of a totalitarian state, *1984*, first appeared. "Politics and the English Language" was included in one of his essay collections, *Shooting an Elephant* (1946). Although the essay was written in 1945, the targets still exist, and the criticism is still valid, making it as poignant today as it was over half a century ago.

1   Most people who bother with the matter at all would admit that the English language is in a bad way, but it is generally assumed that we cannot by conscious action do anything about it. Our civilization is decadent and our language —so the argument runs—must inevitably share in the general collapse. It follows that any struggle against the abuse of language is a sentimental archaism, like preferring candles to electric light or hansom cabs to aeroplanes. Underneath this lies the half-conscious belief that language is a natural growth and not an instrument which we shape for our own purposes.

2   Now, it is clear that the decline of a language must ultimately have political and economic causes: it is not due simply to the bad influence of this or that individual writer. But an effect can become a cause, reinforcing the original cause and producing the same effect in an intensified form, and so on indefinitely. A man may take to drink because he feels himself to be a failure, and then fail all the more completely because he drinks. It is rather the same thing that is happening to the English language. It becomes ugly and inaccurate because our thoughts are foolish, but the slovenliness of our language makes it easier for us to have foolish thoughts. The point is that the process is reversible. Modern English, especially written English, is full of bad habits which spread by imitation and which can be avoided if one is willing to take the necessary trouble. If one gets rid of these habits one can think more clearly, and to think clearly is a necessary first step towards political regeneration: so that the fight against bad English is not frivolous and is not the exclusive concern of professional writers. I will come back to this presently, and I hope that by that time the meaning of what I have said here will have become clearer. Meanwhile, here are five specimens of the English language as it is now habitually written.

3   These five passages have not been picked out because they are especially bad—I could have quoted far worse if I had chosen—but because they illustrate various of the mental vices from which we now suffer. They are a little below the average, but are fairly representative samples. I number them so that I can refer back to them when necessary:

1. I am not, indeed, sure whether it is not true to say that the Milton who once seemed not unlike a seventeenth-century Shelley had not become, out of an experience ever more bitter in each year, more alien [*sic*] to the founder of that Jesuit sect which nothing could induce him to tolerate.

    PROFESSOR HAROLD LASKI (ESSAY IN *FREEDOM OF EXPRESSION*)

2. Above all, we cannot play ducks and drakes with a native battery of idioms which prescribes such egregious collocations of vocables as the Basic *put up with* for *tolerate* or *put at a loss* for *bewilder*.

    PROFESSOR LANCELOT HOGBEN (INTERGLOSSA)

3. On the one side we have the free personality: by definition it is not neurotic, for it has neither conflict nor dream. Its desires, such as they are, are transparent, for they are just what institutional approval keeps in the forefront of consciousness; another institutional pattern would alter their number and intensity; there is little in them that is natural, irreducible, or culturally dangerous. But *on the other side,* the social bond itself is nothing but the mutual reflection of these self-secure integrities. Recall the definition of love. Is not this the very picture of a small academic? Where is there a place in this hall of mirrors for either personality or fraternity?

    ESSAY ON PSYCHOLOGY IN *POLITICS* (NEW YORK)

4. All the "best people" from the gentlemen's clubs, and all the frantic fascist captains, united in common hatred of Socialism and bestial horror of the rising tide of the mass revolutionary movement, have turned to acts of provocation, to foul incendiarism, to medieval legends of poisoned wells, to legalize their own destruction of proletarian organizations, and rouse the agitated petty-bourgeoisie to chauvinistic fervor on behalf of the fight against the revolutionary way out of the crisis.

    COMMUNIST PAMPHLET

5. If a new spirit is to be infused into this old country, there is one thorny and contentious reform which must be tackled, and that is the humanization and galvanization of the B.B.C. Timidity here will bespeak canker and atrophy of the soul. The heart of Britain may be sound and of strong beat, for instance, but the British lion's roar at present is like that of Bottom in Shakespeare's *Midsummer Night's Dream*—as gentle as any sucking dove. A virile new Britain cannot continue indefinitely to be traduced in the eyes, or rather ears, of the world by the effete languors of Langham Place, brazenly masquerading as "standard English." When the Voice of Britain is heard at nine o'clock, better far and infinitely less ludicrous to hear aitches honestly dropped than the pre-

sent priggish, inflated, inhibited, school-ma'amish arch braying of blameless bashful mewing maidens!

LETTER IN *TRIBUNE*

4   Each of these passages has faults of its own, but, quite apart from avoidable ugliness, two qualities are common to all of them. The first is staleness of imagery; the other is lack of precision. The writer either has a meaning and cannot express it, or he inadvertently says something else, or he is almost indifferent as to whether his words mean anything or not. This mixture of vagueness and sheer incompetence is the most marked characteristic of modern English prose, and especially of any kind of political writing. As soon as certain topics are raised, the concrete melts into the abstract and no one seems able to think of turns of speech that are not hackneyed: prose consists less and less of *words* chosen for the sake of their meaning, and more and more of *phrases* tacked together like the sections of a prefabricated hen-house. I list below, with notes and examples, various of the tricks by means of which the work of prose-construction is habitually dodged:

Dying Metaphors

5 A newly invented metaphor assists thought by evoking a visual image, while on the other hand a metaphor which is technically "dead" (e.g., *iron resolution*) has in effect reverted to being an ordinary word and can generally be used without loss of vividness. But in between these two classes there is a huge dump of worn-out metaphors which have lost all evocative power and are merely used because they save people the trouble of inventing phrases for themselves. Examples are: *Ring the changes on, take up the cudgels for, toe the line, ride roughshod over, stand shoulder to shoulder with, play into the hands of, no axe to grind, grist to the mill, fishing in troubled waters, on the order of the day, Achilles' heel, swan song, hotbed.* Many of these are used without knowledge of their meaning (what is a "rift," for instance?), and incompatible metaphors are frequently mixed, a sure sign that the writer is not interested in what he is saying. Some metaphors now current have been twisted out of their original meaning without those who use them even being aware of the fact. For example, *toe the line* is sometimes written *tow the line.* Another example is *the hammer and the anvil,* now always used with the implication that the anvil gets the worst of it. In real life it is always the anvil that breaks the hammer, never the other way about: a writer who stopped to think what he was saying would be aware of this, and would avoid perverting the original phrase.

Operators or Verbal False Limbs

6 These save the trouble of picking out appropriate verbs and nouns, and at the same time pad each sentence with extra syllables which give it an appearance of symmetry. Characteristic phrases are *render inoperative, militate against, make contact with, be subjected to, give rise to, give grounds for, have the effect of, play a leading*

part (role) in, making itself felt, take effect, exhibit a tendency to, serve the purpose of, etc., etc. The keynote is the elimination of simple verbs. Instead of being a single word, such as *break, stop, spoil, mend, kill,* a verb becomes a *phrase,* made up of a noun or adjective tacked on to some general-purpose verb such as *prove, serve, form, play, render.* In addition, the passive voice is wherever possible used in preference to the active, and noun constructions are used instead of gerunds (*by examination* of instead of *by examining*). The range of verbs is further cut down by means of the *-ize* and *de-* formations, and the banal statements are given an appearance of profundity by means of the *not un-* formation. Simple conjunctions and prepositions are replaced by such phrases as *with respect to, having regard to, the fact that, by dint of, in view of, in the interests of, on the hypothesis that*; and the ends of sentences are saved from anticlimax by such resounding common places as *greatly to be desired, cannot be left out of account, a development to be expected in the near future, deserving of serious consideration, brought to a satisfactory conclusion,* and so on and so forth.

Pretentious Diction

7 Words like *phenomenon, element, individual* (as noun), *objective, categorical, effective, virtual, basic, primary, promote, constitute, exhibit, exploit, utilize, eliminate, liquidate,* are used to dress up simple statements and give an air of scientific impartiality to biased judgments. Adjectives like *epoch-making, epic, historic, unforgettable, triumphant, age-old, inevitable, inexorable, veritable,* are used to dignify the sordid processes of international politics, while writing that aims at glorifying war usually takes on an archaic color, its characteristic words being: *realm, throne, chariot, mailed fist, trident, sword, shield, buckler, banner, jackboot, clarion.* Foreign words and expressions such as *cul de sac, ancien régime, deus ex machina, mutatis mutandis, status quo, gleichschaltung, weltanschauung,* are used to give an air of culture and elegance. Except for the useful abbreviations *i.e., e.g.,* and *etc.,* there is no real need for any of the hundreds of foreign phrases now current in English. Bad writers, and especially scientific, political and sociological writers, are nearly always haunted by the notion that Latin or Greek words are grander than Saxon ones, and unnecessary words like *expedite, ameliorate, predict, extraneous, deracinated, clandestine, subaqueous* and hundreds of others constantly gain ground from their Anglo-Saxon opposite numbers.[1] The jargon peculiar to Marxist writing (*hyena, hangman, cannibal, petty bourgeois, these gentry, lacquey, flunkey, mad dog, White Guard,* etc.) consists largely of words and phrases translated from Russian, German, or French; but the normal way of coining a new

---

[1]An interesting illustration of this is the way in which the English flower names which were in use till very recently are being ousted by Greek ones, *snapdragon* becoming *antirrhinum, forget-me-not* becoming *myosotis,* etc. It is hard to see any practical reason for this change of fashion; it is probably due to an instinctive turning-away from the more homely word and a vague feeling that the Greek is scientific.

word is to use a Latin or Greek root with the appropriate affix and, where necessary, the *-ize* formation. It is often easier to make up words of this kind (*deregionalize, impermissible, extramarital, non-fragmentary* and so forth) than to think up the English words that will cover one's meaning. The result, in general, is an increase in slovenliness and vagueness.

Meaningless Words

8 In certain kinds of writing, particularly in art criticism and literary criticism, it is normal to come across long passages which are almost completely lacking in meaning.[2] Words like r*omantic, plastic, values, human, dead, sentimental, natural, vitality,* as used in art criticism, are strictly meaningless, in the sense that they not only do not point to any discoverable object, but are hardly ever expected to do so by the reader. When one critic writes, "The outstanding feature of Mr. X's work is its living quality," while another writes, "The immediately striking thing about Mr. X's work is its peculiar deadness," the reader accepts this as a simple difference of opinion. If words like *black* and *white* were involved, instead of the jargon words *dead* and *living,* he would see at once that language was being used in an improper way. Many political words are similarly abused. The word *Fascism* has now no meaning except in so far as it signifies "something not desirable." The words *democracy, socialism, freedom, patriotic, realistic, justice,* have each of them several different meanings which cannot be reconciled with one another. In the case of a word like *democracy,* not only is there no agreed definition, but the attempt to make one is resisted from all sides. It is almost universally felt that when we call a country democratic we are praising it· consequently the defenders of every kind of regime claim that it is a democracy, and fear that they might have to stop using the word if it were tied down to any one meaning. Words of this kind are often used in a consciously dishonest way. That is, the person who used them has his own private definition, but allows his hearer to think he means something quite different. Statements like *Marshal Pétain was a true patriot, The Soviet Press is the freest in the world, The Catholic Church is opposed to persecution,* are almost always made with intent to deceive. Other words used in variable meanings, in most cases more or less dishonestly, are: *class, totalitarian, science, progressive, reactionary, bourgeois, equality.*

9 Now that I have made this catalogue of swindles and perversions, let me give another example of the kind of writing that they lead to. This time it must of its nature be an imaginary one. I am going to translate a passage of good English into modern English of the worst sort. Here is a well-known verse from *Ecclesiastes:*

---

[2]Example: "Comfort's catholicity of perception and image, strangely Whitmanesque in range, almost the exact opposite in aesthetic compulsion, continues to evoke that trembling atmospheric accumulative hinting at a cruel, an inexorably serene timelessness . . . Wrey Gardiner scores by aiming at simple bull's-eyes with precision. Only they are not so simple, and through this contended sadness runs more than the surface bittersweet of resignation." (*Poetry Quarterly*)

> I returned and saw under the sun, that the race is not to the swift, nor the battle to the strong, neither yet bread to the wise, nor yet riches to men of understanding, nor yet favour to men of skill; but time and chance happeneth to them all.

Here it is in modern English:

> Objective consideration of contemporary phenomena compels the conclusion that success or failure in competitive activities exhibits no tendency to be commensurate with innate capacity, but that a considerable element of the unpredictable must invariably be taken into account.

10   This is a parody, but not a very gross one. Above, for instance, contains several patches of the same kind of English. It will be seen that I have not made a full translation. The beginning and ending of the sentence follow the original meaning fairly closely, but in the middle the concrete illustrations—race, battle, bread—dissolve into the vague phrase "success or failure in competitive activities." This had to be so, because no modern writer of the kind I am discussing—no one capable of using phrases like "objective consideration of contemporary phenomena"—would ever tabulate his thoughts in that precise and detailed way. The whole tendency of modern prose is away from concreteness. Now analyse these two sentences a little more closely. The first contains forty-nine words but only sixty syllables, and all its words are those of everyday life. The second contains thirty-eight words of ninety syllables; eighteen of its words are from Latin roots, and one from Greek. The first sentence contains six vivid images, and only one phrase ("time and chance") that could be called vague. The second contains not a single fresh, arresting phrase, and in spite of its ninety syllables it gives only a shortened version of the meaning contained in the first. Yet without a doubt it is the second kind of sentence that is gaining ground in modern English. I do not want to exaggerate. This kind of writing is not yet universal, and outcrops of simplicity will occur here and there in the worst-written page. Still, if you or I were told to write a few lines on the uncertainty of human fortunes, we should probably come much nearer to my imaginary sentence than to the one from *Ecclesiastes*.

11   As I have tried to show, modern writing at its worst does not consist in picking out words for the sake of their meaning and inventing images in order to make the meaning clearer. It consists in gumming together long strips of words which have already been set in order by someone else, and making the results presentable by sheer humbug. The attraction of this way of writing is that it is easy. It is easier—even quicker, once you have the habit—to say *In my opinion it is not an unjustifiable assumption that* than to say *I think.* If you use ready-made phrases, you not only don't have to hunt about for words; you also don't have to bother with the rhythms of your sentences, since these phrases are generally so arranged as to be more or less euphonious. When you are composing in a hurry—when you are dictating to a stenographer, for instance, or making a public speech—it is natural to fall into a pretentious, Latinized style. Tags like *a consideration which we should do well to bear in mind* or *a conclusion to which all of us would readily assent* will

save many a sentence from coming down with a bump. By using stale metaphors, similes and idioms, you save much mental effort, at the cost of leaving your meaning vague, not only for your reader but for yourself. This is the significance of mixed metaphors. The sole aim of a metaphor is to call up a visual image. When these images clash—as in *The Fascist octopus has sung its swan song, the jackboot is thrown into the melting pot*—it can be taken as certain that the writer is not seeing a mental image of the objects he is naming; in other words he is not really thinking. Look again at the examples I gave at the beginning of this essay: Professor Laski (1) uses five negatives in fifty-three words. One of these is superfluous, making nonsense of the whole passage, and in addition there is the slip *alien* for *akin,* making further nonsense, and several avoidable pieces of clumsiness which increase the general vagueness. Professor Hogben (2) plays ducks and drakes with a battery which is able to write prescriptions, and, while disapproving of the everyday phrase *put up with,* is unwilling to look *egregious* up in the dictionary and see what it means; (3), if one takes an uncharitable attitude towards it, is simply meaningless; probably one could work out its intended meaning by reading the whole of the article in which it occurs. In (4), the writer knows more or less what he wants to say, but an accumulation of stale phrases chokes him, like tea leaves blocking a sink. In (5), words and meaning have almost parted company. People who write in this manner usually have a general emotional meaning—they dislike one thing and want to express solidarity with another—but they are not interested in the detail of what they are saying. A scrupulous writer, in every sentence that he writes, will ask himself at least four questions, thus: What am I trying to say? What words will express it? What image or idiom will make it clearer? Is this image fresh enough to have an effect? And he will probably ask himself two more: Could I put it more shortly? Have I said anything that is avoidably ugly? But you are not obliged to go to all this trouble. You can shirk it by simply throwing your mind open and letting the ready-made phrases come crowding in. They will construct your sentences for you—even think your thoughts for you, to a certain extent—and at need they will perform the important service of partially concealing your meaning even from yourself. It is at this point that the special connection between politics and the debasement of language becomes clear.

12   In our time it is broadly true that political writing is bad writing. Where it is not true, it will generally be found that the writer is some kind of rebel, expressing his private opinions and not a "party line." Orthodoxy, of whatever color, seems to demand a lifeless, imitative style. The political dialects to be found in pamphlets, leading articles, manifestos, White Papers and the speeches of undersecretaries do, of course, vary from party to party, but they are all alike in that one almost never finds in them a fresh, vivid, home-made turn of speech. When one watches some tired hack on the platform mechanically repeating the familiar phrases—*bestial atrocities, iron heel, bloodstained tyranny, free peoples of the world, stand shoulder to shoulder*—one often has a curious feeling that one is not watching a live human being but some kind of dummy: a feeling which suddenly becomes stronger at moments when the light catches the speaker's spectacles and turns them into blank

discs which seem to have no eyes behind them. And this is not altogether fanciful. A speaker who uses that kind of phraseology has gone some distance towards turning himself into a machine. The appropriate noises are coming out of his larynx, but his brain is not involved as it would be if he were choosing his words for himself. If the speech he is making is one that he is accustomed to make over and over again, he may be almost unconscious of what he is saying, as one is when one utters the responses in church. And this reduced state of consciousness, if not indispensable, is at any rate favorable to political conformity.

13   In our time, political speech and writing are largely the defence of the indefensible. Things like the continuance of British rule in India, the Russian purges and deportations, the dropping of the atom bombs on Japan, can indeed be defended, but only by arguments which are too brutal for most people to face, and which do not square with the professed aims of political parties. Thus political language has to consist largely of euphemism, question-begging and sheer cloudy vagueness. Defenceless villages are bombarded from the air, the inhabitants driven out into the countryside, the cattle machine-gunned, the huts set on fire with incendiary bullets: this is called *pacification*. Millions of peasants are robbed of their farms and sent trudging along the roads with no more than they can carry: this is called *transfer of population* or *rectification of frontiers*. People are imprisoned for years without trial, or shot in the back of the neck or sent to die of scurvy in Arctic lumber camps; this is called *elimination of unreliable elements*. Such phraseology is needed if one wants to name things without calling up mental pictures of them. Consider for instance some comfortable English professor defending Russian totalitarianism. He cannot say outright, "I believe in killing off your opponents when you can get good results by doing so." Probably, therefore, he will say something like this:

14   "While freely conceding that the Soviet régime exhibits certain features which the humanitarian may be inclined to deplore, we must, I think, agree that a certain curtailment of the right to political opposition is an unavoidable concomitant of transitional periods, and that the rigors which the Russian people have been called upon to undergo have been amply justified in the sphere of concrete achievement."

15   The inflated style is itself a kind of euphemism. A mass of Latin words falls upon the facts like soft snow, blurring the outlines and covering up all the details. The great enemy of clear language is insincerity. When there is a gap between one's real and one's declared aims, one turns as it were instinctively to long words and exhausted idioms, like a cuttlefish squirting out ink. In our age there is no such thing as "keeping out of politics." All issues are political issues, and politics itself is a mass of lies, evasions, folly, hatred and schizophrenia. When the general atmosphere is bad, language must suffer. I should expect to find—this is a guess which I have not sufficient knowledge to verify—that the German, Russian and Italian languages have all deteriorated in the last ten or fifteen years, as a result of dictatorship.

16   But if thought corrupts language, language can also corrupt thought. A bad usage can spread by tradition and imitation, even among people who should and do know better. The deposed language that I have been discussing is in some ways

very convenient. Phrases like *a not unjustifiable assumption, leaves much to be desired, would serve no good purpose, a consideration which we should do well to bear in mind,* are a continuous temptation, a packet of aspirins always at one's elbow. Look back through this essay, and for certain you will find that I have again and again committed the very faults I am protesting against. By this morning's post I have received a pamphlet dealing with conditions in Germany. The author tells me that he "felt impelled" to write it. I open it at random and here is almost the first sentence that I see: "[The Allies] have an opportunity not only of achieving a radical transformation of Germany's social and political structure in such a way as to avoid a nationalistic reaction in Germany itself, but at the same time of laying the foundations of a co-operative and unified Europe." You see, he "feels impelled" to write—feels, presumably, that he has something new to say—and yet his words, like cavalry horses answering the bugle, group themselves automatically into the familiar dreary pattern. This invasion of one's mind by ready-made phrases (*lay the foundations, achieve a radical transformation*) can only be prevented if one is constantly on guard against them, and every such phrase anaesthetizes a portion of one's brain.

17   I said earlier that the decadence of our language is probably curable. Those who deny this would argue, if they produced an argument at all, that language merely reflects existing social conditions, and that we cannot influence its development by any direct tinkering with words and constructions. So far as the general tone or spirit of a language goes, this may be true, but it is not true in detail. Silly words and expressions have often disappeared, not through any evolutionary process but owing to the conscious action of a minority. Two recent examples were *explore every avenue* and *leave no stone unturned,* which were killed by the jeers of a few journalists. There is a long list of flyblown metaphors which could similarly be got rid of if enough people would interest themselves in the job, and it should also be possible to laugh the *not un-* formation out of existence,[3] to reduce the amount of Latin and Greek in the average sentence, to drive out foreign phrases and strayed scientific words, and, in general, to make pretentiousness unfashionable. But all these are minor points. The defence of the English language implies more than this, and perhaps it is best to start by saying what it does *not* imply.

18   To begin with it has nothing to do with archaism, with the salvaging of obsolete words and turns of speech, or with the setting up of a "standard English" which must never be departed from. On the contrary, it is especially concerned with the scrapping of every word or idiom which has outworn its usefulness. It has nothing to do with correct grammar and syntax, which are of no importance so long as one makes one's meaning clear, or with the avoidance of Americanisms, or with having what is called a "good prose style." On the other hand it is not concerned with fake simplicity and the attempt to make written English colloquial. Nor does it even

---

[3]One can cure oneself of the *not un-* formation by memorizing this sentence: *A not unblack dog was chasing a not unsmall rabbit across a not ungreen field.*

imply in every case preferring the Saxon word to the Latin one, though it does imply using the fewest and shortest words that will cover one's meaning. What is above all needed is to let the meaning choose the word, and not the other way about. In prose, the worst thing one can do with words is to surrender to them. When you think of a concrete object, you think wordlessly, and then, if you want to describe the thing you have been visualizing you probably hunt about till you find the exact words that seem to fit it. When you think of something abstract you are more inclined to use words from the start, and unless you make a conscious effort to prevent it, the existing dialect will come rushing in and do the job for you, at the expense of blurring or even changing your meaning. Probably it is better to put off using words as long as possible and get one's meaning as clear as one can through pictures or sensations. Afterwards one can choose—not simply *accept*—the phrases that will best cover the meaning, and then switch round and decide what impression one's words are likely to make on another person. This last effort of the mind cuts out all stale or mixed images, all prefabricated phrases, needless repetitions, and humbug and vagueness generally. But one can often be in doubt about the effect of a word or a phrase, and one needs rules that one can rely on when instinct fails. I think the following rules will cover most cases:

1. Never use a metaphor, simile or other figure of speech which you are used to seeing in print.
2. Never use a long word where a short one will do.
3. If it is possible to cut a word out, always cut it out.
4. Never use the passive where you can use the active.
5. Never use a foreign phrase, a scientific word or a jargon word if you can think of an everyday English equivalent.
6. Break any of these rules sooner than say anything outright barbarous.

These rules sound elementary, and so they are, but they demand a deep change of attitude in anyone who has grown used to writing in the style now fashionable. One could keep all of them and still write bad English, but one could not write the kind of stuff that I quoted in those five specimens at the beginning of this article.

19   I have not here been considering the literary use of language, but merely language as an instrument for expressing and not for concealing or preventing thought. Stuart Chase and others have come near to claiming that all abstract words are meaningless, and have used this as a pretext for advocating a kind of political quietism. Since you don't know what Fascism is, how can you struggle against Fascism? One need not swallow such absurdities as this, but one ought to recognize that the present political chaos is connected with the decay of language, and that one can probably bring about some improvement by starting at the verbal end. If you simplify your English, you are freed from the worst follies of orthodoxy. You cannot speak any of the necessary dialects, and when you make a stupid remark its stupidity will be obvious, even to yourself. Political language—and with variations this is true of all political parties, from Conservatives to Anarchists—is designed to make lies sound truthful and murder respectable, and to give an appearance of so-

lidity to pure wind. One cannot change this all in a moment, but one can at least change one's own habits, and from time to time one can even, if one jeers loudly enough, send some worn-out and useless phrase—some *jackboot, Achilles' heel, hotbed, melting pot, acid test, veritable inferno* or other lump of verbal refuse—into the dustbin where it belongs.

THINKING CRITICALLY

1. Orwell argues that modern writers are destroying the English language. Explain some of the ways in which they are doing so.

2. What is a *euphemism*? Orwell cites "pacification" as an example from World War II (paragraph 13). Try to find some euphemisms that came out of the 2003 war with Iraq. Name and explain some of the euphemisms common in business today.

3. Orwell lists six rules at the end of the essay (paragraph 18). What does he mean by the last rule?

4. Toward the end of the essay, Orwell writes, "Look back through this essay, and for certain you will find that I have again and again committed the very faults I am protesting against." (paragraph 16). Where in the essay has he broken his own rules?

5 Does Orwell seem to criticize one end of the political spectrum more than the other? Support your answer with references to Orwell's essay.

6. Reread the first four paragraphs. What kind of personality does Orwell project—reasonable, honest, condescending, cynical? Explain.

7. Orwell begins his arguments by citing five writers. How does he use these references throughout the essay?

8. Is there any emotional appeal in this essay? If so, what is it and how is it created?

9. Exactly where in the essay does Orwell begin to talk about politics and the English language? Why does he start his discussion there?

WRITING ASSIGNMENTS

1. Orwell gives five examples of bad writing from his own day. Have things changed much since then? Compile your own list from current newspapers, magazines, and books. How do your findings compare with Orwell's?

2. Orwell takes a passage from Ecclesiastes and "translates" it to illustrate bad writing by his contemporaries. Do the same with a different passage from the Bible or an excerpt from a poem or novel. Use some of the same techniques Orwell employs.

3. Some of the most stunning examples of bloated political language come from campaign speeches. Find a campaign speech from either a local or national figure and evaluate it for the political double-talk Orwell discusses. How does the speech sound without the use of double-talk? Discuss your findings in an essay.

4. Have you ever been the victim of political propaganda? Have you ever voted for something or someone (or would have were you not under age) because of a campaigner's persuasive political language, or given to a cause for the same reason? Write an account of your experience, and try to explain how the language influenced you.

5. Read (or reread) one of the political satires mentioned in the headnote to this article: either *Animal Farm* or *1984*. How does language create power for the rulers in the novel? What kinds of power does Orwell think language can have? Examine what literary critics have said by researching articles about the novel with reference tools such as the *Modern Language Association Bibliography*, *Contemporary Literary Criticism*, or the *Dictionary of Literary Biography*.

The Pep Talk:
Patterns of Persuasion in Political Language
Hugh Rank

Many people have negative impressions of political language because so much of it seems to be doublespeak or lofty rhetoric. Hugh Rank agrees that negative stereotypes of politicians and the language they use are based on some "kernels of truth." He also believes that as responsible citizens, we must be able to critically analyze political language. In the next essay, Rank explains how the "pep talk," a high-pressure, emotional appeal designed to persuade audiences is used by politicians to influence and encourage voters to support political goals and agendas.

Hugh Rank is the author of *Teaching about Public Persuasion: Rationale and a Schema* (1976). Rank won the 1976 Orwell Award presented by the Committee on Public Doublespeak for his essay "Intensifying/Downplaying Schema" in which he observed that all acts of public persuasion are variations of intensifying or downplaying. The following piece is an excerpt from his 1984 book, *The Pep Talk: How to Analyze Political Language*.

1 The term "pep talk" is most commonly associated with the pep rallies before the big football games, or the coach's inspiring speech at half-time in the locker room, or the sales manager's enthusiastic meetings instilling a competitive spirit encouraging the staff to greater efforts to sell more, to do more, or to beat their rivals. But in this essay, the term "pep talk" is going to be used more broadly and metaphorically to suggest a very common pattern in a great deal of social and political persuasion.

2 Political, as used here, suggests not only our domestic party politics (Democrat, Republican; national, state, and local politics) and international political issues (Communism, etc.), but also, in the broadest sense, any grouping together for a goal, a purpose, a cause. Thus, this pattern can usefully help to analyze civil rights and environmental issues, party politics and neighborhood citizen's groups, union strikes and company sales meetings, picket lines and protestors, special interest groups and "single issue" candidates, and often rumors and "junk mail."

3   The "pep talk," as used here, is that pattern of persuasion used to organize and direct the energy of a group toward *committed collective action:* commonly a sequence of (1) the Threat, (2) the Bonding, (3) the Cause, (4) the Response.

4   Whether the cause or the group is "good" or "bad," important or trivial, the pattern will be basically the same. The *intent* of a "pep talk" may be the persuader's malicious exploitation of the naive, or it may be the most genuine altruism and benevolence, but the pattern will be basically the same. The *content* of the "pep talk" may be true or false, accurate or erroneous, but the pattern will be basically the same. The *consequences* may be beneficial or harmful, to the individual or to others, but the pattern will be basically the same.

5   In reality, the "pep talk" is not as tidy, nor as sequential as this 1,2,3,4 pattern. Observers come in at different times, or hear only brief fragments. On one hand, we're probably accustomed to the bonding efforts of our own group (nationality, religious, ethnic, etc.), on the other hand, watching the TV news, we're apt to see only a brief exposure of some other group's "cause" without really knowing much about their whole set of beliefs and attitudes, hopes and fears. Typically, we see bits and fragments of the "pep talk," odds and ends.

6   Here's a basic structure to help sort out these fragments of political language and relate them to their part in a process of purposeful communication. Consider first some of the possible benefits and dangers involved in such "pep talks," then note the qualifications and variations: for example, the differences and overlaps between "the pitch" and "the pep talk."

7   Using simple terms such as "pep talk," (and later, "horror stories" and "atrocity pictures") helps to clarify a complex process. Some people may feel that this informal language is flippant or frivolous. But the intent here is not to minimize the genuine human pain and suffering often related to such "pep talks" in the past, but to innoculate for the future. If, by the use of a simple pattern and memorable phrases, it is possible to clarify and to simplify these basic techniques for large audiences, especially younger audiences, then it would be cynical *not* to do so, or to restrict such information to an elite few.

8   For the past few generations, for the first time in human history, broadcasting can link persuaders with a mass audience. Not only do many corporations seek after this audience, using the "pitch" to sell their products, but also many political groups and "causes" would like to organize and direct the energies of this large audience.

9   In the future, as in the past, people will be asked to join in a good cause, or to fight for God and country, or to defend themselves and to protect others from an evil threat. A "cause" can involve mankind's most noble sentiments. But, our altruistic impulses can also be exploited, manipulated, abused by others.

10   Young people are always the prime target for such a "pep talk": they have a great deal of idealism, enthusiasm—and inexperience. It's useful to know some patterns of persuasion, and to teach them to the young. It helps to clarify choice and decisions. There are times when we may wish to commit ourselves to a cause. If we are aware of some patterns, our decisions may be more based on the merit of the cause rather than on the slick delivery, the skill, the cleverness or the charisma of the persuader. If we know the form, we can concentrate on the substance.

11   The propagandist does not want our thought, our contemplation, our analysis, our advance awareness of the techniques; the propagandist wants a response, action.

12   Some persuasion emphasizes the positive or upbeat: some conservative persuasion, for example, would stress joy, contentment, and satisfaction for the "good" possessed, for the blessings received, as we often hear on Thanksgiving Day, Christmas, Fourth of July; some progressive persuasion, for example, might stress growth, progress, and achievement, the optimistic hopes and dreams of a situation getting better ("I have a dream . . ."). There's a great deal of such ceremonial rhetoric, appropriate to many situations, and we expect it and hear it in many instances in which the audience is to be inspired or praised, calmed or consoled. Similarly, in religious persuasion, some preachers might focus on the glory of God, the beauty of the universe, or heavenly delights. But, other preachers have been known to talk about hellfire and damnation. Perhaps the "pep talk" might be the secular equivalent of such hellfire preaching: starting with a problem, working on the emotions, and leading to solutions being suggested.

13   If there are varieties of religious experience, so also there are varieties of secular experience. Some people would prefer hearing "good news" all the time; others would object to such a thing as being unrealistic and Pollyannish. Some people may not like a "pep talk"—some may object to its negative emphasis, others to its emotional intensity, others to its seeming artificiality. Without denying the virtues of positive inspirational rhetoric, the emphasis in this book is on the negative: the conservative rhetoric stressing anxiety and fear of losing the "good" and the progressive rhetoric stressing anger, resentment, and frustration about not having the "good" or seeking relief from the "bad." The attempt here is not to endorse or condemn what persuaders do, but to observe and describe it.

Good Results, Good Intentions

14   "Pep talks" can be beneficial, can be the means to good effects. There are, genuinely, many "good causes." Many things which need to be done in order to make this a better society can only be done by organized group effort. Individuals working alone simply cannot do some things which people can do collectively. Various methods of organizing people are possible: a business corporation can offer financial rewards, for example; or a powerful government can simply command by force. Yet, even without such inducements as money or guns, human energies can be organized toward collective action simply by skillful combination of words and images, a "pep talk."

15   Assume that all or most "pep talks" are made with *good intentions,* that is, the speakers are sincere believers in the merits of their "good cause." (Some persuaders may not be so; some may be manipulators or con men.) However, "good intentions" do not necessarily guarantee good results. But, if it is assumed that everyone (even scoundrels and rascals) can justify their actions as being based on "good intentions," one need not waste effort trying to establish the persuader's motives; be

concerned instead with the *consequences*. More specifically, be aware of the potentially *bad* effects of "pep talks."

16   "Pep talks" can cause harm to great numbers of people. In a world with very real danger of wars among nations, terrorist assaults by individuals and small groups, and sophisticated weapons easily available, it's very risky to stimulate fears or incite quick responses based on emotional feelings. The obvious, overt danger is that of stirring up hatreds and triggering off the Crazies. The more subtle danger is the general conditioning within a wider society in preparation for officially-sanctioned wars.

17   "Pep talks" can be harmful to individuals. What may benefit the group, may harm the individual. All of us owe some debt of loyalty to the many groups to which we belong because we inherit or share in their benefits. Yet, any time a person gives up responsibility to any group, the person risks a loss of self. Yet, it happens. Some people with low self-esteem find their comfort in belonging to a group, identifying with it, and following it with unquestioning loyalty.

18   Self-righteousness is another danger. People who are "true believers" in the absolute virtue of their own "cause" are, at best, obnoxious; at worst, dangerous. The world has seen too many wars, slaughters and massacres carried out in the name of God or the cause of Justice. The "pep talk" encourages polarized thinking, dichotomies, the "good guys/bad guys" mentality; it encourages people who are narrow and rigid authoritarians to believe that they are the "good guys," the Truth-Possessors with an authority to impose the "right way" on others.

19   Individuals can be harmed emotionally by a constant repetition of the "threats" and warnings given in "pep talks." Just as some young people, for example, can be overstimulated by the acquisitive demands ("buy this . . . get that") of commercial advertising, and end up being always dissatisfied and frustrated, so also some people can be overstimulated by a constant repetition of threats, warnings, bad news, and urgent pleas. A sensitive young person, for example, encountering a daily dose of environmentalist pleas (pictures of dead seals, dead whales, dead birds, dead dogs, etc.) can be overwhelmed by this depressing sight. Often these are undue fears, unreasonable anxieties, because the degree, proportion, or relationship of the harm has been exaggerated out of context. Even though any single ad or any single "pep talk" could be defended as being tolerable, the *cumulative impact* of thousands of single-issue "cause" group ads, each intensifying their own warnings and problems, can be harmful to the sensibilities of the audience which receives them all. Our children grow up not only blitzed by commercial advertising pleasantly promising dreams of the good life, but also saturated with horrible warnings and nightmare images.

20   Cynicism is one result. Sometimes young people completely accept a "pep talk" at face value, literally, without reservations. Later, they may feel that they had been deceived, duped, or exploited. Such disillusionment often causes a bitter reaction: cynicism, apathy, a total rejection of previous beliefs. Problems of credibility also exist when so many extreme warnings are made about so many things that some people simply overload and discount everything. Many people scoff at FDA

warnings about cancer-causing chemicals ("next thing they'll say is that *everything* causes cancer" is the cliché) without recognizing the real complexity. Many people simply disregard, block out, any warnings about nuclear war as being either unthinkable or unbelievable.

21   We not only live in an age of real problems and real threats, but we also live in an age in which the professional persuaders are right with us, daily and constantly, often to warn us about these problems and ask us to do something about them. A hundred years ago, even sixty years ago, the average citizen would seldom experience a skillfully constructed "pep talk" during the course of a lifetime. Today, the average citizen is likely to see bits and fragments of one every time the TV is turned on, and is likely to get a complete "pep talk" daily in the mailbox.

The Pitch, the Pep Talk, and Other Persuasive Attempts

22 Both the "pitch" and the "pep talk" seek a response, but the basic difference between the two is that the "pep talk" seeks a *committed collective action.* That is, the "pitch" leads to a simple response (usually, to buy); the "pep talk" asks a person to *join with others, for a cause.*

23   To relate these techniques with other persuasive attempts, consider first the *timing* of the response, using the terms *Command* propaganda which seeks an immediate response *(Now!)* and *Conditioning* propaganda which seeks to mold public opinions, assumptions, beliefs, attitudes on a long-term basis as the necessary climate or atmosphere for a future response *(Later!)*

24   Both the "pitch" and the "pep talk" are *Command* propagandas, seeking immediate actions. The chart (opposite) relates these two concepts with terms used by others to describe other kinds of persuasive attempts.

25   In reality, such neat categories do not exist. Borderline cases are common, between command and conditioning propagandas, and between the "pitch" and the "pep talk." Adding to the complexity of any real situation are some common basic factors which can be described in terms of *multiples, mixtures,* and *mistakes.*

26   *Multiples.* Multiple persuasion attempts are usually made at the same time, either to the same audience using different pitches, or to different audiences using the same pitch. In auto ads, for example, there may be a dozen different sets of ads prepared for different audiences: some ads stressing a "safety" angle for old folks, "sporty" for young folks; some ads with urban backgrounds, some with rural; some emphasizing economy, others stressing prestige, and all could be talking about the same car. In such an advertising campaign, a basic premise is that most people only notice ads directed at "them" in such smaller sub-categories, and ignore the ads directed at other sub-categories.

27   Multiple association devices are also used in politics. In a typical political campaign, for example, the major parties will create and fund a whole host of various committees and "front organizations" and sub-groups (such as Farmers For Reagan, Polish-Americans For Reagan, Italian-Americans For Reagan, Union Mem-

	"Command propaganda" is the easiest to recognise. Here both the "pitch" and the "pep talk" are types of such persuasions seeking an immediate response.	**"Conditioning propaganda"** is more subtle, harder to analyze or limit; many different names have been used to describe persuasion which seeks to create, shape, mold basic opinions, assumptions, beliefs, attitudes, myths, worldviews.
Timing of Response	NOW! (Command)	LATER (Conditioning)
Kind of Response		"soft sell" "public relations" (PR) "publicity"
action	"THE PITCH"	"institutional advertising" "corporate advertising" "image building" "promotion" "goodwill advertising"
committed collective action	"THE PEP TALK"	"political education" (Lenin) "basic propaganda" (Goebbels) "sub-propaganda" (Ellul) "pre-propaganda" "education" "indoctrination" "awareness" "consciousness raising"

The persuader's goals are to get others . . . *to do* the "right" acts . . . and *to think* the "right" way.

bers for Reagan, etc.) not only to give the illusion of widespread support, but also to appeal to those specific ethnic, occupational, or interest groups. Political protest movements also have a multiplicity of propagandas going on at the same time (e.g., Vietnam Veterans Against the War, Another Mother for Peace, Clergy and Laity United for Peace, Students for Peace, etc.); such diversity is sometimes a genuine grassroots movement, sometimes manipulated by others.

28   *Mixtures.* In any political campaign, there's likely to be a mixture of the "pitch" directed at an outside public, and the "pep talk" directed at an insider audience—the party regulars. In religious persuasion, there's likely to be one kind of evangelizing, spreading the good news, to others, and another kind of preaching to the saved. In both of these examples, we are likely to see a "recruiting sequence": first, the "pitch"

to bring in new members, converts; then, the "pep talk" to keep them bonded and to direct them toward a new action. Or we might find a re-directing sequence; first, a "pep talk" to bond for one cause; then, once bonded, re-directed to another cause. Or we might find an escalation sequence: a series of "pep talks" leading to increasingly more difficult actions, "raising the ante."

29   Thus far, we've been assuming that these patterns and variations can be applied to *truthful* and *sincere* attempts at persuasion; but they can also be applied to *deceitful* and *insincere* "pitches" and "pep talks." A scoundrel, for example, may use a "pep talk" to bond people for a political or religious cause, simply as a prelude to a "pitch" to get the audience to buy something or donate money. Sometimes this is obvious and recognizable—if the politician or minister walks away with bulging pockets stuffed with money. But, more likely, it's difficult to detect, and the real borderline cases will be between clever scoundrels and true believers.

30   Mixed motives are common in almost every human action. Multiple goals are possible, simultaneously, in almost every human endeavor. Consider, for example, the many *reasons* for, and the *results* sought in, "corporate advertising" in such organizations as Mobil, U.S. Steel, Dow Chemical, IBM, Xerox, Union Carbide, and other corporate giants. Such "corporate advertising" (*not* ads for specific consumer products) is also called, by various writers, "public relations," "institutional advertising," "image building," "goodwill advertising," and other related synonyms.

31   Note that all four general purposes (above the line) could exist at the same time; most corporations defend their expenditures (to their stockholders and to the general public) with such explanations. In actual practice, there are no problems with the overlaps among these four categories. Serious "borderline" problems occur however in that vague area between *command* propaganda and *conditioning* propaganda, between "advocacy advertising" and "corporate advertising." Just where is the boundary between spending money to have the public "like" (tolerate, accept) the corporation (or the policies, the goals of the corporation) and spending money to have the public "advocate" (support, endorse) the goals and policies of the corporation. Clarifying the issues at this borderline involves high stakes because of the tax laws and the problems of corporate influence—complex legal problems which do not fit neatly into any existing jurisdiction, but are overlapping concerns of the FTC, FCC, and IRS. (As the first step in approaching this problem, the Senate's Subcommittee on Administrative Practice has published a whopping, 2133 pp., *Sourcebook on Corporate Image and Corporate Advocacy Advertising.*)

32   Another factor which makes it difficult to deal with the borderline between command propaganda, seeking an immediate response, and conditioning propaganda, preparing the way for a future response, is that all of this is an *ongoing process,* constantly in motion. Any particular piece of information may be "news" to the *receivers* or may call for an urgent action, but the *sender* may know months or years ahead about the content and timing of a long-term propaganda campaign.

33   The "pitch" and the "pep talk" may be useful to help understand some of the persuasive messages we receive, but we must be prepared to see the variations and the "surface texture." In the United States alone, for example, there are literally

Mixed Motives in Corporate Advertising

Label	Purpose	Audience
synonyms: "corporate advertising"	to sell, indirectly, consumer products by building awareness (Hi!) and reputation (Trust Me) of parent corporation, brand names, logos.	consumers
"institutional advertising" "public relations"	to encourage new stockholders to invest money, existing stockholders to retain stock.	investors; financial community
"image advertising" "goodwill" "publicity"	to increase employee morale, higher productivity and work quality; to attract good new employees.	employees; potential employees
	to influence, indirectly, legislation and regulation; to get citizens and their representatives friendly and favorably disposed toward the corporation; to ward off taxes, controls, regulations, limits, etc.	citizens: voters, legislators & regulators
"advocacy advertising" is the closely related *Command* propaganda here seeking a specific immediate response.	to influence, directly, legislation or regulation: seeking specific actions, explicit directives: "Write your Senator . . ., Vote for . . ."	citizens: voters, legislators & regulators

several hundred thousand commercial products which advertise, and there are probably more than that number of sources of political, religious, ethnic, and social propagandas. We live in this environment of competing propagandas, and the hubbub of this marketplace of ideas can get confusing at times.

34   *Mistakes.* Because of all of this complexity, persuaders can make mistakes. Every persuader seeks to be effective, but this is not always the result. Sometimes ads come "too close" to us, get palsy-walsy, treating us as if we were already friendly, assuming our interest and involvement, taking our assent for granted. This kind of error in persuasion causes the audience to back off, to reject the over-friendly advances as being offensive, cloying, too saccharine. Sometimes this is caused by a mishandling of the "confidence" (Trust Me) part of the "pitch." Sometimes it's caused by using a "pep talk" instead of a "pitch," in a situation which is not appropriate. Sometimes, in a "pep talk," errors in persuasion can occur because of an incomplete bonding or a premature "response" plea.

35   *Delivery.* Although this book concentrates on patterns and the structure underneath, the "surface" tactics of delivery or execution are equally important. Simply
to point out the pattern doesn't mean that everyone has the skill to do it well. Effectiveness varies with the speaker, the audience, and the situation. Sometimes an attempt at a "pep talk" falls flat; the audience may not be moved or may react against
it as being too "gung ho" or too "rah-rah" or as "laying it on too thick."

36   If the bonding is incomplete, if the audience doesn't genuinely feel a part of the
group, feel threatened by the outside, then the pep talk may be ineffective or back-
fire.

A Borderline Case: The "Scare-and-Sell" Ad

37 In contrast to most advertising which deals with our dreams, promises, and hopes,
some health and safety products (such as fire and life insurance, travelers' checks,
burglar alarms, over-the-counter medicines, deodorants, etc.) often start from our
nightmares, threats, and fears: the *"scare-and-sell"* approach.

38   Thus, the ad may begin with a "threat," and in this way is similar to the beginning of the "pep talk." But the "scare-and-sell" approach *does not* ask for bonding
or commitment to a cause. It's a pitch, a simple sales transaction: "You have a
problem; here's the solution."

39   The problem is emphasized, then the solution is offered ("anxiety arousal and
satisfaction"), but there is no demand on us to give anything other than our money.
It's easiest to recognize this in ads which dramatize physical fears (death, fire, loss
of money, etc.), but we also have emotional fears (loneliness, rejection, etc.) that
are stirred by many ads. The basic "translation" of many ads might read: "You'll be
unloved, unwanted, rejected . . . unless you buy our soap, toothpaste, deodorant,
hairspray, etc."

A Borderline Case: The Selling of the Candidates

40 Following the lead of books such as Daniel Boorstin's *The Image* and Joe McGin-
nis' *The Selling of the President,* and movies such as *The Candidate,* there has been
increasing criticism about the packaging or marketing or selling of modern political
candidates as if they were commercial products: bars of soap, tubes of toothpaste.
Critics cry that "Madison Avenue" has taken over: slick professionals, crass manipulators, PR specialists and media technicians who know how to create and manipulate an "image," a "television personality," a "plastic person" who looks like and
talks like what the polls say the voters want. There has been a great deal of commentary about these media mercenaries or rented rhetoricians.

41   Usually such complaints about modern political campaigns are set in contrast
to romanticized images of old-time party politics—of Fourth of July speeches, political rallies, orators on the gazebos, friendly waving crowds, torchlight parades
and bandwagons, handprinted homemade signs, and all the hoopla and ballyhoo
which we associate with political campaigns in the days before radio and television.

Most of this old time politicing can best be described in terms of the *"pep talk"*: the great emphasis was on the bonding of the group, for a cause. Party politics emphasized the group; later, "issue politics" of the 1960s also could be described in terms of the "pep talk" because of its emphasis on "principles," on the "cause."

42   But the approach of those who are creating the "image" candidates can best be described in terms of the *"pitch."* Most of these ads are *not* asking the voters to join the party, work for the party, commit themselves to a cause, but are simply asking for a one-shot "purchase"—a vote. (And if that purchase isn't satisfactory, there'll be a new improved model for the next election.)

43   We are likely to see more of the "pitch" in future political campaigns because of the decline in political party membership, party loyalty; the increase in uncommitted "Independent" voters; and because it is ultimately cheaper and easier to use the technology of the mass media than to sustain an ongoing organization.

44   In the future, we're still likely to see the "pep talk" given to insiders (usually by means of meetings; rallies, letter mailings, in-house publications), but the use of the "pitch" will increase in messages directed to outsiders—to the uncommitted public—seeking only their vote on election day.

45   However, this new kind of "image" campaigning may always be considered a borderline case between a "pitch" and a "pep talk," because it is likely such "pitches" will have the surface appearance of a "pep talk" by using such *commitment words* ("dedicate yourself . . . join us . . . in our noble cause"), but in fact seeking or specifying *no other response than voting.* When somebody asks us to canvas a neighborhood, ring doorbells, fold envelopes, work hard and give time for the cause, we are likely to be hearing part of a "pep talk"; but when we see the 30-second-spot on TV, we're likely to be seeing the "pitch."

46   Hired Hands and True Believers. No one yet knows the full implications of this new "image" campaigning. Those who use the "pitch" in political advertising are open to charges of being cynical, calculating manipulators; those who use the "pep talk" are feared as zealots, fanatics, extremists. But some political observers are saying that we have passed the era of conflicts between political parties, and of conflicts between opposing ideologies, and now are witnessing the conflict between technicians: which team of specialists can best package the product and sell it.

47   *To recap:* The "pep talk" is used here to label a common pattern of persuasion used to organize and direct the energy of a group toward committed collective action; commonly, the sequence: (1) the Threat; (2) the Bonding; (3) the Cause; (4) the Response. Regardless of intent, consequences, significance, or content, the pattern is basically the same, albeit we often see only bits and fragments as reported and edited by others. "Pep talks" can be beneficial as aids to directing human effort; but "pep talks" can also be harmful to society (inciting hatreds, wars) and to the individual (irresponsibility, self-righteousness, undue fears, cynicism). The "pep talk" is similar to the "pitch" in that both are *command* propagandas seeking a response; but the "pitch" leads to a simple transaction while the "pep talk" asks a person to join with others for a good cause. A static diagram is limited in suggesting the reality of multiple and mixed persuasion techniques and motives (illustrated by

the mixed motives of "corporate ads") and in the reality of mistakes in planning and in delivery. Borderline cases exist: some commercial products using ads stressing fears, the "scare-and-sell" technique; some slick political ads "selling candidates" as if they were commercial products.

THINKING CRITICALLY

1. What is the "pep talk"? Who uses it and why?

2. How does Rank's analysis of the "pep talk" as a form of public persuasion provide insight into the dynamics of what makes a speech compelling to an audience? Explain.

3. Describe the basic pattern of the "pep talk." How does dissecting its patterns help us understand its benefits and dangers? Explain.

4. In what ways can the "pep talk" be beneficial? How can it be used to support good causes? Conversely, how can it be abused?

5. What is the difference between the "pitch" and the "pep talk"? Can you identify examples of each used recently? Explain.

6. Evaluate Rank's own use of language as he describes the structure of the "pep talk." Is he persuasive? Critical? Unbiased and fair? Explain.

7. What similarities exist between political "pep talks" and advertising? Discuss how you think they are similar, or different, drawing from the information outlined by Rank in his essay.

WRITING ASSIGNMENTS

1. Locate a recent speech given by a politician and analyze it using Rank's guidelines for understanding the "pep talk." Discuss your analysis.

2. Describe a situation in which you were deceived or inspired by a "pep talk." What compelled you to believe the speaker? What made the speech effective? Describe the experience and its influence on you.

3. Write your own "pep talk." Prepare a short speech for a political or social cause. After you prepare the speech, deliver it to the class. Be prepared to explain why you chose certain persuasive tactics, and to discuss the effectiveness of the speech as part of a peer review.

Doubts About Doublespeak
William Lutz

It has been said that the only sure (or certain) things we cannot change are death and taxes. Well, that's not exactly right. We can call them "terminal living" and "revenue enhancement" to make people feel better about them. And that, in part, is the nature of what William Lutz rails against here: doublespeak. It is language intended not to reveal but to conceal, not to communicate but to obfuscate. In this essay, Lutz categorizes four kinds of doublespeak, distinguishing annoying though relatively harmless professional jargon from ruthlessly devious coinages such as "ethnic cleansing," which attempt to mask barbaric acts.

William Lutz is a professor of English at Rutgers University. He is the editor of the *Quarterly Review of Doublespeak* as well as author of *Beyond Nineteen Eighty-Four: Doublespeak in a Post-Orwellian Age* (1989) and *Doublespeak: From Revenue Enhancement to Terminal Living* (1990). "Doubts About Doublespeak" first appeared in *State Government News,* in July 1993.

1 During the past year, we learned that we can shop at a "unique retail biosphere" instead of a farmers' market, where we can buy items made of "synthetic glass" instead of plastic, or purchase a "high velocity, multipurpose air circulator," or electric fan. A "waste-water conveyance facility" may "exceed the odor threshold" from time to time due to the presence of "regulated human nutrients," but that is not to be confused with a sewage plant that stinks up the neighborhood with sewage sludge. Nor should we confuse a "resource development park" with a dump. Thus does doublespeak continue to spread.

2 Doublespeak is language which pretends to communicate but doesn't. It is language which makes the bad seem good, the negative seem positive, the unpleasant seem attractive, or at least tolerable. It is language which avoids, shifts or denies responsibility; language which is at variance with its real or purported meaning. It is language which conceals or prevents thought.

3 Doublespeak is all around us. We are asked to check our packages at the desk "for our convenience" when it's not for our convenience at all but for someone else's convenience. We see advertisements for "preowned," "experienced" or "previously distinguished" cars, not used cars and for "genuine imitation leather," "virgin vinyl" or "real counterfeit diamonds." Television offers not reruns but "encore telecasts." There are no slums or ghettos, just the "inner city" or "substandard housing" where the "disadvantaged" or "economically nonaffluent" live and where there might be a problem with "substance abuse." Nonprofit organizations don't make a profit, they have "negative deficits" or experience "revenue excesses." With doublespeak it's not dying but "terminal living" or "negative patient care outcome."

4 There are four kinds of doublespeak. The first kind is the euphemism, a word or phrase designed to avoid a harsh or distasteful reality. Used to mislead or deceive, the euphemism becomes doublespeak. In 1984 the U.S. State Department's annual reports on the status of human rights around the world ceased using the word "killing." Instead the State Department used the phrase "unlawful or arbitrary deprivation of life," thus avoiding the embarrassing situation of government-sanctioned killing in countries supported by the United States.

5 A second kind of doublespeak is jargon, the specialized language of a trade, profession or similar group, such as doctors, lawyers, plumbers or car mechanics. Legitimately used, jargon allows members of a group to communicate with each other clearly, efficiently and quickly. Lawyers and tax accountants speak to each other of an "involuntary conversion" of property, a legal term that means the loss or

destruction of property through theft, accident or condemnation. But when lawyers or tax accountants use unfamiliar terms to speak to others, then the jargon becomes doublespeak.

6   In 1978 a commercial 727 crashed on takeoff, killing three passengers, injuring 21 others and destroying the airplane. The insured value of the airplane was greater than its book value, so the airline made a profit of $1.7 million, creating two problems: the airline didn't want to talk about one of its airplanes crashing, yet it had to account for that $1.7 million profit in its annual report to its stockholders. The airline solved both problems by inserting a footnote in its annual report which explained that the $1.7 million was due to "the involuntary conversion of a 727."

7   A third kind of doublespeak is gobbledygook or bureaucratese. Such doublespeak is simply a matter of overwhelming the audience with words—the more the better. Alan Greenspan, a polished practitioner of bureaucratese, once testified before a Senate committee that "it is a tricky problem to find the particular calibration in timing that would be appropriate to stem the acceleration in risk premiums created by falling incomes without prematurely aborting the decline in the inflation-generated risk premiums."

8   The fourth kind of doublespeak is inflated language, which is designed to make the ordinary seem extraordinary, to make everyday things seem impressive, to give an air of importance to people or situations, to make the simple seem complex. Thus do car mechanics become "automotive internists," elevator operators become "members of the vertical transportation corps," grocery store checkout clerks become "career associate scanning professionals," and smelling something becomes "organoleptic analysis."

9   Doublespeak is not the product of careless language or sloppy thinking. Quite the opposite. Doublespeak is language carefully designed and constructed to appear to communicate when in fact it doesn't. It is language designed not to lead but mislead. Thus, it's not a tax increase but "revenue enhancement" or "tax-base broadening." So how can you complain about higher taxes? Those aren't useless, billion dollar pork barrel projects; they're really "congressional projects of national significance," so don't complain about wasteful government spending. That isn't the Mafia in Atlantic City; those are just "members of a career-offender cartel," so don't worry about the influence of organized crime in the city.

10   New doublespeak is created every day. The Environmental Protection Agency once called acid rain "poorly-buffered precipitation" then dropped that term in favor of "atmospheric deposition of anthropogenically-derived acidic substances," but recently decided that acid rain should be called "wet deposition." The Pentagon, which has in the past given us such classic doublespeak as "hexiform rotatable surface compression unit" for steel nut, just published a pamphlet warning soldiers that exposure to nerve gas will lead to "immediate permanent incapacitation." That's almost as good as the Pentagon's official term "servicing the target," meaning to kill the enemy. Meanwhile, the Department of Energy wants to establish a "monitored retrievable storage site," a place once known as a dump for spent nuclear fuel.

11   Bad economic times give rise to lots of new doublespeak designed to avoid some very unpleasant economic realities. As the "contained depression" continues so does the corporate policy of making up even more new terms to avoid the simple, and easily understandable, term "layoff." So it is that corporations "reposition," "restructure," "reshape," or "realign" the company and "reduce duplication" through "release of resources" that involves a "permanent downsizing" or a "payroll adjustment" that results in a number of employees being "involuntarily terminated."

12   Other countries regularly contribute to doublespeak. In Japan, where baldness is called "hair disadvantaged," the economy is undergoing a "severe adjustment process," while in Canada there is an "involuntary downward development" of the work force. For some government agencies in Canada, wastepaper baskets have become "user friendly, space effective, flexible, deskside sortation units." Politicians in Canada may engage in "reality augmentation," but they never lie. As part of their new freedom, the people of Moscow can visit "intimacy salons," or sex shops as they're known in other countries. When dealing with the bureaucracy in Russia, people know that they should show officials "normal gratitude," or give them a bribe.

13   The worst doublespeak is the doublespeak of death. It is the language, wrote George Orwell in 1946, that is "largely the defense of the indefensible . . . designed to make lies sound truthful and murder respectable, and to give an appearance of solidity to pure wind." In the doublespeak of death, Orwell continued, "defenseless villages are bombarded from the air, the inhabitants driven out into the countryside, the cattle machine-gunned, the huts set on fire with incendiary bullets. This is called pacification. Millions of peasants are robbed of their farms and sent trudging along the roads with no more than they can carry. This is called transfer of population or rectification of frontiers." Today, in a country once called Yugoslavia, this is called "ethnic cleansing."

14   It's easy to laugh off doublespeak. After all, we all know what's going on, so what's the harm? But we don't always know what's going on, and when that happens, doublespeak accomplishes its ends. It alters our perception of reality. It deprives us of the tools we need to develop, advance and preserve our society, our culture, our civilization. It breeds suspicion, cynicism, distrust and, ultimately, hostility. It delivers us into the hands of those who do not have our interests at heart. As Samuel Johnson noted in 18th century England, even the devils in hell do not lie to one another, since the society of hell could not subsist without the truth, any more than any other society.

THINKING CRITICALLY

1. What is doublespeak, according to Lutz? What is its purpose?

2. Lutz divides doublespeak into four types. What are they? Give some of your own examples of each type. As best you can, rank these four types according to which are most offensive or harmful. Explain your choices.

3. In paragraph 4, Lutz classifies euphemisms as a form of doublespeak. In your opinion, are there instances when euphemisms are useful? Explain your answer.

4. Lutz says that "inflated language" is designed to make the ordinary seem extraordinary, as with elevated job titles. In your opinion, is there anything wrong with elevating job titles in this way? Why or why not?

5. In your opinion, is doublespeak as widespread as Lutz claims? Are its effects as serious as he perceives them to be?

6. Examine Lutz's introductory paragraph. How does this paragraph set the tone for the piece? Is it effective?

7. What is the opposing view in this piece? How does Lutz handle it in his argument? Are there counterarguments that Lutz has missed in his essay?

8. Are there any places in the essay where Lutz employs doublespeak in his own writing? If so, what effect does this have on your reading?

9. Consider Lutz's voice in this article. Is he a reliable narrator? Does he provide adequate documentation for his assertions? Cite specific examples from the text to support your answers.

WRITING ASSIGNMENTS

1. Write an essay in which you examine instances of doublespeak in the media, a particular profession, or among your acquaintances. Make a case either for or against its usage.

2. Was there ever a time when doublespeak had an impact on your life? Write a personal narrative reflecting on the effect, positive or negative, that doublespeak has had on your experience. You might consider having been swayed by advertising or political jargon.

3. Lutz defines doublespeak as "language which conceals or prevents thought" and "language which pretends to communicate but doesn't." Write an essay describing an experience wherein you used doublespeak. What was your goal in communicating as such? How was doublespeak useful to you in this situation?

4. Over the course of one day, record all the instances of doublespeak you encounter—from ads, TV shows, news articles, films, menus, and so on. (Whenever possible, photocopy or tape these instances.) In a paper, try to classify the different kinds of doublespeak you found. Analyze the different functions of doublespeak and try to determine its effects on the intended audience.

5. Look through a newspaper or magazine for a short and clear discussion of an interesting topic. Then have some fun rewriting the piece entirely in doublespeak.

■ MAKING CONNECTIONS

1. Locate a political speech from a gubernatorial or presidential candidate. After carefully reading the speech, try to summarize what the candidate is promising the public if he or she is

elected to office. In what ways does the politician tap into common ideology to connect with voters? Is any doublespeak used in the speech? Explain.

2. Compare some of the points made in "How to Detect Propaganda" with Charles Lutz's article, "With These Words I Can Sell You Anything," and Charles O'Neill's article, "The Language of Advertising," in Chapter 6. How are Lutz's "weasel words" similar to the propagandist's attempts to appeal to emotion that the Institute's authors identify? Do you think the Institute's authors would agree with O'Neil that the propaganda of advertising uses language in a way that is special or different from everyday use?

3. Try creating some political language of your own. Imagine you are running for office—president, senator, mayor, or school committee. Using some of the features and tricks of political language discussed in this section, write a campaign speech outlining why you, and not your opponent, should be elected. Have the class critique your speech.

4. Find political speeches from a recent campaign, either local or national. Try the "All Things Political" Web site at <http://dolphin.gulf.net/Political.html> by Washington Weekly for a listing of recent political speeches. Select one and try to identify the ways it manipulates language to sway the public.

■ LANGUAGE AND THE PRESIDENCY

The Rhetorical Presidency
Robert E. Denton, Jr. and Dan F. Hahn

In the next essay, political communication analysts Robert Denton and Dan Hahn assert that the presidency is primarily a rhetorical institution. The president's primary function is of a great communicator. The president is, they explain, "the one man distillation of the American people: their hopes, desires, and majesty." Everything the president says is recorded. Everything he communicates—from phone calls to addresses to Congress—carries meaning and significance.

Robert E. Denton, Jr. is head of the Department of Communications Studies at Virginia Polytechnic Institute and State University. He is the author of many books on political communication, including *Political Communications in America* (with Gary C. Woodward) and *Presidential Communication Ethics, An Oxymoron?* (ed., 2002). The following piece is an excerpt from a book he co-authored with Dan F. Hahn, *Presidential Communication* (1987).

Dan F. Hahn is a visiting professor in the Department of Culture and Communications at New York University. He is the author of many articles and convention papers exploring aspects of political communication. In addition to the book he co-authored with Robert Denton, Jr., Hahn is co-author of *Listening for a President: A Citizen's Campaign Methodology*, written with Ruth Gonchar Brennan.

Public sentiment is everything. With public sentiment nothing can fail, without it nothing can succeed.

Abraham Lincoln

1 Presidents are special beings. When they talk, we listen. We want to know where they are, what they are doing, and how they are doing it. Why are they so special? They are not special physically—we have had fat ones, thin ones, tall ones, short ones, some ugly, some handsome. They are not special intellectually—they have ranged through the many gradations from smart to dumb. They are not special emotionally—some have been strengthened by the pressure, others have cracked under the strain. What makes each and every one special, however, is that they lead us, define us, protect us, and embody us. And they do so, implicitly and explicitly, through communication.

2 If you doubt the significance and importance of presidential public communication, consider the following two examples. The presidential debates of 1960 demonstrated how important public speech can be in influencing the very nature of our society. The debates were heard and watched by over 101 million Americans.[1] The election was decided by a mere 118,550 votes—votes that may well have been determined by the public debate performances of the candidates. Scholars have concluded that those viewing the debates shifted their opinion toward Kennedy and most of his last minute support came from the "undecided" voter. In fact, Kennedy's support gained about 4 percent with each debate.[2]

3 By 1979 Carter's public popularity was at an all time low. He decided to retreat with his advisors to Camp David to review his presidency. Upon reflection, Carter believed that his presidential leadership had missed its mark. He had acted, as he told David Broder, as "the head of the government" rather than as the "leader of the people."[3] He also believed that the nation was experiencing a crisis of spirit or "malaise." The answer—a campaign to wake up the American people. The *Washington Post* announced the campaign with the headline that read "Carter Seeking Oratory to Move an Entire Nation."[4]

4 President Reagan, "the great communicator," has clearly demonstrated that how a president communicates with the public is an important element in governing the nation. The rhetoric of presidents is important on several dimensions. Linguistically, their words shape ideas and stimulate action. Intellectually, their words provide rationales for action and justifications for decisions. Psychologically, their words can inspire, comfort, and motivate the nation. Socially, their words connect us as a social entity, providing the feeling of a human relationship with our leader. Ethically, their words can do good or evil, encourage justice or injustice, selfishness or selflessness. Aesthetically, their words have encompassed our grief (Lincoln's Gettysburg Address), given us hope (Franklin Roosevelt's first inaugural address), and challenged us to address the task at hand (Kennedy's inaugural address).

5 In this essay we consider the importance of the "rhetorical presidency." More specifically, we explore the dependency of modern presidents upon public communication activities and provide a basis for citizen analysis of presidential rhetoric.

Politics and Communication

6 Humans are, according to Aristotle's *Politics,* "political beings" and "he who is without a polis, by reason of his own nature and not of some accident, is either a poor sort of being [a beast] or a being higher than man [a god]."[5] And because nature makes nothing in vain, Aristotle continues, humans "alone of the animals are furnished with the faculty of language."[6] Thus, it was recognized over 2,000 years ago that politics and communication go hand in hand because they are essential parts of human nature. Public communication allows us to deal with our social environment. "There are few tools," according to Roderick Hart and his colleagues, "other than public talk with which to maintain the delicate balance between community and jungle."[7]

7 Indeed, through public speaking by our national, state, and local officials, our values and goals are defined, refined, and articulated. Their words can inspire, move, and articulate but also deceive, destroy, and exploit. Public communication, or rhetoric, serves many purposes. Karlyn Campbell recognizes several general rhetorical purposes that represent an orderly progression in terms of complexity and political utility.[8] First, rhetoric serves to create a "virtual experience." Through rhetoric we experience a range of emotions leading to corresponding behavior. In the process, rhetoric functions to alter perceptions and assist in formulating beliefs. Verbal descriptions by our leaders often serve as rationales, justifications, or motivations for collective action. Finally, much public rhetoric by officials is aimed at maintaining support, action, or the status quo.

8 According to Doris Graber, "politics is largely a word game. Politicians rise to power because they can talk persuasively to voters and political elites. Once in power, their daily activities are largely verbal."[9] Dan Nimmo concurs and argues that the purpose of political talk is to "preserve other talk." In fact, politics and communication are inseparable. "Politics, like communication, is a process, and like communication, politics involves talk. This is not talk in the narrow sense of the spoken word but talk in the more inclusive sense, meaning all the ways people exchange symbols—written and spoken words, pictures, movements, gestures, mannerisms, and dress."[10] From this perspective we may view politics as an activity of communication between persons.

Political Language

9 Political consciousness is dependent upon language, for language can determine the way in which people relate to their environment.[11] At the very least, language should be viewed as the medium for the generation and perpetuation of politically significant symbols. Political consciousness, therefore, results from a largely symbolic interpretation of sociopolitical experience. To control, manipulate, or structure the "interpretation" is a primary goal of politics in general. The language of government, in many ways, is the dissemination of illusion and ambiguity.[12] A successful politician will use rather specific linguistic devices that reinforce popular

beliefs, attitudes, and values. Politically manipulated language can, therefore, promote and reinforce the existing political regime or order.

10 From this brief discussion, it is clear that what makes language political is not the particular vocabulary or linguistic form but the *substance* of the information the language conveys, the *setting* in which the interaction occurs, and the explicit or implicit *functions* the language performs. As Doris Graber observes, "When political actors, in and out of government communicate about political matters, for political purposes, they are using political languages."[13]

Functions of Political Language

11 Graber identifies five major functions of political language: information dissemination, agenda-setting, interpretation and linkage, projection for the future and the past, and action stimulation.[14] It is useful to discuss briefly each of these functions.

12 There are many ways information is shared with the public in political messages. The most obvious, of course, is the sharing of explicit information about the state of the polity. Such dissemination of information is vital to the public's understanding and support of the political system. This is especially true in democratic nations where the public expects open access to the instruments and decision-making of government officials. But the public, being sensitized to uses of language, can obtain "information" by what *is not* stated, *how* something is stated, or *when* something is stated. Often times, especially in messages between nations, the public must "read between the lines" of official statements to ascertain proper meanings and significance of statements. Such inferences are useful in gauging security, flexibility, and sincerity. Sometimes the connotations of the words used communicate more truth than the actual statements. Are our relations with the Soviet Union "open," "guarded," or "friendly?" There are times, especially in tragedy, that the very act of speaking by an official can communicate support, sympathy, or strength. Thus, the act of speaking rather than the words spoken sometimes conveys the meaning of the rhetorical event.

13 The very topics chosen by politicians to discuss channel the public's attention and focus issues to be discussed. The agenda-setting function of political language primarily occurs in two ways. First, before "something" can become an issue, some prominent politician must articulate a problem and hence bring the issue to public attention. The issue can be rather obvious (poverty), in need of highlighting (status of American education), or created (the "Great Society"). A major way political language establishes the national agenda is by controlling the information disseminated to the general public. Within this realm there is always a great deal of competition. There are a limited number of issues that can effectively maintain public interest and attention. While certain "self-serving" topics are favored by one person, party, faction, or group, the same topics may be perceived as meaningless or even harmful to other factions, persons, or groups. While President Nixon wanted to limit discussion and public attention regarding the Watergate break-ins and tapes, rival groups wanted public debates and revelations to continue.

14   The very act of calling the public's attention to a certain issue defines, interprets, and manipulates the public's perception of that issue. Causal explanations are
often freely given. Such explanations may be suspect. Control over the definitions
of a situation is essential in creating and preserving political realities. Participants
in election primaries, for example, all proclaim victory regardless of the number of
votes received. The top vote-getter becomes the "front runner." The second place
winner becomes "the underdog" candidate in an "up-hill battle." The third place
candidate becomes a "credible" candidate and alternative for those "frustrated" or
"dissatisfied" with the "same old party favorites." Political language defines and interprets reality as well as provides a rationale for future collective action.

15   A great deal of political rhetoric and language deals with predicting the future
and reflecting upon the past. Candidates present idealized futures under their leadership and predictions of success if their policies are followed. Some predictions
and projections are formalized as party platforms or major addresses as inaugurals
or state of the union addresses. Nearly all such statements involve promises—
promises of a brighter future if followed or Armageddon if rejected. Past memories
and associations are evoked to stimulate a sense of security, better times, and romantic longings. An important function of political language, therefore, is to link us
to past glories and reveal the future in order to reduce uncertainty in a world of ever
increasing complexity and doubt.

16   Finally, and perhaps most importantly, political language must function to mo-
bilize society and stimulate social action. Language serves as the stimulus, means,
or rationale for social action. Words can evoke, persuade, implore, command, label,
praise, and condemn. Political language is similar to other uses of language. But it
also articulates, shapes, and stimulates public discussion and behavior about the al-
location of public resources, authority, and sanctions.

The Rhetorical Nature of the Presidency

17 George Edwards argues that "the greatest source of influence for the president is
public approval."[15] Today, as never before, presidents want not only to please the
public and avoid irritating them, but also want to formulate and lead public opinion.
In fact, research has shown that the higher the president's approval rating by the
public the more Congress supports presidential policy decisions.[16]

18   The study of presidential rhetoric is the investigation of how presidents gain,
maintain, or lose public support. For Theodore Windt, it is "a study of power, of the
fundamental power in a democracy: public opinion and public support."[17] At the
very least, the words of a president establish the public record of the administration,
reflect the values and goals of the public, and in essence, the vocabulary becomes
the favored policy (that is, New Frontier, Great Society, Star Wars, etc.). It is not
surprising, therefore, that James Ceaser and his colleagues argue that "the rhetorical
presidency is based on words, not power."[18] As Hart observes, the "American citizenry nevertheless require the federal archivists to scurry around behind modern

chief executives and record their remarks for posterity, sparing no expense or tree for the sake of president's speeches perhaps because they have become convinced in a media-saturated age that a president is earning his keep only when he stands in public and talks."[19]

[19]   The speeches of presidents, indeed, differ from those of ordinary citizens or even celebrities in terms of frequency and how they must communicate.[20] In addition, presidents seldom face their entire audience and must always keep in mind the impact of their remarks on various constituencies. Presidents must be able to speak on a wide range of topics with great detail, knowing that their words are recorded and "live forever."

[20]   Despite the notion of the "grand oratory" of the nineteenth century, our early presidents seldom relied upon public address to win public support. George Washington usually gave only one speech a year—the one mandated in the Constitution to address Congress. Prior to 1912, the political parties conducted the presidential campaigns. Woodrow Wilson was the first presidential candidate to engage in active public campaigning.[21] In fact, an argument can be made that the framers of the Constitution did not favor "mass oratory" because it could counter "rational" and "enlightened self-interest" concerns of the citizenry.[22] The government was designed to minimize reliance upon the passions of the people and establish institutions that would be stable, efficient, and effective.

[21]   Between 1945 and 1975, public speeches by presidents increased 500 percent. President Gerald Ford, not a particularly effective speaker, delivered 682 public speeches in 1976 and President Jimmy Carter, also not a particularly effective speaker, averaged one speech a day during his entire term of office.[23] The reasons for the rise of the "rhetorical presidency" have already been identified in the preface of this book. But the importance and impact of modern electoral campaign politics plus the role of the mass media cannot be overemphasized. In addition, Gary Woodward argues that today's presidency is a collection of traditions and rhetorical expectations that each new president inherits. The legacies of past presidencies cannot be ignored. Presidents and their public relations staffs "are sensitive to the rhetorical precedents they have inherited. By the time a leader reaches the oval office he has usually spent the better part of an adult lifetime soaking up its unwritten rules and potent traditions. Most presidents come to power as well-versed students of the institutional presidency."[24]

[22]   James Barber recognizes the importance and impact of presidential rhetoric upon their administration. In his classic, *The Presidential Character,* Barber searches for patterns in behavior of past presidents and, based upon these patterns, classifies presidents into "character types."[25] He believes there are three major influences upon a person that will shape the presidential performance: style, world view, and character. For our purposes the variable "style" is especially relevant. He defines it as "the president's habitual way of performing his three political roles: rhetoric, personal relations, and homework."[26] This means communication—public, small group, and face-to-face—to write, think, record, and articulate thoughts.

23   Although it is clear that presidential speechmaking has increased drastically, the question remains, how does it differ significantly from the speechmaking of other public figures? Hart, in his impressive work entitled *Verbal Style and the Presidency,* provides insight into the question.[27] In comparison to corporate leaders, religious leaders, political candidates, and social activists, presidents mention themselves and their actions with great frequency. In addition, presidential speechmaking tends to be more optimistic, practical, "real," and less complex than addresses by other leaders. "Humanity, practicality, and caution are the special sound of presidential discourse."[28]

24   To talk of the "rhetorical presidency" is to recognize more than the increase of and impact of presidential discourse. It is to identify a way of viewing and analyzing the office.[29] The institution of the American presidency is greater than any individual. The office greatly influences the officeholder, who must confront already established expectations of presidential performance and behavior. The set of expected presidential roles results from the interaction of the office with the public. The role sets are created, sustained, and permeated through interaction comprised of campaigns, socialization, history, and myth. There is a clear, rather systematic process of transformation from candidate to president where the candidate must confront the "political self" and the public definition of the presidential role. Thus, as a result of interacting with the public, historical expectations, and individual views of the office, the person "becomes" president. The office of the presidency, then, dictates the nature and relationship of the president with the public. Rhetoric, broadly defined, is the means of confirming or denying the public's expectations of acceptable role behavior.

25   The presidency is simply a rhetorical institution. For the public, the office is comprised of a "string of public conversations" rather than a "series of private decisions." Presidents, although they have names, are corporate models of historical images and personae created in the public's collective consciousness. Their messages are persuasive in nature and are carefully constructed for a purpose. Thus, how a policy is defined, articulated, and sold may be more important than the policy itself. For presidential rhetoric constitutes social action, provides a context for collective action, and contributes to the oral history and definition of the nation.

26   Recognition of the rhetorical presidency is also recognition of potential abuses and concerns. Presidential rhetoric may emphasize style over substance with the belief that "words presented in stylistic finesse can solve real, difficult, even paradoxical problems."[30] There is the danger that symbols and slogans may replace policy discussions. Presidential rhetoric, although increasing, is becoming more one-way communication than two-way interaction. Thus, increased quantity of addresses in no way insures quality of interaction. Finally, too much time spent speaking, Hart observes, leaves too little time for presidential thinking in private to insure "good" policies and decisions. Speechmaking is both an art and a science, a tool for both good and evil uses.

Notes

1. Frank Stanton, "A CBS View," in *The Great Debates,* ed. Sidney Krans (Bloomington, IN: Indiana University Press, 1962), p. 66.
2. Saul Ben Zeev and Irving White, "Effects and Implications," in *The Great Debates,* ed. Sidney Kraus (Bloomington, IN: Indiana University Press, 1962), p. 334.
3. As quoted in James Ceaser et al., "The Rise of the Rhetorical Presidency," in *Essays in Presidential Rhetoric,* ed. Theodore Windt (Dubuque, IA: Kendall/Hunt, 1983), p. 3.
4. "Carter Seeking Oratory to Move an Entire Nation," *Washington Post,* July 14, 1979, pp. 15–16.
5. Aristotle, *The Politics of Aristotle,* trans. Ernest Barker (New York: Oxford University Press, 1970), p. 5.
6. Ibid., p. 6.
7. Roderick Hart, Gustav Friedrich, and William Brooks, *Public Communication* (New York: Harper & Row, 1975), p. 12.
8. Karlyn Kohrs Campbell, *The Rhetorical Act* (Belmont, CA: Wadsworth, 1982), pp. 8–14.
9. Doris Graber, "Political Language," in *Handbook of Political Communication,* ed. Dan Nimmo and Keith Sanders (Beverly Hills, CA: Sage Publications, 1981), p. 195.
10. Dan Nimmo, *Political Communication and Public Opinion in America* (Santa Monica, CA: Goodyear Publishing, 1978), p. 7.
11. The strongest statement of this notion is provided by Benjamin Lee Whorf. For him, "If a man thinks in one language, he thinks one way; in another language, another way." The structure of language "is itself the shaper of ideas, the program and guide for the individual's mental activity, for his analysis of impressions, for his synthesis of his mental stock in trade." See John Carroll, ed., *Language, Thought, and Reality: Selected Writings of Benjamin Whorf* (New York: John Wiley & Sons, 1956).
12. Murray Edelman, *Politics as Symbolic Action* (Chicago: Markham Publishing, 1971), p. 83.
13. Graber, "Political Language," p. 196.
14. Ibid., pp. 195–224.
15. George C. Edwards, *The Public Presidency* (New York: St. Martin's Press, 1983), p. 1.
16. George C. Edwards, *Presidential Influence in Congress* (San Francisco, CA: W.H. Freeman, 1980), pp. 86–100.
17. Theodore Windt, *Presidential Rhetoric (1961–1980)* (Dubuque, IA: Kendall/Hunt, 1980), p. 2.
18. Ceasar et al., "The Rise of the Rhetorical Presidency," p. 17.
19. Roderick Hart, *Verbal Style and the Presidency* (Orlando, FL: Academic Press, 1984), p. 2.
20. Ibid., p. 8.
21. Ceaser et al., "The Rise of the Rhetorical Presidency," p. 14.
22. Ibid., p. 8.
23. Hart, *Verbal Style and the Presidency,* p. 2.
24. Gary Woodward, "The Presidency: Focusing on the Role of Rhetorical Antecedents" (Paper presented at the Annual Convention of the Eastern Communication Association, Providence, Rhode Island, May 2, 1985), 1–2.
25. See James David Barber, *The Presidential Character,* 2nd ed. (Englewood Cliffs, NJ: Prentice-Hall, 1977).

26. Ibid., p. 7.
27. See Hart, *Verbal Style and the Presidency,* especially pp. 32–42.
28. Ibid., p. 41.
29. See Robert E. Denton, Jr., *The Symbolic Dimensions of the American Presidency* (Prospect Heights, IL: Waveland Press, 1982); Hart, *Verbal Style and the Presidency,* especially pp. 5–7; Theodore Windt, *Essays in Presidential Rhetoric;* and Robert E. Denton, Jr. and Gary Woodward, *Political Communication in America* (New York: Praeger, 1985).
30. Hart, *Verbal Style and the Presidency,* p. 231.

THINKING CRITICALLY

1. What, according to Denton and Hahn, makes presidential communication particularly significant and unique? What separates it from the speech of the ordinary citizen, and why?

2. Denton and Hahn note "It was recognized over 2000 years ago that politics and communication go hand in hand because they are essential parts of human nature." What do they mean? Explore the implications of this statement in your own words.

3. In what ways does the public speech of the president guide national and social values? Explain.

4. What are the general rhetorical purposes of presidential communication? Does the fact that the president's language is so publicly owned preclude the person holding office from ever having a personal or a private voice? Explain.

5. What are the five major functions of political language as outlined by Doris Graber? Explain.

6. What does George Edwards mean by the statement, "the greatest source of influence of the president is public approval"? Do you agree? Explain.

7. In your opinion, what is more critical for effective presidential communication: style or substance? Explain.

WRITING ASSIGNMENTS

1. In paragraph 8, Doris Graber states, "Politics is largely a word game." What makes language political? How is it a "word game"? Expand on these ideas based on information provided in this essay as well as from your own knowledge of politics and government.

2. Is it important that the president be a good speaker? In an essay, define the language skills necessary to be an effective leader, and explain why you think these elements are important. Use examples to support your discussion.

3. Write an essay exploring how presidential communication has changed over the last 100 years. What influence has the media, including television and radio, had on the president's use of language? Do you think the Internet will influence the role of language and the presidency? Explain.

Dubya and Me: We've Got No Idea
Ian Frazier

How important is it to the American people that their president be a good public speaker? Are we forgiving of verbal blunders and linguistic stumbles if we really like the candidate? Can we better relate to a more "human" candidate who mispronounces words and mixes his metaphors? In the next essay, Ian Frazier describes his discomfort listening and watching George W. Bush during the 2000 presidential campaign, perhaps because the president wasn't that different from millions of other American men who "fake it" as they go along. As Frazier explains, "If I don't know what I am doing, and W. Bush doesn't know what he's doing, what does that say for the human species as a whole?"

Ian Frazier is a popular essayist for *The New Yorker*. A celebrated humorist and nonfiction writer, he has published many collections of essays, including the best-selling *Great Plains* (1989), *Coyote v. Acme* (1996), *The Fish's Eye* (2001), and *Family* (2002). This essay first appeared in the May/June 2001 issue of *Mother Jones* magazine.

1 Whenever George W. Bush opened his mouth in public during his presidential campaign, a thrill ran through observers all across the country and beyond. The thrill—not pleasant, but exciting nonetheless—was the thrill that comes over us in the presence of a person who does not know what he is doing. Electronically present to more or less the whole world, Bush kept everybody in a state of fearful uncertainty and expectation. Sometimes the feeling was so strong that it began to grow even before he spoke. Before the presidential debates, people were wondering if he would make it through without some fatal blunder. At every slight fumble or mispronunciation, we held the arms of our chairs: Would this be the one that finally revealed how utterly at sea the man was? Watching a person fake it is so nerve-wracking that I believe whenever he got through these ordeals halfway okay, even his enemies were secretly relieved.

2 In former times, that particular thrill was often aroused by his father's vice president, Dan Quayle. Looking into Quayle's eyes on the TV screen when he had no idea of the answer to a question he'd just been asked—what a spine-tingling experience that was! To glimpse the cluelessness in those eyes! For an instant we were up there with him, in the common nightmare: The audience looks at us in anticipation, but we have lost our speech, forgotten our lines, and improvidently dressed in only our underwear. The Dan Quayle deer-in-headlights clueless stare proved a bit too scary to be exciting, finally. Part of what George W. Bush offered was the old Dan Quayle *frisson,* but in a less concentrated, commercially acceptable form.

3 I am a few years younger, but I belong to the same generation as W. Bush and Quayle. I know how many classes we skipped, how much we partied, how much TV we watched. (What great work, I wonder, do those many hours of "Baretta" and "Hee Haw" prepare you for?) I have a generational sense of the vacancy in their

stare, because I share it. I myself don't know what I am doing a good forty percent of the time. I am now the kind of white-haired, thick-waisted, superficially presentable male who people give huge responsibility to and ask directions of on the street. And often, I'm just making it up. The situation is one I've become quite familiar with—I'm asked a question, no answer presents itself in my brain, and I begin to answer anyway. My mouth moves and words come out, propelled perhaps by pure syntax or by the momentum of the language, while I watch from a distance, as curious as anybody to hear what I'm going to say. And somehow words do emerge, and my listeners accept them as an answer representing thought and knowledge; and I alone, apparently, know that no thought or knowledge was involved.

4   I go into a fancy wine store and buy a good bottle of wine. I stop by the bank and listen to a lady there tell about interest points on my home loan. I see the guy who does my taxes and I have a conversation about the new tax laws. I run into a health-conscious friend who discusses some kind of fatty acid and what it could do for me. I go home and answer a homework question from my son having to do with the surface tension of water. I sit down to dinner and talk to my wife about the purchase of some bathroom tile. At no point during any of these encounters do I have more than the vaguest idea of what I am talking about. Nor do I understand in any clear way what is being said to me; instead I listen to the general sound of the sentences, hoping no one has noticed that I am actually lying down someplace in the back of my head, leafing through an old copy of a magazine. And if, God forbid, I actually have to do something—make a decision, provide real information—I close my eyes and just guess.

5   I won't describe the messes this gets me into. With my almost-teenage daughter, I have agreed to complicated plans that later caused me to curse and fume when I discovered what they actually were. But these are personal disasters, probably of no danger to the public at large. Anybody who watches TV or movies knows that Dad will always be an idiot; but what if Dad is the president? Cluelessness multiplied by power is what puts the secret message of dizzying terror in W. Bush's eyes. (Recently, of course, he has kept to his script and hasn't shown the clueless stare; to see him hiding it only scares me more.)

6   And if I don't know what I'm doing and W. Bush doesn't know what *he's* doing, what does that say for the human species as a whole? Clearly, a lot of human history must have been the result of major world figures drawing a total blank at key moments and simply blurting out the first thing that came to mind. Big events as well as small have turned on a neurological roll of the dice. Thomas Jefferson, for example, seems to have improvised a lot more than the textbooks would have us believe. A friend of mine who teaches a college course on Jefferson has examined his famous "life, liberty, and the pursuit of happiness" statement from the Declaration of Independence, and she concludes that he planned the "life, liberty" part beforehand, but "the pursuit of happiness" part he merely added on the spot to round out the phrase, a flourish at the end. Jefferson himself, she believes, had no intention of mentioning "the pursuit of happiness" until he saw the words flowing from his pen. It may be that for 225 years now we've been trying to live up to a founding

concept of our country that was thrown in at the last minute because it sounded nice and the author couldn't think what else to say. That it happened to be a phrase of poetry and genius was one of the best breaks America ever had.

7   People who don't know what they're doing often get by on their supposed freshness and spontaneity. Indeed, the idea of the New, so central to our lives, sets us up for this trick all the time. To devotees of the New, incompetence and unpreparedness are actually good; what we want is a mind uncluttered by previous experience. As a writer, I sometimes get calls from magazine editors who ask me to write articles on subjects about which I am completely uninformed. When I admit my ignorance, the editors always say that's exactly what they're looking for, because someone who understands the subject can't see it with fresh eyes, and it's actually far better that I know nothing, and so on. Usually I don't take these assignments, but once in a while I do. I've noticed that when I submit the article, the editors never say, "Wow! I loved it! You had no idea what you were talking about at all!"

8   When people believe they're creating the New, they even make a virtue of not knowing what they're doing. And now that everything is new all the time, the most thorough kinds of ignorance are accepted as routine. Not long ago I came across a hint of how this bizarre system first began. It's in the Bible, in the Book of Matthew, just a few pages into the New Testament. Jesus is telling the disciples how they should travel about the land preaching, and he says they should not carry money or supplies or extra clothes, because all will be provided for them as they go; and if they are brought before officials to explain themselves, he says, "Take no thought how or what ye shall speak: for it shall be given you in that same hour what ye shall speak. For it is not ye that speak, but the Spirit of your Father."

9   I can sympathize with someone trying to start a new religion and not wanting to get tangled up in the details. You want your disciples to go out there and preach, instead of wasting time on travel plans. But telling them not to bother making some notes beforehand about what they're going to say . . . that's irresponsible, it seems to me. Imagine the millions of hours of dreadful sermons that particular advice has spawned!

10   Once on an airplane I happened to sit in front of two preachers—Southern evangelicals, on their way to seek souls in Russia—and I heard one say to the other, "I didn't have a sermon prepared, so I just stood up there and started ramble-preaching." Ramble-preaching—they even have a term for it! I have sat through many hours of ramble-preaching, in church and not, and it's an ordeal I cannot bear. The moment I realize the minister is just making it up as he goes along is the moment I look for the door. I feel the same about onstage improvisation of any kind. Please, performers, let's not just see what pops into your head. Give me a wooden, pre-scripted speaker any day.

11   So, naturally, in the presidential race I was for Gore. I loved how stiff and prepped and pat he was. Even the makeup I didn't mind. I found the whole Gore approach wonderfully un-spontaneous and restful. As I so often do, when he spoke

I listened to the sound rather than the meaning while drifting in a pleasant reverie. Then suddenly on the TV screen W. Bush would appear. Somehow I could never avoid looking into those frightened, terrifying eyes. It was as if there were swirly spirals going into them like in a science fiction movie, causing a whirlpool effect into which I feared I'd fall. In his cornered-animal gaze darting back and forth I saw mirrored my own deep unpreparedness for so many of the tasks I'm faced with in life. My Gore reverie evaporated as I unwillingly looked and looked again. With dumb luck, and completely unintentionally, Bush's old-guy Republican handlers had created a compelling piece of reality TV simply by the confusion in their candidate's eyes.

12   W. Bush's visible confusion and lostness during his campaign, oddly enough, may help explain why he did as well in the election as he did. Lost, he may have seemed more real, more live; we watch the tightrope walker more closely when it appears he is about to fall. Bill Clinton, a political prodigy, held our attention by staying one step ahead with hard-to-categorize deeds we kept having to judge and argue about. W. Bush is a more average person, as unremarkable as the generation to which he belongs. It's a generation that doesn't have a lot to show for itself; so far, it hasn't started a new country, ended slavery, won a world war. Maybe we will still accomplish something great. Maybe the best we can hope for is just not to do too much wrong.

THINKING CRITICALLY

1. Why does Frazier find watching George W. Bush stressful? Explain.

2. What is Frazier's tone in this essay? Concerned? Sarcastic? Troubled? Sympathetic? How does his tone connect to his audience and his topic?

3. What do you think Frazier means when he says that Bush is more "commercially acceptable" than Dan Quayle?

4. Have you ever faced a situation where you were making a speech or presenting in a public forum and you weren't quite sure what to say? How did you feel and how did you handle the situation? Explain.

5. In paragraph 5, Frazier wonders, "what if Dad was the president?" Do we expect the president to be different from the rest of us? What do we expect from his language? Explain.

6. What is the "New" Frazier discusses in paragraphs 7 and 8? How does the "New" connect to what we learn, know, and say?

7. In paragraph 8, Frazier refers to a story in the Book of Matthew. How does this citation connect to his essay's theme? Explain.

8. Based on this essay, how do you think Frazier feels about George W. Bush? What does his last paragraph reveal about his feelings? What about his title? Explain.

WRITING ASSIGNMENTS

1. Think about how you answer questions in every day conversation. Do you "wing it," not really sure of what is going to come out of your mouth, or do you consider carefully what you are going to say before you say it? Discuss in a short essay, similar to Frazier's article, the relationship between what you say and how people perceive you.

2. Locate some transcripts or audiotapes of speeches or debates given by George W. Bush before he became president and some following his assumption of office (try <www.whitehouse.gov>). Compare his language before and after he became president. Write an analysis of your research drawing your own conclusions on the linguistic style of the president.

3. In paragraph 6, Frazier conjectures that "Clearly, a lot of human history must have been the result of major world figures drawing a total blank at key moments and simply blurting out the first thing that came to mind." Write an essay exploring this idea. In addition to the Jefferson example he cites, can you think of other historical or political situations that may have hinged on verbal blunders?

The Making of the Speech
D. T. Max

In the previous essay, Ian Frazier discussed the nuances of George W. Bush's language when spontaneously responding to questions while running for office. In the next article, D.T. Max describes the process of preparing a presidential speech, in this case, the president's formal oration before Congress addressing the attacks of September 11. As you read the details of how a speech is prepared for the president, consider the many stages of writing; the audience; sources of information; and details such as setting, tone, and style, that factor into the finished product.

D. T. Max is a writer and a contributing editor of the *Paris Review.* Max's articles have appeared in many journals and newspapers, including *The LA Times Sunday Book Review, Salon* magazine, the *Boston Phoenix,* and the *New York Times.* Max is a frequent contributor to the *New York Times Magazine,* in which this article first appeared in October 2001.

1 The president could not find the right words. Soon after the World Trade Center and the Pentagon were attacked on Sept. 11, he tried to articulate his response. In one week he gave more than a dozen speeches and remarks to comfort, rally and then—when he'd rallied too much—calm the country. To some, his language seemed undisciplined. He called the terrorists "folks" and referred to the coming battle as a "crusade." He called for "revenge," called Osama bin Laden the "prime suspect" and asked for him "dead or alive." He said "make no mistake" at least

eight times in public remarks. When Bush didn't seem lost, he often seemed scared. When he didn't seem scared, he often seemed angry. None of this soothed the public. "It was beginning to look like 'Bring Me the Head of Osama bin Laden,' starring Ronald Colman," one White House official remembered.

2   In a time of national crisis, words are key to the presidency. Too many and people tune out; too few and they think he is hiding. The president knew he had not yet said the right things. He returned from Camp David the weekend after the attacks with an intense desire to make a major speech. His aides agreed. The president needed to reassure Americans while conveying a message of resolve to the world. Shaping a successful speech wouldn't be easy. Karen P. Hughes, the counselor to the president, helped write the straightforward statement the president gave on the night of the attack. The speech, delivered from the Oval Office, was poorly received; it felt too slight, too brief for the great events. Three days later, the president's speechwriting team, led by Michael Gerson, came up with an eloquent meditation on grief and resolution, which the president read at the National Cathedral. "We are in the middle hour of our grief," it began. But the beautiful speech sounded borrowed coming from Bush's mouth. The tone was too literary. The president's next speech had to be grand—but it also had to sound more like him.

3   The White House also had to decide where to give it. Among the choices the president and his advisers had was an address to Congress, which had invited him to speak before a joint session. There is no greater backdrop for a president. But some advisers were reluctant. The president couldn't march up Pennsylvania Avenue without something new to say. And according to his advisers, Bush wasn't sure yet what the administration's response to the attack would be. Some advisers suggested a second Oval Office speech, which would be more intimate and controlled than an address to Congress. Others suggested speaking at a war college. He would look strong there.

4   Karl Rove, the president's chief political adviser, felt strongly that the president did better with a big audience. Applause revved him up. Congress, he thought, was ideal: it would build a sense of national unity. That was important. The speech was a huge political opportunity for Bush. War had given the president a second chance to define himself, an accidental shot at rebirth. Bush's first eight months had been middling. To many, he seemed a little slight for the job. His tax cut had gone through, but the education initiative, the defense transformation and the faith-based initiative were not moving forward well. Americans had still not embraced him as a leader. A strong speech could revive Bush's presidency.

5   The president decided to speak to Congress. But he wasn't sure yet what to say. The main focus of the speech was tricky to define. "He had to speak to multiple audiences," his national security adviser, Condoleezza Rice, later told me. "He was speaking to the American people, foreign leaders, to the Congress and to the Taliban."

6   Karen Hughes met Bush at the White House residence Sunday afternoon to discuss what ground the speech might cover. She jotted down notes: Who are they? Why they hate us? What victory means? How will it be won? On Monday morning, Bush talked to Hughes again. According to Hughes, he told her how to deal with the fact that military action might come anytime. "If we've done something, discuss

what we have done," he told Hughes. "If not, tell people to get ready." He told her he wanted a draft quickly. Hughes called Michael Gerson and told him that he had until 7 P.M. to come up with something.

7   Gerson does not write alone. He has five other writers, two of whom he works closely with, Matt Scully and John McConnell. Scully is wiry and ironic, like a comedy writer. McConnell is more earnest. They help bring Gerson down to earth. Gerson, 37, is an owlish man who fills yellow pads with doodles when you ask him a question. He says he believes that social justice must be central in Republican thought. "The great stories of our time," he told me, "are moral stories and moral commitments: the civil rights movement, the War on Poverty." He and the president get along well. The president calls Gerson "the scribe." They share an intensely felt Christianity.

8   Gerson had written speeches with Scully and McConnell during the campaign. They worked well together. Since then, Gerson has moved up a notch: he now has an office in the basement of the West Wing. The office is prestigious but not great for writing. It is claustrophobic and illuminated by artificial light. McConnell and Scully were in the Old Executive Office Building. If the West Wing, with its plush carpeting and secretaries in heels, resembles a Sun Belt office suite, the O.E.O.B. is by comparison a funky hotel. Every office, no matter how small, had its own couch, yet no office had a matching set of chairs. It was a good place to brainstorm.

9   So Gerson crossed West Executive Avenue to see McConnell and Scully. The three writers sat around the computer in McConnell's office, Gerson in one of the gray suits he wears, bouncing nervously, Scully's feet up on the couch. They began to write, adopting the magisterial tone of presidential speechwriting. These were great events. They deserved great sentiments, a lofty style that Don Baer, a communications director in the Clinton administration, called "reaching for the marble." The three wrote as a team, trying out sentences on each other: "Tonight we are a country awakened to danger. . . ." They went quickly. They knew there would be time to change things and plenty of hands to do it. They assumed that one of the widows of the heroes of United Airlines Flight 93 would be there, so they put in Lyzbeth Glick, the widow of Jeremy Glick, one of the men who apparently fought with the hijackers. (In fact it would be Lisa Beamer, whose husband, Todd, had also been on the plane.) They knew little for certain, and knowing little increased their natural tendency to sound like Churchill, whose writing they all liked. Gerson tried out: "In the long term, terrorism is not answered by higher walls and deeper bunkers." The team kept going: "Whether we bring our enemies to justice or bring justice to our enemies, justice will be done." The computer screen filled with rolling triads. "This is the world's fight; this is civilization's fight; this is the fight of all who believe in progress and pluralism, tolerance and freedom." Words tumbled out.

10   The patriotic riffs were falling in place. But what, and how much, could they tell the country about the administration's plans for bin Laden and Afghanistan? They received some help from John Gibson, another speechwriter. Gibson writes foreign-policy speeches for the president and the National Security Council and

regularly attends meetings with Condoleezza Rice, the national security adviser, and Stephen Hadley, her deputy. Gibson has the odd job of writing public words about the government's most private decisions. He has top-secret security clearance; his hard drive is stored in a safe.

11   Gibson made contact with Richard A. Clarke, the counterterrorism director for the N.S.C. Clarke is a white-haired, stocky man who has been in the job for nearly a decade. He speaks very loudly. "Even his e-mails are blustery," one White House employee told me. Whatever the meetings were, he was still going to them. Gibson e-mailed Clarke questions that unintentionally echoed Hughes's original discussion with Bush: Who is our enemy? What do they want?

12   The e-mailed answer came in a bulleted memo. Who is our enemy? "Al Qaeda." What do they want? "That all Christians and Jews must be driven out of a vast area of the world," and "that existing governments in Islamic countries like Egypt and Saudi Arabia should be toppled. They have issued phony religious rulings calling for the deaths of all Americans, including women and children." Gibson liked the tone and authority of the response. He handed over an edited version to Gerson.

13   Using Gibson's edit, Gerson, Scully and McConnell began on the Taliban. Scully started: "We're not deceived by their pretenses to piety." Gerson wrote: "They're the heirs of all the murderous ideologies of the 20th century. By sacrificing human life to serve their radical visions, by abandoning every value except the will to power, they follow in the path of Fascism and Nazism and imperial Communism." Scully added, "And they will follow that path all the way to where it ends." They paused. Where would it end? They didn't know. But there were plenty of ready-made phrases around. McConnell threw out five or six, like crumbs from his pocket. They liked the idea of predicting the end of the Taliban's reign of terror. "You know, history's unmarked grave," McConnell said. The group bounced the phrase around until McConnell came up with: "It will end in discarded lies." Gerson liked that, too. So the line read, "history's unmarked grave of discarded lies."

14   But if the Taliban were going to wind up on the ash heap of history, then someone had to suggest how this would be accomplished. Would we attack tomorrow? Would we mount a land invasion of Afghanistan? Would we take on Iraq as well? No one knew. Policy and prose work their way on separate tracks at the White House, only meeting at higher levels. Speechwriters sometimes sit around with finished speeches, waiting for the policy person to call and let them know what the whole thing is for. Not knowing what the president was going to announce, Gerson and his team couldn't come up with the right tone for an ending. But they had done what they could, written a joint-session speech in a day. They sent it off to Hughes.

15   Under Secretary of State Colin Powell's guidance, the State Department drafted the language of the goals. Condoleezza Rice walked them into the Oval Office. There, Bush was saying that he liked the speech but the ending wasn't right; the speechwriters and Hughes scribbled notes as he spoke. Bush was enormously excited, Hughes recalled. The speech shouldn't end reflectively, he said. It should end with him leading. Rice then read aloud the demands Powell sent over: deliver the

leaders of Al Qaeda to the United States; release detained foreign nationals and protect those in Afghanistan; close the terrorist camps. Give the United States full inspection access. Bush liked the points. Calling on the Taliban to give up bin Laden in front of Congress would be a moment of some power. He told the speechwriters to translate them from bureaucratese. Rice left her notes with the speechwriters.

16   The speechwriters went back to work. They laid more marble: "This is not, however, just America's fight. And what is at stake is not just America's freedom. This is the world's fight. This is civilization's fight."

17   Hughes took notes and put them into her copy of the speech. She was thinking domestically: these were wrongs Americans could understand. Hughes also amplified language that Gerson's team had written expressing compassion for the Afghan people. What had helped Bush become president were the overtures of compassion in his conservatism. In the days after the attack, he'd been so bellicose that his father called to tell him to tone it down. It was time to bring back the candidate.

18   Gerson, Scully, McConnell and Hughes sat down in Hughes's office on Wednesday at 11 A.M. They grouped around Hughes's computer. In front of her was a little plaque quoting Churchill: "I was not the lion, but it fell to me to give the lion's roar." New material kept coming in. Vice President Dick Cheney sent up a short text with McConnell defining the new cabinet position, director of homeland security. Hughes felt that the speech didn't make the point clearly enough about America's respect for Muslim Americans. The president's rush visit to a mosque had gotten a good response on Monday; it was important to highlight that theme. Hughes changed the phrase "Tonight I also have a message for Muslims in America" to "I also want to speak tonight directly to Muslims throughout the world. We respect your faith." She helped write the sentence "The United States respects the people of Afghanistan." Hughes was taking the speech out of marble and making it concrete. She added "I ask you to live your lives and hug your children." Rove stopped by; as a result of his input, the speechwriters added the line "I know many citizens have fears tonight, and I ask you to be calm and resolute." Rice's deputy, Stephen Hadley, who had to worry about more terrorism, suggested reminding people that there might be more terrorism to come. "Even in the face of a continuing threat" was added to the sentence.

19   All week, the president worked on the speech at night in the residence. He likes his speeches to make a point and for the point to be clear. He hates redundancies. He took a course in American oratory at Yale and remembers how a speech divides into an introduction, main body, peroration. (He once annotated a speech with phrases like "tugs at heartstrings" and "emotional call to arms.") Bush writes his notes with a black Sharpie pen. His edits tend to simplify. He is a parer. "Bush favors active verbs and short sentences," Rove said.

20   The president had strong feelings about the speech's ending. Although they had not yet found a place for it, the writers had suggested including a quote from Franklin Delano Roosevelt in the speech's conclusion: "We defend and we build a way of life, not for America alone, but for all mankind." The president didn't want to quote anyone else. He'd said this to them in emphatic terms at a meeting the day

before, explaining that he saw this as a chance to lead. "I was scribbling notes as fast as I could," Gerson said.

21   The team worked on an ending that would be all Bush. They revisited the phrase "freedom and fear are at war" and gave it a providential spin: "We know that God is not neutral between them." Without hitting it too hard, a religious note would be sounded.

22   At 1 P.M., Gerson's team met with Bush and Hughes. They pulled up their chairs around the desk in the Oval Office. "You all have smiles on your faces; that's good," Bush said. Then, wearing his glasses, he began reading the speech aloud, stopping only for a few edits. He read the new ending aloud. "It is my hope that in the months and years ahead, life will return almost to normal," it said. "Even grief recedes with time and grace." But these comforting words were not all. "I will not forget the wound to our country and those who inflicted it," the speech went on. "I will not yield. I will not rest. I will not relent in waging this struggle for freedom and security for the American people." It echoed William Lloyd Garrison ("And I will be heard!"), but it was his own. Here was his peroration, and it tugged on your heartstrings and called you to arms. The final "freedom and fear" image worked, too. The president said: "Great speech, team. Let's call the Congress." He would give the speech the next night, on Thursday the 20th.

23   The president had to rehearse. It was the first thing he'd thought of after deciding to do the speech. The more time he practices, the better his speeches come off. The downward furl of his mouth relaxes. His tendency to end every phrase with an upward cadence diminishes. The first teleprompter rehearsal was at 6:30 Wednesday night. The president came out in his blue track suit with his baseball cap on. His dog, Spot, ran around the room, nuzzling the writers as they sat listening. The president weighed the sounds in his mouth. He came to lines about the administration's domestic legislative agenda, lines that had been slowly piling up—the energy plan, the faith-based initiative, the patients' bill of rights. "This isn't the time," he said and cut them. Hughes agreed. This was the time for Bush to assert his credentials on foreign policy and not retreat into the domestic sphere.

24   Thursday morning, the day of the speech, Bush rehearsed again. He didn't like the clunky paragraph that contained the list of our allies: the Organization of American States and the European Union, among others. It was too much of a mouthful. They would no longer hear their names spoken. State lost that round.

25   The president took a nap at 4:30, was awakened by an aide and rehearsed one more time. At 5:15 Hughes told Gerson the name of the new director of homeland security. It was Bush's old friend, the governor of Pennsylvania, Tom Ridge. The news had been held back so it wouldn't leak. Tony Blair, the British prime minister, was late arriving for dinner, and the president was offered a chance to rehearse again but said he was ready. The communications office prepared a list of sound bites and distributed them to the press: "The enemy of America is not our many Muslim friends." "Be ready." "Freedom and fear are at war."

26   The president got into his motorcade and went to the Capitol. The vice president stayed behind so they would not be in the Capitol together. It was an unprece-

dented security move. It meant that every time the camera showed Bush, you would think about the meaning of Cheney's absence. You would remember the crisis. Bush walked into the Capitol, a president in wartime. He wore a pale blue tie. He began: "Mr. Speaker, Mr. President pro tempore, members of Congress and fellow Americans." He was interrupted for applause 31 times.

27   A week after the speech, the flag at the White House was back at full mast, waving in the wind. Karen Hughes wore a metal American flag on her lapel, upward streaming too. Was the speech a success? For the president, yes. "He told me he felt very comfortable," Hughes said. "I told him he was phenomenal." Bush had wanted to steady the boat, and he had done it. He had shown leadership. The Congress felt included. "The president's speech was exactly what the nation needed—a message of determination and hope, strength and compassion," Ted Kennedy said. For the writers, there was catharsis: Gerson felt that by working on the speech, he had become connected to "the men digging with shovels in New York." Pundits wrote that the president had said just the right thing in a time of crisis. The Uzbeks were pleased. The Syrians were not enraged. Only the Canadians, of all people, were piqued: their mention, as part of O.A.S., had been cut so the speech wouldn't sag. Even professional speechwriters, tough critics of one another, were impressed. "It was a good, strong speech," said Ted Sorensen, who wrote speeches for John F. Kennedy. "I'm not sure 'freedom versus fear' means much. But it had a nice ring to it, and you can be sure we're on the side of freedom."

28   The very act of the speech suggested that civilized life would continue. The president had just sat around a big war map at Camp David—but instead of first doing something violent, he turned to words. Some of those words were bland. Many were vague. Other than the demands to the Taliban, there was little policy in it. "This was a strategic speech, not tactical," admitted a senior White House official.

29   This wasn't a State of the Union address. It wasn't a moment to look ahead. Bad news could wait. New presidents are terrified of looking indecisive, but this one realized it would be worse to be rash. Who are they? Where are they? How can we strike back? The coming challenge is enormous. By delivering a speech that emphasized reason over wrath, Bush bought himself some time until someone could draw a real map for the first war of the 21st century.

THINKING CRITICALLY

1. In his introduction, Max identifies several unscripted words and phrases Bush used in response to September 11. What was objectionable about these words? Explain.

2. What does Max mean when he says "words are the key to the presidency"? Do you agree? Why or why not?

3. In your opinion, is it expected and acceptable that presidents have speech writing teams? Is there a fine line between being scripted and being assisted? What is your position on presidential speech writing?

4. Describe in brief the multifaceted aspects of creating a presidential speech.

5. What is Karen P. Hughes's role in creating the presidential "voice"? How does the president's voice differ from what his speech writers create? Explain.

6. What is the importance of style in the creation and delivery of a presidential speech? What is the president's style? How does setting factor into the delivery and ultimate reception of his speech? Explain.

7. What is "bureaucratese"? Why does Bush object to it?

8. After reading this description of the etymology of a presidential speech, do you feel more or less respect for the president? Explain your point of view.

WRITING ASSIGNMENTS

1. Max explains that this speech is the one that "changed a presidency." Read about issues connected to the speech at <www.whitehouse.gov/news/releases/2001/09/20010920-8.html>. Read the entire speech that follows, and analyze its language, style, tone, and construction. What makes this particular speech so significant? What factors before and after its delivery contribute to its success in changing the public's perception of George W. Bush? Explain.

2. Write an essay exploring the connection between the president, his language, and public perception of his leadership. Use examples from at least three different presidents from the twentieth century as you formulate your essay.

Address to a Joint Session of Congress and the American People
George W. Bush

On September 20, 2001, President George W. Bush made this address to a joint session of Congress. The etymology of the speech, described in the preceding essay, was a combined effort of writers, advisors, the Presidential Cabinet, and the president himself. For the President, it was more than just a speech—it was a critical opportunity to prove to the American people that he was the leader they needed to guide them through the most shocking terrorist attack in the nation's history. As you read the speech, consider the language, tone, and style employed by the president. Consider also who the president acknowledges, and why. Finally, think about why critics call this particular speech, one that "changed a presidency."

1 THE PRESIDENT: Mr. Speaker, Mr. President Pro Tempore, members of Congress, and fellow Americans:

2 In the normal course of events, Presidents come to this chamber to report on the state of the Union. Tonight, no such report is needed. It has already been delivered by the American people.

3   We have seen it in the courage of passengers, who rushed terrorists to save others on the ground—passengers like an exceptional man named Todd Beamer. And would you please help me to welcome his wife, Lisa Beamer, here tonight. (Applause.)

4   We have seen the state of our Union in the endurance of rescuers, working past exhaustion. We have seen the unfurling of flags, the lighting of candles, the giving of blood, the saying of prayers—in English, Hebrew, and Arabic. We have seen the decency of a loving and giving people who have made the grief of strangers their own.

5   My fellow citizens, for the last nine days, the entire world has seen for itself the state of our Union—and it is strong. (Applause.)

6   Tonight we are a country awakened to danger and called to defend freedom. Our grief has turned to anger, and anger to resolution. Whether we bring our enemies to justice, or bring justice to our enemies, justice will be done. (Applause.)

7   I thank the Congress for its leadership at such an important time. All of America was touched on the evening of the tragedy to see Republicans and Democrats joined together on the steps of this Capitol, singing "God Bless America." And you did more than sing; you acted, by delivering $40 billion to rebuild our communities and meet the needs of our military.

8   Speaker Hastert, Minority Leader Gephardt, Majority Leader Daschle and Senator Lott, I thank you for your friendship, for your leadership and for your service to our country. (Applause.)

9   And on behalf of the American people, I thank the world for its outpouring of support. America will never forget the sounds of our National Anthem playing at Buckingham Palace, on the streets of Paris, and at Berlin's Brandenburg Gate.

10   We will not forget South Korean children gathering to pray outside our embassy in Seoul, or the prayers of sympathy offered at a mosque in Cairo. We will not forget moments of silence and days of mourning in Australia and Africa and Latin America.

11   Nor will we forget the citizens of 80 other nations who died with our own: dozens of Pakistanis; more than 130 Israelis; more than 250 citizens of India; men and women from El Salvador, Iran, Mexico and Japan; and hundreds of British citizens. America has no truer friend than Great Britain. (Applause.) Once again, we are joined together in a great cause—so honored the British Prime Minister has crossed an ocean to show his unity of purpose with America. Thank you for coming, friend. (Applause.)

12   On September the 11th, enemies of freedom committed an act of war against our country. Americans have known wars—but for the past 136 years, they have been wars on foreign soil, except for one Sunday in 1941. Americans have known the casualties of war—but not at the center of a great city on a peaceful morning. Americans have known surprise attacks—but never before on thousands of civilians. All of this was brought upon us in a single day—and night fell on a different world, a world where freedom itself is under attack.

13   Americans have many questions tonight. Americans are asking: Who attacked our country? The evidence we have gathered all points to a collection of loosely af-

filiated terrorist organizations known as al Qaeda. They are the same murderers indicted for bombing American embassies in Tanzania and Kenya, and responsible for bombing the USS Cole.

14   Al Qaeda is to terror what the mafia is to crime. But its goal is not making money; its goal is remaking the world—and imposing its radical beliefs on people everywhere.

15   The terrorists practice a fringe form of Islamic extremism that has been rejected by Muslim scholars and the vast majority of Muslim clerics—a fringe movement that perverts the peaceful teachings of Islam. The terrorists' directive commands them to kill Christians and Jews, to kill all Americans, and make no distinction among military and civilians, including women and children.

16   This group and its leader—a person named Osama bin Laden—are linked to many other organizations in different countries, including the Egyptian Islamic Jihad and the Islamic Movement of Uzbekistan. There are thousands of these terrorists in more than 60 countries. They are recruited from their own nations and neighborhoods and brought to camps in places like Afghanistan, where they are trained in the tactics of terror. They are sent back to their homes or sent to hide in countries around the world to plot evil and destruction.

17   The leadership of al Qaeda has great influence in Afghanistan and supports the Taliban regime in controlling most of that country. In Afghanistan, we see al Qaeda's vision for the world.

18   Afghanistan's people have been brutalized—many are starving and many have fled. Women are not allowed to attend school. You can be jailed for owning a television. Religion can be practiced only as their leaders dictate. A man can be jailed in Afghanistan if his beard is not long enough.

19   The United States respects the people of Afghanistan—after all, we are currently its largest source of humanitarian aid—but we condemn the Taliban regime. (Applause.) It is not only repressing its own people, it is threatening people everywhere by sponsoring and sheltering and supplying terrorists. By aiding and abetting murder, the Taliban regime is committing murder.

20   And tonight, the United States of America makes the following demands on the Taliban: Deliver to United States authorities all the leaders of al Qaeda who hide in your land. (Applause.) Release all foreign nationals, including American citizens, you have unjustly imprisoned. Protect foreign journalists, diplomats and aid workers in your country. Close immediately and permanently every terrorist training camp in Afghanistan, and hand over every terrorist, and every person in their support structure, to appropriate authorities. (Applause.) Give the United States full access to terrorist training camps, so we can make sure they are no longer operating.

21   These demands are not open to negotiation or discussion. (Applause.) The Taliban must act, and act immediately. They will hand over the terrorists, or they will share in their fate.

22   I also want to speak tonight directly to Muslims throughout the world. We respect your faith. It's practiced freely by many millions of Americans, and by millions more in countries that America counts as friends. Its teachings are good and

peaceful, and those who commit evil in the name of Allah blaspheme the name of Allah. (Applause.) The terrorists are traitors to their own faith, trying, in effect, to hijack Islam itself. The enemy of America is not our many Muslim friends; it is not our many Arab friends. Our enemy is a radical network of terrorists, and every government that supports them. (Applause.)

23   Our war on terror begins with [al] Qaeda, but it does not end there. It will not end until every terrorist group of global reach has been found, stopped and defeated. (Applause.)

24   Americans are asking, why do they hate us? They hate what we see right here in this chamber—a democratically elected government. Their leaders are self-appointed. They hate our freedoms—our freedom of religion, our freedom of speech, our freedom to vote and assemble and disagree with each other.

25   They want to overthrow existing governments in many Muslim countries, such as Egypt, Saudi Arabia, and Jordan. They want to drive Israel out of the Middle East. They want to drive Christians and Jews out of vast regions of Asia and Africa.

26   These terrorists kill not merely to end lives, but to disrupt and end a way of life. With every atrocity, they hope that America grows fearful, retreating from the world and forsaking our friends. They stand against us, because we stand in their way.

27   We are not deceived by their pretenses to piety. We have seen their kind before. They are the heirs of all the murderous ideologies of the 20th century. By sacrificing human life to serve their radical visions—by abandoning every value except the will to power—they follow in the path of fascism, and Nazism, and totalitarianism. And they will follow that path all the way, to where it ends: in history's unmarked grave of discarded lies. (Applause.)

28   Americans are asking: How will we fight and win this war? We will direct every resource at our command—every means of diplomacy, every tool of intelligence, every instrument of law enforcement, every financial influence, and every necessary weapon of war—to the disruption and to the defeat of the global terror network.

29   This war will not be like the war against Iraq a decade ago, with a decisive liberation of territory and a swift conclusion. It will not look like the air war above Kosovo two years ago, where no ground troops were used and not a single American was lost in combat.

30   Our response involves far more than instant retaliation and isolated strikes. Americans should not expect one battle, but a lengthy campaign, unlike any other we have ever seen. It may include dramatic strikes, visible on TV, and covert operations, secret even in success. We will starve terrorists of funding, turn them one against another, drive them from place to place, until there is no refuge or no rest. And we will pursue nations that provide aid or safe haven to terrorism. Every nation, in every region, now has a decision to make. Either you are with us, or you are with the terrorists. (Applause.) From this day forward, any nation that continues to harbor or support terrorism will be regarded by the United States as a hostile regime.

31   Our nation has been put on notice: We are not immune from attack. We will take defensive measures against terrorism to protect Americans. Today, dozens of federal departments and agencies, as well as state and local governments, have responsibilities affecting homeland security. These efforts must be coordinated at the highest level. So tonight I announce the creation of a Cabinet-level position reporting directly to me—the Office of Homeland Security.

32   And tonight I also announce a distinguished American to lead this effort, to strengthen American security: a military veteran, an effective governor, a true patriot, a trusted friend—Pennsylvania's Tom Ridge. (Applause.) He will lead, oversee and coordinate a comprehensive national strategy to safeguard our country against terrorism, and respond to any attacks that may come.

33   These measures are essential. But the only way to defeat terrorism as a threat to our way of life is to stop it, eliminate it, and destroy it where it grows. (Applause.)

34   Many will be involved in this effort, from FBI agents to intelligence operatives to the reservists we have called to active duty. All deserve our thanks, and all have our prayers. And tonight, a few miles from the damaged Pentagon, I have a message for our military: Be ready. I've called the Armed Forces to alert, and there is a reason. The hour is coming when America will act, and you will make us proud. (Applause.)

35   This is not, however, just America's fight. And what is at stake is not just America's freedom. This is the world's fight. This is civilization's fight. This is the fight of all who believe in progress and pluralism, tolerance and freedom.

36   We ask every nation to join us. We will ask, and we will need, the help of police forces, intelligence services, and banking systems around the world. The United States is grateful that many nations and many international organizations have already responded—with sympathy and with support. Nations from Latin America, to Asia, to Africa, to Europe, to the Islamic world. Perhaps the NATO Charter reflects best the attitude of the world: An attack on one is an attack on all.

37   The civilized world is rallying to America's side. They understand that if this terror goes unpunished, their own cities, their own citizens may be next. Terror, unanswered, can not only bring down buildings, it can threaten the stability of legitimate governments. And you know what—we're not going to allow it. (Applause.)

38   Americans are asking: What is expected of us? I ask you to live your lives, and hug your children. I know many citizens have fears tonight, and I ask you to be calm and resolute, even in the face of a continuing threat.

39   I ask you to uphold the values of America, and remember why so many have come here. We are in a fight for our principles, and our first responsibility is to live by them. No one should be singled out for unfair treatment or unkind words because of their ethnic background or religious faith. (Applause.)

40   I ask you to continue to support the victims of this tragedy with your contributions. Those who want to give can go to a central source of information, libertyunites.org, to find the names of groups providing direct help in New York, Pennsylvania, and Virginia.

41   The thousands of FBI agents who are now at work in this investigation may need your cooperation, and I ask you to give it.

42   I ask for your patience, with the delays and inconveniences that may accompany tighter security; and for your patience in what will be a long struggle.

43   I ask your continued participation and confidence in the American economy. Terrorists attacked a symbol of American prosperity. They did not touch its source. America is successful because of the hard work, and creativity, and enterprise of our people. These were the true strengths of our economy before September 11th, and they are our strengths today. (Applause.)

44   And, finally, please continue praying for the victims of terror and their families, for those in uniform, and for our great country. Prayer has comforted us in sorrow, and will help strengthen us for the journey ahead.

45   Tonight I thank my fellow Americans for what you have already done and for what you will do. And ladies and gentlemen of the Congress, I thank you, their representatives, for what you have already done and for what we will do together.

46   Tonight, we face new and sudden national challenges. We will come together to improve air safety, to dramatically expand the number of air marshals on domestic flights, and take new measures to prevent hijacking. We will come together to promote stability and keep our airlines flying, with direct assistance during this emergency. (Applause.)

47   We will come together to give law enforcement the additional tools it needs to track down terror here at home. (Applause.) We will come together to strengthen our intelligence capabilities to know the plans of terrorists before they act, and find them before they strike. (Applause.)

48   We will come together to take active steps that strengthen America's economy, and put our people back to work.

49   Tonight we welcome two leaders who embody the extraordinary spirit of all New Yorkers: Governor George Pataki, and Mayor Rudolph Giuliani. (Applause.) As a symbol of America's resolve, my administration will work with Congress, and these two leaders, to show the world that we will rebuild New York City. (Applause.)

50   After all that has just passed—all the lives taken, and all the possibilities and hopes that died with them—it is natural to wonder if America's future is one of fear. Some speak of an age of terror. I know there are struggles ahead, and dangers to face. But this country will define our times, not be defined by them. As long as the United States of America is determined and strong, this will not be an age of terror; this will be an age of liberty, here and across the world. (Applause.)

51   Great harm has been done to us. We have suffered great loss. And in our grief and anger we have found our mission and our moment. Freedom and fear are at war. The advance of human freedom—the great achievement of our time, and the great hope of every time—now depends on us. Our nation—this generation—will lift a dark threat of violence from our people and our future. We will rally the world to this cause by our efforts, by our courage. We will not tire, we will not falter, and we will not fail. (Applause.)

52   It is my hope that in the months and years ahead, life will return almost to normal. We'll go back to our lives and routines, and that is good. Even grief recedes

with time and grace. But our resolve must not pass. Each of us will remember what happened that day, and to whom it happened. We'll remember the moment the news came—where we were and what we were doing. Some will remember an image of a fire, or a story of rescue. Some will carry memories of a face and a voice gone forever.

53   And I will carry this: It is the police shield of a man named George Howard, who died at the World Trade Center trying to save others. It was given to me by his mom, Arlene, as a proud memorial to her son. This is my reminder of lives that ended, and a task that does not end. (Applause.)

54   I will not forget this wound to our country or those who inflicted it. I will not yield; I will not rest; I will not relent in waging this struggle for freedom and security for the American people.

55   The course of this conflict is not known, yet its outcome is certain. Freedom and fear, justice and cruelty, have always been at war, and we know that God is not neutral between them. (Applause.)

56   Fellow citizens, we'll meet violence with patient justice—assured of the rightness of our cause, and confident of the victories to come. In all that lies before us, may God grant us wisdom, and may He watch over the United States of America.

57   Thank you. (Applause.)

THINKING CRITICALLY

1. In the preceding essay, D. T. Max made observations regarding George W. Bush's personal use of language (see paragraphs 17, 18, 23, and 24). Analyze the language of this speech—mindful of Max's remarks—such as the president's use of adjectives and grammar.

2. Are there any phrases in this speech that fit into William Lutz's definition of "doublespeak" (see page 185)? If so, identify them and explain why you think they are examples of doublespeak.

3. Who are "the enemies of freedom"? How does Bush identify these enemies? Explain.

4. Consider how Bush describes the terrorists in this speech. Do you think he is forceful enough? Is he too "politically correct" or cautious? Is he diplomatic? Explain.

5. Do you think Ian Frazier's opinion of the president's command of language would be different if he had heard this address? (His article was written about three months before this speech was delivered.) Why or why not?

6. The White House Web site, where this speech is posted, chose to include areas where this speech was met with applause. Does such inclusion influence your reception and interpretation of the speech? Should such annotations be included? Explain.

7. Who is the audience for this speech? Identify the audience based on the words and delivery of the speech.

8. Bush mentions that he holds a police badge from a fallen police officer who sacrificed his life to save others at the World Trade Center. What is the symbolism of this badge? Why do you think he mentions it?

WRITING ASSIGNMENTS

1. Compare this speech to others given before and after September 11 by Bush. An archive of presidential addresses can be found at <http://www.whitehouse.gov>. After this address, did the president's use of language indeed change? Did he seem more confident in his messages? Explain and cite specific examples gathered from your research.

2. Review the first section of this chapter and compare the points made by the authors in that section to this speech. How would Orwell respond to this speech? Lutz? Explain.

■ MAKING CONNECTIONS

1. Is presidential discourse too influential? Does everything the president says or does indeed carry particular significance or meaning to the general public? If so, what does that mean about who we want to be president, and why?

2. President Harry S. Truman once said, "the principle power that the president has is to bring people in and try to persuade them to do what they ought to do without persuasion." What did Truman mean? Write an essay exploring this statement and your opinion of Truman's assessment of the presidency.

3. Denton and Hahn explain that the president's language serves to motivate, rally, and persuade. Have you ever found yourself influenced by a particular speech made by the president? What was particularly compelling and why? Reflect on the speech and how the language the president used influenced your emotions and opinions.

4. Locate several speeches made by different presidents and compare their style, content, delivery, and message. Using information presented in this section, write an essay exploring the connection between what the president says, and how we perceive his leadership ability.

■ CASE STUDY: TERRORISM AND THE WAR OF WORDS

The Semantics of Murder
Amir Taheri

We would like to think that words have ascribable definitions and meanings. Language and meaning, while organic, should still have stability. However, as Amir Taheri explains, the interpretation of a single word can mean the difference between "unpardonable sin" and "heroic martyr." In the first editorial, Taheri questions the way some Muslims are "playing games with words" to justify suicide attacks.

Amir Taheri is the author of *The Cauldron: Middle East Behind the Headlines* (1988). This editorial was published in the May 8, 2002, edition of the *Wall Street Journal* as part of its editorial section.

1 As President Bush and Israel's prime minister, Ariel Sharon, met in Washington on May 7, 2002, the latest mass murder rocked Tel Aviv. A blast in a pool hall killed at

least 16 people and wounded at least 57 others. So, will the Palestinian who here turned himself into a walking agent of destruction be regarded by his people as a "suicide bomber," a "terrorist" or a "martyr"?

2   Many in the West assume that the Muslim world has already answered by honoring the human bombs as "martyrs." And the chorus of voices from the Muslim world does support that assumption. Foreign ministers from 57 Muslim countries met in Kuala Lumpur, Malaysia, this month with the stated intention of defining terrorism and distancing Islam from terror. Instead, they ended up endorsing the suicide bombers.

3   Iran's former president, Hashemi Rafsanjani, says he would accept the suicide of even 10% of Muslims in a nuclear war to wipe Israel off the map. Algeria's president, Abdelaziz Bouteflika, has described the bombers as "innocent blossoms of martyrdom." Ghazi Algosaibi, Saudi Arabia's ambassador in London and also a poet, has praised the human bombs as a model for Muslim youth in an ode. Ismail Abushanab, the Hamas leader in Gaza, says that 10,000 Palestinians should die while killing 100,000 Israelis as part of a strategy to "put the Jews on the run." And Saddam Hussein says the suicide bombers are "reviving Islam."

4   Many Arab television channels have enlisted their resources in the battle for the hearts and minds of the Arab world, presenting self-styled sheikhs who use sophistry to bestow religious authority on a cynical political strategy. But even these apologists of terror find it difficult to justify the bombers in terms of Islamic ethics.

5   The first difficulty they face is that Islam expressly forbids suicide. Islamic ethics underlines five "unpardonable sins": cannibalism, murder, incest, rape and suicide. The rationale is that these are evil deeds that cannot be undone. To avoid such awkwardness, the apologists of terror recently abandoned the term *entehari* ("suicidal") which was coined for human bombs when they first appeared in Lebanon in 1983.

6   The apologists also know that they cannot use the term *shahid* for the men who self-detonate in civilian areas. This is a complex term. Although it also means "martyr," it must not be confused with the Christian concept of martyrdom. In Islam, Allah himself is the first shahid, meaning "witness" to the unity of creation. The word indicates that individuals cannot decide to become martyrs—that choice belongs only to God.

7   But this is a lofty honor. There are no more than a dozen or so "shahids" in the history of Islam—people who fell in loyal battle in defense of the faith, not in pursuit of political goals. By becoming shahid they bore testimony to the truth of God's message. The Palestinian teenager who says in video-recorded testament that he or she has decided to become a martyr is, in fact, challenging one of Allah's prerogatives.

8   To get around the semantics, terror's apologists now use the word *etsesh'had,* which literally means "affidavit." As a neologism, it means conducting "martyr-like" operations. Thus "martyr-like," the ersatz in place of the real, is used to circumvent the impossibility of regarding suicide bombers as martyrs in Islam.

9   Muslims who implicitly condone terror know they cannot smuggle a new concept into Islamic ethics, where human activities are divided into six categories along a spectrum of good and evil. Most activities fall into a gray area, half of which is described as *mobah* (acceptable though not praiseworthy), the other half as *makruh* (acceptable though best avoided).

10   Suicide bombing falls within the category that is forbidden *(haram)*. To change its status as a concept, its supporters must give a definition *(ta'rif)*, spell out its rules *(ahkam)*, fix its limits *(hodoud)*, find its place in jurisprudence *(shar'e)* and common law *(urf)*. Such an undertaking would require a large measure of consensus *(ijma'a)* among the believers, something the prophets of terror will never secure. And not a single reputable theologian anywhere has endorsed the new trick word *estesh'had,* though some have spoken with forked tongues. The reason is not hard to see.

11   Islam forbids human sacrifice. The greatest Islamic festival is the Eid al-Adha which marks the day God refused Abraham's offer to sacrifice his firstborn and, instead, substituted a lamb. A god who refuses human sacrifice for his cause can hardly sanction the same to promote the strategies of Mr. Abushanab, or Yasser Arafat. Islam also rejects the crucifixion of Christ because it cannot accept that God would claim human sacrifice in atonement of men's sins.

12   Some, like Iran's President Mohammad Khatami, present suicide bombings as acts of individual desperation. This is disingenuous. One of the girls who blew herself up, murdering almost a dozen Israelis, had been recruited at 14 and brainwashed for two years. Mounting a suicide operation needs planning, logistics, surveillance, equipment, money and postoperation publicity—in short, an organization.

13   But then, the recruiters never use their own children. No one related by blood to the leaders of Hamas or Islamic Jihad has died in suicide bombings.

14   Arafat's wife, Suha, says she would offer her son for suicide attacks. Mrs. Arafat, however, has no son, only a daughter, living with her in Paris. It is always someone else's child who must die.

A True Jihad or a Sinful War Against Innocents?
Jim Guirard

Jim Guirard wrote this viewpoint in response to Amir Taheri's editorial. Building upon the ideas expressed in Taheri's essay, Guirard attempts to bring the former's "truth-in-language" thesis even further." Guirard calls for a "heightened focus" on this war of words—a war for "the minds, hearts and souls of hundreds of millions of Muslims."

Jim Guirard is an attorney, government affairs consultant, and lecturer. He served as national affairs director of the American Security Council Foundation. He has written many articles on the language of politics, and currently is affiliated with the TrueSpeak Institute in Washington, D.C. This editorial appeared in the *Wall Street Journal* on May 27, 2002, a few weeks after Taheri's piece was published.

1 Amir Taheri's May 8 editorial-page essay "Semantics of Murder" calls for a heightened focus on the war of words between us and the terrorists—a war for the minds, hearts and souls of hundreds of millions of Muslims and of all too many Westerners as well.

2 Without repeating Mr. Taheri's expert observations about traditional Islam's sharp condemnation of suicide and of the wanton killing of innocents, as well as its highly restrictive definition of "martyrdom," here is a question-and-answer exercise designed to carry his truth-in-language thesis even further.

3 Its purpose is to draw a no-nonsense, bright-line distinction between those who support and rationalize and those who condemn and oppose genocidal terrorism of the al Qaeda, Hamas, Hezbollah, al Fatah and Islamic Jihad varieties.

4 **Question:** Do al Qaeda's actions constitute an authentic, Qur'an-approved *Jihad* (a truly holy war), or do they constitute a Qur'an-prohibited *Hirabah* (a forbidden killing of innocents and a mortally sinful "war against society") instead?

5 **Question:** Are those who conduct such a war the blessed *mujaheddin* (holy warriors) and the "martyrs for Allah" they claim to be, or are they what the Qur'an severely condemns as *mufsidoon* (evildoers) for conducting an unholy Hirabah?

6 **Question:** Are those conducting this suicidal, al Qaeda-type of warfare destined for a maiden-filled Paradise, or are they headed—unless they immediately cease and sincerely repent their evildoing—straight for *jahannam* (eternal hellfire) instead?

7 **Question:** Is this war in full accord with the *Shari'ah* (the traditional Islamic Law), or does it constitute a multi-part *tajdeef* (a gigantic blasphemy) against the peaceful and compassionate Allah, who is clearly portrayed by the Qur'an?

8 **Question:** Is the nature of the war being waged by al Qaeda and its clones a truly godly mission in the name of Allah, or is it a patently evil, destructive and *shaitaniyah* (satanic) enterprise fomented by Satan himself?

9 The five-word answer is quite plain. It is *Hirabah* conducted by *mufsidoon* destined for *jahannam* because of the *tajdeef shaitaniyah*—the satanic blasphemy—they are waging against peaceful Allah and authentic Islam.

THINKING CRITICALLY

1. What is the difference between most of the western world's interpretation of the word *martyr* and the Islamic world's interpretation? Explain.

2. What does *shahid* mean? Why can't this word be used to describe suicide bombers? In what ways is this word in conflict with how suicide bombers view their mission and Islamic ethics?

3. What is Taheri's opinion of the suicide bombings? On what they mean to the West's impression of Islam? Explain.

4. What does *estesh'had* mean? Why are "terror's apologists" using the word to describe the actions of suicide bombers?

5. How does the deliberate use of Arabic words contribute to the message, meaning, and impact of these editorials? Explain.

6. What is the effect of Guirard's use of citing a list of questions? Do they make an effective point? Why or why not?

7. Taheri's editorial is titled "The Semantics of Murder." What does *semantics* mean? How does it apply to interpretations of crucial words such as *terrorism, suicide,* and *murder?* Can you think of other examples in which semantics plays a role in our understanding of critical events or actions?

Fighting Words: The War Over Language
Jon Hooten

Our everyday language is liberally sprinkled with the language of war—we "defend" our positions, "wage price wars" at discount stores, and "battle" termite "invasions." We get "bombed" or "blitzed" at parties. Perhaps we are so free with war language because over half the population has yet to experience a true war. But as we become more removed from the original meanings of the language of war, are we in danger of blurring metaphorical issues with ones of great consequence for humanity?

Jon Hooten is an educational administrator in the School of Communication at the University of Denver. He frequently writes on culture, religion, and environmental issues. He is currently co-authoring a book on value-centered education in the twenty-first century. This essay first appeared in the September 2002 issue of the online magazine, *PopPolitics*.

1 Mine—perhaps, ours—is the first American generation that has yet to experience a full-blown, machine-gun shooting, prisoner-taking, horror-story war.

2 We youngsters sit wide-eyed while our shaky grandfathers and crusty uncles tell tales of enemy occupation, dead buddies, pretty gals and the joy of a fresh Lucky Strike on a rainy afternoon. To those born in the late 1960s and beyond, Nazis are nothing but cultural extremists (of the "femi-" or "soup" varieties), Vietnam makes a good setting for a summer blockbuster, and the Battle of the Bulge is a corny baby boomer punch line. Simply, the realities of the nation's major wars have been lost on one—going on two and three—generations of Americans.

3 That's not to say that my generation has not lived through skirmishes, conflicts and appalling battles. Those of us sitting in high school during the winter of 1991 watched the air strikes on Baghdad through the glassy eyes of CNN, with Peter Ar-

nett and Wolf Blitzer calling the play-by-play. As Desert Storm eventually became known as the "Gulf War," many of us wondered if this was the future of the genre that we had read about in 11th grade-history class.

4   From now on, it seemed, war would be a few nights of superpower smart-bombing and long-range tanks lobbing shells into ragtag militias commanded by egomaniacal dictators. It hardly seemed worthy of the designation "war."

5   Those of us who grew up after Vietnam simply cannot comprehend the dread that shaped older generations of Americans. Our experience of the Gulf War was an acutely sterile encounter. We watched replays of laser-guided missiles entering bunker windows, but seldom were we exposed to the sights of actual human collateral. Though tens—hundreds—of thousands of Iraqi casualties resulted, the televised images of precision war games grossly outnumbered the news clips of war's grisly human cost. Since many of us have not experienced the sights and sounds of war firsthand, we think about war rather thoughtlessly.

6   In our lack of true wartime experience, American culture has learned to deploy the images of war rather casually. The words of war were once the moral and emotional defense of the nation, corresponding with the real memories and motivations of an embattled citizenry. As war became less messy and more distant, the language of war invaded the common lexicon of America. Though you may have never noticed it, the extraordinary metaphor of war has infiltrated our quotidian use of language. (Can you count how many times "war words" are fired at you in this very paragraph?)

7   Our popular culture thinks nothing of invoking the language of conflict to describe most any topic. Pick up the morning's paper and browse through the headlines: "Mayor *Defends* New Budget." "Media *Blitz* Saves Kidnapped Girl." "Farmers *Battle* Summer Drought." "Browser *War* Heats Up." "Champ's Left Hook Right *on Target*."

8   Consider, for instance, the numerous ways in which the word 'bomb' is used: "Frat brothers get bombed on a Saturday night." "Your new car is 'the bomb.'" "Did you see that comedian bomb on Letterman last night?" "The quarterback threw a long bomb to win the game."

9   While we have haphazardly sprinkled our language with war's metaphors, is it possible that we have collectively forgotten how to think clearly about the literal phenomenon? Can the collective linguistic turn from the literal to the metaphorical be without consequence?

10   Throughout history, wars have usually followed a certain pattern: They have generally involved elaborate, enduring campaigns between at least two somewhat equal forces; they have resulted in mass casualties; and—this is the most important part—they have some sort of *conclusion*. Common sense would agree with this characterization, at least in the conventional sense of the phenomenon.

11   With this definition in mind, the latter half of the twentieth century has seen a proliferation of non-war-like wars. The war on poverty that Lyndon Johnson waged in the 1960s was an elaborate public policy initiative. The war on drugs that swelled in the 1970s and 1980s became a tsunami of agencies, non-profit organiza-

tions, police action and international diplomacy. The Cold War, fought with national ideologies, economic posturing and infinite defense budgets, festered without any combat or mass casualties (at least among the superpowers) throughout the latter half of the twentieth century before finally coming to a head in the mid-1980s.

12 Now, after a decade's respite of new wars, we have another one on our hands: the war on terrorism.

13 After that inconceivable morning in September 2001, our media-sated political culture was quick to place the blame on those radicals who have become known as "the terrorists." Soon after, the "war on terror" was a go. President Bush promptly assembled his posse to round up the scoundrels who had done this—"Wanted," we were told by the president, "dead or alive." The weeks and months following that day were a slow and deliberate escalation of the war on terrorism, beginning internally with beefed up airports and FBI round-ups, then spreading—in a violent and explicit way—abroad in Afghanistan.

14 For several weeks, while the United States bombed that impoverished nation, the "war on terrorism" became known as the "war on Afghanistan." Quickly, this new war began to look like a war that the president's father fought ten years earlier. Though similar to the Gulf War in many ways, the mission in Afghanistan was very different. While Bush the Elder relied heavily on turkey-shoot combat fought from above, George W. sent in massive numbers of ground troops to hunt down "the evil ones."

15 A wobbly alliance with the locals in Afghanistan was also formed, so that fewer body bags would be sent back to the States full of our brothers and sisters. (Who knows how many Northern Alliance fighters were buried in their native soil.) And while his father had the modest goal of expelling Iraqi forces from Kuwait, Bush the Younger had grander plans of rounding up all the Al Qaeda and Taliban evil-doers he could find.

16 After the fighting in Afghanistan simmered down, and the immediate goal of capturing top terrorists was not met, the popular rhetoric of national affairs shifted away from geographic specifics to the more general "war on terrorism." No longer involving specific battles or well-defined goals, this war quickly began to look similar to other drawn-out wars with which my generation *is* familiar.

17 In 1981, first lady Nancy Reagan boldly advised us first-graders to "Just Say No to Drugs." (Abbie Hoffman is widely reported to have said, "To tell a drug addict to 'just say no' is like telling a manic depressive to 'just cheer up.'") Soon after, President Reagan instigated the all-out war on druggies. By 1988, the Anti-Drug Abuse Act had set its national sights on both the supply and demand of illegal substances in the United States. Though the DEA had been on the scene since 1973, the Reagans took seriously the evil scourge that they saw infecting America's children. The war on drugs was born, has thrived for more than 15 years, and continues in 2002 with an overall federal budget of $19.2 billion.

18 Last time I checked, however, people still buy and use drugs with relative ease. Though the statistics of drug use wax and wane like a Santa Cruz tide, it is safe to say that the war on drugs has not been won. What's more, the war is not a winnable

affair. The war on drugs is a war on a perpetual opponent. Unlike a conventional war, there will be no Normandy or Hiroshima, no crucial turning point or day of victory when all the pot heads and speed freaks will finally surrender.

19 Returning to our definition above, there is no doubt that the war on drugs largely fits the characterization of conventional war. The national strategy has certainly been a strategic battle of wits between two equally matched opponents (as the drug complex still manages to outfox the government with regularity and sophistication). This war has also lasted for more than two decades, and nobody doubts that real casualties have ensued, both domestically and abroad. The question remains, however, if this war will in fact ever come to completion. Can it be won?

20 If we put our heads to it, we will quickly recognize that a "war" of this type is nothing but a grand metaphor, a riding crop with which to whip patriotic Americans into action. In the case of the drug war, the United States has moved from metaphor to militarized efforts in the attempt to alter human habits. While these symbolic, rhetorical wars may seem to have few negative consequences, the conjuring of war's images, passions and emotions has real damaging effects. We are racing toward a finish line that doesn't exist.

21 The language of war, in all its urgency and obligation, will always motivate the patriotic and righteous. The metaphor necessarily creates an enemy, which, when characterized as such, becomes equally entrenched in the language of offense and defense. At its dark heart, a war demands division and opposition. Right vs. wrong. Good vs. evil.

22 Like the war on drugs, the war on terrorism is another overarching metaphor. Terrorism, like drug use, is an act unique to humanity, an action which will be with us for a long time. To war against terrorism is to war against an enemy that does not exist in only one place, that cannot be controlled by laws, that will perpetually be reborn in creative and cunning ways. Terrorism grows out of the fecund social and cultural and economic and religious and psychological slough that is civilization. Like the drug war, the war on terrorism can never be won.

23 By definition, terrorism is a concept or category that describes human actions. In most any dictionary, you will find no examples of what terrorism must be in order to be considered as such. In the dictionary, you will not find "hostage-taking," "suicide-bombing" and "the throwing of Molotov cocktails" under the definition of terrorism. Rather, you will find it described as systematic and violent acts to advance political ends. To war against terrorism, therefore, is to war against a classification, a description, in essence, a word.

24 How can bombs be dropped on a word?

25 At this point, you may be wondering, Doesn't this guy know that the war on terrorism is actually a war on *terrorists?* That it is a war on their weapons supply, their finances, their training camps and the axis of evil that harbors them? Doesn't he realize that this exercise in logic has nothing to do with the reality of reality?

26 Well, yes. And no. I am well aware that acts of terrorism do not commit themselves. Of course, terrorism requires the personnel, training and weapons that make violence possible; limiting all of that should therefore logically decrease the in-

stances of terrorist acts. However, the United States must realize that this war—while focused against terrorists, their weapons, etc.—is shaped and fought through the way we speak and write about it.

27   Fighting terrorism is different than fighting cavities. It is not a localized menace that can be brushed away, drilled or filled. On Sept. 9, 2001—two days before the events that sparked the Bush's new war—Alan Block wrote in *Pravda,* "When the metaphorical use of the term [war] is common and seldom challenged, resistance to actual war becomes more difficult and uncommon." Eventually, the verbal sparring becomes literal bombing.

28   When we generalize about the evils of terrorism, we shroud the faces, politics and religion behind the acts. That which motivates the militants has become opaqued by the wordiness of bumper sticker aphorisms and campaign stump speeches. While the war on terrorism has set its sights on the perpetrators and mechanisms therein, it has ignored that which initially provokes the violence. As a damning result, the evil, as it were, will always be with us. As long as the seeds of terrorism—ignorance, injustice, exploitation—are perpetually planted by the careless hand of the superpowers, the weeds of violence will continue to steal nutrients from the fruits of civilization.

29   Politicians, prosecutors and preachers alike invoke moving imagery of cosmic battles of good and evil. Yet, many public figures use this language in knowingly figurative ways. I get the sense, though, that President Bush takes seriously his war on evil, that with enough bombs, with plenty of firepower, and if the right people can be killed, then the axis of evil will fall. He does not seem to realize that evil is perennial, that the death of one season's crops will only fertilize the next season's seedlings. By creating martyrs of the evil-doers, he is signing the marching orders of their followers and inspiring a new impassioned generation of freedom fighters.

30   I would like nothing more than to eradicate the horror that is terrorism . . . along with poverty, hunger, ecocide and oppression. But invoking the language of war does more damage than it prevents. To war against anything will eventually allow the metaphors to become realities. If the twentieth century has taught us anything, it is that words have consequences. Words persuade, encourage and tyrannize. They convey power, passion and persecution. When we invoke the language of war, figurative battles against finances become literal battles against financiers. Symbolic warfare against weapons supplies becomes bloody warfare against weapons suppliers. While we arm ourselves for war, the roots of the violence go ignored, growing deeper into the fertile soils of culture and power.

31   In a famous article that was widely distributed on the Internet just before the first Gulf War, linguist George Lakoff wrote, "It is important to distinguish what is metaphorical from what is not. Pain, dismemberment, death, starvation, and the death and injury of loved ones are not metaphorical." Lakoff would agree that acts based on a metaphor will mirror the metaphor. Warring words will become warring deeds. Clearly, the metaphorical war on terrorism might just become a very real attack on Iraq, with real casualties and consequences.

32   When war is accepted in any form, it can be accepted in all forms. Oscar Wilde wrote in 1891, "As long as war is regarded as wicked, it will always have its fasci-

nation. When it is looked upon as vulgar, it will cease to be popular." Only when we choose to not invoke the words of war to address social ills will we begin to solve the problems that lead to violence. More often than not, we are our own worst enemy.

THINKING CRITICALLY

1. How does the fact that generations born after 1970 have not experienced a "full-blown" war influence their use of the "language of war"?

2. At the end of paragraph 6, Hooten asks his readers to count how many "war words" he has used. Identify these words, and discuss how these words have become mainstream in our regular speech.

3. In what ways, according to Hooten, has the pop-culture use of war words influenced our thinking about the "war on terrorism"? Explain.

4. What is the author's tone in this piece? What is he trying to achieve by writing this essay? Explain.

5. According to Hooten, how have the wars of the last twenty years been "nothing but grand metaphors"? Do you agree with his assertions? Explain.

6. In paragraph 23, Hooten states, "By definition, terrorism is a concept or category that describes human actions . . . To war against terrorism, therefore, is to war against a classification, a description, a word." What does Hooten mean by this statement? How does he qualify his claim in the paragraphs that follow?

7. In paragraph 9, Hooten asks, "is it possible that we have collectively forgotten how to think clearly about the literal phenomenon [of war]?" Write a response to his question, presenting your own perspective, while addressing some of the points Hooten raises in his essay.

A Lot to Learn
David Brudnoy

In the days following September 11, 2001, America was unified both by grief and a combined sense of national purpose. Many people sought a silver lining through all the sadness, saying that the nation emerged with a stronger awareness of community, charity, and patriotism. Journalist David Brudnoy, however, explains why he feels little has changed since September 11. Part of the reason is that the words used to describe the event, its perpetrators, and the quest to bring them to justice, are weak and ineffectual. Such "political politeness," he explains, must stop if we are to ever succeed in the "war against terrorism."

David Brudnoy teaches at Boston University in the College of Communication. He is the host of a radio talk program on Boston's WBZ Radio. A recognized television and radio personality in the Boston area, Brudnoy is known as a right-wing conservative. He is the author of *Life is Not a Rehearsal: A Memoir* (1997). His commentaries have appeared in many national publications, including the *National Review*. This article first appeared in the *Boston Phoenix* on September 6, 2002.

1   It was the worst of times. But in our grief, our fury, we made halting efforts to say that maybe September 11 would lead to the best of times. In the aftermath of the Islamic attack maybe America would come together. Maybe we would defeat terrorism. We were wrong.

2   Absorbing the event itself was a Herculean effort. To see the Twin Towers in New York City *vanish,* like some repulsively persuasive special effect in the latest action movie, and then to see them vanish *again* and *again* as we compulsively watched the news footage, became an act of near-religious observance. We felt an obligation to keep watching the destruction in New York, at the Pentagon, in that field in Pennsylvania. Our vigil morphed into a sacrament in all but name, a vicarious participation in the deaths of what we were first told might be more than 10,000 people. It was as if we who were alive couldn't let go of those who had perished unless we latched onto their deaths as if we too had died.

3   In our grief, we grasped at straws. The first was the notion that our anguish would unite us the way the political murders of John and Robert Kennedy and Martin Luther King Jr. had united us in the 1960s. The second was our belief that we would prevent this ever from happening again. That we would strike without hesitation at those who had engineered, financed, and effected this new day. That we would destroy the perpetrators of 9/11 with speed and decisiveness. That there would be a conclusion.

4   Of course, we were wrong. We didn't come together and we didn't destroy the enemy.

5   We learned something, though. We learned that we didn't have the vocabulary to talk about what had happened. Our words were either too anemic or too overblown. We tried to find context for the day by talking of it incessantly, as if by doing so we could knit a protective shield against the agony. In truth, we had no words at all.

6   We noted the . . . *magnificence* of the mayor of New York, Rudy Giuliani. We never said what later became obvious: that while he was superb, any intelligent mayor of New York would have been superb in those circumstances. We were looking not for brilliant speeches but for a fatherly embrace. The mayor (soon dubbed "the mayor of America" and later designated *Time* magazine's Man of the Year) eschewed the brilliant speeches and extended the embrace. He was everywhere, he was one with the city.

7   We noted the . . . *leadership* of the president. A week after the attacks, President Bush delivered a masterful speech, and an embrace too. Thus the man who had been regarded by many as the accidental president and by almost all as minor league became a giant. Again, we never said that while he did his job superbly, the occasion truly made the man.

8   The word *crusade* came and went with the speed of those four planes that took 3000 to their deaths. It was replaced with *war on terrorism.* Which terrorism? We neither set out to rid the world of any of the many known non-Islamic terrorists (the Irish Republican Army, Basque separatists, Peru's communist Shining Path) nor to target those terrorist organizations (Hamas, Hizbollah, Islamic Jihad) overlapping Al Qaeda, the one we had determined was the Enemy.

9   We described the Enemy in politically correct baby talk drained of meaning and vague to the point of inanity. At its worst, this impulse led us to say that the culprits adhered to a renegade brand of Islam, as if a religion is merely what its most cordial advocates say it is rather than what its most zealous devotees show it to be. We talked as if Osama bin Laden's gang were a tiny coterie, ignoring the reality of the worldwide Muslim expression of joy at what happened on September 11.

10   Hoisted on that petard, so beloved by the president, we manufactured an Islam that isn't—hence the president's hyperbolic babbling about Islam as a "religion of peace." We have yet to figure out how to be intellectually honest about the full reality of the Enemy as Islamist lunacy in its many forms: puritanical Wahhabist fanaticism (convert or die, and when converted, follow exactly our interpretations); dictatorial repressiveness; monarchical medievalism; the Palestinian equating of martyrdom with the murder of innocents; scientific development of weapons that, if used, would only unleash a second Holocaust.

11   The notion that we could prattle mindlessly about a kind of all-purpose *war on terrorism,* instead of putting in the necessary adjective *—Islamist—*is an idea fit only for fabulists. The inability even to utter the words *war on Islamist terrorism,* made strategizing this "war" difficult to the point of impossibility. Especially after we had bombed Afghanistan and chased out a large portion of the Taliban who had ruined that country but who had, after all, only *hosted* Osama bin Laden. Because we cannot bear to talk like adults about the task and the Enemy, we cannot conceptualize what we should be doing.

12   Which brings us to the one-year anniversary of the Islamist attack. We are terrorizing ourselves with the creation of absurd "security" devices and Rube Goldberg–like apparatus at our airports, sports stadiums, and many other places. We have accepted with little complaint our Justice Department's substitution of *tattling* for serious espionage and intelligence gathering. We are bemoaning the lousy stockmarket numbers, the apparently stalled economic "recovery," and nestling comfortably, as was inevitable, in partisan quibbling. We're back in the kingdom of Gotcha: *Gotcha,* Dick Cheney, you were a CEO! *Gotcha,* Joe Lieberman, you don't want stock options counted as a liability! *Gotcha,* George W., you owned a profitable baseball team! None of this is more unseemly now than before 9/11, but we had become so wrapped up in our sense of wonderfulness, of the "united" part of our national name, that we actually vowed we would never again descend to business as usual.

13   We had snatches of an artificial unity for a few weeks, but it was gossamer. It was a unity premised on a fantasy, that fury at the monstrous act would give us a common cause. In reality, America is neither the mythic melting pot nor, in the

words of the previous mayor of New York, a gorgeous mosaic. We are a nation of disparate parts, instructed by our leading propagandists and educators to think of ourselves not as Americans but as hyphenated tribes. During the 2000 presidential campaign, Al Gore famously mistranslated *e pluribus unum* as "out of one, many." Maybe his subconscious slip was telling an unhappy truth.

14   Today, our leaders talk as if finding bin Laden will successfully conclude the *war on terrorism*. Or that "taking out" the dictator of Iraq is the same as infusing a maddened and self-destructive region with democratic ideology and democratic institutions. We don't have leaders who talk straight. We bounce around in uncertainty. We confuse the bluster of media stars with profundity. There is no one person or thing to make a whole out of the separate ingredients of our populace. There is no one person or thing to propel us to do what is necessary to defeat Islamist terrorism, which isn't surprising, since most of us are too squeamish to call it by name. No, today we include the grabby ones who think that their loss of a loved one on September 11 entitles them to millions of dollars, although the loss of a soldier brings his or her family paltry thousands. We are the preachy, who tell doubters that if only they believed more in *our* definition of the divinity, they would be saved and welded into an impregnable nation, and *our* divinity will defeat the Enemy's false god, because our divinity roots for *our* team. We have become to some extent laughably juvenile.

15   We are living in a continuous state of apprehension, counting the days until the next attack and repeating the now-standard mantra that we will only unite more when—not if, but when—we're hit again. That we'll strike even harder, more righteously, and more effectively. We have spent a year failing to synchronize the necessary ideas with the necessary actions. Our borders remain scandalously porous: tuck a suitcase bomb into the trunk of your car and drive right in from Canada. We delude ourselves by thinking that a photo ID is proof against evil intent. We allow our e-mails to be invaded by our dubiously named Department of Justice while nests of terrorists undoubtedly continue to thrive in our territory as they do in Europe. We countenance an absurd policy of "random" scrutiny of airplane passengers rather than engage in thoughtful profiling, lest we be accused of racism. Our president spends ample time cozying up to the smarmy representatives of the House of Saud—oil is king—while we require nothing of that monarchy by way of assisting us in locating terrorists. If anything is of use, we eschew it; if something is pointless but looks good on the evening news, we go with it. We have resolved nothing. We have managed to offend those we shouldn't, like the Israelis, by excluding them entirely from our plans to confront Iraq, but not those we should, like the Pakistani government, which countenances terrorist encampments in its territory, and, again, the Saudis, who mount telethons to fund the families of homicide-bombers in Israel, blatantly giving their imprimatur to terrorism. To fear offending an enemy who took down the two towers of the World Trade Center, drilled a hole through the Pentagon, and left a death pit in Pennsylvania is a strange way to bind the nation's wounds.

16   We did not come together after September 11. It wasn't, even in the most metaphoric and hope-filled sense, "the best of times." It was the worst of times. Not

solely because of the death and destruction of that day, but also because of what we've become in its aftermath: preposterously maudlin. Ineffectively incendiary. Painfully earnest. Muddled.

17   We are foolishly polite when we need to be fiercely determined. To give this vaunted "war on terrorism" legitimacy and determination and purpose, we might recall the words of "The Battle Hymn of the Republic," written in 1861, during a time of national crisis like none we've seen till now. The Civil War was waged to save the republic; today's war against Islamist terrorism must be waged to save Western civilization. It requires precisely, in Julia Ward Howe's unparalled image, that "terrible swift sword."

THINKING CRITICALLY

1. What does Brudnoy mean "we learned that we didn't have the vocabulary to talk about what happened"? Does he mean that we literally did not have the words? Explain.

2. In paragraph 9, Brudnoy asserts that we "described the enemy in politically correct baby talk." What is this "baby talk" to which he objects? What words does he think are more appropriate, and why? Do you agree with his perspective? Why or why not?

3. Why does Brudnoy put some words in italics throughout this essay? What is he trying to say about these words? Is this technique of italicizing words an effective way to emphasize his point? What other essays have used this technique?

4. What is Brudnoy's tone in this article? Who is his audience? Evaluate Brudnoy's tone, and its relationship to his argument.

5. Brudnoy stresses that America is not at war with terrorism in general, but is battling specifically *Islamist terrorism*. Is this true? If so, could such an assertive identification be made by politicians and the government? Why or why not?

6. Brudnoy closes his essay with the statement, "we are foolishly polite when we need to be fiercely determined." Why does he say America is being "foolishly polite"? What is the "fierce" determination he claims it must have in order to effectively fight terrorist acts? Do you agree?

Self Evident

Ani Difranco

The events of September 11, 2001, left many people at a loss for words. But soon after the event, singers and songwriters began to form artistic responses to how they felt about what happened. In the next piece, folksinger, poet, and songwriter Ani Difranco expresses her own feelings about September 11. As you read her poem, consider how she uses words to convey her viewpoint. In what ways do her words carry multiple meanings and messages?

Ani Difranco is a folksinger and songwriter who has been producing records since 1990. She was listed in *Ms.* magazine's twenty-fifth anniversary issue as one of the "21 Feminists for the 21st Century." Her most recent albums include *Swing Set* (2000), *Reveling Reckoning* (2001), and *So Much Shouting, So Much Laughter* (2002). This poem can be found on her Web site, at <www.righteousbabe.com>.

self evident

yes,
us people are just poems
we're 90% metaphor
with a leanness of meaning
approaching hyper-distillation
and once upon a time
we were moonshine
rushing down the throat of a giraffe
yes, rushing down the long hallway
despite what the p.a. announcement says
yes, rushing down the long stairs
with the whiskey of eternity
fermented and distilled
to eighteen minutes
burning down our throats
down the hall
down the stairs
in a building so tall
that it will always be there
yes, it's part of a pair
there on the bow of noah's ark
the most prestigious couple
just kickin back parked
against a perfectly blue sky
on a morning beatific
in its indian summer breeze
on the day that america
fell to its knees
after strutting around for a century
without saying thank you
or please

and the shock was subsonic
and the smoke was deafening
between the setup and the punch line
cuz we were all on time for work that day
we all boarded that plane for to fly

and then while the fires were raging
we all climbed up on the windowsill
and then we all held hands
and jumped into the sky

and every borough looked up when it heard the first blast
and then every dumb action movie was summarily surpassed
and the exodus uptown by foot and motorcar
looked more like war than anything i've seen so far
so far
so far
so fierce and ingenious
a poetic specter so far gone
that every jackass newscaster was struck dumb and stumbling
over 'oh my god' and 'this is unbelievable' and on and on
and i'll tell you what, while we're at it
you can keep the pentagon
keep the propaganda
keep each and every tv
that's been trying to convince me
to participate
in some prep school punk's plan to perpetuate retribution
perpetuate retribution
even as the blue toxic smoke of our lesson in retribution
is still hanging in the air
and there's ash on our shoes
and there's ash in our hair
and there's a fine silt on every mantle
from hell's kitchen to brooklyn
and the streets are full of stories
sudden twists and near misses
and soon every open bar is crammed to the rafters
with tales of narrowly averted disasters
and the whiskey is flowin
like never before
as all over the country
folks just shake their heads
and pour

so here's a toast to all the folks who live in palestine
afghanistan
iraq

el salvador

here's a toast to the folks living on the pine ridge reservation
under the stone cold gaze of mt. rushmore

here's a toast to all those nurses and doctors
who daily provide women with a choice
who stand down a threat the size of oklahoma city
just to listen to a young woman's voice

here's a toast to all the folks on death row right now
awaiting the executioner's guillotine
who are shackled there with dread and can only escape into their heads
to find peace in the form of a dream

cuz take away our playstations
and we are a third world nation
under the thumb of some blue blood royal son
who stole the oval office and that phony election
i mean
it don't take a weatherman
to look around and see the weather
jeb said he'd deliver florida, folks
and boy did he ever

and we hold these truths to be self evident:
#1 george w. bush is not president
#2 america is not a true democracy
#3 the media is not fooling me
cuz i am a poem heeding hyper-distillation
i've got no room for a lie so verbose
i'm looking out over my whole human family
and i'm raising my glass in a toast

here's to our last drink of fossil fuels
let us vow to get off of this sauce
shoo away the swarms of commuter planes
and find that train ticket we lost
cuz once upon a time the line followed the river
and peeked into all the backyards
and the laundry was waving
the graffiti was teasing us
from brick walls and bridges
we were rolling over ridges
through valleys
under stars
i dream of touring like duke ellington

in my own railroad car
i dream of waiting on the tall blonde wooden benches
in a grand station aglow with grace
and then standing out on the platform
and feeling the air on my face

give back the night its distant whistle
give the darkness back its soul
give the big oil companies the finger finally
and relearn how to rock-n-roll
yes, the lessons are all around us and a change is waiting there
so it's time to pick through the rubble, clean the streets
and clear the air
get our government to pull its big dick out of the sand
of someone else's desert
put it back in its pants
and quit the hypocritical chants of
freedom forever

cuz when one lone phone rang
in two thousand and one
at ten after nine
on nine one one
which is the number we all called
when that lone phone rang right off the wall
right off our desk and down the long hall
down the long stairs
in a building so tall
that the whole world turned
just to watch it fall

and while we're at it
remember the first time around?
the bomb?
the ryder truck?
the parking garage?
the princess that didn't even feel the pea?
remember joking around in our apartment on avenue D?

can you imagine how many paper coffee cups would have to change their
design
following a fantastical reversal of the new york skyline?

it was a joke, of course
it was a joke

at the time
and that was just a few years ago
so let the record show
that the FBI was all over that case
that the plot was obvious and in everybody's face
and scoping that scene
religiously
the CIA
or is it KGB?
committing countless crimes against humanity
with this kind of eventuality
as its excuse
for abuse after expensive abuse
and it didn't have a clue
look, another window to see through
way up here
on the 104th floor
look
another key
another door
10% literal
90% metaphor
3000 some poems disguised as people
on an almost too perfect day
should be more than pawns
in some asshole's passion play
so now it's your job
and it's my job
to make it that way
to make sure they didn't die in vain
sshhhhhh. . . .
baby listen
hear the train?

THINKING CRITICALLY

1. What do you think is the meaning of Difranco's title, "Self Evident"?

2. How did you feel after reading this poem? Uplifted? Disturbed? Angry? Soothed? What do you think Difranco wanted her poem to do? Who is its intended audience? Explain.

3. Would this poem and its message be as powerful if it were an essay? Explain.

4. Consider the way Difranco's poem is punctuated. Why does she choose to break different lines the way she does? What about her lack of capital letters?

5. Identify three sections of the poem that have particular appeal or seem powerful to you. Why?

6. What other references to terrorism does Difranco make in addition to September 11? Why do you think she cites these other events?

7. In the eleventh stanza of her poem, Difranco cites several "truths." What are these "truths"? Why does she identify these particular ones? How do they connect to the events of September 11? Write a response to each of the "truths" she cites presenting your own perspective.

Nameless Event
William Safire

In the next short piece, language maven William Safire discusses how the events of September 11, 2001, lack a proper name. America seemed, literally, at a loss for adequate words to describe what happened. Unlike other tragedies that center on a single location, September 11, 2001, presents unique circumstances that almost prevent its being satisfactorily named.

Pulitzer-prize-winning writer William Safire is considered one of the most recognized authorities on language today. A former speechwriter for President Richard Nixon, Safire has authored and/or edited more than twenty-five books on language, political speeches and quotations, and wisdom. He is also the author of *Scandalmonger* (2001), a historical novel that traces five political scandals when the United States was still in its infancy. Safire writes a weekly column, "On Language," for the *New York Times Magazine,* from which this piece was excerpted from his October 7, 2001, editorial.

1 The surprise attack on the U.S. fleet in 1941 is remembered by the name of the place where it happened: Pearl Harbor. The bloodiest day in all our wars is also identified by its locale: Antietam creek (though Southerners often identify that battle by the nearby town, Sharpsburg, Md). The shocking murder of a president is known by its victim: *the Kennedy assassination.*

2 But what label is applied to the horrific (more horrid than *horrible,* perhaps because of its less frequent use and similarity in emphasis to *terrific*) events of Sept. 11, 2001?

3 Because the calamities occurred almost simultaneously in two cities, they could not adopt the name of one locality or single structure: taken together, they are not written about in shorthand as *the twin towers destruction* or *the bombing of the Pentagon.* (And *bombing* is a misnomer, since no bomb was dropped.) *Attack* (or *Assault*) *on America* has been a frequent usage, but it seems too general, since Pearl Harbor was also an attack on the U.S.

4 *Terrorist massacre* is accurate, since *massacre* means "indiscriminate killing of large numbers," but that phrase has not been widely adopted. *The recent tragic events* is euphemistic and antiseptic, and *the catastrophe in New York and Washington* too long.

5   We may settle on using the date. Just as F.D.R. vividly identified Dec. 7, 1941, as "a date which will live in infamy," many journalists use "ever since Sept. 11" as shorthand for this new date of infamy. (A further shortening is 9/11, as in "The New York Times 9/11 Neediest Fund," which is also a play on the number punched on a telephone keyboard for emergencies.) In time, however, the nation's choice of the date of Dec. 7 was replaced by the location of the disaster, as Americans "remember Pearl Harbor." On that analogy, perhaps a new designation will appear for the disaster that struck an unsuspecting nation now seeking a return to normalcy.

THINKING CRITICALLY

1. Consider Safire's title describing September 11, 2001. Why does he call it a "nameless event"? What obstacles do we encounter when trying to "name" the day and what happened? Explain.

2. Safire wrote this essay less than one month after September 11, 2001. In paragraph 5, he conjectures, "perhaps a new designation will appear for the disaster." Has a new name emerged? Do you think that the tragedy will be renamed as Pearl Harbor was? Why or why not?

3. How do we name things? What is the significance of a name of an event or circumstance? Think about the names of other important events in American history. How do these names compare to the name Americans have adopted for September 11, 2001? Explain.

4. What name would you give to September 11, 2001? Would you keep the date as the name, or use something else? In addition to the name you chose, explain why you think the title you chose is appropriate and fitting.

■ MAKING CONNECTIONS

1. Try to identify as many war words as possible and their pop-culture uses in today's lexicon. Then, discuss whether the use of these words in common speech has diluted or influenced our view of war itself.

2. Find out more information about some of the words Taheri and Guirard use in their editorials: *shahid, entehari, haram, ta'rif, ahkam, hodoud, mujaheddin, jahannam*, etc. If possible, ask a student who speaks Arabic to help you understand what these words mean. Try to make connections between the words and meanings with Western equivalents. Are some words simply untranslatable? Do the semantics of these words change how different cultures understand terrorism, war, and faith? Explain.

3. Write an essay in which you discuss your personal view of the "war on terrorism" as a label and a policy. Consider what the term means to you. What does it mean to the general population? To people from outside of the United States? Interview a spectrum of people for their viewpoint on what the phrase means, and what their interpretations might mean.

4. As a radio talk-show host, David Brudnoy frequently interviews people to discuss social, political, and economic issues. Create a fictitious dialogue between Brudnoy and another writer featured in this section based on your analysis of their particular essays. If necessary, research both authors for additional background information.

5. Several of the authors in this section, including Taheri, Guirard, and Brudnoy, touch on the issue of what Islam professes, and what its followers seem to believe and support. Research this issue in greater depth in an exploratory essay. In addition to online research, try to interview some students who practice Islam for their perspective on this issue.

6. David Brudnoy, a known political conservative, demands in his essay that politicians stop engaging in "politically correct" language. Write an essay exploring the ways politically correct language has affected international relationships over the last twenty years. Does it make America weaker or stronger—or does it have any impact at all? Has it improved international views of America? Is such linguistic sensitivity reciprocated? Explain.

7. In his article on the language of war, Jon Hooten quotes linguist George Lakoff (paragraph 31), "It is important to distinguish what is metaphorical from what is not." Read the article Lakoff wrote before the Gulf War in 1991 at <http://philosophy.uoregon.edu/metaphor/lakoff-1.htm> and write an essay in which you explore this idea. Why is it important to make such distinctions? What are the implications of the linguistic blurring of real versus metaphorical acts of war?

8. Write your own poem on a political event about which you feel strongly. After you have written your poem, consider the ways poetic expression allows you to creatively articulate and convey your feelings.

4 The Art of Conversation

- Speaking over 6,500 different languages worldwide, human beings are social creatures who depend on language to survive. Consider the ways you use language to communicate. What social, biological, and intellectual influences affect the way you communicate with different people?

He Says, She Says: Differences in Discourse

Some sociologists and psychologists claim that men and women talk differently—either due to social conditioning or basic physiology—and that the "male" form of discourse is the preferred form of communication. With the great interest in communication, a growing number of scholars are attempting to prove that important differences distinguish the way men and women use language. Most researchers present theories that such differences are the results of either discriminatory socialization or genetic disposition. The first two essays in this cluster face off as they address the assumption that woman speak more than men. In "Women Talk Too Much," Janet Holmes explains that the stereotype that women speak more than men is rooted in how our society values speech and claims this stereotype simply isn't true. Tony Kornheiser, however, comparing conversations between himself and his daughter and son asserts, "Women Have More to Say on Everything."

In "Sex Differences," linguist Ronald Macaulay says that although some differences in expression reflect social and cultural conditioning, much of the controversy regarding gender-based linguistic differences are based on myths and age-old stereotypes. Bestselling author and sociolinguist Deborah Tannen takes a different perspective. In "'I'll Explain It to You': Lecturing and Listening," she demonstrates how social and cultural conditioning often creates inequalities in conversations, where men dominate discourse and women let them—causing tension and resentment. Finally, communications professors Teri Kwal Gamble and Michael W. Gamble project the discussion on gender styles to nonverbal behavior, pointing out that how this "gendered" sublanguage is influenced internally by culture and externally by the media.

Let's Talk About It: Conversation in Action

Human beings are social animals. As such, conversation forms the foundation of our social interactions. This section discusses the social elements of conversation, its importance to our very existence, and its role in our culture. Ronald Wardhaugh describes the unspoken, and often unconscious, expectations we bring to everyday conversation. In "The Social Basis of Talk," Wardhaugh explains that trust, shared experience and expectations of universal truths play a vital role in the success of social conversation. Margaret Wheatley discusses how conversation has the power to effect social change in "Some Friends and I Started Talking." And James Gorman takes a humorous look at a curious speech pattern he noticed while conversing with his students in "Like, Uptalk?"

Over the last decade, the Internet has revolutionized how we communicate and view the world and ourselves. The next two essays explore how electronic communication has affected our conversations and our relationships with one another. Robert Kuttner discusses the detrimental effects of the instant nature of e-mail in "The Other Side of E-Mail." In "Come in CQ," Ellen Ullman describes how midnight conversations over the Internet with a coworker developed into an online romance that came to a grinding halt when they had to converse face to face.

■ HE SAYS, SHE SAYS: DIFFERENCES IN DISCOURSE

Women Talk Too Much
Janet Holmes

Do women really talk more than men? Many people seem to think so, but is this assumption based on stereotypes or fact? And who determines how much talk is "too much?" In the next essay, linguist Janet Holmes sets out to debunk the "language myth" that women talk too much. In fact, explains Holmes, women speak less than men do in situations where talk is most "valued." She also asserts that the claim that "women talk too much" is inherently biased because it is men, who tend to hold positions of power, who determine when talk is too much (such as women speaking in informal settings) and when it is appropriate (men speaking in public forums).

Janet Holmes is a professor of sociolinguistics at the Victoria University of Wellington, New Zealand. Her publications include, *An Introduction to Sociolinguistics*, and *Women, Men and Politeness*. She has published many articles on numerous sociolinguistic topics, including spoken New Zealand English, sexist language, humor, and workplace discourse.

1 Do women talk more than men? Proverbs and sayings in many languages express the view that women are always talking:

2 *Women's tongues are like lambs' tails—they are never still. —English*

3 *The North Sea will sooner be found wanting in water than a woman at a loss for words. —Jutlandic*

4 *The woman with active hands and feet, marry her, but the woman with overactive mouth, leave well alone. —Maori*

5 Some suggest that while women talk, men are silent patient listeners.

6 *When both husband and wife wear pants it is not difficult to tell them apart—he is the one who is listening. —American*

7 *Nothing is so unnatural as a talkative man or a quiet woman. —Scottish*

8 Others indicate that women's talk is not valued but is rather considered noisy, irritating prattle:

9 *Where there are women and geese there's noise. —Japanese*

10 Indeed, there is a Japanese character which consists of three instances of the character for the concept 'woman' and which translates as 'noisy'! My favourite

proverb, because it attributes not noise but rather power to the woman speaker is this Chinese one:

11 *The tongue is the sword of a woman and she never lets it become rusty.*

12 So what are the facts? Do women dominate the talking time? Do men struggle to get a word in edgewise, as the stereotype suggests?

The Evidence

13 Despite the widespread belief that women talk more than men, most of the available evidence suggests just the opposite. When women and men are together, it is the men who talk most. Two Canadian researchers, Deborah James and Janice Drakich, reviewed sixty-three studies which examined the amount of talk used by American women and men in different contexts. Women talked more than men in only two studies.

14 In New Zealand, too, research suggests that men generally dominate the talking time. Margaret Franken compared the amount of talk used by female and male 'experts' assisting a female TV host to interview well-known public figures. In a situation where each of three interviewers was entitled to a third of the interviewers' talking time, the men took more than half on every occasion.

15 I found the same pattern analyzing the number of questions asked by participants in one hundred public seminars. In all but seven, men dominated the discussion time. Where the numbers of women and men present were about the same, men asked almost two-thirds of the questions during the discussion. Clearly women were not talking more than men in these contexts.

16 Even when they hold influential positions, women sometimes find it hard to contribute as much as men to a discussion. A British company appointed four women and four men to the eight most highly paid management positions. The managing director commented that the men often patronized the women and tended to dominate meetings:

17 *I had a meeting with a [female] sales manager and three of my [male] directors once . . . It took about two hours. She only spoke once and one of my fellow directors cut across her and said 'What Anne is trying to say Roger is . . .' and I think that about sums it up. He knew better than Anne what she was trying to say, and she never got anything said.*

18 There is abundant evidence that this pattern starts early. Many researchers have compared the relative amounts that girls and boys contribute to classroom talk. In a wide range of communities, from kindergarten through primary, secondary and tertiary education, the same pattern recurs—males dominate classroom talk. So on this evidence we must conclude that the stereotype of the garrulous woman reflects sexist prejudice rather than objective reality.

Looking for an Explanation

19 Why is the reality so different from the myth? To answer this question, we need to go beyond broad generalizations and look more carefully at the patterns identified. Although some teachers claim that boys are 'by nature more spirited and less disciplined,' there is no evidence to suggest that males are biologically programmed to talk more than females. It is much more likely that the explanation involves social factors.

What Is the Purpose of the Talk?

20 One relevant clue is the fact that talk serves different functions in different contexts. Formal public talk is often aimed at informing people or persuading them to agree to a particular point of view (e.g., political speeches, television debates, radio interviews, public lectures, etc.). Public talk is often undertaken by people who wish to claim or confirm some degree of public status. Effective talk in public and in the media can enhance your social status—as politicians and other public performers know well. Getting and holding the floor is regarded as desirable, and competition for the floor in such contexts is common. (There is also some risk, of course, since a poor performance can be damaging.)

21 Classroom research suggests that more talk is associated with higher social status or power. Many studies have shown that teachers (regardless of their gender) tend to talk for about two-thirds of the available time. But the boys dominate the relatively small share of the talking time that remains for pupils. In this context, where talk is clearly valued, it appears that the person with most status has the right to talk most. The boys may therefore be asserting a claim to higher status than the girls by appropriating the majority of the time left for pupil talk.

22 The way women and men behave in formal meetings and seminars provides further support for this explanation. Evidence collected by American, British and New Zealand researchers shows that men dominate the talking time in committee meetings, staff meetings, seminars and task-oriented decision-making groups. If you are sceptical, use a stopwatch to time the amount of talk contributed by women and men at political and community meetings you attend. This explanation proposes that men talk more than women in public, formal contexts because they perceive participating and verbally contributing in such contexts as an activity which enhances their status, and men seem to be more concerned with asserting status and power than women are.

23 By contrast, in more private contexts, talk usually serves interpersonal functions. The purpose of informal or intimate talk is not so much status enhancement as establishing or maintaining social contact with others, making social connections, developing and reinforcing friendships and intimate relationships. Interestingly, the few studies which have investigated informal talk have found that there are fewer differences in the amount contributed by women and men in these contexts (though men still talked more in nearly a third of the informal studies reviewed by Deborah James and Janice Drakich). Women, it seems, are willing to

talk more in relaxed social contexts, especially where the talk functions to develop and maintain social relationships.

24   Another piece of evidence that supports this interpretation is the *kind* of talk women and men contribute in mixed-sex discussions. Researchers analysing the functions of different utterances have found that men tend to contribute more information and opinions, while women contribute more agreeing, supportive talk, more of the kind of talk that encourages others to contribute. So men's talk tends to be more referential or informative, while women's talk is more supportive and facilitative.

25   Overall, then, women seem to use talk to develop personal relationships and maintain family connections and friendships more often than to make claims to status or to directly influence others in public contexts. Of course, there are exceptions, as Margaret Thatcher, Benazir Bhutto and Jenny Shipley demonstrate. But, until recently, many women seem not to have perceived themselves as appropriate contributors to public, formal talk.

26   In New Zealand we identified another context where women contributed more talk than men. Interviewing people to collect samples of talk for linguistic analysis, we found that women were much more likely than men (especially young men) to be willing to talk to us at length. For example, Miriam Meyerhoff asked a group of ten young people to describe a picture to a female and to a male interviewer. It was made quite clear to the interviewees that the more speech they produced the better. In this situation, the women contributed significantly more speech than the men, both to the male and to the female interviewer.

27   In the private but semi-formal context of an interview, then, women contributed more talk than men. Talk in this context could not be seen as enhancing the status of the people interviewed. The interviewers were young people with no influence over the interviewees. The explanation for the results seems to be that the women were being more cooperative than the men in a context where more talk was explicitly sought by the interviewer.

Social Confidence

28 If you know a lot about a particular topic, you are generally more likely to be willing to contribute to a discussion about it. So familiarity or expertise can also affect the amount a person contributes to a particular discussion. In one interesting study the researcher supplied particular people with extra information, making them the 'experts' on the topic to be discussed. Regardless of gender, these 'experts' talked more in the subsequent discussions than their uninformed conversational partners (though male 'experts' still used more talking time in conversation with uninformed women than female 'experts' did with uninformed men).

29   Looking at people's contributions to the discussion section of seminars, I found a similar effect from expertise or topic familiarity. Women were more likely to ask questions and make comments when the topic was one they could claim expert knowledge about. In a small seminar on the current state of the economy, for instance, several women economists who had been invited to attend contributed to

the discussion, making this one of the very few seminars where women's contributions exceeded men's.

30   Another study compared the relative amount of talk of spouses. Men dominated the conversations between couples with traditional gender roles and expectations, but when the women were associated with a feminist organization they tended to talk more than their husbands. So feminist women were more likely to challenge traditional gender roles in interaction.

31   It seems possible that both these factors—expert status and feminist philosophy—have the effect of developing women's social confidence. This explanation also fits with the fact that women tend to talk more with close friends and family, when women are in the majority, and also when they are explicitly invited to talk (in an interview, for example).

Perceptions and Implications

32 If social confidence explains the greater contributions of women in some social contexts, it is worth asking why girls in school tend to contribute less than boys. Why should they feel unconfident in the classroom? Here is the answer which one sixteen-year-old gave:

33 *Sometimes I feel like saying that I disagree, that there are other ways of looking at it, but where would that get me? My teacher thinks I'm showing off, and the boys jeer. But if I pretend I don't understand, it's very different. The teacher is sympathetic and the boys are helpful. They really respond if they can show YOU how it is done, but there's nothing but 'aggro' if you give any signs of showing THEM how it is done.*

34 Talking in class is often perceived as 'showing off', especially if it is girl-talk. Until recently, girls have preferred to keep a low profile rather than attract negative attention.

35   Teachers are often unaware of the gender distribution of talk in their classrooms. They usually consider that they give equal amounts of attention to girls and boys, and it is only when they make a tape recording that they realize that boys are dominating the interactions. Dale Spender, an Australian feminist who has been a strong advocate of female rights in this area, noted that teachers who tried to restore the balance by deliberately 'favouring' the girls were astounded to find that despite their efforts they continued to devote more time to the boys in their classrooms. Another study reported that a male science teacher who managed to create an atmosphere in which girls and boys contributed more equally to discussion felt that he was devoting 90 per cent of his attention to the girls. And so did his male pupils. They complained vociferously that the girls were getting too much talking time.

36   In other public contexts, too, such as seminars and debates, when women and men are deliberately given an equal amount of the highly valued talking time, there is often a perception that they are getting more than their fair share. Dale Spender explains this as follows:

37 *The talkativeness of women has been gauged in comparison not with men but with silence. Women have not been judged on the grounds of whether they talk more than men, but of whether they talk more than silent women.*

38 In other words, if women talk at all, this may be perceived as 'too much' by men who expect them to provide a silent, decorative background in many social contexts. This may sound outrageous, but think about how you react when precocious children dominate the talk at an adult party. As women begin to make inroads into formerly 'male' domains such as business and professional contexts, we should not be surprised to find that their contributions are not always perceived positively or even accurately.

Conclusion

39 We have now reached the conclusion that the question 'Do women talk more than men?' can't be answered with a straight 'yes' or 'no'. The answer is rather, 'It all depends.' It depends on many different factors, including the social context in which the talk is taking place, the kind of talk involved and the relative social confidence of the speakers, which is affected by such things as their social roles (e.g., teacher, host, interviewee, wife) and their familiarity with the topic.

40 It appears that men generally talk more in formal, public contexts where informative and persuasive talk is highly valued, and where talk is generally the prerogative of those with some societal status and has the potential for increasing that status. Women, on the other hand, are more likely to contribute in private, informal interactions, where talk more often functions to maintain relationships, and in other situations where for various reasons they feel socially confident.

41 Finally, and most radically, we might question the assumption that more talk is always a good thing. 'Silence is golden,' says the proverb, and there are certainly contexts in all cultures where silence is more appropriate than talk, where words are regarded as inadequate vehicles for feelings, or where keeping silent is an expression of appreciation or respect. Sometimes it is the silent participants who are the powerful players. In some contexts the strong silent male is an admired stereotype. However, while this is true, it must be recognized that talk is very highly valued in western culture. It seems likely, then, that as long as holding the floor is equated with influence, the complexities of whether women or men talk most will continue to be a matter for debate.

THINKING CRITICALLY

1. How do the proverbs preceding Holmes's essay set the tone for her essay? What is remarkable about these proverbs? Have you heard any of them? Which one do you like or dislike the most, and why?

2. In what ways does the context and setting of the conversation influence men and women's talking patterns? Explain.

3. Holmes explains that in situations where talk is valued—in the classroom or boardroom for instance—males are likely to speak more than females. If this is true, what accounts for the excess of proverbs and sayings regarding women's talk? Explain.

4. In paragraph 32, Holmes cites a 16-year-old girl who explains why she doesn't speak more in class. Evaluate this girl's response in the context of your own social and classroom experiences in high school.

5. What, according to Holmes, are the differences between men and women's use of talk? Do you agree or disagree with her conclusions? Explain.

WRITING ASSIGNMENTS

1. Ben Johnson, a seventeenth-century writer and playwright, wrote a popular play called "'Epicene', or, 'The Silent Woman.'" Locate a copy of this play and write an essay in which you make connections between attitudes toward women's talk three hundred years ago and today. How have things changed, and how are they similar?

2. Several of the authors in this section seem to advocate their own gender's communication style. Write an essay in which you support your gender's communication style, or advocate or analyze the style of the opposite sex. Is one better than the other? Why or why not? Remember to support your perspective with examples.

3. Do you think that understanding gender patterns in conversation will change the way men and women speak to each other? Do you think that such changes are necessary and healthy? Alternatively, do you think that some men and women have a need for the established patterns? Explain.

No Detail Is Too Small for Girls Answering a Simple Question
Tony Kornheiser

A common complaint between the sexes is that men and women just don't speak the same language. In the next piece, columnist and humorist Tony Kornheiser observes the difference in the communication style of his daughter and son, and by extension, women and men. His conclusion is that "women have more to say on everything."

Tony Kornheiser is columnist and sports writer for the *Washington Post*. He also hosts "The Tony Kornheiser Show" on ESPN radio and co-hosts "Pardon the Interruption" with fellow *Post* sports columnist Mike Wilbon on ESPN2. He is the author of several books, including *Pumping Irony* and *Bald as I Want to Be*.

1 The last time I ventured into my favorite column area—differences between men and women—was when the infamous Teen Talk Barbie doll came out. Barbie was given 270 things to say, and one of them was "Math class is tough!" This, of course, is infuriating, because it plays into the damaging sexual stereotype that girls are stupid in math.

2 Well, I got cute and wrote how everyone knows girls are stupid in math. I gave an example of my own daughter, whom I love dearly, and who is a sensitive and caring soul, and how when I ask her, "If a bus leaves Cleveland at 7 p.m. heading for Pittsburgh, 200 miles away, and traveling 50 miles per hour, when will it arrive?" she answers, "Do all the children have seat belts, Daddy?" I thought it was a pretty good line. But I received all kinds of nasty mail, much of it—so help me—from female mathematicians, and female actuaries and female physicists specializing in subatomic particle acceleration. In that same column, I wrote that boys are stupid in English, yet I didn't get a single letter of protest from boys. Obviously, they couldn't read the column.

3 Anyway . . . here we go again.

4 My daughter recently came home from sleep-away camp, where she'd spent five weeks. She looked great. And I was so proud of her, going away by herself.

5 The first question I asked her was "How was camp?"

6 She began by saying, "Well, the day I left, I got on the bus, and I sat next to Ashley, and she brought Goldfish, which was good because I forgot my Now and Laters, and then Shannon came over, and she's from Baltimore, and she gets her clothes at the Gap, and she had a Game Boy, but all she had was Tetris, which I have, so we asked Jenny, who was the counselor, if anybody had Sonic the Hedgehog, but. . . ."

7 She went on like this for a few minutes, still talking about the bus ride up to camp five weeks ago, and I came to the horrifying realization that she was actually going to tell me how camp was, minute by minute. Because this is what girls do (and when they grow up and become women, they do it, too, as any man can vouch for). They gather information and dispense it without discrimination. Everything counts the same! It is not that women lack the ability to prioritize information, it is that they don't think life is as simple as men do, and so they are fascinated by the multiplicity of choices that they see.

8 This is why you have to be very specific with what you ask women. If, for example, you missed a Rams game, and you know a woman who saw it, never, ever ask, "What happened?" Unless you have nowhere to go until Thursday.

9 Ask:

10 1. Who won?

11 2. What was the score?

12 3. Was anyone carried out on a stretcher?

13 You must get them to fast-forward.

14 Left to their own devices, girls go through life volubly answering essay questions. And boys? Multiple choice is way too complicated. Boys restrict themselves to true/false.

15   Boys do not gather and retain information, they focus on results.

16   My son went to camp for six weeks—one week longer than my daughter. As I had with my daughter, I asked him, "How was camp?"

17   He said, "Good. I busted Jason's nose." Short and to the point.

18   This was followed by, "Can we go to McDonald's?"

19   Did I mention the cheers? My daughter came back with cheers. About 187,640 musical cheers, all of which are accompanied by an intricate series of hand, feet and hip movements. She went to camp a 10-year-old, she came back a Vandella.

20   It's amazing, the affinity of girls and cheers. If you've ever been to camp, you know that girls have a special gene for cheers and that even girls who have never been to camp before—or, for that matter, been to America or spoken English before—automatically know all the cheers the moment they step off the bus. As a boy at camp, I used to look at girls in amazement, wondering why they would waste their time like that, when they could be doing useful things like me—memorizing Willie Mays' doubles and sacrifice flies during an entire decade.

21   Boys don't do musical cheers.

22   Even during "color war," that traditional camp competition when cheering is supposed to result in points, here's how boys cheer on the way to the dining hall: They look at the other team and say, "Yo, Green Team, drop dead."

THINKING CRITICALLY

1. Kornheiser, in the context of his daughter's communication style, states that women "gather information and dispense it without discrimination." Respond to Kornheiser's assertion. Is there truth to his stereotypical description of the way men and women relay information? Explain.

2. In his introduction, Kornheiser relates how his joking about girls and math resulted in angry letters from many women, yet his comments about boys and English received no such response. What accounts for this difference? Is it more important to dispel one stereotype than the other? Why or why not?

3. Based on his essay, can you determine which communication style Kornheiser prefers? As a writer and columnist, is Kornheiser more "male" or "female" in his communication style? Explain.

4. How would you characterize Kornheiser's tone and style? What assumptions does he make about his audience? Does his article appeal to both sexes? Why or why not?

WRITING ASSIGNMENTS

1. Many of the authors in this section seem to defend their own gender's communication style. Write an essay in which you support your gender's communication style, or defend or analyze the style of the opposite sex. Is one better than the other? Why or why not? Remember to support your perspective with examples.

2. In his essay, Tony Kornheiser describes the differences between the way his children, one boy and one girl, communicate. How do his observations connect to stereotypes between how men and women communicate? Are these communication styles simply a fact of gender? Explain, using examples from Kornheiser's essay and from other authors in this section, such as Tannen and Gamble.

Sex Differences
Ronald Macaulay

Contrary to popular belief, men and women do not speak different forms of English. Nor are there innate or genetic differences in the way males and females acquire or use language. So argues Ronald Macaulay, a professor of linguistics and an expert on language acquisition. Although social background can generate some differences in the way the sexes speak, it is pure myth and stereotyping that sex differences show up in language patterns. Males do not, for instance, instinctively gravitate to coarse language nor are females preternaturally drawn to the language of nurturing.

Ronald Macaulay is professor of linguistics at Pitzer College. He is the author of *Generally Speaking: How Children Learn Language* (1980), *Locating Dialect in Discourse: The Language of Honest Men and Bonnie Lasses in Ayr* (1991), and *The Social Art: Language and Its Uses* (1996), from which this essay is taken.

I think the English women speak awfy nice. The little girls are very feminine just because they've a nice voice. But the same voice in an Englishman— nae really. I think the voice lets the men down but it flatters the girls.

Aberdeen housewife

1 More nonsense has been produced on the subject of sex differences than on any linguistic topic, with the possible exception of spelling. Perhaps this is appropriate. The relations between the sexes have generally been considered a fit topic for comedy. In his book *Language: Its Nature, Development and Origin,* Otto Jespersen has a chapter entitled "The Woman" in which he manages to include every stereotype about women that was current at the time. It is almost unfair to quote directly but even in the 1920s Jespersen should have known better, particularly since he lived in Denmark where women have traditionally shown an independent spirit. Here are a few examples:

There can be no doubt that women exercise a great and universal influence on linguistic development through their instinctive shrinking from coarse and gross expressions and their preference for refined and (in certain spheres) veiled and indirect expressions.

Men will certainly with great justice object that there is a danger of the language becoming languid and insipid if we are always to content ourselves with women's expressions.

Women move preferably in the central field of language, avoiding everything that is out of the way or bizarre, while men will often either coin new words or expressions or take up old-fashioned ones, if by that means they are enabled, or think they are enabled, to find a more adequate or precise expression for their thoughts. Woman as a rule follows the main road of language, where man is often inclined to turn aside into a narrow footpath or even to strike out a new path for himself. . . .

Those who want to learn a foreign language will therefore always do well at the first stage to read many ladies' novels, because they will there continually meet with just those everyday words and combinations which the foreigner is above all in need of, what may be termed the indispensable small-change of a language.

Woman is linguistically quicker than man: quicker to learn, quicker to hear, and quicker to answer. A man is slower: he hesitates, he chews the cud to make sure of the taste of words, and thereby comes to discover similarities with and differences from other words, both in sound and in sense, thus preparing himself for the appropriate use of the fittest noun or adjective.

The superior readiness of speech of women is a concomitant of the fact that their vocabulary is smaller and more central than that of men.

2   Such stereotypes are often reinforced by works of fiction. Since little information about prosodic features or paralinguistic features is contained in the normal writing system, novelists frequently try to indicate the tone of voice by descriptive verbs and adjectives to introduce dialogue. An examination of several novels revealed an interesting difference between the expression used to introduce men's or women's speech:

MEN	WOMEN
said firmly	said quietly
said bluntly	asked innocently
said coldly	echoed obediently
said smugly	said loyally
urged	offered humbly
burst forth	whispered
demanded aggressively	asked mildly
said challengingly	agreed placidly
cried furiously	smiled complacently
exclaimed contemptuously	fumbled on
cried portentously	implored
grumbled	pleaded

The surprising part is that the two lists are totally distinct. No doubt the novelists intended to be realistic in describing two very different styles of speech but, in doing so, they also reinforce the stereotypes of men and women.

3   In the past twenty years the question of sex differences in language has been a growth industry as scholars have attempted to claim and to counter claims that there are or are not important differences in the ways in which males and females use language. It would, of course, be surprising if there were not. Both men and women will use the forms of language, registers, and styles appropriate to the activities in which they are engaged. To the extent that these activities differ between males and females, it is to be expected that their language will differ. This much is obvious. There is no need to look for a genetic basis for such differences. It is also obvious that those in a position of power often expect to be treated with deference by those over whom they have power. To the extent that in Western industrialized societies men have more often been in positions of power over women rather than the reverse, it is hardly surprising if women are sometimes found to have used deferential language. There have also been certain violent activities, such as fighting or contact sports, that until recently have been exclusively a male province, and there are forms of language appropriate to them that may have been less common among women.

4   Even in making such banal statements, one must qualify them by reference to "Western industrialized societies" or by limiting them to a single section of the community. For example, it is probably true that in Britain until World War I middle-class women were less likely to swear in public than middle-class men, but working-class women were less inhibited. (G. K. Chesterton reported that in an argument with a fishwife he could not compete in obscenities with her but triumphed in the end by calling her "An adverb! A preposition! A pronoun!")

5   In sociolinguistic studies of complex communities such as Glasgow, New York, and Norwich, it has been shown that women in the lower middle class are likely to be closer in their speech to the women in the class immediately above them than are the men, who are likely to be closer to the men in the class immediately below them. It has been suggested that this is because lower-class speech is associated with toughness and virility and the men in the lower middle class choose to identify with this image rather than with the less "masculine" speech of the upper-class men. It may not be unimportant that in these studies the interviewers were all men.

6   There seems, however, to be a deep-seated desire to find essential differences between the speech of men and women that can either be attributed to some discriminatory kind of socialization or, even better, to genetic disposition. This can be seen in many references to sex differences in language development. Popular belief and scholarly opinion has generally maintained that girls are more advanced in language development than boys at the same age. Jespersen, for example, claimed that girls learned to talk earlier and more quickly than boys, and that the speech of girls is more correct than that of boys.

7   For about fifty years after Jespersen this view was maintained in the scholarly literature on children's development. In 1954 Professor Dorothea McCarthy published an article summarizing what was known about children's language development at that time. Her conclusion about sex differences is:

> One of the most consistent findings to emerge from the mass of data accumulated on language development in American white children seems to be a slight difference in favor of girls in nearly all aspects of language that have been studied.

8   What McCarthy actually found, however, was that the differences were not large enough to be statistically significant. Although psychologists are normally very careful not to make claims about differences that could be the result of chance (that is, are not statistically significant), McCarthy was so convinced that girls were more advanced in their speech that she chose to interpret the evidence the way she did. In a survey of the literature up till 1975, I found that none of the studies provided convincing evidence of consistent sex differences in language development. I concluded that the burden of proof remained with those who wished to claim otherwise. To the best of my knowledge, the situation has not changed since then.

9   What I did find were many examples of preconceived notions of sex differences from the assertion that girls have an innate tendency toward sedentary pursuits to claims that it is easier and more satisfying for the girl baby to imitate the mother's speech than it is for the boy baby to imitate the father's. One example will illustrate the kind of attitude:

> The little girl, showing in her domestic play the over-riding absorption in personal relationships through which she will later fulfill her role of wife, mother and "expressive" leader of the family . . . learns language early in order to communicate. The kind of communication in which she is chiefly interested at this stage concerns the nurturant routines which are the stuff of family life. Sharing and talking about them as she copies and "helps" her mother about the house must enhance the mutual identification of mother and child, which in turn . . . will reinforce imitation of the mother's speech and promote further acquisition of language, at first oriented toward domestic and interpersonal affairs but later adapted to other uses as well. Her intellectual performance is relatively predictable because it is rooted in this early communication, which enables her (environment permitting) to display her inherited potential at an early age.

This is contrasted with the interests of boys:

> Their preoccupation with the working of mechanical things is less interesting to most mothers and fathers are much less available.

As a result the boy's language development is slower:

> His language, less fluent and personal and later to appear than the girl's, develops along more analytic lines and may, in favourable circumstances, pro-

vide the groundwork for later intellectual achievement which could not have been foreseen in his first few years.

Girls, of course, are more predictable:

> The girl, meanwhile, is acquiring the intimate knowledge of human reactions which we call feminine intuition. Perhaps because human reactions are less regular than those of inanimate objects, however, she is less likely to develop the strictly logical habits of thought that intelligent boys acquire, and if gifted may well come to prefer the subtler disciplines of the humanities to the intellectual rigour of science.

I am not sure whether the writer considered himself a scientist, but if his writing is an example of intellectual rigor, then give me the subtlety of the humanities any day. What makes his statement all the more incredible is that it comes after describing a longitudinal study of children that showed no important sex differences in language development.

10   One of the problems with attempting to demonstrate differences in language development is that measures of linguistic proficiency, particularly for young children, are extremely crude instruments. Thus it is not surprising that samples of linguistic behaviour will reveal occasional differences between subgroups of the sample. Such sex differences that have shown up on tests are much smaller than those that have been shown to relate to social background. The fact that most studies show no sex differences and that many of the findings of small differences have been contradicted in other studies should be sufficient warning against drawing conclusions about the linguistic superiority of either sex.

11   There are some differences between males and females that do not depend upon unreliable tests of language development. Boys are much more likely to suffer from speech disorders, such as stuttering, than girls. Adult males on average have deeper voices than adult females because the vibrating part of the vocal cords is about a third longer in men. However, there may be social influences on this physiological difference. It has been claimed that in the United States women may speak as if they were smaller than they are (that is, with higher-pitched voices) and men as if they were bigger than they are (that is, with lower-pitched voices). The "Oxford voice" common among Oxford fellows (all male) at one time was remarkably high pitched, and other social groups have adopted characteristic pitch levels that are not totally "natural."

12   It was reported that once during a debate in the French parliament when a delegate pointed out that there were differences between men and women, another delegate shouted out *Vive la difference!* It is not necessary to believe that men and women are the same to be skeptical about claims as to the differences in the way men and women speak. The desire to emphasize the differences seems to be widespread. Jespersen's chapter remains as a warning signal to all who venture into this murky area that one's prejudices may show through. Jesperson obviously believed (and no doubt so did many of his readers) that what he was saying was self-evident.

However, he ends the chapter by observing that "great social changes are going on in our times which may eventually modify even the linguistic relations of the two sexes." Eventually, even scholars following in Jespersen's footsteps may come to see that men and women are simply people and that what they have in common is more important than *la difference,* at least as far as their use of language is concerned.

13   It is, however, disturbing to find in a work published in 1991 the following passage by a distinguished and respected scholar:

> [I]t is clear why, as sociolinguists have often observed, women are more disposed to adopt the legitimate language (or the legitimate pronunciation): since they are both inclined towards docility with regard to the dominant usages both by the sexual division of labour, which makes them specialize in the sphere of consumption, and by the logic of marriage, which is their main if not their only avenue of social advancement and through which they circulate upwards, women are predisposed to accept, from school onwards, the new demands of the market in symbolic goods.

14   It is a salutary reminder that progress is often an illusion.

THINKING CRITICALLY

1. Why does Macaulay refer to much of the work done on sex differences as "nonsense"?

2. Macaulay charges that fiction often reinforces sexual stereotypes, as novelists attempt to introduce men's or women's speech. Are there any problems with the examples he cites? Support your answer.

3. What examples does Macaulay give to indicate how society influences male or female speech patterns?

4. Because Macaulay sees so many flaws in Jespersen's findings, why does he devote such a large portion of his article to discussing and even quoting Jespersen?

5. Does Macaulay feel that a lessening of sexist language indicates that society has made significant progress in the way it views the sexes?

6. Macaulay wrote his essay for a scholarly audience. In your opinion, is the language used in the essay more like that of a class lecture, a textbook, a radio talk, a professional journal, or a conference presentation? Why?

WRITING ASSIGNMENTS

1. Keep a journal of the expressions writers you encounter use to introduce male and female characters' speech. What conclusions can you draw?

2. Watch a television program with a story line (e.g., a situation comedy, a drama, or a full-length movie). Write a brief critique of the program, based on its presentation of linguistic sex differences.

"I'll Explain It to You": Lecturing and Listening
Deborah Tannen

It is easy to assume that because English belongs to those who use it, men and women speak the same language. That may not be the case. There is strong evidence that male and female conversational patterns differ significantly. In fact, using fascinating examples from her own studies, sociolinguist Deborah Tannen shows that men and women use language in essentially different ways based on gender and cultural conditioning. From early childhood, girls use speech to seek confirmation and reinforce intimacy, whereas boys use it to protect their independence and negotiate group status. Carrying these styles into adulthood, men end up lecturing while women nod warmly and are bored. Is there hope for the sexes? Yes, says the author: by understanding each other's gender style, and by learning to use it on occasion to find a common language.

Deborah Tannen is professor of linguistics at Georgetown University. She is the author of many best-selling books on linguistics and social discourse, including *I Only Say This Because I Love You* (2001), *The Argument Culture* (1999), and *You Just Don't Understand* (1997), from which this essay is excerpted. She has been a featured guest on many news programs, including *20/20, 48 Hours,* and the *News Hour with Jim Lehrer.*

1   At a reception following the publication of one of my books, I noticed a publicist listening attentively to the producer of a popular radio show. He was telling her how the studio had come to be built where it was, and why he would have preferred another site. What caught my attention was the length of time he was speaking while she was listening. He was delivering a monologue that could only be called a lecture, giving her detailed information about the radio reception at the two sites, the architecture of the station, and so on. I later asked the publicist if she had been interested in the information the producer had given her. "Oh, yes," she answered. But then she thought a moment and said, "Well, maybe he did go on a bit." The next day she told me, "I was thinking about what you asked. I couldn't have cared less about what he was saying. It's just that I'm so used to listening to men go on about things I don't care about, I didn't even realize how bored I was until you made me think about it."

2   I was chatting with a man I had just met at a party. In our conversation, it emerged that he had been posted in Greece with the RAF during 1944 and 1945. Since I had lived in Greece for several years, I asked him about his experiences:

What had Greece been like then? How had the Greek villagers treated the British soldiers? What had it been *like* to be a British soldier in wartime Greece? I also offered information about how Greece had changed, what it is like now. He did not pick up on my remarks about contemporary Greece, and his replies to my questions quickly changed from accounts of his own experiences, which I found riveting, to facts about Greek history, which interested me in principle but in the actual telling left me profoundly bored. The more impersonal his talk became, the more I felt oppressed by it, pinned involuntarily in the listener position.

3   At a showing of Judy Chicago's jointly created art work *The Dinner Party,* I was struck by a couple standing in front of one of the displays: The man was earnestly explaining to the woman the meaning of symbols in the tapestry before them, pointing as he spoke. I might not have noticed this unremarkable scene, except that *The Dinner Party* was radically feminist in conception, intended to reflect women's experiences and sensibilities.

4   While taking a walk in my neighborhood on an early summer evening at twilight, I stopped to chat with a neighbor who was walking his dogs. As we stood, I noticed that the large expanse of yard in front of which we were standing was aglitter with the intermittent flickering of fireflies. I called attention to the sight, remarking on how magical it looked. "It's like the Fourth of July," I said. He agreed, and then told me he had read that the lights of fireflies are mating signals. He then explained to me details of how these signals work—for example, groups of fireflies fly at different elevations and could be seen to cluster in different parts of the yard.

5   In all these examples, the men had information to impart and they were imparting it. On the surface, there is nothing surprising or strange about that. What is strange is that there are so many situations in which men have factual information requiring lengthy explanations to impart to women, and so few in which women have comparable information to impart to men.

6   The changing times have altered many aspects of relations between women and men. Now it is unlikely, at least in many circles, for a man to say, "I am better than you because I am a man and you are a woman." But women who do not find men making such statements are nonetheless often frustrated in their dealings with them. One situation that frustrates many women is a conversation that has mysteriously turned into a lecture, with the man delivering the lecture to the woman, who has become an appreciative audience.

7   Once again, the alignment in which women and men find themselves arrayed is asymmetrical. The lecturer is framed as superior in status and expertise, cast in the role of teacher, and the listener is cast in the role of student. If women and men took turns giving and receiving lectures, there would be nothing disturbing about it. What is disturbing is the imbalance. Women and men fall into this unequal pattern so often because of the differences in their interactional habits. Since women seek to build rapport, they are inclined to play down their expertise rather than display it. Since men value the position of center stage and the feeling of knowing more, they seek opportunities to gather and disseminate factual information.

8   If men often seem to hold forth because they have the expertise, women are often frustrated and surprised to find that when they have the expertise, they don't necessarily get the floor.

First Me, Then Me

9 I was at a dinner with faculty members from other departments in my university. To my right was a woman. As the dinner began, we introduced ourselves. After we told each other what departments we were in and what subjects we taught, she asked what my research was about. We talked about my research for a little while. Then I asked her about her research and she told me about it. Finally, we discussed the ways that our research overlapped. Later, as tends to happen at dinners, we branched out to others at the table. I asked a man across the table from me what department he was in and what he did. During the next half hour, I learned a lot about his job, his research, and his background. Shortly before the dinner ended there was a lull, and he asked me what I did. When I said I was a linguist, he became excited and told me about a research project he had conducted that was related to neurolinguistics. He was still telling me about his research when we all got up to leave the table.

10   This man and woman were my colleagues in academia. What happens when I talk to people at parties and social events, not fellow researchers? My experience is that if I mention the kind of work I do to women, they usually ask me about it. When I tell them about conversational style or gender differences, they offer their own experiences to support the patterns I describe. This is very pleasant for me. It puts me at center stage without my having to grab the spotlight myself, and I frequently gather anecdotes I can use in the future. But when I announce my line of work to men, many give me a lecture on language—for example, about how people, especially teenagers, misuse language nowadays. Others challenge me, for example questioning me about my research methods. Many others change the subject to something they know more about.

11   Of course not all men respond in this way, but over the years I have encountered many men, and very few women, who do. It is not that speaking in this way is *the* male way of dong things, but that it is *a* male way. There are women who adopt such styles, but they are perceived as speaking like men.

If You've Got It, Flaunt It—or Hide It

12 I have been observing this constellation in interaction for more than a dozen years. I did not, however, have any understanding of *why* this happens until fairly recently, when I developed the framework of status and connection. An experimental study that was pivotal in my thinking shows that expertise does not ensure women a place at center stage in conversation with men.

13   Psychologist H. M. Leet-Pellegrini set out to discover whether gender or expertise determined who would behave in what she terms a "dominant" way—for
example, by talking more, interrupting, and controlling the topic. She set up pairs
of women, pairs of men, and mixed pairs, and asked them to discuss the effects of
television violence on children. In some cases, she made one of the partners an expert by providing relevant factual information and time to read and assimilate it before the videotaped discussion. One might expect that the conversationalist who
was the expert would talk more, interrupt more, and spend less time supporting the
conversational partner who knew less about the subject. But it wasn't so simple. On
the average, those who had expertise did talk more, but men experts talked more
than women experts.

14   Expertise also had a different effect on women and men with regard to supportive behavior. Leet-Pellegrini expected that the one who did not have expertise
would spend more time offering agreement and support to the one who did. This
turned out to be true—*except* in cases where a woman was the expert and her nonexpert partner was a man. In this situation, the women experts showed support—
saying things like "Yeah" and "That's right"—far *more* than the nonexpert men
they were talking to. Observers often rated the male nonexpert as more dominant
than the female expert. In other words, the women in this experiment not only did-
n't wield their expertise as power, but tried to play it down and make up for it
through extra assenting behavior. They acted as if their expertise were something to
hide.

15   And perhaps it was. When the word *expert* was spoken in these experimental
conversations, in all cases but one it was the man in the conversation who used it,
saying something like "So, you're the expert." Evidence of the woman's superior
knowledge sparked resentment, not respect.

16   Furthermore, when an expert man talked to an uninformed woman, he took a
controlling role in structuring the conversation in the beginning *and* the end. But
when an expert man talked to an uninformed man, he dominated in the beginning
but not always in the end. In other words, having expertise was enough to keep a
man in the controlling position if he was talking to a woman, but not if he was talking to a man. Apparently, when a woman surmised that the man she was talking to
had more information on the subject than she did, she simply accepted the reactive
role. But another man, despite a lack of information, might still give the expert a
run for his money and possibly gain the upper hand by the end.

17   Reading these results, I suddenly understood what happens to me when I talk
to women and men about language. I am assuming that my acknowledged expertise
will mean I am automatically accorded authority in the conversation, and with
women that is generally the case. But when I talk to men, revealing that I have acknowledged expertise in this area often invites challenges. I *might* maintain my position if I defend myself successfully against the challenges, but if I don't, I may
lose ground.

18   One interpretation of the Leet-Pellegrini study is that women are getting a bum
deal. They don't get credit when it's due. And in a way, this is true. But the reason

is not—as it seems to many women—that men are bums who seek to deny women authority. The Leet-Pellegrini study shows that many men are inclined to jockey for status, and challenge the authority of others, when they are talking to men too. If this is so, then challenging a woman's authority as they would challenge a man's could be a sign of respect and equal treatment, rather than lack of respect and discrimination. In cases where this is so, the inequality of the treatment results not simply from the men's behavior alone but from the differences in men's and women's styles: Most women lack experience in defending themselves against challenges, which they misinterpret as personal attacks on their credibility.

19   Even when talking to men who are happy to see them in positions of status, women may have a hard time getting their due because of differences in men's and women's interactional goals. Just as boys in high school are not inclined to repeat information about popular girls because it doesn't get them what they want, women in conversation are not inclined to display their knowledge because it doesn't get them what they are after. Leet-Pellegrini suggests that the men in this study were playing a game of "Have I won?" while the women were playing a game of "Have I been sufficiently helpful?" I am inclined to put this another way: The game women play is "Do you like me?" whereas the men play "Do you respect me?" If men, in seeking respect, are less liked by women, this is an unsought side effect, as is the effect that women, in seeking to be liked, may lose respect. When a woman has a conversation with a man, her efforts to emphasize their similarities and avoid showing off can easily be interpreted, through the lens of status, as relegating her to a one-down position, making her appear either incompetent or insecure.

A Subtle Deference

20   Elizabeth Aries, a professor of psychology at Amherst College, set out to show that highly intelligent, highly educated young women are no longer submissive in conversations with male peers. And indeed she found that the college women did talk more than the college men in small groups she set up. But what they said was different. The men tended to set the agenda by offering opinions, suggestions, and information. The women tended to react, offering agreement or disagreement. Furthermore, she found that body language was as different as ever: The men sat with their legs stretched out, while the women gathered themselves in. Noting that research has found that speakers using the open-bodied position are more likely to persuade their listeners, Aries points out that talking more may not ensure that women will be heard.

21   In another study, Aries found that men in all-male discussion groups spent a lot of time at the beginning finding out "who was best informed about movies, books, current events, politics, and travel" as a means of "sizing up the competition" and negotiating "where they stood in relation to each other." This glimpse of how men talk when there are no women present gives an inkling of why displaying knowledge and expertise is something that men find more worth doing than women. What

the women in Aries's study spent time doing was "gaining a closeness through more intimate self-revelation."

22   It is crucial to bear in mind that both the women and the men in these studies were establishing camaraderie, and both were concerned with their relationships to each other. But different aspects of their relationships were of primary concern: their place in a hierarchical order for the men, and their place in a network of intimate connections for the women. The consequence of these disparate concerns was very different ways of speaking.

23   Thomas Fox is an English professor who was intrigued by the differences between women and men in his freshman writing classes. What he observed corresponds almost precisely to the experimental findings of Aries and Leet-Pellegrini. Fox's method of teaching writing included having all the students read their essays to each other in class and talk to each other in small groups. He also had them write papers reflecting on the essays and the discussion groups. He alone, as the teacher, read these analytical papers.

24   To exemplify the two styles he found typical of women and men, Fox chose a woman, Ms. M, and a man, Mr. H. In her speaking as well as her writing, Ms. M held back what she knew, appearing uninformed and uninterested, because she feared offending her classmates. Mr. H spoke and wrote with authority and apparent confidence because he was eager to persuade his peers. She did not worry about persuading; he did not worry about offending.

25   In his analytical paper, the young man described his own behavior in the mixed-gender group discussions as if he were describing the young men in Leet-Pellegrini's and Aries's studies:

> In my sub-group I am the leader. I begin every discussion by stating my opinions as facts. The other two members of the sub-group tend to sit back and agree with me. . . . I need people to agree with me.

Fox comments that Mr. H reveals "a sense of self, one that acts to change himself and other people, that seems entirely distinct from Ms. M's sense of self, dependent on and related to others."

26   Calling Ms. M's sense of self "dependent" suggests a negative view of her way of being in the world—and, I think, a view more typical of men. This view reflects the assumption that the alternative to independence is dependence. If this is indeed a male view, it may explain why so many men are cautious about becoming intimately involved with others: It makes sense to avoid humiliating dependence by insisting on independence. But there is another alternative: *inter*dependence.

27   The main difference between these alternatives is symmetry. Dependence is an asymmetrical involvement: One person needs the other, but not vice versa, so the needy person is one-down. Interdependence is symmetrical: Both parties rely on each other, so neither is one-up or one-down. Moreover, Mr. H's sense of self is also dependent on others. He requires others to listen, agree, and allow him to take the lead by stating his opinions first.

28   Looked at this way, the woman and man in this group are both dependent on each other. Their differing goals are complementary, although neither understands the reasons for the other's behavior. This would be a fine arrangement, except that their differing goals result in alignments that enhance his authority and undercut hers.

Different Interpretations—and Misinterpretations

29 Fox also describes differences in the way male and female students in his classes interpreted a story they read. These differences also reflect assumptions about the interdependence or independence of individuals. Fox's students wrote their responses to "The Birthmark" by Nathaniel Hawthorne. In the story, a woman's husband becomes obsessed with a birthmark on her face. Suffering from her husband's revulsion at the sight of her, the wife becomes obsessed with it too and, in a reversal of her initial impulse, agrees to undergo a treatment he has devised to remove the birthmark—a treatment that succeeds in removing the mark, but kills her in the process.

30   Ms. M interpreted the wife's complicity as a natural response to the demand of a loved one: The woman went along with her husband's lethal schemes to remove the birthmark because she wanted to please and be appealing to him. Mr. H blamed the woman's insecurity and vanity for her fate, and he blamed her for voluntarily submitting to her husband's authority. Fox points out that he saw her as individually responsible for her actions, just as he saw himself as individually responsible for his own actions. To him, the issue was independence: The weak wife voluntarily took a submissive role. To Ms. M, the issue was interdependence: The woman was inextricably bound up with her husband, so her behavior could not be separated from his.

31   Fox observes that Mr. H saw the writing of the women in the class as spontaneous—they wrote whatever popped into their heads. Nothing could be farther from Ms. M's experience as she described it: When she knew her peers would see her writing, she censored everything that popped into her head. In contrast, when she was writing something that only her professor would read, she expressed firm and articulate opinions.

32   There is a striking but paradoxical complementarity to Ms. M's and Mr. H's styles, when they are taken together. He needs someone to listen and agree. She listens and agrees. But in another sense, their dovetailing purposes are at cross-purposes. He misinterprets her agreement, intended in a spirit of connection, as a reflection of status and power: He thinks she is "indecisive" and "insecure." Her reasons for refraining from behaving as he does—firmly stating opinions as facts—have nothing to do with her attitudes toward her knowledge, as he thinks they do, but rather result from her attitudes toward her relationships with her peers.

33   These experimental studies by Leet-Pellegrini and Aries, and the observations by Fox, all indicate that, typically, men are more comfortable than women in giving

information and opinions and speaking in an authoritative way to a group, whereas women are more comfortable than men in supporting others. . . .

Listener as Underling

34 Clearly men are not always talking and women are not always listening. I have asked men whether they ever find themselves in the position of listening to another man giving them a lecture, and how they feel about it. They tell me that this does happen. They may find themselves talking to someone who presses information on them so insistently that they give in and listen. They say they don't mind too much, however, if the information is interesting. They can store it away for future use, like remembering a joke to tell others later. Factual information is of less interest to women because it is of less use to them. They are unlikely to try to pass on the gift of information, more likely to give the gift of being a good audience.

35 Men as well as women sometimes find themselves on the receiving end of a lecture they would just as soon not hear. But men tell me that it is most likely to happen if the other man is in a position of higher status. They know they have to listen to lectures from fathers and bosses.

36 That men can find themselves in the position of unwilling listener is attested to by a short opinion piece in which A. R. Gurney bemoans being frequently "cornered by some self-styled expert who harangues me with his considered opinion on an interminable agenda of topics." He claims that this tendency bespeaks a peculiarly American inability to "converse"—that is, engage in a balanced give-and-take—and cites as support the French observer of American customs Alexis de Tocqueville, who wrote, "An American . . . speaks to you as if he was addressing a meeting." Gurney credits his own appreciation of conversing to his father, who "was a master at eliciting and responding enthusiastically to the views of others, though this resiliency didn't always extend to his children. Indeed, now I think about it, he spoke to us many times as if he were addressing a meeting."

37 It is not surprising that Gurney's father lectured his children. The act of giving information by definition frames one in a position of higher status, while the act of listening frames one as lower. Children instinctively sense this—as do most men. But when women listen to men, they are not thinking in terms of status. Unfortunately, their attempts to reinforce connections and establish rapport, when interpreted through the lens of status, can be misinterpreted as casting them in a subordinate position—and are likely to be taken that way by many men.

What's So Funny?

38 The economy of exchanging jokes for laughter is a parallel one. In her study of college students' discussion groups, Aries found that the students in all-male groups spent a lot of time telling about times they had played jokes on others, and laughing about it. She refers to a study in which Barbara Miller Newman found that high school boys who were not "quick and clever" became the targets of jokes. Practical

joking—playing a joke *on* someone—is clearly a matter of being one-up: in the know and in control. It is less obvious, but no less true, that *telling* jokes can also be a way of negotiating status.

39   Many women (certainly not all) laugh at jokes but do not later remember them. Since they are not driven to seek and hold center stage in a group, they do not need a store of jokes to whip out for this purpose. A woman I will call Bernice prided herself on her sense of humor. At a cocktail party, she met a man to whom she was drawn because he seemed at first to share this trait. He made many funny remarks, which she spontaneously laughed at. But when she made funny remarks, he seemed not to hear. What had happened to his sense of humor? Though telling jokes and laughing at them are both reflections of a sense of humor, they are very different social activities. Making others laugh gives you a fleeting power over them: As linguist Wallace Chafe points out, at the moment of laughter, a person is temporarily disabled. The man Bernice met was comfortable only when he was making her laugh, not the other way around. When Bernice laughed at his jokes, she thought she was engaging in a symmetrical activity. But he was engaging in an asymmetrical one.

40   A man told me that sometime around tenth grade he realized that he preferred the company of women to the company of men. He found that his female friends were more supportive and less competitive, whereas his male friends seemed to spend all their time joking. Considering joking an asymmetrical activity makes it clearer why it would fit in with a style he perceived as competitive. . . .

Mutual Accusations

41 Considering these dynamics, it is not surprising that many women complain that their partners don't listen to them. But men make the same complaint about women, although less frequently. The accusation "You're not listening" often really means "You don't understand what I said in the way that I meant it," or "I'm not getting the response I wanted." Being listened to can become a metaphor for being understood and being valued.

42   In my earlier work I emphasized that women may get the impression men aren't listening to them even when the men really are. This happens because men have different habitual ways of showing they're listening. As anthropologists Maltz and Borker explain, women are more inclined to ask questions. They also give more listening responses—little words like *mhm, uh-uh,* and *yeah*—sprinkled throughout someone else's talk, providing a running feedback loop. And they respond more positively and enthusiastically, for example by agreeing and laughing.

43   All this behavior is doing the work of listening. It also creates rapport-talk by emphasizing connection and encouraging more talk. The corresponding strategies of men—giving fewer listener responses, making statements rather than asking questions, and challenging rather than agreeing—can be understood as moves in a contest by incipient speakers rather than audience members.

44   Not only do women give more listening signals, according to Maltz and Borker, but the signals they give have different meanings for men and women, con-

sistent with the speaker/audience alignment. Women use "yeah" to mean "I'm with you, I follow," whereas men tend to say "yeah" only when they agree. The opportunity for misunderstanding is clear. When a man is confronted with a woman who has been saying "yeah," "yeah," "yeah," and then turns out not to agree, he may conclude that she has been insincere, or that she was agreeing without really listening. When a woman is confronted with a man who does *not* say "yeah"—or much of anything else—she may conclude that *he* hasn't been listening. The men's style is more literally focused on the message level of talk, while the women's is focused on the relationship or metamessage level.

45   To a man who expects a listener to be quietly attentive, a woman giving a stream of feedback and support will seem to be talking too much for a listener. To a woman who expects a listener to be active and enthusiastic in showing interest, attention, and support, a man who listens silently will seem not to be listening at all, but rather to have checked out of the conversation, taken his listening marbles, and gone mentally home.

46   Because of these patterns, women may get the impression that men aren't listening when they really are. But I have come to understand, more recently, that it is also true that men listen to women less frequently than women listen to men, because the act of listening has different meanings for them. Some men really *don't* want to listen at length because they feel it frames them as subordinate. Many women do want to listen, but they expect it to be reciprocal—I listen to you now; you listen to me later. They become frustrated when they do the listening now and now and now, and later never comes.

Mutual Dissatisfaction

47 If women are dissatisfied with always being in the listening position, the dissatisfaction may be mutual. That a woman feels she has been assigned the role of silently listening audience does not mean that a man feels he has consigned her to that role—or that he necessarily likes the rigid alignment either.

48   During the time I was working on this book, I found myself at a book party filled with people I hardly knew. I struck up a conversation with a charming young man who turned out to be a painter. I asked him about his work and, in response to his answer, asked whether there has been a return in contemporary art to figurative painting. In response to my question, he told me a lot about the history of art—so much that when he finished and said, "That was a long answer to your question," I had long since forgotten that I had asked a question, let alone what it was. I had not minded this monologue—I had been interested in it—but I realized, with something of a jolt, that I had just experienced the dynamic that I had been writing about.

49   I decided to risk offending my congenial new acquaintance in order to learn something about his point of view. This was, after all, a book party, so I might rely on his indulgence if I broke the rules of decorum in the interest of writing a book. I asked whether he often found himself talking at length while someone else listened. He thought for a moment and said yes, he did, because he liked to explore ideas in detail. I asked if it happened equally with women and men. He thought again and

said, "No, I have more trouble with men." I asked what he meant by trouble. He said, "Men interrupt. *They* want to explain to *me*."

50   Finally, having found this young man disarmingly willing to talk about the conversation we had just had and his own style, I asked which he preferred: that a woman listen silently and supportively, or that she offer opinions and ideas of her own. He said he thought he liked it better if she volunteered information, making the interchange more interesting.

51   When men begin to lecture other men, the listeners are experienced at trying to sidetrack the lecture, or match it, or derail it. In this system, making authoritative pronouncements may be a way to begin an *exchange* of information. But women are not used to responding in that way. They see little choice but to listen attentively and wait for their turn to be allotted to them rather than seizing it for themselves. If this is the case, the man may be as bored and frustrated as the woman when his attempt to begin an exchange of information ends in his giving a lecture. From his point of view, she is passively soaking up information, so she must not have any to speak of. One of the reasons men's talk to women frequently turns into lecturing is *because* women listen attentively and do not interrupt with challenges, sidetracks, or matching information.

52   In the conversations with male and female colleagues that I recounted at the outset of this chapter, this difference may have been crucial. When I talked to the woman, we each told about our own research in response to the other's encouragement. When I talked to the man, I encouraged him to talk about his work, and he obliged, but he did not encourage me to talk about mine. This may mean that he did not want to hear about it—but it also may not. In her study of college students' discussion groups, Aries found that women who did a lot of talking began to feel uncomfortable; they backed off and frequently drew out quieter members of the group. This is perfectly in keeping with women's desire to keep things balanced, so everyone is on an equal footing. Women expect their conversational partners to encourage them to hold forth. Men who do not typically encourage quieter members to speak up, assume that anyone who has something to say will volunteer it. The men may be equally disappointed in a conversational partner who turns out to have nothing to say.

53   Similarly, men can be as bored by women's topics as women can be by men's. While I was wishing the former RAFer would tell me about his personal experiences in Greece, he was probably wondering why I was boring him with mine and marveling at my ignorance of the history of a country I had lived in. Perhaps he would have considered our conversation a success if I had challenged or topped his interpretation of Greek history rather than listening dumbly to it. When men, upon hearing the kind of work I do, challenge me about my research method, they are inviting me to give them information and show them my expertise—something I don't like to do outside of the classroom or lecture hall, but something they themselves would likely be pleased to be provoked to do.

54   The publicist who listened attentively to information about a radio station explained to me that she wanted to be nice to the manager, to smooth the way for placing her clients on his station. But men who want to ingratiate themselves with

women are more likely to try to charm them by offering interesting information than by listening attentively to whatever information the women have to impart. I recall a luncheon preceding a talk I delivered to a college alumni association. My gracious host kept me entertained before my speech by regaling me with information about computers, which I politely showed interest in, while inwardly screaming from boredom and a sense of being weighed down by irrelevant information that I knew I would never remember. Yet I am sure he thought he was being interesting, and it is likely that at least some male guests would have thought that he was. I do not wish to imply that all women hosts have entertained me in the perfect way. I recall a speaking engagement before which I was taken to lunch by a group of women. They were so attentive to my expertise that they plied me with questions, prompting me to exhaust myself by giving my lecture over lunch before the formal lecture began. In comparison to this, perhaps the man who lectured to me about computers was trying to give me a rest.

55   The imbalance by which men often find themselves in the role of lecturer, and women often find themselves in the role of audience, is not the creation of only one member of an interaction. It is not something that men do to women. Neither is it something that women culpably "allow" or "ask for." The imbalance is created by the difference between women's and men's habitual styles. . . .

Hope for the Future

56 What is the hope for the future? Must we play out our assigned parts to the closing act? Although we tend to fall back on habitual ways of talking, repeating old refrains and familiar lines, habits can be broken. Women and men both can gain by understanding the other gender's style, and by learning to use it on occasion.

57   Women who find themselves unwillingly cast as the listener should practice propelling themselves out of that position rather than waiting patiently for the lecture to end. Perhaps they need to give up the belief that they must wait for the floor to be handed to them. If they have something to say on a subject, they might push themselves to volunteer it. If they are bored with a subject, they can exercise some influence on the conversation and change the topic to something they would rather discuss.

58   If women are relieved to learn that they don't always have to listen, there may be some relief for men in learning that they don't always have to have interesting information on the tips of their tongues if they want to impress a woman or entertain her. A journalist once interviewed me for an article about how to strike up conversations. She told me that another expert she had interviewed, a man, had suggested that one should come up with an interesting piece of information. I found this amusing, as it seemed to typify a man's idea of a good conversationalist, but not a woman's. How much easier men might find the task of conversation if they realized that all they have to do is listen. As a woman who wrote a letter to the editor of *Psychology Today* put it, "When I find a guy who asks, 'How was your day?' and really wants to know, I'm in heaven."

THINKING CRITICALLY

1. Explain the lecturer–listener relationship described in the opening paragraphs. How does Tannen explain this asymmetry in conversations? Is this pattern typical of male–female conversations in your experience—or of your family, or your peers?

2. According to the Leet-Pellegrini study, what typical role patterns evolve in conversations when women are the experts and men the nonexperts? And when men are the experts and women the nonexperts? How does Tannen explain these different reactions?

3. Does Tannen's explanation of why men challenge women's authority (paragraphs 18 and 19) seem valid to you? Or, do you think Tannen lets men off the hook too easily? Imagine you are Ms. M's academic adviser. Would you advise her to maintain or to change her current style of speaking and writing in class? What about Mr. H.?

4. According to the author, what happens when men find themselves being lectured to in a conversation with another man? Does Tannen's analysis ring true to your experience? Explain.

5. Why are men more interested in telling jokes, according to this article? In playing practical jokes? Do you agree? Can you give some exceptions?

6. Tannen closes her piece with advice on how to break old conversational habits: How to talk more if you are a listener, and how to listen more if you are a talker. Do you find her advice helpful? Oversimplified? Too optimistic? Too unrealistic? What obstacles might someone encounter in trying to break old conversational habits?

7. This piece opens with four anecdotes. What points are they making? Are the anecdotes effective? Are there subtle differences, or did you find them repetitious?

WRITING ASSIGNMENTS

1. Try a class experiment. Break into two groups: one half will hold a discussion about a topic of interest, the other half will observe the discussion group to see if the lecturer–listener patterns that Tannen describes emerge or not. What do you make of the results? Discuss your observations in a short essay, citing examples from the class discussion.

2. Many people interested in gender and language complain that communication breaks down because men attempt to dominate women. Tannen maintains that the effect of dominance ". . . is not always the result of an intention to dominate" but the result of the fact that males and females have distinctly different conversational styles based on gender and cultural conditioning. She says that as early as childhood boys learn to use speech as a way of getting attention and establishing status in a group; girls, to the contrary, use speech to confirm and maintain intimacy. Write a paper in which you support or refute Tannen's stand.

3. If you tend to be a lecturer, take the role of listener in a conversation. Or, if you tend to be a listener, experiment by being more outgoing and forceful in a conversation. Did you have difficulties adapting to a different role? Were you able to maintain it? Did you like the change, or were you uncomfortable? Did anybody notice the difference in you? Write a paper describing your experience. As Tannen does, use the summary-and-analysis approach in your discussion.

4. Write a paper explaining why you do or do not think the conversational patterns described by Tannen apply to you. Use some specific details to support your position.

5. Using audio or videotape, record a conversation in which a group of men and women talk. Write a paper analyzing the conversational patterns you see emerging. Does what you see support or contradict Tannen's views?

6. Write a dialogue between a man and woman in which you employ some of the gender patterns Tannen discusses here. Then write the same dialogue so that the two speakers are conversationally equal.

Exploring the Language of **V I S U A L S**

Men Are from Belgium, Women Are from New Brunswick

Roz Chast (cartoon)

In the early 1990s, marriage counselor John Gray published a controversial but best-selling book, *Men Are from Mars, Women Are from Venus: A Guide to Getting What You Want in Your Relationships*. Humorously explaining that men and women come from different planets (Mars and Venus), Gray postulated that the genders must respect their differences to achieve harmony. Although men and women speak a common tongue, their construction of meaning differs. For example, Gray proposed that when a woman suggests to a man that they stop and ask for directions, what he actually hears is her not trusting him to find his way without help. The cartoon by Roz Chast plays with some of Gray's concepts of male/female interpretations of language meaning. Chast's cartoons appear regularly in the *New Yorker* and the *Harvard Review*. She has illustrated several children's books and is the author of a number of cartoon collections, including *Childproof: Cartoons about Parents and Children* (1997).

V I S U A L S
continued ➤

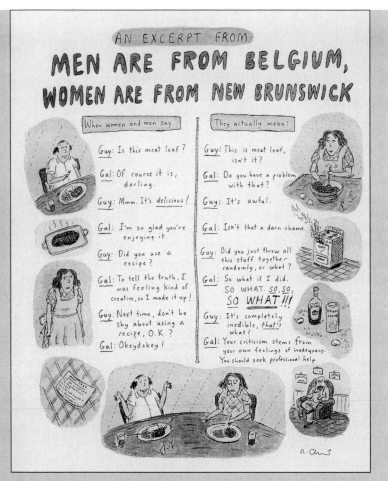

THINKING CRITICALLY

1. What is Chast trying to convey in this cartoon? Does it operate on several levels? Explain.

2. Do you find this cartoon funny? Do you think that it may be more humorous to one gender than another? If so, which gender would find it funnier, and why?

3. Why does Chast claim men are from Belgium and women are from New Bruswick? Why do you think she chose these locations?

4. If you did not know the gender of the author of this cartoon, could you guess? Why or why not? Does gender matter to the success of the cartoon and the points it is trying to make? Explain.

Nonverbal Behavior:
Culture, Gender, and the Media
Teri Kwal Gamble and Michael W. Gamble

Much of this chapter addresses how men and women use written and spoken language. But what about our nonverbal communication skills—the way we "speak" without words? Do men and women use different nonverbal cues? Are smiles and nods a female communication trait, whereas interruptions and touching are a male one? These are just a few of the body-language questions addressed by this essay.

Teri Kwal Gamble is a professor of communication at the College of New Rochelle, and Michael Gamble is a professor of communication at New York Institute of Technology. They have coauthored many books, including *Communication Works* (1990), *Literature Alive!* (1994), and *Public Speaking in the Age of Diversity* (1998). The following article is an excerpt from their latest collaboration, *Contacts: Communicating Interpersonally* (1998).

1 Throughout the world, people use nonverbal cues to facilitate self-expression. To a great extent, however, the culture of a people modifies their use of such cues. For example, individuals who belong to contact cultures, which promote interaction and encourage displays of warmth, closeness, and availability, tend to stand close to each other when conversing, seek maximum sensory experience, and touch each other frequently. In contrast, members of noncontact cultures discourage the use of such behaviors. Saudi Arabia, France, and Italy are countries with contact cultures; their members relish the intimacy of contact when conversing. In contrast, Scandinavia, Germany, England, Japan, and the United States are low or lower-contact cultures whose members value privacy and maintain more distance from each other when interacting.[1]

2 Individuals who grow up in different cultures may display emotion or express intimacy in different ways. It is normal, for example, for members of Mediterranean cultures to display highly emotional reactions that are uninhibited and greatly exaggerated; it is common for them to express grief or happiness with open facial displays, magnified gestures, and vocal cues that support the feelings. On the other hand, neither the Chinese nor the Japanese readily reveal their feelings in public, preferring to display less emotion, maintain more self-control, and keep their feelings to themselves; for these reasons, they often remain expressionless.

3 Even when different cultures use the same nonverbal cues, their members may not give the cues the same meaning. In the United States, for example, a nod symbolizes agreement or consent, while in Japan it means only that a message was received.

4 If we hope to interact effectively with people from different cultures, it is important that we make the effort to identify and understand the many ways culture

shapes nonverbal communication. We need to acknowledge that one communication style is not intrinsically better than any other; it is that awareness that can help contribute to more successful multicultural exchanges.

5   Men and women commonly use nonverbal communication in ways that reflect societal expectations. For example, men are expected to exhibit assertive behaviors that demonstrate their power and authority; women, in contrast, are expected to exhibit more reactive and responsive behaviors. Thus, it should not surprise us that men talk more and interrupt women more frequently than vice versa. [2]

6   Men are also usually more dominant during interactions than women. Visual dominance is measured by comparing the percentage of time spent looking while speaking with the percentage of time spent looking while listening. When compared with women, men display higher levels of looking while speaking than women do, and lower levels than women when they are listening. Thus, the visual dominance ratio of men is usually higher than that of women, and again reflects the use of nonverbal cues to reinforce perceptions of social power. [3]

7   Men and women also differ in their use of space and touch. Men use space and touch to assert their dominance over women. As a result, men are much more likely to touch women than women are to touch men. Women are thus more apt to be the recipients of touching actions than they are to be the initiators of such actions. Men also claim more personal space than women usually do, and they more frequently walk in front of women rather than behind them. Thus, in general, males are the touchers, not the touchees, and the leaders rather than the followers.

8   There are nonverbal behaviors that women display more than men do. Women tend to smile more than men. They also commonly display their feelings more overtly than men. In general, women are more expressive than men and exhibit higher levels of involvement when engaged in person-to-person interaction than men. Women also use nonverbal signals to draw others into conversation to a greater extent than men. While women demonstrate an interest in affiliation, men are generally more interested in establishing the strength of their own ideas and agendas than they are in sharing the floor with others.[4] Women also are better interpreters of nonverbal messages than men.

9   All too often, the media and technology help legitimize stereotypical nonverbal displays. The contents of various media contain a plethora of open sexual appeals, portrayals of women obsessed with men, and male–female interactions that portray the man as physically dominant and the female as subordinate. They also include numerous repetitions of the message that "thin is in." [5]

10   After repeated exposure to such media messages, men and women come to believe and ultimately emulate what they see and hear. Thus, females are primed to devote considerable energy to improving their appearance, preserving their youthfulness, and nurturing others, while males learn to display tougher, more aggressive take-charge cues, trying all the while to control their emotions.

11   Nonverbal power cues echo the male dominance/female subservience-mediated message. In advertisements, for example, men are typically portrayed superior to women, who are usually shown in various stages of undress. In the media, nonverbal behaviors portray women as vulnerable and men in control.[6]

12   The repetition of such myths can make us feel dissatisfied and inadequate. If we rely on the media as a reference point for what is and is not desirable in our relationships and interactions, we may find it difficult to be ourselves.

13   Even mediated vocal cues suggest that it is the male and not the female who is the authority. In up to 90 percent of all advertisements male voices are used in voice-overs—even when the product being sold is aimed at women.

14   Further complicating the situation is the continued growth of the use of computer-generated virtual reality simulations. In addition to allow us to feel as if we were really interacting in different, but make-believe environments and even giving us the opportunity to change our gender, such simulations are also being used to enforce violent gender scenarios resulting in women being threatened and killed. Even when erotic rather than violent, the media offerings all too often reinforce the notion that men have physical control over women.[7]

Notes

1. Peter Andersen, "Exploring Intercultural Differences in Nonverbal Communication," in L. Samovar and R. Porter (eds.), *Interpersonal Communication; A Reader,* 5th ed., Belmont, CA: Wadsworth Publishing, 1988, pp. 272–282.
2. B. Veland, "Tell Me More: On the Fine Art of Listening," *Utne Reader* (1992): 104–109; A. Mulac, "Men's and Women's Talk in Some Gender and Mixed Gender Dyads: Power or Polemic?" *Journals of Language and Social Psychology,* 8 (1989): 249–270.
3. J. F. Dovidio, S. L. Ellyson, C. F. Keating, K. Heltman, and C. E. Brown, "The Relationship of Social Power to Visual Displays of Dominance between Men and Women," *Journal of Personality and Social Psychology,* 54 (1988): 233–242.
4. Julia T. Wood, *Gendered Lives,* Belmont, CA: Wadsworth, 1994, p. 154.
5. See for example, J. Leland and E. Leonard, "Back to Twiggy," *Newsweek,* February 1, 1993, pp. 64–65.
6. Wood, *Gendered Lives,* p. 239.
7. Suzanne Stefanic, "Sex and the New Media," *NewMedia,* (April 1993): 38–45.

THINKING CRITICALLY

1. How does culture influence nonverbal communication? What are contact cultures? How can our understanding of contact cultures likewise improve our understanding of nonverbal communication between genders?

2. In paragraph 5, Gamble and Gamble say "it should not surprise us that men talk more and interrupt women more frequently than vice versa." Why do they feel this statement to be true? Based on your own experience, does it seem like a reasonable assessment? Explain.

3. How can looking and listening behaviors of men and women reinforce perceptions of social power?

4. In the final sentence of paragraph 7, the authors connect the act of touching to the act of leading. "Thus, in general, males are the touchers, not the touchees, and the leaders rather than the followers." Evaluate the accuracy of this connection. Do you agree with their conclusion? Explain.

WRITING ASSIGNMENTS

1. Try to identify some of the differences between the way men and women use language through cues that are connected with language but not necessarily actual words—such as pitch, tone, volume, facial expression, and touch. Write an essay from your own personal perspective analyzing the nonverbal communication of men and women. Are they indeed speaking the same language?

2. The authors theorize that women are better interpreters of nonverbal messages than men are (paragraph 8). Why do you think they make this judgment? Do you agree? How does the media perpetuate gender–power issues? In what nonverbal ways do they communicate gender stereotypes? Write an essay exploring the connection between the media and the nonverbal communication style of men and women.

■ MAKING CONNECTIONS

1. Do you think language itself can be "gendered"? For example, are there certain words that seem "male" and others that seem "female"? Review the essays by Gold and Quindlen and evaluate the words they use to convey their ideas. Write an essay that considers the idea of "gendered" language.

2. Have you ever found yourself at an impasse with a member of the opposite sex because your communication styles were different? For example, did you think the person you were arguing with "just didn't get it" solely because of his or her sex? Explain what accounted for the miscommunication and how you solved it.

3. Many of the authors in this section explain that men and women use language differently. Develop a list of the ways you think men and women use language differently and then develop your own theory, or expound on an existing one, to explain the communication differences. Think about the adjectives they use, their body language, why they speak, and how they present their information. If you wish, you may write about why you feel there is no difference in the ways men and women use language.

4. Record the conversations of some family members or friends as part of an experiment. Explain to the subjects that you are doing a study on language, but do not explain the details of your experiment. Try to record a conversation between two men, two women, and of a mixed group of both genders. Do you notice any differences in the ways men and women converse and use language? Evaluate your results and discuss your findings in class.

5. Nonverbal behavior can be influenced by gender, culture, and media cues that may cause people to misunderstand each other. Explore the ways you rely on nonverbal cues when communicating with others. How much do you depend on the actual words used in a conversation versus the tone, facial expressions, gestures, and mannerisms of the conversationalists? Explain.

6. Much of this section focuses on communication differences between men and women. Do you think language itself can be "gendered"? For example, are there certain words that seem "male" and others that seem to be "female"? Review an essay by a male author and a female author in another chapter of this book and evaluate the words they use to convey their ideas. Do they indeed use language differently to convey their ideas?

■ LET'S TALK ABOUT IT: CONVERSATION IN ACTION

The Social Basis of Talk
Ronald Wardhaugh

Conversation is often naturally spontaneous and informal. But despite its seeming effortlessness, it is still governed by conscious and unconscious rules and principles of language, grammar, and behavior. What we say, how we say it, and to whom is much more complicated than we might think. A great deal depends on our personal expectations, opinions of the people with whom we speak, and our comfort level with the people and subject matter. In the next essay, Ronald Wardhaugh explores the characteristics of talk and the requirements of successful conversations.

Ronald Wardhaugh is a professor of linguistics and director of the Center for Language and Language Behavior at the University of Toronto. He is the author of many books on language, including *Introduction to Sociolinguistics* (1992), *Investigating Language* (1993), *Proper English: Myths and Misunderstandings About Language* (1999), and *How Conversation Works* (1985) from which the following essay is excerpted.

1 Our concern is with talk and the types of language used in talk. The major emphasis will be on conversation, the most generalized form of talk. We will also be concerned with both speakers and listeners, since talk is, as we shall see, essentially a cooperative undertaking. [. . .] The focus of our concern will be what happens when two or more people exchange words for some reason. Why does one person say one thing and the other reply as he or she does?

2 Talk is usually a social activity and therefore a public activity. It involves you with others, and each time you are involved with another person you must consider him or her. You must be aware of that person's feelings about what is happening, and you have some right to require him or her to do the same for you, to be aware of you and your feelings. In this sense talk is a reciprocal undertaking. Involvement in conversation therefore requires the two (or various) parties to be conscious of each other's needs, particularly the need not to be offended. Public life is possible only when the opportunities for being seriously offended are reduced to near zero. If the risks in an activity are great, you may be wise to refrain from that activity unless the potential gains are correspondingly great or you have no alternative. As we shall see, conversation is an activity which makes use of many devices in order to reduce the risks to participants. Consequently, skilled conversationalists rarely get 'hurt'.

3 There remains for most of us, however, a certain element of risk in any conversation. You may be hurt or you may inflict hurt in that one of the participants can emerge from the conversation diminished in some way. While it is unlikely that you insulted someone or you yourself were insulted, many lesser hurts are possible. You may have criticized another or have been criticized yourself; you may have incurred an obligation that you did not seek or made a suggestion that another could

not refuse; someone may have complimented you, thereby requiring you not only to acknowledge acceptance of that compliment but to live up to it; you may have skirted a topic which others expected you to confront, you may have offered an excuse or an apology but be left with the feeling that it was not necessarily accepted completely—someone's sincerity may therefore be suspect. During a conversation some subtle change in relationships between the parties is likely to have occurred; many conversations result in the participants having definite, residual feelings about them: of pleasure, displeasure, ease, frustration, anger, alarm, satisfaction, and so on. We are not loath to judge conversations in such terms. When we do so, we are in an important sense evaluating the risks we took, counting our gains and losses as a result of taking them, and adding everything up on our mental score cards. That we do such things is apparent from the comments we sometimes make following conversations or reporting on them to others, comments such as *He was pretty short with her, You should have heard her go on about it. Why didn't you speak up?, She shouldn't have spoken to me like that, He just grunted, never said a word,* or that sure sign that a relationship is in trouble: *You're not listening; you never listen!*

4   Indeed, if all participants in a conversation are to feel happy with it, each must feel that he or she got out of it what was sought. If you wish to appear as a 'sensitive' participant in a conversation, you will therefore try to make sure that all the participants get to share in the various aspects of the conversation that will make it 'successful': in selecting the topics that will be talked about; in having adequate and timely opportunities to speak; in feeling at ease in saying what needs to be said; in achieving a sense of orderliness and adequacy about what is going on and doing this as one of a group of two or more; and so on. None of these characteristics can be prescribed in advance—unless the conversation is a very formal one, for example, a meeting of some kind—so it is necessary for you at all times to be aware of just what exactly is happening in any conversation in which you participate. You must be aware of both what has gone before and what may come next, as well as where you seem to be at the moment. You must be aware that a complicated array of possibilities exists and that each choice must necessarily preclude others. You must exhibit a certain sensitivity if you are to avoid some choices so that no one may feel arbitrarily cut off either from the topic or from other participants. Your goal must be to see that everyone leaves the conversation satisfied.

5   What we can infer from all this is that if you want to be a successful conversationalist you must command a wide variety of skills. You must have a well developed feeling about what you can (or cannot) say and when you can (or cannot) speak. You must know how to use words to do things and also exactly what words you can use in certain circumstances. And you must be able to supplement and reinforce what you choose to say with other appropriate behaviours: your movements, gestures, posture, gaze, and so on. You must also attune yourself to how others employ these same skills. This is a considerable task for anyone—or *everyone,* as it turns out—to perform, so it is not surprising that individuals vary widely in their ability to be successful in conversation. You can bungle your way through or you

can be witty, urbane, and always sure to say the right thing. And some can even exploit the ability they have for ends that are entirely selfish.

6   The actual requirements will vary from group to group and culture to culture. Some situations may require considerable amounts of silence and others considerable amounts of talk. Others may be partly defined by who gets to talk and in what order, for not everyone necessarily has a right to speak: contrast a state ceremonial with a Quaker meeting. And once speaking has begun, it has to stay within the bounds of the occasion: you do not deliver a lecture at a cocktail party; you do not tell a dirty joke while conveying bad news; and you do not (any longer in many places now) make sexist or racist remarks in public and hope to win or keep public office. In this broad sense linguistic behaviour may be described as appropriate or not, and it is this sense of appropriateness that is the subject of studies by those who work in a discipline known as the ethnography of speaking; the study of who speaks to whom, when, how, and to what ends.

7   Certain basic conditions seem to prevail in all conversation, and many of the details of individual conversations are best understood as attempts that speakers (and listeners) make to meet these conditions. Above all, conversation is a social activity and, as such, it shares characteristics of all social activities. These characteristics we usually take for granted so that it is only their absence we notice. When there is some kind of breakdown in society, we notice the absence of principles, conventions, laws, rules, and so on, which guided or controlled behaviour in better times. Or, alternatively, we become aware of these same principles only when we have too readily accepted certain things as 'normal' and then find out that we have been deceived, as when someone has tricked or 'conned' us by pretending to do one thing (apparently quite normal) but actually doing another.

8   Conversation, like daily living, requires you to exhibit a considerable trust in others. Life would be extremely difficult, perhaps even impossible, without such trust. It is this trust that allows you to put money in a bank in the expectation that you will get it back on demand, to cross the street at a busy intersection controlled by either lights or a policeman, to eat food prepared by others, to plan for the future, and so on. But there is also the more general trust we have in the evidence of our senses, in the recurrence of both natural and other events, and in the essential unchanging and possibly unchangeable nature of the world and of the majority of its inhabitants. Trust in other people is the cornerstone of social living: to survive we must believe that people do not change much, if at all, from day to day and from encounter to encounter, and also that the vast majority do not set out deliberately to deceive or harm us. Indeed, we must believe them to be benevolent rather than malevolent. Without such trust in others and in what they do and say we could not get very far in coping with the world in which we find ourselves. So far as conversation is concerned, we would have little or no shared ground on which to build, and communication would become next to impossible. States of enmity and war or 'not speaking' are good examples of the kinds of conditions that exist when trust is broken. However, it is important to realize that even in such cases there is almost never a complete breakdown, since the antagonists usually continue to observe cer-

tain rules and decencies. Not everything becomes 'fair', which in such a case could mean only that absolutely anything might be possible, a situation therefore in which no rules of any kind would apply, an example of 'savagery' in its mythical, pathological form.

9   We cannot survive without putting trust in others, but it must be a trust tempered with a certain amount of caution. We cannot insist on viewing the world with wide-eyed innocence and hope we will never be disappointed. If you want to survive and minimize the hurts you will experience, you must employ a little bit of common sense too. You must exercise certain powers of judgement and you must make sound decisions constantly. For example, in any encounter with another person, you must try to work out exactly what is going on. That requires you to exhibit characteristics for which terms like 'intelligence' and 'sensitivity' are often used: you must judge the actual words you hear in relation to the possible intentions of the speaker, in order to come up with a decision as to what the speaker really means. In abstract, theoretical terms, the possible permutations of meaning are immense. Fortunately, in reality, most of those possibilities are extremely unlikely. You can rule them out, and you must do so—otherwise you could never decide anything at all: you could never be in any way sure about anything anyone said to you. But that ruling-out is not done haphazardly. Certain basic principles that prevail in most conversations help you to narrow down the possibilities to a manageable set: mutual trust, the sincerity of participants, the validity of everyday appearances, and 'common sense'. A certain scepticism may obtain in our views of life and of human motivation, but it must have 'healthy' limits. We cannot question and doubt everything or suspect every motive and still insist that we be regarded as normal people. We must seriously restrict such questioning, doubt, and suspicion; they are indicators, or markers, of very special kinds of conversation—interviews, psychiatric consultations, seminars, investigations—and such special activities must be clearly 'framed' in some way to indicate their special character. In order to participate in a conversation, you must be a willing party to a certain worldview. In that respect conversation is a collusive activity. You may have reservations about certain matters, but unless you are prepared to meet others on common ground and ignore differences which can only be divisive there is little hope that any kind of meaningful communication will occur.

10   Ethnomethodologists—those who study common-sense knowledge and reasoning as they pertain to social organisation—tell us that we are all parties to an agreement to inhabit a world in which things are what they appear to be and people do not in general go scratching beneath the surface of appearances. Living is largely a collusive activity, one in which you find yourself united with me because we both use our common sense and our goodwill to blind ourselves to things that do not seem to be important: we do not ask tough questions of each other; we do not seek rigid proofs; we do accept contradictions and uncertainty; and we do prefer to go along with others in most circumstances. That is how ordinary life is lived and must be lived.

11   Because conversation necessarily has a social basis, we must try to meet each other on common ground. For example, there is a general unspoken agreement

among people that what we actually inhabit is a consistent, even mundane, world. It is essentially a world of the commonplace and the things in it do not change much, if at all. These 'things' are also what they appear to be; they are not something else. Consequently, we tend to be amused when a 'petrol station' really turns out to be a fast-food restaurant or one of James Bond's cars turns into a submarine and another into an aeroplane. Magicians exploit this kind of amusement. But if such situations and such trickery happened continually we would undoubtedly find them stressful, or, alternatively, we would be forced to recast our image of fast-food outlets, auto-mobiles, and trickery. That world too is one of simple causation: it is a recurrent world in which day follows night and night follows day, and so on. We see our-selves and others as consistent objects within that world; we believe we behave consistently and we tend to grant the same consistency to others.

12   We also tend to accept what we are told, taking any words spoken to us at close to face value unless we appear to have some very good reason for doing otherwise. For example, we seek only occasional clarification of remarks made to us. We are prepared to tolerate a remarkable amount of unclarity and imprecision in what we are told. We hold our peace and trust that everything will eventually work itself out to our satisfaction. So when we listen to interchanges that do involve considerable questioning and commenting, we know we are observing conversations of a special kind: for example, interrogations, psychiatric interviews, exchanges between teach-ers and students, and so on. If you suddenly let flow a stream of questions during what is otherwise just an ordinary conversation, you may effectively stop, or at least change, what is happening. You may well be perceived to be trying to turn something commonplace into an investigation and to be violating the basic condi-tion of trust between participants. If I do not believe what you are telling me, I can challenge your truthfulness or I can start probing your account with questions. In either case you are likely to react in much the same way. You will become 'defen-sive', for your trust in what we were doing *together* will be weakened as you find yourself under attack. I will have violated the normal unspoken agreement that I will believe what you say because in return you will believe what I say. For, after all, are not both of us reasonable, sincere, and honest individuals? Some people re-gard defensive behaviour as 'bad' behaviour or evidence of some kind of guilt; it need be neither, being just a normal reaction to unwarranted offensive behaviour from others.

13   Each party in a social encounter has a certain amount of 'face' to maintain; many of the things that happen are concerned with maintaining appearances. I do not want to attack you in any way nor do I want you to attack me. We are, in a sense, parties to an agreement each to accept the other as the other wishes to ap-pear. We may even go further and try to support a particular appearance the other proposes for himself or herself. If you want to act in a manner which I find some-what peculiar, I may have very great difficulty in 'calling' you on what you are do-ing. It is much more likely that I will go along with your performance and keep my doubts to myself. After all, you may have a good motive unknown to me for your behaviour, so my initial reaction is likely to be to go along with what you are doing, to help you maintain the 'face' you are presenting, rather than to propose some kind

of change in your behaviour. Those individuals who go around trying to 'un-face' others, as it were, may find themselves unwelcome, even to each other, being constantly in violation of this norm that 'good' social behaviour is based on mutual trust in appearances.

14   Conversation proceeds on the basis that the participants are reasonable people who can be expected to deal decently with one another. There must be a kind of reasonableness, a sort of 'commonsenseness', in the actual choice of the words and expressions we employ. There must also be a certain rightness in the quantity as well as the quality of those words. You have to say enough to do the job that must be done: not too little must be said nor, on the other hand, too much. Too little and someone will feel deprived of information; too much and someone will feel either imposed upon or the unwilling beneficiary of a performance rather than of a genuine instance of communication. Unreasonable language may also produce obscurity or even rouse someone to challenge what has been said. It may create problems which the participants can solve only when they have re-established the basic preconditions of trust that are necessary if anything positive is to be accomplished.

15   You must assume, too, that most others with whom you come into contact can deal adequately with the world, just as adequately as you believe you yourself deal with it. You do not readily question another's ability to state simple facts, or to ask and give directions, or to add new information to old. When you ask another person for directions, you expect that he or she will employ a scheme for giving the directions that will be adequate for the occasion. For example, if you have asked for a description of the interior of a house, you expect to get that description according to an acceptable pattern of spatial organization. You also expect certain kinds of information and not other kinds and to get information that is adequate for the purpose you have in mind, if you have made that purpose clear in some way. And that expectation is generally fulfilled. 'Basic' information is fairly easily accessible, but we should notice how difficult it is quite often to gain certain further kinds of information—or to supply that information if we are asked for it. A lot of 'information' that we actually have access to never becomes part of that body of information we rely on for ordinary living and routine communication with others. Police officers, for example, have to be specially trained to observe certain kinds of details that are, indeed, accessible to the general public. But what they observe and report is very different from what we, commonplace actors in a commonplace world, observe and are therefore able to report. We actually see the same things but we do not observe and record them in the same way; there is really no need to do so, for we know that everyday life does not usually require that intensity of observation. The events in our everyday world are necessarily mundane: life would quickly become unbearable if it were not so ordered and predictable and consequently so unworthy of close and continuing attention.

16   The kind of world in which we see ourselves and others existing is also one in which personal behaviour is consistent—or should be. When we meet another person repeatedly, we assume that that person's behaviour is consistent. The other is the 'same' person from encounter to encounter and there is little, if any, fluctuation

in behaviour. When a person is consistently inconsistent, which is therefore a consistent fact in itself, we assume that he will continue to be inconsistent. Indeed, if you notice a change in consistency when you meet someone, you are likely to make a comment to that effect or express some concern, possibly to others rather than to the person himself. You may quietly ask yourself *What is up with him?* or *What have I done to make Sally say that?* Or, having noticed John's 'peculiar' behaviour, you may ask Bill *Why is John behaving the way he is these days?* The relative infrequency of such expressions of concern indicates how 'normal' most continuing encounters are; the everyday sameness of behaviour and routine does not require notice or comment, except perhaps about that very sameness: *What's new? Nothing!*

17   Just as we expect the behaviour of others to be consistent, so we also view the world consistently; our beliefs about it and about how its various bits and pieces relate to one another change slowly, if at all. We tend to have rather fixed ideas about our place within that world, of who we are and how we relate to others, and this observation is true even of those whose world is partly a world of fantasy. Only schizophrenics inhabit more than one world, thereby appearing to inhabit one world inconsistently. Each of us has a picture or self-image of himself or herself and of the various others in our environment, and we seek to keep these pictures consistent. A particular picture may also have more than a single dimension to it: for example, we may have both a public image and a very different private one. If we do, we must try to keep the two apart. The private lives of public figures are of interest to us not only because they show us quite different aspects of character, but also because we can try to judge how successful the individuals are in separating the two existences. We may also be tempted to evaluate one existence, particularly the public one, against what we come to know of the other. Much of the appeal of biographies lies in attempts to reconcile the various images of the subjects.

18   We function in a world of normal appearances and usually do not probe beneath the surface of events, and in general, we believe that everybody else behaves in that respect much as we do, sharing with us a similar approach to daily existence. Those who probe are people like scientists and psychiatrists, but even their probing is restricted to a very narrow range of activities. Indeed, we go further and assume that those with whom we deal share much specific information about the world. One simple way of convincing yourself that this is so, that there is considerable shared background knowledge in any conversation, is to insist that each party make everything quite explicit in the very next conversation you have. That conversation will quickly degenerate: you may find yourself accused of being crazy, pedantic, or disruptive, or you may be assigned some other clearly antisocial label. Tempers are also likely to become frayed. Another way is to attempt to find out from newspapers, magazines, or radio and TV reports what is happening on some issue by using only the actual words you read or hear on a single specific occasion, completely disregarding any previous knowledge you might have of the topic. You will probably not be able to make much sense of what you either read or hear. One of the great difficulties you encounter in reading a local newspaper in a place you happen to be visiting is your lack of the background knowledge necessary to interpret what

you are reading. This lack makes many items of local news either obscure or elusive: you lack knowledge of the people, the events, and the issues and have little or nothing on which to hang any details you are presented with. But the locals do not experience this difficulty.

19   Common knowledge, then—that is, 'what everyone knows'—is necessarily something that is culture-loaded and varies from group to group. Much of what everyone knows is also either scientifically unwarranted or very superficial. For example, there are numerous stereotypes in this kind of knowledge—ideas we have about the 'typical' behaviour and characteristics of people or objects. But that should not surprise us, because, after all, that is essentially what norms themselves are in one sense—abstractions based on certain kinds of experiences which apparently typify some kind of general behaviour. Many people go through life holding the view that common knowledge and stereotypes characterize a sort of truth about the world; others are somewhat more critical and conscious of the complexities that lie behind such a simple belief. What we must not assume, however, is that common knowledge is always false and stereotyping is always bad; social harmony is possible only if there are things we can agree on, and there are measures of agreement. What may be important is how fixed are the measures any society uses, not the existence of the measures themselves.

20   For any particular conversation it is also possible to show that there are differences between the parties in the specific things that they know in contrast to the kinds of background knowledge that they share. No two people have identical backgrounds, so in any conversation the participants will have different kinds of knowledge about almost any topic that is likely to be mentioned. If only two people, Fred and Sally, are involved, there will be certain matters known to both, some because 'everybody knows such things' and others because both Fred and Sally happen to know them. Then there will be matters known to only one of the speakers, so that Fred will know something that Sally does not know, or Sally something that Fred does not know. In addition, there will be partly known information: Fred or Sally, or both, may partly know something or know parts of something, but not necessarily the same parts. And Fred or Sally, or both again, may believe that the other knows something that the other actually does not know. As we can see, there are numerous possible permutations in who knows what, who believes who knows what, and so on.—Again, there are predictable consequences: conversation can proceed only on the basis that the participants share a set of beliefs, that is, certain things must be known to all parties; others may be known; some will have to be explained; questions may be asked for clarification; difficulties will be negotiated or cleared up somehow; people will be understanding and tolerant; and the various processes that are involved will be conducted decently. If only one participant in a conversation refuses to subscribe to these beliefs and to conduct himself or herself accordingly, the others will become irritated, confused, or frustrated, and may well abandon any attempt to continue what they have begun.

21   Since most participants in a conversation usually do share a certain amount of background knowledge about 'proper' behaviour and the 'right' way to do things,

much of what they say can be understood if we, too, are familiar with the knowledge they share. Their references to places, times, and events, and their accounts and descriptions are related to what they know and what they believe the others know. A participant in a conversation must believe that he or she has access to the same set of reference points that all the other participants have access to; all he or she needs do in conversing is use those points for orientation, and listeners will comprehend. And such a belief is largely justified. What is hardly ever necessary in a conversation is to begin at the very beginning of anything and to treat everyone and everything as unique and somehow without antecedents. In a trivial sense every occasion is unique, but procedures exist which minimize novelty and maximize normality—accepted ways of asking and giving directions, rules for regulating who speaks to whom and about what, and basic principles for conducting yourself, for example, with complete strangers.

22   A conversation between familiars offers a very special mix of knowledge. There are matters in it which the parties know but are reluctant to refer to directly, although they may allude to them if necessary. There are matters which are in the conversation by reason of the fact that they are deliberately avoided—their absence is conspicuous. And then there are the actual topics of the conversation. However, these topics are not introduced logically, as it were, but rather in a variety of ways according to the needs of the individuals and of the occasion, with each participant willing to let a topic emerge as seems natural at the time in the expectation that its various bits and pieces will hold together.

23   In general conversation with others it is ordinary, everyday, 'commonsense' knowledge that we assume they share with us. In certain circumstances, as between professionals, we can also assume a sharing of specialized knowledge. We must always take great care when we refer to items outside these shared areas. We cannot rely on others knowing what we know. They may not even share the same assumptions about what it means to 'know' something. A physicist's knowledge of matter is different from a lay person's, and an actor's view of character is unlikely to be the same as that of a psychiatrist. Explanations may well become necessary, and they may not be easily provided. Briefing is one kind of explaining behaviour in such circumstances. But a recurrent difficulty is knowing just how much to say on a particular occasion and then judging how successful we have been in saying it. This is particularly crucial if we then proceed to treat this 'new' information we supply henceforth as part of our listeners' everyday knowledge. It may not be easily incorporated into existing knowledge, as anyone who has ever taught well knows, for it is one thing to teach something and quite another to learn it.

24   Repetition and checking up therefore become a very necessary part of conversation. They are demanded by the general requirement of language and communication that you must always say more than you minimally need to say so that you will not be misunderstood. The person you are talking to also must have checking devices to indicate whether you are being understood: for example, certain kinds of gestures or glances, which, because of the puzzlement they show, require you to offer some further explanation; outright questions; some kinds of denial behaviour;

and so on. In other words, as a speaker you are not free to indulge in a monologue, disregard those who are listening to you, and assume you are being understood. You must work to be understood and you must be sensitive to your audience. One consequence is that sophisticated public communicators are much more likely to seek other ways than formal speeches in order to get their views across to an audience which, by its nature, cannot ask for clarifications—a president's 'fireside chats', press conferences, staged interviews, and appearances before favourable groups or friendly committees.

25 What should be apparent from what we have said is that successful conversations exploit many of the same principles that underlie all forms of social existence. There is really nothing 'special' or unique about conversation in that sense. To get through a week in your life, you must be prepared to accept things for what they appear to be and put your trust in that appearance. You must also assume a certain regularity and continuity of existence. To do otherwise is to be paranoid or act anti-socially. When disaster strikes and the 'normal', consistent world vanishes, people often find themselves unable to cope with the changed circumstances of their lives. They no longer have the necessary reference points on which to pin their existence. Conversation is a form of 'coping' behaviour which relies heavily on just those same sets of assumptions that allow us to drive to work safely, drink water in a restaurant, cash a government cheque, and even go to sleep at night. Saying *Hi* to Sally and expecting Sally to say *Hi* in return is much the same kind of thing, or asking a stranger *Excuse me, do you have the time?* and getting the reply *Yes, it's ten to four.*

26 Without routine ways of doing things and in the absence of norms of behaviour, life would be too difficult, too uncertain for most of us. The routines, patterns, rituals, stereotypes even of everyday existence provide us with many of the means for coping with that existence, for reducing uncertainty and anxiety, and for providing us with the appearance of stability and continuity in the outside world. They let us get on with the actual business of living. However, many are beneath our conscious awareness; what, therefore, is of particular interest is bringing to awareness just those aspects of our lives that make living endurable (and even enjoyable) just because they are so commonly taken for granted.

THINKING CRITICALLY

1. What are our unconscious expectations in social conversation? How do social dimensions of language impact the quality and substances of everyday discourse? Explain.

2. In what ways must we consider the person with whom we converse? What factors do we consciously and unconsciously process as we engage in conversation with another person?

3. How can we hurt others or hurt ourselves during conversation? Describe a situation in which you unintentionally hurt someone or yourself during a conversation.

4. What is the role of trust in everyday conversation? Consider the role of trust in your own conversations. How does the element of trust influence what you say and to whom? Explain.

5. What skills, according to the author, must a successful conversationalist possess?

6. What are the basic conditions that the author identifies as necessary for all conversations to prevail? Explain.

7. What is the author's thesis and how does he support it? How effective are his examples in supporting his claims? Can you think of other areas in the essay where examples would be useful? Explain.

8. In what ways does effective conversational discourse depend on our shared sense of a "mundane" existence?

WRITING ASSIGNMENTS

1. Tape a conversation between two people discussing an everyday topic such as their weekend activities or a current event. Analyze their discussion applying some of the conversational elements Wardbaugh describes. For example, what shared assumptions do the conversationalists hold in common? How do they exhibit trust? Do they risk hurting one another by making a conversational blunder? Explain.

2. Write an essay exploring the concept of trust in conversation. Why is trust so important to the success of social conversation? Describe situations from your own experience in which trust played an important role in the success or failure of a conversation.

Some Friends and I Started Talking: Conversation and Social Change
Margaret J. Wheatley

We spend our lives having conversations. The huge explosion of cell-phone use in the last five years is testimony to how much time and money we are willing to expend in search of conversation. Communication is fundamental to our survival. It not only is used to articulate needs and wants, but also our dreams, desires, fears, and goals. We use conversation to argue, console, share beliefs, develop thoughts, and discover more about each other. And it is from discussion and the exchange of ideas that great social movements are born. In the next essay, Margaret Wheatley explains why conversation can be a compelling tool for change. As Wheatley explains, "all social change begins with a conversation."

Margaret J. Wheatley is a well-known authority on organizational development. She is president of the Berkana Institute in Provo, Utah. She is the author of several books, including *Leadership and the New Science* (1992, co-authored with Myron Kellner-Rogers) and *A*

Simpler Way (1996). The following essay first appeared in the *UTNE Reader* excerpted from her book, *Turning to One Another* (2002).

1 A Canadian woman told me this story. She was returning to Vietnam to pick up her second child, adopted from the same orphanage as her first child. On her visit two years earlier she had seen challenging conditions at the orphanage and had vowed this time to take medical supplies. "They needed Tylenol, not T-shirts or trinkets," she said to a friend one day. The friend suggested that the most useful thing to take would be an incubator. The woman was surprised (she'd been thinking bandages and pills), but she started making calls, looking for an incubator. Weeks later, she had been offered enough pediatric medical supplies to fill four 40-foot shipping containers! And 12 incubators. From a casual conversation between two friends, a medical relief effort for Vietnamese children emerged. And it all began when "some friends and I started talking."

2 Stories like this are plentiful. Nothing has given me more hope recently than to observe how simple conversations give birth to actions that can change lives and restore our faith in the future. There is no more powerful way to initiate significant social change than to start a conversation. When a group of people discover that they share a common concern, that's when the process of change begins.

3 Yet it's not easy to begin talking to one another. We stay silent and apart from one another for many reasons. Some of us never have been invited to share our ideas and opinions. From early school days we've been instructed to be quiet so others can tell us what to think. Others have soured on conversation, having sat through too many meetings that degenerated into people shouting, or stomping out angrily, or taking control of the agenda.

4 But true conversation is very different from those sorts of experiences. It is a timeless and reliable way for humans to think together. Before there were classrooms, meetings, or group facilitators, there were people sitting around talking. When we think about beginning a conversation, we can take courage from the fact that this is a process we all know how to do. We are reawakening an ancient practice, a way of being together that all humans intimately understand.

5 We also can take courage in the fact that many people are longing to converse again. We are hungry for a chance to talk. People want to tell their stories, and are willing to listen to yours. I find that it takes just one person to start a conversation, because everyone else is eager to talk once it has begun. "Some friends and I started talking. . . ." Change doesn't happen from a leader announcing the plan. Change begins from deep inside a system, when a few people notice something they will no longer tolerate, or when they respond to someone's dream of what's possible.

6 It's easy to observe this in recent history. The Solidarity trade union movement in Poland began with conversation—less than a dozen workers in a Gdansk shipyard in 1980 speaking to each other about despair, their need for change, their need for freedom. Within months, Solidarity grew to 9.5 million workers. There was no e-mail then, just people talking to each other about their own needs, and finding

that millions of fellow citizens shared their feelings. In a short time, they shut down the country, and changed the course of history.

7   To make important changes in our communities, our society, our lives, we just have to find a few others who care about the same thing we do. Together we can figure out the first step, then the second, then the next. Gradually, we grow powerful. But we don't have to start with power, only with passion.

8   Even among friends, starting a conversation can take courage. But conversation also *gives* us courage. Thinking together, deciding what actions to take, more of us become bold. As we learn from each other's experiences and interpretations, we see issues in richer detail. This clarity can help us see both when to act and when not to. In some cases, the right timing means doing nothing right now. Talking can be enough for the time being.

9   If conversation is the natural way that humans think together, what gets lost when we stop talking? Paulo Freire, the influential Brazilian educator who used education to support poor people in transforming their lives, said that we "cannot be truly human apart from communication. . . . To impede communication is to reduce people to the status of things."

10   When we don't talk to one another in a meaningful way, Freire believes, we never act to change things. We become passive and allow others to tell us what to do. Freire had a deep faith in every person's ability to be a clear thinker and a courageous actor. Not all of us share this faith, but it is necessary if we are to invite colleagues into conversation. Sometimes it is hard to believe that others have as much to offer as we do in the way of concern and skill. But I have found that when the issue is important to others, they will not disappoint us. If you start a conversation, others will surprise you.

11   Near my home in Utah, I watched a small group of mothers cautiously begin meeting about a problem in the community: They wanted their children to be able to walk to school safely. They were shocked when the city council granted their request for a pedestrian traffic light. Encouraged by this victory, they started other projects, each more ambitious than the last. After a few years, they participated in securing a federal grant for neighborhood development worth tens of millions of dollars. Today, one of those mothers has become an expert on city housing, won a seat on the city council, and completed a term as council chair. When she tells her story, it begins like so many others: "Some friends and I started talking. . . ."

12   For conversation to become a powerful tool in society, we must take it seriously and examine our own role in making it successful. Here are some basic principles I've learned over years of hosting formal conversations around the country.

13   We acknowledge one another as equals. One thing that makes us equal is that we need each other. Whatever any one of us knows alone, it is not enough to change things. Someone else is bound to see things that we need to know.

14   We try to stay curious about each other. I maintain my curiosity by reminding myself that everyone has something to teach me. When others are saying things I

disagree with, or have never thought about, or that I consider foolish or wrong, I remind myself that I really can learn from them—if I stay open and do not shut them out.

15   We recognize that we need each other's help to become better listeners. The greatest barrier to good conversation is that as a culture we're losing the capacity to listen. We're too busy. We're too certain of our own views. We just keep rushing past each other. At the beginning of any conversation I host, I make a point of asking everyone to help each other listen. This is hard work for almost everyone, but if we talk about listening at the start of a conversation, it makes things easier. If someone hasn't been listening to us, or misinterprets what we say, we're less likely to blame that person. We can be a little gentler with the difficulties we experience in a group if we make a commitment at the start to help each other listen.

16   We slow down so we have time to think and reflect. Most of us work in places where we rarely have time to sit together and think. We dash in and out of meetings where we make hurried, not thoughtful, decisions. Working to create conditions for a true spirit of conversation helps rediscover the joy of thinking together.

17   We remember that conversation is the natural way humans think together. Conversation is not a new invention for the 21st century; we're restoring a tradition from earlier human experience. It does, however, take time to let go of our modern ways of being in meetings, to get past the habits that keep us apart— speaking too fast, interrupting others, monopolizing the time, giving speeches or making pronouncements. Many of us have been rewarded for these behaviors, becoming more powerful by using them. But the blunt truth is that they don't lead to wise thinking or healthy relationships.

18   We expect it to be messy at times. Life doesn't move in straight lines; and neither does a good conversation. When a conversation begins, people always say things that don't connect. What's important at the start is that everyone's voice gets heard, that everyone feels invited into the conversation. If you're hosting the conversation, you may feel responsible for pointing out connections between these diverse contributions, but it's important to let go of that impulse and just sit with the messiness. The messy stage doesn't last forever. If we suppress the messiness at the beginning, it will find us later on and be more disruptive. The first stage is to listen well to whatever is being said, forgetting about neat thoughts and categories, knowing that all contributions add crucial elements to the whole. Eventually, we will be surprised by how much we share.

19   The practice of true talking takes courage, faith, and time. We don't always get it right the first time, and we don't have to. We need to settle into conversation: we don't just do it automatically. As we risk talking to each other about things we care about, as we become curious about each other, as we slow things down, gradually we remember this timeless way of being together. Our rushed

and thoughtless behaviors fade away, and we sit quietly in the gift of being to-gether, just as humans have always done.

20   Another surprising but important element of conversation is a willingness to be disturbed, to allow our beliefs and ideas to be challenged by what others think. No one person or perspective can solve our problems. We have to be will-ing to let go of our certainty and be confused for a time.

21   Most of us weren't trained to admit what we don't know. We haven't been re-warded for being confused, or for asking questions rather than giving quick answers. We were taught to sound certain and confident. But the only way to understand the world in its complexity is to spend more time in the state of *not* knowing. It is very difficult to give up our certainties—the positions, beliefs, and explanations that lie at the heart of our personal identities. And I am not saying that we have to give up what we believe. We only need to be curious about what others believe, and to acknowl-edge that their way of interpreting the world might be essential to us.

22   I think it's important to begin a conversation by listening as best you can for what's different, for what surprises you. We have many opportunities every day to be the one who listens, curious rather than certain. If you try this with several people, you might find yourself laughing in delight as you realize how many unique ways there are to be human. But the greatest benefit of all is that listen-ing moves us closer. When we listen with as little judgment as possible, we de-velop better relationships with each other.

23   Sometimes we hesitate to listen for what's different because we don't want to change. We're comfortable with our lives, and if we listened to anyone who raised questions, we might feel compelled to engage in new activities and ways of thinking. But most of us do see things in our lives or in the world that we would like to be different. If that's true, it means we listen more, not less. And we have to be willing to move into the very uncomfortable place of uncertainty.

24   We may simply fear the confusion that comes with new ideas in unsettled forms. But we can't be creative if we refuse to be confused. Change always starts with confusion; cherished interpretations must dissolve to make way for what's new. Great ideas and inventions miraculously appear in the space of not knowing. If we can move through the fear and enter the abyss we are rewarded greatly. We rediscover we're creative.

25   As the world grows more puzzling and difficult, most of us don't want to keep struggling through it alone. I can't know what to do from my own narrow perspective. I need a better understanding of what's going on. I want to sit down with you and talk about all the frightening and hopeful things I observe, and lis-ten to what frightens you and gives you hope. I need new ideas and solutions for the problems I care about. And I know I need to talk to you to discover them. I need to learn to value your perspective, and I want you to value mine. I expect to be disturbed by what I hear from you. I know we don't have to agree with each other in order to think well together. There is no need for us to be joined at the head. We are joined by our human hearts.

THINKING CRITICALLY

1. How does Wheatley's introductory story about the Canadian woman set the tone and theme for the rest of her essay? Explain.

2. Did this essay change the way you think about the power of conversation? About how you listen and how you converse? Explain.

3. Why do we "stay silent and apart from one another" in today's society? What reasons does Wheatley give? Can you think of additional reasons for people's reluctance to engage in conversation?

4. What, according to the author, is "true conversation"? Identify the elements of true conversation. How do your own everyday conversations compare to her definition? Explain.

5. Compare the points Wheatley makes about speaking and listening to the points Deborah Tannen makes about "lecturing and listening" in her essay in the preceding section of this chapter. On what points do they agree? Do you think Tannen would disagree with any of Wheatley's suggestions? Why or why not?

6. What happens when people stop talking? Explain.

WRITING ASSIGNMENTS

1. Wheatley provides several examples of conversations that changed society. Can you think of other examples that would support her thesis? Identify at least two other examples and discuss how conversation and discussion led to change.

2. Among her suggestions for productive conversation, Wheatley states that we also enter conversation with a "willingness to be disturbed," and to have our beliefs challenged. Write about a conversation from your personal experience in which your beliefs were challenged. Did you try to see the other viewpoint? Did you focus on defending your beliefs? After reading this essay, would you try to conduct the conversation differently? Explain.

3. Among the aristocracy of the eighteenth century, salons became the rage. *Salons* were rooms in which people of social or intellectual distinction would gather to discuss topics and exchange ideas. (Salons later gave way to the *parlors* of the nineteenth century. The root word of *parlor* is *parler,* which is old French for "talk.") Many Internet salons have emerged online, reviving this tradition. Visit an Internet salon and read some of the exchanges <http://café.utne.com> or <http://theworldcafe.org>. Write an essay comparing some of the points Wheatley makes in this essay regarding the power of conversation and the dialogues you read online. In what ways are people using Internet cafés to promote social change? Explain.

Like, Uptalk?

James Gorman

Uptalk is a way of speaking practiced by teenagers and young adults in which statements sound like questions through a rising inflection of pitch at the end of the sentence or comment. From the language of teens and twenty-somethings, it has infected the conversational patterns of mainstream society. In the next piece, James Gorman offers some humorous insights on the phenomenon of uptalk, and like—its possible origins, significance, and consequences?

James Gorman teaches journalism at New York University. This article first appeared in the *New York Times Magazine* in August of 1993.

1   I used to speak in a regular voice. I was able to assert, demand, question. Then I started teaching. At a university? And my students had this rising intonation thing? It was particularly noticeable on telephone messages. "Hello? Professor Gorman? This is Albert? From feature writing?"

2   I had no idea that a change in the "intonation contour" of a sentence, as linguists put it, could be as contagious as the common cold. But before long I noticed a Jekyll-and-Hyde transformation in my own speech. I first heard it when I myself was leaving a message. "This is Jim Gorman? I'm doing an article on Klingon? The language? From *Star Trek?*" I realized then that I was unwittingly, unwillingly speaking uptalk.

3   I was, like, appalled?

4   Rising intonations at the end of a sentence or phrase are not new. In many languages, a "phrase final rise" indicates a question. Some Irish, English and Southern American dialects use rises all the time. Their use at the end of a declarative statement may date back in America to the 17th century.

5   Nonetheless, we are seeing, well, hearing, something different. Uptalk, under various names, has been noted on this newspaper's Op-Ed page and on National Public Radio. Cynthia McLemore, a University of Pennsylvania linguist who knows as much about uptalk as anyone, says the frequency and repetition of rises mark a new phenomenon. And although uptalk has been most common among teen-agers, in particular young women, it seems to be spreading. Says McLemore, "What's going on now in America looks like a dialect shift." In other words, what is happening may be a basic change in the way Americans talk.

6   Nobody knows exactly where uptalk came from. It might have come from California, from Valley Girl talk. It may be an upper-middle-class thing, probably starting with adolescents. But everybody has an idea about what uptalk means. Some twenty somethings say uptalk is part of their attitude: cool, ironic, uncommitted.

7   I myself was convinced that uptalk was tentative, testing, oversensitive; not feminine so much as wimpy, detumescent. Imagine how it would sound in certain cocksure, authoritative occupations, like police work:

You're under arrest? You have some rights?

Or surgery:

So, first I'll open up your chest?

8   I also thought how some of the great dead white males of the much maligned canon might sound, reintoned:

It was really dark? Like, on the deep? The face of the deep?

Or:

Hi, I'm Ishmael? I'll be your narrator?

Or:

A horse? A horse? My kingdom for a horse?

9   My speculations have some support; there are linguists who see uptalk as being about uncertainty and deference to the listener. But McLemore scoffs at these ideas. People tend to hear what they want to hear, she says. One can, for instance, take a speech pattern common among women and link it to a stereotype of women. (Uncertain? Deferential?)

10   Deborah Tannen—a linguist at Georgetown, who, with her book *You Just Don't Understand: Women and Men in Conversation,* may have overtaken Noam Chomsky and become the best-known linguist in America—contends that broad theorizing about uptalk is downright foolish. Speech patterns are contagious, she says, and they spread the way fads do. "There's a fundamental human impulse to imitate what we hear," she says. "Teen-agers talk this way because other teen-agers talk this way and they want to sound like their peers."

11   That doesn't mean rises have no function. They can be used as a signal that "more is coming," says Mark Aronoff of the State University of New York at Stony Brook. An adolescent might be signaling "I have more to say; don't interrupt me." McLemore says an early study of telephone conversation suggested that rises may be used as a probe of sorts, to see if the hearer is getting what you are saying.

12   A friend of mine (of no formal linguistic expertise) likes this latter interpretation. He insists that the spread of uptalk indicates the lack of shared knowledge in our society. Our society, he contends, has become so fragmented that no one knows anymore whether another person will have a clue as to what he's saying. We need to test the hearer's level of understanding.

13   *Like, suppose I want to talk about Sabicas? Or Charles Barkley? Or nitric oxide? The molecule of the year? For 1992?*

14   By using the questioning tone, I'm trying to see if my conversational partner knows anything at all about flamenco guitar, professional basketball or neurochemistry.

15   McLemore studied intonation in one very particular context. She observed uses of intonation in a Texas sorority, where uptalk was not at all about uncertainty or deference. It was used most commonly by the leaders, the senior officers. Uptalk

was a kind of accent, or tag, to highlight new information for listeners: "We're having a bake sale? On the west mall? On Sunday?" When saying something like "Everyone should know that your dues should be in," they used a falling intonation at the end of the sentence.

16   The sorority members' own interpretation of uptalk was that it was a way of being inclusive. McLemore's conclusions are somewhat similar. She says the rises are used to connect phrases, and to connect the speaker to the listener, as a means of "getting the other person involved."

17   Since McLemore did her study, people are constantly calling to her attention other uses of uptalk. It seems to be a common speech pattern in Toronto, where, she says, a radio show called "Ask the Pastors" displays uptalk in spades. She also found that on another radio show the Mayor of Austin, Tex., used rises to mark items in a list. Asked to explain why he should maintain bike paths, he said things like: Austin has a good climate? It's good for bike riding? McLemore also observed a second-grade teacher who used rises freely for commands and statements: "Jason? Back to your chair? Thank you?"

18   I confess to ambivalence about uptalk. When I use it, I judge it to mark a character flaw. On the other hand, there are some ritual utterances that could clearly benefit from a change in pitch contour.

19   *Mea culpa? Mea culpa? Mea maxima culpa?*

20   Or, to reflect the true state of matrimony in our society:

21   *I do?*

22   I do not, however, want the speech pattern to spread to airplane pilots. I don't want to hear: *This is Captain McCormick? Your pilot? We'll be flying to Denver? Our cruising altitude will be, like, 30,000 feet?*

23   McLemore, however, says it seems possible that we will be hearing such an intonation among pilots in the future. After all, it looks as if pilots are getting younger every year. Once commercial airline pilots start using uptalk, McLemore notes, it will mean that a full-blown dialect shift has occurred. Uptalk won't be uptalk anymore. It will be, like, American English?

THINKING CRITICALLY

1. How does Gorman define *uptalk?* Are you familiar with this pattern in speech? If so, do you or any of your friends speak in uptalk? From your observations, would you agree that uptalk is on the rise, or fading away from everyday discourse?

2. According to Gorman, what are the possible origins of uptalk? What groups have used uptalk in the past, and who uses it now?

3. In his opening paragraph, Gorman differentiates speech functions: assertions, demands, and questions. In your own words, explain each of these functions as they apply to everyday conversation. How might these functions be "equalized" if common speech indeed embraces this

shift to uptalk? Would such a shift, in your opinion, damage communication? Why or why not?

4. In paragraph 12, Gorman discusses the link between the advent of uptalk and the fragmented nature of contemporary society. What social situations support the use of uptalk in everyday conversation? Summarize, in your own words, the argument being made here. Do you agree with his hypothesis regarding the usefulness of uptalk? Explain.

5. Given that the phenomenon of uptalk is an oral one, how well does Gorman translate it into the essay? Are you able to "hear" what he is talking about? Do his examples serve as effective "translations"? Explain.

6. In what areas of conversation and everyday speech does Gorman not want to hear uptalk, and why?

7. From this essay, can you tell if Gorman is endorsing or condemning the use of uptalk in American discourse? Explain.

WRITING ASSIGNMENTS

1. Gorman says that teenagers and young "twenty-somethings" are the most frequent users of uptalk. Conduct interviews with other students to determine their familiarity with and interpretation of uptalk. Write a paper exploring your findings. Try to determine if different demographic groups have different responses. Also, what different theories do your respondents have as to the cause and meaning of uptalk? Will it indeed become a mainstream speech pattern?

2. Gorman rewrites the opening linings of several literary classics including *Moby Dick*. Pick a famous literary work and rewrite a portion of it, making strategic use of uptalk. Does the meaning shift? Explain.

3. Write a paper in which you question the idea of standard or proper American English. What does the definition mean? What groups or dialects fall outside the standard, and what are the consequences of this? Should there be a language standard in the United States? Explain.

The Other Side of E-Mail
Robert Kuttner

Few people would disagree that e-mail is revolutionizing how we communicate. Individuals who never wrote an ordinary letter before now spend hours online composing and sending electronic messages. We can communicate to virtually every corner of the world with the push of a button. But what is the price of this easy and efficient new mode of communication? Robert Kuttner contends that instead of freeing our time, e-mail is, in fact, a time "thief." He declares that although e-mail has many uses, there is a darker side to it that we must consider when employing this medium.

Founder and co-editor of *The American Prospect*, a bimonthly journal of policy and politics, Robert Kuttner is also one of five contributing columnists to *Business Week*'s "Economic Viewpoint." His work has appeared in many publications including the *New York Times*, the *Atlantic Monthly*, and *Harvard Business Review*. Kuttner is the author of five books, including *The End of Laissez Faire* (1991) and *Everything for Sale: The Virtues and Limits of Markets* (1997). The following editorial appeared in the April 19, 1998, issue of the *Boston Globe*.

1   A few years ago, when my daughter was a college freshman, I wrote a column singing the praises of e-mail. We were, suddenly, corresponding. It was, I decided, the revenge of print on electronics—a whole generation raised on the tube and the phone, rediscovering the lost art of writing letters. How utterly charming.

2   Now I'm not so sure. Like all new media, e-mail has a dark side. To be sure, it saves a great deal of time and paperwork and has facilitated new, unimagined forms of affinity. However, e-mail is also a thief. It steals our time and our privacy. It deceives us into thinking we have endless additional hours in the day to engage in far-flung communications that we may or may not need or want.

3   All of a sudden, on top of everything else we have to do, e-mail is one more garden demanding tending.

4   E-mail brings a kind of pseudo-urgency that demands an instant response. It creates false intimacies. Recently, I got an e-mail message from a perfect stranger, a student who had read one of my articles and wanted help on a term paper. I was touched, but alas, there aren't enough hours in the day. Yet something about the message made me feel I needed to apologize for not being able to do her homework. With e-mail, it's too easy to hit the reply key, with results you may regret. One acquaintance, thinking she was just responding to a note from a close friend, accidentally sent a highly personal message to the friend's entire mailing list.

5   I recently had a painful quarrel triggered by e-mail messages. A dear friend and I were both having a very busy week and imposing on each other's time. Without quite intending to, we ended up firing salvos of e-mail back and forth of escalating testiness until we had quite insulted each other. We apologized, in person.

6   This mishap could not have occurred either by phone or by ordinary mail. When talking to someone, you pay attention to tonality. And when you write a letter, you read it over a few times before sending it. But e-mail is tone-deaf and all too instant. It is ephemeral, yet irrevocable. Once you've banged out your message and sent it into the ether, you can't take it back.

7   E-mail is a great convenience—for the sender. The recipient is presumed to have infinite time and interest. It is the equivalent of endless Christmas letters from boring distant relatives all year long.

8   Bosses get in the habit of sending down incessant e-mail messages from on high, as if anyone cared. (Now hear this . . .) A large corporation with which I am vaguely affiliated sends me more messages than I could possibly want to have, let alone answer.

9   E-mail is also not secure. The magazine that I edit regularly gets highly personal missives, sent by mistake to the wrong e-mail address thanks to a typo. With the phone, you know as soon as you have a wrong number. And mis-addressed letters either get returned or end up in the dead letter office.

10   At one company, two people carrying on an affair were incautiously sending each other intimate e-mail, which a supervisor discovered. To make matters worse, they were making snide comments about the supervisor. Security escorted them from the premises.

11   E-mail is also easily forwarded and deliberately or mistakenly put into mass circulation. Don't e-mail anything private unless you are prepared to see it crop up all over the World Wide Web. E-mail, like talk radio, reduces inhibitions; it is democratic to the point of moronic. And I've not even gotten to mass junk e-mail, known in the trade as spam.

12   I know, I know, the Internet is a marvel. And it is. And, sure, e-mail is great for scheduling meetings, for sending and receiving research materials, for allowing people in remote locations to collaborate on projects. But novelty and low cost tend to breed excess.

13   Like every new tool, from the wheel to nuclear energy, electronic communication will take a while to find its proper etiquette and niche. In the meantime, it is an awkward adolescent that has borrowed the family car, hormones raging and radio blaring, with little regard for the rules of the road.

14   Of course, some fans of e-mail may find these words controversial or offensive. So if you have any comments on this column, my e-mail address is . . . no, actually, send me a letter.

THINKING CRITICALLY

1. According to Kuttner, how does e-mail transcend the generation gap? Can you think of other ways that e-mail bridges gaps between groups of people?

2. How is e-mail a "thief"? Do you agree with Kuttner's assessment? Describe the ways e-mail can make life more complicated, rather than simplify it. Would you have more, or less time, without e-mail access? Explain.

3. How does e-mail "reduce inhibitions" (paragraph 11)? What are the social perils of e-mail? Describe the complications of e-mail that are not found in other communication mediums such as the telephone or ordinary face-to-face conversation.

4. What function does e-mail have in today's society? How have our lives changed because of it? What influence has it had on our communication style and habits?

5. What could be the long-term effects of e-mail on social discourse? On how we converse with each other? Explain.

6. Kuttner compares the Internet to a garden that requires constant tending. How effective is this metaphor? Explain.

WRITING ASSIGNMENTS

1. A popular television commercial for an Internet employment agency features a man writing an insulting letter to his boss only to have a toy fall off his monitor and hit the "enter" key, sending his message. Have you ever had a mishap with e-mail such as the ones described by Kuttner in this article? Describe your experience. How did it influence your use of e-mail in the future?

2. How does e-mail differ from ordinary conversation? Drawing from your personal experience, write a paper in which you predict the influence of e-mail on social discourse and how we converse with each other offline.

3. Visit the chatrooms of several different groups and evaluate the communication style of the participants. Can you distinguish any trends or common behaviors in their language? For example, do teen chatrooms employ more symbolic language than ones frequented by older populations? Is this language more inclusive or exclusive to a new visitor? Write a paper evaluating the differences in Internet communication as demonstrated by various populations in specific chatrooms.

Come in CQ: The Body on the Wire
Ellen Ullman

Often called the great connector, the Internet links everything from organizations, libraries, and universities, to social groups and individuals. The versatility of the Internet allows people to interact at their own comfort level. You can be a nameless visitor to an online museum, or you can have a very personal interaction with another individual via e-mail or a chatroom. For many people, the Internet is the only place they truly feel comfortable meeting people and making conversation. Some even fall in love online. But what happens when an online romance is brought outside the virtual world and into the restaurant down the street? In the next article, Ellen Ullman describes the comfort of late night conversation that leads to romance, and how face-to-face dialogue for such lovebirds can be awkward once away from their keyboards.

A software engineer by trade, Ellen Ullman's articles have appeared in computer industry publications, *Harper's* magazine, and in her 1997 book, *Close to the Machine: Technophilia and Its Discontents.* She is also a regular contributor to the online business magazine, *The Red Herring.* This essay appeared in *Wired Women* (1997).

1   When I was growing up, the boy next door was a ham radio operator. His name was Eugene. He was fat, went to Bronx High School of Science to study engineering, and sat evenings in the basement of his house beaming a signal off into the atmosphere. The heart of Eugene's world was the radio room: a dim box filled with equipment, all of it furnished with dials and toggles and switches. It was there he spent his Saturday nights, alone in the dark, lit only by small red lights and a flex-arm lamp bent low over his operator's guide.

2   I grew up in the shadow of Eugene's radio. Over time, his antenna became more and more elaborate, and my family kept giving him permission to add anchors

to the roof of our house. From a simple T-bar arrangement, the antenna sprouted new masts and crossbeams, and finally a wide circular thing that could be positioned with a motor. This whole complicated structure whirred when the motor was engaged, vibrated in the wind, was twice reduced to dangling pieces by hurricanes. Mostly, it just sat there and cast an electronic shadow over our house, which is how I came to know everything about Eugene's secret life in the basement.

3   On Saturday nights, when my parents and sister were out, I could hear Eugene and "see" him on the wire. Perry Como would be singing on the TV set, and then, suddenly, the loud white noise of electronic snow. Through the snow came a pattern like the oscilloscope on *Outer Limits,* which I came to think of as the true physical presence of Eugene, the real Eugene, the one he was meant to be beyond his given body. He always seemed to be broadcasting the same message: "CQ, CQ. Come in, CQ. This is K3URS calling CQ. Come in, CQ." K3URS were his call letters, his license number, his handle. CQ meant anyone. *Come in, CQ:* Anyone out there, anyone at all, if you're there, please respond. To this day, nothing reminds me of engineering loneliness so much as that voice calling CQ through the snow.

4   Sometimes Eugene actually made contact. Breaking through the television signal came both sides of their "conversation." What they did, it seemed, was compare radios. All those massive structures rising over neighborhoods, all that searching the night sky for another soul on the air, and then they talked about—equipment. One talked—my amp, my mike, over; then the other—my filter, my voltage regulator, over. This "talk" seemed to make them happy. I could hear them laughing: a particularly wide pattern of amplitude, a roiling wave across the screen. If CQ was the representation of loneliness, then this pattern was the look of engineering fulfillment. It reassured the boys in the basement: All that hardware has a purpose, it said. It can indeed bring you company.

5   Thirty-five years later, I have insomnia, but down the hall my three computers are sleeping. Not sure what I'm looking for, I go wake them up. The Mac PowerBook is really sleeping: Some hours ago, I put it in "sleep mode," and now its small green light is blinking as steadily as a baby's breathing. The portable Sun workstation, Voyager, shows a blank screen. But the touch of a key puts it right back where I left off five hours ago. One small window opens to show a clock. I know the clock is digital, but for some reason, I'm glad it's been given a face, a big hand and a little hand and a secondhand sweep, all of which now say it's 2:05 a.m. PST. The last machine, the PC, is primitive. It doesn't really know how to go to sleep. Like a cranky child, it needed diversions and tactics to be put down for the night: a screen saver that knows when to come on, a human who remembers to hit the right off buttons.

6   The room is filled with the sound of fans and disk drives spinning to life. Two big 21-inch monitors give off a flickering light. Still, flicker and all, I admit I'm happy. I *like* sitting in a humming room surrounded by fine machinery. I dial up my three Internet accounts one after the other. The net is full of jabber and postings from around the globe. But now I know what I'm looking for, and it's not there. I'd like to find someone still up and working on a program, someone I know—a colleague on my node or one nearby, who'll get my mail virtually "now."

7   Sometimes I do find someone. Although almost no one answers mail in real time during the day, a kind of license prevails in the middle of the night. "What are you doing on at 2 a.m.?" the colleague writes, finding my mail when the signal he's set on his machine beeps to say there's "incoming." He knows, but here, online at 2 a.m. one does not say *I'm alone, I'm awake, Come in, CQ.* What am I doing on in the middle of the night? I know his workstation has the same small window holding a clock with a face. "Same as you," I reply.

8   The next morning we see each other at a meeting. We don't mention we've met in the middle of the night. Daytime rules prevail: We're about to have a no-rules battle over a design issue. We can't possibly think about the person who was lonely and looking for company. That life, the one where our insomniac selves met, exists in a separate universe from this one, here in this room, where we're sitting next to each other at a conference table and about to do technical battle. Some implosion may occur, some *Star Trek*–like breach of containment fields may happen, if the two universes meet. No, the persona online must not touch the person at the table. As the meeting starts, I'm distracted, I want to ask him, "How are you? Did you get some rest?" He's inches from me, but in what way am I permitted to *know* him? And which set of us is the more real: the sleepless ones online, or these bodies in the daylight, tired, primed for a mind-fight?

9   Somehow, in the thirty-five years between Eugene's ham radio and my middle-of-the-night email, the search for electronic companionship has become a sexy idea. I'm not sure how this happened. One year I found myself exchanging messages with a universe of Eugenes, and the next, journalists were calling me up and asking if I would be an informant for a "phenomenological study of email."

10   I fell in love by email. It was as intense as any other falling in love—no, more so. For this love happened in my substitute body, the one online, a body that stays up later, is more playful, more inclined to games of innuendo—all the stuff of romantic love.

11   I must stress from the outset there was nothing in this online attraction of "sexual harassment" or "environments hostile to women." Neither was it some anonymous, fetishistic Internet encounter. We knew each other. We'd worked on the same project off and on for years. But it was a project that took place almost entirely via Internet. Even the software was distributed through FTP sites; we "knew" our customers by their Internet addresses. I was separated from the development team by some fifty miles of crowded freeway, and I saw actual human beings perhaps once every two months. If I were going to fall in love on this project, there was no choice: It would have to be by email.

12   I'll call the object of my affections "him" or "Karl," but these are only disguises. I'll describe coastlines and places that sound like San Francisco, but such descriptions may or may not be accurate. The only thing you can know for sure is that something like this did indeed happen, and that the "I" in the story is I, myself, contractor on the project.

13   The relationship began after a particularly vicious online battle. The thread went on for weeks, and the mail became progressively more bitter, heedless of feel-

ings, sarcastic. My work was the object of scorn. I say "my work," but the team made no nice distinction between "me" and "my work." One wrote, "Wrong, wrong, wrong, wrong! Completely dumb!" Said another, "What's the objective? Just to produce some piece of shit to satisfy the contract?" If I hadn't been working around people like this for years, I surely would have quit. As it was, I said to myself, "Whoa. Remember they treat each other this way. It's just the far end of the scale on arrogance."

14   After I had been run through the gauntlet, Karl did this amazing thing: He posted to the group alias a story about the time he made a cut-and-paste error and therefore became "the official project whipping boy." He described how it felt to be the object of ridicule, and ended with the report of yet another stupid mistake he had just made. I watched this posting roll up my screen in amazement. In all my experience, no male engineer had ever posted such a letter to his colleagues.

15   To the group alias, I sent the following reply:

> Thank you, Karl, for sharing the whipping energies with me. Your company at the post was much appreciated.

16   Even as I typed a period at the beginning of a clear line and hit the Return key—sending this mail off to the entire project group—I was aware of a faint whiff of exhibitionism. His reply only enhanced the thrill:

> Delighted. Anytime.

17   Then we abandoned the group alias.

18   What followed were months of email that rode back and forth between us with increasing speed. Once a day, twice a day, hourly. It got so I had to set a clock to force myself to work uninterruptedly for an hour then—ring!—my reward was to check my mail. We described our lives, interests, favorite writers, past work projects and, finally, past lovers. Once we got to lovers, the deed was done. It was inevitable that we would have to go out, *see* each other. Yet we delayed. We wanted to stay where we were: in the overwhelming sensation of words, machine, imagination.

19   It's tempting to think of these email exchanges as just another epistolary romance—*The Sorrows of Young Werther* with phone lines. But the "mail" in electronic mail is just a linguistic artifact. Lasers can be described in terms of candle power, but there's no flicker, no slow hot drop of wax in laser light; and there's not much "mail" left in email. I have in my desk drawer a piece of paper on which Karl has written the title and author of a book. Here is his writing: precise and printlike, standing straight upward, as lean and spare as his body. Having this piece of paper, I know what the email lacks: the evidence of his flesh, the work of his *hand.*

20   And, although we seem to be delaying, prolonging the time of imagination, the email is rushing us. I read a message. The prompt then sits there, the cursor blinking. It's all waiting for me to type "r" for "reply." The whole system is designed for it, is pressing me, is sitting there pulsing, insisting, *Reply. Reply right now.* Before I know it, I've done it: I've type "r." Immediately, the screen clears, a heading appears, "From:" my Internet address, "To:" Karl's address, "Re:" Karl's subject. And now I reply. Even though I meant to hold the message a while, even though I

wanted to treat it as if it were indeed a letter—something to hold in my hand, read again, mull over—although my desire is to wait, I find it hard to resist that voice of the software urging, *Reply, reply now.*

21   There's a text editor available. I can fix mistakes, rethink a bit here and there. But there'll be no evidence of my changes, which makes edited email appear rather studied and, well, edited. No, the system wants a quick reply, and, according to some unspoken protocol, no one wants to look as if he or she had actually spent much time composing. So the ironic effect of the text editor is to discourage anyone from using it. It's best if the reply has the look of something fired off, full of spelling errors and typos. Dash it off, come to the beginning of a clean line, type a period, hit the Return key, and it's gone: done, replied to.

22   What's missing now is geography. There's no delightful time of imagination as my letter crosses mountains and oceans. In the world of paper mail, now is when I should be hearing my own words in my lover's mind, envisioning the receipt of the envelope, the feeling at seeing the return address, the opening, the reading. But my email is already there. And my lover has the same pressures to type "r" as I did. Before I know it, it's back. "Re:" the same subject. Even though we're both done with the subject and haven't mentioned it for weeks, the subject heading lingers, back and forth, marker of where this thread of messages began.

23   Still, Karl and I do manage to forge a relationship out of this environment designed for information exchange. He meticulously types out passages from Borges, which we only admire, never analyze. We share a passion about punctuation. He sends me his dreams. I send him pieces of articles I'm working on. An electronic couple, a "we," begins to evolve: "We think that way," he writes once; "You and I feel that way," he says later. Suddenly, we change our signatures. He ends his messages with—K, I respond as—E, like adulterous correspondents who fear discovery.

24   *But* soon we come to the first communications problem of our relationship: interpolation. The email software we are using allows the recipient to copy the contents of the received message into the reply. At the beginning of an empty line, the recipient enters "~m" and the machine answers, "interpolating message number *nnn.*" The result is something like the following:

> There's something in this team's working process that's really broken. [I write in the original message]
> I couldn't agree more. [Karl interpolates his reply]
> I think it's because they evaluate the messenger, not the ideas. I mean, when someone makes a suggestion, the immediate reaction is not to consider the idea but to decide if the person is worthy to be commenting on their work.
> Interesting. I've felt alienated for a long time, but perhaps it takes an outsider to see exactly what's making us such a dysfunctional group.
> I've never seen such a ruthless development team.
> It's the sort of thing that makes me wonder what I'm doing in the profession.

25   At first it seems like an attentive gesture—he is responding to my every line—but soon I feel as though I am living with an echo. Not only do I get a response back

in a hurry, but what I get back are *my own words*. I would rather see what he remembered of my mail. I would like to know the flow of his mind, how it leaps from one paragraph to the next. But instead I get interpolations. I don't feel answered; I feel commented upon. I get irritated, should say something, as one should in any relationship. But I let it go, just break a thread (I don't type "r," dropping his subject on the "Re:" line) to signal my displeasure.

26   Months go by. Slowly, without ever talking about it, we work out the interpolation problem. We get good at it, use it. I write to thank him for recommending a book, and he interpolates his reply:

> Thanks again for the book. I don't want to finish it.
> My pleasure.
> I like having it by my bedside.
> My pleasure.
> —E
> —K

Meanwhile, our daylight life moves in a separate, parallel track. When we "speak" in the group alias, it's without overtones. I even report a bug in Karl's code as I would in anyone's. When I have to write to him directly about some work matter, I always "CC" the lead engineer. The "CC" is the signal: Watch out, pretend you know nothing.

27   Only once does our private world intersect with our work. I have to get a technical particular from Karl; mail would be too slow, I use the phone. I say my name, and our voices drop to a soft low tone. I am talking about a program—"So it becomes 'root' then calls 'setuid' to get read/write/execute permissions on the file"—but I am murmuring. In my mouth, "root" and "call" and "permissions" become honeyed words. He responds slowly. "Yes. That's what it does." Pause. Low talk: "All permissions. Yes."

28   Exquisite as delay has been, we can't put off meeting indefinitely. The email subject heading for the past month has been "Dinner?" and we both know we can't keep writing messages under this topic and never actually have dinner. Perhaps it's simply the way words have power over our software-engineered lives: The dinner date sits there as a mail header, and we have no choice but to fulfill it. There are real and good reasons we should resist the header, why we should stay where we are and just send mail. We work together. We're both just out of long-term relationships (which we've discussed).

29   Still, there is a momentum by now, a critical mass of declared "we-ness" that is hurtling us towards each other. It must be done: We will have dinner.

30   By the time he is to arrive, my body is nearly numb. Part of my body turns off as the time for his actual presence comes nearer. He calls. He's going to be late— bug in a program, traffic. I hear the fear in his voice. It's the same fear as mine: We will have to speak. We will have to know when to talk and when to listen. Panic. We have no practice in this. All we know is we must type "r" and reply, reply right now. Without the press of the system, how will we find the auditory, physical rhythm of speech?

31   We should not have worried. We sit down in the restaurant, and our "conversation" has an all too familiar feel. One talks, stops; then the other replies, stops. An hour later, we are still in this rhythm. With a shock, I realize that we have finally gone out to dinner only to *exchange email.* I can almost see the subject headings flying back and forth. I can even see the interpolations: "About what you said about. . . ." His face is the one of my imaginings, the same serious attention; deep voice, earnest manner with an occasional smile or tease. But, in some odd way, it's as if his face is not there at all, it has so little effect on the flow of "talk." I look at our hands lying near each other's on the table: They might as well be typing.

32   We close the restaurant—they have to vacuum around us. It's nearly midnight on a Tuesday, and he gives off the cues of a man who has no interest in going home. He says "Yes, the beach" before I can even get to the alternatives of the Marina, the new pier at the Embarcadero, a South of Market club. Yes, the beach.

33   A storm is coming in off the Pacific. The air is almost palpable, about to burst with rain. The wind has whipped up the ocean, and breakers are glowing far out from the beach. The world is conspiring around us. All things physical insist we pay attention. The steady rush of the ocean. The damp sand, the tide coming in to make us scuttle up from the advancing edge. The sandpipers busy at the uncovered sand. The smell of salt, of air that has traveled across the water all the way from Japan. The feel of continent's end, a gritty beach at the far edge of a western city.

34   Yet we talk, talk, talk. My turn, over; your turn. He walks, briskly, never adjusting his pace to mine, and he talks, talks, talks. Finally, I can't stand it. I just stop. I put my hands in my pockets, face the ocean, and watch the waves setting up in the dark. I feel my whole body saying, "Touch me. Put your arm around me. Only brush my shoulder. Even just stand next to me, your hands in your pockets, but our jacket sleeves grazing each other."

35   Still we march up and down the beach. He clearly doesn't want to leave. He wants to stay, talk, walk at that relentless, never-adjusting pace. Which should I believe: his staying with me at midnight on a deserted stormy beach or this body-absent talk?

36   Across the road from the beach is an old windmill that doesn't turn, a *folie* of the 1890s. Naturally he is interested, he wants to go there, walk, see everything. I tell him I think it once worked, something about an acquifer under the park and the windmill used to pump up water. We think it over. It's consoling, this engineer talk, this artifact of a thing that once did actually useful labor, handiwork of the Progressive Era, great age of engineering.

37   Surrounding the windmill are tulips, white, and a bench. I want to sit quietly on the bench, let my eyes adjust to the dark until the tulips glow like breakers. I imagine us sitting there, silent, in the lee of a windmill that doesn't turn in the wind.

38   But I look up to the top of the windmill, and I can't help myself.

39   "A dish!" I exclaim. What appears to be a small satellite dish is perched in the spokes of the mill.

40   He looks up. "Signal repeater," he says.

41   "Not a dish?"

42   "No, signal repeater."

43   It is kind of small for a dish. He's probably right. "I wonder what signal it's repeating," I say.

44   We're finally quiet for a moment. We look up and wonder over the signal being repeated from somewhere to somewhere across the ocean.

45   "Navigation aid?" I hazard. "Marine weather?"

46   "Depends," he says. "You know, signal strength, receiving station location."

47   I think: antennas, receiving stations. Spectre of hardware. World of Eugenes.
Bits and protocols on air and wire. Machines humming alone all night in the dark.
"Yeah," I say, remembering the feel of CQ through electric snow, giving up on the
evening, "signal strength."

48   Near dawn, I'm awakened by the sound of drenching rain. The storm has come
in. My cat is cold, scratches at the top sheet for me to let her in. We fall back to
sleep like litter mates.

49   For a few hours the next morning, I let myself feel the disappointment. Then,
before noon, the email resumes.

50   He writes. His subject heading is "Thank you!" He thanks me for the "lovely,
wonderful" evening. He says he read the article I gave him before going to bed. He
wanted to call me in the morning but didn't get to sleep until 2 a.m. He woke up
late, he says, rushed from meeting to meeting. I write back to thank him. I say that,
when we walked on the beach, I could smell and feel the storm heading for us
across the Pacific. How, when the rain's ruckus awakened me in the night, I didn't
mind; how I fell back to sleep thinking to the rain, I was expecting you.

51   Immediately, the body in the machine has returned us to each other. In this interchange there is the memory of the beach, its feel and smell, mentions of beds and
sleep. Bed, a word we would never say in actual presence, a kind of touch by word
we can only do with our machines. We're programmers. We send mail. It's no use
trying to be other than we are. Maybe the facts of our "real" lives—his ex-
girlfriend, my ex-boyfriend, all the years before we met in the group alias—mean
we won't touch on deserted shorelines or across dinner tables. If so, our public
selves will go on talking programs and file permissions in a separate and parallel
track. If so, we're lucky for the email. It gives us a channel to each other, at least, an
odd intimacy, but intimacy nonetheless.

52   He ends with, "We should do it again soon . . ." I reply, "Would love to." *Love
to.* Who knows. The world is full of storms and beaches, yes? Below, I leave the
two interpolated signatures:

    —K
    —E

THINKING CRITICALLY

1. Who is CQ? What parallels does Ullman make between the ham radio operator and the late-
    night e-mail user? In what ways does Ullman connect to Eugene and CQ?

2. Why do you think Ullman's co-worker inches away from her at a meeting after they had spent e-mail time together in the early hours of the morning (paragraph 8)? How does this behavior confuse her?

3. Assess Ullman's use of e-mail threads throughout her essay to relay to the reader a sense of being online. Would our impression of their correspondence change if she merely paraphrased this material?

4. Why does Ullman say that falling in love online via the texual world of the Internet is more intense than falling in love "in person"? What role does language play in Ullman and Karl's relationship?

5. What happens when Karl and Ellen meet for a real-life date? How do they communicate? How does their online courtship influence their real-life interaction?

6. Are there differences between the "daytime" and "nighttime" Internet conversations? Do you communicate differently online at night as compared to your daytime interaction? If so, explain.

WRITING ASSIGNMENT

1. Evaluate your own e-mail relationships. Are you a different person online than you are in "real" life? Does the time of day you are online influence your communication style? Have you, like Ullman, ever experienced the feeling that a person you knew online was very different offline?

2. We often read about people who meet and fall in love via the Internet. Some people even marry based on their online relationships. Write a paper conjecturing how the Internet could change the way we conduct romantic relationships. Is it realistic to expect that this kind of courtship style will grow more popular and common?

3. Ullman opens her essay with the story of CQ, a lonely boy who desparately tries to connect with the outside world via a ham radio. Write a creative story that brings CQ full circle. CQ is now an adult. Develop his character, profession, and social self. Your description can be serious, funny, or dramatic, but try to work with the few facts presented by Ullman about her neighbor.

■ MAKING CONNECTIONS

1. Write a paper in which you examine the effects of certain dialects or speech patterns on the perception of those who use and/or hear it. How are stereotypes created by speech patterns? Explain.

2. Write a response to one of the authors in this section in which you explain why you agree, disagree, or partially agree with their observations on conversation. Support your response with examples from your own experience, outside research using resources from the supplemental Web site, and other arguments presented in this section.

3. Select two issues of the same popular magazine, one from thirty years ago, and one from the last six months. *Time, Newsweek, Playboy, People, Ladies Home Journal, Mademoiselle,*

Vogue, etc. Describe differences you notice in the language of the advertising and articles between the past and present. Include observations about sexist language, references to children and teenagers, social interaction, etc.

4. What effect has "political correctness" had on our everyday conversation? What issues of trust do we now harbor with politically correct language? Explain.

5. What nonverbal cues do you project to others? In a few paragraphs, analyze yourself and the "vibes" you give to those around you through your body language, the way you walk, your facial expressions, dress style, and mental attitude.

The language of humor is highly interpretative and can be very personal. Humor touches our lives daily in many different ways. We may softly chuckle at the Sunday funny pages, smile at the sarcasm of a coworker, laugh at a well-told joke, or double over in tears watching a stand-up comedian's routine. What we find humorous may vary widely as well. Some people prefer the satire of political skits and cartoons, others like social commentary, and still others enjoy the so-called "tasteless" humor of ethnic and sexual jokes. We may even find ourselves resorting to humor in the most difficult of times, taking the expression "you can either laugh or cry" to heart.

Despite the very important role humor plays in our lives, we often take it for granted as a communication medium. The truth is, the language of humor may well be one of the most powerful forms of language that we have. It can be the sugar-coated pill of social commentary. It can be a venue for change, lending comedians a forum in which to discuss social, political, religious, and sexual issues safely. And humor can help us get through unspeakable difficulties by reducing the faceless monsters of our imaginations by talking about them.

What's Funny?

We begin the chapter with the first of three essays that examines how humor is used as a means for social protest and change. In the first article, "Outsiders/Insiders," Boston University professor Joseph Boskin explains how marginalized groups of people—Jews, Irish immigrants, and later, African-Americans, Hispanics, homosexuals, and women—have used humor as a way to voice injustice, mock social conventions, and gain respect. As these groups gained both voice and recognition, their humor changed from introspective examinations to looking outward at how their situations fit into a larger social context. Next is an excerpt from a Latins Anonymous comic play, "The LA LA Awards," which attacks Hollywood stereotypes of Latinos, demonstrating Boskin's points on how "outsider" groups can employ comedy as a weapon against prejudice. In the poem, "In Answer to the Question: Have You Ever Considered Suicide?" African-American writer Kate Rushin demonstrates how to employ humor to dispel cruel realities. And Dave Barry presents an alternative to William Safire's column on language with "Mr. Language Person Takes a Hammer to Grammar."

Case Study: Political and Editorial Cartoons

The second section in this chapter explores the way editorial and political cartoons convey meaning, make us laugh, and comment on American life. Cartoons depend a great deal on a common social consciousness. Using nonverbal cues, symbolism, and carefully selected wording, cartoonists must pull all these elements together to present a punch line in a small area of space. Unlike comedians who can gauge their audience based on intuition and reaction, cartoonists release their work to a faceless public and hope for the best. Like stand-up comedians, the comedic nature of cartoonists is very diverse. Some are content to depict the lighter side of American life, but others use cartoons as a forum to challenge the boundaries of political correctness, social issues, and public decorum. As you read this section, consider the different ways cartoonists communicate their humor and how much they rely on the common expectations and experiences of their audience. How do they use symbolism and tap into popular consciousness? Consider also the differences between the types of cartoons and their subject matter and how this unique form of language influences us. A sampling of cartoons from September 11, 2001, and its aftermath follow the section.

■ WHAT'S SO FUNNY?

Outsiders/Insiders
Joseph Boskin

Trying to determine what makes us laugh seems like a futile task, because different people laugh at different things. What's funny to one person may draw a blank stare from another and a grimace from somebody else. But as Joseph Boskin explains in the introduction of his book, *The Humor Prism* (1997), the "study of humor is essentially an exploration of a particular type of cultural language. . . . [L]ike all languages, humor organizes and correlates experience by seeking and creating order and meaning . . . creating a communal consciousness while at the same time enabling each person a singular connection." One way humor organizes experience is to create a polarity of opposites—in particular, what Boskin categorizes in the following essay as "outsiders and insiders." Out of such a dichotomy we come to express emotions, frustrations, and observations about our society and ourselves that we otherwise would keep silent. In this next essay, Boskin relates this taboo slant of humor to one of the most shaping forces of American humor, social minorities—those traditional outsiders whose marginalized experiences have broken the boundaries and redefined our collective funny bone.

For over 30 years Boskin has taught history and African-American Studies at Boston University, where he is also the director of the Urban Studies and Public Policy Program. Throughout his career, Boskin has devoted much time and research to the study of American humor and its relationship to historical events and social change. He is the author of many books, including *Humor and Social Change in the Twentieth Century* (1979), *Sambo: The Rise and Demise of an American Jester* (1986), and *Rebellious Laughter: People's Humor in American Culture* (1997), from which this next essay was taken.

1 Humor's peculiarity lies in its elastic polarity: it can operate for or against, deny or affirm, oppress or liberate. On the one hand, it reinforces pejorative images; on the other, it facilitates the inversion of such stereotypes. Just as it has been utilized as a weapon of insult and persecution, so, too, has humor been implemented as a device of subversion and protest. In the absence of cosmological affirmation, humor fills a

void. "When no other strategy is to be found to avoid the pitfalls of life," wrote Daniel Royot, "humor is the ultimate substitute for faith."[1] Yet it cannot be a faith in itself.

2   Nowhere in American humor has this duality, this refractory set of opposites, been more sharply delineated than in the experience of minority groups. America's outsiders—Jews, African-Americans, women, Hispanics, gays and lesbians—represent this paradigm. Their marginal presence, highlighted against the backdrop of the American Dream, has, as much as any factor, reshaped the configurations of American humor.

3   "The comic spirit," wrote critic Eric Bentley in *The Life of the Drama,* "tries to cope with the daily, hourly, inescapable difficulty of being. For if everyday life has an undercurrent or cross-current of the tragic, the main current is material for comedy."[2] Struggling on the knife edge of urban environments, their jokes and routines offering an ongoing summons, minorities have recast the language, character, and tempo of national humor. Nineteenth-century Irish immigrants, later joined by incoming Jews, migrant African-Americans, and women and other groups after the 1950s, forged a style and practice of comedy that was subversively wicked and sly, prodding and absurdist, indirect and undercutting. A mélange of masks—the trickster, the con man, the affable rogue, the role-reversing jokester—emerged as minorities coped with discriminatory practices and stereotypes, turning negative features into virtues.[3]

4   Protest and resistance have constantly fueled outsider comedy. Concomitantly sustaining morale while resisting encroachment, minorities have woven their way through society's obstacles with raillery. Indeed, long before the rise of multiculturalist politics, there was already in place a well-honed pluralistic comedy. Offering a social commentary that comically displayed the harshness of industrial life, on occasion employing slapstick and satire that plunged into anarchy, the outsiders frequently accomplished the "corrective laugh."[4] By the latter decades of the century, the corrective laugh had finally forced native American culture to take stock of its oppressive policies.

5   It was a combination of the Irish and Eastern European Jews that first pried open the boundaries of entertainment humor. Because the nascent entertainment industry—burlesque and vaudeville, nickelodeons and films—was held in such low esteem, minority performers and producers gravitated to its ranks. Jewish comics and entrepreneurs quickly rose in eminence and command. Isaac Deutscher astutely observed that Jews, having "dwelt on the borderlines" of various civilizations, took refuge in the nooks and crannies of society. "Each of them was in society, yet not in it, of it yet not of it. It was this that enabled them to rise in thought above their societies, above their nations, above their times and generations, and to strike out mentally into wide new horizons and far into the future."[5]

6   A stockpile of folk humor tangling and combining with urban experiences created a new comedic vitality. "The earthiness of their wit, the tautness of their one-liners—uttered as if in preparation for flight—the extravagance of their routines,

and the brio and agility of their deliveries constituted a new comic style—comic modernism—that simply outpaced the droll and folksy humor associated with the likes of Mark Twain and Will Rogers, and in more recent times, Garrison Keillor of *A Prairie Home Companion*."[6] So dominant were Jewish entertainers in vaudeville, radio, theater, television, and the nightclub circuit before the 1970s, that though they constituted less than 3 percent of the population, Jews made up about 80 percent of all professional comedians. That percentage would drop considerably in the following decades as African-Americans, women, Hispanics, Asian-Americans, and some Native Americans poured into the profession of comedy. Even then, the preponderance of Jewish writers and producers in the centers of entertainment remained high by century's end.

7   Segregated in the "Chitlin Circuit," by contrast, black humor and its performers were little known. There were white jazz musicians, folklorists, and the members of the cultural left who were privy to the tales, jokes, witticisms, and skits of black culture, who on occasion had witnessed a routine, but they were few in number or had no power. Black humor flowed into society in the performances and writings of whites, in the guise of Joel Chandler Harris's *Uncle Remus,* the black-faced songs of Al Jolson, and the radio comedy *Amos 'n' Andy.* While offering idiomatic nuances, these presentations were distanced from the original.

8   Authentic black humor, however, did make its way into the mainstream from the segregated black minstrel shows, musicals, songs, stage routines, and more widely read short stories and novels—though it was rarely acknowledged or recognized as such. Then in 1960, at a Playboy Club in Chicago, the first black comic finally made it onstage before a largely white audience. Dick Gregory's arrival and brilliant, provocative performances signaled one of the most consequential changes in entertainment history, comparable in effect with Jackie Robinson's appearance in a Brooklyn Dodgers uniform at Ebbets Field in 1947. (The thirteen years separating these two events signified the power of ridicule: segregation walls came tumbling down much faster in sports than in humor. By the 1980s black humor, like black music, had become a considerable part of mainstream American culture.)[7]

9   Like other oppressed groups, African-Americans quickly learned the lesson of laughing out of earshot of their detractors. A Southern black man in the late 1960s recalled a special "box" in his childhood town: "In my hometown there was a laughing box. Any time a Negro wanted to laugh, he had to run to the box, stick his head into it, laugh, and proceed home. If you lived too far from the box, you could put the laugh into an envelope and mail it, or put it into a bag and take it to the box."[8] More often than not, "the laughter was dark and removed."[9]

10   When Stokely Carmichael uttered his thunderous phrase during the Meredith March in 1966—"We Want Black Power! We Want Black Power!"—whites were already being publicly mauled and subjected to revengeful jokes and satirical jibes. Trotting his heavyset frame onto stages, a puffing Godfrey Cambridge would exclaim to the largely white audiences, "I hope you noticed how I rushed up here. No more shuffle after the Revolution. We gotta be agile." A chorus of militant humorous acts greeted whites as legal and psychological barriers came down. Dick Gre-

gory playfully threatened to picket the Weather Bureau until it named a hurricane "Beulah," which in fact it eventually did. Dr. Martin Luther King, Jr., ended his "I Have a Dream" speech at the March on Washington in 1963 with an old slave witticism: "We ain't what we ought to be and we ain't what we're going to be, but thank God we ain't what we was." Amiri Baraka and several friends in the 1960s mocked the watermelon stereotype by sitting and eating melons on a busy Washington, D.C., thoroughfare during rush hour. At the height of the Watts Revolt in 1965, blacks placed two white mannequins in an obscene position in the middle of a street.

11   Comics on the nightclub and concert circuits kept up the assault, and though many of their routines reflected idiosyncratic styles, portions derived from a vast body of folk experience. "The remarkable thing about this gift of ours," wrote Jessie Fauset about black laughter in the 1920s, "is that it has its rise, I am convinced, in the very woes which beset us. . . . It is our emotional salvation."[10] The emergence of old-style comedians—"Moms" Mabley, "Pigmeat" Markham, Redd Foxx, Nipsey Russell—together with the rise of a younger generation of performers—Gregory, Cambridge, Bill Cosby, Flip Wilson, Richard Pryor, and Eddie Murphy—reflected the insistent challenge to the social structure.

12   By the later decades of the century, major elements of Jewish and black cultures' comedic styles and content had worked their way into the national lexicon. Stand-up comedy, novels, films, and jokes refracted their diverse genres and approach. In the wake of their gallows humor, for example, came the novel *Catch–22,* the film *Dr. Strangelove,* good news/bad news jokes, and the sick and disaster cycles to some extent.

13   Perched on the edge of personal destruction, gallows humor confronts a seemingly hopeless situation. It is an unmistakable index of group morale, an élan of resistance; its absence reveals either resigned indifferences or a breakdown of the will to resist.

14   Psychiatrist Victor E. Frankl, incarcerated for three years at Auschwitz and other Nazi concentration camps, remarked that a stranger would be surprised to find art in the concentration camp barracks and "even more astonished to hear that one could find a sense of humor there as well—[if] only the faint trace of one," and "then only for a few seconds or minutes." Gallows humor, in short, has its limitations. Nonetheless, Frankl described humor as a "soul weapon" in the struggle for self-preservation: "It is well known that humor, more than anything else in the human makeup, can afford an aloofness and an ability to rise above any situation, even if only for a few seconds."[11]

15   Outsider tales invariably evoked expiration. "Well, what's new today?" asked Simon of a friend during the Nazi period. "At last," replied Nathan, "I do have something new. I have just heard a brand new Nazi joke. What do I get for telling it?" "Don't you know by this time?" Simon quickly fired back. "Six months in a concentration camp." A similar African-American version of what the critic Touré called "making light of personal horror": "Can you tell me where the Negroes hang

out in this town?" a black man asked a policeman shortly after his arrival in a Southern town in the 1930s. "Yes," said the officer. "Do you see that tall tree over there?"[12]

16   A whimsical fatalism coursed through both cultures. A Jewish version:

> Three men lay dying in a hospital ward. Their doctor, making the rounds, went up to the first and asked him his last wish. The patient was a Catholic. "My last wish," he murmured, "is to see a priest and make confession." The doctor assured him he would arrange it, and moved on.
>
> The second patient was a Protestant. When asked his last wish, he replied, "My last wish is to see my family and say goodbye." The doctor promised he would have them brought, and moved on.
>
> The third patient was, of course, a Jew. "And what is your last wish?" the doctor asked.
>
> "My last wish," came the feeble, hoarse reply, "is to see another doctor."[13]

A comparable black rendering:

> Two black men were visited by a fairy who told them she would grant them their fondest wish. The first man turned to his friend and exclaimed, "I'm going to buy me a white suit, white shirt, white shoes, white Cadillac, and drive to Miami Beach and lay in the white sand."
>
> He then asked his friend what wish he desired most. His friend quickly replied, "I'm going to buy me a black suit, black shoes, black Cadillac, and drive to Miami Beach and watch them hang your black ass."[14]

17   In dealing with their oppressors, both groups worked language as a weapon to offset suspicion of improper thought and hostile action. The ironic curse, an intent concealed by a statement meaning the opposite, pervades Jewish folklore; the double entendre and triple entendre function in African-American communities. Jews sarcastically refer to their detractor's welfare: "My enemy, he should live so long" or "He should live and be well!"; alluding to his illness, "It couldn't happen to a nicer person!" To blacks, all whites are the heavy, *The Man.* "The Man has it all" is its summation.

18   Viewed with contemptible amusement was the ineptitude, if not downright stupidity, of their oppressors. A *goyishe mind* is the ultimate Jewish put-down; for blacks, it is *dumb.* Nicknames and insults are crucial ploys. Before the acronym WASP came into extensive usage in the 1970s and 1980s, the word *goy* encompassed the Christian majority. Far more inventive have been black terms: Ofay, Mr. Charlie, Miss Ann, honky, splib, vanilla, dude, pig.

19   Each group in its own way assailed social and economic restrictions. For Jews the assault was directed against representations of authority, as expressed in Groucho Marx's classic refusal to join a club that would have him as a member. Assaulting the system was this black joke:

> "Good morning, ladies and gentlemen," announced the first black pilot of a major commercial airline company. "Welcome aboard Flight #606, bound for New York. We will be taking off in a few minutes, after we receive the go-ahead from the tower. Our flight plan is to fly at an altitude of 38,000 feet. Right now the weather across the country looks good and we anticipate no major turbulence. I will point out interesting sights [along] the way. Should you need anything, our stewardesses will be more than happy to make your trip as comfortable as possible. Now, if you will please fasten your seatbelts and observe the 'no smoking' sign, I'll see if I can get this motherfucker off the ground."[15]

20   Maneuvering against stereotypes, both Jews and African-Americans developed a high degree of self-mockery. It was poet Marianne Moore who observed that one's sense of humor is "a clue to the most serious part of one's nature."[16] And the most serious part of one's nature, argued Spanish philosopher Miguel de Unamuno, involves coping with ridicule. "The greatest height of heroism to which an individual, like a people, can attain is to know how to face ridicule; better still, to know how to make oneself ridiculous and not shrink from the ridicule."[17]

21   Throughout the centuries Jews have deployed subtle forms of self-derision as a means of deflecting criticism and inverting ridicule. Several versions from the 1970s and 1980s:

How do you say 'fuck you' in Yiddish?

Trust me.

How many New Yorkers does it take to screw in a lightbulb?

None of your goddamn business.

How can you prove Jesus Christ was Jewish?

He lived at home until he was thirty.

His mother thought he was a god.

He went into his father's business.

He thought his mother was a virgin.[18]

22   One of the most potent black jokes played off the African past with American urban existence. Sitting on a curb after an exhausting day of seeking work, an unemployed black man winds up in a conversation with God:

"Tell me, Lord, how come I'm so black?"

"YOU'RE BLACK SO YOU COULD WITHSTAND THE HOT RAYS OF THE SUN IN AFRICA."

"Tell me, Lord, how come my hair is so nappy?"

"YOUR HAIR IS NAPPY SO THAT YOU WOULD NOT SWEAT UNDER THE HOT RAYS OF THE SUN IN AFRICA."

"Tell me, Lord, how come my legs are so long?"

"YOUR LEGS ARE LONG SO THAT YOU COULD ESCAPE FROM THE WILD BEASTS IN AFRICA."

"Then tell me, Lord, what the hell am I doing in Chicago?"[19]

23   Just as black humor swept into the national consciousness, so did women's. If Jews and blacks can be said to have been historically entwined, so, too, in a curious way were blacks and women. Without question, no other group in American society has been so stigmatized for so long as natural buffoons. Only a handful of social clusters have been so depicted as being comical without intent. For women there existed an even more insidious perception, one that centered on creating and articulating humor itself. As Germaine Greer asserted in *The Female Eunuch* (1970), "Her expression must betray no hint of humor, curiosity or intelligence."[20]

24   Ann Beatts, one of the very few women who wrote for the comedy trade in the 1970s, dissected the rationale undergirding this notion. "Humor is aggression [and] aggression is 'hard.' Women have always been supposed to be nice to men." Beatts caustically noted that "it is more than a myth; it is a rule to live by: women have no sense of humor—though [men] might prefer to phrase it, 'Chicks just ain't funny.'"[21]

25   The belief that women lacked a sense of humor made them particularly open to ridicule. Images in print and electronic media, cartoons and comic strips, invariably displayed females as silly, verbose, intellectually lacking, and mechanically dependent. Paradoxically, the situation was ludicrous because women were also required to provide an appreciative audience for male joking: How could they possibly know when to laugh if they lacked comic facility?

26   Psychologically sentenced to humorlessness, largely denied access as writers and performers, in effect comedically invisible, women thus played largely to themselves. Dorothy Parker, Mae West, Lucille Ball, and Erma Bombeck were the exceptions to the rule and had a measurable influence on mass media.

27   In *A Very Serious Thing: Women's Humor and American Culture* (1988), a pioneering work on the subject, Nancy A. Walker wrote that in initiating a scholarly study she "ventured into uncharted territory. Studies of American humor abounded, but, as is the case in so much traditional scholarship, the women were left out or relegated to footnotes." Naturally curious about such an egregious exclusion, Walker noted that it came down to the stereotypical canard: "Women aren't supposed to have a sense of humor. Time and again, in sources from the mid-nineteenth century to very recently, I encountered writers (male) commenting—and sometimes lamenting—that women were incapable of humor, and other writers (female) explaining that they knew women weren't *supposed* to have a sense of humor and then proceeding to be very funny indeed."[22]

28   Excluded from the mainstream of political and economic power, women's humor took its cue from the domestic realm, from immersion in the homestead that involved children and community, and from male-female relationships. It was a humor concertedly more inwardly rebellious than retaliatory.[23] Being removed from power did not mean that women shied from exploring humor's impact on them-

selves or others. Rather, women's critique of American society was indirectly couched, "with authors and *personae* adopting a less confrontational and frequently an apparently self-deprecatory stance more in keeping with women's traditional status."[24]

29   By the late 1970s, however, the focus dramatically shifted away from the self-deprecatory. Like blacks, women regaled themselves with hostile and aggressive joking, intent on making men squirm. "Do you know how sex and a snowstorm are alike? *You never know how long it's going to last or how many inches you're going to get.*" Females chuckled as men squirmed.[25]

30   In a special issue in 1979 devoted to women's laughter, the editors of the radical journal *Cultural Correspondence* wrote that "the precise forms of the new women's humor are still in the process of creation."[26] Within a decade, however, women had redefined the script. Deriding patriarchal institutions, ridiculing male sexual behavior, plunging into taboos such as menstruation, lesbianism, and abortion, they vastly extended the humor landscape.[27] Explicit retorts and jokes excoriating males crisscrossed the country, highlighting the differences between the sexes.

> Stanley was on his knees, entreating his love to marry him. "Be my wife," he beseeched her, "and for you I will climb mountains and swim the torturous seas."
>
> Shaking her head, she said, "I don't think you'll do. I want a husband who'll stay home and carry out the garbage."[28]

31   Dependence on men was particularly scorned. A popular graffito made the rounds: "A Woman Without a Man Is Like a Fish Without a Bicycle." And a story jiving male weakness:

> Vernon's wife died. At her burial he wept and wailed. He was beside himself with grief. After the funeral, a friend said to him, "Vernon, I know how attached you were to your wife. I can understand your grief. But you are still young. Wounds heal. You'll meet another woman and in due time you will marry again."
>
> Tears streaming down his face, Vernon blubbered, "Yes, I know. I know. But what am I supposed to do for a wife until then?"[29]

32   Not all humor was confined to rebellion and revelation. Ideology called into question the social basis of humor itself. Positing the difference between "female" and "feminist" humor, Gloria Kaufman in *Pulling Our Own Strings: Feminist Humor and Satire* (1980) struck a responsive chord when she noted that women "are ridiculing a social system that can be, that must be changed. *Female* humor may ridicule a person or a system from an accepting point of view ('that's life'), while the *nonacceptance* of oppression characterizes feminist humor and satire."[30]

33   Feminist humor confronted, as did female humor, but it sought major transformation. It demanded an end to stereotypical formulas in the popular culture along

with the creation of a distinct consciousness and sense of empowerment. A graffito exchange symbolizing the message appeared in a college bathroom in the 1980s:

> Initial Statement: "I don't know what to do. I'm married to Benjy. But I'm in love with Mike. I'll die if I can't have Mike."

> First Response: "Run away with Mike. Love conquers all."

> Second Response: "Have an affair with a third guy and you'll love Benjy again. It worked for me."

> Final Response: "Don't die for love. Live for love. Have an affair with a woman."[31]

34   By the 1990s, confrontation with traditional male values and the hierarchal structure became commonplace: "We are all equal in the eyes of the Goddess."[32] Viewing this challenge as a substantial threat to their status, men counterattacked by accusing feminists of "lacking a sense of humor" and promptly launched a revival of the "dumb blonde" jokes in the 1990s. The tactic failed as women retaliated with "dumb male" jokes, totally silencing the opposition.

35   "An essential purpose of humor is to call the norm into question," wrote Nancy Walker in 1988.[33] By challenging traditional cultural values and seeking empowerment within the institutions of entertainment, the early outsiders provided founts of humor. Although early in the century each group had its own agenda, each nonetheless countermanded entrapping stereotypes and outsider status, and their routines and jokes paved the way for the emergence of others—Hispanics, Native Americans, Asia-Americans, gays and lesbians—who further enlarged the multicultural perspective.

Notes

1. Daniel Royot, "Humor in Transit: Aspects of a Common Language," in Yves Carlet and Michelle Granges, eds., *Confluences Americaines* (Nancy, France: Presses Universitaires, 1990), 183.
2. Eric Bentley, *The Life of the Drama* (New York: Atheneum, 1970), 306.
3. Larry Mintz, "Standup Comedy as Social and Cultural Mediation," in Arthur P. Dudden, ed., *American Humor* (New York: Oxford Univ. Press, 1987), 92–93.
4. Henri Bergson, "Laughter," in Wylie Sypher, ed., *Comedy* (New York: Doubleday, 1956), 187.
5. Issac Deutscher, *The Non-Jewish Jew and Other Essays* (New York: Oxford Univ. Press, 1969), 27.
6. Mark Shechner, "Jewish Comics: Stage & Screen," unpublished MS, 1.
7. Mel Watkins, *On the Real Side* (New York: Simon & Schuster, 1994), 23.
8. Author's notes. Recounted by Solomon Jones, UCLA graduate student, Apr. 1970. "Laughing box" is sometimes a "laughing barrel."
9. John A. Williams and Dennis A. Williams, *If I Stop I'll Die: The Comedy and Tragedy of Richard Pryor* (New York: Thunder's Mouth Press, 1991), 90.
10. Jessie Fauset, "The Gift of Laughter," in Alain Locke, ed., *The New Negro* (New York: Albert and Charles Boni, 1925), 166.

11. Victor E. Frankl, *Man's Search for Meaning: An Introduction to Logotherapy* (New York, Pocket Books, 1963), 68–69.
12. S. Felix Mendelsohn, *Let Laughter Ring* (Philadelphia: Jewish Publication Society of America, 1941), 109; author's notes, Sept. 1966; Touré, "Snoop Dogg's Gentle Hip-Hop Growl," *New York Times,* Nov. 21, 1993, H32.
13. Richard Raskin, *Life Is Like a Glass of Tea; Studies of Classic Jewish Jokes* (Aarhus, Denmark: Aarhus Univ. Press, 1992), 186–89, cites no fewer than ten versions of the joke and provides the texts. See also Harvey Mindess, *Laughter and Liberation* (Los Angeles: Nash Printing, 1971), 238.
14. Author's notes. Los Angeles, Apr. 1968.
15. Author's notes. Los Angeles, Oct. 1971.
16. Morton D. Zabel II, ed., *Literary Opinion in America* (New York: Harper Torchbooks, 1962), 401.
17. Miguel de Unamuno, *The Tragic Sense of Life* (1921; repr. Dover Books, 1954), 315.
18. Author's notes. Boston, 1980s.
19. Author's notes. Los Angeles, Aug. 1972.
20. Germaine Greer, *The Female Eunuch* (New York: McGraw-Hill, 1971), 52.
21. Ann Beatts, "Can a Woman Get a Laugh and a Man Too?" *Mademoiselle,* Nov.–Dec. 1975), 140, 182–86.
22. Nancy A. Walker, *A Very Serious Thing: Women's Humor and American Culture* (Minneapolis: Univ. of Minnesota Press, 1988), ix.
23. Lisa Sulewski, "Feminist Humor: A Call for a Women's Ghetto," unpublished MS, Jan. 1992, 3.
24. Walker, *A Very Serious Thing,* 35.
25. Carol Mitchell, "Hostility and Aggression Toward Males in Female Joke Telling," *Frontiers* 3 (Fall 1978): 19–21. A similar version from Bradford, England, is reported in Nigel Rees, *Graffiti* 4 (London: Unwin Paperbacks, 1982), 121: "Sex is like a snow-storm—you never know how many inches you'll get or how long it will last."
26. "Sex Roles & Humor," *Cultural Correspondence* 9 (Spring 1979): 6.
27. Nancy A. Walker and Zita Dresner, *Redressing the Balance: American Women's Literary Humor from Colonial Times to the Present* (Jackson: Univ. Press of Mississippi, 1988), xxxi–xxxii.
28. Author's notes. Oct. 1983.
29. Ibid.
30. Gloria Kaufman and Mary Kay Blakely, *Pulling Our Own Strings: Feminist Humor and Satire* (Bloomington: Indiana Univ. Press, 1980), 13.
31. Author's notes. From William Zehv, Oct. 1983.
32. Katherine Bishop, "With a Résumé in Hand and a Ring in the Nose," *New York Times,* Feb. 13, 1992, A18.
33. Walker, *A Very Serious Thing,* 71.

THINKING CRITICALLY

1. In Boskin's introduction, he explains that humor "on the one hand . . . reinforces pejorative images, on the other, it facilitates the inversion of such stereotypes." Evaluate this statement. How can humor do both?

2. Boskin states that America's "outsiders"—Jews, African-Americans, women, Hispanics, and homosexuals—best represent the duality of American humor. Why does humor appeal to these groups? How have they used humor to "reshape the configurations of American humor"?

3. Must you be on the fringe of society to tap into the collective consciousness of American humor? Is it a necessary prerequisite of humor to be on the "outside" of the social mainstream? Explain.

4. What, according to Boskin, is "the corrective laugh"? How did it shape American humor in the twentieth century?

5. How can humor be used as a weapon? Who uses this weapon and for what purpose? Can you think of any situations in which you witnessed the use of humor to fight back? Explain.

6. Define *gallows humor.* How has such humor shaped our cultural perspective of what is funny? Can you cite some examples of your own of this type of humor?

7. Evaluate poet Marianne Moore's statement that humor is "a clue to the most serious part of one's nature." Explain this in your own words.

8. What unique obstacles have female comics had to overcome? What accounts for the cultural attitude towards women and humor? Boskin comments that by the late 1970s, female humor had "dramatically shifted away from the self-deprecatory" (paragraph 29). What caused this shift at this time?

WRITING ASSIGNMENTS

1. Analyze the language of one or two comics from the "outsider" categories Boskin discusses in this essay. Try to identify the types of humor Boskin describes—gallows humor, self-depreciation, and so on. Write about your research connecting it to Boskin's observations as well as your own conclusions about humor and American culture.

2. Boskin comments that for many years, women were stigmatized as being unfunny, that they, in fact, collectively lacked a sense of humor. Analyze the differences between male and female stand-up comics. Does one gender seem more accessible to you than the other? Apply the nuances of male and female comedy to Boskin's title of "Outsiders/Insiders."

3. Recall a joke that you have heard in recent weeks that you thought was really funny. Write down the joke, and analyze it. What makes it funny? Does it make fun of a group of people, a culture, or a religion? Does it make light of an unfortunate situation, such as blindness, an accident, or a handicap? Make copies of the joke to bring to class for group discussion. With your group, try to identify the roots of American humor and its connection to our social consciousness.

Excerpt from the LA LA Awards
Latins Anonymous

The Latino comedy group "Latins Anonymous" burst onto the comedy-theater scene in 1987. Their insights into social constructions of Latino life, viewed both from the inside and outside, brought a mixture of "irreverence, energy, and confidence" to the ethnic comedy circuit. With *Saturday Night Live* finesse and style, the troop highlighted the foibles of Latino society and the stereotypes associated with Latin culture. The artists who made up the original troops of Latins Anonymous—Luisa Leschin, Armando Molina, Rich Najera, and Diane Rodriguez—wished to present a comedic analysis of the contemporary Latino condition. The show was a critical and commercial success.

The following excerpt from the group's play, "The LA LA Awards" (1996), tackles the way the media perpetuate negative and stereotypical representations of Latinos. As one critic recognizing the true face behind the humor mask said, "this show knows what ails Latinos and prescribes comedy as its 'medicine.'" A full compilation of skits presented by Latins Anonymous is available from Arte Publico Press.

1 ANNOUNCER: Welcome, *damas y caballeros.* Tonight's LA LA Awards are being broadcast via satellite to 25,000,000 Latinos in Aztechnicolor and Lopezsound . . . "¡Oye como va!" (*We hear the "THX" chord swell into El Chicano's "Oye como va" translation: Get into the vibes. A slide is projected a la "THX": Lopez Sound . . . "Oye como va." Drum roll into opening number.*) And to start our phantasmagoria of ethnic excess, the Chicano-Latino "chicklat" dancers. (*The Chicklat Dancers enter and flail their bodies to the salsa rhythms of the opening theme. Dressed only in spangles and tights, they leap about the stage with little regard for the laws of taste or decorum. Screaming typical Spanish expressions of excitement, such as "andale" and "arriba," the trio throw their bodies beneath the giant LA LA Award statue stage right, finally ending their dance / ritual by kneeling and worshipping it with pagan abandon, as if it were a golden calf. They are awakened from their gyrating trance-like state by the introduction of the first host.*) And now, ladies and gentlemen, introducing one of the most successful Latinos in the history of entertainment . . . star of film, television and eight-track . . . Mr. Cheech Marin County!

Cheech Marin County

2 The Chicklat Dancers *quickly exit, giving* Cheech *the "high five." Wearing a tuxedo and an American-flag headband, a long-haired, mustached, burned-out hippie-type in his late forties,* Cheech Marin County *steps up to the podium with a king-size reefer in hand.*

3 **CHEECH:** (*Sounding a little stoned.*) Wow, man! *Orale,* what's happening? I'm Cheech Marin County. To all my *amigos, buenas noches,* and to all you surfer-types, "bogus nachos."

4 With so many awards shows like the Grammy's, the Tony's, the Chuey's, we thought we'd award ourselves. So welcome to "ta-da . . ." (*Indicate the statue.*) The Los Angeles Lifetime Achievement Awards, or "The LA LA Awards" . . . not to be confused with the Cuban American Community Awards or the "CA CA Awards." First joke the white folks won't get.

5   How many Latinos in the house tonight? Wow! The whole cast of "Mi Familia" is here. Is there anyone here who doesn't speak any Spanish? (*If someone raises his hand, speak directly to him or her. If no one raises a hand, confront someone who looks like they can handle a little audience abuse.*) And you paid full price? Okay, we gotta help you out, that dude/dudette next to you, he/she will be your translator. Just know that when we're all laughing and having fun . . . we're laughing at you. And there'll be a lot to laugh at because tonight we honor all those Latino-Chicano-Hispanics who have achieved the heights of visibility and the pinnacles of success in all fields—particularly in the fields of Fresno and Bakersfield ("*Or your local field.*").

6   It's really exciting backstage, every Latino star is here . . . all five of them. You will be seeing greats, near greats and people who are just grateful to be alive and working in Hollywood, which is Spanish for "Latinos need not apply."

7   And we owe this success and our stellar image to those fabulous film classics: "Tony and the Greaser," "The Greaser's Revenge" and "Die Greasier." And not only in films; we're getting a lot of visibility today. We're everywhere, every off-ramp, every yard . . . (*Poses like the "alien crossing" sign.*) crossing every highway. So put on your Galavision glasses and let *el show* begin.

8   And to celebrate our role as the snag in the fabric of American Society, here are the Chicano-Latino or Chicklat Dancers in our salute to the International Moment of the Latino. Maestro? Tape!

The International Moment of the Latino

9   *SFX: Music. The Chicklat Dancers enter with much attitude, wearing banners reading: LA LA Awards.*

10 **CHEECH:** Miss Puerto Rico!

11 **MISS PUERTO RICO:** (*Heavy Puerto Rican accent.*) I'm from the capital of Puerto Rico: Manhattan.

12 **CHEECH:** Miss Cuba.

13 **MISS CUBA:** (*Heavy Cuban-American accent.*) I'm from the capital of Cuba . . . Miami.

14 **CHEECH:** Mr. Mexico.

15 **MR. MEXICO:** I'm from the capital of Mexico . . . Los Angeles, California. (*They parade off-stage waving and blowing kisses to the adoring audience.*)

16 **CHEECH:** There they are, ladies and gentlemen, Latin America's greatest export: its people! That's the international picture. Moving closer to home, let's welcome our local beauties! (Cheech *leads the audience in giving a big hand to the same trio. Still waving and blowing kisses, they return to the stage wearing the same outfits and fake smiles.*) Aren't they lovely! Miss Taco Shell!

17 **MISS TACO SHELL:** They love our food, but they can't stomach us.

18 **CHEECH:** Make a run for the border! Miss Bilingual U.S.A.!

19 **MISS BILINGUAL U.S.A.:** I live in Los Angeles, drive a Fiesta, work on La Cienega, eat Loco Pollo and drink margaritas. Why are we so afraid of Spanish? We speak it already.

20 **CHEECH:** Can we say, "¿Dónde esta la biblioteca?" Mr. Old El Paso Salsa!

21 **MR. OLD EL PASO SALSA:** (*With a western twang.*) Salsa's now the most eaten condiment in the United States. And remember, if you want safe snacks, use a condiment.

22 **CHEECH:** Preferably, fiesta colored! Miss Hispanic Market!

23 **MISS HISPANIC MARKET:** With a buying power of over five billion dollars, you think they'd try to sell us something!

24 **CHEECH:** And that's a lot of *churros.* Mister Free Trade Agreement.

25 **MR. FREE TRADE AGREEMENT:** It's the good neighbor policy. America gains jobs by sending them south, Mexico makes money by selling themselves cheap. Makes sense to me!

26 **CHEECH:** What did he say? I gotta take Remedial NAFTA 101. Here's Miss Media Statistics!

27 **MISS MEDIA STATISTICS:** The *L.A. Times* states that there are more extraterrestrials and dinosaurs appearing on television than there are Latinos.

28 **CHEECH:** Hey, we've got dinosaurs . . . Haven't you heard of a Barriosaures-Mex? And our final contestant, Mr. Latino Voter! (*No one enters.*) Ms. Latino Voter? (*No one enters.*) Mr. Latino Voter doesn't appear to be with us. Maybe he thinks there's too many of us to fit into a voting booth. I vote we go to a commercial. (*All exit. Crossfade to . . .*)

Chican O's

29 Oscar de la Hoya *shadow boxing in trunks, gloves, and Olympic medal dangling around his neck. Near him is a table with a large box of cereal, with the front turned upstage, a large spoon and a container filled with guacamole (It can be cottage cheese mixed with green food coloring.)*

30 **ANNOUNCER:** Hey, Olympic Gold Medalist Oscar de la Hoya, what's your favorite breakfast cereal?

31 **OSCAR:** (*He shadowboxes over to the table, flashes a toothy grin, picks up the cereal box and turns it around. It says: "Chican O's Cereal."*) Right! CHICAN O'S! (*Quickly pours a lot of cereal into the bowl.*) The breakfast of Mexicans. Little brown toasted CHICAN O'S taste great with milk or guacamole! (*Quickly pours guacamole over the cereal.*) CHICAN O'S! (*He joyously eats a mouthful of the awful stuff. Blackout.*)

Cheech Continued

32 **CHEECH:** (*Returning.*) Personally, I like Cholo Charms. You know, "Pink Chevy's, green cards, yellow spray cans. They're Hispanically delicious!" And now the awards. For our first category, Best Latino Game Show. And the nominees are: "The Ten Trillion Peso Pyramid," that's like four bucks, "The Price is Right On" . . . if it's at Pic'N'Save. And "Wheel of Fresno" (*Or your local city everyone wants to leave.*). I guess the winner gets to leave. But the winner is "The Aztec Dating Game" . . . the game where we find new love in the new world. And now for a live re-enactment clip . . . *(He exits also . . .)*

Aztec Studs

33 *Slides of the bloody conquest of Mexico are projected as* Running Jaw, *a fast-talking game-show host, enters. He wears a bright up-scale three-piece suit and small headdress. He bangs a traditional Aztec drum to punctuate jokes and to get the crowd excited.*

34 **RUNNING JAW:** Moyolo-chocoyotzin tlateo-matini! That's Nahuatl for "Hi, warriors and virgins." I'm your host, Running Jaw, and welcome to Meso-America's number one game show . . . Aztec Studs.

35 It's time to meet our first Aztec Stud. He is a graduate of the Institute of Aztecnology, where he majored in irrigation. He dates primarily during the dry season. He's ruler absolute, direct descendant of our Sun God, Quetzalcoatl, and a great guy. Let's all say Moyolo-chocoyotzin-tlateo-matini and give a great big Aztec Studs welcome to . . . Moctezuma! (Moctezuma, *leader of the Aztecs, enters decked out in giant headdress, holding a blood-stained machete. Running Jaw drops to his knees before him.*)

36 **MOCTEZUMA:** (*To* Running Jaw.) You may live.

37 **RUNNING JAW:** "Mocte," why don't you tell the tribe a little about yourself?

38 **MOCTEZUMA:** My turn-ons are older women, . . . And my turn-offs are vengeful gods. (*Waving a fist at the air.*) Why I ought to . . .

39 **RUNNING JAW:** Are you pumped for the game?

40 **MOCTEZUMA:** Well, I'm having a bad-feather day, but aside from that . . . (*Gives the okay sign.*)

41 **RUNNING JAW:** Our next stud hails from the Old World, *España.* He enjoys traveling, meeting new people and conquering them. Let's all say Moyolo-chocowatza-Boom chucka-boom-chuck-lucka to Hernando Cortez! (Cortez *enters wearing full conquistador armor and bulging codpiece.*)

42 **RUNNING JAW:** Yo, Hernando!

43 **CORTEZ:** (*Lisping heavily.*) ¡Saludoth! Eth un gran plather, esthar aqui con uthtedes esta noche.

44   **RUNNING JAW:** Thuffering Thucotash! Now let's meet our three lovely virgins. Here are Fertile Frog, Passion Lizard and that human Thomas Guide who is about to sell her people down the river, Malinche! (*Only* Malinche, *a budding Aztec babe, enters.*) Where are the other girls?

45   **MALINCHE:** Bummer, they got sacrificed.

46   **RUNNING JAW:** The Gods must be crazy! You all know how we play the game. Our contestants have all gone out with each other. Whoever gets the most questions right about their "get-to-know-you date," marries Malinche, wins cash prizes and gets to rule the Americas! Gents, you all pumped for the game?

47   **ALL:** Yeah!

48   **ORTEZ:** *¡Theguro!*

49   **RUNNING JAW:** Who was Malinche talking about when she said, "He had dried snake's breath."

50   **MOCTEZUMA:** Guilty. That's gotta be me.

51   **RUNNING JAW:** (*Tossing a bloody "heart."*) Correctamundo, you win a human heart.

52   **MOCTEZUMA:** Not expecting a romantic interlude, I forgot my Toltec Tic-Tacs.

53   **MALINCHE:** Romance? There wasn't much chemistry . . . there wasn't even astronomy. I wasn't impressed with how he planned the date. We climbed 539 steps up the Pyramid of the Sun, and the disco was closed, bummer!

54   **MOCTEZUMA:** It wasn't closed, it was "All-Mayan Night."

55   **MALINCHE:** Excuse me, I'm an *Aztec* Princess and I expect to be treated like one. . . .

56   **MOCTEZUMA:** So 500 years of Aztec supremacy are ancient history because Spanish shorty here just bats his baby blues?

57   **MALINCHE:** That's right, something like that. You little dweeb! (Moctezuma *and* Malinche *start to arm wrestle, she quickly overcomes him, sending him to the floor.*)

58   **RUNNING JAW:** We've got tribal disunity, what a great game! But, let's move on to the next question. About whom was Malinche talking when she said, "He put the 'kiss' in 'conquistador.'"

59   **CORTEZ:** Running Jawbone, she's ethpeaking about me.

60   **RUNNING JAW:** (*Tossing* Cortez *a 'human heart.'*) That's right! And the game is tied.

61   **CORTEZ:** Ick! Well, "R.J.," she was some hot Aztec love kitten. (*The rest of the cast pull out bags of popcorn, with ears of corn still sticking out, and loudly munch as* Cortez *launches into a Tony Award-winning soliloquy.*) I came to the New World to conquer the Aztec Empire, but instead, Malinche, that Tempting Translator, conquered me. Oh! The *señorita* gives great headdress . . . Let me tell thee, life at sea is no picnic. Sure my cabin boy looks great in garters and a wig, and does a great

Dolores Del Río impression . . . but nothing compares with the real thing. Alack, I am fortune's fool and Malinche's, too! Ohhhhhhhhh!

62 **RUNNING JAW:** (*All return to their places, as* Running Jaw *leads the audience in applause.*) Wow, that was better than "El Cid." Let's hear it for the spic, folks. Is that a great story or what? So, Malinche, did . . . claim you for Spain?

63 **MALINCHE:** R.J., I never knew I was into white men until I saw him . . . So I just . . . said "Moyolo chocoyotzin tlateo matini," that's Nahuatl for "'Allo love.' Let's play Magellan, you circumnavigate my globes and I'll prove the world's not flat!"

64 **CORTEZ:** Oh! . . . Come with me, darling, I'll give you everything! Syphilis. Smallpox. Uptight Catholic kids and a lifetime of servitude.

65 **MOCTEZUMA:** No, come with me! I'll give you tribal disunity, bloody sacrifices, short, dark, flat-nosed kids and paintings of Elvis on black velvet.

66 **MALINCHE:** (*Directing* Cortez *to kill* Moctezuma.) Kill 'im! (*A fight ensues,* Moctezuma *whips out his machete, does some fancy sword work.* Cortez *takes out his musket and fires at* Moctzuma, *mortally wounding him.*)

67 **MOCTEZUMA:** (*SFX: thunder and lightning throughout.*) You'll pay for this. (*To audience.*) You're *all* gonna pay for this. *Hamana, hamana!* (*Does a Gleason death.*) I'm gonna curse you from here to 1999. Your names will be mispronounced for five-hundred years. You'll work really hard, but everyone will think you're lazy. You're gonna live in the City of Angels, but it's gonna be hell, and you and all your half-breed Mestizo brats will be cursed with anonymity until the year 2000. That's two (*He clutches his heart and sways back and forth in pain.*) oh-oh-oh. (*He falls silent to the floor . . . then sits up.*) And you, Hernando Cortez, I have *one* word for you: *Generalísimo* Franco. (*He dies.*)

68 **RUNNING JAW:** Wow, the curse of Moctezuma. Heavy stuff. But that means you two win! And all you out there can watch our new *telenovela,* "Moctezuma's Revenge." We think it's gonna run about 500 years. Let's say good-bye. (*They blow the audience a "Dating Game" type kiss.*) Moyolochocoyotzin Tlateo Matini. We'll see you all in the New World! (*They exit as lights cross fade to . . .)*

69 **ANNOUNCER:** And now, ladies and gentlemen, the king of *carnales,* the prince of pachucos! Saint Edward James Almost!

THINKING CRITICALLY

1. What type of comedy is used in the skits by Latins Anonymous? What comedic devices can you identify? Provide some examples from the excerpted skits to support your response.

2. What is the tone of the skits presented in Latins Anonymous? Explain.

3. The skits presented here are liberally sprinkled with Spanish and Spanglish words. Evaluate this mixing of languages. How does it work with the comedic intentions of the troupe? Does it present any problems to the non–Spanish-speaking audience?

4. Latins Anonymous accentuates and enlarges Latino stereotypes in an effort to diffuse their power. Identify the stereotypes satirized in these skits, and discuss why these stereotypes exist. Is humor an effective way to address the problem of stereotyping cultures and peoples?

5. How does Latins Anonymous tap into our collective consciousness of symbols and signs to convey meaning? How much of the humor in this piece is dependent on spoken language, and how much on visual cues? Explain.

WRITING ASSIGMENTS

1. In small groups, write a skit featuring two or three characters satirizing a stereotyped ethnic or regional element of American life. For example, you could follow the cue of Latins Anonymous and write a skit featuring your Polish grandparents, people from a particular region of the country, or other stereotyped group (*Saturday Night Live* had a famous skit featuring four guys from Chicago paying homage to their team "Da Bears"). As you write, consider the fine line between humor and ridicule. Share, or even perform, your skits with the class for discussion and analysis.

2. Write an essay analyzing ethnic humor. What role does this type of humor have in our society? Does it contribute to or diffuse stereotypes and ethnic intolerance?

3. How would you react if you were in an ethnically mixed gathering of peers and one of them told a joke about a race or culture that was not his or her own? What if it was about your own ethnicity or culture? Would your feelings change if the joke teller were of the same background? Explain.

In Answer to the Question: Have You Ever Considered Suicide?
Kate Rushin

Many of the authors in this section discuss how people use humor to make light of serious situations—how humor is used as a device of survival. By voicing grim realities, humorists defuse the situation and raise it up for closer scrutiny. The next selection features a poem by African-American poet Kate Rushin dealing with the realities of urban life. As you read the poem, consider carefully the language she uses to frame her response to the "question," her use of repeated words and phrases, and her tone.

Currently a professor and poet-in-residence at Wesleyan University, Kate Rushin received her MFA in Creative Writing from Brown University. Active in the Boston literary and political scene, her work has been widely anthologized for its ability to capture the voices, personalities, and stories of African-American women, society, and history. She is the author of a published work of poetry *The Black Back-ups* (1993). This poem also appeared in *Honey, Hush! An Anthology of African American Women's Humor* (1998).

Suicide??!!
Gurl, is you crazy?
I'm scared I'm not gonna live long enough
As it is

I'm scared to death of high places
Fast cars
Rare diseases
Muggers
Drugs
Electricity
And folks who work roots

Now what would I look like
Jumping off of something
I got everything to do

And I ain't got time for that
Let me tell you
If you ever hear me
Talking about killing my frail self
Come and get me
Sit with me until that spell passes
Cause it will
And if they ever
Find me laying up somewhere
Don't let them tell you it was suicide
Cause it wasn't

I'm scared of high places
Fast-moving trucks
Muggers
Electricity
Drugs
Folks who work roots
And home-canned string beans

Now with all I got
To worry about
What would I look like
Killing myself

THINKING CRITICALLY

1. Evaluate Rushin's tone in this poem. How does her tone contribute to the humor? What signals does she give to her readers to let them know that this poem is meant to be "tongue in cheek"? Explain.

2. Review Rushin's refrain (the second and fourth stanzas). How does this refrain contribute to the poem as a whole? What are its differences and similarities? What "fears" does she repeat? What, in your opinion, is the meaning of this list of fears?

3. In the third stanza of her poem, Rushin tells her readers that if they think she is contemplating doing harm to her "frail self" to sit with her a while until she is better. Why does Rushin refer to herself in these words? Does the description match her lists of fears? Explain.

4. Analyze Rushin's final stanza. What is she really saying here?

5. This poem was featured in an anthology of African-American women's humor. Why do you think the editors chose it for the volume? What does the poem say about being African-American; about being a woman? Explain.

6. What is the meaning of Rushin's title? Why do you think she chose it? How does it work with the humor and meaning of the poem?

WRITING ASSIGNMENTS

1. Write a poem of your own in which you address a serious issue with a hint of humor. You may wish to use sarcasm, irony, gallows humor, or any humoristic literary device in your poem.

2. Have you ever made light of a serious situation? If so, what type of humor did you use, and in what context did you use it? Write about the situation, your use of humor, and your reasons for applying humor to the situation.

Mr. Language Person Takes a Hammer to Grammar
Dave Barry

In the next piece, humorist Dave Barry pokes fun at the silly rules and hang-ups we harbor with language and grammar. Barry's "Mr. Language Person" essays have long been a recurring theme in his weekly column. In the next piece, consider how Barry uses language and shared ideology to appeal to his audience's sense of humor.

Dave Barry has been described as "America's most preposterous newspaper columnist," a man "incapable of not being funny." A Pulitzer Prize-winning humorist with a column appearing in more than 500 newspapers, he is the author of many books including *Dave Barry in Cyberspace* (1996), *Dave Barry Turns 50* (1999), and most recently, *Tricky Business* (2002). The following article first appeared in the *Miami Herald* on September 30, 2001.

Welcome to another episode of "Ask Mister Language Person," the column written by the language expert who recently won the World Wrestling Federation Grammar Smackdown when he kneed William Safire right in the gerunds.

Our first language question comes from an extremely high federal official, who asks:

Q. What are the mandatorical parts of speech that is required to be in a sentence?

A. To be grammatorically correct, a sentence must have three basic elements: (1) A SUBJECT, which is a noun that can be either a person, place or mineral; (2) A VERB, which is a word that describes an action, such as "kung fu"; and (3) AN OBJECT, which is a noun that weighs two or more pounds. Let's see how these elements combine to form this example sentence, written by Marcel Proust:

"Being late at night, Earl failed to check his undershorts for lipstick stains, which is why he was awokened at 6:30 a.m. by Lurleen whanging him upside his head with a object."

Q. Speaking of Marcel Proust, what can the letters in his name be rearranged to spell?

A. "Rump Locaters."

Q. I am a top business executive writing an important memo, and I wish to know if the following wording is correct: "As far as sales, you're figures do not jive with our parameters."

A. You have made the common grammatical error of using the fricative infundibular tense following a third-person corpuscular imprecation. The correct wording is: "As far as sales, you're fired."

Q. I am a foreign person from abroad visiting the United States, and I would like to know how to speak so I can "fit in" with the locals.

A. This depends on where you are. For example, suppose that somebody says "hello" to you:

CORRECT RESPONSE IN THE MIDWEST: "You can make a bet on that! It is not presenting any problems!"

CORRECT RESPONSE IN URBAN AREAS: "Are you talking? To me? Forget all about it, bagful of dirt!"

CORRECT RESPONSE IN THE SOUTH: "I am fixing to experience a hankering for a pig organ such as chitlings, you all!"

Q. I am a member of the United States House of Representatives, and recently, following an incident that was totally not my fault involving an underage Shetland pony, I was charged with "moral turpitude." My question is: Is that bad? If so, would IMMORAL turpitude be good? Also, is there a rock band called "Marcel and the Turpitudes?"

A. There certainly should be.

Q. You know how, when you're waiting on hold for Customer Service, they have a recorded voice tell you that "your call may be monitored?" Who, exactly, may be monitoring it?

A. Keanu Reeves.

Q. In the song "I Shot the Sheriff," how come the singer keeps loudly announcing that he shot the sheriff, but he did NOT shoot the deputy? Is he in some weird municipality where it's a serious criminal offense to shoot a deputy, but if you shoot the actual sheriff, hey, no problem?

A. Your question is very important to us.

Q. Is it time to pad out this column with true examples of strong language usage sent in by alert readers?

A. It most surely is:

- Paul Briggs sent in an Associated Press article concerning a referendum to ban alcohol sales in Fairhope Township, Pa., in which a resident is quoted as making the following allegation about the town's only bar, Hillbilly Haven: "Some nights, I think they have those teriyaki songs."
- Marcia Berner and Charlie Dallas sent in a newsletter from the Musselman Funeral Home in Lemoyne, Pa., that has two front-page articles, one headlined "Cremation Around the World," and the other headlined, "Outdoor Grilling Tips."
- Ann Stanley sent in an article from *The Winston-Salem Journal* that begins: "An attacker shot and killed a Spanish newspaper executive seven times yesterday. . . ."
- Dan Lothringer sent in an article from *The Houston Chronicle* that begins: "Texans used to enjoying a frosty brew inside their car may soon find themselves slapped with a hefty ticket, with a bill banning open containers of alcohol in cars speeding to the governor's desk."
- Sharon Canada sent in an English-language driver's manual for foreigners in the Republic of Korea, which contains this statement: "Drivers must not allow passengers to make noise or disorder such as dancing on vehicles to the degree of interrupting safe driving."

Q. Does that mean that a certain amount of dancing on vehicles is OK?

A. Yes, under the right circumstances, such as when the vehicle is speeding toward the governor's desk and everyone is singing teriyaki songs.

TODAY'S TIP FOR "PROFESSIONAL" WRITERS: When writing poetry, be sure to express angst.

WRONG: Jack fell down, and broke his crown.

RIGHT: Jack fell down, and experienced a bunch of angst.

GOT A QUESTION FOR MISTER LANGUAGE PERSON? Speak directly into the newspaper. Keanu is monitoring you.

THINKING CRITICALLY

1. In his first sentence, why does Barry specifically refer to William Safire? Who is Safire? How does this allusion to him set the tone for the rest of the article?

2. How would Joseph Boskin categorize Barry's humor? Is it "outsider" or "insider" in nature? Explain.

3. How would you characterize Barry's tone? What assumptions does he seem to make about his audience? Is his article funny to all generations? Explain.

4. How does Barry's shared assumptions of his audience contribute to the humor of his article? How much does his humor rely on a common sense of pop culture and social memory? Explain.

5. Describe Barry's style and use of voice in this article. Does it sound like a column? A TV show? A comedy routine? How does his style contribute to the success of his humor?

WRITING ASSIGNMENTS

1. Barry's humor is considered unique and geared to the baby-boomer generation. Read some more of his editorials online at <www.davebarry.com> or at <www.miami.com/mld/miamiherald/living/columnists/dave_barry/> and write a short essay analyzing his humor. Who is his audience and how can you tell? Is his humor accessible to all ages? Why or why not?

2. Write your own column in which you use humor to make fun of a grammatical convention or language rule that seemed to make no sense or had little relevance to "real world" language. Use Barry's article (look at some more Barry articles for a bit more background, at <www.miami.com/mld/miamiherald/living/columnists/dave_barry/> as a starting point, but try to use your own voice and style.

■ MAKING CONNECTIONS

1. Identify some jokes that make fun of serious subject matter, such as war, famine, natural event, or tragic death. Analyze the jokes. In what context were they told? Who told them? Who found the jokes funny, and why? After answering these questions, share your insights with the class in a discussion on how we make humor out of tragedy and/or horror.

2. Do some people have a right to certain joke topics while others do not? For example, is it permissible for Jews to make Holocaust jokes, but not for people of German descent? Or for African-Americans to make lynching jokes (see Boskin) but not for people of other ethnicities? Respond to this question using supporting information from this section as well as from your personal experience.

3. What makes something funny? Drawing from Boskin, the other authors in this section, and your own personal perspective, outline the things we find funny in American society and why. Address the following features in your response: shock, superiority, surprise, anger, trickery, exaggeration, situation, body, accident, irony, sarcasm, insight, and word play.

4. Have you ever known someone who just can't tell a good joke? Their timing is off, they forget punch lines, or they just aren't funny. Analyze the different elements that must come together to create effective comedy.

5. Go to the Comedy Central Web site at <http://www.comedycentral.com>. Select a comedian to profile and write about what makes that particular person so funny. Conversely, you may choose to write about why you feel that a particular comedian is not funny. Try to incorporate some of the points covered by the authors in this section to your analysis.

6. Consider the different comedic requirements for various types of comedy—stand-up, comic strips, slapstick, sitcoms, or jokes. In a group, try to identify the elements necessary to make different types of comedy work. You may wish to refer to the list supplied in question 3 as you address this question.

7. How do you think Boskin would analyze the humor of each of the authors featured in this section? Would he categorize them as outsiders or insiders (or both)? What makes someone an outsider or insider? How is where someone comes from important to their comedy?

8. It is said that there is a fine line between humor and ridicule. Apply this concept to the authors or articles in this section.

■ CASE STUDY: POLITICAL AND EDITORIAL CARTOONS

Editorial cartoons have been a part of American life for more than a century. They are a mainstay feature on the editorial pages in most newspapers—those pages reserved for columnists, contributing editors, and illustrators to present their views in words and pen and ink. As in the nineteenth century, when they first started to appear, such editorial cartoons are political in nature, holding political and social issues up for public scrutiny and sometimes ridicule. For most of the nineteenth century, cartoons were political in nature, holding political and social issues up for public scrutiny and sometimes ridicule. The political art of Thomas Nast, famous for his cartoons in *Harper's*, set the standard for decades to follow—and his artwork is often still featured in history books. He is perhaps best known for his characterizations of the Santa Claus we recognize today and for his battle with political corruption connected to the Boss Tweed/Tammany Hall ring fought with his pen-and-ink drawings.

A stand-alone editorial cartoon—as opposed to a strip of multiple frames—is a powerful and succinct form of communication that combines pen-and-ink drawings with dialogue balloons and captions. They're not just visual jokes, but visual humor that comments on social/political issues while drawing on viewers' experience and knowledge. They often depict a moment in the flow of familiar current events. And the key words here are *moment* and *familiar*. Although a cartoon captures a split instant in time, it also infers what came before and, perhaps, what may happen next—either in the next moment or in some indefinite future.

For a cartoon to be effective, it must make the issue clear at a glance and it must establish where it stands on the argument. To convey less obvious issues and figures in a glance, cartoonists resort to images that are instantly recognizable, that we don't have to work at to grasp. Locales are determined by give-away props: airports will show an airplane out the window; the desert is identified by a cactus and cattle skull; an overstuffed armchair and TV represents the standard living room. Likewise, human emotions are instantly conveyed: pleasure is a huge toothy grin; fury is steam blowing out of a figure's ears; love is two figures making goo-goo eyes with floating hearts. People themselves may have exaggerated features to emphasize a point or emotion.

In his essay "What Is a Cartoon?" Mort Gerberg says that editorial cartoons rely on such visual clichés to instantly convey their messages. That is, they employ stock figures for their representation—images instantly recognizable from cultural stereotypes—the fat-cat tycoon, the mobster thug, the sexy female movie star. And these come to us in familiar outfits and props that give away their identities and profession. The cartoon judge has a black robe and gavel; the prisoner wears striped overalls and a ball and chain; the physician dons a smock and forehead light; the doomsayer is a scrawny longhaired guy carrying a sign saying, "The end is near." These are visual clichés known by the culture at large, and we get them.

In this Case Study, we look at the visual language and symbolism features of editorial and political cartoons—that is, how they convey meaning, entertain, and influence American life. We will also examine how cartoonists present whole concepts in only a single picture—instant communication in a box.

What Is a Cartoon?
Mort Gerberg

We begin this case study with an in-depth discussion of the essential elements of a cartoon. A professional cartoonist himself, Mort Gerberg provides insight into how the various components of a cartoon work together to communicate ideas to the audience.

Mort Gerberg is a longtime contributor to publications such as *The New Yorker* and *Playboy,* as well as the author of many books on the art of cartooning, including *Cartooning: The Art and the Business* (1987), which has served as the leading instructional/reference work on cartooning for over twelve years. The following article is a chapter from his book *The Arbor House Book of Cartooning* (1983).

1 Cartoons? They're the first thing you read when you open a new issue of *The New Yorker.* Or *Playboy.* They pull your eye to print ads and television commercials.

You find them Scotch-taped to refrigerators, pinned up on office bulletin boards and sometimes in a letter from a friend, covered with the scrawl, "Oh, Harry, this is so *you!*" Cartoons are the most powerful, the pithiest form of human communication, used everywhere and in many forms. They are an integral part of the American culture and you want to learn to "do" them.

2   A cartoon is totally familiar to you, but do you really know what it is? Webster defines a cartoon as "a drawing, as in a newspaper or magazine, caricaturing or symbolizing, often satirically, some action, situation or person of topical interest." Accurate enough, but if you're looking for guidelines in creating one, ask a cartoonist.

3   Mischa Richter defines a cartoon as "a visual humorous comment about something that's familiar to all of us." Ed Koren sees a cartoon as "a combination of visual and verbal jokes—Buster Keaton and Henny Youngman—a convention of life turned on end, done quickly and succinctly. If you don't get a cartoon right away, you don't hang around to find out why." Arnie Levin thinks of a cartoon as "basically a story—a moment that's been singled out as different from the next one." For Jules Feiffer, "a cartoon is a form of therapy."

4   Henry Martin calls a cartoon a "marriage of a funny idea with a funny drawing." According to Chuck Saxon, "I don't think it's a joke-telling thing . . . a carton is primarily a comment or a revelation . . . that shows some of the foibles and ridiculousness about normal life." Dana Fradon says it's "something that is first and foremost funny . . . that illustrates a skeptical attitude . . . a laugh at the truth, contrasted to the sham that people live by." And in Jack Ziegler's view, "my definition of a cartoon is a drawing that tickles me."

5   As you see, the definitions say the same thing, but differently, varying with the approach of each cartoonist. I'll define a cartoon as *instant communication of a funny idea.* It is designed so that a reader will get its message in a glance, in the flip of a magazine page. It's about a six-second experience for the average reader, but if it's a great cartoon, the experience may echo through a lifetime.

6   A cartoon is a split second in time—the one precise moment in some continuous action that not only perfectly describes that action, but also tells us what immediately preceded it, and perhaps implies what will happen next. We experience a mini-drama, represented by a single picture. The drawing does not move, but it surely is not a still life.

7   It's simple looking, but difficult doing. To be successful, the cartoon must be the *right* freeze frame from the movie. If Modell had drawn a preceding frame when, perhaps, the lawyer was objecting to the judge, it might not have worked. The humor here, as always, depends greatly on timing and tension.

8   In creating a cartoon, the challenge is not only to envision the correct moment, but to reproduce it so readers can see it, too. It's helpful to recognize that within the single-panel cartoon are found familiar elements commonly associated with art and drama. I offer them here only as aids to defining a cartoon and as guidelines for what can go into its creation. The practical approaches will follow.

9   To begin with, there's the *cast,* the people who perform in the cartoon; the actors. Cartoon characters must be of a very specific type. They are people we imme-

diately recognize from life, people we *know*, like Saxon's surburbanites. Cartoon people must *look* the part. Gangsters, professors, salesmen, tycoons must be unmistakably identifiable. To cast the right actor, the cartoonist functions as a casting director and holds "auditions," sketching perhaps thirty faces before he finds the right one. (Sometimes the first is the one that works best, which is why magazines occasionally publish the rough sketch instead of a finished version.) Ed Frascino "auditioned" at least two dozen ladies before he found the two he liked. Want to guess who got the part?

10   Cartoon actors are more than pretty faces, though; they speak *dialogue,* in the form of captions. Here the cartoonist is a dramatist, putting a well-turned phrase into his character's mouth. A cartoon caption is super-disciplined writing—about twelve words painstakingly chosen for their meaning, imagery and sound, then polished and strung together in a rhythm that puts the beat on the funny part. Carl Rose's classic little girl frowning at her plate: "I say it's spinach, and I say the hell with it!" Lee Lorenz's departing churchgoer to the minister: "Just between us, Doctor, how much of that stuff is cast in cement?" Or Donald Reilly's fourteenth-century nobleman looking critically at his portrait and telling the artist, "Give me more angels and make them gladder to see me."

11   Cartoon actors not only look and speak the part, they move in character. This is the element of *gesture,* the facial expressions and body language, the physical acting which helps convey the sense and mood of the cartoon, even before you "get" the situation. A mere glance at Modell's lawyer and judge convinces you they're annoyed. Look at the postures of Saxon's couple, with arms and legs crossed, chins in hand. You *know* they've been having a quarrel. Their gestures provide a solid frame for the caption.

12   The action of a cartoon is always located in some specific place—the consideration of *setting.* The cartoonist chooses the stage which is most appropriate to his situation, where the idea works funniest and most naturally—a bar, an airport, an office, anyplace in time or space. He not only decides *where* his scene is to be played, he draws only the most characteristic features that make it instantly recognizable to readers. Convincing settings play a major role in Saxon's cartoons. Drawing environments is "my pleasure," he says. And, "certainly, environment tells as much about the people as facial expressions." The same holds true for the chaotic clutter of George Price's rooms, the selected litter on George Booth's lawns or the surreal landscapes of Ziegler and Kliban. Settings may also be minimal.

13   The element of setting includes a consideration of costumes and props. The manner in which characters are dressed and what they carry are visual tipoffs to their profession, their net worth and any number of pertinent things about their personality. In a cartoon, says Saxon, "the reader has to see what you're doing immediately, and you can do that far more than the way people dress . . ." Clothing distinguishes the panhandler from the passerby. A cartoon doctor has a stethoscope hung around his neck. Professors wear glasses and smoke pipes. Tycoons chew big cigars. Gangsters wear dark shirts and white ties. Stereotypes, of course, but they work.

14   Now in order for a cartoon to communicate instantly, its components must be artfully arranged within the frame so the reader sees them in a particular sequence. The cartoon's *composition* presents elements in proper order and holds them together. It is the cartoonist functioning importantly as director. Imagine that you're telling a joke at a party. You begin, "There was an old man who couldn't sleep . . ." And you go on to tell what the son said and how the doctor replied, and so on until finally the last thing you utter is the punch line. And everybody laughs. You hope.

15   Composition in a cartoon is the means by which you tell your story to your audience without personally standing in front of them. Composition is remote control. . . .

16   And underneath all of this, one simple principle is operating: *A cartoon violates some cliché in life*. A cliché is anything which is so familiar to us that we automatically accept it, almost without notice. "Patterns of life . . . natural rhythms," says Arnie Levin.

17   Visual clichés are stop signs, escalators, bicycles, telephones. Clichés are also phrases like "How are you," "Have a nice day," "Glad to meet you," "Thanks for coming." Or situations, like people watching television, sitting in a bar, driving a car, dining in a restaurant. Cartoon clichés are all the clichés of real life, plus those from memory, like well-known fairy tales, history, mythology, literature—and the imagination, which we can thank for the well-worn desert-island situation.

18   The cliché is the vehicle of instant communication. The cartoonist uses it to send his message. And the message is in twisting it, turning the cliché around. Adding a new association. Violating the cliché. Like Sam Gross's amusement park scooter ride, which you recognize, but then a blink later you notice that instead of scooters there are tanks cruising around. Or Bud Handelsman's highway scene, with traffic inching past a group of road workers standing around a "Men Working" sign. Except that the sign reads, "Men Chatting." Here is my own contemporary variation of a caught-in-the-act cliché.

19   The cliché is the cartoonist's trap. He attracts the reader's interest with the familiar and then fools him by changing it just enough to make it a surprise—and funny. In words as well as pictures. Like my own galley slave in chains at the oars, replying to a slave driver holding a clipboard, "My vacation? How about the first two hours in August?"

20   The cliché is also operative in all the elements of the cartoon. The cartoonist casts the actors who most look as though they belong in a particular situation. In captions the cartoonist uses colloquialisms and catchphrases currently fashionable. He directs his actors in gestures and facial expressions that exactly typify the action. And for his settings he uses backgrounds and props that are immediately identified with the scene. The cliché, in effect, is the cartoonist's shorthand.

21   So much for defining what a cartoon is. Obviously, all cartoons can't be described in these terms, just as cartooning can't be learned easily by following any

set of rules; it's too elusive an art form. So don't consider these definitions as chiseled in stone; they're merely points of departure and reference for further study and practice.

THINKING CRITICALLY

1. Gerberg defines a cartoon as "the instant communication of an idea." How does a cartoon communicate and convey meaning? What different features constitute the "language" of the cartoon?

2. Consider the various responses to the question "What is a cartoon?" offered by Richter, Koren, Levin, Feiffer, Martin, Saxon, and the many other humorists quoted in this article. What do these definitions have in common, and how are they different? After considering their responses, formulate your own answer to the question.

3. If cartoon humor can be reduced to a single principle, Gerberg feels it is that "a cartoon violates some cliché in life." What does he mean by this statement? Evaluate the role of cliché in cartoon humor. Why is it so important? Explain.

4. After reading Gerberg's article, collect three or four cartoons from magazines, newspapers, or Internet sources such as from *The New Yorker*'s Cartoon Bank at <http://cartoonbank.com>. For this exercise, avoid strip cartoons with more than one panel. How do the elements of effective cartoons described by Gerberg apply to your cartoon selection? Try to identify as many elements as you can for each cartoon.

Editorial Cartoonists—An Endangered Species?
Doug Marlette

As mentioned in the introduction to this Case Study, the first cartoons were political or social in nature. Before the advent of photography, such "editorial cartoons" were the only illustrations for most newspapers and journals. Today, these single-frame drawings grace the editorial pages of most major newspapers, as well as literary and social journals such as *The New Yorker,* and the *Atlantic.* The turn of the twentieth century also witnessed the rise of comic strips in newspapers. But soon political cartooning became recognized as an art form distinct from these newer strips, constituting a separate genre. Gradually, some artists began to merge the editorial cartoon with the comic strip, developing institutions such as "Doonesbury," "Kudzu," and "Bloom County." However, we still recognize the difference between the political cartoon on the editorial pages from the strip cartoon on the funny pages. In the next article, editorial cartoonist Doug Marlette, creator of "Kudzu" and of many single-frame cartoons, discusses the dying art of the editorial cartoonist. Increasingly viewed as expensive and "emotionally messy," these cartoons face an uncertain future in a politically correct, self-conscious America, he laments.

Doug Marlette is a Pulitzer Prize-winning artist who has worked for *The Charlotte Observer,* the *Atlanta Constitution,* and *New York Newsday.* He is the author of numerous books including *Shred This Book: The Scandalous Cartoons of Doug Marlette* (1988), *Gone With the Kudzu* (1995), and *I Feel Your Pain* (1996). NBC's *Sunday Today Show* regularly animates his editorial cartoons to highlight current events. This article was first published in the spring 1997 issue of *Media Studies Journal.*

1   The problem with editorial cartoons," said Max Frankel, then editor of the *New York Times,* who was sitting across from me at the Pulitzer Prize luncheon at Columbia University, "is you can't edit them."

2   "Why would you want to?" asked my wife.

3   Good question. How do you edit a slam dunk? A great political cartoon is a monster jam, a scud missile, a drive-by shooting. It's also a poem, a prayer, a religious experience. It can strike at the heart like a lightning bolt from above and change the way you see and think and feel.

4   Who can ever forget Bill Mauldin's cartoon of the Lincoln Memorial with head bowed in hands over news of the Kennedy assassination, David Levine's Lyndon Johnson showing his appendectomy scar in the shape of a map of Vietnam, or Herblock's image of Nixon crawling out of a sewer?

5   My own personal test for greatness in cartoonists is simple. Can you remember their cartoons? It's amazing how quickly and efficiently that little test separates the sheep from the goats. We remember the cartoonists of previous decades who singed our synapses, but who's been nailing it in the '90s? Who'll be the Herblocks, Mauldins, Wrights, Conrads, MacNellys and Peters of the 21st century? Lately editorial cartoons seem to have lost their fizz. They're less substantive, less passionate, less like a surgical strike and more like a topical anesthetic that deadens us to the pain of thinking and puts us to sleep.

6   What happened?

7   To begin with, bad times for the Republic are great times for satire. Professionally, I feel lucky to have come of age at the time and place I did. Personally, the '60s were a painful time for me—my father in Vietnam, my mother falling apart emotionally at home—and a tortured time for our nation. But they were a splendid time to learn my trade. Political cartoons are custom-made for such times of tumult when everyone was wearing their hearts and brains on their sleeves, and a good cartoon was as bracing as a whiff of tear gas. At the time I thought I was smack-dab in the middle of nowhere, on the margins of the universe, stuck in Snuffdip, North Carolina, and Bass Ackwards, Mississippi. But there on the red clay piney woods battlefields of the civil rights movement, with a number 10 in the Vietnam draft lottery, my sensibilities were being forged in the fires of the moral and political questions facing America. And with a grandmother bayoneted by a national guardsman in a mill strike during the '30s, I couldn't have asked for a better pedigree to become a professional troublemaker. It was nearly impossible at the time not to have

a political viewpoint. Politics, then, was not an abstraction. Politics tore us apart, divided families and split our guts over the supper table at night. Political cartoons felt to me like the most natural, visceral response to the madness of those times available to me, as natural as going to jail or burning a draft card or sitting in at a lunch counter.

8   I'll never forget being handed a leaflet at an anti-war demonstration emblazoned with a Don Wright cartoon showing a ghostly battalion of Vietnam casualties pointing accusatory fingers at a guilty Nixon with the caption "The Silent Majority." Here was an artist's cry of protest, his dazzling insight passed along hand to hand, like the mimeographed underground scribbles of the French Resistance or the Soviet samizdat. I was hooked. That's what I wanted to do. . . .

9   By the time my generation—Jeff MacNelly, Mike Peters, Garry Trudeau, Paul Szep, Tony Auth—broke onto the scene, the rules had changed, ushering in a renaissance in graphic satire. We were the first generation raised on television. *Mad Magazine* made us question authority and the world of grown-ups. And that was something we could imagine doing for a living. We also were blessed with politicians who looked like their policies—LBJ, Richard Nixon, Spiro Agnew, Henry Kissinger—all living gargoyles who personified what was wrong in civil rights, Vietnam and Watergate. Such leadership ratified our killer instinct. Journalism itself had become a cauldron of insurrection. I.F. Stone, Woodward and Bernstein, and Bob Greene at *Newsday* were retooling the investigative tradition. At magazines like Harold Hayes' *Esquire* and Willie Morris's *Harper's* and Gonzo Guerilla Hunter S. Thompson's *Rolling Stone,* the New Journalism made tidal waves; their backwash showed up in cartoons.

10   Meanwhile, Garry Trudeau was making the comic pages safe for democracy with Doonesbury. Trudeau, inspired by Feiffer's existential soliloquies, used a comic strip format for his editorial commentary. He put words into the mouths of White House officials while his characters became baby-boomer archetypes and proxies for the Woodstock generation. The comics had always played host to right-wing Cold War sentiments from Steve Canyon and Little Orphan Annie; liberal opinion had been a staple of Walt Kelly's Pogo and Al Capp's Li'l Abner for years, but there was something about Trudeau's pungent liberal bias that cut against the generational grain and got him banished from the comics and onto some newspaper editorial pages, and won for him the first Pulitzer Prize awarded a comic strip. . . .

11   Editorial cartoonists are an endangered species. Increasingly, we're seen as a costly indulgence. The *Greensboro* (N.C.) *Daily News* (now the *News and Record*), a paper with an unusually rich cartooning tradition—Bill Sanders, Hugh Haynie and Bob Zschiesche—got started there—no longer has its own cartoonist. The *St. Petersburg* (Fla.) *Times* fired one of its two cartoonists two years ago and has not rehired. The *Los Angeles Times* has not replaced Paul Conrad since he went into semiretirement three years ago.

12   Granted, uncertain economic times at newspapers do not embolden editors and publishers. And in a newspaper culture increasingly obsessed with the bottom line, where a computer-generated pie chart passes for an exciting graphic, it's no acci-

dent that I have had more cartoons killed over the last couple of years than in the previous 25. Today, editors think like publishers, cartoonists think like editors, and they all think like marketing directors. They find the messy emotions that good cartoons raise threatening, untidy, unseemly—and worse, unquantifiable. They want mush. And cartoonists whose ambition outweighs their talent or conscience are delighted to give it to them.

13   Has mandatory sensitivity helped geld us? Irreverence is not appreciated in an atmosphere of public piety. Interestingly, over the years I have had far more cartoons killed by liberal secular humanists than by bible-thumpers. When it comes to free speech I have found liberals more cowardly and more easily intimidated by pressure groups—perhaps because they are more guilt-driven, and easily guilt-tripped by sanctimonious special interests. If it's no longer open season for satire, if some groups are deemed exempt as fair game, if we're not all lampoonable regardless of race, creed, color, gender, whatever, then there is no free speech.

14   Could it be that no one needs satirists in a tabloid age when real life becomes a parody and sleaze dominates the headlines—with O.J., Michael Jackson's baby, Roseanne and the Bobbitts? Twenty-five years ago issues at the core of who we were as a nation and a people were at center stage—civil rights, Vietnam, Watergate. Now sideshows dominate, and the result is wide-scale cynicism and trivialization. Even our response to the most demented of people—John Wayne Gacy, Jeffrey Dahmer—is fascination rather than revulsion. We are too hip to be appalled, too knowing to be ashamed. That which is missing in our national ethos is missing in our editorial cartoons—passion and a sense of outrage.

15   Some of the most incisive editorial cartooning around today, to my eye, can be found on the pages of *The New Yorker*. Whatever the reason—perhaps due to Tina Brown ordering her cartoonists to think topical, or the ascent of Art (Maus) Spiegelman as art editor—the shift is noticeable and bracing. In *The New Yorker* I find what's missing in so many of today's editorial cartoons: something instinctive, unpredictable and up from the depths.

16   Young cartoonists seem to be struggling to find themselves, but instead of breaking new ground, creative energies are spent in rival bashing and crass self-promotion, achieving new levels of smarminess. Some cartoonists go so far as to contact newsmagazines to learn what their lead stories will be that week, the better to tailor their cartoons accordingly and increase chances for reprints. So much for fire in the belly.

17   If we're not an endangered species, we're certainly working hard at thinning the herd. We snipe at each other at cartoonists' conventions, whine incessantly about the successes of others and air the perennial complaint that syndication is a sellout, that the only good cartoon is a local cartoon. We spin elaborate but paper-thin self-justifications and rationalizations of our own personal failures. We make grand displays of removing ourselves from national competition, protecting our wounded pride from further humiliation, then loudly defend our neurosis on panels and in articles, like talk-show trailer trash, making a virtue of our emotional immaturity.

18   Cartoonists seem especially susceptible to the kamikaze allures of self-defeat. We're constantly looking for ways to take time off, cash in our chips, remove ourselves from the game. Self-abnegation is all the rage. With comic strippers Bill Watterson, Berke Breathed and Gary Larson deleting themselves to great fanfare, quitting is seen as a reasonable choice, even a source of pride. As we stand on the bridge to the 21st century, it's clear that as our culture devalues and co-opts the individual, the artist is neutered and the independent spirit is vanquished. So the great cartoonists may be a dying breed, either by forces beyond their control or by their own hands.

19   Yet the way we treat our artists, our exposed nerve endings, reveals something essential about ourselves and our nation. A great democracy needs great cartoonists because theirs is a special kind of vision.

20   "No eyes in your head . . ." we marvel with King Lear at blind Gloucester, "yet you see how this world goes."

21   "I see it feelingly," replies Gloucester.

THINKING CRITICALLY

1. Consider the way Marlette describes an editorial cartoon as "a monster jam, a scud missile, a drive-by shooting . . . a poem, a prayer, and a religious experience" (paragraph 3). How can a political cartoon be all these things? Answer this question drawing from Marlette's article as well as from your own personal experience.

2. Marlette names some notable editorial cartoonists in paragraph 4. How many of them have you heard of? Can you name an equal number of strip cartoonists? What do you think may account for the lack of fame of political cartoonists among the general public? Explain.

3. According to Marlette, why are editorial cartoonists an "endangered species"? Do you agree?

4. How has our social consciousness of what we can and cannot say or communicate influenced editorial cartooning? Explain.

Defiantly Incorrect: The Humor of John Callahan
Timothy Egan

Mort Gerberg claims that cartoons violate a cliché in life—that something we have come to expect as routine and normal is suddenly betrayed. The next article is about a cartoonist actively seeking outrage by pushing the boundaries of cartoon humor. Highlighting some of the most controversial issues of our times, John Callahan challenges the "politically correct" status quo with cartoons featuring the handicapped, the homeless, and the addicted. And as a recovering alcoholic and quadriplegic himself, Callahan is perhaps one of the few cartoonists who can get away with such humor. But his work raises the question of just how far a cartoon can go before it crosses the line.

Timothy Egan is a correspondent for the *New York Times*, where this article first appeared in June 1992.

1   The parade of personality disorders, all the men who hate women and the women who love them, marches on in the talk shows of America. Each day brings new revelations, darker and more embarrassing than the previous ones, the kind of details that were once confined to an analyst's couch but now fuel the self-confession racket practiced by Oprah, Geraldo, Donahue and a half-dozen others. John Callahan sits in this small basement apartment in Portland, Ore., his television tuned to the so-called reality shows, and he is inspired.

2   He draws a small, streetside restaurant, the door shut, no one inside. And in the window, he puts a sign: "The Anorexic Cafe, Now Closed 24 Hours a Day."

3   Another day, another image comes to mind. Callahan sketches a blind man and his Seeing Eye dog, walking on an airport Tarmac toward a plane, escorted by a flight attendant. "We've arranged a window seat for your dog so you can enjoy the view," the stewardess says to the blind man.

4   Callahan imagines a twist on a classic story, and draws four small islands, each with a person sitting on it frowning. He labels the cartoon "The Dysfunctional Family Robinson."

5   Finally, he turns on the medium itself. A condemned man sits tied to an electric chair, awaiting the end. Next to him, behind a desk, is a talk-show host. "So," the host asks, "where do you go from here?"

6   Anorexia, blindness, dysfunctional families and the death penalty—in a good week, all of those topics can find their way into the cartoons of John Callahan. Reality, as presented in the tell-all talk shows, provides a steady flow of ideas. He drew a cartoon in March, showing Geraldo Rivera on his knees saying his bedtime prayers. "Thank you, God, for all the tragedy, wretchedness and perversion in the world," Geraldo says.

7   But for his ongoing source of inspiration, Callahan does not need television; for that, he has himself. Abandoned at birth by his mother, he was educated by Roman Catholic nuns of the old-style school of guilt and harsh discipline, became an alcoholic by the age of 12 and then was paralyzed in an auto accident shortly after his 21st birthday. On any given day, Callahan may call on his family isolation, his religion, his alcoholism or the view from his wheelchair to bring life to a blank sheet of paper.

8   At age 41, he finds himself at the center of a debate raging in editorial offices across the country over how far to push the edge of humor in the venerable American craft of cartooning. His 1989 autobiography, *Don't Worry, He Won't Get Far on Foot,* published by William Morrow, was a critical and commercial hit, intro-

ducing a voice that had rarely been heard among the volumes of stories about people overcoming physical disasters. It was inspirational, the critics said, but not in the traditional sense of such works. When the actor William Hurt purchased the rights to make a movie about Callahan's life, based on the book, the cartoonist had one reservation, "Just don't call it 'Children of a Lesser Quad,'" he said.

9　The books of cartoons, "Do Not Disturb Any Further" and "Digesting the Child Within," and weekly syndication in more than 40 newspapers have helped to establish Callahan among the new breed of quirky sketch-and-gag artists like Gary Larson, creator of the phenomenally popular "Far Side," and Berke Breathed, who won a Pulitzer Prize in 1987 for "Bloom County," a strip he has since discontinued in favor of a new cartoon. "Doonesbury" may trouble editors for its political satire, but Callahan is often accused of doing something that many readers consider more sinister: making fun of invalids and animals.

10　Callahan has yet to achieve the sort of mass-market fame of his friend Larson, who lives in Seattle, or that of another cartoonist and former Portland resident, Matt Groening, the creator of "The Simpsons" on Fox Broadcasting and "Life in Hell," a syndicated strip.

11　In all likelihood, his drawings will never end up on every other coffee cup because they are so polarizing. He is either brilliant and savagely honest, as many fans, in and out of wheelchairs, have told him in letters and phone calls. Or he is sick, making fun of the most vulnerable people in society, as some organizations that represent the disabled have told him.

12　This year [1992] is a landmark for the 43 million Americans whom the Government classifies as physically or mentally impaired. The Americans with Disabilities Act, some of which went into effect in January, forbids bias in hiring and requires businesses and public offices to accommodate the disabled. It has been called the most sweeping, anti-discrimination law since the Civil Rights Act of 1964. For all the liberating intent of the new law, Callahan would add another dimension, one that defies legislation: the freedom of the disabled to laugh at themselves.

13　Not that being crippled, blind or diseased is inherently funny. Obviously it is not. But, says Callahan, that does not mean pity should monopolize all feelings for or about the disabled.

14　"I'm sick and tired of people who presume to speak for the disabled," says Callahan, wheeling down the street in Portland, where he is a celebrity. "The question of what is off-limits should not be defined by some special interest group. The audience, the readers, should decide."

15　Just as Lenny Bruce broke the rules of stand-up comedy in the early 1960s, Callahan sees himself as a rebel force against politically correct views and people who are trying to narrow the boundaries of appropriate humor. The last thing he wants is to be called by one of the new euphemisms for people with disabilities, terms like "vertically challenged," for dwarfs or "otherly abled" for someone in a wheelchair.

16　"Call me a gimp, call me a cripple, call me paralyzed for life, but just don't call me something that I'm not," he says. "I'm not differently abled. I can't walk.

But I also hate it when people say 'wheelchair-bound.' People who can walk are not car-bound."

17   Callahan's words, which can seem bitter and harsh at times, are softened by the way he talks. He drops one-liners, throwaway jokes and self-deprecatory remarks about himself in between barbs aimed at his critics. On an otherwise gloomy, recent visit to the doctor, he says, "Why couldn't I have walking pneumonia?"

18   He has a mop of fading red hair, a ruddy complexion scarred by adolescent acne and a large body, 6 foot 3, that seems uncomfortably tied onto his wheelchair. He struggles with his weight. A cartoon of his reflects the strain of trying to exercise. The drawing shows an aerobics class for quadriplegics. The instructor says, "O.K., let's get those eyeballs moving."

19   The tools of his artistry are simple, pen and sketch pad, but the mechanics are not. Unable to move all his fingers, he draws by clutching a pen in his right hand and then guiding it slowly across the page with his left. He produces 3 to 10 cartoons a week.

20   A few years ago, just as Callahan's cartoons were starting to catch on nationally, he found himself in trouble over one particular drawing. It showed a dark-skinned beggar in the street, wearing a sign that read: "Please help me. I am blind and black, but not musical."

21   Letters poured in to some of the papers that carry Callahan, most of which are on the West Coast. How dare he make fun of blind people, or blacks, or both, the letter writers insisted. Callahan was a bit taken aback by the critics, some of whom accused him of racism. In the midst of the controversy, Callahan says a black man approached him in a restaurant.

22   "Did you draw that black and blind strip?" the man asked, according to Callahan's recollection. The cartoonist nodded. Then, he said, the man shook his hand and thanked him.

23   A similar situation arose over a cartoon about a double amputee. The drawing showed a bartender refusing to pour another drink for a man who had two prosthetic hooks in place of hands. "Sorry Sam," says the bartender, "you can't hold your liquor." Callahan says he was at a concert shortly after the panel appeared, when a man who had lost his hands in Vietnam approached him and thanked him profusely.

24   "My only compass for whether I've gone too far is the reaction I get from people in wheelchairs, or with hooks for hands," says Callahan. "Like me, they are fed up with people who presume to speak for the disabled. All the pity and patronizing. That's what is truly detestable."

25   When pressed by critics, Callahan will rarely defend himself with drawn-out explanations or appeals to reason. Instead, he falls back on a simple answer: "It's funny."

26   Of late, other people have been doing the defending for him. The American Civil Liberties Union of Oregon last year gave Callahan its Free Expression Award. He was cited for a "history of facing challenge to artistic and intellectual freedom." Last fall, he was honored by the Media Across Office in Los Angeles, a disability information center for the entertainment industry.

27   "From my experience, I would say about 90 percent of the people who find John's work questionable are able-bodied," says Royce Hamrick, a paraplegic who is president of the San Diego chapter of the National Spinal Cord Injury Association. "In the disabled community, we make a lot of jokes that stay within that community. What John is doing is bringing those out to everyone else."

28   But for every compliment and accolade, there is a fresh controversy. Last year, Callahan drew a cartoon called "The Alzheimer Hoedown," which showed confused couples at a square dance. They were scratching their heads, unable to follow the instructions to "return to the girl that you just left." In an angry letter to Callahan, Kathleen Higley, executive director of the St. Louis chapter of the Alzheimer's Association, said the drawing had deeply upset some of her members.

29   "Four million Americans suffer from this mind-robbing disease," Higley wrote in the letter. The victims, she said, "should be treated with dignity and compassion, not ridicule."

30   A paper in California, *The Coast Weekly* of Carmel, canceled Callahan after a storm of protest over one cartoon. It showed a dog, lying on its back, with a windowpane imbedded inside its chest. A passer-by asks, "How much is that window in the doggie?" The cartoon has proved to be one of Callahan's most popular, and he has since adapted it into an animated short film.

31   "A lot of people thought the cartoon was just a bit too distasteful," says Bradley Zeve, editor and publisher of *The Coast Weekly*. "Of course, the editors thought it was hilarious."

32   Callahan says there is a double standard for humor in this country. Virtually within hours of the space shuttle accident five years ago, he says people were making jokes. But when Callahan takes the same impulse that drives street humor about popular events and puts it into print he's vilified.

33   "There is humor in all parts of life, families suffering from Alzheimer's or cancer, have their own private jokes as a way of coping with the pain," he says. "So why is it a crime to share the joke in print?" But applying that same standard to, say, racial humor, would likely put Callahan on shaky ground with fans who are otherwise more tolerant. The question with all gallows humor is whether it dehumanizes its subject or helps to cover pain and break down false pretense.

34   Callahan's best weapon with his critics, of course, is his own disability. He can say things that others may be thinking, and usually gets away with it, precisely because he is quadriplegic. "People always say, 'How can he make fun of the handicapped?'" Callahan says. "And then an editor will usually write back and say that I'm in a wheelchair. Their attitude changes immediately."

35   While Callahan's defenders have used his disability to defuse critics, he says he does not want special treatment because he is in a wheelchair. His cartoons, he points out, do not carry a note to readers that the artist is crippled.

36   "Being in a wheelchair has nothing to do with why he can do the things he does," says Sam Gross, a veteran cartoonist whose drawings appear regularly in *The New Yorker, The National Lampoon* and other publications. "He is in the vein of sick humor—but sick humor that's funny. He's intelligent and witty—that is why he gets away with it." . . .

37   By the mid–80's, magazines like *Penthouse* were running Callahan, as was *The Williamette Week,* an alternative weekly in Portland that was also one of the first papers to run Matt Groening and Lynda Barry. Many of Callahan's cartoons went right after the liberal readers of the Portland papers. One drawing, titled "The Politically Appropriate Brain," shows a pie chart inside a man's head. Guilt makes up 40 percent, whales 10 percent, rain forests 10 percent, apartheid 10 percent and comfortable sandals 30 percent. It is the favorite cartoon of Bud Clark, Portland's Mayor.

38   "John is very politically incorrect," says Mark Zusman, editor and co-owner of *The Williamette Week.* "But over the years, everybody has gotten used to him. I remember being taken aback by his answering machine. You'd call and his voice would say, 'Hi, this is John. I'm really depressed right now so I can't come to the phone. Please leave a message after the gunshot.'"

39   Callahan developed a style in which he would take a cliché and turn it on its head. An early cartoon, for example, showed two cowboys getting ready to draw their guns. One of the men is without arms. The other says, "Don't be a fool, Billy."

40   Deborah Levin, a California talent manager who had helped to launch both Groening and Barry into syndication, heard about Callahan while on a Portland visit six years ago. She was responsible for his national syndication, but only after long explanations to the editors of different papers. Readers in south Florida, where Callahan is run in *The Miami Herald,* recently voted him more popular than Dave Barry, the Miami humor columnist.

41   Two of Callahan's longer cartoons, a narrative labeled "The Lighter Side of Being Paralyzed for Life" and a later one called "How to Relate to Handicapped People," have been widely reprinted in magazines and circulars used by the disabled. He wrote in the latter panel that people overcompensate when they meet someone in a wheelchair, usually acting overfriendly or patronizing or directing questions to a friend of the handicapped person. Access Living, a United Way organization in Chicago, has issued a poster of Callahan's satires on attitudes toward the disabled, and the city government of Milpitas, California, wants to use some of this work in educational presentations.

42   Callahan's work has also recently caught on in gift shops of recovery centers, according to Levin. She has also sold his cartoons for T-shirts and postcards. When asked if this spurt of marketing could take away Callahan's edge, Levin says: "It hasn't changed him yet. But he's maturing."

43   Even with new income from books and commercial sales, Callahan lives a spartan life in the Portland studio apartment. He draws from bed, with straps and cables hanging overhead, a cat nearby and the television usually on. The costs of a full-time attendant and medical care have drained much of his earnings, he says.

44   Despite his dismissive remarks, Callahan, who has had a series of girlfriends over the last 20 years, would like to get married and have a family. Some day. But even when speaking in rare solemn tones about his dreams for the future, he cannot resist a self-cutting line: "I think it would be fun to hear the whir of little wheels around the house."

THINKING CRITICALLY

1. Callahan comments that when readers discover that he is a quadriplegic, they are more accepting of his cartoon subject matter. Why do you think this is so? Explain.

2. Egan notes that although John Callahan will probably grow in popularity and syndication, he will probably never achieve the level of fame of Gary Larson or other cartoonists with "bizarre" expressions of cartoon humor. Do you agree with this statement? Explain.

3. Callahan, himself disabled, resents the politically correct names non–physically challenged individuals give to the handicapped. In fact, he is exasperated that such people try to protect the handicapped with their outrage at "sick" cartoon humor. Many of the authors in this chapter comment that humor defuses unpleasant situations and makes the uncomfortable more acceptable. Why do people seem to deny the handicapped the outlets permitted to other marginalized groups?

4. In addition to the cartoons included here, Callahan's Web site, <www.callahanonline.com>, features many of his cartoons. Go to this site and try to evaluate his humor. Are any of his cartoons offensive to you? Would they be offensive to other people? Explain your answer.

Exploring the Language of **VISUALS**

Callahan Cartoon (Wheelchair Posse)
John Callahan

Few cartoonists would dare to make fun of the handicapped. However, John Callahan's "politically incorrect" cartoons regularly depict subjects considered taboo to other artists, such as the handicapped, alcoholics, anorexics, and criminals. Callahan, himself a quadriplegic, explains that admitting that such things have a "sick humor" to them allows us to confront these issues more openly in our society. Says Callahan, "Call me a gimp, call me a cripple, call me paralyzed for life, but just don't call me something that I am not."

THINKING CRITICALLY

1. What is politically incorrect about this cartoon? Is your first impulse to laugh or to protest? Or do you experience a combination of responses? Would your reception of the cartoon and your personal reaction to it change if you knew (or didn't know) that the cartoonist is a quadriplegic? Why or why not?

2. After reading the preceding article on John Callahan, apply what you know about the author to this cartoon. How does knowing about the cartoonist help you understand his perspective and his humor?

3. Why does this cartoon make people uncomfortable? Why would Callahan want to confront this discomfort? Explain.

When Cartoonists Were at Their Wit's End

James Ricci

In the introduction to this case study, we explained that for an editorial cartoon to be effective it must make the issue clear at a glance and it must establish where it stands on the argument. Its success is often dependent on its audience sharing the cartoonist's political perspective on the issue, situation, or people it is trying to depict. On September 11, 2001, America, and indeed the world, all had a common shared experience. But if commentators and writers were at a loss for words, editorial cartoonists faced an even more daunting challenge—how to sensitively, adequately, and succinctly draw what a nation was feeling. In the next piece, James Ricci describes how some editorial cartoonists responded with pen and ink.

James Ricci is a writer for the *Los Angeles Times*, in which this article first appeared on November 25, 2001.

1 The terrorist attacks of September 11 sorely tested one category of American commentators whose stock in trade is the ready gibe, the pitiless lampoon, the summary smirk. Faced with the reality of collapsing skyscrapers and thousands of murdered innocents, the country's editorial cartoonists faced a dilemma: How to express an overwhelming sickness of soul before which their usual cutlery seemed without point.

2 Think back to that day and your own loss for words; to that speechlessness that suddenly was a national language. Now imagine having to sit down and draw a simple, understandable picture that might have relevance to thousands of other dumbstruck and grief-ridden people.

3 The first challenge some of the cartoonists had to overcome was their own disinclination to even function. "My mood on the 11th was one of shock and sadness and fright and grief," says Steve Breen of the *San Diego Union-Tribune*. "I didn't feel like working. All I wanted to do was talk to family and friends and watch CNN."

4 In the end, Breen depicted a weeping Statue of Liberty—shades of the famous Bill Mauldin cartoon (the statue of Lincoln at the Lincoln Memorial with his face buried in his hands) after the assassination of John F. Kennedy.

5 Many other cartoonists also drew tearful Lady Liberties that first day and shortly afterward. The version that probably will prove most memorable was turned out by Pulitzer laureate Mike Luckovich of the *Atlanta Journal Constitution*. In his rendering, a tear drops from the statue's eyes, in which are reflected the stricken World Trade Center towers.

6 Luckovich hated the cartoon. "I really felt like I had screwed up," he says. "I was so emotional that day—sadness, anger and so many different things. I guess because I had this swirl of emotion I felt [the cartoon] didn't capture every emotion

I was feeling. But I realized later I couldn't put into one cartoon everything I was feeling."

7   In the minds of some of the cartoonists, the figure of 77-year-old Paul has loomed large. Since the death of Herbert "Herblock" Block of the *Washington Post*, Conrad is the only living three-time Pulitzer winner. He drew for the *L.A. Times* for years, and now works for a syndicate. He serves as a kind of standard for some younger cartoonists as they assay the terrorist attacks and all that flows from them. Perhaps his strongest work in the show is a cartoon of George Washington wearing a gas mask.

8   "Cartoonists of my generation have always envied guys like Conrad, who were around during Vietnam and Watergate, because they were doing cartoons on really important issues," Luckovich says. "Now we realize we need to rise to the occasion. We're not just commenting on Gary Condit or the semen-stained Lewinsky dress anymore. This is something that is really life and death and has fundamentally changed our country."

9   Cartoonists, like everyone else, had the wind knocked out of them by the attacks. Gasping to comprehend, trying to digest an indigestible immensity, they instinctively "reverted to familiar iconic imagery." Then the work tended to take on an affirmative, cheerleading tone (Breen's drawing of a bald eagle sharpening its talons, syndicated cartoonist Bob Gorrell's depiction of a muscular Uncle Sam holding a small U.S. flag and wearing an "I♥NY" T-shirt). Even Luckovich found himself "trying to use patriotism, and to comfort, and those are two things I've never done in my editorial cartooning."

10   You can't blame the cartoonists. Their art form was inevitably overmatched by the awful reality of September 11. Then again, it's hard to imagine what art, except for Samuel Barber's Adagio for Strings or Verdi's Requiem, could speak truth to the sickened soul just then. As the days and weeks passed, cartoonists recovered their wind. They began drawing more pointed fare aimed at specific aspects of the burgeoning crisis that followed the attacks. They started ridiculing lax airport security, satirizing the CIA and FBI for being caught unawares, highlighting the complexity of bringing to justice those responsible for the destruction.

11   Not all of them waited long to do so, either. In only his second drawing after the attacks, *Pittsburgh Post-Gazette* Pulitzer finalist Rob Rogers ridiculed anti-Arab bigots, eschewing "blind, jingoistic patriotism because it can become too easily hatred for a whole people." Gallery owner Josh Needle contends "cartoonists were in the forefront of expressing all points of view."

12   The truth about editorial cartooning is that it is and always will be at its most delicious a negative art. It is weak and predictable and veers too easily toward the maudlin when it tries to reassure or uplift. It is powerful and original when it ridicules and provokes. Its soul is delinquent wit, not emotion, no matter how much the latter seems in order.

THINKING CRITICALLY

1. What particular difficulties did editorial cartoonists face in expressing the horror of September 11? Explain.

2. What advantages do older political cartoonists such as Paul Conrad have over younger ones?

3. What is *iconic imagery*? Identify the iconic imagery used by many cartoonists in their drawings immediately following September 11. What is the significance of this iconic imagery? Explain.

4. How did editorial cartoons change over the first weeks following September 11? Look up some additional political cartoons from this time period online at <www.cagle.slate.msn .com> and discuss how the subject matter changed. What accounts for this shift?

5. Why is political cartooning a "negative" art? Explain.

Exploring the Language of V I S U A L S

Editorial Cartoons: *September 11 and its aftermath*

The editorial cartoons that follow comment on September 11, 2001, and its aftermath. As you view the cartoons, consider how they each make a claim and harbor certain assumptions about their audience. What "stand" is the cartoonist taking on the issue, event, or situation he or she depicts? And what evidence does the cartoon offer to support this position?

Mike Luckovich
Atlanta Journal Constitution

Weeping Lady Liberty

Mike Luckovich, *Atlanta Journal Constitution,* Sept. 12, 2001, Creators Syndicate.

VISUALS
continued ➤

1. What cultural assumptions does this cartoon make? What does its viewer need to know in order to understand it?

2. When he first submitted the cartoon, Mike Luckovich felt that he had "failed miserably" in his task to depict what he was feeling about September 11. What is your personal reaction to this cartoon, and why?

3. This cartoon uses no words to describe what is happening. Are words necessary? Why or why not?

4. View other cartoons featuring "Lady Liberty" reacting to the attack on the World Trade Center in New York at <http://www.hereandthere.com/2001-September11-LadyLiberty/ladyliberty.htm>. What do the cartoons have in common? How are they different? What makes Luckovich's cartoon stand out?

Jeff Danziger
Tribune Media Services

Uncle Sam

1. What is the effect of depicting Uncle Sam's sleeves rolled up? Is it a strong image? What does his clothing symbolize? How do his actions reinforce this symbolism?

2. What other icons are featured in the drawing. What is left standing in the picture, and why?

3. What is the effect of the figure in Uncle Sam's arms? Whom does she represent? Would the picture be as effective if Uncle Sam were carrying a man? Explain.

4. Many cartoonists drew pictures of either Uncle Sam or Lady Liberty. What do each represent? Do they carry the same symbolism? Explain.

VISUALS
continued ➤

Jeff Stahler
The Cincinnati Post

Cell Phone

Jeff Stahler, *The Cincinnati Post,* Sept. 14, 2001. Jeff Stahler reprinted by permission of Newspaper Enterprise Association, Inc.

1. What is happening in this cartoon? Who is the speaker? What do you need to know about what the cartoon depicts in order to appreciate its message?

2. Summarize your overall feelings regarding this editorial cartoon. What message did you receive as a viewer? What does Stahler "say" through his artwork? Explain.

Jeff Parker
Florida Today

We Are All New Yorkers

IN LIGHT OF RECENT EVENTS, WE'RE ALL NEW YORKERS...

Jeff Parker, *Florida Today*, Sept. 14, 2001.

1. How does the cartoonist use visual clichés to tell a story in this cartoon? What symbols are present? What background does the viewer need in order to understand the cartoon?

2. Would this cartoon be as effective without the caption at the bottom? Would it be stronger? No difference? Explain.

VISUALS
continued ➤

Corky Trinidad
Honolulu Star

Muslims from Iowa

Corky Trinidad, *Honolulu Star,* Sept. 16, 2001.

1. What is happening in this cartoon? What message is the cartoonist trying to convey? What "evidence" does the cartoonist provide to support his position.

2. Examine the characters in this cartoon. What is the effect of depiction of the man as opposed to the little girl? Explain.

3. Although this cartoon was drawn in the context of the events following September 11, 2001, would it be equally effective years later?

■ **MAKING CONNECTIONS**

1. Have you ever read a political cartoon that offended you? What was the nature of the cartoon and why did it bother you? Explain.

2. One of life's little frustrations is reading a cartoon you just "don't get." You ask friends and family to explain the cartoon to you, with little success. Locate a cartoon that you have difficulty understanding and bring it to class. In groups, discuss the cartoons and their possible meanings. If possible, suggest ways to clarify the joke either by refining the drawing or changing the wording.

3. Apply some of the principles of cartooning to some editorial cartoons. Evaluate how the elements Gerberg describes contribute to the overall quality of the cartoons. Select a cartoon and analyze it. In your analysis, address the ways the cartoon communicates its point, its social function, and why you think it is funny.

4. Is there a particular editorial cartoonist whose work you particularly admire? Explain why you like the work of this particular artist. Cite specific cartoons in your response. You may wish to complement your article with some examples of some of the cartoons you are describing.

5. Discuss the role editorial cartoons play in American culture. How are they used as a communication medium? How do they entertain? Refer to specific examples in your response. Are they indeed, as Marlette fears, endangered?

6. Take a look at more political cartoons drawn after September 11 at <http://cagle.slate .msn.com>. How did different cartoonists draw a cartoon that had "relevance to thousands of other dumbstruck and grief-ridden people"? In what ways did cartooning provide an expressive outlet for both artists and readers?

Language of the Mass Media and Advertising

6

■ This image perfectly encapsulates the language of mass media and advertising. What you see is NBC's giant Astrovisions screen telecasting NBC's news and other programming to the crowds. No doubt you recognize Times Square from the advertising billboards that act as place markers here and around the world.

Much of what we know about the world comes from what the media tell us through television, radio, newspapers, magazines, and movies. Similarly, how we perceive that world is influenced by the media's presentation of it. Underwriting most of that media is advertising. Nearly $200 billion is spent every year on television commercials and print ads—more than the gross national product of many countries in the world—accounting for a quarter of each television hour and the bulk of most newspapers and magazines. Tremendous power lies in the hands of those who control the media and write the ads. In this chapter, we will examine the tremendous power of television media and advertising—and explore how each uses and abuses the power of words.

As Seen on TV

At the beginning of the twentieth century, the written word was the prime mover of information and mass entertainment. Books, newspapers, literary journals, and tabloids were the way people got information, shared the latest fashions, and were entertained. Now, a century later, we are a culture dependent on the spoken word—to each other face-to-face, on telephones, radio, television, and film. But what does this shift mean for language? Some critics claim that language is becoming slovenly and unimaginative as media attempt to reach mass audiences. Creative use of language is being lost in an effort to reach the "lowest common denominator."

With today's rabid competition for audience and revenue, the evening news, some say, has become just another form of entertainment—high-power visuals and low-power English. In "TV News: All the World in Pictures," Neil Postman and Steve Powers eloquently argue that TV news, with its heavy reliance on dramatic and dynamic images, has been packaged to suit the requirements of show biz rather than journalism—the result being the corruption of our knowledge and views of world affairs. But it isn't just the news that has become more graphic. Many people also complain that television language aims to shock. The next two pieces take a closer look at television's increasing level of "bad language" and how people are responding to this censorship shift. Deborah Tannen describes how television's love affair with conflict and confrontation is filtering into everyday conversation, in "Taking TV's 'War of Words' Too Literally." The section ends with an essay by Tom Shachtman called "The Entertained Culture." He asserts television's quest to reach wide audiences means scriptwriters must tailor their language to "aim lower." The result, he fears, is that slimmer scripts and elementary-level language will have a negative impact on our linguistic future.

The Language of Advertising

Advertising is everywhere—television, newspapers, magazines, the Internet, the exterior of buses, and highway billboards; it's printed on T-shirts, hot dogs, postage stamps, and even license plates. It is the driving force of our consumer economy. It's everywhere people are, and its appeal goes right to the quick of our fantasies: happiness, material wealth, eternal youth, social acceptance, sexual fulfillment, and power. And it does so in carefully selected images and words. It is the most pervasive form of persuasion in America and, perhaps, the single manufacturer of meaning in our consumer society. Yet, most of us are so accustomed to advertising that we hear it without listening and see it without looking. But if we stopped to examine how it works, we might be amazed at just how powerful and complex a psychological force advertising is. In this chapter we examine how a simple page in a magazine or a fifteen-second TV spot feeds our fantasies and fears with the sole intention of separating us from our money.

By its very nature the language of advertising is a very special language—one that combines words cleverly and methodically. On that point the authors of the next two essays are in agreement. But beyond that, their views diverge widely. In the first piece, "With These Words, I Can Sell You Anything," language-watcher William Lutz argues that advertisers tyrannically twist simple English words so that they appear to promise just what the consumer desires. Taking a defensive posture in "The Language of Advertising," Charles O'Neill, a professional advertiser, admits that the language of ads can be very appealing. With reference to some recent ads, he nonetheless makes a persuasive argument that no ad can force consumers to lay their money down. Marketing guru Herschell Gordon Lewis takes a closer look at some of the words and techniques described by Lutz and O'Neill in "Language Abuse."

While most of us are aware that commercials and advertisements are trying to sell us something, we may be less aware of spots that promote propaganda. Just as ads sell products and services, they can also sell ideas and concepts. The next piece examines how some ads after September 11 aimed to "sell America." Sandra Silberstein discusses how such ads promoted messages of tolerance and freedom to a diverse audience in a time of fear and anxiety. Two ads from this advertising campaign follow her essay.

We conclude this chapter with three recently published magazine ads for sports utility vehicles (SUV). Each of the ads is from a different manufacturer, each takes a different approach to selling its SUV, and each is followed by a set of questions to help you analyze how advertising language and visuals work their appeal.

■ AS SEEN ON TV

TV News: All the World in Pictures
Neil Postman and Steve Powers

Ideally, the news media should be concerned exclusively with facts, logic, and objective analysis. For the most part, major American newspapers and wire services strive to fulfill those ideals. But what about television news? How can a medium whose fast-paced and dynamic images are intended for viewing pleasure deliver unbiased news? According to Neil Postman and Steve Powers, it can't. In this essay, the authors argue that nightly news is a visual entertainment package that creates the illusion of keeping the public informed. They argue that broadcast news shows are, on the contrary, "re-creations" that reveal the world as a series of incoherent and meaningless fragments.

Neil Postman is a critic, writer, communication theorist, and chairman of the Department of Communication Arts at New York University. He is the author of nineteen books, including *Amusing Ourselves to Death* (1985) and *Conscientious Objections* (1992). Steve Powers is an award-winning journalist with more than thirty years of experience in broadcast news, including serving as a correspondent for Fox Television News and the ABC Information Radio Network. They are coauthors of the book, *How to Watch TV News* (1992), from which this essay is excerpted.

1 When a television news show distorts the truth by altering or manufacturing facts (through re-creations), a television viewer is defenseless even if a re-creation is properly labeled. Viewers are still vulnerable to misinformation since they will not know (at least in the case of docudramas) what parts are fiction and what parts are not. But the problems of verisimilitude posed by re-creations pale to insignificance when compared to the problems viewers face when encountering a straight (no monkey-business) show. All news shows, in a sense, are re-creations in that what we hear and see on them are attempts to represent actual events, and are not the events themselves. Perhaps, to avoid ambiguity, we might call all news shows "re-presentations" instead of "re-creations." These re-presentations come to us in two forms: language and pictures. The question then arises: what do viewers have to know about language and pictures in order to be properly armed to defend themselves against the seductions of eloquence (to use Bertrand Russell's apt phrase)? . . .

2 [Let us look at] the problem of pictures. It is often said that a picture is worth a thousand words. Maybe so. But it is probably equally true that one word is worth a thousand pictures, at least sometimes—for example, when it comes to understanding the world we live in. Indeed, the whole problem with news on television comes down to this: all the words uttered in an hour of news coverage could be printed on one page of a newspaper. And the world cannot be understood in one page. Of course, there is a compensation: television offers pictures, and the pictures move. Moving pictures are a kind of language in themselves, but the language of pictures differs radically from oral and written language, and the differences are crucial for understanding television news.

3 To begin with, pictures, especially single pictures, speak only in particularities. Their vocabulary is limited to concrete representation. Unlike words and sentences, a picture does not present to us an idea or concept about the world, except as we use language itself to convert the image to idea. By itself, a picture cannot deal with the unseen, the remote, the internal, the abstract. It does not speak of "man," only of *a*

man; not of "tree," only of *a* tree. You cannot produce an image of "nature," any more than an image of "the sea." You can only show a particular fragment of the here-and-now—a cliff of a certain terrain, in a certain condition of light; a wave at a moment in time, from a particular point of view. And just as "nature" and "the sea" cannot be photographed, such larger abstractions as truth, honor, love, and falsehood cannot be talked about in the lexicon of individual pictures. For "showing of" and "talking about" are two very different kinds of processes: individual pictures give us the world as object; language, the world as idea. There is no such thing in nature as "man" or "tree." The universe offers no such categories or simplifications; only flux and infinite variety. The picture documents and celebrates the particularities of the universe's infinite variety. Language makes them comprehensible.

4   Of course, moving pictures, video with sound, may bridge the gap by juxtaposing images, symbols, sound, and music. Such images can present emotions and rudimentary ideas. They can suggest the panorama of nature and the joys and miseries of humankind.

5   Picture—smoke pouring from the window, cut to people coughing, an ambulance racing to a hospital, a tombstone in a cemetery.

6   Picture—jet planes firing rockets, explosions, lines of foreign soldiers surrendering, the American flag waving in the wind.

7   Nonetheless, keep in mind that when terrorists want to prove to the world that their kidnap victims are still alive, they photograph them holding a copy of a recent newspaper. The dateline on the newspaper provides the proof that the photograph was taken on or after that date. Without the help of the written word, film and videotape cannot portray temporal dimensions with any precision. Consider a film clip showing an aircraft carrier at sea. One might be able to identify the ship as Soviet or American, but there would be no way of telling where in the world the carrier was, where it was headed, or when the pictures were taken. It is only through language—words spoken over the pictures or reproduced in them—that the image of the aircraft carrier takes on specific meaning.

8   Still, it is possible to enjoy the image of the carrier for its own sake. One might find the hugeness of the vessel interesting; it signifies military power on the move. There is a certain drama in watching the planes come in at high speeds and skid to a stop on the deck. Suppose the ship were burning: that would be even more interesting. This leads to an important point about the language of pictures. Moving pictures favor images that change. That is why violence and dynamic destruction find their way onto television so often. When something is destroyed violently it is altered in a highly visible way; hence the entrancing power of fire. Fire gives visual form to the ideas of consumption, disappearance, death—the thing that burned is actually taken away by fire. It is at this very basic level that fires make a good subject for television news. Something was here, now it's gone, and the change is recorded on film.

9   Earthquakes and typhoons have the same power. Before the viewer's eyes the world is taken apart. If a television viewer has relatives in Mexico City and an earthquake occurs there, then he or she may take a special interest in the images of

destruction as a report from a specific place and time; that is, one may look at television pictures for information about an important event. But film of an earthquake can be interesting even if the viewer cares nothing about the event itself. Which is only to say, as we noted earlier, that there is another way of participating in the news—as a spectator who desires to be entertained. Actually to see buildings topple is exciting, no matter where the buildings are. The world turns to dust before our eyes.

10   Those who produce television news in America know that their medium favors images that move. That is why they are wary of "talking heads," people who simply appear in front of a camera and speak. When talking heads appear on television, there is nothing to record or document, no change in process. In the cinema the situation is somewhat different. On a movie screen, closeups of a good actor speaking dramatically can sometimes be interesting to watch. When Clint Eastwood narrows his eyes and challenges his rival to shoot first, the spectator sees the cool rage of the Eastwood character take visual form, and the narrowing of the eyes is dramatic. But much of the effect of this small movement depends on the size of the movie screen and the darkness of the theater, which make Eastwood and his every action "larger than life."

11   The television screen is smaller than life. It occupies about 15 percent of the viewer's visual field (compared to about 70 percent for the movie screen). It is not set in a darkened theater closed off from the world but in the viewer's ordinary living space. This means that visual changes must be more extreme and more dramatic to be interesting on television. A narrowing of the eyes will not do. A car crash, an earthquake, a burning factory are much better.

12   With these principles in mind, let us examine more closely the structure of a typical newscast, and here we will include in the discussion not only the pictures but all the non-linguistic symbols that make up a television news show. For example, in America, almost all news shows begin with music, the tone of which suggests important events about to unfold. The music is very important, for it equates the news with various forms of drama and ritual—the opera, for example, or a wedding procession—in which musical themes underscore the meaning of the event. Music takes us immediately into the realm of the symbolic, a world that is not to be taken literally. After all, when events unfold in the real world, they do so without musical accompaniment. More symbolism follows. The sound of teletype machines can be heard in the studio, not because it is impossible to screen this noise out, but because the sound is a kind of music in itself. It tells us that data are pouring in from all corners of the globe, a sensation reinforced by the world map in the background (or clocks noting the time on different continents). The fact is that teletype machines are rarely used in TV news rooms, having been replaced by silent computer terminals. When seen, they have only a symbolic function.

13   Already, then, before a single news item is introduced, a great deal has been communicated. We know that we are in the presence of a symbolic event, a form of theater in which the day's events are to be dramatized. This theater takes the entire globe as its subject, although it may look at the world from the perspective of a sin-

gle nation. A certain tension is present, like the atmosphere in a theater just before the curtain goes up. The tension is represented by the music, the staccato beat of the teletype machines, and often the sight of news workers scurrying around typing reports and answering phones. As a technical matter, it would be no problem to build a set in which the newsroom staff remained off camera, invisible to the viewer, but an important theatrical effect would be lost. By being busy on camera, the workers help communicate urgency about the events at hand, which suggests that situations are changing so rapidly that constant revision of the news is necessary.

14   The staff in the background also helps signal the importance of the person in the center, the anchor, "in command" of both the staff and the news. The anchor plays the role of host. He or she welcomes us to the newscast and welcomes us back from the different locations we visit during the filmed reports.

15   Many features of the newscast help the anchor to establish the impression of control. These are usually equated with production values in broadcasting. They include such things as graphics that tell the viewer what is being shown, or maps and charts that suddenly appear on the screen and disappear on cue, or the orderly progression from story to story. They also include the absence of gaps, or "dead time," during the broadcast, even the simple fact that the news starts and ends at a certain hour. These common features are thought of as purely technical matters, which a professional crew handles as a matter of course. But they are also symbols of a dominant theme of television news: the imposition of an orderly world—called "the news"—upon the disorderly flow of events.

16   While the form of a news broadcast emphasizes tidiness and control, its content can best be described as fragmented. Because time is so precious on television, because the nature of the medium favors dynamic visual images, and because the pressures of a commercial structure require the news to hold its audience above all else, there is rarely any attempt to explain issues in depth or place events in their proper context. The news moves nervously from a warehouse fire to a court decision, from a guerrilla war to a World Cup match, the quality of the film most often determining the length of the story. Certain stories show up only because they offer dramatic pictures. Bleachers collapse in South America: hundreds of people are crushed—a perfect television news story, for the cameras can record the face of disaster in all its anguish. Back in Washington, a new budget is approved by Congress. Here there is nothing to photograph because a budget is not a physical event; it is a document full of language and numbers. So the producers of the news will show a photo of the document itself, focusing on the cover where it says "Budget of the United States of America." Or sometimes they will send a camera crew to the government printing plant where copies of the budget are produced. That evening, while the contents of the budget are summarized by a voice-over, the viewer sees stacks of documents being loaded into boxes at the government printing plant. Then a few of the budget's more important provisions will be flashed on the screen in written form, but this is such a time-consuming process—using television as a printed page—that the producers keep it to a minimum. In short, the budget is not televisable, and for that reason its time on the news must be brief. The bleacher collapse will get more time that evening.

17   While appearing somewhat chaotic, these disparate stories are not just dropped in the news program helter-skelter. The appearance of a scattershot story order is really orchestrated to draw the audience from one story to the next—from one section to the next—through the commercial breaks to the end of the show. The story order is constructed to hold and build the viewership rather than place events in context or explain issues in depth.

18   Of course, it is a tendency of journalism in general to concentrate on the surface of events rather than underlying conditions; this is as true for the newspaper as it is for the newscast. But several features of television undermine whatever efforts journalists may make to give sense to the world. One is that a television broadcast is a series of events that occur in sequence, and the sequence is the same for all viewers. This is not true for a newspaper page, which displays many items simultaneously, allowing readers to choose the order in which they read them. If newspaper readers want only a summary of the latest tax bill, they can read the headline and the first paragraph of an article, and if they want more, they can keep reading. In a sense, then, everyone reads a different newspaper, for no two readers will read (or ignore) the same items.

19   But all television viewers see the same broadcast. They have no choices. A report is either in the broadcast or out, which means that anything which is of narrow interest is unlikely to be included. As NBC News executive Reuven Frank once explained:

> A newspaper, for example, can easily afford to print an item of conceivable interest to only a fraction of its readers. A television news program must be put together with the assumption that each item will be of some interest to everyone that watches. Every time a newspaper includes a feature which will attract a specialized group it can assume it is adding at least a little bit to its circulation. To the degree a television news program includes an item of this sort . . . it must assume that its audience will diminish.

20   The need to "include everyone," an identifying feature of commercial television in all its forms, prevents journalists from offering lengthy or complex explanations, or from tracing the sequence of events leading up to today's headlines. One of the ironies of political life in modern democracies is that many problems which concern the "general welfare" are of interest only to specialized groups. Arms control, for example, is an issue that literally concerns everyone in the world, and yet the language of arms control and the complexity of the subject are so daunting that only a minority of people can actually follow the issue from week to week and month to month. If it wants to act responsibly, a newspaper can at least make available more information about arms control than most people want. Commercial television cannot afford to do so.

21   But even if commercial television could afford to do so, it wouldn't. The fact that television news is principally made up of moving pictures prevents it from offering lengthy, coherent explanations of events. A television news show reveals the world as a series of unrelated, fragmentary moments. It does not—and cannot be expected to—offer a sense of coherence or meaning. What does this suggest to a

TV viewer? That the viewer must come with a prepared mind—information, opinions, a sense of proportion, an articulate value system. To the TV viewer lacking such mental equipment, a news program is only a kind of rousing light show. Here a falling building, there a five-alarm fire, everywhere the world as an object, much without meaning, connections, or continuity.

THINKING CRITICALLY

1. According to Postman and Powers, how are still pictures like language? How are still pictures different?

2. How do juxtapositions with other images, symbols, sound, music, or printed or verbal language help present the meaning of moving images (paragraph 4)? For each example in paragraphs 5–7, describe how these juxtapositions supply meaning to the moving images.

3. According to the authors, why are violence and destruction so often part of TV news stories? How are violence and destruction better suited for TV than other stories? How do TV screens make such stories more suited to TV than other stories?

4. Why are music, machine sounds, and news workers routinely included in TV news broadcasts? How do these nonessential cues help make news broadcasts seem interesting and important?

5. What devices do news broadcasters use to make them seem in control of "the disorderly flow of events"? Why are stories placed in a particular sequence? How might such a sequence affect audience viewing habits?

6. Why do TV news stories concentrate on "the surface of events rather than underlying conditions"? Why do broadcasters sometimes omit stories that are important but that would interest (or be understood by) only a minority of viewers?

7. What attitude do Postman and Powers convey in their first paragraph about television news shows? What kind of judgments about TV news did you expect to find throughout the rest of the article? What analogies and phrases help you identify the authors' attitude?

8. What attitude is conveyed in comparing TV news to theater? Beyond the aspect of spectacle, what additional denotations or connotations are implicit in the term *theater*? How do these suggest the authors' distrust of TV as a reliable, accurate source of news information? (See paragraph 13.)

9. What kinds of "important" news events are overwhelmed or lost by TV's visual reportage? How significant are such stories to the purpose(s) of news reporting? Do the authors convince you of the urgency of such stories? Would their point seem less urgent if they had focused on sports and weather reporting, for example?

WRITING ASSIGNMENTS

1. Using a family photograph, or a photo of friends, describe how this still picture conveys only a limited idea of what it shows. Did anything happen before or after the photo was snapped to

make it especially important to you? Was anyone in the picture faking pleasure or caught in an uncharacteristic posture? In short, what might a stranger miss in this photo?

2. How do you think Postman and Powers would analyze the effect of closed captioning on television? Do you think they would include closed captioning as a visual element? Support your answer.

3. Videotape a network or local television newscast. First, watch the newscast with the sound (and/or closed captioning) turned off; then, watch the whole newscast with the sound (and/or closed captioning) turned on. Select three stories near the beginning of the broadcast and record your impressions about how important each was. Did you have different impressions when the sound (or closed captioning) accompanied the pictures? Why or why not?

4. Discuss the impact and role of TV news reporting on topics such as the Vietnam War, the civil rights movement, school shootings, the destruction of the Twin Towers of the World Trade Center, suicide bombings in Israel, or some other highly visible current event. How does television news, particularly the images it uses, help to create news rather than just retell it?

Oh, the Profanity!
Paul Farhi

As audiences demand television fare that is raw and "honest," networks are promoting shows that use language to reflect tough subject matter. Gritty cop shows, mafia families, and fast-paced hospital dramas seem to be testing the linguistic boundaries of television concore. But is this tough language necessary? Or is it simply reflecting the language used in the real world, by real people? In the next piece, Paul Farhi takes a look at how some popular television programs are pulling out all the stops.

Paul Farhi is a staff writer for the *Washington Post*, in which this article first appeared on April 21, 2002.

1 Detective Vic Mackey is not a very nice man. A rogue TV cop in the grand tradition of rogue TV cops, Mackey (Michael Chiklis) dispenses his own brand of street justice, roughing up perps, intimidating informants, even stealing his colleagues' HoHos. And gosh oh golly, can he ever swear.

2 On "The Shield," a popular new series on cable's FX network, Mackey bags the bad guys with a vocabulary that would shock Dirty Harry. He describes a drug suspect as a certain bodily orifice. He uses a common expletive, twice, and refers to a sex act with a word that rhymes with "snowing."

3 And this is well before the first commercial break on the first episode. That "The Shield" is a weekly series on basic cable, available in almost 80 percent of U.S. television homes, says something about the state of profanity on television.

Mostly it is this: Just when it seems that TV networks are drawing the line, they move the line again.

4   In "A Season on the Brink," a made-for-TV movie carried on ESPN last month, basketball coach Bobby Knight (played by Brian Dennehy) drops the F-word 15 times in the first 15 minutes. When Disney-owned ABC aired "Saving Private Ryan" last November, it left the movie's harsh soldier talk unbleeped. MTV's "The Osbournes," about a real-life family, is so riddled with crude words that the bleeps almost outnumber the audible words. In recent months, a crass word for "jerk" has popped up on "The Practice," "NYPD Blue" and "ER"; the ever-popular "bull[bleep]" has been heard on "Nightline" and "60 Minutes."

5   Viewers who subscribe to HBO may be used to such things, what with that network's foulmouthed gangsters, convicts and single gals ("The Sopranos," "Oz," "Sex and the City," respectively). But HBO's customers pay monthly fees to receive programs that are more explicit than those on the rest of TV. The news here is that the rest of TV is closing the gap: Basic cable and broadcast—the most widely available form of television—are getting increasingly down and dirty, too.

6   Even the previously sacrosanct "family hour" (8–9 p.m.) isn't inviolate. Between 1996 and 2001, the frequency of profanities such as "bastard," "son of a bitch" and worse roughly tripled on the leading networks during the hour once set aside for feel-good fare like "Little House on the Prairie," according to the Parents Television Council, an organization that monitors TV content. Fox rang up almost four crude words per hour on average, most among the Big Four (Fox, CBS, NBC and ABC), the PTC said.

7   "This is all about the coarsening of the culture, the dumbing down of America," said Melissa Caldwell, who conducted the PTC's research. "There used to be a stigma about using certain words. Unfortunately, those standards are eroding."

8   What was taboo on Monday certainly can become acceptable by Friday (as Cole Porter noted in 1934 in "Anything Goes": "Good authors too who once knew better words / Now only use four-letter words / Writing prose / Anything goes"). TV is no different. Archie Bunker caused uneasy ripples when he salted his tirades on "All in the Family" with "hells" and "damns" in the 1970s—language that seems tame now. The most publicity a forgotten CBS sitcom called "Uncle Buck" got in 1990 was when a child character declared, "That sucks!" Nowadays that term is common, too.

9   "Words that people never thought they'd hear on the air make it on now all the time," said S. Robert Lichter, president of the Center for Media and Public Affairs, a Washington think tank that analyzes TV programming. "I think in five years bull[excrement] will be as common as 'crap.' "

10   Some believe the process has been driven by "Sopranos" envy—a desire by producers to mimic the critically acclaimed HBO series. The groundbreaking show is casually laced with the kinds of words that George Carlin once said could never be mentioned on TV.

11   "Honestly, there's a real frustration among writers and directors that they don't get to play with the same toys as those in pay TV," said Bryce Zabel, a producer

who is chairman of the Academy of Television Arts and Sciences. "The fact is, creative artists want to express themselves in as creative and accurate a way as they can. . . . They want to tell the truth."

12 But Dick Wolf, producer of the "Law & Order" programs on NBC, rejects that argument: "It all comes back to storytelling," he said. "There are no bad words in Shakespeare, and he seems to have done all right."

13 Caught in the middle, network executives say what's acceptable is necessarily a moving target, etched in sand, not stone. As social mores evolve, they say, television is always hustling to keep up.

14 "In the last [few] years, certain words have become more a part of the culture," said Martin Franks, the CBS executive who oversees the network's standards and practices department. "In a world in which eighth- and ninth-grade schoolyards are filled with many more words than we'd allow on our air, at some point you have to ask who is protecting whom, and from what."

15 That is, in fact, much the way the federal government sees it. When he was asked recently at a broadcast industry convention whether the Federal Communications Commission had been lax in enforcing regulations aimed at "indecent" speech on radio and TV, FCC Chairman Michael Powell responded: "This is an increasingly diverse society. Claiming there is just one community today is just not true. . . . Our society is supposed to be strong enough to sustain" a diversity of views.

16 Up till the early 1980s, the three leading networks subscribed to a common code, making TV content reasonably uniform in tone. But this was abandoned under antitrust pressure from the federal government and independent broadcasters. Since then, each network has been free to define its own notions of acceptable behavior and language. The process has become increasingly complicated by competition; each network now has to weigh its decisions against those of dozens of competitors.

17 Fox's prime-time viewers are younger than CBS's and therefore, the network says, more tolerant of profanity. "In the proper context, if some [swear word] is well motivated and germane to the story, there is an acceptance by our core audience," said Roland McFarland, Fox's chief censor. McFarland said context, experience and audience expectations guide Fox's review of scripts. The rule of thumb: Don't surprise or jar viewers with something they didn't expect to hear.

18 During its broadcast of the World Trade Center documentary "9-11" last month, for instance, CBS decided to leave intact many utterances of the F-word by firefighters responding to the attack. Franks said network brass briefly discussed the language but decided it was appropriate, considering the circumstances. "It would have been more offensive if we had taken it out," he said.

19 But determining the proper context can be tricky. When CBS permitted a teenage character in a live prime-time broadcast of the play "On Golden Pond" to say "bull[bleep]," David Letterman seized on the incident to highlight his network's alleged double standard. After airing an uncensored clip of the play on his show, Letterman commented that it was "bull[bleep]" for the network to prohibit him from using the same word during late-night hours. Letterman's comments were sanitized—thereby proving his point (the word still isn't printable in this newspaper).

20   Franks said Letterman's use of the word was "gratuitous," while the play's use was justified by "artistic merit." But he noted: "I wish I could say looking back over 10 years that we've always been semantically precise and crisp and tight. Of course it's subjective."

21   The Comedy Central animated series "South Park" pushed this particular envelope last year, in an episode in which the characters used a well-known word for excrement 162 times in 30 minutes—all duly recorded by an on-screen tally. "The notion that [the word] isn't said every day, everywhere, is ridiculous," said Tony Fox, the network's spokesman. "The point was, these are words everyone uses. Why are they so taboo on TV?"

22   In fact, viewers hardly seem exercised by the increasing trash talk. Network representatives say offensive language ranks low on the list of things that viewers complain about—far behind the two biggest bugaboos, program preemptions and cancellations.

23   Apart from an occasional letter-writing campaign (organized by advocacy groups such as the Parents Television Council), Fox's McFarland said, the network will draw no more than "two, three or five" letters of complaint a week about the language used in a program. CBS's Franks said "a huge response" is 75 letters, calls and e-mails—still minuscule considering that millions of people are watching. Both said this indicates that their networks are in sync with their viewers' sensibilities. (Advertisers could be a different story. Several have pulled out of "The Shield," citing objectionable content.)

24   ESPN's experience with "Season on the Brink" suggests that audiences may be ready for even more profanity. ESPN showed two versions of its movie simultaneously—one uncut on ESPN, another on ESPN2 with the salty language excised. The network warned viewers about the rough language at the start of the program, and after each commercial break. It also flagged the parallel ESPN2 version.

25   The result: Viewers chose the foulmouthed Bobby Knight over his bleeped-out twin by a margin of nearly 7 to 1.

26   "We were surprised at the response," said Chris LaPlaca, a network spokesman. "We thought [the language] was going to be a bigger deal than it was. But I think people recognized it wasn't in there gratuitously. It was for accuracy and authenticity."

27   Is everything up for grabs? Actually, no. McFarland reported that strong taboos remain in place against racist or sexist insults. "That is where we truly draw the line," he said. "We take great care in eliminating that" from Fox programs.

28   While few people think television will ever go back to where it once was, contemplating the future can sometimes be a little chilling. Bryce Zabel, the producer, remembers writing a script for a TV pilot about a violent, Rollerball-style game of the future. In it, the TV announcers on this anything-goes sport casually used the full Carlin arsenal to describe the goings-on.

29   "The idea was that everyone had seen it all and heard it all and no one cared anymore about that kind of language," Zabel said. Pausing to consider his words, he added, "I don't think that scenario is unrealistic."

THINKING CRITICALLY

1. Should foul or offensive language on television be banned? Why or why not?

2. In paragraph 7, Melissa Caldwell of the Parents Television Council asserts that the increased foul language on television is "all about the coarsening of the culture, the dumbing down of America." Do you agree with Caldwell's assessment? Why or why not? Explain.

3. What role has the popular HBO series *The Sopranos* played in the increase of coarse language on television? Explain.

4. This article was written for a newspaper, and uses a standard reporting style. Can you tell how the author feels about this issue? If so, cite examples from the article that reveal his opinion.

5. Throughout most of his article Farhi refers to various obscenities as the "S-word," the "A-word," and the "F-word." Why do you think he chose not to use the actual obscenities? What does this tell you about the role of obscenity censorship in the print media? Explain.

6. In paragraph 13, Farhi states that network executives say that what is acceptable language is "etched in sand, not stone. As social mores evolve, television is always hustling to keep up." Respond to this statement in your own words. Are social mores "evolving" or are censorship rules merely more lax than they were in the past? Explain.

7. What language forces television censors to really "draw the line"? Are there degrees of offensive language? If some of it Is allowed, should all of it be permissible? Why or why not?

WRITING ASSIGNMENTS

1. Farhi cites several programs that are testing the limits of taboo language on television. Brainstorm a list of shows that seek to "push the envelope" in terms of foul language, watch one or two of these shows, and then write a critique of them noting how the language contributes or detracts from the program. For example, would *South Park* be funny if its characters did not use taboo language? Would *The Sopranos* seem less edgy and raw? Explain.

2. Farhi points out that producers of raw television programs argue that the obscenities in their programs are necessary in order to create realistic characters. What is your opinion about this issue? Is it important for characters in movies to sound like "real people," or as an art form, should movies seek to transcend merely holding up a mirror to reality?

Is Bad Language Unacceptable on TV?
BBC Online

In the previous article, Paul Farhi reports on the shifting rules of taboo language on television. The next section takes a closer look at this subject. Readers of the BBC Online discussion forum, "Talking Point," were asked, "Is bad language unacceptable on TV . . . or have swear words and offensive language become an accepted part of TV output?" As you read the responses posted on the discussion board, consider the different arguments posed, and how you personally feel about the subject.

1 Is bad language unacceptable on TV?

2   The use of racially abusive language on television and radio is an area of increasing concern among viewers and listeners, a new study has revealed. The report also suggests most adults with children want their homes to be expletive free. Stephen Whittle, Director of the Broadcasting Standards Commission in England, says there is an acceptance that swearing and offensive language is used in daily life, and may be appropriate if a program is aimed at adults.

3   But he says people "would prefer their homes to remain an expletive deleted zone for children." Is swearing still a matter of major concern to you? Or have swear words and offensive language become an accepted part of TV output? Here are some responses to this question featured on the *BBC Online*'s "Talking Point:"

4   There's a simple answer to all those complaining. If you don't like it then don't watch it. There is nothing more annoying than listening to outraged people complain about what they had to watch the night before. No one makes you watch them so if you hear bad language/see sex scenes/view violence then change the channels instead of watching all three hours and then complaining about it afterwards. YOU DON'T HAVE TO WATCH IT. It's true that at times in films/programs it seems the language is used purely to shock rather than as part of the script/plot/characters but if you sit and watch it all instead of turning over/switching off then you can't then blame your shock and outrage on the program makers.

JAMES, UK

5   There is no justification to the use of bad language on TV. It is unacceptable. How can a parent positively correct a child who uses bad language if all they hear on TV is filthy language every minute?

RUSKIN KWOFIC, USA

6   Not only is swearing wrong and extremely offensive, even worse than that is the constant blasphemy on TV. This is especially hurtful to a Christian like myself when it is done to make people laugh. We should not be blaspheming or condoning this when we laugh or otherwise accept it passively or actively. It is too easy to say, ". . . use the off switch . . .," this is not the answer. Does any parent want to encourage their child to swear and adopt negativity? Rather it would be more constructive to teach them the values of right and wrong. To sum up, all who own a television licence are entitled to be informed and entertained by its purchase and that means all.

K. D., WALES

7   Protecting children is a big chunk of what responsible parenting is about, and protecting their minds and emotions is just as important as physical protection, if not more so. Of course they'll come across it elsewhere, but it's clear that the extent

will be increased or decreased by the levels of exposure of their peers. As a parent I find the so-called watershed is no guarantee at all that my kids won't hear swearing on the television. Please can we have a consistently regulated watershed?

TOM RICHARDS, UK

8   I consider the television to be a guest. I would not allow a visitor to my house to use swearing and foul language in front of me or my children. I consider the television to be a guest, and when it offends, off it goes!

J. HERBERT, UK

9   It really is stupid to campaign for protecting young people against swearing on TV. By the time you reach 12 years old you've heard every word under the sun a million times in the playground. Anyone who fails to realize this is just completely ignorant.

DARREN MEALE, UK

10   Bad language is nothing compared to all the violent shows on so many series. I prefer to hear someone pronounce a four-letter word than to see them beaten to death or killed in a TV series. Bad language is part of the everyday life of most people. Violence is not.

LUC MASUY, BELGIUM

11   The use of bad language in TV or cinema is not a reflection of society, but rather an excuse by writers and actors to hide the fact that they can no longer produce real drama or real emotion. The use of swearing to emphasize a point is only there to mask the lack of understanding and talent. Media twenty years ago didn't need to use bad language—the skill in presenting drama and emotion was there anyway. Sorry, no swearing on TV or cinema at all for me.

STEVE GITTINS, UK

12   In writing drama one of the first rules is to make your characters believable. Censorship of bad language could lead to some of the most unbelievable characters ever portrayed on television. People swear. For instance, a prison drama in which no one ever swore would be ridiculous. What sort of programs you allow your children to watch is up to you. But they will hear swearing in the real world—you can't censor that.

COLIN WRIGHT, UK

13   Why is it necessary? Surely we can use descriptive adjectives without resorting to bad language. It is not enough to say it is a part of life. We have the power to adopt better social attitudes; instead many people seem content with debasing everything.

JILL DOE, WALES

14   All drama revolves around conflict and jeopardy so bad language in itself is not wrong, it all depends on the context it is used in. Imagine if Shakespeare or Chaucer had been prevented from writing and performing their work without the "bawdy" language, the swearing of their day. As long as it doesn't become meaninglessly used and the watershed is observed to my eyes at least, it is acceptable.

JAMES NEWMAN, UK

15   Please keep it off our screens. You only have to listen to children going to school to see how commonplace it has become.

GERRY, SCOTLAND

16   It may be the duty of our media/entertainment outlets to reflect the standards and behavior of our society and culture, but they surely also have some responsibility to set the standard. By merely reflecting, because they permeate every level of society, they take the lead in the general debasement of "generally accepted standards of behavior." I am not prudish or offended by bad language/behavior on TV and radio, per se, but it often makes me wince!

MARK M. NEWDICK, USA

17   As a relatively liberal minded young person, I am not outraged by occasional bad language on television, but at the same time, I do not think that it is necessary. Bad language is neither amusing nor particularly effective in stressing a point. It is just fashion—and a very cheap fashion at that. It's best to leave it in the cinemas (if it is really required there) and edit the more stronger language out before it appears on television. Personally, I have never found that a movie is lacking punch just because a few profanities have been deleted. Indeed, this should be the test to see whether a film is worth its weight at all.

ROBERT KIDD, AUSTRALIA

18   My personal experience of working in an environment where swearing was the norm was to swear more. When I changed jobs where swearing was banned I stopped. The best thing to do is to avoid swearing in the main but keep a little to be realistic, and hence cut down on the excessive use of profanities in society.

GAVIN PEARSON, USA

19   As adults, we can accept bad language on TV programs, as long as it relates to the program in question (i.e., drama series or films). However, children should not have to hear that sort of language. I'm not a prude by any means, but I find it really depressing when I hear children from toddler age and up using foul language. Of course, they may learn this from their parents and other family members, but let's minimize their exposure by keeping it out of children's programs.

KAREN, UK

20   The simple fact of the matter is if you don't like the swearing then turn over! Anything that your children may or may not hear on TV they are certainly going to hear in the real world. People need to wake up and understand that the censorship of television is going beyond a joke. I'm all for restricting bad language before a time when children are likely to be up but can someone please explain to me the necessity to cut swear words from a film at 10:30 or 11:00. People can say they are offended as much as they like but the simple fact is that you control what you watch, if you're offended by swearing then turn it off. Welcome to the real world people, people swear!

RICHARD TYACKE, ENGLAND

THINKING CRITICALLY

1. What is your personal opinion of bad language on television? Is it no big deal? A fact of life? Or is it unacceptable?

2. Is the reality that people swear—as one posting claims—valid support that it should be acceptable television fare? Why or why not?

3. Several respondents to this question state that if you don't like bad language on television, turn off the set. Respond to this statement in your own words.

4. Several forum participants qualify their responses with "I'm not a prude." What are the implications of the word *prude*? Is it prudish to object to bad language? Why or why not?

5. Select one or two of the postings featured in this article and write a response to it, addressing the points it raises.

WRITING ASSIGNMENTS

1. One forum participant comments that while the entertainment industry should reflect society and culture, they also have some responsibility to "set the standard." What should the standard be? Write an essay exploring the responsibility of the entertainment industry to the cultural standards of a society.

2. One respondent, James Newman, points out that bad language depends on the context in which it was used. "Imagine if Shakespeare or Chaucer had been prevented from writing and performing their work without 'bawdy' language, the swearing of their day." Research this assertion. What sort of bawdy language did these two writers use and how did it contribute to the flavor of their work? How would their work be different if they were restricted to neutral language? In this context, does Newman make a valid point?

Taking TV's "War of Words" Too Literally
Deborah Tannen

In this essay, linguistic professor Deborah Tannen examines the ways in which we approach arguments and debates in our society. If ratings are any indication of American's viewing tastes, our culture prefers angry conflict to patient discussion. Tannen describes her personal experience on a television talk show, a program on which she hoped thoughtful deliberation with other participants would help promote a meaningful dialogue. Instead, she found herself the unwilling participant in an aggressive shouting match. Beyond mere entertainment, what is this style of television teaching viewers about the way we address conflict and solve problems?

Deborah Tannen is a professor of linguistics at Georgetown University. She has been a featured guest on many news programs, including *20/20, 48 Hours*, and the *News Hour with*

Jim Lehrer. Tannen is the author of many best-selling books on linguistics and social discourse, most recently *The Argument Culture* (1999), and *I Only Say This Because I Love You* (2001). This article appeared in the weekly edition of the *Washington Post* on March 23, 1998.

1   I was waiting to go on a television talk show a few years ago for a discussion about how men and women communicate, when a man walked in wearing a shirt and tie and a floor-length skirt, the top of which was brushed by his waist-length red hair. He politely introduced himself and told me that he'd read and liked my book *You Just Don't Understand,* which had just been published. Then he added, "When I get out there, I'm going to attack you. But don't take it personally. That's why they invite me on, so that's what I'm going to do."

2   We went on the set and the show began. I had hardly managed to finish a sentence or two before the man threw his arms out in gestures of anger, and began shrieking—briefly hurling accusations at me, and then railing at length against women. The strangest thing about his hysterical outburst was how the studio audience reacted: They turned vicious—not attacking me (I hadn't said anything substantive yet) or him (who wants to tangle with someone who screams at you?) but the other guests: women who had come to talk about problems they had communicating with their spouses.

3   My antagonist was nothing more than a dependable provocateur, brought on to ensure a lively show. The incident has stayed with me not because it was typical of the talk shows I have appeared on—it wasn't, I'm happy to say—but because it exemplifies the ritual nature of much of the opposition that pervades our public dialogue.

4   Everywhere we turn, there is evidence that, in public discourse, we prize contentiousness and aggression more than cooperation and conciliation. Headlines blare about the Star Wars, the Mommy Wars, the Baby Wars, the Mammography Wars; everything is posed in terms of battles and duels, winners and losers, conflicts and disputes. Biographies have metamorphosed into demonographies whose authors don't just portray their subjects warts and all, but set out to dig up as much dirt as possible, as if the story of a person's life is contained in the warts, only the warts, and nothing but the warts.

5   It's all part of what I call the argument culture, which rests on the assumption that opposition is the best way to get anything done: The best way to discuss an idea is to set up a debate. The best way to cover news is to find people who express the most extreme views and present them as "both sides." The best way to begin an essay is to attack someone. The best way to show you're really thoughtful is to criticize. The best way to settle disputes is to litigate them.

6   It is the automatic nature of this response that I am calling into question. This is not to say that passionate opposition and strong verbal attacks are never appropriate. In the words of Yugoslavian-born poet Charles Simic, "There are moments in life when true invective is called for, when it becomes an absolute necessity, out of a deep sense of justice, to denounce, mock, vituperate, lash out, in the strongest possible language." What I'm questioning is the ubiquity, the knee-jerk nature of approaching almost any issue, problem or public person in an adversarial way.

7   Smashing heads does not open minds. In this as in so many things, results are also causes, looping back and entrapping us. The pervasiveness of warlike formats and language grows out of, but also gives rise to, an ethic of aggression: We come to value aggressive tactics for their own sake—for the sake of argument. Compromise becomes a dirty word, and we often feel guilty if we are conciliatory rather than confrontational—even if we achieve the result we're seeking.

8   Here's one example. A woman called another talk show on which I was a guest. She told the following story: "I was in a place where a man was smoking, and there was a no-smoking sign. Instead of saying 'You aren't allowed to smoke in here. Put that out!' I said, 'I'm awfully sorry, but I have asthma, so your smoking makes it hard for me to breathe. Would you mind terribly not smoking?' When I said this, the man was extremely polite and solicitous, and he put his cigarette out, and I said, 'Oh, thank you, thank you!' as if he'd done a wonderful thing for me. Why did I do that?"

9   I think the woman expected me—the communications expert—to say she needs assertiveness training to confront smokers in a more aggressive manner. Instead, I told her that her approach was just fine. If she had tried to alter his behavior by reminding him of the rules, he might well have rebelled: "Who made you the enforcer? Mind your own business!" She had given the smoker a face-saving way of doing what she wanted, one that allowed him to feel chivalrous rather than chastised. This was kinder to him, but it was also kinder to herself, since it was more likely to lead to the result she desired.

10   Another caller disagreed with me, saying the first caller's style was "self-abasing." I persisted: There was nothing necessarily destructive about the way the woman handled the smoker. The mistake the second caller was making—a mistake many of us make—was to confuse ritual self-effacement with the literal kind. All human relations require us to find ways to get what we want from others without seeming to dominate them.

11   The opinions expressed by the two callers encapsulate the ethic of aggression that has us by our throats, particularly in public arenas such as politics and law. Issues are routinely approached by having two sides stake out opposing positions and do battle. This sometimes drives people to take positions that are more adversarial than they feel—and can get in the way of reaching a possible resolution. [. . .]

12   The same spirit drives the public discourse of politics and the press, which are increasingly being given over to ritual attacks. On Jan. 18, 1994, retired admiral Bobby Ray Inman withdrew as nominee for Secretary of Defense after several news stories raised questions about his business dealings and his finances. Inman, who had held high public office in both Democratic and Republican administrations, explained that he did not wish to serve again because of changes in the political climate—changes that resulted in public figures being subjected to relentless attack. Inman said he was told by one editor, "Bobby, you've just got to get thicker skin. We have to write a bad story about you every day. That's our job."

13   Everyone seemed to agree that Inman would have been confirmed. The news accounts about his withdrawal used words such as "bizarre," "mystified" and "extraordinary." A New York Times editorial reflected the news media's befuddlement:

"In fact, with the exception of a few columns, . . . a few editorials and one or two news stories, the selection of Mr. Inman had been unusually well received in Washington." This evaluation dramatizes how run-of-the-mill systematic attacks have become. With a wave of a subordinate clause ("a few editorials . . ."), attacking someone personally and (from his point of view) distorting his record are dismissed as so insignificant as to be unworthy of notice.

14   The idea that all public figures should expect to be criticized ruthlessly testifies to the ritualized nature of such attack: It is not sparked by specific wrongdoing but is triggered automatically.

15   I once asked a reporter about the common journalistic practice of challenging interviewees by repeating criticism to them. She told me it was the hardest part of her job. "It makes me uncomfortable," she said. "I tell myself I'm someone else and force myself to do it." But, she said she had no trouble being combative if she felt someone was guilty of behavior she considered wrong. And that is the crucial difference between ritual fighting and literal fighting: opposition of the heart.

16   It is easy to find examples throughout history of journalistic attacks that make today's rhetoric seem tame. But in the past such vituperation was motivated by true political passion, in contrast with today's automatic, ritualized attacks—which seem to grow out of a belief that conflict is high-minded and good, a required and superior form of discourse.

17   The roots of our love for ritualized opposition lie in the educational system that we all pass through.

18   Here's a typical scene: The teacher sits at the head of the classroom, pleased with herself and her class. The students are engaged in a heated debate. The very noise level reassures the teacher that the students are participating. Learning is going on. The class is a success.

19   But look again, cautions Patricia Rosof, a high school history teacher who admits to having experienced just such a wave of satisfaction. On closer inspection, you notice that only a few students are participating in the debate; the majority of the class is sitting silently. And the students who are arguing are not addressing subtleties, nuances or complexities of the points they are making or disputing. They don't have that luxury because they want to win the argument—so they must go for the most dramatic statements they can muster. They will not concede an opponent's point—even if they see its validity—because that would weaken their position.

20   This aggressive intellectual style is cultivated and rewarded in our colleges and universities. The standard way to write an academic paper is to position your work in opposition to someone else's. This creates a need to prove others wrong, which is quite different from reading something with an open mind and discovering that you disagree with it. Graduate students learn that they must disprove others' arguments in order to be original, make a contribution and demonstrate intellectual ability. The temptation is great to oversimplify at best, and at worst to distort or even misrepresent other positions, the better to refute them.

21   I caught a glimpse of this when I put the question to someone who I felt had misrepresented my own work: "Why do you need to make others wrong for you to

be right?" Her response: "It's an argument!" Aha, I thought, that explains it. If you're having an argument, you use every tactic you can think of—including distorting what your opponent just said—in order to win.

22 Staging everything in terms of polarized opposition limits the information we get rather than broadening it.

23 For one thing, when a certain kind of interaction is the norm, those who feel comfortable with that type of interaction are drawn to participate, and those who do not feel comfortable with it recoil and go elsewhere. If public discourse included a broad range of types, we would be making room for individuals with different temperaments. But when opposition and fights overwhelmingly predominate, only those who enjoy verbal sparring are likely to take part. Those who cannot comfortably take part in oppositional discourse—or choose not to—are likely to opt out.

24 But perhaps the most dangerous harvest of the ethic of aggression and ritual fighting is—as with the audience response to the screaming man on the television talk show—an atmosphere of animosity that spreads like a fever. In extreme forms, it rears its head in road rage and workplace shooting sprees. In more common forms, it leads to what is being decried everywhere as a lack of civility. It erodes our sense of human connection to those in public life—and to the strangers who cross our paths and people our private lives.

THINKING CRITICALLY

1. Do you agree with Tannen's assertion that our public discussions about controversial issues have turned into "battles and duels" by the media? Explain why or why not. Look through several current newspapers or magazines to see if you can find evidence supporting an argument for or against this trend. Do other forms of media such as radio also encourage this approach?

2. What is Tannen's purpose in this essay? Restate her claims in your own words and explain whether you agree or disagree with her thesis and why.

3. In paragraphs 8 and 9, Tannen describes a woman who dealt with a conflict by being conciliatory and even apologetic. Although her approach worked, she and other listeners felt that she should have been more assertive and demanding in her approach. What is your own opinion of how the woman dealt with the situation, and why?

4. What impact does the popularity of "argument culture" television programming have on our language and conversation styles? Explain.

5. Tannen notes in paragraphs 18–20 that students who engage in confrontational-style discourse get more attention from teachers than students who do not. In your own experience, do you agree or disagree with this observation?

6. Is there anything wrong with "argument culture" style communication? Is it indeed a cause for concern, or is it simply a way to solve problems and disagreements? Are arguments really based on winning or losing a position? Should they be? Explain.

WRITING ASSIGNMENTS

1. Watch several television talk-show programs and consider how the "argument culture" is affecting our ability to resolve controversial issues. How do the participants of the programs listen to the words of other people on the program? Are they responding to what is actually said on the program, or merely restating their own opinions? Do they shout, threaten, or interrupt? If so, what effect does this behavior have on the other participants, the audience, and even the host? Explain.

2. In your opinion, has the prevalence of talk shows supporting an argumentative conflict-resolution format filtered into common discourse? In other words, do these television programs influence our culture as a whole? Explain.

3. Write an essay in which you explore the role language plays in solving disagreements. Why is language important to the way our culture addresses conflict? In what ways do we fail to consider language when we argue? In what ways do we use language to our advantage? Explain.

The Entertained Culture
Tom Shachtman

"We have become a country of mass audiences," observes Tom Shachtman in the next essay. Shachtman explains that in an effort to reach as broad an audience as possible, the language used by television media is usually aimed at the lowest linguistic level. This "dumbing down" of language, fears Shachtman, ultimately erodes the grace and fluidity of our language as a whole.

Tom Shachtman teaches writing at New York University. He is the author of several books of fiction and nonfiction, including *Skyscraper Dreams: The Great Real Estate Dynasties of New York* (1991), and *Terrors and Marvels: How Science and Technology Changed the Character and Outcome of World War II* (2002). The following essay is excerpted from his 1995 book, *The Inarticulate Society: Eloquence and Culture in America.*

1 A published novelist moved to Hollywood to join her fiancé and looked for employment in the area's main industry. After she had cut her scriptwriting teeth on occasional television series episodes, she was asked to join the writing staff of a new situation comedy commissioned by a major network. She arrived at the first script meeting brimming over with innovative and quirky ideas for plots, character traits, lines of dialogue. The senior creators heard her out for a few minutes, then enjoined her to remember: "This is television—aim lower."

2 She was perturbed and a bit shocked by that directive, but she should not have been surprised, because aiming lower is what the creators have come to believe is usually required in order to reach the inordinately large audience necessary to keep a prime-time network television show on the air. And part of aiming lower has been

to restrict substantially the vocabulary, sentence structure, word usage, and cultural referents in television scripts.

3   We have become a country of mass audiences. The average American spends half of his or her daily waking hours watching, reading, or listening to some product of the mass media. Most Americans watch thirty hours of television a week, or 1,550 hours a year (during which, according to one estimate, they encounter 37,822 commercials), listen to the radio 1,160 hours a year, spend 180 hours a year reading some part of a newspaper and 110 hours a year reading magazines. We each buy fifteen books a year, and although this appears to be a substantial number, most of the books purchased are considered to be in the category of trashy novels. Surveys conclude that the "most read" portion of any newspaper is Ann Landers's advice column and that the most frequently read magazine is *TV Guide*. The vocabulary and sentence-difficulty level of such readings is quite low, not much above grade-school level. In 1992 Americans spent $12 billion to buy or rent videos, a figure that translates into 49.5 rentals per family a year, about one video each week. Add in a few hours for going to the movies or listening to audio cassettes and CDs, and the total number of hours that the average American spends attending to mass media products comes to more than fifty per week, more time than the average American spends on the job or at school, more hours than he or she devotes to any single activity other than sleeping.[1]

4   A trend toward convergence of the entertainment and news/information industries has made certain that the language practices of one sector largely reproduce the practices of the other, and both aim lower, with dire consequences for articulateness. Because television has tremendous power to influence its viewers, it is legitimate to be concerned with the nature and the accuracy of the medium's representations of reality. Meticulous studies of program content and viewing habits conducted over the course of several decades by George Gerbner and his associates at the Annenberg School have reached the unsurprising conclusion that both fictional and nonfictional broadcasts give viewers inaccurate and misleading representations of reality. Among their findings: Crime is ten times more prevalent on television than it is in the FBI's annual statistics on criminal activity. More than half of television's fictional characters are involved in a violent confrontation each week. Habitual television watchers—defined as those who turn their sets on for more than four hours a day—come to believe the skewed version of reality that is broadcast and to disbelieve reality itself. Not only do such "heavy viewers" perceive crime unrealistically, with a serial killer lurking behind every tree, but they also develop other misperceptions about our society: Their sense of reality comes to reflect television's inaccurate portrayal of who we are and what we do. On prime-time television, nine out of every ten characters are middle-class, less than 1 percent are lower-class, and only one-quarter have blue-collar jobs. On television, only one out of every ten characters is married; women age quickly—there are many youthful female characters and some recognizably older ones, but few are in their middle years. Conversely, the facts show that two out of every three jobs in this country are classified as blue collar, and most women in the country are married and middle-

aged. While 80 percent of the convicted criminals in the United States are young, male and largely from a minority background, the villains seen on television are even more disproportionately young, male, lower-class, minority or foreign-born or mentally ill. "Losers" on television programs are mostly likely to be female, old, unmarried, and/or poor. Similarly, heavy viewers overestimate the number of people in this country employed as doctors, lawyers, and managers, and hold such mistaken beliefs as that the older population of the country is sick, ineffectual, and makes up less of the whole than do the young people whose counterparts fill the bulk of the roles on popular television shows.

5   What do these misrepresentations have to do with the decline in articulate speech? The answer lies in a further investigation into the nature of the misrepresentations, for they are not accidental. Rather, they are a result of marketing analysis, which consistently advises the creators of television programs to aim lower in order to reach broader audiences. That has precipitated the industry into a self-perpetuating cycle of infinite regression, a cycle in which the most effective product is always the one aimed lower than the previous one.

6   Must the need to ensure a large audience automatically mean that the makers of mass media entertainments should trim their creative sails? Clearly, the industry itself has concluded that an entertainment product cannot be both widely popular and of high quality, but there is no intrinsic reason why quality and sales appeal cannot be combined. One of the more popular programs in the early days of commercial television was *Omnibus,* a program of decidedly elite culture but aimed at a mass audience presumed to want to be led upward rather than downward. Other, occasional broadcasts also aimed higher. In a 1950s program designed for young audiences, Leonard Bernstein electrified a generation of viewers and listeners with his demonstration of why an orchestra needs a conductor. Bernstein and the producers of the program assumed that most children—indeed, most people in the viewing audience—had never been to a live concert, but that did not deter the program's creators from making an intelligent point. The composer began at the podium, started the orchestra on a familiar classical theme, and then walked away, leaving the orchestra to its own devices; within a minute, the music turned dissonant and sour, as each instrument player followed his or her own beat. When Bernstein returned to explain what precisely a conductor does, very few in the home mass audience dared turn to another channel.

7   It had been the function of entertainment producers for many centuries to adhere to elite standards and to assume that part of their task was to bring wider and wider audiences up to those standards. That task was most overtly pursued in the age of Addison, Steele, and Henry Fielding, who wrote popular plays and novels. Many of their works were transparently about the spoken word. They offered readers choice phrases to repeat as well as models of good and bad speech. Television now provides models of words to say and how to say them; however, the models are too often based on the worst uses of language. Rather than use their reserves of ingenuity to entertain, today's producers totally abandon any adherence to high standards or to educating as well as titillating audiences and fall back on the most

basic elements at their disposal—an attitude that fosters appeals to base instincts, the too ready exclusion of references to anything other than pop culture, and the endless recycling of familiar material. Circuitous marketing logic becomes self-fulfilling prophecy, and it is heresy to suggest that the intellectually more complicated products of the foreign film industry or the highbrow programs seen on public television might fare better in commercial terms if they had the same financial and promotional backing and the same wide distribution as the products of the mainstream. "Nobody ever went broke underestimating the taste of the American public" goes the phrase attributed to H. L. Mencken. He meant it as an indictment; today's pop culture purveyors treat it as a directive.

8   This directive implies a high degree of contempt for the audience. It expresses a belief that the audience is infinitely malleable and easily led, that it has no intelligence at all, or not enough to see through marketing tricks. It tries to turn audiences into mere consumers who have no more choice in how they react to a stimulus than do hungry animals confronted with food. As Theodor Adorno and the other members of the Frankfurt School pointed out fifty years ago, one of the main purposes of mass culture is to keep the consumer's responses at an infantile level, and thereby to manipulate the consumer with false promises of libidinal gratification.[2] In the ensuing half-century, the purveyors have only become more skilled at their task. The corollary of the directive about taste is that a product will make a great deal of money if it is aimed low. That belief—for it is only a guess—has become the engine of Hollywood, affecting every part of motion picture and television production, from casting to script development to the props on the set. The fact is that Hollywood producers cannot predict with any degree of certainty what will or will not make money. Out of fear of not making money, they resort to the elements that seem most likely to ensure that the product makes money. Certain stars are labeled as "bankable" because such a star's agreement to play a major role in a movie enables the producer to obtain funding for it. A star's bankability, in turn, derives from the presumed (and unproved) relationship between the degree of success of the star's most recent picture and his or her performance.

9   The marketing mentality also skews the writing process. To make a point about just this, one of the most successful American scriptwriters, William Goldman, cites in his memoir a pithy line from Joseph Mankiewicz's *The Barefoot Contessa,* which starred Humphrey Bogart and Ava Gardner. "What she's got, you couldn't spell, and what you've got, you *used* to have." In 1954, Goldman argues, that line could be put in the mouth of a minor character, Bogart's wife, but today it would have to be said by one of the stars, or it would be cut from the script: "Giving that line to the wife, in today's movie world, is not just incorrect screenwriting, it is lethal. Today, you must give the star everything."[3] Giving the star everything contributes to the downward spiral by centering movies more and more on the star's bankable presence. In similar moves based on marketing and appealing to base instincts, beautiful women and handsome men are always cast in the leading roles on the assumption that no one will want to gaze at a less than pretty face. When Farrah Fawcett was asked if it was the acting abilities of herself and the two other top

models in starring roles that ensured the success of the television series *Charlie's Angels,* she reportedly replied that it was more likely to have been the fact that none of the women wore brassieres.

10   Classic behavioral psychology experiments have repeatedly demonstrated that when image and sound are presented concurrently, a subject is better able to recall the image than the sound and retains that image in memory for a longer time. Producers seize on this, too, as rationale to get rid of words and to rely only on the visual nature of moving pictures. Where filmmakers err is in assuming that audiences always prefer the visual to the verbal or that film is only visual. There has always been tension between literacy and the visual image in films, but in the talking films of the 1930s and 1940s, dialogue was considered supremely important. The verbal byplay of Nick and Nora Charles in the *Thin Man* series of mystery films was one of its glories; by comparison, the character of the supposedly literate mystery novelist played by Angela Lansbury in *Murder, She Wrote* on television is entirely witless. The notion that a picture is worth a thousand words has wreaked insidious and far-reaching havoc in Hollywood, for now the film and television industries have embraced visual storytelling without pausing to determine which words a picture can or should replace. As most film and videotape editors will readily admit, the ultra-rapid cutting between images best exemplified by MTV videos, which has already taken over commercials and is creeping into all Hollywood feature and television production, is incapable of telling complex or subtle stories; it is most appropriately used in conveying emotional impact. The end result of choosing only pictures to tell stories is products in which rapidly changing images convey information in ways that are often deliberately illogical, disorienting, and surreal.

11   The need for writing good dialogue has been obviated by the producers' belief that audiences prefer physical action to words. Filmmakers are urged to give the audience more and more physical action, fewer and fewer words, and characters who are even less inclined to speech than the audience itself. Sylvester Stallone—more precisely, the roles in which he has achieved his greatest commercial success—is a prime example of the current generation of inarticulate screen heroes who make John Wayne's strong-and-silent cowboys and soldiers seem loquacious by comparison. Stallone's Rocky Balboa and John Rambo, and the appallingly similar characters played by Arnold Schwarzenegger, by Clint Eastwood as Dirty Harry, by Mel Gibson in the *Lethal Weapon* series, by Bruce Willis in the *Die Hard* films, and even by John Travolta in *Saturday Night Fever* or *Pulp Fiction* speak in fragments or incomplete sentences when they voice words at all, and employ a severely stunted, reflexively profane vocabulary. Equally important, they and virtually all the other characters in these films are ignorant of history and make no references to literature, art, or anything else except other recent products of popular culture, such as commercial advertisements. When they have a choice between physical and verbal solutions to a given problem, they unhesitatingly go for the blow. If they have any breath to spare, they accompany it with a wisecrack.

12   To have characters speak lines that are brief, pithy, and memorable is one of the goals of all Hollywood films and the source of the scriptwriter's imperative to

"write short." Never say in ten words what you can get across in five. Linda Seger, a script doctor, gives this advice in *Making a Good Script Great:* After a writer prunes the script so that it focuses mainly on the images and actions of the story, the writer should reexamine what has been removed. "If these sections were long speeches, see if you can reduce the pertinent information to a sentence or two. . . . If some of [the scenes] reveal character through talk, try to find an image or an action you can substitute for the dialogue."[4] The imperative has corollaries, such as never have a character who overexplains, and never continue a scene past a trenchant "button line." William Goldman, the screenwriter of *Butch Cassidy and the Sundance Kid,* a movie well regarded for its quips, quotes in his memoir the scene in which Butch walks up to a modern-looking, heavily barred bank and asks a guard, "What was the matter with the old bank this town used to have? It was beautiful." The guard says that people kept robbing it, and Butch walks off, saying, "That's a small price to pay for beauty." Seventeen years after the movie, Goldman reprints the dialogue in his memoir, and comments:

> I happen not to believe Butch's final retort—I don't think he'd say it and I think it's smart-ass. There's a lot about the screenplay I don't like, the smart-assness just being one of them. I also find that there are too many reversals and that the entire enterprise suffers, on more than one occasion, from a case of the cutes.[5]

13   The idealization of writing short and cute in movies is the logical result of competition with television and its cult of the one-liner, the quotable joke that enlivens situation comedies. Each sitcom character must respond to any comment with a single, snappy, mirth-provoking line; just in case we miss the joke, it is highlighted by a laugh track that reminds us to join in the fun. Let us cheerfully admit that the writing in sitcoms is frequently funny—I myself cannot watch a good sitcom without being often moved to laughter, and neither can you. The problem is that the producer's compulsive need to make the audience chortle at every second or third line is, for the writer, a smotherer of invention. Plot and character development, or the interplay of themes and ideas, must be forgone in the all-consuming quest for the perfect retort.

14   In the era before cable television, the prevailing theory of programming was based on the view that Americans wanted to watch something, few choices were available, and the least objectionable program, or LOP, would be the most widely watched. Now that the menu of viewing choices has been expanded, the LOP has been replaced by the LCD—the lowest common denominator. This principle operates, for example, in the decision to schedule the most sensational made-for-television and feature movies during May and November. In those "sweeps" periods, viewership is measured and ratings are established, and they become the basis for the advertising rates on which the networks' and syndicators' revenues depend. Among the principal ingredients in the offerings made especially for sweeps period are larger than usual doses of violence. Violence is hip right now, and highly commercial. For instance, violence is an accepted sales tool for the breakfast cereals

and toys advertised on children's cartoon programs. A recent study by Gerbner and associates tallied 7.8 violent acts per children's program, or 32 per hour—more such acts per hour than in any other form of programming. The National Coalition on Television Violence says that the leader in showcasing violence is the cable network MTV, with 29 instances of "violent or hostile imagery" per hour, and with one-third of its videos containing some violent elements.[6]

15   A controversy rages over whether depicted violence in entertainment has any direct relationship to the raising of the level of violence in individuals or in society as a whole. What is more relevant to this discussion is the dire effect that the producers' craving for violence has on writers and other creators of entertainment. The creative difficulty lies in the fact that violence is often so visually and emotionally compelling that it tends to overshadow any other dramatic element. When Shakespeare wrote his *Henry V,* he made sure that the battle of Agincourt took place offstage, and he invoked a "muse of fire" to help his audience properly imagine it. In Laurence Olivier's film adaptation of the play, made almost fifty years ago, the battle appears on screen but in a relatively tasteful and limited way; in Kenneth Branagh's much lauded 1992 film version, the battle takes up many minutes, during which Branagh fills the screen with slow-motion shots of swords and spears impaling bodies amid mud and flying gobs of blood and bone—so much detail that the battle sequence nearly overwhelms the original text.

16   Violence takes focus. Violence is more quickly depicted than verbal action, and in films and television, every second counts. Violence obscures plots that make no sense and characters that have no depth. Violence does not require good actors and actresses, or even performers who have good speaking voices. Two other LCD elements are on the rise in commercial broadcasting, overt sex and profanity, and the same charges can be leveled against them: They take focus, serve to obscure silly plots and weak characters, are more easily portrayed, and do not require deft performers.

17   The 1993 fall television season, according to the critic Tom Shales, reflected an "obsession" with sex that "seems to have been cranked up to a new high." Shales reprinted examples of smutty jokes and profanity from pilots he had watched, including bits from such new programs as *Family Album, It Had To Be You,* and *The Trouble With Larry* (CBS); *Daddy Dearest* and *Living Single* (Fox); *The John Larroquette Show* (NBC); and *Grace Under Fire* (ABC).[7] By common consent, the worst offender of the fall 1993 season was not a sitcom but an hour-long drama, *N.Y.P.D. Blue* (ABC), which featured nudity and language previously considered too obscene for prime-time network television. The admired producer Steven Bochco, whose company created the series, told reporters that he had deliberately incorporated those elements because he is in a struggle for viewers with cable television, which runs full-length motion pictures with "adult" content. "I don't think we can at ten o'clock with our hour dramas effectively compete any longer unless we can paint with some of the same colors that you can paint with when you make a movie," he stated.[8] The shock value of the nudity and profanity attracted some

viewers and repelled others, but those "colors" were toned down after the first few episodes. Later reviews, which were quite enthusiastic, stressed the series' good stories and believable characters. Indeed, *N.Y.P.D. Blue* has gone on to become a critical and commercial success, and many critics and viewers have wondered why the creators considered it important in the first place to pander to base instincts. It appears that nudity and profanity were deemed essential at the outset because the creators and the ABC network executives were somehow afraid not to include LCD elements, lest their enterprise fail commercially for lack of them. They were also enamored of the publicity generated by the controversy over the nudity and profanity. Heightening viewer interest through controversy is a well-known tool in the marketer's belt. With these craven (and possibly unnecessary) actions on the part of the creators and the network, the downward regressive cycle took another turn for the worse.

Notes

1. Figures from Anthony R. Pratkanis and Eliot Aronson, *Age of Propaganda,* 1992; Kathleen Hall Jamieson and Karlyn Kohrs Campbell, *The Interplay of Influence,* 1988; Peter M. Nichols, "Home Video" column, *New York Times,* July 30, 1993. *Newsweek,* August 2, 1993, reports that Nielsen Media Research estimates the average daily viewing time for television as six hours and forty-six minutes.
2. See Martin Jay, *The Dialectical Imagination: A History of the Frankfurt School and the Institute of Social Research, 1923–1950,* 1973.
3. William Goldman, *Adventures in the Screen Trade,* 1983.
4. Linda Seger, *Making a Good Script Great,* 1987.
5. Goldman, *Adventures in Screen Trade.*
6. Statistics reported in "Kiddie TV Packs the Most Punch," an Associated Press story in *New York Post,* January 28, 1993, and Don Feder, "MTV = Mindless TV," *New York Post,* April 22, 1993.
7. Tom Shales, "Saturated with Sex," *New York Post,* September 13, 1993.
8. Elizabeth Kolbert, "Not Only Bochco's Uniforms Are Blue," *New York Times;* July 26, 1993.

THINKING CRITICALLY

1. Discuss how Shachtman's opening paragraphs establish the tone and theme for his essay. Is his choice of the story of the novelist-turned-screenwriter an effective way to introduce his topic? Explain.

2. What does "aiming lower" mean for television scripts and language? Does this principle have implications for spoken language as a whole? Why or why not?

3. How does Shachtman's use of the history of television dialogue and language support his argument regarding television today? Are his comparisons relevant? Explain.

4. What is the relationship between the skewed reality depicted on television and the decline of articulate speech? Explain.

5. What is the author advocating in this essay? Who is his audience? Cite specific examples from the text that reveal his assumptions about his audience.

6. What is the connection between advertising and marketing interests and television language? How has advertising influenced scripts and television programming? In your opinion, has advertising had a detrimental influence on television language? Why or why not?

7. In several parts of this essay, the author speaks directly to his readers. Evaluate this writing technique.

WRITING ASSIGNMENTS

1. In this essay, the author explains how television presents viewers with a skewed sense of reality. Write an essay exploring this issue. Should television more accurately depict reality—the people, places, and circumstances of life? What are the possible consequences when television exaggerates reality such as crime? Support your essay with information from the essay and your personal experience.

2. Shachtman compares television dialogue from the past and present. Conduct your own analysis of television language. Watch several television programs from the 1950s or 1960s, and from current offerings. Try to watch programs that deal with similar subject matter, such as family comedies, or detective or crime programs. Has television dialogue and the general use of language changed over the last forty years? If so, in what ways?

■ MAKING CONNECTIONS

1. Over the course of a week, watch several different local newscasts and consider the ways they support or refute Postman's and Power's assertions on TV news broadcasts. How are the programs similar and different? How do the programs distinguish themselves from each other? Or do they? How are the stories they present similar or different? Explain.

2. How has bad language infiltrated the film and television industry over the last decade? Using library resources or the Internet, research what laws or codes guided the use of language in the television industry over the last fifty years. How have standards changed over time? Once you have gathered your research, write an essay about which standards or codes seem most appropriate for today's audiences.

3. You are a television news producer who must develop a local news broadcast program for a local network. Conduct a survey on what people want to watch on the television news. Consider your questions carefully. After gathering your information, design your newscast and explain in detail the rationale behind your program's design. How much does your program resemble others already on the air? What distinguishes your program? Or do you rely on popular conventions already in place? Explain.

4. The BBC's *Talking Point* forum invited readers to respond with their personal opinion of bad language on television. Take an informal poll of your own regarding foul language on television and see if your results are similar to the ones posted by the *BBC Online*, or quite different. Be sure to poll people of different ages, since only asking young people may skew your re-

sults. Brainstorm a list of about ten questions to include in your poll. You may want to ask for information such as: age, sex, and how much television the respondent watches in an average week in addition to the questions about language.

5. Brainstorm a list of shows that seek to "push the envelope" in terms of foul language; watch one or two of these shows, and then write a critique of these programs asserting your personal viewpoint on this issue.

Two-Headed Monsters
From the Columbia Journalism Review

Words are the business of journalism, and accuracy of usage is undoubtedly the pride of any newspaper. Occasionally, however, words may turn against the meaning intended, as is the case when printer's devils plague the presses. The result is news gone askew. Such was the case in the real headlines that follow, in which unforeseen misprints, double entendres, and grammatical goofs turned into news that did not fit the print. The *Columbia Journalism Review,* a watchdog magazine of the media, has a department called "The Lower Case" that gathers such gaffes; these examples were originally reprinted there.

Chinese general donated to Clinton campaign
The Pantagraph (Bloomington-Normal, Ill.) 4/5/99

Death to be explained
Home News Tribune (East Brunswick, N.J.) 4/16/98

Litigant has no right to lay adviser in chambers
London Times 3/8/99

Judge dismisses charges against duck protecting non-hunter
The Knoxville News-Sentinel 2/24/99

Breast implants prominent
The Olathe (Kan.) *Daily News* 2/2/99

Clinton takes credit for drop in unwed birth rate
The Ashland (Ore.) *Daily Tidings* 10/5/96

Shooting witness helps build murder case
The Times (Northwest Ind.) 7/10/98

Experts suggest education standards might be to lofty

The Courier-News (N.J.) 1/25/99

Steamed pudding and crap dip

The Sacramento Beef 12/27/98

FBI adds to reward for killing suspects

The Olympian (Olympia, Wash.) 7/15/98

Socks Lower in Tokyo

The New York Times 8/17/98

Lamb Retiring From USU Animal Department

The Times (Northwest Ind.) 7/10/98

Giant women's health study short of volunteers

Aruba Today (Caribbean) 7/13/97

U.S., Brits agree to bomb trial at Hague

Jefferson City Post-Tribune (Mo.) Daily News 08/24/98

Call for Ban on Toys For Tots Made of Vinyl

San Francisco Chronicle 11/20/98

Toxic street residents storm out of public meeting

Daily News (Nanaimo, B.C.) 08/13/98

Doctor discusses his action with infant

Seattle Post-Intelligencer 09/07/98

School testing mushrooms

Marshfield News-Herald (Wis.) 08/25/98

Hitler used to sell potato chips

The New Mexican 6/2/98

Dog rules on agenda in Old Orchard

Portland (Maine) Press Herald 5/18/99

Pope remembers shooting victims

The New World (Chicago) 4/25/99

Mattel recalls eating dolls

The Burlington (Vt.) *Free Press* 1/7/97

UMaine women selling fast in Portland

Morning Sentinel (Waterville, Me.) 12/18/96

Banana faces sodomy charges

The Examiner (Cork, Ireland) 5/9/97

Great night for Trojans

Terra Linda girls on fire

Marin Independent Journal (Calif.) 2/22/96

Man kills himself hours before appearing in court

Richmond Hill-Bryan County News (Ga.) 8/6/97

Will women in combat stop sexual misconduct?

New Holstein (Wis.) *Reporter* 12/19/96

Police patrol vandalized site nearly 40 times

The Orlando Sentinel 4/17/99

9 hammers in home of hooker attack suspect

San Francisco Examiner 10/24/97

■ THE LANGUAGE OF ADVERTISING

With These Words, I Can Sell You Anything
William Lutz

In "Politics and the English Language," featured in Chapter Three, George Orwell writes that the "great enemy of clear language is insincerity." To fill the gap "between one's real and one's declared aims," he explains, one simply resorts to inflated language to give importance to the insignificant. Of course, Orwell is talking about the irresponsible habit of government officials who use language to exploit and manipulate. But he could just as well have been talking about the language of advertisers. At least that's the opinion of William Lutz, who assails the linguistic habits of hucksters. In his essay below, he alerts readers to the special power of "weasel words"—those familiar and sneaky critters that "appear to say one thing when in fact they say the opposite, or nothing at all."

William Lutz has been called the George Orwell of the 1990s. Chair of the Committee on Public Doublespeak of the National Council of Teachers of English, Lutz edits the *Quarterly Review of Doublespeak*, a magazine dedicated to the eradication of misleading official statements. He also teaches in the English department at Rutgers University. He is the author of *Beyond Nineteen Eighty-Four* (1989), *Doublespeak* (1989), from which this essay is taken, and most recently, *Doublespeak Defined* (1999).

1 One problem advertisers have when they try to convince you that the product they are pushing is really different from other, similar products is that their claims are subject to some laws. Not a lot of laws, but there are some designed to prevent fraudulent or untruthful claims in advertising. Even during the happy years of non-regulation under President Ronald Reagan, the FTC did crack down on the more blatant abuses in advertising claims. Generally speaking, advertisers have to be careful in what they say in their ads, in the claims they make for the products they advertise. Parity claims are safe because they are legal and supported by a number of court decisions. But beyond parity claims there are weasel words.

2 Advertisers use weasel words to appear to be making a claim for a product when in fact they are making no claim at all. Weasel words get their name from the way weasels eat the eggs they find in the nests of other animals. A weasel will make a small hole in the egg, suck out the insides, then place the egg back in the nest. Only when the egg is examined closely is it found to be hollow. That's the way it is with weasel words in advertising: Examine weasel words closely and you'll find that they're as hollow as any egg sucked by a weasel. Weasel words appear to say one thing when in fact they say the opposite, or nothing at all.

"Help"—The Number One Weasel Word

3 The biggest weasel word used in advertising doublespeak is "help." Now "help" only means to aid or assist, nothing more. It does not mean to conquer, stop, eliminate, end, solve, heal, cure, or anything else. But once the ad says "help," it can say just about anything after that because "help" qualifies everything coming after it. The trick is that the claim that comes after the weasel word is usually so strong and so dramatic that you forget the word "help" and concentrate only on the dramatic claim. You read into the ad a message that the ad does not contain. More importantly, the advertiser is not responsible for the claim that you read into the ad, even though the advertiser wrote the ad so you would read that claim into it.

4 The next time you see an ad for a cold medicine that promises that it "helps relieve cold symptoms fast," don't rush out to buy it. Ask yourself what this claim is really saying. Remember, "helps" means only that the medicine will aid or assist. What will it aid or assist in doing? Why, "relieve" your cold "symptoms." "Relieve" only means to ease, alleviate, or mitigate, not to stop, end, or cure. Nor does the claim say how much relieving this medicine will do. Nowhere does this ad claim it will cure anything. In fact, the ad doesn't even claim it will *do* anything at all. The ad only claims that it will aid in relieving (not curing) your cold symptoms,

which are probably a runny nose, watery eyes, and a headache. In other words, this medicine probably contains a standard decongestant and some aspirin. By the way, what does "fast" mean? Ten minutes, one hour, one day? What is fast to one person can be very slow to another. Fast is another weasel word.

5　　Ad claims using "help" are among the most popular ads. One says, "Helps keep you young looking," but then a lot of things will help keep you young looking, including exercise, rest, good nutrition, and a facelift. More importantly, this ad doesn't say the product will keep you young, only "young *looking*." Someone may look young to one person and old to another.

6　　A toothpaste ad says, "Helps prevent cavities," but it doesn't say it will actually prevent cavities. Brushing your teeth regularly, avoiding sugars in foods, and flossing daily will also help prevent cavities. A liquid cleaner ad says, "Helps keep your home germ free," but it doesn't say it actually kills germs, nor does it even specify which germs it might kill.

7　　"Help" is such a useful weasel word that it is often combined with other action-verb weasel words such as "fight" and "control." Consider the claim, "Helps control dandruff symptoms with regular use." What does it really say? It will assist in controlling (not eliminating, stopping, ending, or curing) the *symptoms* of dandruff, not the cause of dandruff nor the dandruff itself. What are the symptoms of dandruff? The ad deliberately leaves that undefined, but assume that the symptoms referred to in the ad are the flaking and itching commonly associated with dandruff. But just shampooing with *any* shampoo will temporarily eliminate these symptoms, so this shampoo isn't any different from any other. Finally, in order to benefit from this product, you must use it regularly. What is "regular use"—daily, weekly, hourly? Using another shampoo "regularly" will have the same effect. Nowhere does this advertising claim say this particular shampoo stops, eliminates, or cures dandruff. In fact, this claim says nothing at all, thanks to all the weasel words.

8　　Look at ads in magazines and newspapers, listen to ads on radio and television, and you'll find the word "help" in ads for all kinds of products. How often do you read or hear such phrases as "helps stop . . . ," "helps overcome . . . ," "helps eliminate . . . ," "helps you feel . . . ," or "helps you look . . . "? If you start looking for this weasel word in advertising, you'll be amazed at how often it occurs. Analyze the claims in the ads using "help," and you will discover that these ads are really saying nothing.

9　　There are plenty of other weasel words used in advertising. In fact, there are so many that to list them all would fill the rest of this book. But, in order to identify the doublespeak of advertising and understand the real meaning of an ad, you have to be aware of the most popular weasel words in advertising today.

Virtually Spotless

10　　One of the most powerful weasel words is "virtually," a word so innocent that most people don't pay any attention to it when it is used in an advertising claim. But watch out. "Virtually" is used in advertising claims that appear to make specific, definite promises when there is no promise. After all, what does "virtually" mean? It means "in essence of effect, although not in fact." Look at that definition again. "Virtually" means *not in fact*. It does *not* mean "almost" or "just about the same as," or anything else. And before you dismiss all this concern over such a small word, remember that small words can have big consequences.

11   In 1971 a federal court rendered its decision on a case brought by a woman who became pregnant while taking birth control pills. She sued the manufacturer, Eli Lilly and Company, for breach of warranty. The woman lost her case. Basing its ruling on a statement in the pamphlet accompanying the pills, which stated that, "When taken as directed, the tablets offer virtually 100% protection," the court ruled that there was no warranty, expressed or implied, that the pills were absolutely effective. In its ruling, the court pointed out that, according to *Webster's Third New International Dictionary*, "virtually" means "almost entirely" and clearly does not mean "absolute" (*Whittington* v. *Eli Lilly and Company,* 333 F. Supp. 98). In other words, the Eli Lilly company was really saying that its birth control pill, even when taken as directed, *did not in fact* provide 100 percent protection against pregnancy. But Eli Lilly didn't want to put it that way because then many women might not have bought Lilly's birth control pills.

12   The next time you see the ad that says that this dishwasher detergent "leaves dishes virtually spotless," just remember how advertisers twist the meaning of the weasel word "virtually." You can have lots of spots on your dishes after using this detergent and the ad claim will still be true, because what this claim really means is that this detergent does not *in fact* leave your dishes spotless. Whenever you see or hear an ad claim that uses the word "virtually," just translate that claim into its real meaning. So the television set that is "virtually trouble free" becomes the television set that is not in fact trouble free, the "virtually foolproof operation" of any appliance becomes an operation that is in fact not foolproof, and the product that "virtually never needs service" becomes the product that is not in fact service free.

New and Improved

13 If "new" is the most frequently used word on a product package, "improved" is the second most frequent. In fact, the two words are almost always used together. It seems just about everything sold these days is "new and improved." The next time you're in the supermarket, try counting the number of times you see these words on products. But you'd better do it while you're walking down just one aisle, otherwise you'll need a calculator to keep track of your counting.

14   Just what do these words mean? The use of the word "new" is restricted by regulations, so an advertiser can't just use the word on a product or in an ad without meeting certain requirements. For example, a product is considered new for about six months during a national advertising campaign. If the product is being advertised only in a limited test market area, the word can be used longer, and in some instances has been used for as long as two years.

15   What makes a product "new"? Some products have been around for a long time, yet every once in a while you discover that they are being advertised as

"new." Well, an advertiser can call a product new if there has been "a material functional change" in the product. What is "a material functional change," you ask? Good question. In fact it's such a good question it's being asked all the time. It's up to the manufacturer to prove that the product has undergone such a change. And if the manufacturer isn't challenged on the claim, then there's no one to stop it. Moreover, the change does not have to be an improvement in the product. One manufacturer added an artificial lemon scent to a cleaning product and called it "new and improved," even though the product did not clean any better than without the lemon scent. The manufacturer defended the use of the word "new" on the grounds that the artificial scent changed the chemical formula of the product and therefore constituted "a material functional change."

16   Which brings up the word "improved." When used in advertising, "improved" does not mean "made better." It only means "changed" or "different from before." So, if the detergent maker puts a plastic pour spout on the box of detergent, the product has been "improved," and away we go with a whole new advertising campaign. Or, if the cereal maker adds more fruit or a different kind of fruit to the cereal, there's an improved product. Now you know why manufacturers are constantly making little changes in their products. Whole new advertising campaigns, designed to convince you that the product has been changed for the better, are based on small changes in superficial aspects of a product. The next time you see an ad for an "improved" product, ask yourself what was wrong with the old one. Ask yourself just how "improved" the product is. Finally, you might check to see whether the "improved" version costs more than the unimproved one. After all, someone has to pay for the millions of dollars spent advertising the improved product.

17   Of course, advertisers really like to run ads that claim a product is "new and improved." While what constitutes a "new" product may be subject to some regulation, "improved" is a subjective judgment. A manufacturer changes the shape of its stick deodorant, but the shape doesn't improve the function of the deodorant. That is, changing the shape doesn't affect the deodorizing ability of the deodorant, so the manufacturer calls it "improved." Another manufacturer adds ammonia to its liquid cleaner and calls it "new and improved." Since adding ammonia does affect the cleaning ability of the product, there has been a "material functional change" in the product, and the manufacturer can now call its cleaner "new," and "improved" as well. Now the weasel words "new and improved" are plastered all over the package and are the basis for a multimillion-dollar ad campaign. But after six months the word "new" will have to go, until someone can dream up another change in the product. Perhaps it will be adding color to the liquid, or changing the shape of the package, or maybe adding a new dripless pour spout, or perhaps a———. The "improvements" are endless, and so are the new advertising claims and campaigns.

18   "New" is just too useful and powerful a word in advertising for advertisers to pass it up easily. So they use weasel words that say "new" without really saying it. One of their favorites is "introducing," as in, "Introducing improved Tide," or "Introducing the stain remover." The first is simply saying, here's our improved soap: the second, here's our new advertising campaign for our detergent. Another favorite is "now," as in, "Now there's Sinex," which simply means that Sinex is

available. Then there are phrases like "Today's Chevrolet," "Presenting Dristan," and "A fresh way to start the day." The list is really endless because advertisers are always finding new ways to say "new" without really saying it. If there is a second edition of this book, I'll just call it the "new and improved" edition. Wouldn't you really rather have a "new and improved" edition of this book rather than a "second" edition?

Acts Fast

19 "Acts" and "works" are two popular weasel words in advertising because they bring action to the product and to the advertising claim. When you see the ad for the cough syrup that "Acts on the cough control center," ask yourself what this cough syrup is claiming to do. Well, it's just claiming to "act," to do something, to perform an action. What is it that the cough syrup does? The ad doesn't say. It only claims to perform an action or do something on your "cough control center." By the way, what and where is your "cough control center"? I don't remember learning about that part of the body in human biology class.

20   Ads that use such phrases as "acts fast," "acts against," "acts to prevent," and the like are saying essentially nothing, because "act" is a word empty of any specific meaning. The ads are always careful not to specify exactly what "act" the product performs. Just because a brand of aspirin claims to "act fast" for headache relief doesn't mean this aspirin is any better than any other aspirin. What is the "act" that this aspirin performs? You're never told. Maybe it just dissolves quickly. Since aspirin is a parity product, all aspirin is the same and therefore functions the same.

Works Like Anything Else

21 If you don't find the word "acts" in an ad, you will probably find the weasel word "works." In fact, the two words are almost interchangeable in advertising. Watch out for ads that say a product "works against," "works like," "works for," or "works longer." As with "acts," "works" is the same meaningless verb used to make you think that this product really does something, and maybe even something special or unique. But "works," like "acts," is basically a word empty of any specific meaning.

Like Magic

22 Whenever advertisers want you to stop thinking about the product and to start thinking about something bigger, better, or more attractive than the product, they use that very popular weasel word, "like." The word "like" is the advertiser's equivalent of a magician's use of misdirection. "Like" gets you to ignore the product and concentrate on the claim the advertiser is making about it. "For skin like peaches and cream" claims the ad for a skin cream. What is this ad really claiming? It doesn't say this cream will give you peaches-and-cream skin. There is no verb in

this claim, so it doesn't even mention using the product. How is skin ever like "peaches and cream"? Remember, ads must be read literally and exactly, according to the dictionary definition of words. (Remember "virtually" in the Eli Lilly case.) The ad is making absolutely no promise or claim whatsoever for this skin cream. If you think this cream will give you soft, smooth, youthful-looking skin, you are the one who has read that meaning into the ad.

23   The wine that claims "It's like taking a trip to France" wants you to think about a romantic evening in Paris as you walk along the boulevard after a wonderful meal in an intimate little bistro. Of course, you don't really believe that a wine can take you to France, but the goal of the ad is to get you to think pleasant, romantic thoughts about France and not about how the wine tastes or how expensive it may be. That little word "like" has taken you away from crushed grapes into a world of your own imaginative making. Who knows, maybe the next time you buy wine, you'll think those pleasant thoughts when you see this brand of wine, and you'll buy it. Or, maybe you weren't even thinking about buying wine at all, but now you just might pick up a bottle the next time you're shopping. Ah, the power of "like" in advertising.

24   How about the most famous "like" claim of all, "Winston tastes good like a cigarette should"? Ignoring the grammatical error here, you might want to know what this claim is saying. Whether a cigarette tastes good or bad is a subjective judgment because what tastes good to one person may well taste horrible to another. Not everyone likes fried snails, even if they are called escargot. (*De gustibus non est disputandum,* which was probably the Roman rule for advertising as well as for defending the games in the Colosseum.) There are many people who say all cigarettes taste terrible, other people who say only some cigarettes taste all right, and still others who say all cigarettes taste good. Who's right? Everyone, because taste is a matter of personal judgment.

25   Moreover, note the use of the conditional, "should." The complete claim is, "Winston tastes good like a cigarette should taste." But should cigarettes taste good? Again, this is a matter of personal judgment and probably depends most on one's experiences with smoking. So, the Winston ad is simply saying that Winston cigarettes are just like any other cigarette: Some people like them and some people don't. On that statement R. J. Reynolds conducted a very successful multimillion-dollar advertising campaign that helped keep Winston the number-two-selling cigarette in the United States, close behind number one, Marlboro.

Can It Be Up to the Claim

26 Analyzing ads for doublespeak requires that you pay attention to every word in the ad and determine what each word really means. Advertisers try to wrap their claims in language that sound concrete, specific, and objective, when in fact the language of advertising is anything but. Your job is to read carefully and listen critically so that when the announcer says that "Crest can be of significant value . . ." you know immediately that this claim says absolutely nothing. Where is the doublespeak in this ad? Start with the second word.

27   Once again, you have to look at what words really mean, not what you think they mean or what the advertiser wants you to think they mean. The ad for Crest only says that using Crest "can be" of "significant value." What really throws you off in this ad is the brilliant use of "significant." It draws your attention to the word "value" and makes you forget that the ad only claims that Crest "can be." The ad doesn't say that Crest *is* of value, only that it is "able" or "possible" to be of value, because that's all that "can" means.

28   It's so easy to miss the importance of those little words, "can be." Almost as easy as missing the importance of the words "up to" in an ad. These words are very popular in sale ads. You know, the ones that say, "Up to 50% Off!" Now, what does that claim mean? Not much, because the store or manufacturer has to reduce the price of only a few items by 50 percent. Everything else can be reduced a lot less, or not even reduced. Moreover, don't you want to know 50 percent off of what? Is it 50 percent off the "manufacturer's suggested list price," which is the highest possible price? Was the price artificially inflated and then reduced? In other ads, "up to" expresses an ideal situation. The medicine that works "up to ten times faster," the battery that lasts "up to twice as long," and the soap that gets you "up to twice as clean" all are based on ideal situations for using those products, situations in which you can be sure you will never find yourself.

Unfinished Words

29 Unfinished words are a kind of "up to" claim in advertising. The claim that a battery lasts "up to twice as long" usually doesn't finish the comparison—twice as long as what? A birthday candle? A tank of gas? A cheap battery made in a country not noted for its technological achievements? The implication is that the battery lasts twice as long as batteries made by other battery makers, or twice as long as earlier model batteries made by the advertiser, but the ad doesn't really make these claims. You read these claims into the ad, aided by the visual images the advertiser so carefully provides.

30   Unfinished words depend on you to finish them, to provide the words the advertisers so thoughtfully left out of the ad. Pall Mall cigarettes were once advertised as "A longer, finer and milder smoke." The question is, longer, finer, and milder than what? The aspirin that claims it contains "Twice as much of the pain reliever doctors recommend most" doesn't tell you what pain reliever it contains twice as much of. (By the way, it's aspirin. That's right; it just contains twice the amount of aspirin. And how much is twice the amount? Twice of what amount?) Panadol boasts that "nobody reduces fever faster," but, since Panadol is a parity product, this claim simply means that Panadol isn't any better than any other product in its parity class. "You can be sure if it's Westinghouse," you're told, but just exactly what it is you can be sure of is never mentioned. "Magnavox gives you more" doesn't tell you what you get more of. More value? More television? More than they gave you before? It sounds nice, but it means nothing, until you fill in the claim with your own words, the words the advertisers didn't use. Since each of us fills in

the claim differently, the ad and the product can become all things to all people, and not promise a single thing.

31   Unfinished words abound in advertising because they appear to promise so much. More importantly, they can be joined with powerful visual images on television to appear to be making significant promises about a product's effectiveness without really making any promises. In a television ad, the aspirin product that claims fast relief can show a person with a headache taking the product and then, in what appears to be a matter of minutes, claiming complete relief. This visual image is far more powerful than any claim made in unfinished words. Indeed, the visual image completes the unfinished words for you, filling in with pictures what the words leave out. And you thought that ads didn't affect you. What brand of aspirin do you use?

32   Some years ago, Ford's advertisements proclaimed "Ford LTD—700% quieter." Now, what do you think Ford was claiming with these unfinished words? What was the Ford LTD quieter than? A Cadillac? A Mercedes Benz? A BMW? Well, when the FTC asked Ford to substantiate this unfinished claim, Ford replied that it meant that the inside of the LTD was 700% quieter than the outside. How did you finish those unfinished words when you first read them? Did you even come close to Ford's meaning?

Combining Weasel Words

33   A lot of ads don't fall neatly into one category or another because they use a variety of different devices and words. Different weasel words are often combined to make an ad claim. The claim, "Coffee-Mate gives coffee more body, more flavor," uses Unfinished Words ("more" than what?) and also uses words that have no specific meaning ("body" and "flavor"). Along with "taste" (remember the Winston ad and its claim to taste good), "body" and "flavor" mean nothing because their meaning is entirely subjective. To you, "body" in coffee might mean thick, black, almost bitter coffee, while I might take it to mean a light brown, delicate coffee. Now, if you think you understood that last sentence, read it again, because it said nothing of objective value; it was filled with weasel words of no specific meaning: "thick," "black," "bitter," "light brown," and "delicate." Each of those words has no specific, objective meaning, because each of us can interpret them differently.

34   Try this slogan: "Looks, smells, tastes like ground-roast coffee." So, are you now going to buy Taster's Choice instant coffee because of this ad? "Looks," "smells," "and "tastes" are all words with no specific meaning and depend on your interpretation of them for any meaning. Then there's that great weasel word "like," which simply suggests a comparison but does not make the actual connection between the product and the quality. Besides, do you know what "ground-roast" coffee is? I don't, but it sure sounds good. So, out of seven words in this ad, four are definite weasel words, two are quite meaningless, and only one has any clear meaning.

35   Remember the Anacin ad—"Twice as much of the pain reliever doctors recommend most"? There's a whole lot of weaseling going on in this ad. First, what's

the pain reliever they're talking about in this ad? Aspirin, of course. In fact, any time you see or hear an ad using those words "pain reliever," you can automatically substitute the word "aspirin" for them. (Makers of acetaminophen and ibuprofen pain relievers are careful in their advertising to identify their products as nonaspirin products.) So, now we know that Anacin has aspirin in it. Moreover, we know that Anacin has twice as much aspirin in it, but we don't know twice as much as what. Does it have twice as much aspirin as an ordinary aspirin tablet? If so, what is an ordinary aspirin tablet, and how much aspirin does it contain? Twice as much as Excedrin or Bufferin? Twice as much as a chocolate chip cookie? Remember those Unfinished Words and how they lead you on without saying anything.

36   Finally, what about those doctors who are doing all that recommending? Who are they? How many of them are there? What kind of doctors are they? What are their qualifications? Who asked them about recommending pain relievers? What other pain relievers did they recommend? And there are a whole lot more questions about this "poll" of doctors to which I'd like to know the answers, but you get the point. Sometimes, when I call my doctor, she tells me to take two aspirin and call her office in the morning. Is that where Anacin got this ad?

Read the Label, or the Brochure

37 Weasel words aren't just found on television, on the radio, or in newspaper and magazine ads. Just about any language associated with a product will contain the doublespeak of advertising. Remember the Eli Lilly case and the doublespeak on the information sheet that came with the birth control pills. Here's another example.

38   In 1983, the Estée Lauder cosmetics company announced a new product called "Night Repair." A small brochure distributed with the product stated that "Night Repair was scientifically formulated in Estée Lauder's U.S. laboratories as part of the Swiss Age-Controlling Skincare Program. Although only nature controls the aging process, this program helps control the signs of aging and encourages skin to look and feel younger." You might want to read these two sentences again, because they sound great but say nothing.

39   First, note that the product was "scientifically formulated" in the company's laboratories. What does that mean? What constitutes a scientific formulation? You wouldn't expect the company to say that the product was casually, mechanically, or carelessly formulated, or just thrown together one day when the people in the white coats didn't have anything better to do. But the word "scientifically" lends an air of precision and promise that just isn't there.

40   It is the second sentence, however, that's really weasely, both syntactically and semantically. The only factual part of this sentence is the introductory dependent clause—"only nature controls the aging process." Thus, the only fact in the ad is relegated to a dependent clause, a clause dependent on the main clause, which contains no factual or definite information at all and indeed purports to contradict the independent clause. The new "skincare program" (notice it's not a skin cream but a "program") does not claim to stop or even retard the aging process. What, then,

does Night Repair, at a price of over \$35 (in 1983 dollars) for a .87-ounce bottle do? According to this brochure, nothing. It only "helps," and the brochure does not say how much it helps. Moreover, it only "helps control," and then it only helps control the "*signs* of aging," not the aging itself. Also, it "encourages" skin not to *be* younger but only to "look and feel" younger. The brochure does not say younger than what. Of the sixteen words in the main clause of this second sentence, nine are weasel words. So, before you spend all that money for Night Repair, or any other cosmetic product, read the words carefully, and then decide if you're getting what you think you're paying for.

Other Tricks of the Trade

41 Advertisers' use of doublespeak is endless. The best way advertisers can make something out of nothing is through words. Although there are a lot of visual images used on television and in magazines and newspapers, every advertiser wants to create that memorable line that will stick in the public consciousness. I am sure pure joy reigned in one advertising agency when a study found that children who were asked to spell the word "relief" promptly and proudly responded "r-o-l-a-i-d-s."

42 The variations, combinations, and permutations of doublespeak used in advertising go on and on, running from the use of rhetorical questions ("Wouldn't you really rather have a Buick?" "If you can't trust Prestone, who can you trust?") to flattering you with compliments ("The lady has taste." "We think a cigar smoker is someone special." "You've come a long way baby."). You know, of course, how you're *supposed* to answer those questions, and you know that those compliments are just leading up to the sales pitches for the products. Before you dismiss such tricks of the trade as obvious, however, just remember that all of these statements and questions were part of very successful advertising campaigns.

43 A more subtle approach is the ad that proclaims a supposedly unique quality for a product, a quality that really isn't unique. "If it doesn't say Goodyear, it can't be polyglas." Sounds good, doesn't it? Polyglas is available only from Goodyear because Goodyear copyrighted that trade name. Any other tire manufacturer could make exactly the same tire but could not call it "polyglas," because that would be copyright infringement. "Polyglas" is simply Goodyear's name for its fiberglass-reinforced tire.

44 Since we like to think of ourselves as living in a technologically advanced country, science and technology have a great appeal in selling products. Advertisers are quick to use scientific doublespeak to push their products. There are all kinds of elixirs, additives, scientific potions, and mysterious mixtures added to all kinds of products. Gasoline contains "HTA," "F–130," "Platformate," and other chemical-sounding additives, but nowhere does an advertisement give any real information about the additive.

45 Shampoo, deodorant, mouthwash, cold medicine, sleeping pills, and any number of other products all seem to contain some special chemical ingredient that allows them to work wonders. "Certs contains a sparkling drop of Retsyn." So what?

What's "Retsyn"? What's it do? What's so special about it? When they don't have a secret ingredient in their product, advertisers still find a way to claim scientific validity. There's "Sinarest. Created by a research scientist who actually gets sinus headaches." Sounds nice, but what kind of research does this scientist do? How do you know if she is any kind of expert on sinus medicine? Besides, this ad doesn't tell you a thing about the medicine itself and what it does.

Advertising Doublespeak Quick Quiz

46 Now it's time to test your awareness of advertising doublespeak. (You didn't think I would just let you read this and forget it, did you?) The following is a list of statements from some recent ads. Your job is to figure out what each of these ads really says:

DOMINO'S PIZZA: "Because nobody delivers better."

SINUTAB: "It can stop the pain."

TUMS: "The stronger acid neutralizer."

MAXIMUM STRENGTH DRISTAN: "Strong medicine for tough sinus colds."

LISTERMINT: "Making your mouth a cleaner place."

CASCADE: "For virtually spotless dishes nothing beats Cascade."

NUPRIN: "Little. Yellow. Different. Better."

ANACIN: "Better relief."

SUDAFED: "Fast sinus relief that won't put you fast asleep."

ADVIL: "Advanced medicine for pain."

PONDS COLD CREAM: "Ponds cleans like no soap can."

MILLER LITE BEER: "Tastes great. Less filling."

PHILIPS MILK OF MAGNESIA: "Nobody treats you better than MOM (Philips Milk of Magnesia)."

BAYER: "The wonder drug that works wonders."

CRACKER BARREL: "Judged to be the best."

KNORR: "Where taste is everything."

ANUSOL: "Anusol is the word to remember for relief."

DIMETAPP: "It relieves kids as well as colds."

LIQUID DRANO: "The liquid strong enough to be called Drāno."

JOHNSON & JOHNSON BABY POWDER: "Like magic for your skin."

PURITAN: "Make it your oil for life."

PAM: "Pam, because how you cook is as important as what you cook."

IVORY SHAMPOO AND CONDITIONER: "Leave your hair feeling Ivory clean."

TYLENOL GEL-CAPS: "It's not a capsule. It's better."

ALKA-SELTZER PLUS: "Fast, effective relief for winter colds."

The World of Advertising

47 In the world of advertising, people wear "dentures," not false teeth; they suffer from "occasional irregularity," not constipation; they need deodorants for their "nervous wetness," not for sweat; they use "bathroom tissue," not toilet paper; and they don't dye their hair, they "tint" or "rinse" it. Advertisements offer "real counterfeit diamonds" without the slightest hint of embarrassment, or boast of goods made out of "genuine imitation leather" or "virgin vinyl."

48 In the world of advertising, the girdle becomes a "body shaper," "form persuader," "control garment," "controller," "outerwear enhancer," "body garment," or "anti-gravity panties," and is sold with such trade names as "The Instead," "The Free Spirit," and "The Body Briefer."

49 A study some years ago found the following words to be among the most popular used in U.S. television advertisements: "new," "improved," "better," "extra," "fresh," "clean," "beautiful," "free," "good," "great," and "light." At the same time, the following words were found to be among the most frequent on British television: "new," "good-better-best," "free," "fresh," "delicious," "full," "sure," "clean," "wonderful," and "special." While these words may occur most frequently in ads, and while ads may be filled with weasel words, you have to watch out for all the words used in advertising, not just the words mentioned here.

50 Every word in an ad is there for a reason; no word is wasted. Your job is to figure out exactly what each word is doing in an ad—what each word really means, not what the advertiser wants you to think it means. Remember, the ad is trying to get you to buy a product, so it will put the product in the best possible light, using any device, trick, or means legally allowed. Your only defense against advertising (besides taking up permanent residence on the moon) is to develop and use a strong critical reading, listening, and looking ability. Always ask yourself what the ad is *really* saying. When you see ads on television, don't be misled by the pictures, the visual images. What does the ad *say* about the product? What does the ad *not* say? What information is missing from the ad? Only by becoming an active, critical consumer of the doublespeak of advertising will you ever be able to cut through the doublespeak and discover what the ad is really saying.

51 Professor Del Kehl of Arizona State University has updated the Twenty-third Psalm to reflect the power of advertising to meet our needs and solve our problems. It seems fitting that this chapter close with this new psalm.

The Adman's 23rd

The Adman is my shepherd;
I shall ever want.
He maketh me to walk a mile for a Camel;

He leadeth me beside Crystal Waters
   In the High Country of Coors;
He restoreth my soul with Perrier.
He guideth me in Marlboro Country
For Mammon's sake.
Yea, though I walk through the Valley of the
   Jolly Green Giant,
In the shadow of B.O., halitosis, indigestion,
   headache pain, and hemorrhoidal tissue,
I will fear no evil,
For I am in Good Hands with Allstate;
Thy Arid, Scope, Tums, Tylenol, and Preparation H—
They comfort me.
Stouffer's preparest a table before the TV
In the presence of all my appetites;
Thou anointest my head with Brylcream;
My Decaffeinated Cup runneth over.
Surely surfeit and security shall follow me
All the days of Metropolitan Life,
And I shall dwell in a Continental Home
With a mortgage forever and ever.
Amen.

THINKING CRITICALLY

1. How did *weasel words* get their name? Does it sound like an appropriate label? Why, according to Lutz, do advertisers use them?

2. What regulations restrict the use of the word *new*? How can these regulations be sidestepped according to the author? In your opinion, do these regulations serve the interests of the advertiser or the consumer?

3. Do you think that most people fail to comprehend how advertising works on them? When you read or watch ads, do you see through the gimmicks and weasel words?

4. Take a look at Lutz's Doublespeak Quick Quiz. Select five items and write a language analysis explaining what the ad really says.

5. According to the author, how can consumers protect themselves against weasel words?

6. The author uses "you" throughout the article. Do you find the use of the second person stylistically satisfying? Do you think it is appropriate for the article?

7. What do you think of Lutz's writing style? Is it humorous? Informal? Academic? What strategies does he use to involve the reader in the piece?

8. Evaluate the conclusion of this piece. Did you think Lutz's choice of the updated version of the Twenty-third Psalm was appropriate? Did you find it funny? Did it suit the theme of the essay?

WRITING ASSIGNMENTS

1. The essays in this section deal with advertising language and its effects on consumers and their value systems. Describe how understanding the linguistic strategies of advertisers—as exemplified here by Lutz—will or will not change your reaction to advertising.

2. As Lutz suggests, look at some ads in a magazine and newspaper (or television and radio commercials). Then make a list of all uses of "help" you find over a twenty-four hour period. Examine the ads to determine exactly what is said and what the unwary consumer thinks is being said. Write up your report.

3. Invent a product and have some fun writing an ad for it. Use as many weasel words as you can to make your product shine.

4. Undertake a research project on theories of advertising: Find books by professional advertisers or texts for courses in advertising and marketing. Then go through them trying to determine how they might view Lutz's interpretation of advertising techniques. How would the authors view Lutz's claim that advertising language is loaded with "weasel words"?

The Language of Advertising
Charles A. O'Neill

Taking the minority opinion is a former advertising executive Charles A. O'Neill, who disputes the criticism of advertising language by William Lutz and other critics of advertising. While admitting to some of the craftiness of his profession, O'Neill defends the huckster's language—both verbal and visual—against claims that it debases reality and the values of the consumer. Examining some familiar television commercials and recent print ads, he explains why the language may be seductive but far from brainwashing.

This essay, originally written for *Exploring Language,* has been updated for this text. Charles O'Neill is an independent marketing consultant.

1 In 1957, a short dozen years after World War II, many people had good reason to be concerned about Science. On the one hand, giant American corporations offered the promise of "Better Living Through Chemistry." Labs and factories in the U.S. and abroad turned out new "miracle" fabrics, vaccines, and building materials. Radar and other innovative technology developed during the War had found important applications in the fast-growing, surging crest of consumer-centric, late 1950s America.

2   But World War II American Science had also yielded The Bomb. Specialists working in a secret desert laboratory had figured out how to translate the theoretical work of Dr. Einstein, and others, into weapons that did exactly what they were intended to do, incinerating hundreds of thousands of civilian Japanese men, women and children in the process. The USSR and the USA were locked in an arms race. Americans were told the Soviets held the advantage. Many families built bomb shelters in the yard, and millions of school children learned to "Duck and Cover."

3   So when Vance Packard wrote a book about a dark alliance of social scientists with product marketers and advertisers, an alliance forged in order to gain a better understanding of "people's subsurface desires, needs, and drives," to "find their points of vulnerability," he struck a resonant chord. The scientists who had brought us the weapons that helped win the war had now, apparently, turned their sights on the emerging consumer society. By applying the principles of laboratory experimentation and scientific reasoning to learn about the fears, habits and aspirations of John and Mary Public, they would help businesses create products whose sales would be fueled by ever-more powerful advertising. In the view of Virginia Postrel, (writing in the *Wall Street Journal* in August 1999), the book "envisions consumers as passive dupes who never catch on even to the most obvious manipulations." Among many examples cited, Mr. Packard noted that what he called "depth probers" had learned that "fear of stern bankers was driving borrowers to more expensive loan companies. Banks began training their employees to be nice so as to attract more business." We were led to believe the banker's smile was a form of manipulation, a contrived courtesy. The book was itself a bestseller.

4   In fairness to Mr. Packard, the decade of the 1950s did offer numerous examples of consumer excess. Cars from the era sported tail fins stretched to new extremes, for no aerodynamic or practical purpose. And it is impossible to miss the overtly sexual reference in the jutting chrome bumpers of the era's most flamboyant road machines. The story of manufactured excess could be extended through all product categories. Of course, it could also be extended through all decades, including our own. Just as Mr. Packard's book so well reflected the uncertainty and angst of the times, cars and other products reflected American popular culture—a world in which jet planes and the race to space dominated headlines. It was also a world in which Big was best, in starlets as well as the family car.

5   Mr. Packard is certainly not alone as a critic of advertising. Every decade has brought a new generation of critics. We recognize the legitimacy—even the value—of advertising, but on some level we can't quite fully embrace it as a "normal" part of our experience. At best, we view it as distracting. At worst, we view it as dangerous to our health and a pernicious threat to our social values. Also lending moral support to the debate about advertising is no less an authority than the Vatican. In 1997, the Vatican issued a document prepared by the Pontifical Council, titled "Ethics in Advertising." Along with acknowledgment of the positive contribution of advertising (e.g., provides information, supports worthy causes, encourages competition and innovation), the report states, as reported by the *Boston Globe,* "In the competition to attract ever larger audiences . . . communicators can find them-

selves pressured . . . to set aside high artistic and moral standards and lapse into superficiality, tawdriness and moral squalor."

6   How does advertising work? Why is it so powerful? Why does it raise such concern? What case can be made for and against the advertising business? In order to understand advertising, you must accept that it is not about truth, virtue, love, or positive social values. It is about money. Ads play a role in moving customers through the sales process. This process begins with an effort to build awareness of a product, typically achieved by tactics designed to break through the clutter of competitive messages. By presenting a description of product benefits, ads convince the customer to buy the product. Once prospects have become purchasers, advertising is used to sustain brand loyalty, reminding customers of all the good reasons for their original decision to buy.

7   But this does not sufficiently explain the ultimate, unique power of advertising. Whatever the product or creative strategy, advertisements derive their power from a purposeful, directed combination of images. Images can take the form of words, sounds, or visuals, used individually or together. The combination of images is the language of advertising, a language unlike any other.

8   Everyone who grows up in the Western world soon learns that advertising language is different from other languages. We may have forgotten the sponsors, but we certainly know these popular slogans[1] "sound like ads."

> "Where's the Beef?" (Wendy's restaurants, 1984)
> "Please, Don't Squeeze the Charmin." (Charmin bathroom tissue, 1964)
> "I Can't Believe I Ate the Whole Thing." (Alka-Seltzer, 1977)
> "M'm! M'm! Good!" (Campbell's Soup, 1950)
> "I've Fallen, and I Can't Get Up!" (Lifecall, 1990)

Edited and Purposeful

9 In his book, *Future Shock,* Alvin Toffler described various types of messages we receive from the world around us each day. Much of normal, human experience is merely sensory, "not designed by anyone to communicate anything." In contrast, the language of advertising is carefully engineered, ruthlessly purposeful. Advertising messages have a clear purpose; they are intended to trigger a specific response.

10   The response may be as utterly simple as "Say, I *am* hungry. Let's pull right on up to the drive-through window and order a big, juicy Wendy's burger, fast!"

11   In the case of some advertising, our reactions may be more complex. In 1964, the Doyle Dane Bernbach agency devised an elegantly simple television ad for President Lyndon Johnson's campaign against his Republican challenger, Barry Goldwater. A pretty young girl is shown picking petals from a daisy, against the background of a countdown. The ad ends with the sound of an explosion. This ad, ranked number 20, among *TV Guide*'s assessment of the 50 greatest TV commer-

---

[1]*TV Guide* July 3–9, 1999, "Our picks for the 10 catchiest ad lines"

cials of all time, was broadcast once, but it had succeeded in underscoring many voters' greatest fear: a vote for the GOP was a vote for nuclear war; a vote for Johnson was a vote for peace. The ad's overwhelming, negative message was too much even for President Johnson, who ordered it replaced.

12   This short TV spot reached well beyond hunger—"Fast food—yummy!"—into a far more sacred place: "Honey, they want to kill our kids!"

Rich and Arresting

13 Advertisements—no matter how carefully "engineered"—cannot succeed unless they capture our attention. Of the hundreds of advertising messages in store for us each day, very few will actually command our conscious attention. The rest are screened out. The people who design and write ads know about this screening process; they anticipate and accept it as a premise of their business.

14   The classic, all-time favorite device used to breach the barrier is sex. The desire to be sexually attracted to others is an ancient instinct, and few drives are more powerful. A magazine ad for Ultima II, a line of cosmetics, invites readers to "find everything you need for the sexxxxiest look around . . ." The ad goes on to offer other "Sexxxy goodies," including "Lipsexxxxy lip color, naked eye color . . . Sunsexxxy liquid bronzer." No one will accuse Ultima's marketing tacticians of subtlety. In fact, this ad is merely a current example of an approach that is as old as advertising. After countless years of using images of women in various stages of undress to sell products, ads are now displaying men's bodies as well. A magazine ad for Brut, a men's cologne, declares in bold letters, "MEN ARE BACK"; in the background, a photograph shows a muscular, shirtless young man preparing to enter the boxing ring—a "manly" image indeed; an image of man as breeding stock.

15   Every successful advertisement uses a creative strategy based on an idea that will attract and hold the attention of the targeted consumer audience. The strategy may include strong creative execution or a straightforward presentation of product features and customer benefits.

- An ad for Clif Bars, an "energy bar," is clearly directed to people who want to snack but wouldn't be caught dead in a coffee house eating ginger spice cake with delicate frosting, much less ordinary energy bars—the kind often associated with the veggie and granola set: The central photograph shows a gristled cowboy-character, holding a Clif Bar, and asking, in the headline, "What 'n the hell's a carbohydrate?" Nosiree. This here energy bar is "bound to satisfy cantakerous folk like you."
- Recent cigar ads attract attention through the use of unexpected imagery. An ad for Don Diego cigars, for example, shows a bejeweled woman in an evening dress smoking a cigar, while through the half-open door her male companion asks, "Agnes, have you seen my Don Diegos?"
- A two-page ad for Diesel clothing includes a photo showing the principal participants in the famous Yalta conference in 1945 (Churchill, Roosevelt, and Stalin) with one important difference: Young models in Diesel clothing have

been cleverly added and appear to be flirting with the dignitaries. The ad is presented as a "Diesel historical moment" and "the birth of the modern conference." This unexpected imagery is engaging and amusing, appealing to the product's youthful target audience.

Even if the text contains no incongruity and does not rely on a pun for its impact, ads typically use a creative strategy based on some striking concept or idea. In fact, the concept and execution are often so good that many successful ads entertain while they sell.

16   Consider, for example, the campaigns created for Federal Express. A campaign was developed to position Federal Express as the company that would deliver packages, not just "overnight," but "by 10:30 A.M." the next day. The plight of the junior executive in "Presentation," one early TV ad in the campaign, is stretched for dramatic purposes, but it is, nonetheless, all too real: The young executive, who is presumably to try to climb his way up the corporate ladder, is shown calling another parcel delivery service and all but begging for assurance that he will have his slides in hand by 10:30 the next morning. "No slides, no presentation," he pleads. Only a viewer with a heart of stone can watch without feeling sympathetic as the next morning our junior executive struggles to make his presentation *sans* slides. He is so lost without them that he is reduced to using his hands to perform imitations of birds and animals in the shadows on the movie screen. What does the junior executive *viewer* think when he or she sees the ad?

1. Federal Express guarantees to deliver packages "absolutely, positively overnight."
2. Federal Express packages arrived early in the day.
3. What happened to that fellow in the commercial will absolutely not happen to me, now that I know what package delivery service to call.

17   A sound, creative strategy supporting an innovative service idea sold Federal Express.

18   Soft drink and fast-food companies often take another approach. "Slice of life" ads (so-called because they purport to show people in "real-life" situations) created to sell Coke or Pepsi have often placed their characters in Fourth of July parades or other family events. The archetypical version of this ad is filled-to-overflowing with babies frolicking with puppies in the sunlit foreground while their youthful parents play touch football. On the porch, Grandma and Pops are seen quietly smiling as they wait for all of this affection to transform itself in a climax of warmth, harmony, and joy. In part, these ads work through repetition: How-many-times-can-you-spot-the-logo-in-this-commercial?

19   These ads seduce us into feeling that if we drink the right combination of sugar, preservatives, caramel coloring, and secret ingredients, we'll join the crowd that—in the words of Coca-Cola's ad from 1971—will help "teach the world to sing . . . in perfect harmony." A masterstroke of advertising cemented the impression that Coke was hip: not only an American brand, but a product and brand for all peace-loving peoples everywhere!

20   If you don't buy this version of the American Dream, search long enough and you are sure to find an ad designed to sell you what it takes to gain prestige within whatever posse you do happen to run with. As reported by the *Boston Globe,* "the malt liquor industry relies heavily on rap stars in delivering its message to inner-city youths, while Black Death Vodka, which features a top-hatted skull and a coffin on its label, has been using Guns N' Roses guitarist Slash to endorse the product in magazine advertising." A malt liquor company reportedly promotes its 40-ounce size with rapper King T singing, "I usually drink it when I'm just out clowning, me and the home boys, you know, be like downing it . . . I grab me a 40 when I want to act a fool." A recent ad for Sasson jeans is a long way from Black Death in execution, but a second cousin in spirit. A photograph of a young, blonde (they do have more fun, right?) actress appears with this text: "Baywatch actress Gene Lee Nolin Puts On Sasson. OOLA-LA. Sasson. Don't put it on unless it's Sasson."

21   Ads do not often emerge like Botticelli's Venus from the sea, flawless and fully grown. Most often, the creative strategy is developed only after extensive research. "Who will be interested in our product? How old are they? Where do they live? How much money do they earn? What problem will our product solve?" Answers to these questions provide the foundation on which the creative strategy is built.

Involving

22 We have seen that the language of advertising is carefully engineered; we have discovered a few of the devices it uses to get our attention. Coke and Pepsi have caught our eye with visions of peace and love. An actress offers a winsome smile. Now that they have our attention, advertisers present information intended to show us that their product fills a need and differs from the competition. It is the copywriter's responsibility to express, exploit, and intensify such product differences.

23   When product differences do not exist, the writer must glamorize the superficial differences—for example, differences in packaging. As long as the ad is trying to get our attention, the "action" is mostly in the ad itself, in the words and visual images. But as we read an ad or watch it on television, we become more deeply involved. The action starts to take place in us. Our imagination is set in motion, and our individual fears and aspirations, quirks, and insecurities, superimpose themselves on that tightly engineered, attractively packaged message.

24   Consider, once again, the running battle among the low-calorie soft drinks. The cola wars have spawned many "look-alike" advertisements, because the product features and consumer benefits are generic, applying to all products in the category. Substitute one cola brand name for another, and the messages are often identical, right down to the way the cans are photographed in the closing sequence. This strategy relies upon mass saturation and exposure for impact.

25   Some companies have set themselves apart from their competitors by making use of bold, even disturbing, themes and images. For example, it was not uncommon not long ago for advertisers in the fashion industry to make use of gaunt, lan-

guid models—models who, in the interpretation of some observers, displayed a certain form of "heroin chic." Something was most certainly unusual about the models appearing in ads for Prada and Calvin Klein products. A young woman in a Prada ad projects no emotion whatsoever; she is hunched forward, her posture suggesting that she is in a trance or drug-induced stupor. In a Calvin Klein ad, a young man, like the woman in the Prada ad, is gaunt beyond reason. He is shirtless. As if to draw more attention to his peculiar posture and "zero body fat" status, he is shown pinching the skin next to his navel. One well-recognized observer of public morality, President Clinton, commented on the increasing use of heroin on college campuses, noting that "part of this has to do with the images that are finding their way to our young people." One industry maven agreed, asserting that "people got carried away by the glamour of decadence."

26   Do such advertisers as Prada and Calvin Klein bear responsibility—morally, if not legally—for the rise of heroin use on college campuses? Does "heroin chic" and its depiction of a decadent lifestyle exploit certain elements of our society—the young and clueless, for example? Or did these ads, and others of their ilk, simply reflect profound bad taste? In fact, on one level, all advertising is about exploitation: the systematic, deliberate identification of our needs and wants, followed by the delivery of a carefully constructed promise that Brand X will satisfy them.

27   Symbols offer an important tool for involving consumers in advertisements. Symbols have become important elements in the language of advertising, not so much because they carry meanings of their own, but because we bring meaning to them. One example is provided by the campaign begun in 1978 by Somerset Importers for Johnnie Walker Red Scotch. Sales of Johnnie Walker Red had been trailing sales of Johnnie Walker Black, and Somerset Importers needed to position Red as a fine product in its own right. Their agency produced ads that made heavy use of the color red. One magazine ad, often printed as a two-page spread, is dominated by a close-up photo of red autumn leaves. At lower right, the copy reads, "When their work is done, even the leaves turn to Red." Another ad—also suitably dominated by a photograph in the appropriate color—reads: "When it's time to quiet down at the end of the day, even a fire turns to Red." Red. Warm. Experienced. Seductive.

28   Advertisers make use of a great variety of techniques and devices to engage us in the delivery of their messages. Some are subtle, making use of warm, entertaining, or comforting images or symbols. Others, like Black Death Vodka and Ultima II, are about as subtle as MTV's "Beavis and Butt-head." Another common device used to engage our attention is old but still effective: the use of famous or notorious personalities as product spokespeople or models. Advertising writers did not invent the human tendency to admire or otherwise identify themselves with famous people. Once we have seen a famous person in an ad, we associate the product with the person: "Britney Spears drinks milk. She's a hottie. I want to be a hottie, too. 'Hey Mom, Got Milk?'" "Guns 'N Roses rule my world, so I will definitely make the scene with a bottle of Black Death stuck into the waistband of my sweat pants." "Gena Lee Nolin is totally sexy. She wears Sasson. If I wear Sasson, I'll be sexy,

too." The logic is faulty, but we fall under the spell just the same. Advertising works, not because Britney is a nutritionist, Slash has discriminating taste, or Gena knows her jeans, but because we participate in it. In fact, we charge ads with most of their power.

A Simple Language

29 Advertising language differs from other types of language in another important respect; it is a simple language. To determine how the copy of a typical advertisement rates on a "simplicity index" in comparison with text in a magazine article, for example, try this exercise: Clip a typical story from the publication you read most frequently. Calculate the number of words in an average sentence. Count the number of words of three or more syllables in a typical 100-word passage, omitting words that are capitalized, combinations of two simple words, or verb forms made into three-syllable words by the addition of *–ed* or *–es*. Add the two figures (the average number of words per sentence and the number of three-syllable words per 100 words), then multiply the result by .4. According to Robert Gunning, if the resulting number is 7, there is a good chance that you are reading *True Confessions.*[2] He developed this formula, the "Fog Index," to determine the comparative ease with which any given piece of written communication can be read.

30   Let's apply the Fog Index to the complete text of Britney Spears' 1999 ad for the National Fluid Milk Processing Board ("Got Milk?")

> "Baby, one more time isn't enough.
> 9 out of 10 girls don't get enough calcium. It takes about 4 glasses of milk every day. So when I finish this glass, fill it up, baby. Three more times."

The average sentence in this ad is 7.4 words. There is only one three-syllable word, *calcium.* Counting *isn't* and *don't* as two words each, the ad is 40 words in length. The average number of three syllable words per hundred is 2.5.

7.4 words per sentence
+ 2.5 three syllable words/100
9.9
×.4
3.96

According to Gunning's scale, this ad is about as hard to read as a comic book. But of course the text is only part of the message. The rest is the visual; in this case, a photo of pop star Britney Spears sprawled across a couch, legs in the air, while she talks on the phone. A plate holding cookies and a glass of milk is set next to her.

31   Why do advertisers generally favor simple language? The answer lies with the consumer: The average American adult is subject to an overwhelming number of

---

[2]Curtis D. MacDougall, *Interpretive Reporting* (New York: Macmillan, 1968), p. 94.

commercial messages each day. As a practical matter, we would not notice many of these messages if length or eloquence were counted among their virtues. Today's consumer cannot take the time to focus on anything for long, much less blatant advertising messages. Every aspect of modern life runs at an accelerated pace. Overnight mail has moved in less than ten years from a novelty to a common business necessity. Voice mail, pagers, cellular phones, e-mail, the Internet—the world is always awake, always switched on, and hungry for more information, now. Time generally, and TV-commercial time in particular, is now dissected into increasingly smaller segments. Fifteen-second commercials are no longer unusual.

32   Advertising language is simple language; in the ad's engineering process, difficult words or images—which in other forms of communication may be used to lend color or fine shades of meaning—are edited out and replaced by simple words or images not open to misinterpretation. You don't have to ask whether King T likes to "grab a 40" when he wants to "act a fool," or whether Gena wears her Sassons when she wants to do whatever it is she does.

Who Is Responsible?

33 Some critics view the advertising business as a cranky, unwelcomed child of the free enterprise system—a noisy, whining, brash kid who must somehow be kept in line, but can't just yet be thrown out of the house. In reality, advertising mirrors the fears, quirks, and aspirations of the society that creates it (and is, in turn, sold by it). This factor alone exposes advertising to parody and ridicule. The overall level of acceptance and respect for advertising is also influenced by the varied quality of the ads themselves. Some ads, including a few of the examples cited here, seem deliberately designed to provoke controversy. For example, it is easy—as President Clinton and others charged—to conclude that clothing retailers deliberately glamorized the damaging effects of heroin addiction. But this is only one of the many charges frequently levied against advertising:

1. Advertising encourages unhealthy habits.
2. Advertising feeds on human weaknesses and exaggerates the importance of material things, encouraging "impure" emotions and vanities.
3. Advertising sells daydreams—distracting, purposeless visions of lifestyles beyond the reach of the majority of the people who are most exposed to advertising.
4. Advertising warps our vision of reality, implanting in us groundless fears and insecurities.
5. Advertising downgrades the intelligence of the public.
6. Advertising debases English.
7. Advertising perpetuates racial and sexual stereotypes.

34   What can be said in advertising's defense? Advertising is only a reflection of society. A case can be made for the concept that advertising language is an accept-

able stimulus for the natural evolution of language. Is "proper English" the language most Americans actually speak and write, or is it the language we are told we should speak and write?

35   What about the charge that advertising debases the intelligence of the public? Those who support this particular criticism would do well to ask themselves another question: Exactly how intelligent is the public? Sadly, evidence abounds that "the public" at large is not particularly intelligent, after all. Johnny can't read. Susie can't write. And the entire family spends the night in front of the television, channel surfing for the latest scandal—hopefully, one involving a sports hero or political figure said to be a killer or a frequent participant in perverse sexual acts.

36   Ads are effective because they sell products. They would not succeed if they did not reflect the values and motivations of the real world. Advertising both reflects and shapes our perception of reality. Consider several brand names and the impressions they create: Ivory Snow is pure. Federal Express won't let you down. Absolut is cool. Sasson is sexxy. Mercedes represents quality. Our sense of what these brand names stand for may have as much to do with advertising as with the objective "truth."

37   Advertising shapes our perception of the world as surely as architecture shapes our impression of a city. Good, responsible advertising can serve as a positive influence for change, while generating profits. Of course, the problem is that the obverse is also true: Advertising, like any form of mass communication, can be a force for both "good" and "bad." It can just as readily reinforce or encourage irresponsible behavior, ageism, sexism, ethnocentrism, racism, homophobia, heterophobia—you name it—as it can encourage support for diversity and social progress. People living in society create advertising. Society isn't perfect. In the end, advertising simply attempts to change behavior. Do advertisements sell distracting, purposeless visions? Occasionally. But perhaps such visions are necessary components of the process through which our society changes and improves.

38   Perhaps, by learning how advertising works, we can become better equipped to sort out content from hype, product values from emotions, and salesmanship from propaganda.

THINKING CRITICALLY

1. O'Neill's introduction describes the "alliance" between science and consumer marketing during the 1950s especially as it connected to the automotive industry. Evaluate the alliance he describes. Review some automobile advertisements from the 1950s and 1960s to help you formulate your response. How would you assess this relationship between science and marketing today?

2. O'Neill says that advertisers create in consumers a sense of need for products. Do you think it is ethical for advertisers to create such a sense when their products are "generic" and do not differ from those of the competition? Consider ads for gasoline, beer, and instant coffee.

3. Toward the end of the essay, O'Neill anticipates potential objections to his defense of advertising. What are some of these objections? What does he say in defense of advertising? Which set of arguments do you find stronger?

4. O'Neill describes several ways in which the language of advertising differs from other kinds of language. Briefly list the ways he mentions. Can you think of any other characteristics of advertising language that set it apart?

5. O'Neill says in paragraph 27 that "[symbols] have become important elements in the language of advertising." Can you think of some specific symbols from the advertising world that you associate with your own life? Are they effective symbols for selling? Explain your answer.

6. In paragraph 28, O'Neill claims that celebrity endorsement of a product is "faulty" logic. Explain what he means. Why do people buy products sold by famous people?

7. William Lutz teaches English and writes books about the misuse of language. Charles O'Neill is a professional advertiser. How do their views about advertising reflect their occupations? Which side of the argument do you agree with?

8. How effective do you think O'Neill's introductory paragraphs are? How well does he hook the reader? What particular audience might he be appealing to early on? What attitude toward advertising is established in the introduction?

WRITING ASSIGNMENTS

1. Obtain a current issue of each of the following publications: *The New Yorker, Time, GQ, Vogue,* and *People.* Choose one article from each periodical and calculate its Fog Index according to the technique described in paragraphs 29 and 30. Choose one ad from each periodical and figure out its Fog Index. What different reading levels do you find among the publications? What do you know about the readers of these periodicals from your survey of the reading difficulty of the articles? Write up your findings in a paper.

2. O'Neill believes that advertising language mirrors the fears, quirks, and aspirations of the society that creates it. Do you agree or disagree with this statement? Explain in a brief essay.

3. Working with a group of classmates, develop a slogan and advertising campaign for one of the following products: sneakers, soda, a candy bar, or jeans. How would you apply the principles of advertising, as outlined in O'Neill's article, to market your product? After completing your marketing strategy, "sell" your product to the class. If time permits, explain the reasoning behind your selling technique.

Language Abuse
Herschell Gordon Lewis

The next essay, written by one of the most prolific marketing writers of the twentieth century, takes a humorous, but candid look at the marketing language used by copywriters to get us to part with our money. As Lewis explains in this piece written for an advertising audience, unimaginative language and worn-out clichés alienate consumers and dilute our language as a whole.

Herschell Gordon Lewis is the author of over 20 books on marketing and advertising, including *Herschell Gordon Lewis on the Art of Writing Copy* (1988) and *Marketing Mayhem*, (2001) from which this essay is excerpted. His columns on marketing and copywriting have appeared in many advertising publications.

1 Today's marketers throw terms the way they'd throw confetti . . . and with just about as much impact.

2 Yes, yes, of course we have "Free" and "New" and "Important" used so often and so unrelated to a specific offer we have the feeling some child has hit a macro button on a computer keyboard or, worse, the computer is operating without human intervention.

3 Here's an ad in a free-standing insert in the Sunday paper: Great news! Metab-o-lite now has a full line of products for extra energy and increased metabolism!" By golly, they're right on the money. We haven't had such great news since Gutenberg. Here's a mailing from a company selling hams by mail. It's labeled. "Urgent!" By golly, *they're* right on the money too. We'd better act now or they'll run out of hams. Then where would we be?

4 (Parenthetically, "Act now!" is another phrase that ought to be sent to that great Lexicographical Purgatory.)

5 We have offers from credit cards—dozens of credit cards, all leaning on the same everlasting arms of credit reporting bureaus—telling us we've been pre-approved . . . and then asking us for so much financial information or warning us that we may *not* be pre-approved that we wonder whether one person wrote the envelope copy, went on vacation, and was replaced by another person who wrote the deadly-warning text while unaware of the commitment the envelope made.

6 One of the most puzzling aspects of marketing mayhem is the plethora of inde-cipherable automobile names. Who, oh, who, decided to call the Cheap Cadillac "Catera"? The initial campaign for that status-busting car has (thankfully) been dis-continued, but we should remember "The Caddy that zigs" as a no-brain totem. De-nali, Escalade, Allante—who came up with these? What image is the car supposed to project?

7 And our tired old standby "Free" is reduced to limping, in The Age of Skep-ticism. Certainly more than half the offers that begin with a huge "Free!" are fol-lowed by an "if . . ." or "when . . ." condition. What we've done to that poor word is criminal, and what makes the criminality worse is that so many uses of free are the result of desperation. We don't have anything else to say, so we drag in "Free!" and because it doesn't fit, we have to saddle it with conditions and exclu-sions and exceptions.

8 The language abusers don't care. They throw terms, they invent unpronounce-able product names, they assault us with cliché after cliché. Response slides. And can you believe it, they're actually surprised to see their own murder victim die.

9   What we really need is an uprising, a revolution, a mutiny in which we organize and fight the deadly marketing-murdering forces of term-throwing. We need to impose a gigantic penalty on the use of "Important" and "Free" and "0% APR" . . . until and unless those terms once again run pure.

10   With that imprecation, take a look at some case histories:

The Importance of Saying "Important"

11   I'm getting more and more steamed at hit-and-run copywriters.

12   Who or what are hit-and-runners? They're the ones who know a couple of action words but don't know what damage they're doing by using these words and not justifying them.

13   Some of the words:

- Important
- Urgent
- Personal
- Hurry
- Rush

14   I've left off the mandatory exclamation points . . . although adding one after "Personal" is an Open Sesame to anyone other than the target, to peek inside (and be the first one to be disappointed).

15   What's wrong with all these imperatives? you ask. Not a thing—IF what follows *is* important or urgent or personal or legitimizes the demand for fast action.

16   But here's an envelope—a 9" x 12" jumbo—from a publication in the meetings and conventions field. In big stencil type on the envelope is the word "URGENT."

17   Urgent, huh? Then why does the postal indicia say "Bulk Rate"? How come it's urgent for me but not for you?

18   And what's inside? No letter. You're reading right, *no letter*. Bulk rate urgency without any semi-personal communication? Gee, that'll do a lot for the credibility of everybody else's direct response.

19   What *was* enclosed was a beautifully-printed brochure, on whose cover is the cryptic message:

> *Can You Imagine Having the Power*
> *To Increase the Value of Gold?*

20   Yeah, yeah, it's not only too prettily laid out to be "urgent"; it's also too lyrical. (The eventual reference: Gold awards for the best hotels and resorts and golf courses.)

21   Look: Stay in character. How easy all this is if you STAY IN CHARACTER.

22   Aw, but I know what happened. Some consultant told them to put "Urgent" on the envelope. He or she was hired only for the day, so there wasn't time to explain that if we cry, "Wolf!" we'd better show them a wolf.

23   "Urgent" isn't the abused word winner. By far the most abused word we have—even surpassing "Free" and "New"—is "Important."

24   Hey, guys, *Important* isn't a stand-alone. Every time you kick it in the head, you weaken it a little more for the rest of us.

Important To Whom?

25   Here's an envelope. It says, all caps: *IMPORTANT FINANCIAL DOCUMENT EN-CLOSED.* Yes, it's a manila envelope with those fake "Instructions to postmaster" instructions we've all used. Yes, the window shows "Pay to the order of" next to my name. But I *know,* as I open the envelope, the importance is to the sender, not the recipient.

26   Yep. It's a standard fake check, with the words "This is not a check" printed on it. It offers me a home equity loan, if I qualify. A reply card lets me choose between bill consolidation, home improvements, major purpose, refinancing an existing loan, or other. Okay, I choose other—a not-for-profit campaign to stamp out unau-thorized use of the word "Important." Where's the importance here? It's a flat, stan-dard financial offer every homeowner gets two or three times a week. That key mis-used word on the envelope has no backup inside.

27   Another problem: The "Important" infection has spread so it's now an epi-demic. Two competitive mailings, mailed within a week or two of this one, use the same fake check gimmick and the same claim of importance. One tells me: "IM-PORTANT: Your Single Family Residence has been reviewed."

28   Gee, I guess that *is* important. It isn't every day that my Single Family Resi-dence is not only given caps/l.c. treatment but is also reviewed. I qualify for $35,000 more (than what?).

29   The American Express Platinum Card is never far behind. It shucks its mantle of dignity but manages to water down the promise:

> IMPORTANT
> INFORMATION
> For Automatic Flight
> Insurance Enrollees

30   I hadn't known I enrolled for this, but maybe it was a negative option. Any-way, the "Important" information is that I can upgrade my coverage "to the highest level of accident protection." Now, is that elite status, or what!

31   One "Important Information Enclosed" fibber adds a deadline date and "Final Notice" in a second window. Uh-oh! (And of course it has the boiler-plate "Post-master . . ." imperative.) Final notice? What have I done? Or not done? Aha! It's my last chance "to upgrade your present vehicle to a brand-new Honda or KIA." Hey, fellas, I hate to rain on your parade, but I'm driving a Jaguar convertible. How about having a clue about who you're selling to?

32 What's the next one? A plain white jumbo window envelope with "IMPOR-TANT INFORMATION ENCLOSED" in red above the window. Of course, the Bulk Rate indicia, in the same red, rides serenely above this legend.

33 Inside is one of the most impenetrable documents I've ever tried to look at. It's a prospectus for Fidelity Advisor Funds Class A, Class T, and Class B. No letter. No indication of what makes this important. Every indication of why the word "Bulk" is more apt than the word "Important."

34 And on we go, into this pseudo-psychological jungle. The Discover Card takes a stern parental position:

> *Important:*
> Please open at once.
> DO NOT DISCARD.

35 Yeah, guys, but you've joined the "Bulk rate" parade. Oh, what the heck—even though it parallels the dire warning on the tags attached to pillows and mattresses, I'll open it.

36 I wish I hadn't.

37 The message from Discover (I haven't used this card since 1992, when Costco wouldn't accept any others) tells me, "Enclosed are four Discover® Card Checks just for you. Use them to . . ." Naturally, that "®" symbol destroys any rapport, but this doesn't bother me because I've built up an immunity to ® and ᵀᴹ symbols, legal necessities for immediate identification and pomposities when overused.

A Simple Little Rule

38 I have a theory: Somebody writes the envelope copy, goes on vacation, and is eaten by a shark. Somebody else rushes in to write the enclosures; in the heat of getting these out, whatever is written on the envelope is overlooked.

39 How simple it is!

40 I have a little rule I've both preached and employed ever since the Fake Importance Syndrome showed up and developed into a Nile virus-like plague:

> *If you claim importance, prove it.*

41 See how uncomplicated those six words are? They *force* the creative team out of the hit-and-run bunker, onto the open battlefield.

42 So when Sprint sends me a letter (presorted first class . . . I'm moving up!) with the legend "Important news about your telephone service," I first take a deep breath, hoping it won't be a stupid message tied to Candace Bergen or Sela Ward, then open it to find what I expected to find: "Now your small business can get the same quality and value you enjoy on long distance, for all your *local toll* calls, too."

43 Is a puzzlement. My business isn't that small (should I be insulted?), and Sprint isn't our long distance provider. I wouldn't expect a company with the creative depth they have to die in the heading with limp words such as *quality* and

value. Those are peculiarities, but they aren't germane to the point here, which is: What's so important? Couldn't the creative team have adapted envelope copy to intrigue me rather than generate just another weak cliché?

44 Hey, Sprint and Discover and AmEx and all you Honda dealers out there: Want to add some octane to your messages? *If you claim importance, prove it.*

45 Remember that, will you? It's important.

"Free at Last"? Well, Sort of . . . Except . . .

46 One of the great wonders of our time is that the word "Free" survives.

47 We've kicked it in the head, stomped on it with golf shoes, strangled it with adjectival qualifiers, drowned it in a sea of asterisks, maimed it with "if" phrases, and suffocated it with cheap rhetorical varnish . . . and still it survives.

48 As any resident of the former Yugoslavia might point out: Survival isn't equivalent to thriving.

49 Today's target doesn't accept "Free!" as really free, the way his or her forebears did a generation ago. Today's "What's the angle?" hesitation is often precursor to a consultation with one of those lawyers slathering for the typical unreasonable percentage of a class action settlement. We can be next in line for that reaction.

50 **"It isn't 'Free,' you dummy. It's 'Complimentary.'**

51 **Or it's 'No extra charge.' But it isn't 'free.'"**

52 **"Oh."**

53 Writing for credit card companies and financial institutions, I often encounter the warning: "We can't say it's free. We can only say it's complimentary or at no extra charge."

54 That a difference in perception between "free" and "complimentary" exists (and only the sedate marketers heed that difference in perception) is an indication of the litigious, looking-for-trouble early 21st century societal structure. That one of the mailings coming to me spelled the word *complementary*—a word that has a totally different meaning—is an indication of the borderline literacy of some of our confrères.

55 Anybody who has practiced advertising, marketing, or basic salesmanship for more than 20 minutes is aware of the idiosyncrasies surrounding the word "Free." For example, we all refer to "Free Gift." Now, come on, have we ever heard of a gift that isn't free? That isn't the point. The redundancy "Free Gift" pulls. That's what matters, because we deal in response, not logic.

56 So I suppose we'll expand to "Totally Free Gift" and then to "100% Totally Free Gift." Does that make us charlatans? Certainly not. It makes us salespeople, sensitive to what motivates our targets.

57 When I was about six years old, living near Pittsburgh, I visited relatives in Detroit. Detroit had a paper called *The Free Press.* Gee, I wondered, how could they make any money? (The last few years have proved me right. Apparently they

can't.) My aunt didn't disabuse me of the notion, and I was lucky that I didn't just grab a paper off the newsstand: After all, it was free.

58   So was Radio Free Europe. The magic of the word has been inescapable. In David Ogilvy's *Confessions of an Advertising Man,* published two generations ago, he singled out *Free* as one of the powerful motivators. That power still drives the marketing engine, though it no longer purrs on all twelve cylinders.

59   Why has *free* begun to sputter, running so roughly it even backfires now and then? Because of a venerable monolith of a rule affecting all forms of force-communication:

> *Sameness = boredom.*
> *Overuse = abuse.*

60   We lean on "free" the way a cripple leans on a crutch. It may not save us, but it supports us. But it doesn't support us as profoundly as it supported our predecessors a generation ago.

61   A generation ago, a free offer wasn't a novelty but neither was it a daily occurrence. Today, we fish around for something in an offer, something we can isolate so we can say we're including it free.

62   The creeping cynicism among those who read, see, or hear our messages is based on two factors. They're responsible for the first one and we're the generators of the second. Theirs:

63   A universal "I want mine" attitude has replaced the kinder, gentler "Gee, thanks!" of earlier times.

64   Ours:

65   To work the magical word into the mix, we hedge—"Free with your third shipment," "Free when you've collected the complete set," "Free if yours is one of the first 50 replies we receive."

66   And we have the old dependable "Buy one, get one free," which usually outpulls "Two for the price of one" or "Buy two and get 50% off." So even though the clock is ticking, even though worn spots are showing, even though the FCC occasionally growls, the Old Dependable still churns out response for us.

67   Understand, please: I keep score the same way I hope you do: by response, not by critical accolades or art directors' awards. So I'm in there, milking our favorite word just as you are. I'm not going to let pride stand in the way of response.

68   But I'm glad I'm operating during this generation. By the next one, we may have damaged our durable crutch so deeply it may not support those who follow us in our most noble profession.

New and Improved: A Good Old-fashioned Home-made Original

69 How big a house do you need to make "home-made" ice cream?

70   If you have one of those electric gadgets that can turn out a pint of mushy ice cream for about eleven dollars' worth of ingredients, you can prepare that pint in a

studio apartment. But you'd need every room in a mansion to supply a chain of stores.

71   My son Bob took his two little daughters out for some ice cream. He chuckled when he told me about it:

72   "It's called 'Kemp's Home-Made ice cream,'" he said. "They sell it in a couple of hundred stores. I'd like to go to their house and watch Mrs. Kemp wrestling with half a ton of chocolate syrup."

73   The "home-made" conceit set me to thinking about all the phrases we in the force-communication universe corrupt in our mindless grappling for attention and sales.

74   One of the most obvious . . . and it also applies to ice cream . . . is "old-fashioned." Curious, isn't it, in the rocket-speed Internet era, that we venerate the past when we're describing a space-age pistachio-nut concoction. Oh, we understand the sales pitch behind the label: Contemporary products, they tell us, are loaded with ersatz ingredients such as sawdust and iron filings and camel dung; theirs come from cows whose udders are massaged with Jergen's Lotion.

75   So okay, "old-fashioned" can be a smart (if semi-subliminal) marketing ploy. But please, please, refuse to buy any item advertising itself as "old-fashion." Truncating the phrase is the work of semi-literates, and if you patronize them what does that say about *you?*

76   Two curious descriptions are "original" and "new and improved." Even more curious is the oxymoron resulting from combining them—a symbol of copywriting desperation. (My old friend Don Logay points out that the two terms are mutually exclusive—something can't be both "new" and "improved.")

77   What benefit does the word "original" transmit? In one of its purer interpretations, the word means *unchanged.* First (original) definition, American Heritage Dictionary: "Preceding all others in time." Would you want to be writing or handling a layout or doing a spreadsheet with your *original* computer, which in 1986 was the wonder of its time with 20 megabytes of memory and 4 megabytes of RAM? Would you want to submit yourself to the *original* treatment for many illnesses—heated cups stuck onto your back by the local barber?

78   "New and improved" is a nondescript non-description. In what way? I remember without any particular fondness reading that phrase on containers of the semi-tasteless orange drink Tang. Oh, yeah, I had to admire the honesty behind it—"The previous formulation wasn't very good but we marketed it anyway."

79   "New and improved" somehow parallels a sign on a failed business: "Under new management." So what? Those of us whose incomes depend on success in driving customers or clients through the door certainly ought to know that *benefit* outsells thin chest-thumping. In what way is it new? In what way is it improved? Or is the claim a hope that dissatisfied buyers will ignore their previous disgruntlement?

80   Yeah, I'm being wry, but the conclusion isn't wry: Whatever use we make of "original" and "new and improved," we have better expressions at our command; or, at least, as professionals we *should* have better expressions at our command.

Adding to the List

81 Let's add two massive entries to our list: "heavy duty" and "heavyweight." I admit to being a sometime patron of "heavy duty"; but after buying some "heavy duty" AA batteries at Walgreens, I no longer can accept the term without challenging it as puffery. Wouldn't it be nice if our bureau-crazed government added one more: The Department of Heavy Duty Evaluation?

82 "Heavyweight" doesn't carry as heavy a burden as "heavy duty," so let's consider this just a preliminary warning, a caution: If you describe something as a heavyweight, meaning anything other than avoirdupois, accompany that claim with an explanation.

83 Which brings us to "discount." Living in Florida, I've become immunized to the word, which attaches itself leechlike to stores and space ads and mailings and Web offerings, often mindlessly and often duplicitously. Oh, it still works on the unaware. For those of us whose skepticism it regularly feeds, the word needs validation. Who has been responsible for the latter-day rash of unbacked claims of "discount"? Wal-Mart? No, Wal-Mart's prices actually are discounted. A simple demand: Discounted from *what?*

84 What else? "King-size." For beds and bedding, it's a measurable absolute. For a claim from the clouds, it conjures up the image of getting something bigger and/or more intense than we're paying for. We see the intensification at work in "King-size discount." The Mother of all discounts? Based on the typical shouter of the phrase, it should only be.

85 A recent addition—in fact, I'd place it from 1998 upward—is "Enterprise." Now, this isn't the original *enterprise* as we've always known it; nor is it the starship. No, no, it's the new and improved *Enterprise* with a capital "E," grasped to the bosom of electron-lovers. We see magazine columns and entire books with the "Enterprise Computing" title. What does it mean? I've asked several who inhabit that half-world to explain the term; invariably the answer is something like, "It's the whole thing . . . the entire . . . well, the entire enterprise." Oh. Thanks.

86 One more for now: "World class." I have no idea whence this phrase came; somehow I associate it with that marvel of corruption, the Olympic Games. But maybe I'm wrong. Our shrunken globe rubber-banded into a tight little ball by jet aircraft and discounted (for real) fares, has eliminated many of the peaks and valleys we used to assume were there, between Texas and Tajikistan. So "world class" already may be on the route to join "23 skiddoo" and "hooch inspector" and "cuspidor" as a once-active expression.

87 Aw, enough already. Are these the only candidates? Even as you read this, you undoubtedly have others to contribute. If you have some favorites, tell me so and we might immortalize them and you in another book of harangues. But don't give me "ultimate" or "your partner in. . . ." I'm saving those.

THINKING CRITICALLY

1. Describe the voice you hear in this essay. How does Lewis balance humor and a sense of concern regarding the ineffective use of language in advertising today? Cite examples from the essay to support your conclusion.

2. What is the connection between language abuses made by advertising copywriters and consumer apathy? How do language abuses made by advertising writers "weaken" language? Explain.

3. What, according to Lewis, is the most "abused" word used in marketing today? Why does he feel that this word surpasses other overused words such as "free" and "new"? Do you agree with his assessment?

4. What advice does Lewis give marketing writers to prevent the distribution of boring or ineffectual copy? As a consumer, do you agree with his advice?

5. Does the fact that Lewis is an experienced marketing writer influence your reception of his argument? Why or why not?

6. How does Lewis use examples to support his criticisms of language abuse in advertising? Explain.

7. Is there a difference between "free" and "complimentary"? Explain. What is the legal difference? Explain.

WRITING ASSIGNMENTS

1. In this essay, Lewis highlights some marketing ploys that he finds particularly annoying and ineffective. Identify some commercials or advertisements that especially annoyed you. Why exactly did they bother you? Try to locate any cultural, linguistic, social, or intellectual reasons behind your annoyance or distaste. How do these commercials compare to the marketing criticisms expressed in Lewis's article?

2. Lewis draws several examples of language abuses from companies such as Sprint, Discover, and Wal-Mart. Examine a few of these companies' marketing campaigns in detail. Write an essay that compares the language in these ads to the language Lewis describes. Discuss whether or not you find any of the ads you have gathered effective.

Selling America
Sandra Silberstein

When we think of advertising, we tend to think of marketers trying to sell us something. But it isn't only products that advertising aims to promote. Sometimes ads and commercials pitch ideas and concepts, such as quitting smoking or the merits of volunteering. In the aftermath of the September 11 tragedy, the Ad Council produced an ad campaign that promoted messages of tolerance, patriotism, and diversity. This "selling of America" is the subject of the next essay.

Sandra Silberstein is a linguist and professor of English at the University of Washington in Seattle. She focuses on the role of language in creating national identity and public consciousness. The next piece is an excerpt from her book, *War of Words: Language, Politics and 9/11* (2002).

Make Alan Greenspan proud; buy something.

DALLAS BILLBOARD SELLING CLASSIFIED ADS

1 The Ad Council of America was founded as the War Advertising Council in 1942, in the wake of the attack on Pearl Harbor.[1] It is the group that has brought America some of its most powerful slogans, from the World War II "Loose Lips Sink Ships"[2] to Smokey the Bear's "Only You Can Prevent Forest Fires," to "Friends Don't Let Friends Drive Drunk."[3] The council is a private, nonprofit agency whose mission remains today as it was articulated in 1942:

> To identify a select number of significant public issues and to stimulate action on those issues through communications programs which make a measurable difference in society.[4]

2 After the attacks of 9/11, the Ad Council undertook to provide messages of tolerance and patriotism. The Ad Council's campaign was a manifestation of nation building as it sold America on itself, building loyalty to values of tolerance and diversity.

America Responds to the Crisis

3 In the aftermath of September 11, the Ad Council developed an extensive media campaign titled, "America Responds to the Crisis: Messages That Can Help and Heal."

4 In its government partnerships and access to the American people, the Ad Council is as close as the U.S. comes to having a national propaganda organ; it is responsible for many of the public service announcements Americans encounter on television and radio, in print, and now on the Internet. The messages of the "Crisis" campaign stressed the civic virtues of tolerance and social responsibility. But what can be seen by many as ideologically neutral public service announcements can be read quite differently by others, depending on the worldview they bring to the task.

5 Like all texts, these ads allowed for a range of readings, as recipients were able to project their own perspectives onto them. A few preliminary examples below will quickly underscore the complex task facing the Ad Council as it launched its most famous PSA, "I am an American." This potential for diverse readings can be seen first in brief examples from the Web. Ad Council Internet campaigns urge Web masters to add council banners to their sites. Examples include two reproduced below. While on the screen, each line flashes, then is replaced, in a continual loop, by the next.

6   Whatever race
Whatever country
Whatever religion
All families worry about the same thing

Talk to your children about terrorism
Talk to your children about tolerance

7   Turning to the last message first, we see that these very abbreviated banners require a great deal of "filling in." This is an ad campaign that asks viewers to supply familiar cultural themes and common-sense reactions to potent terms. What is the connection between talking about terrorism and talking about tolerance? Is it causal? If so, in which direction? To demonstrate the multiple possibilities, here are a few possible interpretations, together with a pair of contrasting glosses for the banner. Readers will no doubt be able to generate many others.

- *Terrorism is caused by a lack of tolerance. Inoculate your children against terrorism; teach tolerance.* As a native speaker of "Americanese," I rather think that this is at least close to an intended, first-order message. But other possibilities abound.
- *Terrorism is caused by a lack of tolerance. If we don't teach tolerance we would become vulnerable to recruitment by terrorists.* This meaning is slightly different from the first, but plausible. It works particularly if one enters the loop seeing *tolerance* first, then *terrorism.*

8   Here are quite different possibilities:

- *Tolerance is a liberal term that doesn't address the underlying roots of terrorism. Explain to your children why people turn to terrorism when despair overtakes hope.*
- *Tolerance is a liberal term that doesn't address the underlying roots of terrorism. It asks the victim to embrace tolerance while being savaged. Talk to your children about the necessity of terrorism now that despair has overtaken hope.*

9   Finally, here are two alternative glosses:

- *This is a message that Americans write to assume moral superiority over the world's desperate and poor.*
- *This is the kind of message that would save the world if everyone could see it and be schooled in it.*

10   As we can see, ad campaigns cannot guarantee a single response from a diverse audience. There is presumably an infinite number of "readings" of, and reactions to, this banner. The job of advertisers is to position targeted readers as closely as possible to at least a range of desired reactions. Those sympathetic to terrorism were presumably not the targeted audience. Predicting viewer response is a challenge, but it is also the special task of advertising. A similar set of readings could arise from the first banner:

Whatever race
Whatever country
Whatever religion
All families worry about the same thing

11   The most obvious reading in the U.S. is the universalist one: *Don't lose sight of the commonalities of being human.* But this is not the only reaction. There is also the racist one: *This sentiment is the luxury of those who are relatively safe; "those people" don't care about their families or they wouldn't send them off to kill us and die.* And there is the reading of the desperate: *We don't have the luxury of worrying about the physical safety of a single person; we are fighting for the survival of our people* or *homeland* or *culture.*

12   The common-sense civic virtues that the Ad Council propounds will not resonate universally. But they do appeal to a range of readers in the U.S. Within the complex and contradictory rhetoric of the nation, these ads draw on an internal discourse of what is considered the best of America. They sell the nation to itself. They remind America of its multicultural identity at a time when that could be threatened.

13   One of the print ads was particularly powerful. On the skyline of New York, where the Twin Towers had been, two long columns read as follows:

WILL HATE BRING IT ALL BACK? WILL IT BRING BACK THE INNOCENCE? THE SENSE OF SECURITY? WILL IT BRING BACK THE HUS BANDS AND WIVES AND SONS AND DAUGHTERS? WILL HATE MAKE US BETTER THAN THOSE WHO HATE US? OR MERELY BRING US CLOSER TO THEM? WILL HATE HELP US DESTROY OUR ENEMIES? OR WILL IT LAUGH AS WE DESTROY OURSELVES? THERE ARE THOSE WHO SAY WE DON'T KNOW WHO OUR ENEMY IS, BUT WE DO. OUR ENEMY IS A NEIGHBORHOOD MOSQUE DEFACED BY VANDALS. AN ARAB-AMERICAN STOREKEEPER IN FEAR OF REPRISAL. A SCARED MUSLIM CHILD BULLIED BECAUSE SHE IS DIFFERENT. HATE IS OUR ENEMY. AND WHEN WE START TO HATE OTHER AMERICANS, WE HAVE LOST EVERYTHING. HATE HAS TAKEN ENOUGH FROM US ALREADY. DON'T LET IT TAKE YOU.

14   The ad identifies an enemy worse than the terrorists of 9/11, that is, the scourge of hate. But what does the slogan, "Americans Stand United" mean? On the one hand, it means that Americans are united against an internal enemy, in this case, hate. On the other hand, calls to stand united are a fairly standard wartime exhortation, and the U.S. was at war. Another possible reading of the full ad focuses on an external enemy: America will not be able to fully unite in the War on Terrorism if it

is internally fractured by divisive hate. And at a distance, the ad scans like typical patriotism, urging unity in support of the current war. This combination of themes, inclusion, unity and traditional patriotism (along with the diverse readings they allow), became the Ad Council signature in several ads.

15   The[se] complex decisions of how to best unify a diverse nation (of viewers) within secular virtues are best exemplified in one of the council's TV spots.

I Am an American

16 Perhaps the most widely circulated ad was the television spot, "I am an American," which seemed to appear almost immediately after 9/11. It was created by staffers of an Austin-based ad agency who'd been in Washington, DC, on September 11. On the long drive home, they hatched the plan for the PSA, which they donated to the Ad Council. The council was able to distribute it to 3,000 media outlets nationwide.[5]

17   Americans found the PSA very powerful, and beautifully produced. A concise description came from the *Houston Chronicle:*

> The commercial shows people from the melting pot—including a firefighter, children and adults of many ethnicities—facing the camera and saying simply, "I am an American." The screen then flashes the nation's venerable motto, *e pluribus unum,* a Latin phrase that means "out of many, one."[6]

18   In fact, the ad showed more than 40 individuals—from a nun, to a police officer, to firefighters—with fully diverse skin tones and accents. Some were native speakers of a variety of English dialects, others clearly had first languages other than English. One speaker was in a wheelchair, another used sign language. Speakers stood in urban areas, including New York and San Francisco, as well as in gardens and fields. Each delivery of "I am an American" was a bit different, as the ad captured the variety of individual cadences.

19   The reaction to the ad was so rich that the Ad Council developed a Web page titled, "What people are saying about 'I am an American'." It is here that we can gain some insight into the varied receptions of this most widely distributed selling of America. We know from media coverage the intent of the ad's makers. It was designed as "a gift to the American people from the advertising industry."[7] Ad agency president, Roy Spence, reported: "We wanted to make sure that when we strike back, we don't strike back at one of our own."[8]

20   Many of the responses on the "What People are Saying" Web page were laudatory. Here are typical sentiments:

> Just thought you'd like to hear about this. I was flying out of Atlanta on Friday, September 28th. Your "I am an American" PSA came on the television monitors as I was passing through a terminal. What followed was something I've never seen in an airport before. I stopped to watch the PSA, and like others was very moved by it. As the PSA played, more and more people stopped to watch. By the time the PSA was over, there were at least 40 people gathered around just the one monitor.

With smiles on our faces, we broke up and went about our business. I just want to congratulate you on such a successful campaign and thank you for helping make the day a little bit brighter. (Chris)

Kudos. This ad captures precisely what America should be. I hope it becomes etched in every American's brain. (Robert)

Your "I am an American" television ad stirs the deepest emotions of my American soul. When I see your ad at my age of 40 years it brings tears of sadness and joy to my eyes. Sadness that an unparalleled tragedy had to occur for such an ad to have meaning in our country, but joy in that I think the time may have finally arrived when not just whites and blacks can come together but—all Americans. If I had a million dollars, I'd buy as much ad time as I could for the ad. (Norm)

Thank you for your campaign. The most destructive impact of 9/11 could well be what it turns us into. I believe your campaign will play a part in assuring that we turn into a better nation. Thanks. (Petrops)

Thanks for your ad. Very little air time in the last two weeks has been more valuable. God bless us all. (Franca, Baltimore, MD.)

21   There is, even in this ad, however, an ambiguity. Does the ad celebrate the achievement of a diverse unity of Americans or is it trying to create this? Put more starkly: Is the ad meant to celebrate or protect nonwhite Americans; does the majority need to be reminded that minorities are members of the community when the wagons are circled? The stated goals of the campaign actually lean toward the latter interpretation—"to assure that we don't strike out at one of our own."

22   The statements above respond to a rather romanticized viewing. People saw the ad as a reaffirmation of, perhaps a tutorial on, what America could be. But there was a spectrum of responses when viewers rated the ad in its portrayal of diversity. This range of responses indicates that viewers bring with them divergent ingredients from the narrative stew that is public discourse. At the risk of getting carried away with a metaphor: you are what you eat. Many people saw a refreshing range of people on the screen (perhaps because their world is not so diverse?). Within that group, Bob wrote, "It is clear that you intended everyone to be included." Margaret wrote, "the commercial . . . represents all countries and all types, shapes and colors of faces." Several writers, however, noted limitations on that diversity (perhaps because they are closer to issues of exclusion):

Your PSA is quite powerful and very useful. However, it does not include any Muslim man in Islamic Dress and any Muslim woman in Islamic Dress with the head hijab. Diversification without Muslims is indeed incomplete; Muslims are also American. (Ilyas)

With the recent aftermath of the NY and Washington bombings, male Sikhs in particular and Muslim women have faced the brunt of the backlash. I was hoping that a male Sikh with a turban and beard could be added to this ad. This would speed up the rebuilding process of our great nation and help people understand the differences between various religions and races. (Manny)

> I am American and I have been watching your latest campaign on TV with a feeling of admiration, but also a profound feeling of being insulted. You failed to show a single member of the Armed Forces. How utterly thoughtless of you at a time when brave noble brothers and sisters are putting their lives at risk for all of the freedom loving people of this earth. (William)

> I love ur ad . . . it is wonderful . . . but being an American citizen and wearing a headscarf i don't see myself there pleez have somebody like me too in the ad or if u need assistance i know many people who would be willing to be in it . . . hope to hear from u sooooon. (Saniya)

23   These diverse responses confirm that public service announcements, like all texts, are interpreted through a complex interaction of their content and the preexisting perspective of the viewer. Several final responses make this abundantly clear.

24   > I just saw your "I am An American" ad, and while I can appreciate the sentiment, I found it deeply distressing and highly offensive that no European Americans were included in the segment. (Joe)

25   It is fascinating that fully half the faces (approximately 20) are likely European American. Clearly for viewers who are either unaccustomed to faces of color and/or uncomfortable with these images, it is possible for an equal representation to be completely misperceived. For this viewer, past some threshold, every face became one of color. This is perhaps an extreme example of what is surely universal—seeing ads through the lens of one's particular concerns. One viewer noticed in the ads her "pet peeve":

> I really liked your diversity PSA. It addresses a pet peeve of mine. As an Asian American, I find myself constantly correcting my less enlightened Asian friends when they talk about so-and-so's "American" spouse. What do you mean by "American"? Aren't YOU American too? Maybe I can get off the soap box now . . . thanks. (R. Louie)

26   The last segments discussed here address assimilation. Randy, of Pennsylvania, wrote of the ads:

> They Are The Best!!! Finally, people are standing up and saying that they are Americans, period. Thank you for taking the "hyphen" out of being an American. I never thought it should have been there in the first place. . . .

27   It's not the least bit clear that the folks in these ads do not think of themselves as hyphenated Americans, or that they do not take great pride in their ethnic or cultural origins. Nor is it clear that the ad makers intended a message along the lines that to be American, one has to give up hyphenated identities. But for Randy, who was presumably moved by the ad, to assert Americanism is to forego a hyphen.

28   Earl, from Pennsylvania, saw a distancing from "political correctness" in the ad:

> I want to compliment you on your TV ad: "I am an American." After years of insane political correctness it is uplifting to me to see people of different ethnic backgrounds unite as one instead of using hyphens and asking for victim group hand outs. Thankfully, Clinton's "Our strength is our diversity" defiance of common sense did not affect everyone. We do have an American culture, and the nation is strong because the immigrants that came here united in to one people. Your ad reflects my beliefs and I want to thank you for placing it on TV.

29   Like all viewers, Earl read the ad through the lens of his experience and concerns. While the ad makers might well see "our strength is our diversity" as the perfect gloss for this spot, for Earl the PSA was a corrective to that sentiment. It also appears to Earl to be a denunciation of affirmative action ("victim group hand outs") and an endorsement of assimilation. For other viewers (I daresay most), the ad embraced diversity. Judy wrote from Houston, "Thanks for making Americans aware that 'we' are made up of many nationalities That's what 'America' is," David, writing from South Carolina, spoke of the "collaboration of our nation's diversity and its unity."

30   But perhaps the single most important endorsement the Ad Council could have received was Earl's final testimonial, "Your ad reflects my beliefs." In a sense the ad did. It allowed a range of viewers to position themselves as appreciative participants in a racially diverse America. For some viewers that diversity was only visual; they read the ad with an assimilationist tinge. For many others, the ad ratified a society united in its appreciation of diversity. In its ability to allow for both of those readings, "I am an American" became a vehicle for all stripes of patriotism.

31   David, in Washington, wrote to say that he had responded as "a quiet and grateful patriot." Chris in Canada wrote to say "I haven't seen anything come close, since the tragedy, to expressing so clearly and poignantly what it is we are trying to defend. This ad will cause our enemies consternation." And David, from Pennsylvania, wrote:

> I am a navy veteran of WWII and I still remember the poster with "Loose Lips Sink Ships" on them. I am still impressed with that phrase and happy to learn that you will be adding your know-how to the upcoming struggle. That should help the American people maintain their resolve during the years to come.

32   While a good deal more complex than "Loose Lips Sink Ships," "I am an American" nonetheless worked the same side of the street: to unite a diverse country in common cause at a time of war.

Notes

1. Ad Council of America, "Message From the President of the Ad Council of America," www.adcouncil.org/crisis/index.htm.

2. Claire Cozens, "American Ad Body in Call to Arms," *Guardian Unlimited,* October 2, 2001.
3. Greg Hassell, "Altruistic Ads Try to Unite Americans," *Houston Chronicle,* September 25, 2001.
4. Ad Council.
5. Hassell
6. Ibid.
7. Ibid.
8. Ibid.

THINKING CRITICALLY

1. What was the motivation behind the Ad Council's advertising campaign "I am an American"?

2. What is the author's personal opinion of the "I am an American" campaign? Is she admiring? Critical? Concerned? Supportive? Explain.

3. How did the Ad Council use the Internet as part of the "I am an American" campaign? What opportunities does the Web provide advertisers in promoting messages? What made this campaign suitable for the Internet? Explain.

4. Silberstein explains that the television commercial for "I am an American" elicited a wide scope of "readings." That is, different people had different reactions to the ad. What were these readings and what accounted for the broad responses?

5. The author provides several interpretations of the Internet ad promoting tolerance. Respond to her analysis in your own words. Specifically, which interpretations seem to make sense to you, and which seem off target, and why? Are there any other obvious interpretations that the author missed?

6. How did the Ad Council "sell" America in the "I am an American" campaign? In your opinion, was the campaign a success? Explain.

WRITING ASSIGNMENTS

1. Visit the Ad Council's Web site at <www.adcouncil.org>, and evaluate another public service announcement (PSA) campaign. Analyze the campaign's message, audience, and slogans. What is the campaign trying to "sell"? How does it appeal to its audience? Does it allow for multiple readings? Does it reach its intended public? Explain.

2. Response to the television ad "I am an American" was so overwhelming that the Ad Council set up a Web site to allow people to express their opinions. Access the Ad Council's Web site at <www.adcouncil.org> and view the "I am an American" television commercial cosponsored by the Arab American Institute. Write a response to the ad expressing your own opinion of the message and meaning of the ad. How did it make you feel? What "reading" do you ascribe to the commercial? How does your response compare to those expressed in the essay?

Americans Stand United

In the preceding essay, Sandra Silberstein described this ad sponsored by the Arab American Institute and the Ad Council and designed by the Brokaw Agency to encourage tolerance during the aftermath of September 11. As you view the ad below, consider how the ad uses symbolism, language, and emotion to reach its audience and promote its message.

THINKING CRITICALLY

1. If you were leafing through a magazine and saw this ad, would you stop to read it? Would you read the entire message? Why or why not?

2. How does this ad use symbolism to promote its message? Is it an appropriate use of symbolism? Explain.

3. What time of day is it? Is there any significance to the time of day featured in the ad? Would this ad be more effective if it pictured the New York skyline at a different time of day?

4. Consider the final line floating in the water, "Americans Stand United." What do these words mean to you? Are there other meanings in addition to your first impression?

5. What trademark logos are included in the ad? Where are they placed? Why are they there?

6. Analyze the language that makes up the Twin Towers. How accessible is it? Does it engage the audience? Explain.

Exploring the Language of **VISUALS**

Two Sample Ads

Take a look at the following two magazine advertisements for sports utility vehicles (SUVs). Although some people will say that most SUVs are alike, each of the two manufacturers wants you to believe that its vehicle is for you. Thus, the sales pitches and marketing techniques take different slants—some relying on hard-sell copy, others hoping to arrest your attention with creative visuals; some taking the informative, even chatty approach, and others making an appeal to emotions. Following each ad is a list of questions to help you analyze the individual spreads and comparative strategies. These questions should help stimulate class discussion and provide ideas for future papers.

VISUALS
continued ➤

JEEP. WRANGLER

Take a ride in a rugged Jeep Wrangler and you'll see the world like never before. And the world will see you like never before. That's because Wrangler says a lot about you, on the road and off. Your passion for discovery. Your quest for fun.

In fact, fun is what Wrangler is all about. So it's easy to overlook important features like Command-Trac® shift-on-the-fly four-wheel drive, axle ratios geared low enough for rock crawling, and Quadra-Coil™ suspension for literally soaking up the bumps.

Is Wrangler the original go-anywhere vehicle? Of course. Is it the most fun? Definitely!

Exclamation point well taken.

Jeep Wrangler. From the most award-winning brand of 4x4s on Earth. For all the details, visit us online at www.jeep.com or call 1-800-925-JEEP.

Jeep

THERE'S ONLY ONE

Always use seat belts. Remember, a backseat is the safest place for children. Rearward-facing child seats can be used in the front seat only with the passenger air bag turned off. Jeep is a registered trademark of DaimlerChrysler.

Jeep Wrangler Ad

1. Examine this advertisement carefully. What is the effect of placing an exclamation point after the image of the Jeep Wrangler?
2. How does the setting and the use of boulders to construct the exclamation point promote the product? How do these elements tap into audience expectations about the product?
3. Would you know what this ad was selling if there were no copy in the ad? Explain.
4. If you were leafing through a magazine and saw this ad, would you stop to read it? Why or why not?
5. This advertisement features a great deal of printed material under the picture. Does the copy detract from the simplicity of the photograph or complement it?
6. Explain how this advertisement plays with language and our understanding of the conventions of expression.

VISUALS
continued ➤

Chevy Blazer Ad

1. Compare this advertisement to the ad for Jeep Wrangler. What elements do the two ads have in common? How are they different?
2. What is the effect of featuring the SUV on top of a lighthouse? What message does it send to the reader? Explain.
3. How does the written copy featured at the bottom of the ad complement the photograph? How does it reinforce the message of the photo and of the slogan, "A little security in an insecure world"?
4. Would this ad be less effective if it fetured people in the photograph?
5. Who do you think is the target audience for this advertisement? How do you think a child would respond to it? A woman? A man? Explain.
6. Evaluate how symbolism serves as an unspoken form of language. How does symbolism work in this advertisement to sell the product?

■ MAKING CONNECTIONS

1. Clip three ads for products that use sex as a selling device, yet have no sexual connotations whatsoever. Explain how sex helps sell the products. Would feminists consider these ads demeaning to women?

2. Choose a brand-name product you use regularly and one of its competitors—one whose differences are negligible, if they exist at all. Examine some advertisements for each brand. Write a short paper explaining what really makes you prefer your brand.

3. Herschell Gordon Lewis complains how ads employ "in your face" tactics to sell products. Brainstorm a list of "aggressive" ads that you have seen in magazines or on TV and discuss whether or not you find their tactics effective. Be sure to refer to specific details of the ads (particularly the language used) to support your claims.

4. Sandra Silberstein explains that in most of the ads presented by the Ad Council in their campaigns, the language they used was ambiguous enough for different audiences with disparate points of view and experience to come away with their own, positive, spin on the ads' messages. Take a look at some other slogans presented by other advertising agencies to see if this element of ambiguity exists in other types of advertising.

5. William Lutz characterizes the language used in ads as "weasel words," that is, language that pretends to do one thing, while really doing another. Explore your campus for examples of weasel words. Look not only at ads, but at material such as university brochures and pamphlets that are sent to prospective students, and/or any political contests taking place (i.e., students running for the student government or candidates for office speaking at your campus). Write down all examples of weasel words and report back to your classmates.

Censorship and Free Speech

7

■ We saw Margaret Sanger gagged in Chapter 1. Here, an artist uses the same gag imagery and a symbol of liberty to make a point about free speech in America. Just what are the limits of our First Amendment rights? (Rohan Van Twest, photographer)

*"C*ongress shall make no law . . . abridging the freedom of speech, or of the press."* With these simple words, the writers of the Constitution created one of the pillars of our democratic system of government—the First Amendment guarantee of every American's right to the free exchange of ideas, beliefs, and political debate. Most Americans passionately support their right to express themselves without fear of government reprisal. However, over the years questions have arisen about whether limits should be imposed on our right to free expression when the exercise of that right imposes hardship or pain on others. What happens when the right of one person to state his or her beliefs conflicts with the rights of others to be free from verbal abuse? What happens when free expression runs counter to community values? At what point does the perceived degree of offensiveness warrant censorship? And at what point does censorship threaten to undermine our constitutional rights? In this chapter we look at two particular areas that have generated debate and dialogue recently: censorship and books and censorship of campus speech.

Censorship and Books

The censorship of books challenges the rights guaranteed by the First Amendment on two fronts: the right to express ideas freely and the right to have access to the ideas of others. In "The Freedom to Read," the American Library Association (ALA) and the Association of American Publishers explore the effects of censorship attempts on Americans' freedom to read and affirm the importance of making all viewpoints available for public scrutiny, even when the ideas are unpopular and offensive. The next two pieces present different points of view on the issue of banned books. Jeff Jacoby, in "Book Banning, Real and Imaginary" takes the position that there is no "book banning" threat in the United States, merely a bunch of parents who want a voice in what their children read in school. Author Judy Blume, however, explains in her editorial, "Is Harry Potter Evil?" that book censorship is harmful, both to children and our free society.

Perhaps no other piece of American literature has stirred up more debates about book banning than Mark Twain's 1885 classic, *Adventures of Huckleberry Finn.* It was immediately banned by the Concord, Massachusetts, Public Library the year it was published and, according to the ALA, it continues to be banned today in libraries throughout America—but for very different reasons. In tribute to the book's fame, we have reproduced an early cover of the classic for analysis and discussion. We conclude this section with an "afterword" of sorts by renowned science fiction author Ray Bradbury, who presents a rather lively perspective on the question of editing literary works to accommodate popular notions of political correctness.

Censorship and Free Speech on Campus

The free and open exchange of ideas seems critical to the goals of higher education. However, when the ideas expressed are racist, sexist, or otherwise offensive toward specific groups on campus, do universities and colleges have the right to censor and punish that form of speech? This case study takes a look at this issue in depth, presenting multiple points of view. For example, in "Regulating Racist Speech on Campus," Charles R. Lawrence argues that verbal harassment violates student victims' rights to an education. Colleges and universities must act to prevent such harassment from happening by restricting this form of speech, he believes. Taking the opposite side, Alan Charles Kors and Harvey A. Silverglate find this form of censorship objectionable and dangerous, arguing that it chills freedom of expression and opinion. Alternatively, Stanley Fish argues that truly free speech doesn't really exist, on campus or anywhere else—it is merely a rhetorical construct used by those in power to forward political agendas. The case study ends with an examination of a recent free speech controversy at Harvard Law School.

■ CENSORSHIP AND BOOKS

The Freedom to Read
American Library Association

The American Library Association, founded in 1876, is the oldest and largest national library association in the world. Addressing the needs of state, public, school, and academic libraries, it has over 55,000 members across the country. Dedicated to preserving the freedom of information distribution and assuring the access to information for all, the ALA has even written its own "Bill of Rights." The following document was originally drafted and adopted in 1953. It was later revised in 1991, in response to increasing pressure from special interest groups to censure or limit the distribution of certain books to American libraries and schools. What follows represents its most recent revision in July of 2000.

1   The freedom to read is essential to our democracy. It is continuously under attack. Private groups and public authorities in various parts of the country are working to remove or limit access to reading materials, to censor content in schools, to label "controversial" views, to distribute lists of "objectionable" books or authors, and to purge libraries. These actions apparently rise from a view that our national tradition of free expression is no longer valid; that censorship and suppression are needed to avoid the subversion of politics and the corruption of morals. We, as citizens devoted to reading and as librarians and publishers responsible for disseminating ideas, wish to assert the public interest in the preservation of the freedom to read.

2   Most attempts at suppression rest on a denial of the fundamental premise of democracy: that the ordinary citizen, by exercising critical judgment, will accept the good and reject the bad. The censors, public and private, assume that they should determine what is good and what is bad for their fellow citizens.

3   We trust Americans to recognize propaganda and misinformation, and to make their own decisions about what they read and believe. We do not believe they need the help of censors to assist them in this task. We do not believe they are prepared to sacrifice their heritage of a free press in order to be "protected" against what others think may be bad for them. We believe they still favor free enterprise in ideas and expression.

4   These efforts at suppression are related to a larger pattern of pressures being brought against education, the press, art and images, films, broadcast media, and the Internet. The problem is not only one of actual censorship. The shadow of fear cast by these pressures leads, we suspect, to an even larger voluntary curtailment of expression by those who seek to avoid controversy.

5   Such pressure toward conformity is perhaps natural to a time of accelerated change. And yet suppression is never more dangerous than in such a time of social tension. Freedom has given the United States the elasticity to endure strain. Freedom keeps open the path of novel and creative solutions, and enables change to come by choice. Every silencing of a heresy, every enforcement of an orthodoxy, diminishes the toughness and resilience of our society and leaves it less able to deal with controversy and difference.

6   Now as always in our history, reading is among our greatest freedoms. The freedom to read and write is almost the only means for making generally available ideas or manners of expression that can initially command only a small audience. The written word is the natural medium for the new idea and the untried voice from which come the original contributions to social growth. It is essential to the extended discussion that serious thought requires, and to the accumulation of knowledge and ideas into organized collections.

7   We believe that free communication is essential to the preservation of a free society and a creative culture. We believe that these pressures toward conformity present the danger of limiting the range and variety of inquiry and expression on which our democracy and our culture depend. We believe that every American community must jealously guard the freedom to publish and to circulate, in order to preserve its own freedom to read. We believe that publishers and librarians have a profound responsibility to give validity to that freedom to read by making it possible for the readers to choose freely from a variety of offerings. The freedom to read is guaranteed by the Constitution. Those with faith in free people will stand firm on these constitutional guarantees of essential rights and will exercise the responsibilities that accompany these rights.

8   We therefore affirm these propositions:

9   1. *It is in the public interest for publishers and librarians to make available the widest diversity of views and expressions, including those that are unorthodox or unpopular with the majority.*

Creative thought is by definition new, and what is new is different. The bearer of every new thought is a rebel until that idea is refined and tested. Totalitarian systems attempt to maintain themselves in power by the ruthless suppression of any concept that challenges the established orthodoxy. The power of a democratic system to adapt to change is vastly strengthened by the freedom of its citizens to choose widely from among conflicting opinions offered freely to them. To stifle every nonconformist idea at birth would mark the end of the democratic process. Furthermore, only through the constant activity of weighing and selecting can the democratic mind attain the strength demanded by times like these. We need to know not only what we believe but why we believe it.

10   2. *Publishers, librarians, and booksellers do not need to endorse every idea or presentation they make available. It would conflict with the public interest for them to establish their own political, moral, or aesthetic views as a standard for determining what should be published or circulated.*

Publishers and librarians serve the educational process by helping to make available knowledge and ideas required for the growth of the mind and the increase of learning. They do not foster education by imposing as mentors the patterns of their own thought. The people should have the freedom to read and consider a broader range of ideas than those that may be held by any single librarian or publisher or government or church. It is wrong that what one can read should be confined to what another thinks proper.

11   3. *It is contrary to the public interest for publishers or librarians to bar access to writings on the basis of the personal history or political affiliations of the author.*

No art or literature can flourish if it is to be measured by the political views or private lives of its creators. No society of free people can flourish that draws up lists of writers to whom it will not listen, whatever they may have to say.

12   4. *There is no place in our society for efforts to coerce the taste of others, to confine adults to the reading matter deemed suitable for adolescents, or to inhibit the efforts of writers to achieve artistic expression.*

To some, much of modern expression is shocking. But is not much of life itself shocking? We cut off literature at the source if we prevent writers from dealing with the stuff of life. Parents and teachers have a responsibility to prepare the young to meet the diversity of experiences in life to which they will be exposed, as they have a responsibility to help them learn to think critically for themselves. These are affirmative responsibilities, not to be discharged simply by preventing them from reading works for which they are not yet prepared. In these matters values differ, and values cannot be legislated; nor can machinery be devised that will suit the demands of one group without limiting the freedom of others.

13   5. *It is not in the public interest to force a reader to accept with any expression the prejudgment of a label characterizing it or its author as subversive or dangerous.*

The ideal of labeling presupposes the existence of individuals or groups with wisdom to determine by authority what is good or bad for the citizen. It presupposes that individuals must be directed in making up their minds about the ideas they examine. But Americans do not need others to do their thinking for them.

14   6. *It is the responsibility of publishers and librarians, as guardians of the people's freedom to read, to contest encroachments upon that freedom by individuals or groups seeking to impose their own standards or tastes upon the community at large.*

It is inevitable in the give and take of the democratic process that the political, the moral, or the aesthetic concepts of an individual or group will occasionally collide with those of another individual or group. In a free society individuals are free to determine for themselves what they wish to read, and each group is free to determine what it will recommend to its freely associated members. But no group has the right to take the law into its own hands, and to impose its own concept of politics or morality upon other members of a democratic society. Freedom is not freedom if it is accorded only to the accepted and the inoffensive.

15   7. *It is the responsibility of publishers and librarians to give full meaning to the freedom to read by providing books that enrich the quality and diversity of thought and expression. By the exercise of this affirmative responsibility, they can demonstrate that the answer to a "bad" book is a good one, the answer to a "bad" idea is a good one.*

The freedom to read is of little consequence when the reader cannot obtain matter fit for that reader's purpose. What is needed is not only the absence of restraint, but the positive provision of opportunity for the people to read the best that has been thought and said. Books are the major channel by which the intellectual inheritance is handed down, and the principal means of its testing and growth. The defense of the freedom to read requires of all publishers and librarians the utmost of their faculties, and deserves of all citizens the fullest of their support.

16   We state these propositions neither lightly nor as easy generalizations. We here stake out a lofty claim for the value of the written word. We do so because we believe that it is possessed of enormous variety and usefulness, worthy of cherishing and keeping free. We realize that the application of these propositions may mean the dissemination of ideas and manners of expression that are repugnant to many persons. We do not state these propositions in the comfortable belief that what people read is unimportant. We believe rather that what people read is deeply important; that ideas can be dangerous; but that the suppression of ideas is fatal to a democratic society. Freedom itself is a dangerous way of life, but it is ours.

THINKING CRITICALLY

1. What attempts at suppression of information is the ALA concerned about? Do the authors provide any examples? Are examples necessary to support their argument? Explain.

2. In paragraph 5, the document states that "suppression is never more dangerous than in such a time of social tension." What do the authors mean by this statement? How do you think opponents to this declaration would respond?

3. Can you think of any attempts by certain groups to control the accessibility of written material (besides pornography) because it is unacceptable? Explain the circumstances and the reaction to their censorship attempt.

4. The writers mention the labeling of books. To what are they objecting? Are they against all types of labels? Explain.

5. How do the writers use the First Amendment and the Constitution to support their argument? Is this an effective means of persuasion? Explain.

WRITING ASSIGNMENTS

1. Analyze the seven "declarations" of the ALA document and formulate a response to each. What questions do you have about them? What exceptions to these "declarations" can you anticipate?

2. Can you think of any type of publication, besides pornography, that should be suppressed? If so, write a letter to the authors of the ALA in which you explain your reasoning. In your letter, make clear the kinds of negative consequences that could result should such a publication be publicly available.

The 100 Most Frequently Challenged Books of 2000

This list represents the top 100 books reported challenged to the Office for Intellectual Freedom, who compiled this list. According to the ALA Office for Intellectual Freedom, research suggests that for each challenge, of which there were over 6,300 in 2000, there are as many as four or five others that go unreported. The list is periodically updated and posted online at the American Library Association's Web site at <www.ala.org>.

1. *Scary Stories* (Series) by Alvin Schwartz
2. *Daddy's Roommate* by Michael Willhoite
3. *I Know Why the Caged Bird Sings* by Maya Angelou
4. *The Chocolate War* by Robert Cormier
5. *Adventures of Huckleberry Finn* by Mark Twain
6. *Of Mice and Men* by John Steinbeck
7. *Harry Potter* (Series) by J. K. Rowling
8. *Forever* by Judy Blume
9. *Bridge to Terabithia* by Katherine Paterson
10. *Alice* (Series) by Phyllis Reynolds Naylor
11. *Heather Has Two Mommies* by Leslea Newman
12. *My Brother Sam is Dead* by James Lincoln Collier and Christopher Collier
13. *The Catcher in the Rye* by J. D. Salinger
14. *The Giver* by Lois Lowry
15. *It's Perfectly Normal* by Robie Harris

16. *Goosebumps* (Series) by R. L. Stine
17. *A Day No Pigs Would Die* by Robert Newton Peck
18. *The Color Purple* by Alice Walker
19. *Sex* by Madonna
20. *Earth's Children* (Series) by Jean M. Auel
21. *The Great Gilly Hopkins* by Katherine Paterson
22. *A Wrinkle in Time* by Madeleine L'Engle
23. *Go Ask Alice* by Anonymous
24. *Fallen Angels* by Walter Dean Myers
25. *In the Night Kitchen* by Maurice Sendak
26. *The Stupids* (Series) by Harry Allard
27. *The Witches* by Roald Dahl
28. *The New Joy of Gay Sex* by Charles Silverstein
29. *Anastasia Krupnik* (Series) by Lois Lowry
30. *The Goats* by Brock Cole
31. *Kaffir Boy* by Mark Mathabane
32. *Blubber* by Judy Blume
33. *Killing Mr. Griffin* by Lois Duncan
34. *Halloween ABC* by Eve Merriam
35. *We All Fall Down* by Robert Cormier
36. *Final Exit* by Derek Humphry
37. *The Handmaid's Tale* by Margaret Atwood
38. *Julie of the Wolves* by Jean Craighead George
39. *The Bluest Eye* by Toni Morrison
40. *What's Happening to My Body? Book for Girls: A Growing-Up Guide for Parents & Daughters* by Lynda Madaras
41. *To Kill a Mockingbird* by Harper Lee
42. *Beloved* by Toni Morrison
43. *The Outsiders* by S. E. Hinton
44. *The Pigman* by Paul Zindel
45. *Bumps in the Night* by Harry Allard
46. *Deenie* by Judy Blume
47. *Flowers for Algernon* by Daniel Keyes
48. *Annie on My Mind* by Nancy Garden
49. *The Boy Who Lost His Face* by Louis Sachar
50. *Cross Your Fingers, Spit in Your Hat* by Alvin Schwartz
51. *A Light in the Attic* by Shel Silverstein
52. *Brave New World* by Aldous Huxley
53. *Sleeping Beauty Trilogy* by A. N. Roquelaure (Anne Rice)
54. *Asking About Sex and Growing Up* by Joanna Cole
55. *Cujo* by Stephen King
56. *James and the Giant Peach* by Roald Dahl
57. *The Anarchist Cookbook* by William Powell
58. *Boys and Sex* by Wardell Pomeroy

59. *Ordinary People* by Judith Guest
60. *American Psycho* by Bret Easton Ellis
61. *What's Happening to My Body? Book for Boys: A Growing-Up Guide for Parents & Sons* by Lynda Madaras
62. *Are You There, God? It's Me, Margaret* by Judy Blume
63. *Crazy Lady* by Jane Conly
64. *Athletic Shorts* by Chris Crutcher
65. *Fade* by Robert Cormier
66. *Guess What?* by Mem Fox
67. *The House of Spirits* by Isabel Allende
68. *The Face on the Milk Carton* by Caroline Cooney
69. *Slaughterhouse-Five* by Kurt Vonnegut
70. *Lord of the Flies* by William Golding
71. *Native Son* by Richard Wright
72. *Women on Top: How Real Life Has Changed Women's Fantasies* by Nancy Friday
73. *Curses, Hexes and Spells* by Daniel Cohen
74. *Jack* by A.M. Homes
75. *Bless Me, Ultima* by Rudolfo A. Anaya
76. *Where Did I Come From?* by Peter Mayle
77. *Carrie* by Stephen King
78. *Tiger Eyes* by Judy Blume
79. *On My Honor* by Marion Dane Bauer
80. *Arizona Kid* by Ron Koertge
81. *Family Secrets* by Norma Klein
82. *Mommy Laid An Egg* by Babette Cole
83. *The Dead Zone* by Stephen King
84. *The Adventures of Tom Sawyer* by Mark Twain
85. *Song of Solomon* by Toni Morrison
86. *Always Running* by Luis Rodriguez
87. *Private Parts* by Howard Stern
88. *Where's Waldo?* by Martin Hanford
89. *Summer of My German Soldier* by Bette Greene
90. *Little Black Sambo* by Helen Bannerman
91. *Pillars of the Earth* by Ken Follett
92. *Running Loose* by Chris Crutcher
93. *Sex Education* by Jenny Davis
94. *The Drowning of Stephen Jones* by Bette Greene
95. *Girls and Sex* by Wardell Pomeroy
96. *How to Eat Fried Worms* by Thomas Rockwell
97. *View from the Cherry Tree* by Willo Davis Roberts
98. *The Headless Cupid* by Zilpha Keatley Snyder
99. *The Terrorist* by Caroline Cooney
100. *Jump Ship to Freedom* by James Lincoln Collier and Christopher Collier

Book-Banning, Real and Imaginary

Jeff Jacoby

Each year, usually during the fourth week of September, the American Library Association observes "National Banned Book Week." To promote dialogue on the issue of censorship and book banning, the ALA publishes a list of books that have been banned by various libraries and schools (see list on pp. 449–451). Its goal is to raise national consciousness regarding what the association perceived to be an escalating problem nationwide. This view, however, is skewed says Jeff Jacoby. Our nation, he explains, isn't facing a book banning crisis. Jacoby explains that the "banned books" on the ALA list are really books that have been merely considered "objectionable," usually by parents. And objecting to certain books isn't censorship.

Jeff Jacoby is often called the "conservative voice" of the *Boston Globe* where he is an editorial columnist. This editorial first appeared in the Boston Globe on September 21, 2001.

1 SO YOU'RE PROUD TO BE AN AMERICAN? GLAD TO LIVE IN THIS SWEET LAND OF LIBERTY, A COUNTRY FANATICS HATE BECAUSE OF ITS FREEDOM, PLURALISM, AND OPENNESS TO NEW IDEAS? WELL, JUST IN TIME TO POP THAT ILLUSION, THE AMERICAN LIBRARY ASSOCIATION IS BACK THIS WEEK WITH BANNED BOOKS WEEK, ITS ANNUAL ATTEMPT TO CONVINCE US THAT CENSORSHIP IS ALIVE AND WELL AND EATING AWAY AT OUR INTELLECTUAL RIGHT TO CHOOSE.

2 Not to worry. Your freedom to read isn't under attack. No censors are stalking you, no library is being stripped. On the contrary: Never have more books by more authors on more subjects been more readily available to more people. Americans have things to worry about these days, but **book-banning** isn't among them. For a "banned book," it turns out, doesn't mean a book that has been banned. It means a book about which somebody, usually a parent, has raised an objection—typically that it is too violent or sexually explicit or that it is not age-appropriate. The vast majority of these complaints deal with books assigned in school classes or found in school libraries. And as even the ALA acknowledges, the complaints usually go nowhere and the books stay where they are.

3 In short, the fanatics and book-burners against whom Banned Books Week is meant to keep us vigilant are mostly parents who raise questions about their kids' reading material. In the world according to the American Library Association, moms and dads are the enemy.

4 And the books this enemy is trying to ban? No. 1 on the ALA's current list is J. K. Rowling's *Harry Potter* series. No. 5 is John Steinbeck's *Of Mice and Men.* No. 6 is Maya Angelou's *I Know Why the Caged Bird Sings.* Those books can be found in 98 percent of the nation's bookstores and 99 percent of its libraries. They can be bought over the Web, listened to on tape, and read in a host of foreign languages. This is censorship?

5   Of course not every complaint about a book is reasonable. Parents who want to keep *Huckleberry Finn* and *Native Son* out of students' hands deserve to get short shrift. But not every complaint is unreasonable, either. Some books do contain vile language or graphic sex and violence; some books are inappropriate for younger readers. A parent who asks the local library to limit her 11-year-old's access to *The Turner Diaries* because she doesn't want him reading neo-Nazi literature is hardly a fanatic. Yet the ALA makes no allowance for common sense. Anyone who challenges any book for any reason is "banning books."

6   Unless they work for a library or bookstore, that is. Nowhere does the ALA warn against, say, the bookstore buyer who refuses to stock a book because he doesn't like its message or the librarian who suppresses works by authors he disagrees with. "The selection criteria that librarians use may not always be what everybody wants," says spokeswoman Larra Clark. "I don't see that it's a real problem."

7   She ought to meet Tom Spence. He is the president of Spence Publishing Company, a small press dedicated to books on cultural and social issues written from a conservative outlook. Among its current offerings are A. J. Conyers's history of toleration, *The Long Truce*; *Shows About Nothing*, a study of film and TV by Boston College philosopher Thomas Hibbs; David Horowitz's bracing polemic on racial politics, *Hating Whitey*; and *Love and Economics: Why the Laissez-Faire Family Doesn't Work*, by the economist (and Forbes columnist) Jennifer Roback Morse. Serious books by serious authors, in other words, and presumably of interest to serious bookstores and libraries.

8   But consider some of the responses Spence received after mailing his Spring 2001 catalog.

9   From the director of a state university bookstore:

> I wish to be REMOVED from your mailing list. I find some of your titles to be offensive and outright simple minded. I will not sell your titles in any of my stores so please do not promote these ridiculous books to me!

10   From the manager at a Berkeley, Calif., bookstore:

> Please take me off your mailing list. . . . We do NOT sell fascist publications.

11   From the books editor at a major Midwestern daily, after receiving a review copy of *Love and Economics*.

> Please take me off of your contact list. If you want to reach a narrowminded audience, try the small-town rags.

12   Then there was the public library in West Haven, Conn., that ordered Spence not to send any more catalogs. When the publisher called to ask why, the librarian hung up on him—four times.

13   Bookstores, libraries, and newspapers can't acquire or review every new book, of course. But should entire catalogs be blackballed or publishers insulted because of the ideological prejudice of the librarian or books editor? Isn't that a form of "book banning?" Maybe the ALA ought to take a closer look.

THINKING CRITICALLY

1. Consider the word *banned* and the word *challenged*. Do they mean the same thing? Is the American Library Association inflaming or exaggerating the issue of objectionable books by calling the week they discuss this issue "Banned Books Week"? Would the phrasing "Challenged Books Week" be more accurate? Less effective? Explain.

2. What is Jacoby's argument against the ALA's Banned Books Week? Does he support his argument with reasonable evidence? Explain.

3. Jacoby comments that the books the "enemy" is trying to ban are found in 98 percent of the nation's bookstores and 99 percent of the nation's libraries. He then asks, "Is this censorship?" (paragraph 4). Answer his question in your own words.

4. According to Jacoby, what objections to books are "unreasonable"? Does the fact that he qualifies some objections as unthreatening, and others unreasonable, undermine his argument?

5. Consider Jacoby's closing comments regarding librarians and bookstore owners who refuse to stock certain titles, usually conservative ones, with which they do not agree. Is this simply another form of censorship? Explain.

WRITING ASSIGNMENTS

1. Is censorship of written materials ever permissible? If so, under what conditions? If not, why not? Write up your thoughts in an essay.

2. Have you ever encountered or heard of the banning of books in schools? If so, who proposed the censorship and why was it enforced? Write about the experience in an essay.

Is Harry Potter Evil?
Judy Blume

In the preceding article, editorial columnist Jeff Jacoby notes that the most objected to books in 2001 (and 2002) were the Harry Potter series. In 2000, as the 100 Most Frequently Challenged Books list indicates, Harry Potter books were the sixth most challenged reading material. In the next editorial, author Judy Blume (who has no less than five books on the Challenged Books list) explains that it is dangerous to shrug off book censorship. Objecting to books such as the Harry Potter series harms not just the children who do not understand all the fuss, but also free society, which we treasure.

Judy Blume is the author of more than twenty books, including the frequently challenged *Are You There God? It's Me, Margaret*, *Tiger Eyes*, *Then Again, Maybe I Won't*, and *Blubber*. She is the editor of *Places I Never Meant to Be: Original Stories by Censored Writers*. This editorial first appeared in the *New York Times* on October 22, 1999.

---

1 I happened to be in London last summer on the very day *Harry Potter and the Prisoner of Azkaban,* the third book in the wildly popular series by J. K. Rowling, was published. I couldn't believe my good fortune. I rushed to the bookstore to buy a copy, knowing this simple act would put me up there with the best grandmas in the world. The book was still months away from publication in the United States, and I have an 8-year-old grandson who is a big Harry Potter fan.

2 It's a good thing when children enjoy books, isn't it? Most of us think so. But like many children's books these days, the Harry Potter series has recently come under fire. In Minnesota, Michigan, New York, California and South Carolina, parents who feel the books promote interest in the occult have called for their removal from classrooms and school libraries.

3 I knew this was coming. The only surprise is that it took so long—as long as it took for the zealots who claim they're protecting children from evil (and evil can be found lurking everywhere these days) to discover that children actually like these books. If children are excited about a book, it must be suspect.

4 I'm not exactly unfamiliar with this line of thinking, having had various books of mine banned from schools over the last 20 years. In my books, it's reality that's seen as corrupting. With Harry Potter, the perceived danger is fantasy. After all, Harry and his classmates attend the celebrated Hogwarts School of Witchcraft and Wizardry. According to certain adults, these stories teach witchcraft, sorcery and satanism. But hey, if it's not one "ism," it's another. I mean Madeleine L'Engle's *A Wrinkle in Time* has been targeted by censors for promoting New Ageism, and Mark Twain's *Adventures of Huckleberry Finn* for promoting racism. Gee, where does that leave the kids?

5 The real danger is not in the books, but in laughing off those who would ban them. The protests against Harry Potter follow a tradition that has been growing since the early 1980's and often leaves school principals trembling with fear that is then passed down to teachers and librarians.

6 What began with the religious right has spread to the politically correct. (Remember the uproar in Brooklyn last year when a teacher was criticized for reading a book entitled *Nappy Hair* to her class?) And now the gate is open so wide that some parents believe they have the right to demand immediate removal of any book for any reason from school or classroom libraries. The list of gifted teachers and librarians who find their jobs in jeopardy for defending their students' right to read, to imagine, to question, grows every year.

7 My grandson was bewildered when I tried to explain why some adults don't want their children reading about Harry Potter. "But that doesn't make any sense!" he said. J. K. Rowling is on a book tour in America right now. She's probably befuddled by the brouhaha, too. After all, she was just trying to tell a good story.

8 My husband and I like to reminisce about how, when we were 9, we read straight through L. Frank Baum's Oz series, books filled with wizards and witches. And you know what those subversive tales taught us? That we loved to read! In those days I used to dream of flying. I may have been small and powerless in real life, but in my imagination I was able to soar.

9   At the rate we're going, I can imagine next year's headline: "'Goodnight Moon' Banned for Encouraging Children to Communicate With Furniture." And we all know where that can lead, don't we?

THINKING CRITICALLY

1. How does Blume engage her audience? What techniques does she use to connect with her readers and encourage them to see her point of view? Explain.

2. What is a "zealot"? Why does Blume use this word to describe people who don't want their children to read certain books, including the Harry Potter series?

3. What is the "perceived danger" of the Harry Potter books? How does the author react to this "danger"? Do you think the fact that her own books have been banned influenced her reaction to objections to the Harry Potter books? Why or why not?

4. Consider Blume's concluding statements on book censorship. What is the tone of her hypothetic example of a headline featuring *Goodnight Moon?* Is it an effective ending to her editorial? Why or why not?

WRITING ASSIGNMENT

1. Do parents have the right to object to certain books being used as reading material in school? Write an essay exploring the rights of parents to determine what their children read.

Exploring the Language of **V I S U A L S**

Huckleberry Finn Banned!

Even when it was first published in 1885, Mark Twain's *Adventures of Huckleberry Finn* was the topic of controversy. That year, the public library in Concord, Massachusetts, banned it as "rude, coarse, and inelegant." More than 100 years later, with its revealing description of racism and slavery, it is still the most frequently challenged book in American schools. The classic novel describes the journey and revelations of a young man who decides to escape the rules of society by floating on a raft down the Mississippi River with an escaped slave named Jim. Although considered by many scholars to be a "staunchly anti-racist novel," African American writer Toni Morrison conjectures that it unsettles people because it realistically depicts race relations—including the liberal use of the word *nigger*—in the pre–Civil War South to a society that is still divided along racial lines.

Nonetheless, most educators believe, as Ernest Hemingway expresses in the cover quotation, that Twain's work is a fundamental and shaping work of American literature essential to our understanding of the American experience. Attempts to ban the book raise many questions. Do we ignore the parts of American history that make us feel uncomfortable? Should books be banned if parents or teachers object to their content and if so, what content is considered "dangerous" or "harmful"? Finally, who decides what is acceptable for students to read? Although this issue raises many questions, the one thing that we do know, however, is that the Huckleberry Finn controversy will continue for many decades to come.

VISUALS
continued ➤

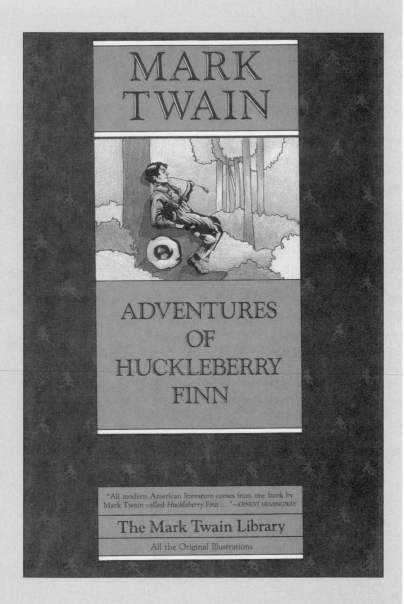

THINKING CRITICALLY

1. Does the cover of this edition of *Adventures of Huckleberry Finn* reveal anything about the controversy associated with it? Does the cover seem appropriate to the story and its theme? Explain.

2. Did you have to read *Adventures of Huckleberry Finn* in school? If so, what were your impressions of the story? Do you recall any objections you, your peers, your parents, or your teachers had to the novel? If the book was banned in your school, discuss the school committee's reasons for doing so and how you feel about such a measure.

3. Respond to the quote by Ernest Hemingway featured on the front jacket of this edition of *Adventures of Huckleberry Finn*. Do you agree with Hemingway's assessment? Why or why not?

4. Many of the people who call for the banning of *Adventures of Huckleberry Finn* from public libraries are concerned about the exposure of racial epithets to children. But what do you make of the fact that some of these same people were once part of the Free Speech Movement of the 1960s? Do you see this turnabout as justified or as hypocritical? Has political correctness gone too far? Or do you think that the "racial" material of the Twain classic is unsuitable for children?

5. Go to the University of Virginia's Mark Twain archives at <http://etext.lib.virginia.edu/twain/huckfinn.html> and examine some of the reviews and illustrations of the first edition of *Adventures of Huckleberry Finn*. Discuss these reviews and illustrations in context of society both then and now.

Author's Afterword from *Fahrenheit 451*

Ray Bradbury

First published in 1953, the classic science fiction novel, *Fahrenheit 451*, by Ray Bradbury depicts a future in which books forbidden by a totalitarian government are burned. In the novel firemen don't put out fires—they start them, burning books in giant bonfires. By controlling information, the government creates a society in which the appearance of happiness is the highest goal—a place where trivial information is good, and knowledge and ideas are bad. The novel raises questions, including what is the price of censorship "protection" and who decides what is acceptable to read? The statement that follows is a recent response to readers and editors suggesting that Bradbury edit his stories to, ironically, make them more "acceptable" to certain audiences.

Ray Bradbury is the author of more than 500 short stories, novels, plays, and poems, including *The Martian Chronicles* and *The Illustrated Man*. He has won numerous awards for his writing, including the Grand Master Award from the Science Fiction Writers of America.

1   About two years ago, a letter arrived from a solemn young Vassar lady telling me how much she enjoyed reading my experiment in space mythology, *The Martian Chronicles*.

2   But, she added, wouldn't it be a good idea, this late in time, to rewrite the book inserting more women's characters and roles?

3   A few years before that I got a certain amount of mail concerning the same Martian book complaining that the blacks in the book were Uncle Toms and why didn't I "do them over"?

4   Along about then came a note from a Southern white suggesting that I was prejudiced in favor of the blacks and the entire story should be dropped.

5   Two weeks ago my mountain of mail delivered forth a pipsqueak mouse of a letter from a well-known publishing house that wanted to reprint my story "The Fog Horn" in a high school reader.

6   In my story, I had described a lighthouse as having, late at night, an illumination coming from it that was a "God-Light." Looking up at it from the viewpoint of any sea-creature one would have felt that one was in "the Presence."

7   The editors had deleted "God-Light" and "in the Presence."

8   Some five years back, the editors of yet another anthology for school readers put together a volume with some 400 (count 'em) short stories in it. How do you cram 400 short stories by Twain, Irving, Poe, Maupassant and Bierce into one book?

9   Simplicity itself. Skin, debone, demarrow, scarify, melt, render down and destroy. Every adjective that counted, every verb that moved, every metaphor that weighed more than a mosquito—out! Every simile that would have made a sub-

moron's mouth twitch—gone! Any aside that explained the two-bit philosophy of a first-rate writer—lost!

10   Every story, slenderized, starved, bluepenciled, leeched and bled white, resembled every other story. Twain read like Poe read like Shakespeare read like Dostoevsky read like—in the finale—Edgar Guest. Every word of more than three syllables had been razored. Every image that demanded so much as one instant's attention—shot dead.

11   Do you begin to get the damned and incredible picture?

12   How did I react to all of the above?

13   By "firing" the whole lot.

14   By sending rejection slips to each and every one.

15   By ticketing the assembly of idiots to the far reaches of hell.

16   The point is obvious. There is more than one way to burn a book. And the world is full of people running about with lit matches. Every minority, be it Baptist/Unitarian, Irish/Italian/Octogenarian/Zen Buddhist, Zionist/Seventh-day Adventist, Women's Lib/Republican, Mattachine/Four Square Gospel feels it has the will, the right, the duty to douse the kerosene, light the fuse. Every dimwit editor who sees himself as the source of all dreary blanc-mange plain porridge unleavened literature, licks his guillotine and eyes the neck of any author who dares to speak above a whisper or write above a nursery rhyme.

17   Fire-Captain Beatty, in my novel *Fahrenheit 451,* described how the books were burned first by minorities, each ripping a page or a paragraph from this book, then that, until the day came when the books were empty and the minds shut and the libraries closed forever.

18   "Shut the door, they're coming through the window, shut the window, they're coming through the door," are the words to an old song. They fit my lifestyle with newly arriving butcher/censors every month. Only six weeks ago, I discovered that, over the years, some cubby-hole editors at Ballantine Books, fearful of contaminating the young, had, bit by bit, censored some 75 separate sections from the novel. Students, reading the novel which, after all, deals with censorship and book-burning in the future, wrote to tell me of this exquisite irony. Judy-Lynn Del Rey, one of the new Ballantine editors, is having the entire book reset and republished this summer with all the damns and hells back in place.

19   A final test for old Job II here: I sent a play, *Leviathan 99,* off to a university theater a month ago. My play is based on the "Moby Dick" mythology, dedicated to Melville, and concerns a rocket crew and a blind space captain who venture forth to encounter a Great White Comet and destroy the destroyer. My drama premiers as an opera in Paris this autumn. But, for now, the university wrote back that they hardly dared do my play—it had no women in it! And the ERA ladies on campus would descend with ballbats if the drama department even tried!

20   Grinding my bicuspids into powder, I suggested that would mean, from now on, no more productions of *Boys in the Band* (no women), or *The Women* (no men). Or, counting heads, male and female, a good lot of Shakespeare that would never

be seen again, especially if you count lines and find that all the good stuff went to the males!

21   I wrote back maybe they should do my play one week, and *The Women* the next. They probably thought I was joking, and I'm not sure that I wasn't.

22   For it is a mad world and it will get madder if we allow the minorities, be they dwarf or giant, orangutan or dolphin, nuclear-head or water-conversationalist, pro-computerologist or Neo-Luddite, simpleton or sage, to interfere with aesthetics. The real world is the playing ground for each and every group, to make or unmake laws. But the tip of the nose of my book or stories or poems is where their rights end and my territorial imperatives begin, run and rule. If Mormons do not like my plays, let them write their own. If the Irish hate my Dublin stories, let them rent typewriters. If teachers and grammar school editors find my jawbreaker sentences shatter their mushmilk teeth, let them eat stale cake dunked in weak tea of their own ungodly manufacture. If the Chicano intellectuals wish to re-cut my "Wonderful Ice Cream Suit" so it shapes "Zoot," may the belt unravel and the pants fall.

23   For, let's face it, digression is the soul of wit. Take philosophic asides away from Dante, Milton or Hamlet's father's ghost and what stays is dry bones. Laurence Sterne said it once: Digressions, incontestably, are the sunshine, the life, the soul of reading! Take them out and one cold eternal winter would reign in every page. Restore them to the writer—he steps forth like a bridegroom, bids them all-hail, brings in variety and forbids the appetite to fail.

24   In sum, do not insult me with the beheadings, finger-choppings or the lung-deflations you plan for my works. I need my head to shake or nod, my hand to wave or make into a fist, my lungs to shout or whisper with. I will not go gently onto a shelf, degutted, to become a non-book.

25   All you umpires, back to the bleachers. Referees, hit the showers. It's my game. I pitch, I hit, I catch. I run the bases. At sunset I've won or lost. At sunrise, I'm out again, giving it the old try.

26   And no one can help me. Not even you.

THINKING CRITICALLY

1. According to Bradbury, what happens when books are edited to make them more "acceptable" to audiences? Do you agree with him? Explain.

2. Bradbury compares himself to Job. What is the effect of this comparison? Why does he use it? How might it be ironic?

3. Consider the tone Bradbury uses in this essay. Is he angry, defiant, sarcastic, or resigned? How does his tone influence the audience's reception of his points? What does he hope to impress upon his readers?

4. What is the impact of Bradbury's final statement? Explain.

WRITING ASSIGNMENT

1. In paragraph 22, Bradbury proclaims, ". . . it is a mad world and it will get madder if we allow the minorities . . . to interfere with aesthetics." Do you agree with him, or do you think he protests too much? Do you think there are works—including Bradbury's—that could, or should, be rewritten to better reflect or appeal to a more diversified audience? Write Ray Bradbury a letter explaining why you agree or disagree with his views.

■ MAKING CONNECTIONS

1. Is censorship of written materials ever permissible? If so, under what conditions? If not, why not? Write your thoughts in an essay.

2. Have you ever encountered or heard of the banning of books in schools? If so, who proposed the censorship and why was it enforced? Write about the experience in an essay.

3. As violence in and outside of school has escalated in recent years, complaints about reading material for children have shifted from outrage about sexual matters to concern about violence. Although recent efforts to pass legislation making it a felony to expose children to books, movies, and video games that contain explicit sex or violence have failed, the debate lingers among the book stacks of public and school libraries. Some argue that reading about violence is not the same as watching movie mayhem. Others say both have the same detrimental effects on young people. What do you think? Write an essay in which you explore the effects of graphic violence in books versus violence on the screen. The following titles have recently been singled out for criticism: *Of Mice and Men* by John Steinbeck (1937), *A Time to Kill* by John Grisham (1989), *More Scary Stories to Tell in the Dark* by Alvin Schwartz (1984), *I Know What You Did Last Summer* by Lois Duncan (1973), *The Devil's Storybook* by Natalie Babbitt (1974), and *Hannibal* by Thomas Harris (1999).

4. Was *Adventures of Huckleberry Finn* banned in your elementary or high school? Were any other books? If so, which ones and why? If you are not sure, contact your old schools to find out. Were students aware of the forbidden books, or was the subject not an issue? Were students more eager to read the banned books?

5. Take an opinion poll on book-banning in your area. Ask individuals from different age groups for their perspective on book-banning. If a respondent is in favor of restricting book access, ask for a list of books to be banned. Can you draw any conclusions from your research?

6. In 1996, a publishing company printed the book, *Hit Man: A Technical Manual for Independent Contractors,* which explained how to hire a hit man to murder someone. Public outcry against the book resulted in its going out of publication, but the publishers defended their decision to print the book, citing the principles of freedom of speech and the First Amendment. Access the Northwestern University Web site, which addresses the issues of freedom of speech and the book at <http://faculty-web.at.nwu.edu/ commstud/freespeech/cont/cases/hitman.html>. After accessing the page and exploring its contents, draft a response to the publishers of the book. Support your response with information gathered from the site, as well as from your own perspective.

■ CASE STUDY: CENSORSHIP AND FREE SPEECH ON CAMPUS

The Betrayal of Liberty on America's Campuses
Alan Charles Kors

In the following essay, Alan Charles Kors argues that instituting sanctions on speech is a direct violation of students' right to free expression. Exactly where should the line be drawn as to what constitutes "hate speech"? The ambiguity of many university codes, says Kors, leads to sanctioning students for ridiculous and outrageous reasons. When students must consider every word they say, and even how they say it, they are prevented from engaging in honest intellectual inquiry, debate, and dialogue.

Alan Charles Kors is a professor of history at the University of Pennsylvania. He is the co-author with Harvey Silverglate of *The Shadow University: The Betrayal of Liberty on America's Campuses* (1998). Together with Silverglate, he founded The Foundation for Individual Rights in Education (FIRE), a non-profit organization that addresses individual liberty and rights issues on campuses. The following essay was a feature of the Bradley Lecture Series of the American Enterprise Institute for Public Policy Research in October 1998.

1 Those things that threaten free and open debate and those things that threaten academic freedom are the direct enemy of liberty. Such threats exist most dangerously at universities not in curriculum and scholarship, but in the new university *in loco parentis* (the university standing in the place of parents), where our nation's colleges and universities, across the board, are teaching contempt for liberty and its components: freedom of expression and inquiry; individual rights and responsibilities over group rights and entitlements; equal justice under law; and the rights of private conscience. *That* assault upon liberty is occurring not in the sunlight of open decisions and advertised agendas, but in the shadows of an unaccountable middle-administration that has been given coercive authority over the lives, speech, consciences, and voluntary individuation and association of students.

2 Almost all colleges and universities, for example, have "harassment" policies that prohibit selective "verbal behavior" or "verbal conduct," but almost none has the honesty to call these "speech codes." These policies, adopted from employment law and catastrophic for universities, are applied to faculty and students, the latter not even being employees of a university, but, in fact, its clients. The core of these codes is the prohibition of the creation of "a hostile or offensive environment," with the remarkable variations and embellishments that follow from Hobbes's observation that to the learned it is given to be learnedly foolish. Within very recent times, Bowdoin College chose to outlaw jokes and ways of telling stories "experienced by others as harassing." Brown University banned verbal behavior that produced "feelings of impotence . . . anger . . . or disenfranchisement . . . [whether] inten-

tional or unintentional." Colby prohibited speech that caused loss of "self-esteem." The University of Connecticut prohibited "inconsiderate jokes," "stereotyping," and even "inappropriately directed laughter." Indeed, a student at Sarah Lawrence College recently was convicted of laughing at something that someone else said, and was ordered as a condition of remaining in the college, for his laughter, to read a book entitled *Homophobia on Campus,* see a movie about "homophobia," and write a paper about "homophobia." Rutgers University included within the forbidden and "heinous act" of harassment, "communication" that is "in any manner likely to cause annoyance or alarm," which causes *me* a great deal of annoyance *and* alarm. The University of Maryland—College Park outlaws not only "idle chatter of a sexual nature" and "comments or questions about the sensuality of a person," but pointedly explains that these verbal behaviors "do not necessarily have to be specifically directed at an individual to constitute sexual harassment." Expression goes well beyond the verbal, however, because the University of Maryland also prohibits "gestures . . . that are expressive of an idea, opinion, or emotion," including "sexual looks such as leering and ogling with suggestive overtones; licking lips or teeth; holding or eating food provocatively."

3   At Carnegie Mellon University, a student called his female opponent in an election for the Graduate Student Organization a "megalomaniac." He was charged with sexual harassment. The Dean of Students explained the deeper meaning of calling a woman a megalomaniac, citing a vast body of what he termed feminist "victim theory" on the plaintiff's behalf, and the associate provost submitted a brief that stated, "I have no doubt that this has created a hostile environment which impacts Lara's productivity as a student leader and as a graduate student."

4   Many universities, such as Berkeley itself, no less, adopted speech codes that outlawed "fighting words." That term is taken from the U.S. Supreme Court decision of the 1940s, *Chaplinsky* v. *New Hampshire* (a decision surely mooted by later Supreme Court decisions), in which, leftists take note, the unprotected fighting word was, of all things, "fascist." Many universities also leave the determination of whether something was a fighting word or created a hostile environment to the plaintiff. Thus, the University of Puget Sound states that harassment "depends on the point of view of the person to whom the conduct is unwelcome." The City University of New York warns that "sexual harassment is not defined by intentions, but by its impact on the subject." "No one," Bowdoin College warns, "is entitled to engage in behavior that is experienced by others as harassing." At the University of Connecticut, criticising someone's limits of tolerance toward the speech of others is itself harassment: its code bans "attributing objections to any of the above [instances of harassment] to 'hypersensitivity' of the targeted individual or group."

5   West Virginia University prohibited, among many other things, "insults, humor, jokes, and anecdotes that belittle or demean an individual's or a group's sexuality or sex," and, try this one on for vagueness, "inappropriate displays of sexually suggestive objects or pictures which may include but are not limited to posters, pin-ups, and calendars." If applied equally, of course, such a policy would leave no sex or race safe in its conversations or humor, let alone in its artistic taste, but such

policies never are applied equally. Thus, students at West Virginia received the official policies of the "Executive Officer for Social Justice," who stated the institutional orthodoxy about "homophobia" and "sexism." The Officer of Social Justice warned that "feelings" about gays and lesbians could not become "attitudes": "Regardless of how a person feels about others, negative actions or attitudes based on misconceptions and/or ignorance constitute prejudice, which contradicts everything for which an institution of higher learning stands." Among those prejudices it listed "heterosexism . . . the assumption that everyone is heterosexual, or, if they aren't, they should be." This, of course, outlawed specific religious inner convictions about sexuality. Because everyone had the right to be free from "harassment," the policy specified "behaviors to avoid." These prohibitions affected speech and voluntary associations based upon beliefs. Thus, "DO NOT [in capital letters] tolerate 'jokes' which are potentially injurious to gays, lesbians and bisexuals. . . . DO NOT determine whether you will interact with someone by virtue of his or her sexual orientation." The policy also commanded specific prescriptions: "value alternate lifestyles . . . challenge homophobic remarks . . . [and] use language that is not gender specific. . . . Instead of referring to anyone's romantic partner as 'girlfriend' or 'boyfriend,' use positive generic terms such as a 'friend,' 'lover,' or 'partner.' Speak of your own romantic partner similarly." The "homophobia" policy ended with the warning that "harassment" or "discrimination" based on sexual preference was subject to penalties that ranged "from reprimand . . . to expulsion and termination, and including public service and educational remediation." "Educational remediation," note well, is an academic euphemism for thought reform. Made aware of what their own university was doing, a coalition of faculty members threatened to expose West Virginia University for its obvious violations of the state and federal constitutions, and to sue the administration if need be. As I talk, the University has removed the offending codes from its freshmen orientation packages and from its website. We shall see if it has removed them from its operational policies.

6   When federal courts struck down two codes restricting "verbal behavior" at public universities and colleges, namely, at the University of Michigan and the University of Wisconsin, other public colleges and universities—even in those jurisdictions where codes had been declared unconstitutional—did not seek to abolish their policies. Thus, Central Michigan University, after the University of Michigan code had been struck down, maintained a policy whose prohibitions included "any intentional, unintentional, physical, verbal, or nonverbal behavior that subjects an individual to an intimidating, hostile or offensive educational . . . environment by demeaning or slurring individuals through . . . written literature because of their racial or ethnic affiliation or using symbols, epitaphs [sic, we hope] or slogans that infer [sic] negative connotations about an individual's racial or ethnic affiliation."

7   In 1993, this policy was challenged, successfully, in Federal District Court. The Court noted that the code applied to "all possible human conduct," and, citing internal University documents, ruled that Central Michigan intended to apply it to speech "which a person 'feels' has affronted him or some group, predicated on race or ethnicity." The Court ruled that if the policy's words had meaning, it banned,

precisely, protected speech. If someone's "treatise, term paper or even . . . cafeteria bull session" about the Middle East, the Court observed, blamed one group more than another on the basis of "some ancient ethnic traditions which give rise to barbarian combativeness or . . . inability to compromise," such speech, the Court found, "would seem to be a good fit with the policy language." In fact, the Court ruled, "Any behavior, even unintentional, that offends any individual is to be prohibited under the policy. . . . If the speech gives offense it is prohibited." When the President of Central Michigan University offered assurances that the policy was not intended to be enforced in such a way as to "interfere impermissibly with individuals' rights to free speech," the Court declared itself "emphatically unimpressed" by such a savings clause, and it observed: "The university . . . says in essence, 'trust us; we may interfere, but not impermissibly.' The Court is not willing to entrust . . . the First Amendment to the tender mercies of this institution's discriminatory harassment/affirmative action enforcer."

8   Many in the academy insist that the entire phenomenon labeled "political correctness" is the mythical fabrication of opponents of "progressive" change. The authors of an American Association of University Professors' special committee report, the "Statement on the 'Political Correctness' Controversy" (1991), insisted, without irony, that claims of "political correctness" were merely smokescreens to hide the true agenda of such critics—a racist and sexist desire to thwart the aspirations of minorities and women in the academic enterprise.

9   It is, in fact, almost inconceivable that anyone of good faith could live on a college campus unaware of the repression, legal inequality, intrusions into private conscience, and malignant double standards that hold sway there. In the Left's history of McCarthyism, the firing or dismissal of one professor or student, the inquisition into the private beliefs of one individual, let alone the demands for a demonstration of fealty to community standards stand out as intolerable oppressions that coerced people into silence, hypocrisy, betrayal, and tyranny.

10   In fact, in today's assault on liberty on college campuses, there is not a small number of cases, speech codes, nor apparatuses of repression and thought reform. Number aside, however, a climate of repression succeeds not by statistical frequency, but by sapping the courage, autonomy, and conscience of individuals who otherwise might remember or revive what liberty could be.

11   Most students respect disagreement and difference, and they do not bring charges of harassment against those whose opinions or expressions "offend" them. The universities themselves, however, encourage such charges to be brought. At almost every college and university, students deemed members of "historically oppressed groups"—above all, women, blacks, gays, and Hispanics—are informed during orientations that their campuses are teeming with illegal or intolerable violations of their "right" not to be offended. To believe many new-student orientations would be to believe that there was a racial or sexual bigot, to borrow the mocking phrase of McCarthy's critics, "under every bed." At almost every college and university, students are presented with lists of a vast array of places to which they should submit charges of such verbal "harassment," and they are promised "victim

support," "confidentiality," and sympathetic understanding when they file such complaints.

12   What an astonishing expectation to give to students: the belief that, if they belong to a protected category and have the correct beliefs, they have a right to four years of never being offended. What an extraordinary power to give to administrative tribunals: the prerogative to punish the free speech and expression of people to whom they assign the stains of historical oppression, while being free, themselves, to use whatever rhetoric they wish against the bearers of such stains. While the world looks at issues of curriculum and scholarship, above all, to analyze and evaluate American colleges and universities, it is, in fact, the silencing and punishment of belief, expression, and individuality that ought to concern yet more deeply those who care about what universities are and could be. Most cases never reach the public, because most individuals accused of "verbal" harassment sadly (but understandably) accept plea-bargains that diminish their freedom but spare them Draconian penalties, including expulsion. Those settlements almost invariably involve "sensitivity training," an appalling term, "training," to hear in matters of the human mind and spirit. Even so, the files on prosecutions under speech codes are, alas, overflowing.

13   "Settlements," by the way, are one of the best-kept and most frightening secrets of American academic life, almost always assigned with an insistence upon confidentiality. They are nothing less than an American version of thought reform from benighted offender into a politically correct bearer, in fact or in appearance, of an ideology that is the regnant orthodoxy of our universities *in loco parentis*.

14   From this perspective, American history is a tale of the oppression of all "others" by white, heterosexual, Eurocentric males, punctuated by the struggles of the oppressed. "Beneficiaries" see their lives as good and as natural, and falsely view America as a boon to humankind. Worse, most "victims" of "oppression" accept the values of their oppressors. A central task of education, then, is to "demystify" such arbitrary power. Whites, males, and heterosexuals must recognize and renounce the injustice of their "privilege." Nonwhites, women, gays, and lesbians must recognize and struggle against their victimization, both in their beliefs and in their behaviors.

15   Such "demystification" has found a welcome home in a large number of courses in the humanities and social sciences, but for the true believers, this is insufficient, because most courses remain optional, many professors resist the temptation to proselytize, and students, for the most part, choose majors that take them far from oppression studies.

16   Indeed, students forever disappoint the ideologues. Men and women generally see themselves neither as oppressor nor oppressed, and, far from engaging in class warfare, often quite love each other. Most women refuse to identify themselves as "feminists." Group-identity centers—although they can rally support at moments of crisis—attract few students overall, because invitees busily go about the business of learning, making friends, pursuing interests, and seeking love—all the things that 18-to–22-year-olds have done from time immemorial. Attendance at group-identity

organizations is often miniscule as a percentage of the intended population, and militant leaders complain endlessly about "apathy." Whites don't feel particularly guilty about being white, and almost no designated "victims" adopt truly radical politics. Most undergraduates unabashedly seek their portion of American freedom, legal equality, and bounty. What to do with such benighted students? Increasingly, the answer to that question is to use the *in loco parentis* apparatus of the university to reform their private consciences and minds. For the generation that once said, "Don't trust anyone *over* 30," the motto now is "Don't trust anyone *under* 30." Increasingly, Offices of Student Life, Residence Offices, and residence advisors have become agencies of progressive social engineering whose mission is to bring students to mandatory political enlightenment.

17   Such practices violate more than honest education. Recognition of the sanctity of conscience is the single most essential respect given to individual autonomy. There are purely practical arguments for the right to avoid self-incrimination or to choose religious (or other) creeds, but there is none deeper than restraining power from intruding upon the privacy of the self. Universities and colleges that commit the scandal of sentencing students (and faculty) to "sensitivity therapy" do not even permit individuals to choose their therapists. The Christian may not consult his or her chosen counselor, but most follow the regime of the social worker selected by the Women's Center or by the Office of Student Life. . . .

18   Imagine a campus on which being denounced for "irreligious bigotry" or "un-Americanism" carried the same stigma that being denounced for "racism," "sexism," and "homophobia" now carries in the academic world, so that in such hearings or trials, the burden of proof invariably fell upon the "offender." The common sign at pro-choice rallies, "Keep your rosaries off our ovaries," would be prima facie evidence of language used as a weapon to degrade and marginalize, and the common term of abuse, "born-again bigot," would be compelling evidence of the choice to create a hostile environment for evangelicals. What panegyrics to liberty and free expression we would hear in opposition to any proposed code to protect the "religious" or the "patriotic" from "offense" and "incivility." Yet what deafening silence we have heard, in these times, in the campus acceptance of the speech provisions of so-called harassment codes.

19   The goal of a speech code, then, is to suppress speech one doesn't like. The goal of liberty and equal justice is to permit us to live in a complex but peaceful world of difference, disagreement, debate, moral witness, and efforts of persuasion—without coercion and violence. Liberty and legal equality are hard-won, precious, and, indeed—because the social world is often discomforting—profoundly complex and troublesome ways of being human. They require, for their sustenance, men and women who would abhor their own power of censorship and their own special legal privileges as much as they abhor those of others. In enacting and enforcing speech codes, universities, for their own partisan reasons, have chosen to betray the human vision of freedom and legal equality. It was malignant to impose or permit such speech codes; to deny their oppressive effects while living in the midst of those effects is beyond the moral pale.

20   On virtually any college campus, for all of its rules of "civility" and all of its prohibitions of "hostile environment," assimilationist black men and women live daily
with the terms "Uncle Tom" and "Oreo" said with impunity, while their tormenters
live with special protections from offense. White students daily hear themselves,
their friends, and their parents denounced as "racists" and "oppressors," while their
tormenters live with special protections from offense. Believing Christians hear their
beliefs ridiculed and see their sacred symbols traduced—virtually nothing, in the
name of freedom, may not be said against them in the classroom, at rallies, and in
personal encounters—while their tormenters live with special protection from offense. Men hear their sex abused, find themselves blamed for all the evils of the
world, and enter classrooms whose very goal is to make them feel discomfort, while
their tormenters live with special protections from "a hostile environment."

21   It is our liberty, above all else, that defines us as human beings, capable of
ethics and responsibility. The struggle for liberty on American campuses is one of
the defining struggles of the age in which we find ourselves. A nation that does not
educate in freedom will not survive in freedom, and will not even know when it has
lost it. Individuals too often convince themselves that they are caught up in moments of history that they cannot affect. That history, however, is made by their
will and moral choices. There is a moral crisis in higher education. It will not be resolved unless we choose and act to resolve it.

22   It is easy, however, to identify the vulnerabilities of the bearers of this worst
and, at the time, most marginal legacy of the '60s: they loathe the society that they
believe should support them generously in their authority over its offspring; they
are detached from the values of individual liberty, legal equality, privacy, and the
sanctity of conscience toward which Americans essentially are drawn; and, for both
those reasons, they cannot bear the light of public scrutiny. Let the sunlight in.

THINKING CRITICALLY

1. Why does Kors believe racist and inflammatory speech should be protected by the First
   Amendment? What examples does he use to prove his point? Do you agree? Can you think of
   circumstances in which racist speech should not be protected? Explain.

2. How has this article affected your thinking on the subject of free speech and censorship?
   Has it changed your mind about the use of racially or sexually abusive language? Explain
   your perspective.

3. How are colleges and university administrators dealing with incidents of verbal abuse on
   American campuses? What is Kors's reaction to their handling of such problems? According
   to Kors, how are students being manipulated by university censorship rules?

4. Explain what Kors means when he says, "Many in the academy insist that the entire phenomenon labeled 'political correctness' is the mythical fabrication of opponents of 'progressive'
   change" (paragraph 8). Do you agree with this view?

5. Consider the author's voice in this essay. What sense do you get of Kors as an individual?
   Write a paragraph characterizing the author. Take into consideration his stand in the essay,

his style and tone of writing, and the examples he uses to support his view and how he presents them.

Regulating Racist Speech on Campus
Charles R. Lawrence III

Recent years have witnessed a disturbing rise in racist and sexist language on college campuses. Some administrations have dealt with the problem by banning outright offensive language on the grounds that racial slurs are violent verbal assaults that interfere with students' rights to an education. Others fear that placing sanctions on racist speech violates the First Amendment guarantee of free expression. In the following essay law professor Charles R. Lawrence III argues for the restriction of free speech by citing the U.S. Supreme Court's landmark decision in the case of *Brown* v. *Board of Education.*

Charles R. Lawrence teaches law at Georgetown University. He is the co-author of *We Won't Go Back: Making the Case for Affirmative Action* (1997), written with his wife and fellow Georgetown professor Mari J. Matsuda. Lawrence is best known for his work in antidiscrimination law, equal protection, and critical race theory. He is also a former president of the Society of American Law Teachers.

1   I have spent the better part of my life as a dissenter. As a high-school student, I was threatened with suspension for my refusal to participate in a civil-defense drill, and I have been a conspicuous consumer of my First Amendment liberties ever since. There are very strong reasons for protecting even racist speech. Perhaps the most important of these is that such protection reinforces our society's commitment to tolerance as a value, and that by protecting bad speech from government regulation, we will be forced to combat it as a community.

2   But I also have a deeply felt apprehension about the resurgence of racial violence and the corresponding rise in the incidence of verbal and symbolic assault and harassment to which blacks and other traditionally subjugated and excluded groups are subjected. I am troubled by the way the debate has been framed in response to the recent surge of racist incidents on college and university campuses and in response to some universities' attempts to regulate harassing speech. The problem has been framed as one in which the liberty of free speech is in conflict with the elimination of racism. I believe this has placed the bigot on the moral high ground and fanned the rising flames of racism.

3   Above all, I am troubled that we have not listened to the real victims, that we have shown so little understanding of their injury, and that we have abandoned those whose race, gender, or sexual preference continues to make them second-class citizens. It seems to me a very sad irony that the first instinct of civil libertarians has been to challenge even the smallest, most narrowly framed efforts by

universities to provide black and other minority students with the protection the Constitution guarantees them.

4   The landmark case of *Brown* v. *Board of Education* is not a case that we normally think of as a case about speech. But *Brown* can be broadly read as articulating the principle of equal citizenship. *Brown* held that segregated schools were inherently unequal because of the *message* that segregation conveyed—that black children were an untouchable caste, unfit to go to school with white children. If we understand the necessity of eliminating the system of signs and symbols that signal the inferiority of blacks, then we should hesitate before proclaiming that all racist speech that stops short of physical violence must be defended.

5   University officials who have formulated policies to respond to incidents of racial harassment have been characterized in the press as "thought police," but such policies generally do nothing more than impose sanctions against intentional face-to-face insults. When racist speech takes the form of face-to-face insults, catcalls, or other assaultive speech aimed at an individual or small group of persons, it falls directly within the "fighting words" exception to First Amendment protection. The Supreme Court has held that words which "by their very utterance inflict injury or tend to incite an immediate breach of the peace" are not protected by the First Amendment.

6   If the purpose of the First Amendment is to foster the greatest amount of speech, racial insults disserve that purpose. Assaultive racist speech functions as a preemptive strike. The invective is experienced as a blow, not as a proffered idea, and once the blow is struck, it is unlikely that a dialogue will follow. Racial insults are particularly undeserving of First Amendment protection because the perpetrator's intention is not to discover truth or initiate dialogue but to injure the victim. In most situations, members of minority groups realize that they are likely to lose if they respond to epithets by fighting and are forced to remain silent and submissive.

7   Courts have held that offensive speech may not be regulated in public forums such as streets where the listener may avoid the speech by moving on, but the regulation of otherwise protected speech has been permitted when the speech invades the privacy of the unwilling listener's home or when the unwilling listener cannot avoid the speech. Racist posters, fliers, and graffiti in dormitories, bathrooms, and other common living spaces would seem to clearly fall within the reasoning of these cases. Minority students should not be required to remain in their rooms in order to avoid racial assault. Minimally, they should find a safe haven in their dorms and in all other common rooms that are a part of their daily routine.

8   I would also argue that the university's responsibility for insuring that these students receive an equal educational opportunity provides a compelling justification for regulations that insure them safe passage in all common areas. A minority student should not have to risk becoming the target of racially assaulting speech every time he or she chooses to walk across campus. Regulating vilifying speech that cannot be anticipated or avoided would not preclude announced speeches and rallies—situations that would give minority-group members and their allies the chance to organize counter-demonstrations or avoid the speech altogether.

9   The most commonly advanced argument against the regulation of racist speech proceeds something like this: we recognize that minority groups suffer pain and injury as the result of racist speech, but we must allow this hate mongering for the benefit of society as a whole. Freedom of speech is the lifeblood of our democratic system. It is especially important for minorities because often it is their only vehicle for rallying support for the redress of their grievances. It will be impossible to formulate a prohibition so precise that it will prevent the racist speech you want to suppress without catching in the same net all kinds of speech that it would be unconscionable for a democratic society to suppress.

10   Whenever we make such arguments, we are striking a balance on the one hand between our concern for the continued free flow of ideas and the democratic process dependent on that flow, and, on the other, our desire to further the cause of equality. There can be no meaningful discussion of how we should reconcile our commitment to equality and our commitment to free speech until it is acknowledged that there is real harm inflicted by racist speech and that this harm is far from trivial.

11   To engage in a debate about the First Amendment and racist speech without a full understanding of the nature and extent of that harm is to risk making the First Amendment an instrument of domination rather than a vehicle of liberation. We have not known the experience of victimization by racist, misogynist, and homophobic speech, nor do we equally share the burden of the societal harm it inflicts. We are often quick to say that we have heard the cry of the victims when we have not.

12   The *Brown* case is again instructive because it speaks directly to the psychic injury inflicted by racist speech by noting that the symbolic message of segregation affected "the hearts and minds" of Negro children "in a way unlikely ever to be undone." Racial epithets and harassment often cause deep emotional scarring and feelings of anxiety and fear that pervade every aspect of a victim's life.

13   *Brown* also recognized that black children did not have an equal opportunity to learn and participate in the school community if they bore the additional burden of being subjected to the humiliation and psychic assault contained in the message of segregation. University students bear an analogous burden when they are forced to live and work in an environment where at any moment they may be subjected to denigrating verbal harassment and assault. The same injury was addressed by the Supreme Court when it held that sexual harassment that creates a hostile or abusive work environment violates the ban on sex discrimination in employment of Title VII of the Civil Rights Act of 1964.

14   Carefully drafted university regulations would bar the use of words as assault weapons and leave unregulated even the most heinous of ideas when those ideas are presented at times and places and in manners that provide an opportunity for reasoned rebuttal or escape from immediate injury. The history of the development of the right to free speech has been one of carefully evaluating the importance of free expression and its effects on other important societal interests. We have drawn the line between protected and unprotected speech before without dire results. (Courts

have, for example, exempted from the protection of the First Amendment obscene speech and speech that disseminates official secrets, that defames or libels another person, or that is used to form a conspiracy or monopoly.)

15   Blacks and other people of color are skeptical about the argument that even the most injurious speech must remain unregulated because, in an unregulated marketplace of ideas, the best ones will rise to the top and gain acceptance. Our experience tells us quite the opposite. We have seen too many good liberal politicians shy away from the issues that might brand them as being too closely allied with us.

16   Whenever we decide that racist speech must be tolerated because of the importance of maintaining societal tolerance for all unpopular speech, we are asking blacks and other subordinated groups to bear the burden for the good of all. We must be careful that the ease with which we strike the balance against the regulation of racist speech is in no way influenced by the fact that the cost will be borne by others. We must be certain that those who will pay that price are fairly represented in our deliberations and that they are heard.

17   At the core of the argument that we should resist all government regulation of speech is the ideal that the best cure for bad speech is good, that ideas that affirm equality and the worth of all individuals will ultimately prevail. This is an empty ideal unless those of us who would fight racism are vigilant and unequivocal in that fight. We must look for ways to offer assistance and support to students whose speech and political participation are chilled in a climate of racial harassment.

18   Civil rights lawyers might consider suing on behalf of blacks whose right to an equal education is denied by a university's failure to insure a nondiscriminatory educational climate or conditions of employment. We must embark upon the development of a First Amendment jurisprudence grounded in the reality of our history and our contemporary experience. We must think hard about how best to launch legal attacks against the most indefensible forms of hate speech. Good lawyers can create exceptions and narrow interpretations that limit the harm of hate speech without opening the floodgates of censorship.

19   Everyone concerned with these issues must find ways to engage actively in actions that resist and counter the racist ideas that we would have the First Amendment protect. If we fail in this, the victims of hate speech must rightly assume that we are on the oppressors' side.

THINKING CRITICALLY

1. What reasons does Lawrence offer for protecting racist speech from governmental restrictions? Do you agree? How are university restrictions different from those imposed by the government?

2. According to the author, how in the debate over racist language does the fight against racism conflict with the fight for free speech? What fundamental problem does Lawrence have with this conflict? Are his reasons convincing?

3. Why, according to Lawrence, is racist speech "undeserving of First Amendment protection" (paragraph 6)? Do you agree? If not, why not? If so, can you think of any circumstances when racist speech should be protected?

4. Have you ever been the victim of abusive speech—speech that victimized you because of your race, gender, religion, ethnicity, or sexual preference? Do you agree with Lawrence's argument regarding "psychic injury" (paragraph 12)? Explain.

5. How convincingly does Lawrence argue that racist speech should not be protected by the First Amendment? What is the logic of his argument? What evidence does he offer as support?

6. Select one of Lawrence's arguments that you think is especially strong or especially weak, and explain why you think so.

7. Lawrence opens his essay saying that he has a long history as a "dissenter." What is his strategy? What assumptions does he make about his audience? What does his refusal to participate in a civil-defense drill have to do with the essay's central issues?

There's No Such Thing as Free Speech, and It's a Good Thing, Too
Stanley Fish

The first two readings in this case study present different points of view regarding campus speech codes and free speech. In the next essay, academic and law professor Stanley Fish argues that there really is no such thing as free speech. Free speech is, he explains, "just the name we give to verbal behavior that serves the substantive agendas we wish to advance." Free speech is, in his opinion, simply a "political prize." As a social construct, free speech has always had "qualifiers" depending on who wielded power. And Fish thinks that the liberal left should realize that this reality isn't such a bad thing.

Stanley Fish is Arts and Sciences Professor of English and a professor of law at Dartmouth University. His many academic works include, *Is There a Text in This Class?* (1984), and *Professional Correctness: Literary and Political Change* (1995). The following essay first appeared in the *Boston Review* and was later republished in his book of the same title, *There's No Such Thing as Free Speech, and It's a Good Thing, Too* (1994).

1 Lately, many on the liberal and progressive left have been disconcerted to find that words, phrases, and concepts thought to be their property and generative of their politics have been appropriated by the forces of neoconservatism. This is particularly true of the concept of free speech, for in recent years First Amendment rhetoric has been used to justify policies and actions the left finds problematical if not abhorrent: pornography, sexist language, campus hate speech. How has this happened? The answer I shall give in this essay is that abstract concepts like free speech do not have any "natural" content but are filled with whatever content and direction one can manage to put into them. "Free speech" is just the name we give to verbal behavior that serves the substantive agendas we wish to advance; and we give our preferred verbal behaviors *that* name when we can, when we have the power to do so, because in the rhetoric of American life, the label "free speech" is

the one you want your favorites to wear. Free speech, in short, is not an independent value but a political prize, and if that prize has been captured by a politics opposed to yours, it can no longer be invoked in ways that further your purposes, for it is now an obstacle to those purposes. This is something that the liberal left has yet to understand, and what follows is an attempt to pry its members loose from a vocabulary that may now be a disservice to them.

2   Not far from the end of his *Areopagitica,* and after having celebrated the virtues of toleration and unregulated publication in passages that find their way into every discussion of free speech and the First Amendment, John Milton catches himself up short and says, of course I didn't mean Catholics, them we exterminate:

> I mean not tolerated popery, and open superstition, which as it extirpates all religious and civil supremacies, so itself should be extirpate . . . that also which is impious or evil absolutely against faith or manners no law can possibly permit that intends not to unlaw itself.

3   Notice that Milton is not simply stipulating a single exception to a rule generally in place; the kinds of utterance that might be regulated and even prohibited on pain of trial and punishment constitute an open set; popery is named only as a particularly perspicuous instance of the advocacy that cannot be tolerated. No doubt there are other forms of speech and action that might be categorized as "open superstitions" or as subversive of piety, faith, and manners, and presumably these too would be candidates for "extirpation." Nor would Milton think himself culpable for having failed to provide a list of unprotected utterances. The list will fill itself out as utterances are put to the test implied by his formulation: would this form of speech or advocacy, if permitted to flourish, tend to undermine the very purposes for which our society is constituted? One cannot answer this question with respect to a particular utterance in advance of its emergence on the world's stage; rather, one must wait and ask the question in the full context of its production and (possible) dissemination. It might appear that the result would be ad hoc and unprincipled, but for Milton the principle inheres in the core values in whose name individuals of like mind came together in the first place. Those values, which include the search for truth and the promotion of virtue, are capacious enough to accommodate a diversity of views. But at some point—again impossible of advance specification—capaciousness will threaten to become shapelessness, and at that point fidelity to the original values will demand acts of extirpation.

4   I want to say that all affirmations of freedom of expression are like Milton's, dependent for their force on an exception that literally carves out the space in which expression can then emerge. I do not mean that expression (saying something) is a realm whose integrity is sometimes compromised by certain restrictions but that restriction, in the form of an underlying articulation of the world that necessarily (if silently) negates alternatively possible articulations, is constitutive of expression. Without restriction, without an inbuilt sense of what it would be meaningless to say or wrong to say, there could be no assertion and no reason for asserting it. The exception to unregulated expression is not a negative restriction but a positive hollow-

ing out of value—we are for *this,* which means we are against *that*—in relation to which meaningful assertion can then occur. It is in reference to that value—constituted as all values are by an act of exclusion—that some forms of speech will be heard as (quite literally) intolerable. Speech, in short, is never a value in and of itself but is always produced within the precincts of some assumed conception of the good to which it must yield in the event of conflict. When the pinch comes (and sooner or later it will always come) and the institution (be it church, state, or university) is confronted by behavior subversive of its core rationale, it will respond by declaring "of course we mean not tolerated ———, that we extirpate," not because an exception to a general freedom has suddenly and contradictorily been announced, but because the freedom has never been general and has always been understood against the background of an originary exclusion that gives it meaning.

5   This is a large thesis, but before tackling it directly I want to buttress my case with an example taken from the charter and case law of Canada. Canadian thinking about freedom of expression departs from the line usually taken in the United States [in ways that bring that country very close to the *Areopagitica* as I have expounded it.] The differences are fully on display in a recent landmark case, *R.* v. *Keegstra.* James Keegstra was a high school teacher in Alberta who, it was established by evidence, "systematically denigrated Jews and Judaism in his classes." He described Jews as treacherous, subversive, sadistic, money loving, power hungry, and child killers. He declared them "responsible for depressions, anarchy, chaos, wars and revolution" and required his students "to regurgitate these notions in essays and examinations." Keegstra was indicted under Section 319(2) of the Criminal Code and convicted. The Court of Appeal reversed, and the Crown appealed to the Supreme Court, which reinstated the lower court's verdict.

6   Section 319(2) reads in part, "Every one who, by communicating statements other than in private conversation, willfully promotes hatred against any identifiable group is guilty of . . . an indictable offense and is liable to imprisonment for a term not exceeding two years." In the United States, this provision of the code would almost certainly be struck down because, under the First Amendment, restrictions on speech are apparently prohibited without qualification. To be sure, the Canadian charter has its own version of the First Amendment, in Section 2(b): "Everyone has the following fundamental freedoms . . . (b) freedom of thought, belief, opinion, and expression, including freedom of the press and other media of communication." But Section 2(b), like every other section of the charter, is qualified by Section 1: "The Canadian Charter of Rights and Freedoms guarantees the rights and freedoms set out in it subject only to such reasonable limits prescribed by law as can be demonstrably justified in a free and democratic society." Or in other words, every right and freedom herein granted can be trumped if its exercise is found to be in conflict with the principles that underwrite the society.

7   This is what happens in *Keegstra* as the majority finds that Section 319(2) of the Criminal Code does in fact violate the right of freedom of expression guaranteed by the charter but is nevertheless a *permissible* restriction because it accords with the principles proclaimed in Section 1. There is, of course, a dissent that

reaches the conclusion that would have been reached by most, if not all, U.S. courts; but even in dissent the minority is faithful to Canadian ways of reasoning. "The question," it declares, "is always one of balance," and thus even when a particular infringement of the charter's Section 2(b) has been declared unconstitutional, as it would have been by the minority, the question remains open with respect to the next case. In the United States the question is presumed closed and can only be pried open by special tools. In our legal culture as it is now constituted, if one yells "free speech" in a crowded courtroom and makes it stick, the case is over.

8   Of course, it is not that simple. Despite the apparent absoluteness of the First Amendment, there are any number of ways of getting around it, ways that are known to every student of the law. In general, the preferred strategy is to manipulate the distinction, essential to First Amendment jurisprudence, between speech and action. The distinction is essential because no one would think to frame a First Amendment that began "Congress shall make no law abridging freedom of action," for that would amount to saying "Congress shall make no law," which would amount to saying "There shall be no law," only actions uninhibited and unregulated. If the First Amendment is to make any sense, have any bite, speech must be declared not to be a species of action, or to be a special form of action lacking the aspects of action that cause it to be the object of regulation. The latter strategy is the favored one and usually involves the separation of speech from consequences. This is what Archibald Cox does when he assigns to the First Amendment the job of protecting "expressions separable from conduct harmful to other individuals and the community." The difficulty of managing this segregation is well known: speech always seems to be crossing the line into action, where it becomes, at least potentially, consequential. In the face of this categorical instability, First Amendment theorists and jurists fashion a distinction within the speech/action distinction: some forms of speech are not really speech because their purpose is to incite violence or because they are, as the court declares in *Chaplinsky* v. *New Hampshire* (*1942*), "fighting words," words "likely to provoke the average person to retaliation, and thereby cause a breach of the peace."

9   The trouble with this definition is that it distinguishes not between fighting words and words that remain safely and merely expressive but between words that are provocative to one group (the group that falls under the rubric "average person") and words that might be provocative to other groups, groups of persons not now considered average. And if you ask what words are likely to be provocative to those nonaverage groups, what are likely to be *their* fighting words, the answer is anything and everything, for as Justice Holmes said long ago (in *Gitlow* v. *New York*), every idea is an incitement to somebody, and since ideas come packaged in sentences, in words, every sentence is potentially, in some situation that might occur tomorrow, a fighting word and therefore a candidate for regulation.

10   This insight cuts two ways. One could conclude from it that the fighting words exception is a bad idea because there is no way to prevent clever and unscrupulous advocates from shoveling so many forms of speech into the excepted category that the zone of constitutionally protected speech shrinks to nothing and is finally with-

out inhabitants. Or, alternatively, one could conclude that there was never anything in the zone in the first place and that the difficulty of limiting the fighting words exception is merely a particular instance of the general difficulty of separating speech from action. And if one opts for this second conclusion, as I do, then a further conclusion is inescapable; insofar as the point of the First Amendment is to identify speech separable from conduct and from the consequences that come in conduct's wake, there is no such speech and therefore nothing for the First Amendment to protect. Or, to make the point from the other direction, when a court invalidates legislation because it infringes on protected speech, it is not because the speech in question is without consequences but because the consequences have been discounted in relation to a good that is judged to outweigh them. Despite what they say, courts are never in the business of protecting speech per se, "mere" speech (a nonexistent animal); rather, they are in the business of classifying speech (as protected or regulatable) in relation to a value—the health of the republic, the vigor of the economy, the maintenance of the status quo, the undoing of the status quo—that is the true, if unacknowledged, object of their protection.

11   But if this is the case, a First Amendment purist might reply, why not drop the charade along with the malleable distinctions that make it possible, and declare up front that total freedom of speech is our primary value and trumps anything else, no matter what? The answer is that freedom of expression would only be a primary value if it didn't matter what was said, didn't matter in the sense that no one gave a damn but just liked to hear talk. There are contexts like that, a Hyde Park corner or a call-in talk show where people get to sound off for the sheer fun of it. These, however, are special contexts, artificially bounded spaces designed to assure that talking is not taken seriously. In ordinary contexts, talk is produced with the goal of trying to move the world in one direction rather than another. In these contexts—the contexts of everyday life—you go to the trouble of asserting that X is Y only because you suspect that some people are wrongly asserting that X is Z or that X doesn't exist. You assert, in short, because you give a damn, not about assertion—as if it were a value in and of itself—but about what your assertion is about. It may seem paradoxical, but free expression could only be a primary value if what you are valuing is the right to make noise; but if you are engaged in some purposive activity in the course of which speech happens to be produced, sooner or later you will come to a point when you decide that some forms of speech do not further but endanger that purpose.

12   Take the case of universities and colleges. Could it be the purpose of such places to encourage free expression? If the answer were "yes," it would be hard to say why there would be any need for classes, or examinations, or departments, or disciplines, or libraries, since freedom of expression requires nothing but a soapbox or an open telephone line. The very fact of the university's machinery—of the events, rituals, and procedures that fill its calendar—argues for some other, more substantive purpose. In relation to that purpose (which will be realized differently in different kinds of institutions), the flourishing of free expression will in almost all circumstances be an obvious good; but in some circumstances, freedom of ex-

pression may pose a threat to that purpose, and at that point it may be necessary to discipline or regulate speech, lest, to paraphrase Milton, the institution sacrifice itself to one of its *accidental* features.

13   Interestingly enough, the same conclusion is reached (inadvertently) by Congressman Henry Hyde, who addressed these very issues in an offered amendment to Title VI of the Civil Rights Act. The first section of the amendment states its purpose, to protect "the free speech rights of college students" by prohibiting private as well as public educational institutions from "subjecting any student to disciplinary sanctions solely on the basis of conduct that is speech." The second section enumerates the remedies available to students whose speech rights may have been abridged; and the third, which is to my mind the nub of the matter, declares as an exception to the amendment's jurisdiction any "educational institution that is controlled by a religious organization," on the reasoning that the application of the amendment to such institutions "would not be consistent with the religious tenets of such organizations." In effect, what Congressman Hyde is saying is that at the heart of these colleges and universities is a set of beliefs, and it would be wrong to require them to tolerate behavior, including speech behavior, inimical to those beliefs. But insofar as this logic is persuasive, it applies across the board, for all educational institutions rest on some set of beliefs—no institution is "just there" independent of any purpose—and it is hard to see why the rights of an institution to protect and preserve its basic "tenets" should be restricted only to those that are religiously controlled. Read strongly, the third section of the amendment undoes sections one and two—the exception becomes, as it always was, the rule—and points us to a balancing test very much like that employed in Canadian law: given that any college or university is informed by a core rationale, an administrator faced with complaints about offensive speech should ask whether damage to the core would be greater if the speech were tolerated or regulated.

14   The objection to this line of reasoning is well known and was reformulated by Benno Schmidt, former president of Yale University. According to Schmidt, speech codes on campuses constitute "well intentioned but misguided efforts to give values of community and harmony a higher place than freedom" (*Wall Street Journal,* May 6, 1991). "When the goals of harmony collide with freedom of expression," he continues, "freedom must be the paramount obligation of an academic community." The flaw in this logic is on display in the phrase "academic community," for the phrase recognizes what Schmidt would deny, that expression only occurs in communities—if not in an academic community, then in a shopping mall community or a dinner party community or an airplane ride community or an office community. In these communities and in any others that could be imagined (with the possible exception of a community of major league baseball fans), limitations on speech in relation to a defining and deeply assumed purpose are inseparable from community membership.

15   Indeed, "limitations" is the wrong word because it suggests that expression, as an activity and a value, has a pure form that is always in danger of being compromised by the urgings of special interest communities; but independently of a community context informed by interest (that is, purpose), expression would be at once

inconceivable and unintelligible. Rather than being a value that is threatened by limitations and constraints, expression, in any form worth worrying about, is a *product* of limitations and constraints, of the already-in-place presuppositions that give assertions their very particular point. Indeed, the very act of thinking of something to say (whether or not it is subsequently regulated) is already constrained— rendered impure, and because impure, communicable—by the background context within which the thought takes its shape. (The analysis holds too for "freedom," which in Schmidt's vision is an entirely empty concept referring to an urge without direction. But like expression, freedom is a coherent notion only in relation to a goal or good that limits and, by limiting, shapes its exercise.)

16   Arguments like Schmidt's only get their purchase by first imagining speech as occurring in no context whatsoever, and then stripping particular speech acts of the properties conferred on them by contexts. The trick is nicely illustrated when Schmidt urges protection for speech "no matter how obnoxious in content." "Obnoxious" at once acknowledges the reality of speech-related harms and trivializes them by suggesting that they are *surface* injuries that any large-minded ("liberated and humane") person should be able to bear. The possibility that speech-related injuries may be grievous and *deeply* wounding is carefully kept out of sight, and because it is kept out of sight, the fiction of a world of weightless verbal exchange can be maintained, at least within the confines of Schmidt's carefully denatured discourse.

17   To this Schmidt would no doubt reply, as he does in his essay, that harmful speech should be answered not by regulation but by more speech; but that would make sense only if the effects of speech could be canceled out by additional speech, only if the pain and humiliation caused by racial or religious epithets could be ameliorated by saying something like "So's your old man." What Schmidt fails to realize at every level of his argument is that expression is more than a matter of proffering and receiving propositions, that words do work in the world of a kind that cannot be confined to a purely cognitive realm of "mere" ideas.

18   It could be said, however, that I myself mistake the nature of the work done by freely tolerated speech because I am too focused on short-run outcomes and fail to understand that the good effects of speech will be realized, not in the present, but in a future whose emergence regulation could only inhibit. This line of reasoning would also weaken one of my key points, that speech in and of itself cannot be a value and is only worth worrying about if it is in the service of something with which it cannot be identical. My mistake, one could argue, is to equate the something in whose service speech is with some locally espoused value (e.g., the end of racism, the empowerment of disadvantaged minorities), whereas in fact we should think of that something as a now-inchoate shape that will be given firm lines only by time's pencil. That is why the shape now receives such indeterminate characterizations (e.g., true self-fulfillment, a more perfect polity, a more capable citizenry, a less partial truth); we cannot now know it, and therefore we must not prematurely fix it in ways that will bind successive generations to error.

19   This forward-looking view of what the First Amendment protects has a great appeal, in part because it continues in a secular form the Puritan celebration of millenarian hopes, but it imposes a requirement so severe that one would except more

justification for it than is usually provided. The requirement is that we endure whatever pain racist and hate speech inflicts for the sake of a future whose emergence we can only take on faith. In a specifically religious vision like Milton's, this makes perfect sense (it is indeed the whole of Christianity), but in the context of a politics that puts its trust in the world and not in the Holy Spirit, it raises more questions than it answers and could be seen as the second of two strategies designed to delegitimize the complaints of victimized groups. The first strategy, as I have noted, is to define speech in such a way as to render it inconsequential (on the model of "sticks and stones will break my bones, but . . ."); the second strategy is to acknowledge the (often grievous) consequences of speech but declare that we must suffer them in the name of something that cannot be named. The two strategies are denials from slightly different directions of the *present* effects of racist speech; one confines those effects to a closed and safe realm of pure mental activity; the other imagines the effects of speech spilling over into the world but only in an ever-receding future for whose sake we must forever defer taking action.

20   I find both strategies unpersuasive, but my own skepticism concerning them is less important than the fact that in general they seem to have worked; in the parlance of the marketplace (a parlance First Amendment commentators love), many in the society seemed to have bought them. Why? The answer, I think, is that people cling to First Amendment pieties because they do not wish to face what they correctly take to be the alternative. That alternative is *politics,* the realization (at which I have already hinted) that decisions about what is and is not protected in the realm of expression will rest not on principle or firm doctrine but on the ability of some persons to interpret—recharacterize or rewrite—principle and doctrine in ways that lead to the protection of speech they want heard and the regulation of speech they want heard and the regulation of speech they want silenced. (That is how George Bush can argue *for* flag-burning statutes and *against* campus hate-speech codes.) When the First Amendment is successfully invoked, the result is not a victory for free speech in the face of a challenge from politics but a *political victory* won by the party that has managed to wrap its agenda in the mantle of free speech.

21   It is from just such a conclusion—a conclusion that would put politics *inside* the First Amendment—that commentators recoil, saying things like "This could render the First Amendment a dead letter," or "This would leave us with no normative guidance in determining when and what speech to protect," or "This effaces the distinction between speech and action," or "This is incompatible with any viable notion of freedom of expression." To these statements (culled more or less at random from recent law review pieces) I would reply that the First Amendment has always been a dead letter if one understood its "liveness" to depend on the identification and protection of a realm of "mere" expression distinct from the realm of regulatable conduct; the distinction between speech and action has always been effaced in principle, although in practice it can take whatever form the prevailing political conditions mandate; we have never had any normative guidance for marking off protected from unprotected speech; rather, the guidance we have has been fash-

ioned (and refashioned) in the very political struggles over which it then (for a time) presides. In short, the name of the game has always been politics, even when (indeed, especially when) it is played by stigmatizing politics as the area to be avoided.

22   In saying this, I would not be heard as arguing either for or against regulation and speech codes as a matter of general principle. Instead my argument turns away from general principle to the pragmatic (anti)principle of considering each situation as it emerges. The question of whether or not to regulate will always be a local one, and we can not rely on abstractions that are either empty of content or filled with the content of some partisan agenda to generate a "principled" answer. Instead we must consider in every case what is at stake and what are the risks and gains of alternative courses of action. In the course of this consideration many things will be of help, but among them will not be phrases like "freedom of speech" or "the right of individual expression," because, as they are used now, these phrases tend to obscure rather than clarify our dilemmas. Once they are deprived of their talismanic force, once it is no longer strategically effective simply to invoke them in the act of walking away from a problem, the conversation could continue in directions that are now blocked by a First Amendment absolutism that has only been honored in the breach anyway. To the student reporter who complains that in the wake of the promulgation of a speech code at the University of Wisconsin there is now something in the back of his mind as he writes, one could reply, "There was always something in the back of your mind, and perhaps it might be better to have this code in the back of your mind than whatever was in there before." And when someone warns about the slippery slope and predicts mournfully that if you restrict one form of speech, you never know what will be restricted next, one could reply. "Some form of speech is always being restricted, else there could be no meaningful assertion; we have always and already slid down the slippery slope; someone is always going to be restricted next, and it is your job to make sure that the someone is not you." And when someone observes, as someone surely will, that antiharassment codes chill speech, one could reply that since speech only becomes intelligible against the background of what isn't being said, the background of what has already been silenced, the only question is the political one of which speech is going to be chilled, and, all things considered, it seems a good thing to chill speech like "nigger," "cunt," "kike," and "faggot." And if someone then says, "But what happened to free-speech principles?" one could say what I have now said a dozen times, free-speech principles don't exist except as a component in a bad argument in which such principles are invoked to mask motives that would not withstand close scrutiny.

23   An example of a wolf wrapped in First Amendment clothing is an advertisement that ran in the Duke University student newspaper, the *Chronicle*. Signed by Bradley R. Smith, well known as a purveyor of anti-Semitic neo-Nazi propaganda, the ad is packaged as a scholarly treatise: four densely packed columns complete with "learned" references, undocumented statistics, and an array of so-called authorities. The message of the ad is that the Holocaust never occurred and that the

German state never "had a policy to exterminate the Jewish people (or anyone else) by putting them to death in gas chambers." In a spectacular instance of the increasingly popular "blame the victim" strategy, the Holocaust "story" or "myth" is said to have been fabricated in order "to drum up world sympathy for Jewish causes." The "evidence" supporting these assertions is a slick blend of supposedly probative facts—"not a single autopsied body has been shown to be gassed"—and sly insinuations of a kind familiar to readers of *Mein Kampf* and *The Protocols of the Elders of Zion.* The slickest thing of all, however, is the presentation of the argument as an exercise in free speech—the ad is subtitled "The Case for Open Debate"—that could be objected to only by "thought police" and censors. This strategy bore immediate fruit in the decision of the newspaper staff to accept the ad despite a long-standing (and historically honored) policy of refusing materials that contain ethnic and racial slurs or are otherwise offensive. The reasoning of the staff (explained by the editor in a special column) was that under the First Amendment advertisers have the "right" to be published. "American newspapers are built on the principles of free speech and free press, so how can a newspaper deny these rights to anyone?" The answer to this question is that an advertiser is not denied his rights simply because a single media organ declines his copy so long as other avenues of publication are available and there has been no state suppression of his views. This is not to say that there could not be a case for printing the ad, only that the case cannot rest on a supposed First Amendment obligation. One might argue, for example, that printing the ad would foster healthy debate, or that lies are more likely to be shown up for what they are if they are brought to the light of day, but these are precisely the arguments the editor *disclaims* in her eagerness to take a "principled" free-speech stand.

24   What I find most distressing about this incident is not that the ad was printed but that it was printed by persons who believed it to be a lie and a distortion. If the editor and her staff were in agreement with Smith's views or harbored serious doubts about the reality of the Holocaust, I would still have a quarrel with them, but it would be a different quarrel; it would be a quarrel about evidence, credibility, documentation. But since on these matters the editors and I are in agreement, my quarrel is with the reasoning that led them to act in opposition to what they believed to be true. That reasoning, as I understand it, goes as follows: although we ourselves are certain that the Holocaust was a fact, facts are notoriously interpretable and disputable; therefore nothing is ever really settled, and we have no right to reject something just because we regard it as pernicious and false. But the fact—if I can use that word—that settled truths can always be upset, at least theoretically, does not mean that we cannot affirm and rely on truths that according to our present lights seem indisputable; rather, it means exactly the opposite: in the absence of absolute certainty of the kind that can only be provided by revelation (something I do not rule out but have not yet experienced), we must act on the basis of the certainty we have so far achieved. Truth may, as Milton said, always be in the course of emerging, and we must always be on guard against being so beguiled by its present shape that we ignore contrary evidence; but, by the same token, when it happens

that the present shape of truth is compelling beyond a reasonable doubt, it is our moral obligation to act on it and not defer action in the name of an interpretative future that may never arrive. By running the First Amendment up the nearest flagpole and rushing to salute it, the student editors defaulted on that obligation and gave over their responsibility to a so-called principle that was not even to the point.

25   Let me be clear. I am not saying that First Amendment principles are inherently bad (they are *inherently* nothing), only that they are not always the appropriate reference point for situations involving the production of speech, and that even when they are the appropriate reference point, they do not constitute a politics-free perspective because the shape in which they are invoked will always be political, will always, that is, be the result of having drawn the relevant line (between speech and action, or between high-value speech and low-value speech, or between words essential to the expression of ideas and fighting words) in a way that is favorable to some interests and indifferent or hostile to others. This having been said, the moral is not that First Amendment talk should be abandoned, for even if the standard First Amendment formulas do not and could not perform the function expected of them (the elimination of political considerations in decisions about speech), they still serve a function that is not at all negligible: they slow down outcomes in an area in which the fear of overhasty outcomes is justified by a long record of abuses of power. It is often said that history shows (itself a formula) that even a minimal restriction on the right of expression too easily leads to ever-larger restrictions; and to the extent that this is an empirical fact (and it is a question one could debate), there is some comfort and protection to be found in a procedure that requires you to jump through hoops—do a lot of argumentative work—before a speech regulation will be allowed to stand.

26   I would not be misunderstood as offering the notion of "jumping through hoops" as a new version of the First Amendment claim to neutrality. A hoop must have a shape—in this case the shape of whatever binary distinction is representing First Amendment "interests"—and the shape of the hoop one is asked to jump through will in part determine what kinds of jumps can be regularly made. Even if they are only mechanisms for slowing down outcomes, First Amendment formulas by virtue of their substantive content (and it is impossible that they be without content) will slow down some outcomes more easily than others, and that means that the form they happen to have at the present moment will favor some interests more than others. Therefore, even with a reduced sense of the effectivity of First Amendment rhetoric (it can not assure any particular result), the counsel with which I began remains relevant: so long as so-called free-speech principles have been fashioned by your enemy (so long as it is *his* hoops you have to jump through), contest their relevance to the issue at hand; but if you manage to refashion them in line with your purposes, urge them with a vengeance.

27   It is a counsel that follows from the thesis that there is no such thing as free speech, which is not, after all, a thesis as startling or corrosive as may first have seemed. It merely says that there is no class of utterances separable from the world of conduct and that therefore the identification of some utterances as members of

that nonexistent class will always be evidence that a political line has been drawn rather than a line that denies politics entry into the forum of public discourse. It is the job of the First Amendment to mark out an area in which competing views can be considered without state interference; but if the very marking out of that area is itself an interference (as it always will be), First Amendment jurisprudence is inevitably self-defeating and subversive of its own aspirations. That's the bad news. The good news is that precisely *because* speech is never "free" in the two senses required—free of consequences and free from state pressure—speech always matters, is always doing work; because everything we say impinges on the world in ways indistinguishable from the effects of physical action, we must take responsibility for our verbal performances—*all* of them—and not assume that they are being taken care of by a clause in the Constitution. Of course, with responsibility comes risks, but they have always been our risks, and no doctrine of free speech has ever insulated us from them. They are the risks, respectively, of permitting speech that does obvious harm and of shutting off speech in ways that might deny us the benefit of Joyce's *Ulysses* or Lawrence's *Lady Chatterly's Lover* or Titian's paintings. Nothing, I repeat, can insulate us from those risks. (If there is no normative guidance in determining when and what speech to protect, there is no normative guidance in determining what is art—like free speech a category that includes everything and nothing—and what is obscenity.) Moreover, nothing can provide us with a principle for deciding which risk in the long run is the best to take. I am persuaded that at the present moment, right now, the risk of not attending to hate speech is greater than the risk that by regulating it we will deprive ourselves of valuable voices and insights or slide down the slippery slope toward tyranny. This is a judgment for which I can offer reasons but no guarantees. All I am saying is that the judgments of those who would come down on the other side carry no guarantees either. They urge us to put our faith in apolitical abstractions, but the abstractions they invoke—the marketplace of ideas, speech alone, speech itself—only come in political guises, and therefore in trusting to them we fall (unwittingly) under the sway of the very forces we wish to keep at bay. It is not that there are no choices to make or means of making them; it is just that the choices as well as the means are inextricable from the din and confusion of partisan struggle. There is no safe place.

THINKING CRITICALLY

1. How does Fish establish his thesis in his opening paragraphs? Why does he assert that there really isn't such a thing as "free speech"? Explain.

2. In his first paragraph, Fish explains that his essay is an attempt to "pry" the liberal left "loose from a vocabulary that may now be a disservice to them." What is the "vocabulary" of the argument in support of free speech? Why does he feel that the liberal left's defense of free speech may be a "disservice"?

3. How does Fish's example of *R. v. Keegstra* in Canada support his argument? How does he feel about the Canadian interpretation of free speech? What is your own opinion of it? Explain.

4. In paragraph 9, Fish explains that one way lawyers circumvent the First Amendment is to manipulate the distinction between speech and action. What role does language play in this distinction? Explain.

5. What are "fighting words"? What is the author's position on "fighting words"? What complications do "fighting words" lend to the First Amendment's protections?

6. Evaluate Fish's argument regarding the role of colleges and universities and free speech. What is the purpose of higher education? How does free speech connect to this purpose, or does it?

7. Fish asserts that arguments in support of absolute free speech occur "in no context whatsoever." He makes a distinction between theoretical free speech and the real world. Respond to this part of his argument in your own words.

8. Fish cites an example of "a wolf wrapped in First Amendment clothing" in which neo-Nazi propagandist Bradley R. Smith manipulated student newspapers into printing an ad on the Holocaust that was "patently false" under the guise that he was asserting his right to free speech. What is Fish's position on publishing this material? Why does he feel that it shouldn't be protected by the First Amendment? In your opinion, were student newspapers manipulated? Should they have published the ad? Why or why not?

Muzzling Free Speech
Harvey A. Silverglate

In an effort to curtail criticism of campus speech codes, some colleges and universities have designated "free speech zones" on campus where students may assemble, speak, and protest. In most cases, students must request permission in advance from the administration to use these zones. Harvey Silverglate argues that such zones do not solve the issue of restricted speech. Instead, he asserts, they have a "chilling effect" on campus discourse, and are a dangerous threat to ideals of free speech.

Harvey Silverglate is a partner at the law firm of Silverglate and Good in Boston. He is the co-author with Alan Charles Kors of *The Shadow University: The Betrayal of Liberty on America's Campuses* (1998). Together with Kors, he founded The Foundation for Individual Rights in Education (FIRE), a non-profit organization that addresses individual liberty and rights issues on campus. This article was published in the October 2002 issue of *The National Law Journal*, written with Joshua Gewolb, a special projects coordinator at FIRE.

1   In the last five years, free speech zones have become the trendiest weapon in campus administrators' war on free expression. More than 20 colleges and universities have established speech-zone systems relegating protests, demonstrations and all other forms of student speech to a handful of places on campus. In June 2002, the University of Houston (UH) joined a growing number of colleges and universities that have turned their campuses into censorship zones while restricting unfettered expression to a few tiny "free speech zones."

2   The speech-zones movement presents a major threat to the ideals of free thought and free inquiry to which colleges and universities should be devoted. Free expression, however, means freedom to choose where and when and to whom to speak, not just what to say.

3   College administrators have used every trick in the book to try to limit student speech: Content-based speech codes were the weapon of choice against "offensive" speech on campuses in the early 1980s, but universities were forced to abandon these codes after courts uniformly struck them down. Since then, administrators have used racial and sexual harassment rules to create de facto speech codes. Though these rules have had a chilling effect on campus discourse, recent court opinions finding it unconstitutional to classify as "harassment" speech that is merely offensive (but not physically threatening), reduce the utility of such rules in suppressing speech.

4   College speech zones are the rage because they have not yet faced a court test. When they do, however, they will almost certainly be declared unconstitutional on public campuses. The law requires that government infringements on First Amendment rights be narrowly tailored to accomplish a specific, legitimate purpose— which speech zones are not. Public universities can restrict the "time, place and manner of speech" to avoid disturbing, say, sleeping or studying students, but regulations aimed at forcing students to shut up or move to where they won't be heard and seen are constitutionally verboten.

Houston, We Have a Problem

5   Ironically, UH established its draconian new speech-zone system almost immediately after a court ruled that its previous policy was unconstitutional. The old policy allowed free expression everywhere on campus, but gave Dean William Munson authority to relegate "potentially disruptive" events to four designated areas. In March, the university allowed a large anti-abortion traveling exhibit on the main campus green. The display proved uneventful. But when a second student group, the Pro-Life Cougars, sought to bring the exhibition back for a second run in June, Munson refused permission, citing its potential disruptiveness.

6   The Pro-Life Cougars students sued. On June 24, 2002, the U.S. District Court for the Southern District of Texas declared Munson's actions and UH's speech policy unconstitutional. The court held that the lack of objective standards in UH's policy invited arbitrary prior restraints, and issued a preliminary injunction order-

ing UH to let the Cougars erect their display and barring the university from imposing restrictions on speech in the plaza.

7   The next day, UH's president established the new, more restrictive, zone policy, limiting free speech events on campus to the four zones previously designated for potentially disruptive speech. Students must now register 10 days in advance for even minor protests. Spontaneous demonstrations are relegated to one additional area where amplified sound and signs mounted on sticks are prohibited. Exceptions are only at the dean's discretion.

8   The new policy appears to seek to avoid the unbridled-discretion problem that was fatal to its predecessor. But the administration apparently has not noted the court's warning that even a content-neutral regulation of speech in a public forum must be narrowly tailored to serve a significant government interest and must leave open ample alternative channels of communication. Simply put, there is no legitimate government interest in moving speech from the heart of campus to more peripheral areas.

9   Though free speech zones are on the rise at some universities, several schools, including Penn State and the University of Wisconsin, have revoked their freshly minted zone regulations. In May 2002, speech-zone opponents convinced West Virginia University to liberalize a policy that restricted free expression to two classroom-sized areas. The school is now testing a new policy that, though it does not go far enough, lets small groups stage protests anywhere on campus, at any time, without advance permission.

10   It will take determined advocacy to keep speech zones from invading the rest of America's college and universities. But the recent successes at West Virginia University and elsewhere suggest that the censorship zone movement may burn out as precipitously as it has caught fire. There is a growing recognition, especially by students and civil libertarians, that our entire country is a free speech zone, and that our campuses of higher education, of all places, cannot be an exception.

THINKING CRITICALLY

1. What are "free speech zones"? What purpose do they serve? Are they a fair concession to campus free speech, or a violation of the First Amendment? Explain.

2. In paragraph 3, Silverglate states "college administrators have used every trick in the book to try and limit student speech." What "tricks" according to the author, have they used? Why does Silverglate object to limiting student speech? Has your own campus administration employed any of the speech codes he describes?

3. Silverglate cites several universities that have employed free speech zones, including the University of Houston, Penn State, and West Virginia University. As a class, research the arguments for and against free speech zones as expressed in university publications available online at each of these universities. Discuss your research with the class. If your own campus has a free speech zone, include it in your discussion.

4. Summarize Sliverglate's argument in one paragraph. Include the key points of his discussion and his concluding observations.

SPEECH CODES AT HARVARD LAW SCHOOL?

The next two articles take a close look at a controversial and well-publicized call for a campus speech code at Harvard Law School in 2002. In November of 2002, following some racial incidents earlier that year on campus, the Black Law Students' Association (BLSA) demanded that the administration come up with a "racial harassment policy." While the administration seemed to support the BLSA's requests, protests against violations of free speech were heard from campus and across the country. "Racial harassment" policies, it was argued, were merely another name for a campus speech code. Should Harvard Law School enforce a speech code? Or should all speech, even objectionable, hurtful speech, be protected under the First Amendment?

The first article, by *Wall Street Journal* editorial writer Dorothy Rabinowitz, describes some of the events that led to the BSLA's call for action as well as expresses her concern that speech codes at a law school go counter to what a legal education should teach. The second piece, which appeared as a letter to the editor of Harvard Law School's student newspaper *The Record,* presents third-year law student Austin Bramwell's opinions on this controversial issue. Both articles appeared during the third week of November 2002.

Difficult Conversations
Dorothy Rabinowitz

1 In 1973, film audiences were captivated by "The Paper Chase," a drama about the travails of a first year student at Harvard Law School. His performance as the mercilessly demanding Professor Kingsfield secured an Oscar for John Houseman, a television series based on the film, and left Americans and a good part of the rest of the world with a vivid impression of the fearful intellectual rigors of life at Harvard Law.

2 Current Harvard Law students may have a hard time reconciling this picture with the realities of life at their school today, a time, after all, when a Kingsfield would surely face accusations that he had created a discomfiting learning environment for one group or another. Certain of the newer aspects of life and learning at Harvard Law would also have come as a surprise, to put it mildly, to its renowned longtime dean, the late Erwin Griswold.

3 "Look to the right of you, look to the left of you," the famously tough Griswold was known to advise first year students: "One of you isn't going to be here by the end of the year." The students had entered a world—and this was still true as recently as the 1980s—in which intellectual rigor, skill in logic and harsh argumentation were prized. Harvard had pioneered the Socratic method of case studies emulated by all other law schools: a combative intellectual exercise requiring students to counter torrents of relentless questions designed to drive them into a corner,

much like the kind the devilish Kingsfield asked. And much like those they might encounter from justices of an appellate court.

4   At Harvard Law today, skill in hard combative argument is no longer prized, nor even considered quite respectable. Indeed, first year law students can hardly fail to notice the pall of official disapproval now settled over everything smacking of conflict and argument. That perception can only have been strengthened by a new program for freshmen, called "Managing Difficult Conversations."

5   In the lesson books provided, students learn the importance of empathy. "Emotions need to be acknowledged and understood before people can problem solve," another lesson teaches. In a book by the program's chief creators we learn that "A Difficult Conversation Is Anything You Find It Hard To Talk About." Not the sort of wisdom that would have taxed the minds of the students. Still, the purpose of the three-hour sessions did elude one otherwise accepting attendee, who reports that the discussion leaders seemed to circle around specific issues, and that he had the feeling there was a real subject here not yet clear or acknowledged.

6   He was not the only one wondering about the substance of these meetings. The freshman had just gained entry to the most elite of the nation's law schools. For upward of $32,000 a year tuition, he could learn that a difficult conversation is anything a person finds hard to talk about, and that "logic/reason" have to be combined with "emotions and personal experience" in order to be persuasive. He would not have learned, at such a session, that all the negotiating strategies, all the emphases on emotion and personal history and subtext being advanced at these workshops, was exactly opposite of what legal training was supposed to teach. He would not learn here that the law deals in objective truth that it is concerned with fact. That what is said is determinative, not what is left unsaid, not subtexts, not emotions, expressed or other, not personal history.

7   The student's feeling that the sessions concerned more than the art of difficult conversations was correct. In March, a freshman summarizing a court decision on racial covenants had put his class notes on the Web, which included two references to "Nigs"—abbreviations that caused an uproar. The offender, a Filipino from Hawaii, apologized profusely. Another first year law student weighed in next, this one from Poland. In an anonymous, extremely unpleasant e-mail, he claimed the right to use the N-word, in the interests of free speech. He, too, apologized.

8   The Harvard Black Law Students Association reponded with declarations charging the Law School administrators with willful inaction in the face of "racial outrages." High on their list of perpetrators was senior law professor Charles Nesson, who had offered, as a kind of pedagogic exercise, a mock trial of the anonymous e-mailer, with himself as defense counsel. Arguing that this was an outrage even at a mock trial, the BLSA demanded that Mr. Nesson be barred from teaching mandatory first-year classes.

9   Prof. David Rosenberg was similarly named as a perpetrator of racial outrages. "Marxists, feminists and the blacks had contributed nothing to torts," he is alleged to have told his class. From the context of the class discussion it was clear that the reference to "the blacks" was to the school of legal scholars, known as the Crits—

critics whose viewpoints were based on radical black and feminist perspectives, who had, in Mr. Rosenberg's view, contributed nothing to tort law. This explanation was unacceptable to the BLSA, which demanded that he, too, be barred from teaching mandatory first-year classes, and that the administration publicly reprimand him (along with Mr. Nesson) in the Harvard Law Bulletin and the Harvard Crimson.

10   The answer from law school dean Robert Clark was a model of responsiveness. The Nesson course would be taught by an assistant dean—Mr. Nesson having volunteered, publicly, to remove himself. As for Mr. Rosenberg, his classes would be tape-recorded, so that students who felt he might insult them need not suffer the discomfort of sitting in his class.

11   Dean Clark next announced plans for a "Committee on Healthy Diversity," along with suggestions that a racial harassment policy might be enacted at the school. There was to be, in addition, "a responsive training program for incoming students and faculty." So did it happen that first-year Harvard law students found themselves in workshops on managing difficult conversations.

12   One senior member of the faculty marveled that the school was now training law students to stigmatize conflict. Just before his own class went off to attend the workshops, he slipped them all pieces of paper—these filled with quotes from Supreme Court Justices's opinions holding that free speech is supposed to invite dispute.

13   Boston attorney Harvey Silverglate, who tracks assaults on free speech at universities, describes the workshops as "an exercise in thought reform disguised as an effort to help students improve their negotiation skills." Dean Todd Rakoff, the program's overseer, stands foursquare behind it, nonetheless. The students needed these skills for their careers, he argues. As to free speech, "We are absolutely in favor of uninhibited debate, in a workable fashion."

14   Why the school's administration yielded to the pressure to punish two senior professors charged with racism, one because of a misunderstanding of his meaning, another because of an attempt to turn an ugly episode into an educational one—instead of standing by them—remains unexplained. Nor has anyone in that administration explained why, instead of a rational assessment of these hysterically inflated incidents, the school's dean was moved to give instant implicit assent to the strange notion that racism was running riot at Harvard Law. Both of these subjects would, of course, make for difficult conversations.

Censor This?
Austin Bramwell

1   To the Editor:

2   Like many, I am concerned that a speech code would chill valuable speech on campus. In particular, I wonder whether Diversity Committee members would discipline the author of any of the following opinions:

3   1.   Only the most hyperbolic imagination could believe that racism remains a problem at Harvard. Indeed, the threat of being called a racist does more to chill speech on campus than the use of racial slurs.

4   2.   However uncouth the two racist incidents of last spring, most adults, to say nothing of aspiring attorneys, learn to withstand such petty contumely. Even if they can't, the incidents did not merit public demonstrations, months of campus angst, petitions, demands from the administration, and, now, a speech code.

5   3.   The two students responsible for the racist incidents of last spring have already suffered public obloquy, ostracism, discipline from the administration, withdrawn job offers, and may have had their legal careers ruined. A regime which visits even more punishment upon others like them verges on cruelty.

6   4.   The effect, if not the purpose, of "Diversity Fairs," "Ethnic Counselors," and other programs of "Sensitivity Training" is to augment racial differences and exacerbate racial tensions. If the administration really wanted to promote understanding between races, it would eliminate all such programs and add no more.

7   5.   African-Americans at Harvard are far more likely to have their speech chilled by fellow African-Americans than anyone else, as the savage treatment that Clarence Thomas receives attests. Given that groups like BLSA reinforce the assumption that African-Americans speak univocally, an administration serious about encouraging African-Americans to speak up would withdraw its imprimatur from BLSA and all other ethnic student groups.

8   6.   African-Americans may very well feel disproportionately intimidated at Harvard Law School, but that is more likely a function of affirmative action, which creates a presumption that blacks on campus are less qualified, than systemic racism on campus.

9   7.   BLSA's habit last spring of capitalizing the first letter of "black" in its literature has undeniably racialist overtones. Certainly no group could get away with calling whites "Whites."

10   I welcome any thoughts on which of the above opinions, if any, should be silenced.

THINKING CRITICALLY

1. Review the incidents that led to the Black Law Students' Association's demands to the administration to create and enforce a campus racial harassment policy and speech code. (For more information on the BLSA's demands and the incidents leading up to it, review the archives of Harvard Law School's student newspaper, *The Record,* at <www.hlrecord.org>.) Are the BLSA's demands reasonable? Or are they an infringement of free speech? Explain, citing references from the two articles published here and additional outside research on the issue.

2. In paragraph 4 of her editorial, Rabinowitz states that at Harvard Law School, it seems as if "skill in hard combative argument is no longer prized." Is her argument valid? Would a speech code, in addition to curtailing free speech, harm students of the law when they face the real world? Explain.

3. What is Rabinowitz's position on a campus speech code or harassment policy at Harvard Law? How would Fish respond to her editorial? Kors and Silverglate? Explain.

4. Rabinowitz expresses the concern that if professors fear upsetting students with controversial issues and sensitive topics, education as a whole will suffer. Explore this idea in your own words.

5. Rabinowitz quotes Harvard Law Dean Todd Rakoff, "We are absolutely in favor of uninhibited debate, in a workable fashion." Why do you think she chose this quote? What is Rakoff saying? In light of the disciplinary action taken against professors and students at Harvard Law School, is the administration encouraging uninhibited debate? Explain.

6. Evaluate Bramwell's points in his letter to the editor of *The Record*. How do his points address the current controversy at Harvard Law School?

7. What is Bramwell's tone in his letter? Do you think he faced a risk in sending it? Explain.

8. Write a response to Bramwell's letter in which you either support or refute his points.

■ MAKING CONNECTIONS

1. Suppose that a leader of a known hate group were invited to your campus, someone certain to speak in inflammatory racist language. Would you defend that person's right to address the student body? Why or why not? Should the person be protected under the First Amendment? Why or why not?

2. Write a letter to the editor of your school newspaper advocating restricted or unlimited speech on campus. In your letter, explain your viewpoint and provide supporting material. How do you think your letter would be received by the student body? Explain.

3. Imagine that a condition of acceptance to your school was signing an agreement that you would refrain from using racist, sexist, or otherwise abusive language on campus. Weighing the social benefits of such a measure against the restrictions on freedom of expression, write a paper in which you explain why you would or would not sign such an agreement.

4. Some of the essays in this section discuss censorship codes limiting racist or hate speech on campus. Write a code to be implemented at your college or university. Consider students' rights to free speech, what constitutes hate speech, and what limits can be placed on hate speech. Write a prologue to your code explaining and supporting its tenets.

5. In 1996, Robert B. Chatelle, co-chair of the Political Issues Committee National Writers Union, wrote a letter to Wesleyan University President Douglas Bennet to express concern about a Wesleyan student who had been suspended by the university's student judicial board for violating the Wesleyan speech code. Read Chatelle's argument at <http://users.rcn.com/kyp/schools/bennet2.html>. After identifying both sides of the conflict, write your own views in an essay. Support yourself using information from the readings in this chapter, as well as from your own personal experience.

6. In a January 2003 article in *Boston Magazine,* Harvey Silverglate stated that the First Amendment should protect your right to say what you wish, but that you are not immune to what happens after that. You may be subjected to angry retorts, public shunning, and social pressure, but you should not be officially punished for your language. Write a response to Silverglate expressing your own opinion on this assessment of the First Amendment.

Political Correctness and Hate Speech

8

- The saying "sticks and stones can break my bones but names will never hurt me," doesn't seem to ring true for many people who have been subjected to hateful and demeaning language. Sometimes a symbol can carry as much meaning—and hurt—as a word. As you read the articles in this chapter, think about the ways language can be used as a weapon to injure, as well as a means to convey respect.

America is the most diverse society on earth, home to people of every race, nation, religion, and creed. Because of this incomprehensible mix, our ability to comprehend all that "otherness" is overwhelmed, and we may fall into the trap of reducing different people to handy but offensive labels. In this chapter we will explore efforts to create tolerance such as political correctness, and inclusive language. We will also examine slurs and stereotypes—words that hurt.

Politically Correct Language

The language issue known as *political correctness* has generated intense social, cultural, and political debate. According to William Safire, the term made its first major appearance in 1975 in a statement by Karen DeCrow, then president of the National Organization for Women (NOW), as an assertion of NOW's progressive activities. Picking up momentum from the feminist movement, the term became attached to the celebration of America's rapidly growing multiculturalism and efforts aimed at making people more sensitive to built-in language prejudices against racial and ethnic minorities. By the late 1980s, the new sensitivity grew to encompass language biases based on gender as well as sexual preference, age, class, and physical disability. But around 1990, *politically correct,* abbreviated to *p.c.,* turned into a controversial expression, especially for conservatives who turned the term into a battle cry against the perceived regimentation in language and thought by liberals. The readings in this section take a closer look at the language political correctness has sought to change, and at differing opinions regarding this linguistic effort.

The first reading takes a close look at "hate speech" and "political correctness." Linguist Robin Lakoff examines the connection between hate speech, and the First Amendment from right and left political viewpoints. Then, author of a popular "politically correct" language handbook, Rosalie Maggio describes how English subtly perpetuates prejudice and offers some simple guides for avoiding offensive stereotypes and exclusionary expressions. Arguing with Maggio's position is literary critic and journalist Michiko Kakutani, whose "The Word Police" vehemently condemns such "language-laundering" efforts. In the final essay in this section, Dr. Bernard Rimland, an authority on autistic children, argues that politically correct taboo words such as "retarded" and "handicapped" have produced absurd euphemisms such as "differently-abled" while masking the limitations of handicapped people.

Case Study: Words That Hurt

Racial epithets, ethnic slurs, and other words meant to demean or denigrate others are collectively known as the language of prejudice. Forged by ignorance, fear, and intolerance, these words that hurt damningly reduce people to nothing more than a race, religion, gender, or body type. Such words aim to make the victim seem less than human, less worthy of respect. In this case study, we examine some such words and how they hurt.

■ CASE STUDY: POLITICAL CORRECTNESS

Hate Speech
Robin Tomach Lakoff

While the First Amendment protects free speech, not all speech is truly protected. You cannot, for example, yell "fire" in a crowded theater just for kicks, threaten someone with bodily harm, commit perjury, or knowingly slander another individual. Less clear are attitudes toward "fighting words"—words that are "so very bad that, upon hearing them, an ordinary person must strike out" and words that hurt such as racial epithets. This is the language that gave birth to the "politically correct"—or p.c.—movement. In the next article, linguist Robin Tomach Lakoff takes a look at both sides of the p.c. "hate speech" debate. Should hate speech be protected under the First Amendment? As Lakoff explains, how we feel about this issue is closely connected to how we view the power of language itself.

Robin Tomach Lakoff is a professor of linguistics at the University of California Berkeley. She is the author of several books on language and politics, most recently *Talking Power: The Politics of Language in Our Lives* (1990) and *The Language War* (2000), from which this essay is excerpted.

1   The jewel in the anti-p.c. crown is the First Amendment, newly claimed by the right as its own. Historically the First Amendment was a thorn in the conservative side: it offered protection to nonmajoritarian views, lost causes, and the disenfranchised— not to mention, of course, Communists and worse. From the Sedition Act of the Adams administration to continual attempts to pass a constitutional amendment banning flag-desecration, conservatives have always tried to impose sanctions on free expression, while liberals have tried to keep the "marketplace of ideas" open to all traders. For most of this century it has been the liberal wing of the Supreme Court that has struck down constraints on expression, from Nazi marches to antiwar protests, and the conservative wing that has tried to keep them in effect. But when the shoe is on the other foot and language control is passing from them, conservatives rethink that position. If p.c. can be framed as an attempt to wrest from *us* our historical right to use whatever language we want, whenever we want, to whomever we want, its proponents can be made out to be opponents of free speech and— voilà—we are metamorphosed into all-American defenders of the First Amendment against the infidel Hun, or the p.c. professoriate.

2   No one is expressly demanding the right to make use of hateful slurs. As Mari Matsuda notes, those with media access, the educated upper classes, need not stoop so low: "The various implements of racism find their way into the hands of different dominant-group members. Lower- and middle-class white men might use violence against people of color, whereas upper-class whites might resort to private clubs or righteous indignation against 'diversity' and 'reverse discrimination'" (in Matsuda et al. 1993, 23). So a member of a higher caste might never actually be ex-

posed to virulent racist or sexist language among his associates, and therefore might be able to claim that it didn't exist any more or need not be taken seriously (because *we* don't have to encounter it in its more distasteful forms). And while there do exist epithets to be hurled at males and whites ("phallocrat," "honky"), they lack the sting of slurs against women, blacks, Latinos, and Asians. That is because, according to Matsuda, "racist speech proclaims racial inferiority and denies the personhood of target-group members. All members of the target group are at once considered alike and inferior" (36).

3   But a proclamation of inferiority is meaningful, or even possible, only if it can piggyback on an older stereotype of one race (or gender) as inferior: the "Snark Rule," which states that repetition makes a statement "true." Judith Butler defines hate speech as working through the repetition of similar prior speech acts: "hate speech is an act that recalls prior acts, requiring a future repetition to endure" (1997, 20). So if your group, or you as an individual member of that group, have never been subjected to epithets in the past, no words directed at you, however irritating, can have the full noxious effect of true hate speech. That is not to say that such language is benign. But if you are not a member of a historically submerged group, "you just don't get it," since you don't have a visceral understanding of the harm such speech can do. So it's relatively easy for you to see racist and sexist language and behavior as "just kidding" or "childish horseplay" and not demand a remedy for it.

4   Those who don't have personal reasons to feel that hateful epithets are damaging and who at the same time feel that any challenge to the right to use such speech is a serious threat to the First Amendment are apt to feel not only permitted but obligated, as a sacred duty, to oppose any attempts to legislate language control—at least those that come from the other side and attempt to constrain *our* preferred linguistic possibilities. Laws that might constrain *theirs* are still unproblematic. Hence the right's continuing attempts to outlaw flag-burning, and the loud ruckus on the right that followed the 1989 five-to-four Supreme Court decision (*Texas v. Johnson*) that flag-burning constituted permissible expression under the First Amendment.[1]

5   To listen to some born-again First Amendment advocates, you would believe that its guarantee of free speech is and has always been absolute. But that is far from the case. Courts have always recognized the validity of competing claims: "clear and present danger," "falsely shouting 'fire' in a crowded theater," imminent threat, "fighting words," national interest, libel, threats, subornation of perjury, perjury itself, and others. Even some speech rights we consider uncontroversial today—including the right to provide birth control information or the right to protest the government's involvement in a war—were guaranteed only after arduous struggles. Even if hate speech regulations were to be enforced, that would not be the first curtailment of the absolute right to say anything, under any circumstances. In pondering the need for legislation against hate speech, the first question to address is the validity of competing interests. Does the right to enjoy speech that is as free as possible outweigh the right to "the equal protection of the laws" guaranteed to each of us under the Fourteenth Amendment, or vice versa?

6   This argument pits supporters of the Fourteenth Amendment (Critical Race Theorists and anti-pornography feminists like Catharine MacKinnon) against the odd couple composed of card-carrying ACLU liberals and conservative First Amendment supporters. Everyone agrees that hate speech is deplorable, and no reasonable person would ever indulge in any form of it. But the sides differ on what is to be done and on the consequences of what is done. Is racism so pervasive across this country and on college campuses, and other remedies so ineffectual, that speech codes must be enforced to guarantee to all the equal protection mandated by the Fourteenth Amendment? Or is the problem exaggerated—are there other ways to combat it, and does the need for preserving the First Amendment outweigh the responsibility to enforce the Fourteenth?

7   As a card-carrying ACLU member who is also a member of a couple of historically targeted groups, and as a member of a profession that abhors an unqualified statement, I naturally straddle the line. Others are more decisive. The CRTists tend to see hate speech as deeply pervasive, an increasing "epidemic" that can only be stopped by the immunization of speech codes. In the introduction to *Words That Wound,* its four authors argue that "Incidents of hate speech and racial harassment are reported with increasing frequency and regularity, particularly on American college campuses, where they have reached near epidemic proportions" (Matsuda et. al. 1993, I).

8   Since no figures are given, it is difficult to assess the accuracy of the claim. Even reports of an increasing number of acts of hate speech on college campuses would not necessarily show that hate speech had reached "epidemic" proportions— and might not even be an unequivocally bad thing. First, the larger numbers might merely be the result of more such acts being reported, a sign that minorities are being listened to more and taken more seriously than they used to be and that they now feel safe enough to complain. Even if there actually are more acts committed, that might merely mean that the presence of more minorities and women in places where they previously had not had entree creates more readily available targets, and arouses more resentment. But even if the authors of *Words That Wound* have identified a real problem of endemic racism and sexism in America, the remedy is still not obvious: to some it is not even apparent that any remedy is needed, much less what remedy will work and occasion the least interference with freedom of speech.

Language: Thought or Action?

9 Once again language is the problem. We don't know how to legislate hate speech, because we don't really know how to classify any kind of speech, which we would have to do before we could safely legislate against it. We are pretty clear on other kinds of human activity. Most of us would agree that thought cannot be an object of legislation and should not become one even if science could develop ways to peer into our minds. On the other hand, overt actions are always subject to control by law, and we would agree that they have to be, if we are to live together more or less peaceably in a state of civilization. We may argue about what kinds of actions

should be punishable, and how, but punished bad actions must be. Language is intermediate between thought and action: it is thought made observable. It straddles the line between the abstract and the concrete, the ethereal and the corporeal. Which of its aspects—the ethereal or the physical—should be the basis of our legal understanding of the capacity of language to do harm? Is language inconsequential and therefore immune to legislation? Or is language equivalent to action—world-changing and so capable of harm—in which case legal notice must be taken of injurious linguistic behavior?

10   We teach our children the proverb "Sticks and stones may break my bones, but words will never harm me." Do we offer this saying as truth or as wishful magic: believe it and the pain will go away? Probably we would not be so quick to teach our children these words if we did not fear that the opposite was true. In our natural desire to save our children from pain, we encourage them to deny their feelings. But denial doesn't make it so.

11   We have only recently become a psychologically conscious society. Only in the last hundred years or so have we talked about psychic *wounds* and mental *diseases.* We are never sure whether we mean those expressions as literal descriptions or metaphors. We know that an autopsy on someone suffering from psychic trauma would reveal no physical evidence of that "wound." Yet there now exist physical interventions in the form of drugs that "cure" these traumas, and this possibility of physical "cure" argues for the physical reality of the symptoms.

12   When our legal system was established, it seemed clear that words were not deeds, so only physical misbehaviors were legally actionable. The legal systems of all societies specify punishments or remedies for physical harm. The wound is visible; witnesses may have observed exactly what occurred. There may be disagreement among the parties about the interpretation of the events: Did the victim do anything to provoke the act? Did the perpetrator perform it intentionally? Did he mean to do harm? To do as much harm as he did? Are there other extenuating circumstances? But all participants can agree that something took place that changed the physical world.

13   But what about "words that wound"? Is that expression even meaningful? Are those who feel verbally wounded describing a real interaction with real and adjudicable consequences, or are they merely oversensitive souls who should grow up and take it like a man? If outsiders can't observe the damage, how can anyone prescribe a legal remedy for it?

14   If observers can agree on the amount and kind of force employed to make a physical wound, they can agree on the amount of damage probably sustained by the victim: their conclusions are based on scientifically demonstrable physical laws. But words mean different things to different people in different contexts: a word that would shock and intimidate a woman uttered by a strange man on a dark street at night might be a delightful expression of intimacy between her and someone she loves and trusts. African Americans can call one another "nigger" with relative impunity under specific conditions, but a white person cannot do the same. Language by nature is ambiguous and sensitive to context. The law by necessity strives to be

precise and decontextualized. There is a discontinuity between the two words in the expression "language crime." Yet the law recognizes several: threats, defamation, offers of bribes, and perjury, for example. To make these concepts workable, we need to reach a formal understanding of language and its relation to action.

Speech Acts: "Only Theory" or Reality?

15 Relevant here is the discussion of J. L. Austin's theory of performative speech acts. Austin concluded that language was equivalent to action, in that all utterances were performative and all performatives were world-changing—that is, actions. That theory has had important consequences for several academic fields: philosophy and linguistics (naturally), as well as literary theory, anthropology, and education. As long as it is confined safely within academia, it is mere theory that applies only to ideas, with few actual consequences. But in recent years, it has been incorporated into the discourse of the law, by both legal scholars (as in several papers of Peter Tiersma [1986, 1987]) and sociolinguists (see, for example, Shuy 1993). But nowhere does speech act theory have such concrete and far-reaching consequences as in the definitions of hate speech and its legal status.

16   Those who believe in Austin's formulation are likely to follow it to its logical conclusion: that linguistic misbehavior is a type of bad action and should be treated as such by the law, criminally and civilly. A strict Austinian is likely to support speech codes. If problems of enforceability arise based on the vagueness or ambiguity of language, it is the job of the codifiers to rewrite their statutes clearly enough to solve the problem. Those who disagree with Austin are apt to treat words very differently from actions, beyond the reach of legal remedy in most or even all cases.

17   There are many mixed positions and evasions, depending on the ability to draw and maintain a distinction between those kinds of language that constitute action-equivalents and others that are closer to thought-equivalents. Since the 1920's First Amendment law has divided utterances along those lines: language that constitutes "expression" and receives a high degree of protection under the First Amendment, versus language that constitutes "conduct" and doesn't. A political opinion like "the Republicans deserve to win" will be counted in the first set and be protected, while a threat (even in indirect form) like, "I have a gun and I know how to use it" will under many circumstances be judged "conduct" and treated as a criminal action.

18   A crucial concept is that of "fighting words," as addressed in the 1942 Supreme Court decision *Chaplinsky v. New Hampshire,* which established the category of "fighting words" as unprotected action-equivalents. Chaplinsky, a Jehovah's Witness, got into a verbal altercation with the town marshal of Rochester, New Hampshire, in the course of which he used language considered very shocking in its time, calling the marshal a "Goddamned racketeer" and a "damned Fascist."[2] He was arrested and found guilty under the town's speech code, which prohibited "fighting words." The case was appealed up to the U.S. Supreme Court, which

found for the state. In its unanimous opinion, the Court defined "fighting words"; "There are certain well-defined and narrowly limited classes of speech, the prevention and punishment of which have never been thought to raise any Constitutional problem. These include the lewd and obscene, the profane, the libelous, and the insulting or 'fighting' words—those which by their very utterance inflict injury or tend to incite an immediate breach of the peace."

19   Significantly *Chaplinsky,* as well as later decisions citing it as precedent, locate the justification for the "fighting words" exception in the government's duties to prevent injury to citizens and keep the peace. The former has been essentially negated by later opinions, while the latter has provided appellate courts with an enduring can of worms. If the danger of "fighting words" is that the addressee is apt to lose control and breach the peace (the "breach" is accomplished, in this perspective, only via actions, not via the offensive utterance itself), why not hold the breacher, not the utterer, responsible? The Court's assumption is that some words are so very bad that on hearing them, an ordinary person *must* strike out (as reflexively as, when the doctor taps your knee with a hammer, you *have* to jerk your leg). No psychological or other evidence is cited in support of this proposition.

20   *Chaplinsky* would seem to suggest that verbal aggressors should pick their targets carefully. Persons with less testosterone are known to be less likely than those with more to react physically to provocation. So, presumably, insulting women is more likely to be constitutional under *Chaplinsky* than insulting men, and it's probably better to insult someone smaller than you (who will be less likely to "breach the peace") than someone larger. Scholars who try to justify speech codes these days, like the authors of *Words That Wound,* avoid the morass by thinking in terms of psychic rather than physical trauma. But the "fighting words" exception was not meant to cover psychic wounds, and even if it were determining whether psychic trauma has occurred is—if possible at all—not the business of a court of law and a lay jury.

21   As fond as linguists are of Austinian doctrine (if words are actions, then what we linguists do is important), we must recognize that in fact words are not the same as actions. Most people given the choice between a vile epithet and a punch in the nose would opt for the former. Arguably this is because the second has immediate and obvious painful consequences, while the effects of the first take longer to emerge and are harder to link directly to their cause. If, as the judge said in admitting *Ulysses* into the country, no woman was ever seduced by a book, so no one was ever killed by a word. If language is world-changing, the way it works is different from that of direct action, and less accessible to legal investigation.

22   Franklyn Haiman, in *"Speech Acts" and the First Amendment* (1993), proposes that language is "mediated" action. Austin is not quite right, he suggests, in equating performativity with action. When I give an order, you have to perform the mental act of *deciding* or *willing* to obey me. Even in the clearer case of excommunication, the recipient must determine that the appropriate conditions are met and decide to behave as an excommunicated person in the future, for it to succeed. The words alone, Haiman points out, are meaningless: they derive force through the

agreement by all participants on the nature of the real-world circumstances in which they find themselves.

23   But Haiman is not quite right to dismiss the word-as-action theory entirely. While words are not directly as world-changing as actions are, they are indirectly or psychologically world-changing. If I make a promise to you, that utterance forever alters our relationship and the way I think about it and behave toward you, and you toward me, in the future. To say that speech is not action is to fall into the logical error of drawing a sharp distinction between mind and body.

24   How we feel about hate speech and the First Amendment reflects our view of language itself. If we believe that words are not world-changing, we are apt to be comfortable with an interpretation of the First Amendment that permits much more freedom of speech than is permitted to action. But this leeway comes at the price, ironically, of devaluing language—seeing it as non-action, essentially harmless.

Notes

1. At this writing, an anti–flag desecration law has passed the House of Representatives and is considered likely to pass the Senate.
2. Chaplinsky admitted making the basic statement, but said that as a Jehovah's Witness, he would never have uttered the d-word.

THINKING CRITICALLY

1. This article, and several others in the preceding chapter, comment on "right" and "left" attitudes toward the First Amendment. To what are these authors referring? In what ways have the political left and right used the First Amendment to forward their own agendas? Explain.

2. In several places in this essay, Lakoff strategically puts certain words in italics, including pronouns. Why does she do this? How does her use of italics contribute to what she is trying to relay to the reader? Explain.

3. What is the author's personal position on politically correct language and hate speech codes? When does her position become clear? Does she fairly describe both sides of the issue? Explain.

4. Why does Lakoff say some racial epithets are worse than others? For example, are "phallocrat" and "honkey" parallel to other racial slurs? Why or why not?

5. What is the "Snark rule"? How does it relate to the impact of hate speech on a population?

6. In paragraph 4, Lakoff cites several examples of kinds of speech *not* protected by the First Amendment. How can her examples be used to support both sides of the hate speech argument? Explain.

7. In her discussion of *Chaplinksy v. New Hampshire* (paragraphs 16–18), Lakoff concludes that the ruling on the case "would seem to suggest that verbal aggressors should pick their targets carefully . . . So, presumably, insulting women is more likely to be constitutional than insulting men. . . ." Describe the case and how Lakoff draws such a conclusion. Do you agree? Why or why not?

8. In paragraph 19, Lakoff explains why she feels that words are not actions. On what does she base her assessment? Why does she feel that Austin and Haiman are incorrect in their presumption that action and speech are corollaries? Explain.

9. In her closing comments, Lakoff comments that how we feel about hate speech has a great deal to do with how we feel about language. In your own words, explain what she means by this statement.

WRITING ASSIGNMENTS

1. In your experience, has anyone called you, or a member of a group to which you belong, a name you found offensive? How did that incident make you feel? What was your response? Write a paper based on your answer.

2. In this essay, Lakoff notes that individuals or groups who do not have a history of hearing hate speech "just don't get it." It is the historical repetition and legacy of such language that give racial and sexist epithets their sting. Write an essay exploring this idea from your own viewpoint.

Bias-Free Language: Some Guidelines
Rosalie Maggio

The growing reality of America's multiculturalism has produced a heightened sensitivity to language offensive to members of minority groups. In response, a number of bias-free language guides have been written—guides that caution against terms that might offend not only racial and ethnic groups but women, gays, senior citizens, the handicapped, animal lovers, and the overweight. One of the most successful guides is Rosalie Maggio's *The Dictionary of Bias-Free Usage: A Guide to Nondiscriminatory Language* (1991). In the following excerpt from that guide's introduction, the author discusses how to evaluate and recognize language bias, and why it should be avoided.

Rosalie Maggio is also the author of *The Nonsexist Word Finder* (1987), *How to Say It: Words, Phrases, Sentences, and Paragraphs for Every Situation* (1990), and *The Music Box Christmas* (1990). She has edited many college textbooks and published hundreds of stories and articles in educational publications and children's magazines. Her work has received several literary honors and awards for children's fiction and research on women's issues.

1 Language both reflects and shapes society. The textbook on American government that consistently uses male pronouns for the president, even when not referring to a specific individual (e.g., "a president may cast his veto"), reflects the fact that all

our presidents have so far been men. But it also shapes a society in which the idea of a female president somehow "doesn't sound right."

2   Culture shapes language and then language shapes culture. "Contrary to the assumption that language merely reflects social patterns such as sex-role stereotypes, research in linguistics and social psychology has shown that these are in fact facilitated and reinforced by language" (Marlis Hellinger, in *Language and Power,* ed., Cheris Kramarae et al.).

3   Biased language can also, says Sanford Berman, "powerfully harm people, as amply demonstrated by bigots' and tyrants' deliberate attempts to linguistically dehumanize and demean groups they intend to exploit, oppress, or exterminate. Calling Asians 'gooks' made it easier to kill them. Calling blacks 'niggers' made it simpler to enslave and brutalize them. Calling Native Americans 'primitives' and 'savages' made it okay to conquer and despoil them. And to talk of 'fishermen,' 'councilmen,' and 'longshoremen' is to clearly exclude and discourage women from those pursuits, to diminish and degrade them."

4   The question is asked: Isn't it silly to get upset about language when there are so many more important issues that need our attention?

5   First, it's to be hoped that there are enough of us working on issues large and small that the work will all get done—someday. Second, the interconnections between the way we think, speak, and act are beyond dispute. Language goes hand-in-hand with social change—both shaping it and reflecting it. Sexual harassment was not a term anyone used twenty years ago; today we have laws against it. How could we have the law without the language; how could we have the language without the law? In fact, the judicial system is a good argument for the importance of "mere words"; the legal profession devotes great energy to the precise interpretation of words—often with far-reaching and significant consequences.

6   On August 21, 1990, in the midst of the Iraqi offensive, front-page headlines told the big story: President Bush had used the word *hostages* for the first time. Up to that time, *detainee* had been used. The difference between two very similar words was of possible life-and-death proportions. In another situation—also said to be life-and-death by some people—the difference between *fetal tissue* and *unborn baby* (in referring to the very same thing) is arguably the most debated issue in the country. So, yes, words have power and deserve our attention.

7   Some people are like George Crabbe's friend: "Habit with him was all the test of truth, / it must be right: I've done it from my youth." They have come of age using *handicapped, black-and-white, leper, mankind,* and pseudogeneric *he*; these terms must therefore be correct. And yet if there's one thing consistent about language it is that language is constantly changing; when the *Random House Dictionary of the English Language: 2nd Edition* was published in 1988, it contained 50,000 new entries, most of them words that had come into use since 1966. There were also 75,000 new definitions. (Incidentally, *RHD-II* asks its readers to "use gender-neutral terms wherever possible" and it never uses *mankind* in definitions where *people* is meant, nor does it ever refer to anyone of unknown gender as *he*.)

However, few supporters of bias-free language are asking for changes; it is rather a matter of choice—which of the many acceptable words available to us will we use?

8   A high school student who felt that nonsexist language did demand some changes said, "But you don't understand! You're trying to change the English language, which has been around a lot longer than women have!"

9   One reviewer of the first edition commented, "There's no fun in limiting how you say a thing." Perhaps not. Yet few people complain about looking up a point of grammar or usage or checking the dictionary for a correct spelling. Most writers are very fussy about finding the precise best word, the exact rhythmic vehicle for their ideas. Whether or not these limits "spoil their fun" is an individual judgment. However, most of us accept that saying or writing the first thing that comes to mind is not often the way we want to be remembered. So if we have to think a little, if we have to search for the unbiased word, the inclusive phrase, it is not any more effort than we expend on proper grammar, spelling, and style.

10   Other people fear "losing" words, as though there weren't more where those came from. We are limited only by our imaginations; vague, inaccurate, and disrespectful words can be thrown overboard with no loss to society and no impoverishment of the language.

11   Others are tired of having to "watch what they say." But what they perhaps mean is that they're tired of being sensitive to others' requests. From childhood onward, we all learn to "watch what we say": we don't swear around our parents; we don't bring up certain topics around certain people; we speak differently to friend, boss, cleric, English teacher, lover, radio interviewer, child. Most of us are actually quite skilled at picking and choosing appropriate words; it seems odd that we are too "tired" to call people what they want to be called.

12   The greatest objection to bias-free language is that it will lead us to absurdities. Critics have posited something utterly ridiculous, cleverly demonstrated how silly it is, and then accounted themselves victorious in the battle against linguistic massacre. For example: "So I suppose now we're going to say: He/she ain't heavy, Father/Sister; he/she's my brother/sister." "I suppose next it will be 'ottoperson'." Cases have been built up against the mythic "woperson," "personipulate," and "personhole cover" (none of which has ever been advocated by any reputable sociolinguist). No grist appears too ridiculous for these mills. And, yes, they grind exceedingly small. Using a particular to condemn a universal is a fault in logic. But then ridicule, it is said, is the first and last argument of fools.

13   One of the most rewarding—and, for many people, the most unexpected—side effects of breaking away from traditional, biased language is a dramatic improvement in writing style. By replacing fuzzy, overgeneralized, cliché-ridden words with explicit, active words and by giving concrete examples and anecdotes instead of one-word-fits-all descriptions you can express yourself more dynamically, convincingly, and memorably.

14   "If those who have studied the art of writing are in accord on any one point, it is on this: the surest way to arouse and hold the attention of the reader is by being

specific, definite, and concrete" (Strunk and White, *The Elements of Style*). Writers who talk about *brotherhood* or *spinsters* or *right-hand men* miss a chance to spark their writing with fresh descriptions; they leave their readers as uninspired as they are. Unthinking writing is also less informative. Why use the unrevealing *adman* when we could choose instead a precise, descriptive, inclusive word like *advertising executive, copywriter, account executive, ad writer,* or *media buyer?*

15   The word *manmade,* which seems so indispensable to us, doesn't actually say very much. Does it mean artificial? Handmade? Synthetic? Fabricated? Machine-made? Custom-made? Simulated? Plastic? Imitation? Contrived?

16   Communication is—or ought to be—a two-way street. A speaker who uses *man* to mean *human being* while the audience hears it as *adult male* is an example of communication gone awry.

17   Bias-free language is logical, accurate, and realistic. Biased language is not. How logical is it to speak of the "discovery" of America, a land already inhabited by millions of people? Where is the accuracy in writing "Dear Sir" to a woman? Where is the realism in the full-page automobile advertisement that says in bold letters, "A good driver is a product of his environment," when more women than men influence car-buying decisions? Or how successful is the ad for a dot-matrix printer that says, "In 3,000 years, man's need to present his ideas hasn't changed. But his tools have," when many of these printers are bought and used by women, who also have ideas they need to present? And when we use stereotypes to talk about people ("isn't that just like a welfare mother/Indian/girl/old man"), our speech and writing will be inaccurate and unrealistic most of the time.

Definition of Terms

Bias/Bias-Free

18 Biased language communicates inaccurately about what it means to be male or female; black or white; young or old; straight, gay, or bi; rich or poor; from one ethnic group or another; disabled or temporarily able-bodied; or to hold a particular belief system. It reflects the same bias found in racism, sexism, ageism, handicappism, classism, ethnocentrism, anti-Semitism, homophobia, and other forms of discrimination.

19   Bias occurs in the language in several ways.

1. Leaving out individuals or groups. "Employees are welcome to bring their wives and children" leaves out those employees who might want to bring husbands, friends, or same-sex partners. "We are all immigrants in this country" leaves out Native Americans, who were here well before the first immigrants.

2. Making unwarranted assumptions. To address a sales letter about a new diaper to the mother assumes that the father won't be diapering the baby. To write "Anyone can use this fire safety ladder" assumes that all members of the household are able-bodied.

3. Calling individuals and groups by names or labels that they do not choose for themselves (e.g., *Gypsy, office girl, Eskimo, pygmy, Bushman, the elderly, colored man*) or terms that are derogatory (*fairy, libber, savage, bum, old goat*).
4. Stereotypical treatment that implies that all lesbians/Chinese/women/people with disabilities/teenagers are alike.
5. Unequal treatment of various groups in the same material.
6. Unnecessary mention of membership in a particular group. In a land of supposedly equal opportunity, of what importance is a person's race, sex, age, sexual orientation, disability, or creed? As soon as we mention one of these characteristics—without a good reason for doing so—we enter an area mined by potential linguistic disasters. Although there may be instances in which a person's sex, for example, is germane ("A recent study showed that female patients do not object to being cared for by male nurses"), most of the time it is not. Nor is mentioning a person's race, sexual orientation, disability, age, or belief system usually germane.

20   Bias can be overt or subtle. Jean Gaddy Wilson (in Brooks and Pinson, *Working with Words*) says, "Following one simple rule of writing or speaking will eliminate most biases. Ask yourself: Would you say the same thing about an affluent, white man?"

Inclusive/Exclusive

21 Inclusive language includes everyone; exclusive language excludes some people. The following quotation is inclusive: "The greatest revolution of our generation is the discovery that human beings, by changing the inner attitudes of their minds, can change the outer aspects of their lives" (William James). It is clear that James is speaking of all of us.

22   Examples of sex-exclusive writing fill most quotation books: "Man is the measure of all things" (Protagoras). "The People, though we think of a great entity when we use the word, means nothing more than so many millions of individual men" (James Bryce). "Man is nature's sole mistake" (W. S. Gilbert).

Sexist/Nonsexist

23 Sexist language promotes and maintains attitudes that stereotype people according to gender while assuming that the male is the norm—the significant gender. Nonsexist language treats all people equally and either does not refer to a person's sex at all when it is irrelevant or refers to men and women in symmetrical ways.

24   "A society in which women are taught anything but the management of a family, the care of men, and the creation of the future generation is a society which is on the way out" (L. Ron Hubbard). "Behind every successful man is a woman—with nothing to wear" (L. Grant Glickman). "Nothing makes a man and wife feel closer, these days, than a joint tax return" (Gil Stern). These quotations display var-

ious characteristics of sexist writing: (1) stereotyping an entire sex by what might be appropriate for some of it; (2) assuming male superiority; (3) using unparallel terms (*man and wife* should be either *wife and husband/husband and wife* or *woman and man/man and woman*).

25   The following quotations clearly refer to all people: "It's really hard to be roommates with people if your suitcases are much better than theirs" (J. D. Salinger). "If people don't want to come out to the ball park, nobody's going to stop them" (Yogi Berra). "If men and women of capacity refuse to take part in politics and government, they condemn themselves, as well as the people, to the punishment of living under bad government" (Senator Sam J. Ervin). "I studied the lives of great men and famous women, and I found that the men and women who got to the top were those who did the jobs they had in hand, with everything they had of energy and enthusiasm and hard work" (Harry S Truman).

Gender-Free/Gender-Fair/Gender-Specific

26 Gender-free terms do not indicate sex and can be used for either women/girls or men/boys (e.g., *teacher, bureaucrat, employee, hiker, operations manager, child, clerk, sales rep, hospital patient, student, grandparent, chief executive officer*).

27   Writing or speech that is gender-fair involves the symmetrical use of gender-specific words (e.g., *Ms. Leinwohl/Mr. Kelly, councilwoman/councilman, young man/young woman*) and promotes fairness to both sexes in the larger context. To ensure gender-fairness, ask yourself often: Would I write the same thing in the same way about a person of the opposite sex? Would I mind if this were said of me?

28   If you are describing the behavior of children on the playground, to be gender-fair you will refer to girls and boys an approximately equal number of times, and you will carefully observe what the children do, and not just assume that only the boys will climb to the top of the jungle gym and that only the girls will play quiet games.

29   Researchers studying the same baby described its cries as "anger" when they were told it was a boy and as "fear" when they were told it was a girl (cited in Cheris Kramarae, *The Voices and Words of Women and Men*). We are all victims of our unconscious and most deeply held biases.

30   Gender-specific words (for example, *alderwoman, businessman, altar girl*) are neither good nor bad in themselves. However, they need to be used gender-fairly; terms for women and terms for men should be used an approximately equal number of times in contexts that do not discriminate against either of them. One problem with gender-specific words is that they identify and even emphasize a person's sex when it is not necessary (and is sometimes even objectionable) to do so. Another problem is that they are so seldom used gender-fairly.

31   Although gender-free terms are generally preferable, sometimes gender-neutral language obscures the reality of women's or men's oppression. *Battered spouse* implies that men and women are equally battered; this is far from true.

Parent is too often taken to mean *mother* and obscures the fact that more and more fathers are very much involved in parenting; it is better here to use the gender-specific *fathers and mothers or mothers and fathers* than the gender-neutral *parents*.

Generic/Pseudogeneric

32 A generic is an all-purpose word that includes everybody (e.g., *workers, people, voters, civilians, elementary school students*). Generic pronouns include: *we, you, they.*

33 A pseudogeneric is a word that is used as though it included all people, but that in reality does not. *Mankind, forefathers, brotherhood,* and *alumni* are not generic because they leave out women. When used about Americans, *immigrants* leaves out all those who were here long before the first immigrants. "What a christian thing to do!" uses *christian* as a pseudogeneric for *kind* or *good-hearted* and leaves out all kind, good-hearted people who are not Christians.

34 Although some speakers and writers say that when they use *man* or *mankind* they mean everybody, their listeners and readers do not perceive the word that way and these terms are thus pseudogenerics. The pronoun *he* when used to mean *he and she* is another pseudogeneric.

35 Certain generic nouns are often assumed to refer only to men, for example, *politicians, physicians, lawyers, voters, legislators, clergy, farmers, colonists, immigrants, slaves, pioneers, settlers, members of the armed forces, judges, taxpayers.* References to "settlers, their wives, and children," or "those clergy permitted to have wives" are pseudogeneric.

36 In historical context it is particularly damaging for young people to read about settlers and explorers and pioneers as though they were all white men. Our language should describe the accomplishments of the human race in terms of all those who contributed to them.

Sex and Gender

37 An understanding of the difference between sex and gender is critical to the use of bias-free language.

38 Sex is biological: people with male genitals are male, and people with female genitals are female.

39 Gender is cultural: our notions of "masculine" tell us how we expect men to behave and our notions of "feminine" tell us how we expect women to behave. Words like *womanly/manly, tomboy/sissy, unfeminine/unmasculine* have nothing to do with the person's sex; they are culturally acquired, subjective concepts about character traits and expected behaviors that vary from one place to another, from one individual to another.

40 It is biologically impossible for a woman to be a sperm donor. It may be culturally unusual for a man to be a secretary, but it is not biologically impossible. To say "the secretary . . . she" assumes all secretaries are women and is sexist because the

issue is gender, not sex. Gender describes an individual's personal, legal, and social status without reference to genetic sex; gender is a subjective cultural attitude. Sex is an objective biological fact. Gender varies according to the culture. Sex is a constant.

41   The difference between sex and gender is important because much sexist language arises from cultural determinations of what a woman or man "ought" to be. Once a society decides, for example, that to be a man means to hide one's emotions, bring home a paycheck, and be able to discuss football standings while to be a woman means to be soft-spoken, love shopping, babies, and recipes, and "never have anything to wear," much of the population becomes a contradiction in terms—unmanly men and unwomanly women. Crying, nagging, gossiping, and shrieking are assumed to be women's lot; rough-housing, drinking beer, telling dirty jokes, and being unable to find one's socks and keys are laid at men's collective door. Lists of stereotypes appear silly because very few people fit them. The best way to ensure unbiased writing and speaking is to describe people as individuals, not as members of a set.

Gender Role Words

42 Certain sex-linked words depend for their meanings on cultural stereotypes: *feminine/masculine, manly/womanly, boyish/girlish, husbandly/wifely, fatherly/motherly, unfeminine/unmasculine, unmanly/unwomanly,* etc. What a person understands by these words will vary from culture to culture and even within a culture. Because the words depend for their meanings on interpretations of stereotypical behavior or characteristics, they may be grossly inaccurate when applied to individuals. Somewhere, sometime, men and women have said, thought, or done everything the other sex has said, thought, or done except for a very few sex-linked biological activities (e.g., only women can give birth or nurse a baby, only a man can donate sperm or impregnate a woman). To describe a woman as unwomanly is a contradiction in terms; if a woman is doing it, saying it, wearing it, thinking it, it must be—by definition—womanly.

43   F. Scott Fitzgerald did not use "feminine" to describe the unforgettable Daisy in *The Great Gatsby.* He wrote instead, "She laughed again, as if she said something very witty, and held my hand for a moment, looking up into my face, promising that there was no one in the world she so much wanted to see. That was a way she had." Daisy's charm did not belong to Woman: it was uniquely hers. Replacing vague sex-linked descriptors with thoughtful words that describe an individual instead of a member of a set can lead to language that touches people's minds and hearts.

Naming

44 Naming is power, which is why the issue of naming is one of the most important in bias-free language.

Self-Definition

45 People decide what they want to be called. The correct names for individuals and groups are always those by which they refer to themselves. This "tradition" is not always unchallenged. Haig Bosmajian (*The Language of Oppression*) says, "It isn't strange that those persons who insist on defining themselves, who insist on this elemental privilege of self-naming, self-definition, and self-identity encounter vigorous resistance. Predictably, the resistance usually comes from the oppressor or would-be oppressor and is a result of the fact that he or she does not want to relinquish the power which comes from the ability to define others."

46   Dr. Ian Hancock uses the term *exonym* for a name applied to a group by outsiders. For example, Romani peoples object to being called by the exonym *Gypsies*. They do not call themselves Gypsies. Among the many other exonyms are: the elderly, colored people, homosexuals, pagans, adolescents, Eskimos, pygmies, savages. The test for an exonym is whether people describe themselves as "redmen," "illegal aliens," "holy rollers," etc., or whether only outsiders describe them that way.

47   There is a very small but visible element today demanding that gay men "give back" the word *gay*—a good example of denying people the right to name themselves. A late-night radio caller said several times that gay men had "stolen" this word from "our" language. It was not clear what language gay men spoke.

48   A woman nicknamed "Betty" early in life had always preferred her full name, "Elizabeth." On her fortieth birthday, she reverted to Elizabeth. An acquaintance who heard about the change said sharply, "I'll call her Betty if I like!"

49   We can call them Betty if we like, but it's arrogant, insensitive, and uninformed: the only rule we have in this area says we call people what they want to be called.

"Insider/Outsider" Rule

50 A related rule says that insiders may describe themselves in ways that outsiders may not. "Crip" appears in *The Disability Rag*; this does not mean that the word is available to anyone who wants to use it. "Big Fag" is printed on a gay man's T-shirt. He may use that expression; a non-gay may not so label him. One junior-high student yells to another, "Hey, nigger!" This would be highly offensive and inflammatory if the speaker were not African American. A group of women talk about "going out with the girls," but a co-worker should not refer to them as "girls." When questioned about just such a situation, Miss Manners replied that "people are allowed more leeway in what they call themselves than in what they call others."

"People First" Rule

51 Haim Ginott taught us that labels are disabling; intuitively most of us recognize this and resist being labeled. The disability movement originated the "people first" rule,

which says we don't call someone a "diabetic" but rather "a person with diabetes." Saying someone is "an AIDS victim" reduces the person to a disease, a label, a statistic; use instead "a person with/who has/living with AIDS." The 1990 Americans with Disabilities Act is a good example of correct wording. Name the person as a person first, and let qualifiers (age, sex, disability, race) follow, but (and this is crucial) only if they are relevant. Readers of a magazine aimed at an older audience were asked what they wanted to be called (elderly? senior citizens? seniors? golden agers?). They rejected all the terms; one said, "How about 'people'?" When high school students rejected labels like kids, teens, teenagers, youth, adolescents, and juveniles, and were asked in exasperation just what they would like to be called, they said, "Could we just be people?"

Women as Separate People

52 One of the most sexist maneuvers in the language has been the identification of women by their connections to husband, son, or father—often even after he is dead. Women are commonly identified as someone's widow while men are never referred to as anyone's widower. Marie Marvingt, a Frenchwoman who lived around the turn of the century, was an inventor, adventurer, stunt woman, superathlete, aviator, and all-around scholar. She chose to be affianced to neither man (as a wife) nor God (as a religious), but it was not long before an uneasy male press found her a fit partner. She is still known today by the revealing label "the Fiancée of Danger." If a connection is relevant, make it mutual. Instead of "Frieda, his wife of seventeen years," write "Frieda and Eric, married for seventeen years."

53 It is difficult for some people to watch women doing unconventional things with their names. For years the etiquette books were able to tell us precisely how to address a single woman, a married woman, a divorced woman, or a widowed woman (there was no similar etiquette on men because they have always been just men and we have never had a code to signal their marital status). But now some women are Ms. and some are Mrs., some are married but keeping their birth names, others are hyphenating their last name with their husband's, and still others have constructed new names for themselves. Some women—including African American women who were denied this right earlier in our history—take great pride in using their husband's name. All these forms are correct. The same rule of self-definition applies here: call the woman what she wants to be called.

THINKING CRITICALLY

1. Maggio begins her article with a discussion of the ways language has real effects on people's attitudes and actions. What are some of the examples she supplies? How does language create desirable or undesirable consequences?

2. What are the four excuses people make to avoid using unbiased language? How does Maggio counter those excuses? What additional counterargument does she supply in defense of nonbiased language?

3. What main idea links all the different ways in which bias can occur (see paragraph 18)? Does biased language refer to individuals or to groups of people? Would the following statement be an example of biased (or stereotyped) language? "Mary is wearing her hair in a French braid today, so she'll no doubt wear it that way tomorrow."

4. What are the categories Maggio specifically names as subject to biased language? Can you supply additional categories?

5. Maggio uses the term *symmetrical* several times (e.g., paragraphs 23 and 27). What does this term mean? Does Maggio want to encourage or discourage the use of symmetrical language? Does *symmetry* refer only to gender bias, or can it refer to other kinds of bias too?

6. What is the difference between gender-free, gender-fair, and gender-specific language in paragraphs 26 through 31? What examples does Maggio supply for each one? When is each kind of nonbiased language appropriate?

7. How can the principles of gender-free, gender-fair, and gender-specific language be applied to language that is biased about handicap, religion, race, age, or other group characteristics? Supply one example for each principle and include a phrase that contains biased language and a revision resolving the problem.

8. What does Maggio mean by a "generic" word? A "pseudogeneric" word? How might pseudo-generic references harm people?

9. What is an *exonym*? Are exonyms ever appropriate, according to Maggio's discussion? Did you recognize all the words Maggio lists in paragraph 46 as exonyms? Can you supply substitutes for all the exonyms? If not, what problems did you encounter? Can you supply examples of other exonyms from your own experience?

10. Why do you think Maggio considers naming "one of the most important [issues] in bias-free language" (paragraph 44)? What is so important about the ability to choose a name? What do you think the woman in paragraph 48 is communicating by choosing to be called Elizabeth? Why do you think Maggio links this announcement to the woman's fortieth birthday celebration?

11. What did the high school student in paragraph 8 really mean to say? Why do you think Maggio includes this statement? What point is she trying to make? Do you think that this student was male or female? Would it make a difference? Why doesn't Maggio specify?

WRITING ASSIGNMENTS

1. Locate an article in a contemporary newspaper that you think displays one or more of the biases Maggio describes. In a letter to the editor (no more than 500 words), persuade the newspaper editors to avoid such biased language in future articles. Remember that your writing will be more effective if you write in a calm, reasonable tone, use specific examples, and explain clearly the benefits of unbiased language.

2. Look back at Susanne K. Langer's essay, "Language and Thought" (page 27). How is Maggio's understanding of biased language, and the harm it can create, based on an understanding of language as "symbol" (as Langer uses that term)? What are the distinguishing features of language as symbol that biased language uses? Pay special attention to Maggio's treat-

ment of naming, because Langer claims that "names are the essence of language" (in Langer's paragraph 19).

3. How would you go about designing an advertising campaign for the magazine that Maggio says is "aimed at an older audience"? What words would you use to avoid offensive labeling and to avoid the vagueness of the broadly generic noun "people" (which is the same term the high school students ask to be designated by)?

The Word Police
Michiko Kakutani

Not everybody applauds the efforts of those hoping to rid the language of offensive terms. To detractors, all such linguistic sensitivity is no more than a symptom of political correctness—a kind of be-sensitive-or-else campaign. They complain that unlike standard dictionaries, which are meant to help people use words, the so-called *cautionary* guides warn people against using them. Such is the complaint of Michiko Kakutani, who specifically targets Rosalie Maggio's *The Bias-Free Word Finder* as an example of the menace of hypersensitivity. She complains that in the name of the "politics of inclusion," proponents hunt down users of "inappropriate" language like the thought police from George Orwell's *1984*. And, claims Kakutani, they fill the English language with sloppy, pious euphemisms.

Michiko Kakutani is a staff writer for the *New York Times*, where this article first appeared in January 1993.

---

1 This month's inaugural festivities, with their celebration, in Maya Angelou's words, of "humankind"—"the Asian, the Hispanic, the Jew/ The African, the Native American, the Sioux,/ The Catholic, the Muslim, the French, the Greek/ The Irish, the Rabbi, the Priest, the Sheik,/ The Gay, the Straight, the Preacher,/ The privileged, the homeless, the Teacher"—constituted a kind of official embrace of multiculturalism and a new politics of inclusion.

2 The mood of political correctness, however, has already made firm inroads into popular culture. Washington boasts a store called Politically Correct that sells pro-whale, anti-meat, ban-the-bomb T-shirts, bumper stickers and buttons, as well as a local cable television show called "Politically Correct Cooking" that features interviews in the kitchen with representatives from groups like People for the Ethical Treatment of Animals.

3 The Coppertone suntan lotion people are planning to give their longtime cover girl, Little Miss (Ms?) Coppertone, a male equivalent, Little Mr. Coppertone. And even Superman (Super-person?) is rumored to be returning this spring, reincarnated as four ethnically diverse clones: an African-American, an Asian, a Caucasian and a Latino.

---

4   Nowhere is this P.C. mood more striking than in the increasingly noisy debate over language that has moved from university campuses to the country at large—a development that both underscores Americans' puritanical zeal for reform and their unwavering faith in the talismanic power of words.

5   Certainly no decent person can quarrel with the underlying impulse behind political correctness: a vision of a more just, inclusive society in which racism, sexism and prejudice of all sorts have been erased. But the methods and fervor of the self-appointed language police can lead to a rigid orthodoxy—and unintentional self-parody—opening the movement to the scorn of conservative opponents and the mockery of cartoonists and late-night television hosts.

6   It's hard to imagine women earning points for political correctness by saying "ovarimony" instead of "testimony"—as one participant at the recent Modern Language Association convention was overheard to suggest. It's equally hard to imagine people wanting to flaunt their lack of prejudice by giving up such words and phrases as "bull market," "kaiser roll," "Lazy Susan," and "charley horse."

7   Several books on bias-free language have already appeared, and the 1991 edition of the Random House *Webster's College Dictionary* boasts an appendix titled "Avoiding Sexist Language." The dictionary also includes such linguistic mutations as "womyn" (women, "used as an alternative spelling to avoid the suggestion of sexism perceived in the sequence m-e-n") and "waitron" (a gender-blind term for waiter or waitress).

8   Many of these dictionaries and guides not only warn the reader against offensive racial and sexual slurs, but also try to establish and enforce a whole new set of usage rules. Take, for instance, *The Bias-Free Word Finder: A Dictionary of Nondiscriminatory Language* by Rosalie Maggio (Beacon Press)—a volume often indistinguishable, in its meticulous solemnity, from the tongue-in-cheek *Official Politically Correct Dictionary and Handbook* put out last year by Henry Beard and Christopher Cerf (Villard Books). Ms. Maggio's book supplies the reader intent on using kinder, gentler language with writing guidelines as well as a detailed listing of more than 5,000 "biased words and phrases."

9   Whom are these guidelines for? Somehow one has a tough time picturing them replacing Fowler's *Modern English Usage* in the classroom, or being adopted by the average man (sorry, individual) in the street.

10   The "pseudogeneric 'he,'" we learn from Ms. Maggio, is to be avoided like the plague, as is the use of the word "man" to refer to humanity. "Fellow," "king," "lord" and "master" are bad because they're "male-oriented words," and "king," "lord" and "master" are especially bad because they're also "hierarchical, dominator society terms." The politically correct lion becomes the "monarch of the jungle," new-age children play "someone on the top of the heap," and the "Mona Lisa" goes down in history as Leonardo's "acme of perfection."

11   As for the word "black," Ms. Maggio says it should be excised from terms with a negative spin: she recommends substituting words like "mouse" for "black eye," "ostracize" for "blackball," "payola" for "blackmail" and "outcast" for "black sheep." Clearly, some of these substitutions work better than others: somehow the

"sinister humor" of Kurt Vonnegut or "Saturday Night Live" doesn't quite make it; nor does the "denouncing" of the Hollywood 10.

12   For the dedicated user of politically correct language, all these rules can make for some messy moral dilemmas. Whereas "battered wife" is a gender-biased term, the gender-free term "battered spouse," Ms. Maggio notes, incorrectly implies "that men and women are equally battered."

13   On one hand, say Francine Wattman Frank and Paula A. Treichler in their book *Language, Gender, and Professional Writing* (Modern Language Association), "he or she" is an appropriate construction for talking about an individual (like a jockey, say) who belongs to a profession that's predominantly male—it's a way of emphasizing "that such occupations are not barred to women or that women's concerns need to be kept in mind." On the other hand, they add, using masculine pronouns rhetorically can underscore ongoing male dominance in those fields, implying the need for change.

14   And what about the speech codes adopted by some universities in recent years? Although they were designed to prohibit students from uttering sexist and racist slurs, they would extend, by logic, to blacks who want to use the word "nigger" to strip the term of its racist connotations, or homosexuals who want to use the word "queer" to reclaim it from bigots.

15   In her book, Ms. Maggio recommends applying bias-free usage retroactively: she suggests paraphrasing politically incorrect quotations, or replacing "the sexist words or phrases with ellipsis dots and/or bracketed substitutes," or using "sic" "to show that the sexist words come from the original quotation and to call attention to the fact that they are incorrect."

16   Which leads the skeptical reader of *The Bias-Free Word Finder* to wonder whether *All the King's Men* should be retitled *All The Ruler's People; Pet Semetary, Animal Companion Graves; Birdman of Alcatraz, Birdperson of Alcatraz;* and *The Iceman Cometh, The Ice Route Driver Cometh?*

17   Will making such changes remove the prejudice in people's minds? Should we really spend time trying to come up with non-male-based alternatives to "Midas touch," "Achilles' heel," and "Montezuma's revenge"? Will tossing out Santa Claus—whom Ms. Maggio accuses of reinforcing "the cultural male-as-norm system"—in favor of Belfana, his Italian female alter ego, truly help banish sexism? Can the avoidance of "violent expressions and metaphors" like "kill two birds with one stone," "sock it to 'em" or "kick an idea around" actually promote a more harmonious world?

18   The point isn't that the excesses of the word police are comical. The point is that their intolerance (in the name of tolerance) has disturbing implications. In the first place, getting upset by phrases like "bullish on America" or "the City of Brotherly Love" tends to distract attention from the real problems of prejudice and injustice that exist in society at large, turning them into mere questions of semantics. Indeed, the emphasis currently put on politically correct usage has uncanny parallels with the academic movement of deconstruction—a method of textual analysis that focuses on language and linguistic pyrotechnics—which has become firmly established on university campuses.

19   In both cases, attention is focused on surfaces, on words and metaphors; in both cases, signs and symbols are accorded more importance than content. Hence, the attempt by some radical advocates to remove the *Adventures of Huckleberry Finn* from curriculums on the grounds that Twain's use of the word "nigger" makes the book a racist text—never mind the fact that this American classic (written in 1884) depicts the spiritual kinship achieved between a white boy and a runaway slave, never mind the fact that the "nigger" Jim emerges as the novel's most honorable, decent character.

20   Ironically enough, the P.C. movement's obsession with language is accompanied by a strange Orwellian willingness to warp the meaning of words by placing them under a high-powered ideological lens. For instance, the "Dictionary of Cautionary Words and Phrases"—a pamphlet issued by the University of Missouri's Multicultural Management Program to help turn "today's journalists into tomorrow's multicultural newsroom managers"—warns that using the word "articulate" to describe members of a minority group can suggest the opposite, "that 'those people' are not considered well educated, articulate and the like."

21   The pamphlet patronizes minority groups, by cautioning the reader against using the words "lazy" and "burly" to describe any member of such groups; and it issues a similar warning against using words like "gorgeous" and "petite" to describe women.

22   As euphemism proliferates with the rise of political correctness, there is a spread of the sort of sloppy, abstract language that Orwell said is "designed to make lies sound truthful and murder respectable, and to give an appearance of solidity to pure wind." "Fat" becomes "big boned" or "differently sized"; "stupid" becomes "exceptional"; "stoned" becomes "chemically inconvenienced."

23   Wait a minute here! Aren't such phrases eerily reminiscent of the euphemisms coined by the Government during Vietnam and Watergate? Remember how the military used to speak of "pacification," or how President Richard M. Nixon's press secretary, Ronald L. Ziegler, tried to get away with calling a lie an "inoperative statement"?

24   Calling the homeless "the underhoused" doesn't give them a place to live; calling the poor "the economically marginalized" doesn't help them pay the bills. Rather, by playing down their plight, such language might even make it easier to shrug off the seriousness of their situation.

25   Instead of allowing free discussion and debate to occur, many gung-ho advocates of politically correct language seem to think that simple suppression of a word or concept will magically make the problem disappear. In the *Bias-Free Word Finder,* Ms. Maggio entreats the reader not to perpetuate the negative stereotype of Eve. "Be extremely cautious in referring to the biblical Eve," she writes; "this story has profoundly contributed to negative attitudes toward women throughout history, largely because of misogynistic and patriarchal interpretations that labeled her evil, inferior, and seductive."

26   The story of Bluebeard, the rake (whoops!—the libertine) who killed his seven wives, she says, is also to be avoided, as is the biblical story of Jezebel. Of Jesus Christ, Ms. Maggio writes: "There have been few individuals in history as com-

pletely androgynous as Christ, and it does his message a disservice to overinsist on his maleness." She doesn't give the reader any hints on how this might be accomplished; presumably, one is supposed to avoid describing him as the Son of God.

27   Of course the P.C. police aren't the only ones who want to proscribe what people should say or give them guidelines for how they may use an idea; Jesse Helms and his supporters are up to exactly the same thing when they propose to patrol the boundaries of the permissible in art. In each case, the would-be censor aspires to suppress what he or she finds distasteful—all, of course, in the name of the public good.

28   In the case of the politically correct, the prohibition of certain words, phrases and ideas is advanced in the cause of building a brave new world free of racism and hate, but this vision of harmony clashes with the very ideals of diversity and inclusion that the multi-cultural movement holds dear, and it's purchased at the cost of freedom of expression and freedom of speech.

29   In fact, the utopian world envisioned by the language police would be bought at the expense of the ideals of individualism and democracy articulated in "The Gettysburg Address." "Fourscore and seven years ago our forefathers brought forth on this continent a new nation, conceived in liberty and dedicated to the proposition that all men are created equal."

30   Of course, the P.C. police have already found Lincoln's words hopelessly "phallocentric." No doubt they would rewrite the passage: "Fourscore and seven years ago our foremothers and forefathers brought forth on this continent a new nation, formulated with liberty, and dedicated to the proposition that all humankind is created equal."

THINKING CRITICALLY

1. What kinds of people are mentioned in the lines of Maya Angelou's inauguration poem? What do these people symbolize, according to Kakutani? How many of these groups are represented in your classroom right now?

2. What specific substitutions of words does Kakutani complain about in paragraph 10? Can you supply the "biased" term that the "politically correct" phrase has replaced in the second half of the paragraph?

3. What are the three "messy moral dilemmas" Kakutani points out in paragraphs 12–14? Why does she tag the examples she cites as *dilemmas*? Why does she object to following politically correct guidelines in each case?

4. What is wrong, according to Kakutani in paragraphs 15 and 16, with Maggio's recommendation that unbiased language be applied retroactively? Rewrite one or two of the titles using Maggio's suggestions as quoted by Kakutani in paragraph 15—that is, use ellipses, brackets, and so on. How well do these suggestions work?

5. What examples of euphemism does Kakutani provide in paragraphs 22–24? What objections does she raise about these euphemisms? Why does she compare the new politically correct terms with terms from Watergate?

6. Describe the tone in Kakutani's first three paragraphs of the article. Do you think this piece is going to be serious, playful, or sarcastic? What evidence did you base your response on?

7. Look closely at the wording of Kakutani's first sentence in paragraph 22. Why doesn't she say outright that political correctness causes "sloppy, abstract language"? What do you think Maggio would say about the cause-and-effect relationship of political correctness and language?

8. Kakutani interrupts herself twice to insert a "correction"—to substitute a politically correct term for an incorrect term she has inadvertently let slip. These appear in paragraphs 9 and 26. What's going on here—didn't she have enough time to edit her article?

WRITING ASSIGNMENTS

1. Compare the views about language of Rosalie Maggio in "Bias-Free Language" and Kakutani in this article. What powers does each author believe language has? What power does language not have? Cite specific evidence from each author for your comparison.

2. Despite Kakutani's attack on Maggio's book, she agrees with at least some of Maggio's underlying assumptions—for example, about language and power, about the need to end prejudice, and other points. Identify and discuss at least three assumptions or values that both authors would agree on; then, discuss why they believe that different actions are appropriate.

3. Examine some samples of your own writing from earlier in the term, or from previous terms. Where have you struggled with politically correct language use? Have you always been successful in using it? What substitutions or changes did you try that, on rereading, seem less than satisfactory?

Beware the Advozealots: Mindless Good Intentions Injure the Handicapped
Bernard Rimland

What kind of language should be used to discuss people with disabilities has long been a controversial topic. Such terms as *cripple, dumbie, and idiot,* once widely used, are now seen as crude and offensive. Yet some people feel that attempts to use language that is sensitive to people with disabilities has gone too far. Is it accurate to say that mentally handicapped people are "differently abled"? Or is this simply a euphemism that seeks to ignore the reality of the person's difficulties or limitations? In the following essay, Dr. Bernard Rimland, an authority on the treatment of autistic and hyperactive children, argues that "advozealots"—people who demand that only certain kinds of "politically correct" language be used when discussing the disabled—are misguided and dangerous. As you read the essay, see where you stand on this difficult and "touchy" issue.

1 In recent years our society has increasingly been directed—often to the great detriment of the handicapped—by ideas that are based on good wishes and fantasies rather than on factual information and rational thought. People who should know better have subscribed to the idea that if you pretend that the handicapped are not really handicapped, the handicaps will disappear and everyone will live happily ever after. The legions of mentally ill homeless, seen shivering in doorways and rummaging for food in dumpsters, are a prime example of what can happen when ideology overrules common sense. People who are unable to care for themselves, and were once sheltered, fed and protected from criminal assault in institutions, are now living in wretched conditions in "the community."

2 How was this accomplished? In part by the manipulation of language. All institutions were characterized as inherently oppressive, and "the community" as *invariably* loving and supportive.

3 The people who wrought such great harm on the institutionalized mentally ill are still at work. Now they are destroying the institutions needed for the most severely retarded and autistic people. Under the banners of "empowerment," "human rights," and "full inclusion," they have also set out to destroy the special education system created by decades of advocacy and hard work on the part of the families of mentally handicapped children.

4 I have coined the word "advozealot" to characterize the people who purport to be advocates for the handicapped but are in fact zealous advocates of their own Alice in Wonderland ideology, in which handicaps can simply be assumed out of existence.

5 A major weapon of the advozealots is "politically correct" (PC) language. There are many forbidden words. They insist that words such as "autistic," "retarded" and "handicapped" not be used. They insist that the silly euphemism "challenging" be used to describe severely self-injurious or assaultive behavior.

6 Professionals working in the field of severe mental handicap have in recent years been subjected to ridicule, censorship, and even intimidation to compel them to comply with the politically correct language insisted upon by the advozealots, who are certain that their way is the *only* way.

7 One of the major contentions of the advozealots, the self-appointed spokesmen for the handicapped, is that the mentally handicapped be referred to by means of "people first" terminology. One, for example, must say "children with autism," rather than "autistic children." Professionals who do not comply with these purportedly benign edicts have been threatened with refusal to publish their books and papers, with rejection of their grant proposals, and even with the loss of their jobs.

8 Even the federal government has succumbed. In Office of Education Regulations issued on September 29, 1992, "technical changes" are announced which include deleting all references to "handicapped children" in the regulations and substituting "children with disabilities." Why are our tax dollars used to promote such nonsense?

9 Insistence upon the use of PC terminology is a violation of the rights of speakers and writers to exercise their freedom of expression. If *you* wish to say "children

with autism" rather than "autistic children," go right ahead. BUT do not insist that I do so.

10   Although at first glance the matter may seem inconsequential—merely quibbling about words—the issue has real implications about real people in the real world. It is no coincidence that those who insist on people-first language are also those who insisted upon closing institutions and farm residences, so "community" living in urban jungles is forced upon the handicapped. These are the people who insist that special education be discarded so that "full inclusion" is forced on the handicapped, and on normal people as well—very often to the detriment of both groups. Research evidence does not support these goals. It is strictly an ideological campaign.

11   But why are the people-first people so zealous in demanding compliance? The answer brings us to the crucial reason for rejecting the terminology being foisted upon us by the purveyors of PC. Underlying the PC terminology is an insidious and deeply pernicious ideology that is based solely on a naive view which I call the fantasy assumption: if enough people join the fantasy, by choice or by coercion, the fantasy will come true. In the present instance, the advozealots appear to believe that if one deliberately trivializes the difference between mentally handicapped and non-handicapped persons, the differences will somehow disappear, and thus no one will be handicapped. Reality does not work that way. Closing down institutions for the mentally handicapped on the assumption that there really was no difference between people inside and outside those institutions has not worked. It has resulted in the displacement of tens of thousands of now homeless mentally handicapped people to the streets where they must fend for themselves. Playing "let's pretend" is a game that's fun for children. Playing let's pretend when the lives of people—especially mentally handicapped people—are at stake, can lead to senseless tragedy.

12   Contrary to what the advozealots want us to believe, being a "person with autism" or a "person with retardation" is not like being "a person with a plaid jacket" or "a person with a cane." Autism, mental retardation, and other mental handicaps pervade and permeate every moment of a person's life. You can't shed autism, or retardation, like a plaid jacket or sunglasses. The PC people are trying to brainwash us into believing, as they seem to, that there is no real difference between the mentally handicapped and the rest of us, but there is. To deny the difference is to reject the disability, to paper over the distinction. It deprives the handicapped of their most valuable asset—the recognition of their disability by the rest of us. It annuls their right to our compassion and to the special treatment they need if they are to live secure and fulfilling lives. Pretending the handicapped are not really handicapped robs them of the respect they deserve for the tremendous effort they must exert to achieve the small accomplishments that come easily to the rest of us.

13   Douglas Biklen, in his book on facilitated communications, *Communication Unbound,* devotes the last of the seven chapters to "Ending the Ability/Disability Dichotomy." He entreats us to abandon the "blinders of disability." He believes (or at least appeared to when he wrote the book) that the supposed ability of virtually

all the handicapped to communicate via facilitated communications proves that the handicaps were not real: handicaps are merely a myth. Biklen's ideas are specious. Yes, there are people on the borderline between normal and handicapped. Does that mean that no one is handicapped? Yes, there are shades of gray. Does that mean there is no black and white? Does twilight disprove the difference between day and night?

14   You can't solve problems by hiding from them, or trying to smother them in a fog of murky words. You are much more likely to solve problems by recognizing them explicitly and thinking about them clearly. In a talk given earlier this year, Clarence Sundram expressed the situation with great clarity: ". . . we have tended to be seduced by the power of these new ideas of equality, autonomy and inclusion to the point that we have relied more upon hope and belief than upon good judgment and careful planning to help make these ideas a reality. In the process we seem to be replacing the old stereotype of people who are mentally retarded as hopelessly dependent, with the new stereotype of a rugged individualist, capable of coping with a hostile and dangerous world, if only given the chance. Both stereotypes contain serious misconceptions and fail to confront the reality that . . . mentally retarded . . . embraces a broad range of functioning capability and includes people with significant areas of incapacity as well."

15   How do we combat these seductive but pernicious ideas, which are being implemented so uncritically?

16   Do not meekly accept the advozealots' arrogant assumption of the moral high ground. Experience and common sense should carry at least as much weight as the strident repetition of PC buzzwords. Do not betray the handicapped by accepting the "people first"/"challenging behavior"/"in the community" ideology, nor any other ideology which is intended to trivialize the difficulties which beset the handicapped. Speak out: do not be afraid to exercise your freedom of expression, and freedom of thought. The advozelots, some with a hidden agenda and others with the best of intentions, have done much harm. If you are truly concerned with the welfare of the handicapped, resist!

THINKING CRITICALLY

1. Discuss Rimland's opening paragraph. How would you characterize his tone? Who are the "people who should know better" that Rimland refers to?

2. What is an advozealot? What two words has Rimland combined to make this word? What are these words' connotations?

3. What evidence does Rimland offer to support his claims about the advozealots' influence? Would you characterize his argument as one that appeals more to "head" or to "heart"?

4. In paragraph 7, Rimland complains that advozealots insist on terms like *children with autism*, rather than *autistic children*. Discuss the differences between the meanings of these two terms. Do you agree with Rimland that the term *children with autism* is in some way misleading? Why or why not?

5. In paragraph 8, Rimland calls it "nonsense" to spend money on changing the term *handicapped children* to children with disabilities in government documents. Do you agree? Why or why not?

6. In paragraph 10, Rimland uses the term *urban jungles*. What does this term suggest about Rimland's world view? Does this term strengthen or weaken his argument? Why?

7. What, according to Rimland, drives the advozealots to want to erase the difference between the abled and the disabled?

WRITING ASSIGNMENTS

1. Write a personal narrative describing how you were taught by parents and teachers to treat handicapped people. What language did they use to describe different disabilities? Do you think language influenced your perception of people with handicaps? Explain.

2. Rimland feels that politically correct language is changing how society treats handicapped people, to their harm. Is politically correct language simply an attempt to "assume [handicaps] out of existence"? Or is it an attempt to promote sensitivity for those who have disabilities? Read an alternative point of view by Kathy Snow at http://www.modmh.state.mo.us/sikeston/people.htm. Then, write an essay expressing your own perspective on this issue, referring to points made in both Rimland's and Snow's essays.

■ MAKING CONNECTIONS

1. Bernard Rimland, Rosalie Maggio, and Michiko Kakutani all take strong positions on the issue of "politically correct" language, while Lakoff takes a more neutral position. Maggio could be described as the most "p.c.," whereas Rimland falls at the other end of the spectrum, with Kakutani and Lakoff falling somewhere in between. Create a conversation between two or more of these authors that discusses the issues of language use. (Your conversation will be more effective if you focus on a particular topic/issue—perhaps choose a controversy in the news, a controversial TV program or movie, or anything to do with your school's speech/behavior codes.)

2. Many of those who feel "p.c." language has gone too far have made a point of collecting examples of the "p.c. police" in action. Using the Internet, your school library, and friends and classmates as sources, collect a list of stories that illustrate political correctness that has gone too far. Pay special attention to the source of these stories' origins. Can you find proof that these events actually occurred, or do they seem to be stories circulated by anti-p.c. individuals/groups in order to undercut the ideals of "political correctness"?

3. Look at some of the parodies of political correctness such as *Bedtimes Stories for Politically Correct Children* or the *Official Politically Correct Dictionary and Handbook.* Choose one of these types of books or go to a humor Web site that parodies politically correct language or groups. Write a critique of the text you choose. Do you find the humor amusing? Why or why not? Do you find it in any way disturbing or offensive? Explain your answer.

4. The issues of hate speech and politically correct language seem to be deeply intertwined. Write an essay in which you explore the connection between the two and likely outcomes for

the future. Will the words "politically correct" drop from our lexicon, as more sensitive forms of speech become the norm? Will hate speech become a thing of the past if speech codes preventing it are instituted and enforced? Why or why not?

■ CASE STUDY: WORDS THAT HURT

Racial epithets, ethnic slurs, and other words meant to inflict emotional injury serve as ugly reminders of our capacity to use language as a weapon to demean and denigrate others. Born of ignorance, fear, and intolerance, these words that hurt dehumanize their victims either intentionally or inadvertently. In this case study, we examine some such words and how they hurt.

Perhaps the most offensive and unacceptable racial/ethnic slur in the English language is *nigger,* a word that this case study gives particular consideration. No other word condenses racial prejudice so powerfully. And, yet, as best-selling author Gloria Naylor explains, she grew up hearing it used by other black Americans as a term of endearment. But when a white boy hurled the term at her as an insult, the word suddenly turned bad.

While some words are immediately identifiable as hurtful, such as racial, sexist, or ethnic slurs, others may be used inadvertently. It is not simply the words themselves that cause harm, but the tone and context in which they are used. For example, while the word "retarded" is a clinically correct definition for individuals with significant developmental disabilities, it can be used inappropriately to demean or debase people with learning difficulties. And everyday words, such as "fat" and "blimp" can sting when spoken with scorn or malice to someone who is overweight.

As you read the articles featured in this case study, consider how words have been used against you to demean or insult you. Perhaps you have used some of them yourself, even inadvertently. Think about the negative power of this type of language, and how words, subtly and sometimes unconsciously, shape social and cultural attitudes of prejudice.

"Nigger": The Meaning of a Word
Gloria Naylor

Context can be everything when it comes to the meaning of a word, even a word recognized as an ugly epithet. As Gloria Naylor explains, when she was a little girl, the word *nigger* was spoken comfortably in front of her by relatives and family friends. She had heard it dozens of times, viewing it as a term of endearment. But she really didn't "hear" the term until it was "spit out" of the mouth of a white boy in her third-grade class.

Gloria Naylor, a native of New York City, is an accomplished writer whose first novel, *The Women of Brewster Place* (1982), won an American Book Award. She is also the author of *Linden Hills* (1985), *Mama Day* (1988), and *Bailey's Cafe* (1992). This essay first appeared in the *New York Times* in February 1986.

1 Language is the subject. It is the written form with which I've managed to keep the wolf away from the door and, in diaries, to keep my sanity. In spite of this, I consider the written word inferior to the spoken, and much of the frustration experienced by novelists is the awareness that whatever we manage to capture in even the most transcendent passages falls far short of the richness of life. Dialogue achieves its power in the dynamics of a fleeting moment of sight, sound, smell and touch.

2 I'm not going to enter the debate here about whether it is language that shapes reality or vice versa. That battle is doomed to be waged whenever we seek intermittent reprieve from the chicken and egg dispute. I will simply take the position that the spoken word, like the written word, amounts to a nonsensical arrangement of sounds or letters without a consensus that assigns "meaning." And building from the meanings of what we hear, we order reality. Words themselves are innocuous; it is the consensus that gives them true power.

3 I remember the first time I heard the word nigger. In my third-grade class, our math tests were being passed down the rows, and as I handed the papers to a little boy in back of me, I remarked that once again he had received a much lower mark than I did. He snatched his test from me and spit out that word. Had he called me a nymphomaniac or a necrophiliac, I couldn't have been more puzzled. I didn't know what a nigger was, but I knew that whatever it meant, it was something he shouldn't have called me. This was verified when I raised my hand, and in a loud voice repeated what he had said and watched the teacher scold him for using a "bad" word. I was later to go home and ask the inevitable question that every black parent must face—"Mommy, what does 'nigger' mean?"

4 And what exactly did it mean? Thinking back, I realize that this could not have been the first time the word was used in my presence. I was part of a large extended family that had migrated from the rural South after World War II and formed a close-knit network that gravitated around my maternal grandparents. Their ground-floor apartment in one of the buildings they owned in Harlem was a weekend mecca for my immediate family, along with countless aunts, uncles and cousins who brought along assorted friends. It was a bustling and open house with assorted neighbors and tenants popping in and out to exchange bits of gossip, pick up an old quarrel or referee the ongoing checkers game in which my grandmother cheated shamelessly. They were all there to let down their hair and put up their feet after a week of labor in the factories, laundries and shipyards of New York.

5 Amid the clamor, which could reach deafening proportions—two or three conversations going on simultaneously, punctuated by the sound of a baby's crying

somewhere in the back rooms or out on the street—there was still a rigid set of rules about what was said and how. Older children were sent out of the living room when it was time to get into the juicy details about "you-know-who" up on the third floor who had gone and gotten herself "p-r-e-g-n-a-n-t!" But my parents, knowing that I could spell well beyond my years, always demanded that I follow the others out to play. Beyond sexual misconduct and death, everything else was considered harmless for our young ears. And so among the anecdotes of the triumphs and disappointments in the various workings of their lives, the word nigger was used in my presence, but it was set within contexts and inflections that caused it to register in my mind as something else.

6   In the singular, the word was always applied to a man who had distinguished himself in some situation that brought their approval for his strength, intelligence or drive:

7   "Did Johnny *really* do that?"

8   "I'm telling you, that nigger pulled in $6,000 of overtime last year. Said he got enough for a down payment on a house."

9   When used with a possessive adjective by a woman—"my nigger"—it became a term of endearment for husband or boyfriend. But it could be more than just a term applied to a man. In their mouths it became the pure essence of manhood—a disembodied force that channeled their past history of struggle and present survival against the odds into a victorious statement of being: "Yeah, that old foreman found out quick enough—you don't mess with a nigger."

10   In the plural, it became a description of some group within the community that have overstepped the bounds of decency as my family defined it: Parents who neglected their children, a drunken couple who fought in public, people who simply refused to look for work, those with excessively dirty mouths or unkempt households were all "trifling niggers." This particular circle could forgive hard times, unemployment, the occasional bout of depression—they had gone through all of that themselves—but the unforgivable sin was a lack of self-respect.

11   A woman could never be a "nigger" in the singular, with its connotation of confirming worth. The noun girl was its closest equivalent in that sense, but only when used in direct address and regardless of the gender doing the addressing. "Girl" was a token of respect for a woman. The one-syllable word was drawn out to sound like three in recognition of the extra ounce of wit, nerve or daring that the woman had shown in the situation under discussion.

12   "G-i-r-l, stop. You mean you said that to his face?"

13   But if the word was used in a third-person reference or shortened so that it almost snapped out of the mouth, it always involved some element of communal disapproval. And age became an important factor in these exchanges. It was only between individuals of the same generation, or from an older person to a younger (but never the other way around), that "girl" would be considered a compliment.

14   I don't agree with the argument that use of the word nigger at this social stratum of the black community was an internalization of racism. The dynamics were

the exact opposite: the people in my grandmother's living room took a word that whites used to signify worthlessness or degradation and rendered it impotent. Gathering there together, they transformed "nigger" to signify the varied and complex human beings they knew themselves to be. If the word was to disappear totally from the mouths of even the most liberal of white society, no one in that room was naïve enough to believe it would disappear from white minds. Meeting the word head-on, they proved it had absolutely nothing to do with the way they were determined to live their lives.

15   So there must have been dozens of times that the "nigger" was spoken in front of me before I reached the third grade. But I didn't "hear" it until it was said by a small pair of lips that had already learned it could be a way to humiliate me. That was the word I went home and asked my mother about. And since she knew that I had to grow up in America, she took me in her lap and explained.

THINKING CRITICALLY

1. Does Naylor think that written or spoken words are more powerful? Why? What does she mean when she says that it is "consensus that gives [words] true power"?

2. What did Naylor do as a response to hearing the word *nigger?* In your judgment, were her actions appropriate and effective ways of handling the situation?

3. List four different meanings that Naylor says she has heard adults apply to the word *nigger.* How are these four meanings different from what she believed the boy in her class meant? Are all four meanings positive?

4. Why can't a woman be referred to as a *nigger?* What other term is used for a woman that achieves meaning similar to the term *nigger* for a man?

5. Does Naylor approve of her family and friends' use of the word *nigger?* Why or why not? Does she approve of white people using the word? Why or why not?

6. Naylor relates in some detail the circumstances surrounding the first time she heard the word *nigger.* Why does she paint such an elaborate picture? Why doesn't she simply list her age and the fact that she heard it used as an insult? What do you think prompted the boy to use this word?

7. Why does Naylor compare the word *nigger* specifically to *nymphomaniac* and *necrophiliac?* Why these words? How are they similar? How different? (Look them up in your dictionary if you are not sure what they mean.)

8. In paragraphs 4 and 5, Naylor provides a detailed discussion of her extended family: where they lived, how they were related, what kind of atmosphere these people created, and what kinds of discussion children were permitted to eavesdrop on. How is this information related to the subject of Naylor's essay, the meaning of the word *nigger?*

The Etymology of the International Insult
Charles F. Berlitz

In the preceding section on politically correct language, authors discuss the ways language has the power to slant the way we see the world and to prejudice the way we think. Perhaps no aspect of language is more slanted and prejudiced than that of ethnic, racial, sexist, and religious insults. In this essay, Charles F. Berlitz, founder of the internationally known Berlitz School of Languages, takes a look at international insults. Instead of exploring moral issues, he objectively examines the origins of these insults, some of which are surprisingly inoffensive. As you read, consider how these words, some with rather benign origins, linguistically shift into insults.

1   "What is a kike?" Disraeli once asked a small group of fellow politicians. Then, as his audience shifted nervously, Queen Victoria's great Jewish Prime Minister supplied the answer himself. "A kike," he observed, "is a Jewish gentlemen who has just left the room."

2   The word kike is thought to have derived from the ending *-ki* or *-ky* found in many names borne by the Jews of Eastern Europe. Or, as Leo Rosten suggests, it may come from *kikel,* Yiddish for a circle, the preferred mark for name signing by Jewish immigrants who could not write. This was used instead of an *X,* which resembles a cross. Kikel was not originally pejorative, but has become so through use.

3   Yid, another word for Jew has a distinguished historic origin, coming from the German *Jude* (through the Russian *zhid*). *Jude* itself derives from the tribe of Judah, a most honorable and ancient appellation. The vulgar and opprobrious word "Sheeny" for Jew is a real inversion, as it derives from *shaine* (Yiddish) or *schön* (German), meaning "beautiful." How could beautiful be an insult? The answer is that it all depends on the manner, tone or facial expression or sneer (as our own Vice President[1] has trenchantly observed) with which something is said. The opprobrious Mexican word for an American—*gringo,* for example, is essentially simply a sound echo of a song the American troops used to sing when the Americans were invading Mexico—"Green Grow the Lilacs." Therefore the Mexicans began to call the Americans something equivalent to "los green-grows" which became Hispanized to *gringo.* But from this innocent beginning to the unfriendly emphasis with which many Mexicans say *gringo* today there is a world of difference—almost a call to arms, with unforgettable memories of past real or fancied wrongs, including "lost" Texas and California.[2]

4   The pejorative American word for Mexicans, Puerto Ricans, Cubans and other Spanish-speaking nationals is simply *spik,* excerpted from the useful expression

---

[1]A reference to Spiro Agnew, who served as Vice President to Richard Nixon. (Ed.)
[2]Other linguists theorize the term "gringo" derives from the seventeenth-century Spanish *griego* for Greek, a term used widely in Latin America, not just Mexico.

"No esspick Englitch." Italians, whether in America or abroad, have been given other more picturesque appellations. *Wop,* an all-time pejorative favorite, is curiously not insulting at all by origin, as it means, in Neapolitan dialect, "handsome," "strong" or "good looking." Among the young Italian immigrants some of the stronger and more active—sometimes to the point of combat—were called *guappi,* from which the first syllable, "wop," attained an "immediate insult" status for all Italians.

5   "Guinea" comes from the days of the slave trade and is derived from the African word for West Africa. This "guinea" is the same word as the British unit of 21 shillings, somehow connected with African gold profits as well as New Guinea, which resembled Africa to its discoverers. Dark or swarthy Italians and sometimes Portuguese were called *Guineas* and this apparently spread to Italians of light complexion as well.

6   One of the epithets for Negroes has a curious and tragic historic origin, the memory of which is still haunting us. The word is *"coons."* It comes from *baracoes* (the o gives a nasal *n* sound in Portuguese), and refers to the slave pens or barracks (*"baracoons"*) in which the victims of the slave trade were kept while awaiting transshipment. Their descendants, in their present emphasizing of the term "black" over "Negro," may be in the process of upgrading the very word "black," so often used pejoratively, as in "black-hearted," "black day," "black arts," "black hand," etc. Even some African languages use "black" in a negative sense. In Hausa "to have a black stomach" means to be angry or unhappy.

7   The sub-Sahara African peoples, incidentally, do not think that they are black (which they are not, anyway). They consider themselves a healthy and attractive "people color," while whites to them look rather unhealthy and somewhat frightening. In any case, the efforts of African Americans to dignify the word "black" may eventually represent a semantic as well as a socio-racial triumph.

8   A common type of national insult is that of referring to nationalities by their food habits. Thus "Frogs" for the French and "Krauts" for the Germans are easily understandable, reflecting on the French addiction to *cuisses de grenouilles* (literally "thighs of frogs") and that of the Germans for various kinds of cabbage, hot or cold. The French call the Italians *"les macaronis"* while the German insult word for Italians is *Katzenfresser* (Cateaters), an unjust accusation considering the hordes of cats among the Roman ruins fed by individual cat lovers—unless they are fattening them up? The insult word for an English person is "limey," referring to the limes distributed to seafaring Englishmen as an antiscurvy precaution in the days of sailing ships and long periods at sea.

9   At least one of these food descriptive appellations has attained a permanent status in English. The word "Eskimo" is not an Eskimo word at all but an Algonquin word unit meaning "eaters-of-flesh." The Eskimos naturally do not call themselves this in their own language but, with simple directness, use the word *Inuit*—"the men" or "the people."

10   Why is it an insult to call Chinese "Chinks"? Chink is most probably a contraction of the first syllables of *Chung-Kuo-Ren*—"Middle Country Person." In Chinese there is no special word for China, as the Chinese, being racially somewhat

snobbish themselves (although *not* effete, according to recent reports), have for thousands of years considered their land to be the center or middle of the world. The key character for China is therefore the word *chung* or "middle" which, added to *kuo,* becomes "middle country" or "middle kingdom"—the complete Chinese expression for "China" being *Chung Hwa Min Kuo* ("Middle Flowery People's Country"). No matter how inoffensive the origin of "Chink" is, however, it is no longer advisable for everyday or anyday use now.

11   Jap, an insulting diminutive that figured in the . . . [1968] national U.S. election (though its use in the expression "fat Jap" was apparently meant to have an endearing quality by our Vice President) is a simple contraction of "Japan," which derives from the Chinese word for "sun." In fact the words "Jap" and "Nip" both mean the same thing. "Jap" comes from Chinese and "Nip" from Japanese in the following fashion: *Jihpen* means "sun origin" in Chinese, while *Ni-hon* (Nippon) gives a like meaning in Japanese, both indicating that Japan was where the sun rose. Europeans were first in contact with China, and so originally chose the Chinese name for Japan instead of the Japanese one.

12   The Chinese "insult" words for whites are based on the observations that they are too white and therefore look like ghosts or devils, *fan kuei* (ocean ghosts), or that their features are too sharp instead of being pleasantly flat, and that they have enormous noses, hence *ta-bee-tsu* (great-nosed ones). Differences in facial physiognomy have been fully reciprocated by whites in referring to Asians as "Slants" or "Slopes."

13   Greeks in ancient times had an insult word for foreigners too, but one based on the sound of their language. This word is still with us, though its original meaning has changed. The ancient Greeks divided the world into Greeks and "Barbarians"—the latter word coming from a description of the ridiculous language the stranger was speaking. To the Greeks it sounded like the "baa-baa" of a sheep—hence "Barbarians"!

14   The black peoples of South Africa are not today referred to as Negro or Black but as Bantu—not in itself an insult but having somewhat the same effect when you are the lowest man on the totem pole. But the word means simply "the men," *ntu* signifying "man" and *ba* being the plural prefix. This may have come from an early encounter with explorers or missionaries when Central or South Africans on being asked by whites who they were may have replied simply "men"—with the implied though probably unspoken follow-up questions, "And who are you?"

15   The basic and ancient idea that one's group are the only people—at least the only friendly or non-dangerous ones—is found among many tribes throughout the world. The Navajo Indians call themselves *Diné*—"the people"—and qualify other tribes generally as "the enemy." Therefore an Indian tribe to the north would simply be called "the northern enemy," one to the east "the eastern enemy," etc., and that would be the *only* name used for them. These ancient customs, sanctified by time, of considering people who differ in color, customs, physical characteristics and habits—and by enlargement all strangers—as potential enemies is something mankind can no longer afford, even linguistically. Will man ever be able to rise

above using insult as a weapon? It may not be possible to love your neighbor, but by understanding him one may be able eventually to tolerate him. Meanwhile, if you stop calling him names, he too may eventually learn to dislike *you* less.

THINKING CRITICALLY

1. Knowing how racial and ethnic insults originate, do you find that you can more easily accept them? That they are even more objectionable? Explain.

2. In the first paragraph, Berlitz quotes Disraeli. What do you think was the meaning of Disraeli's definition of *kike*?

3. Berlitz gives etymological meanings of the following words: *Jude, wop, schön, guappi,* and *Chung-Kuo-Ren.* What similarities do the meanings of these words have?

4. Explain the relationship between national insults and national eating habits. Can you think of others not mentioned by Berlitz?

5. Why do so many tribal peoples refer to themselves as "the people"? What does that say about people's habits of insulting others of different ethnic or racial origins?

6. What does Berlitz mean in the last paragraph when he warns that even linguistically, humanity can no longer afford to consider different races and customs as enemies?

7. Berlitz begins this essay with an anecdote. How effective is it? What is the relationship of the anecdote to the rest of the essay?

8. For the most part, Berlitz is objective in his discussion. Can you find instances where he expresses his attitude toward the use of international insults?

The "R" Word: How Do You Avoid Saying "Retarded"?
John Cook

The word *retarded* has a clinical definition of "impaired intellectual function that results in an inability to cope with the normal responsibilities of life" (American Medical Association). Recently, however, advocacy groups have been calling for a less pejorative word to be used to describe individuals with developmental disabilities. Why has this clinical word become a negative one? One reason is due to schoolyard epithets in which the word was flung unkindly at children with all sorts of disabilities and medical conditions—from cerebral palsy to Down syndrome—some of which involve no cognitive impairment at all. Other codified words that describe degrees of mental impairment such as *moron, imbecile,* and *idiot* have become part of our general lexicon. In the next piece, John Cook examines why *retarded* carries pejorative connotations, and wonders what word could possibly take its place.

The following article first appeared in *Slate* magazine in July 2001.

1 We've been hearing an awful lot about retarded people lately. More precisely, we've been hearing about a certain subset of mentally retarded people who live on death row. The recent interest in the fate of mentally retarded convicts has launched a bevy of headlines like this from the *New York Times* in June: "Jeb Bush Signs Bill Barring Executing the Retarded." On television, we've heard Ed Bradley, filling in for Dan Rather on the *CBS Evening News* earlier this month, refer to "retarded killer Johnny Penry" and "retarded criminals."

2   What's striking about all this attention is that the word "retarded" has fallen from favor—and not just among the PC crowd. Though it's still a clinical term used, somewhat begrudgingly, by psychologists to describe people who score lower than 70 on IQ tests, almost everyone in the developmental-disability field thinks it's demeaning and wants a new word. In May 2001, for instance, the American Association on Mental Retardation, the leading advocacy group for the, um, mentally retarded, voted to change its name. But no one could agree on the replacement, so the group simply pledged to change it to something better—less pejorative, less likely to bring schoolyard epithets to mind. And in August at the American Psychological Association's annual convention, the group's panel on Mental Retardation and Developmental Disabilities (called Division 33), will likely drop the "R" word from its name. "There will be a discussion," says Philip Davidson, Division 33's president-elect, "and I suspect it will be put to a vote and that it will pass." The smart bets for an eventual successor are on "intellectual disability," the term used in Europe. But competitors abound (many dislike the word "disability"), and the issue is far from settled.

3   "I don't think there are any questions about the moral and ethical side to this," says Davidson. "I think everyone recognizes that mentally retarded is a negative term." Of course, it's a step up from "moron," "imbecile," or "idiot," which were actually codified as appropriate technical terms in 1910 by the AAMR, then known as the Association of Medical Officers of American Institutions for Idiots and Feeble-Minded Persons. (Morons were the brightest, followed by idiots and imbeciles.) The AAMR replaced those terms with "mild," "moderate," and "severe" retardation in 1959, but the old words did not go quietly: Davidson recalls attending a guest lecture in graduate school in the 1970s where the speaker, an esteemed professor in the field, discoursed on "low-grade imbeciles." (The professor was not invited back.)

4   There are fine gradations of usage when it comes to the term "mental retardation," and some are more cringe-inducing than others. The lowest of the low is the simple "retard." You will never hear Ed Bradley say, "Jeb Bush signed a bill barring the execution of retards." The least worrisome version is the abstract: "the mentally retarded" or "mental retardation." Activists and physicians also prefer what they call "People First Language," which is supposed to emphasize a person's individuality: People aren't mentally retarded, they are individuals with mental retardation. Yet these subtleties still tend to escape even advocates on behalf of people with mental retardation. Davidson recently consulted on an amicus curiae brief the American Psychological Association has filed with the Supreme Court in the case of a mentally retarded North Carolina death-row inmate named Ernest P.

McCarver. "In the McCarver brief, every single time the lawyers referred to developmental disability, they said 'the mentally retarded,'" he says. "I said, 'Come on guys, you gotta change this.' And they did."

5   If everybody hates the word, why is it still around? Is anybody pounding on the table in support of "retarded"? Well, yes. Changing the name, many point out, could create problems for the government programs that serve the mentally retarded. For instance, people who have been diagnosed as mentally retarded currently qualify for Supplemental Security Income. Will they still qualify if their doctor changes the diagnosis to intellectual disability? "I don't think we're going to accomplish anything other than screw[ing] up our public programs that help these people," says James A. Mulick, an Ohio State University pediatrics professor and Division 33 member who opposes changing the name. The APA's Davidson supports getting rid of "retarded" in popular parlance, but wants to continue using the word in diagnostic circles for the same reason. "'What's intellectual disability?'" he says, impersonating a hypothetical HMO executive. "'We only cover mental retardation.'"

6   Three years ago, organizations involved in serving the needs of the mentally retarded, including the AAMR, Division 33, and the Social Security Administration, formed an ad hoc committee—rather creepily called the Consortium on Language, Image, and Public Education—to hash out just such issues and come up with a plan for moving away from "retarded." The group announced in May that, for the time being, there's no better clinical term than "mental retardation," but that "retarded" should be dropped from popular parlance and replaced with something better (a particular term, not surprisingly, is not forthcoming). The consortium is now devising a media campaign to persuade two crucial consituencies—pre-teens and copy editors—to strike "retarded" from the insult registries and stylebooks.

7   But any psychologist will point out that changing the name is, in the end, folly. Whatever new term comes into favor today will seem insensitive, or worse, tomorrow. A nation of 10-year-olds has pretty much exhausted the pejorative power of "retarded" and is eagerly awaiting a new state-of-the-art insult. (The AAMR actually went through this before: In 1973, it switched its name from the American Association on Mental Deficiency to its current appellation because "deficiency" implied, well, deficiency. And retarded, at the time, did not.) The current frontrunner, "intellectual disability," even contracts nicely to ID, which can become a cousin of LD (for learning disability), which served as a choice epithet among the circles I ran in in fifth grade. Steven Warren, the president of the soon-to-be-differently-named AAMR, admits that whatever term his organization comes up with, all the little boys who have crushes on little girls and so call them "retarded" will be quick on its heels. In other words, the AAMR will almost certainly be going through an identity crisis again in 20 years, just to stay ahead of the game.

THINKING CRITICALLY

1. What objections do advocacy groups have to the word, *retarded*? What objections do they have for the European alternative, *intellectual disability*?

2. What arguments do some groups make in favor of retaining the label "mentally retarded"? In your opinion, how strong are these arguments?

3. When you were growing up, did you ever hear the word *retarded* used as an insult? Was it used against someone who indeed had a developmental disability? What was the effect of the word?

4. According to Cook, what is the most "cringe-inducing" gradation of usage of the word *retarded*? Why is this wording so bad? Do you agree? Explain.

5. Review Bernard Rimland's article in the preceding section in this chapter. How do you think he would react to this editorial?

Crimes Against Humanity
Ward Churchill

As this chapter illustrates, many racial stereotypes are unfortunately built into American popular culture. To Ward Churchill, a man of Creek and Cherokee blood, none has been so damning as those regarding Native Americans. In this essay, Churchill argues that professional sports teams that take Indian names or use Indian cultural images and symbols as mascots, as logos, and for advertising, ultimately defame Native Americans. In fact, he argues that such seemingly innocent practices perpetuate the crimes committed against Native Americans.

Churchill is the coordinator of the American Indian Movement for the state of Colorado. He is the author of several books on Native Americans including *Fantasies of the Master Race: Literature, Cinema, and the Colonization of American Indians* (1992), *Indians Are Us* (1993), and most recently *From a Native Son: Selected Essays on Indigenism, 1985–1995* (1996). He teaches in the Center for Studies of Ethnicity and Race in America at the University of Colorado, Boulder. This essay originally appeared in *Z Magazine* in March 1993.

1 During the past couple of seasons, there has been an increasing wave of controversy regarding the names of professional sports teams like the Atlanta "Braves," Cleveland "Indians," Washington "Redskins," and Kansas City "Chiefs." The issue extends to the names of college teams like Florida State University "Seminoles," University of Illinois "Fighting Illini," and so on, right on down to high school outfits like the Lama (Colorado) "Savages." Also involved have been team adoption of "mascots" replete with feathers, buckskins, beads, spears and "warpaint" (some fans have opted to adorn themselves in the same fashion), and nifty little "pep" gestures like the "Indian Chant" and "Tomahawk Chop."

2 A substantial number of American Indians have protested that use of native names, images and symbols as sports team mascots and the like is, by definition, a virulently racist practice. Given the historical relationship between Indians and non-Indians during what has been called the "Conquest of America," American Indian Movement leader (and American Indian Anti-Defamation Council founder) Russell Means has compared the practice to contemporary Germans naming their

soccer team the "Jews," "Hebrews," and "Yids," while adorning their uniforms with grotesque caricatures of Jewish faces taken from the Nazis' anti-Semitic propaganda of the 1930s. Numerous demonstrations have occurred in conjunction with games—most notably during the November 15, 1992 match-up between the Chiefs and Redskins in Kansas City—by angry Indians and their supporters.

3   In response, a number of players—especially African Americans and other minority athletes—have been trotted out by professional team owners like Ted Turner, as well as university and public school officials, to announce that they mean not to insult but to honor native people. They have been joined by the television networks and most major newspapers, all of which have editorialized that Indian discomfort with the situation is "no big deal," insisting that the whole thing is just "good, clean fun." The country needs more such fun, they've argued, and "a few disgruntled Native Americans" have no right to undermine the nation's enjoyment of its leisure time by complaining. This is especially the case, some have argued, "in hard times like these." It has even been contended that Indian outrage at being systematically degraded—rather than the degradation itself—creates "a serious barrier to the sort of intergroup communication so necessary in a multicultural society such as ours."

4   Okay, let's communicate. We are frankly dubious that those advancing such positions really believe their own rhetoric, but, just for the sake of argument, let's accept the premise that they are sincere. If what they say is true, then isn't it time we spread such "inoffensiveness" and "good cheer" around among *all* groups so that *everybody* can participate *equally* in fostering the round of national laughs they call for? Sure it is—the country can't have too much fun or "intergroup involvement"—so the more, the merrier. Simple consistency demands that anyone who thinks the Tomahawk Chop is a swell pastime must be just as hearty in his or her endorsement of the following ideas. The same logic used to defend the defamation of American Indians should help us all start yukking it up.

5   First, as a counterpart to the Redskins, we need an NFL team called "Niggers" to honor Afro-Americans. Half-time festivities for fans might include a simulated stewing of the opposing coach in a large pot while players and cheerleaders dance around it, garbed in leopard skins and wearing fake bones in their noses. This concept obviously goes along with the kind of gaiety attending the Chop, but also with the actions of the Kansas City Chiefs, whose team members—prominently including black members—lately appeared on a poster looking "fierce" and "savage" by way of wearing Indian regalia. Just a bit of harmless "morale boosting," says the Chiefs' front office. You bet.

6   So that the newly-formed Niggers sports club won't end up too out of sync while expressing the "spirit" and "identity" of Afro-Americans in the above fashion, a baseball franchise—let's call this one the "Sambos"—should be formed. How about a basketball team called the "Spearchuckers"? A hockey team called the "Jungle Bunnies"? Maybe the "essence" of these teams could be depicted by images of tiny black faces adorned with huge pairs of lips. The players could appear on TV every week or so gnawing on chicken legs and spitting watermelon seeds at one another. Catchy, eh? Well, there's "nothing to be upset about," according to

those who love wearing "war bonnets" to the Super Bowl or having "Chief Illini-wik" dance around the sports arenas of Urbana, Illinois.

7   And why stop there? There are plenty of other groups to include. Hispanics? They can be "represented" by the Galveston "Greasers" and San Diego "Spics," at least until the Wisconsin "Wetbacks" and Baltimore "Beaners" get off the ground. Asian Americans? How about the "Slopes," "Dinks," "Gooks," and "Zipper-heads"? Owners of the latter teams might get their logo ideas from editorial page cartoons printed in the nation's newspapers during World War II: slant-eyes, buck teeth, big glasses, but nothing racially insulting or derogatory, according to editors and artists involved at the time. Indeed, this Second World War–vintage stuff can be seen as just another barrel of laughs, at least by what current editors say are their "local standards" concerning American Indians.

8   Let's see. Who's been left out? Teams like the Kansas City "Kikes," Hanover "Honkies," San Leandro "Shylocks," Daytona "Dagos," and Pittsburgh "Polacks" will fill a certain social void among white folk. Have a religious belief? Let's all go for the gusto and gear the Milwaukee "Mackerel Snappers" and Hollywood "Holy Rollers." The Fighting Irish of Notre Dame can be rechristened the "Drunken Irish" or "Papist Pigs." Issues of gender and sexual preference can be addressed through creation of teams like the St. Louis "Sluts," Boston "Bimbos," Detroit "Dykes," and the Fresno "Fags." How about the Gainesville "Gimps" and Richmond "Re-tards," so the physically and mentally impaired won't be excluded from our fun and games?

9   Now, don't go getting "overly sensitive" out there. None of this is demeaning or insulting, at least not when it's being done to Indians. Just ask the folks who are doing it, or their apologists like Andy Rooney in the national media. They'll tell you—as in fact they *have* been telling you—that there's been no harm done, re-gardless of what their victims think, feel, or say. The situation is exactly the same as when those with precisely the same mentality used to insist that Step 'n' Fetchit was okay, or Rochester, on the Jack Benny Show, or Amos and Andy, Charlie Chan, the Frito Bandito, or any of the other cutesy symbols making up the lexicon of American racism. Have we communicated yet?

10   Let's get just a little bit real here. The notion of "fun" embodied in rituals like the Tomahawk Chop must be understood for what it is. There's not a single non-In-dian example used above which can be considered socially acceptable in even the most marginal sense. The reasons are obvious enough. So why is it different where American Indians are concerned? One can only conclude that, in contrast to the other groups at issue, Indians are (falsely) perceived as being too few, and therefore too weak, to defend themselves effectively against racist and otherwise offensive behavior.

11   Fortunately, there are some glimmers of hope. A few teams and their fans have gotten the message and have responded appropriately. Stanford University, which opted to drop the name "Indians" from Stanford, has experienced no resulting drop-off in attendance. Meanwhile, the local newspaper in Portland, Oregon recently de-cided its long-standing editorial policy prohibiting use of racial epithets should in-

clude derogatory team names. The Redskins, for instance, are now referred to as "the Washington team," and will continue to be described in this way until the franchise adopts an inoffensive moniker (newspaper sales in Portland have suffered no decline as a result).

12   Such examples are to be applauded and encouraged. They stand as figurative beacons in the night, proving beyond all doubt that it is quite possible to indulge in the pleasure of athletics without accepting blatant racism into the bargain.

13   On October 16, 1946, a man named Julius Streicher mounted the steps of a gallows. Moments later he was dead, the sentence of an international tribunal composed of representatives of the United States, France, Great Britain, and the Soviet Union having been imposed. Streicher's body was then cremated, and—so horrendous were his crimes thought to have been—his ashes dumped into an unspecified German river so that "no one should ever know a particular place to go for reasons of mourning his memory."

14   Julius Streicher had been convicted at Nuremberg, Germany of what were termed "Crimes Against Humanity." The lead prosecutor in his case—Justice Robert Jackson of the United States Supreme Court—had not argued that the defendant had killed anyone, nor that he had personally committed any especially violent act. Nor was it contended that Streicher had held any particularly important position in the German government during the period in which the so-called Third Reich had exterminated some 6,000,000 Jews, as well as several million Gypsies, Poles, Slavs, homosexuals, and other untermenschen (subhumans).

15   The sole offense for which the accused was ordered put to death was in having served as publisher/editor of a Bavarian tabloid entitled *Der Sturmer* during the early-to-mid 1930s, years before the Nazi genocide actually began. In this capacity, he had penned a long series of virulently anti-Semitic editorials and "news" stories, usually accompanied by cartoons and other images graphically depicting Jews in extraordinary derogatory fashion. This, the prosecution asserted, had done much to "dehumanize" the targets of his distortion in the mind of the German public. In turn, such dehumanization had made it possible—or at least easier—for average Germans to later indulge in the outright liquidation of Jewish "vermin." The tribunal agreed, holding that Streicher was therefore complicit in genocide and deserving of death by hanging.

16   During his remarks to the Nuremberg tribunal, Justice Jackson observed that, in implementing its sentences, the participating powers were morally and legally binding themselves to adhere forever after to the same standards of conduct that were being applied to Streicher and the other Nazi leaders. In the alternative, he said, the victorious allies would have committed "pure murder" at Nuremburg—no different in substance from that carried out by those presumed to judge—rather than establishing the "permanent bench-mark for justice" which was intended.

17   Yet in the United States of Robert Jackson, the indigenous American Indian population had already been reduced, in a process which is ongoing to this day, from perhaps 12.5 million in the year 1500 to fewer than 250,000 by the beginning of the 20th century. This was accomplished, according to official sources, "largely

through the cruelty of [Euro-American] settlers," and an informal but clear governmental policy which had made it an articulated goal to "exterminate these red vermin," or at least whole segments of them.

18   Bounties had been placed on the scalps of Indians—any Indians—in places as diverse as Georgia, Kentucky, Texas, the Dakotas, Oregon, and California, and had been maintained until resident Indian populations were decimated or disappeared altogether. Entire peoples such as the Cherokee had been reduced to half their size through a policy of forced removal from their homelands east of the Mississippi River to what were then considered less preferable areas in the West.

19   Others, such as the Navajo, suffered the same fate while under military guard for years on end. The United States Army had also perpetrated a long series of wholesale massacres of Indians at places like Horseshoe Bend, Bear River, Sand Creek, the Washita River, the Marias River, Camp Robinson, and Wounded Knee.

20   Through it all, hundreds of popular novels—each competing with the next to make Indians appear more grotesque, menacing, and inhumane—were sold in the tens of millions of copies in the U.S. Plainly, the Euro-American public was being conditioned to see Indians in such a way as to allow their eradication to continue. And continue it did until the Manifest Destiny of the U.S.—a direct precursor to what Hitler would subsequently call Lebensraumpolitik (the politics of living space)—was consummated.

21   By 1900, the national project of "clearing" Native Americans from their land and replacing them with "superior" Anglo-American settlers was complete; the indigenous population had been reduced by as much as 98 percent while approximately 97.5 percent of their original territory had "passed" to the invaders. The survivors had been concentrated, out of sight and mind of the public, on scattered "reservations," all of them under the self-assigned "plenary" (full) power of the federal government. There was, of course, no Nuremberg-style tribunal passing judgment on those who had fostered such circumstances in North America. No U.S. official or private citizen was ever imprisoned—never mind hanged—for implementing propagandizing what had been done. Nor had the process of genocide afflicting Indians been completed. Instead, it merely changed form.

22   Between the 1880s and the 1980s, nearly half of all Native American children were coercively transferred from their own families, communities, and cultures to those of the conquering society. This was done through compulsory attendance at remote boarding schools, often hundreds of miles from their homes, where native children were kept for years on end while being systematically "deculturated" (indoctrinated to think and act in the manner of Euro-Americans rather than as Indians). It was also accomplished through a pervasive foster home and adoption program—including "blind" adoptions, where children would be permanently denied information as to who they were/are and where they'd come from—placing native youths in non-Indian homes.

23   The express purpose of all this was to facilitate a U.S. governmental policy to bring about the "assimilation" (dissolution) of indigenous societies. In other words, Indian cultures as such were to be caused to disappear. Such policy objectives are

directly contrary to the United Nations 1948 Convention on Punishment and Prevention of the Crime of Genocide, an element of international laws arising from the Nuremberg proceedings. The forced "transfer of the children" of a targeted "racial, ethnical, or religious group" is explicitly prohibited as a genocidal activity under the Convention's second article.

24   Article II of the Genocide Convention also expressly prohibits involuntary sterilization as a means of "preventing births among" a targeted population. Yet, in 1975, it was conceded by the U.S. government that its Indian Health Service (IHS), then a subpart of the Bureau of Indian Affairs (BIA), was even then conducting a secret program of involuntary sterilization that had affected approximately 40 percent of all Indian women. The program was allegedly discontinued, and the IHS was transferred to the Public Health Service, but no one was punished. In 1990, it came out that the IHS was inoculating Inuit children in Alaska with Hepatitis-B vaccine. The vaccine had already been banned by the World Health Organization as having a demonstrated correlation with the HIV-Syndrome which is itself correlated to AIDS. As this is written, a "field test" of Hepatitis-A vaccine, also HIV-correlated, is being conducted on Indian reservations in the northern plains region.

25   The Genocide Convention makes it a "crime against humanity" to create conditions leading to the destruction of an identifiable human group, as such. Yet the BIA has utilized the government's plenary prerogatives to negotiate mineral leases "on behalf of" Indian peoples paying a fraction of standard royalty rates. The result has been "super profits" for a number of preferred U.S. corporations. Meanwhile, Indians, whose reservations ironically turned out to be in some of the most mineral-rich areas of North America, which makes us, the nominally wealthiest segment of the continent's population, live in dire poverty.

26   By the government's own data in the mid–1980s, Indians received the lowest annual and lifetime per capita incomes of any aggregate population group in the United States. Concomitantly, we suffer the highest rate of infant mortality, death by exposure and malnutrition, disease, and the like. Under such circumstances, alcoholism and other escapist forms of substance abuse are endemic in the Indian community, a situation which leads both to a general physical debilitation of the population and a catastrophic accident rate. Teen suicide among Indians is several times the national average.

27   The average life expectancy of a reservation-based Native American man is barely 45 years; women can expect to live less than three years longer.

28   Such itemizations could be continued at great length, including matters like the radioactive contamination of large portions of contemporary Indian Country, the forced relocation of traditional Navajos, and so on. But the point should be made: Genocide, as defined in international law, is a continuing fact of day-to-day life (and death) for North America's native peoples. Yet there has been—and is—only the barest flicker of public concern about, or even consciousness of, this reality. Absent any serious expression of public outrage, no one is punished and the process continues.

29   A salient reason for public acquiescence before the ongoing holocaust in Native North America has been a continuation of the popular legacy, often through more effective media. Since 1925, Hollywood has released more than 2,000 films, many of them rerun frequently on television, portraying Indians as strange, perverted, ridiculous, and often dangerous things of the past. Moreover, we are habitually presented to mass audiences one-dimensionally, devoid of recognizable human motivations and emotions; Indians thus serve as props, little more. We have thus been thoroughly and systematically dehumanized.

30   Nor is this extent of it. Everywhere, we are used as logos, as mascots, as jokes: "Big Chief" writing tablets, "Red Man" chewing tobacco, "Winnebago" campers, "Navajo" and "Cherokee" and "Pontiac" and "Cadillac" pickups and automobiles. There are the Cleveland "Indians," the Kansas City "Chiefs," the Atlanta "Braves" and the Washington "Redskins" professional sports teams—not to mention those in thousands of colleges, high schools, and elementary schools across the country— each with their own degrading caricatures and parodies of Indians and/or things Indian. Pop fiction continues in the same vein, including an unending stream of New Age manuals purporting to expose the inner works of indigenous spirituality in everything from pseudo-philosophical to do-it-yourself styles. Blond yuppies from Beverly Hills amble about the country claiming to be reincarnated 17th century Cheyenne Ushamans ready to perform previously secret ceremonies.

31   In effect, a concerted, sustained, and in some ways accelerating effort has gone into making Indians unreal. It is thus of obvious importance that the American public begin to think about the implications of such things the next time they witness a gaggle of face-painted and war-bonneted buffoons doing the "Tomahawk Chop" at a baseball or football game. It is necessary that they think about the implications of the grade-school teacher adorning their child in turkey features to commemorate Thanksgiving. Think about the significance of John Wayne or Charleton Heston killing a dozen "savages" with a single bullet the next time a western comes on TV. Think about why Land-o-Lakes finds it appropriate to market its butter with the stereotyped image of an "Indian princess" on the wrapper. Think about what it means when non-Indian academics profess—as they often do—to "know more about Indians than Indians do themselves." Think about the significance of charlatans like Carlos Castaneda and Jamake Highwater and Mary Summer Rain and Lynn Andrews churning out "Indian" bestsellers, one after the other, while Indians typically can't get into print.

32   Think about the real situation of American Indians. Think about Julius Streicher. Remember Justice Jackson's admonition. Understand that the treatment of Indians in American popular culture is not "cute" or "amusing" or just "good, clean fun."

33   Know that it causes real pain and real suffering to real people. Know that it threatens our very survival. And know that this is just as much a crime against humanity as anything the Nazis ever did. It is likely that the indigenous people of the United States will never demand that those guilty of such criminal activity be punished for their deeds. But the least we have the right to expect—indeed, to demand—is that such practices finally be brought to a halt.

THINKING CRITICALLY

1. Before you read this essay, did you feel that the use of Native American names, mascots, and symbols by sports teams and car manufacturers was denigrating and insulting to Native Americans? Did this essay change your way of thinking? Explain your answer.

2. How did the press react to the protests by Native Americans of their degradation by professional sports teams? How might the media's reaction have been more appropriate? Does Churchill supply any examples of suitable responses?

3. To make his point, Churchill suggests other racial and ethnic groups for sports teams' names and halftime activities. What specific racial stereotypes does he offer for different groups? What is the tone of his suggestions? Would you say his analogies are an effective part of his argument? Explain.

4. In paragraph 13, Churchill mentions Julius Streicher. Who was Streicher? How did Streicher's trial and execution serve as a "permanent benchmark for justice" (paragraph 16)? What point does Churchill make by placing this historical information immediately after his satire of team names?

5. According to Churchill, why has society gotten away with offensive stereotypes of Native Americans but not with stereotypes of other groups?

6. Now that you have read Churchill's essay, do you agree that it is time for a change, that the use of Native American names, images, caricatures, symbols, and so on for sports teams perpetuates crimes against this segment of humanity? Explain.

7. How well does the title of the essay fit the discussion? Explain, citing details from the text.

8. Beginning in paragraph 17, Churchill offers a brief historical survey of the crimes against Native Americans. Did you find this too much of a digression from the rest of his argument? Or do you think it was necessary for Churchill to bolster his argument regarding the cultural denigration of Native Americans by names for teams and products? Explain.

Queer
Lillian Faderman

Not long ago, the word *queer* was used as a slur against homosexuals and lesbians. But similar to African Americans who in the 1960s learned that it was possible to take a one-time taboo word, *black*, and reclaim it with pride, many gays and lesbians have taken back the enemy's prime insult, *queer*, and "valorized it," as Lillian Faderman explains below. Although not all gays and lesbians easily embrace the old taboo label, some have realized the political power that is inherent in renaming oneself, and the effectiveness of taking a word and diffusing its sting through claiming it as your own.

Lillian Faderman is a professor of English at California State University, Fresno; and the author of many articles and books on women's relationships including *Surpassing the Love of*

Men (1981) and *Odd Girls and Twilight Lovers: A History of Lesbian Life in Twentieth Century America* (1991). This article first appeared in the *Boston Globe* in 1991.

1   When I was in elementary school in East Los Angeles during the late 1940s, playground lore had it that Thursday was queer day. I had no idea what "queer" meant, but I knew it was something you did not want to be. I was 16 when I had my first relationship with another female, who told me that in the Midwestern elementary school she had attended, Friday was queer day, and that what we had just done together made me a queer. I think that was the only time, until a couple of years ago, that I had heard that word used by a lesbian, though I did hear drag queens use it when they were camping it up in the gay bars of the 1950s and 1960s: "Hello, Miss Thing, Hello, Duchess Ding-a-Ling, Hello, all you queers."

2   However, most of us gays and lesbians hated that word, not only because "queer" was the term straight people were most likely to hurl at us as an insult for our sexuality, but also because it had nonsexual connotations—weird, eccentric, suspicious—that were disturbing to us in our desire to fit in and to be just like heterosexuals in all ways but what we did in bed. In fact, long before the word "queer" became a pejorative for "homosexual," it meant bad things. In Old German (whence it eventually evolved into English) *queer* denoted "oblique," "perverse," "odd." Its meanings deteriorated in English. In the 1600s, for example, a "queer mort" was a syphilitic harlot. A 1796 "Dictionary of the Vulgar Tongue" lists 23 uses of the word "queer," all of them negative, but none of them denoting a person who loves the same sex. In the 19th century, "queer bub" was bad liquor," a "queer chant" was a false name or address. To "shove the queer" meant to pass counterfeit money.

3   According to Eric Partridge, the slang lexicographer, it was not until 1910 in the United States and 1915 in the British Empire that the term queer was first used to refer to "sexually degenerate men or boys." Hugh Rawson in "Wicked Words" traces the word back a bit earlier. He cites an ad placed in a 1902 issue of "The Blue Book," a directory of the red-light district of New Orleans, that seems to suggest (though ambiguously) a homosexual definition of the word: The ad copy says of Diana and Norma, "Their names have become known on both continents, because everything goes as it will, and those that cannot be satisfied there must surely be of a queer nature."

4   It's possible, also, that the term had some early, less hostile, usage among homosexuals themselves, perhaps as a code word (like "gay") that few heterosexuals would have understood. For example, in Gertrude Stein's 1903 manuscript about lesbian relationships, "QED," Helen invites Adele to meet Jane Fairfield by saying, "She is queer and will interest you and you are queer and will interest her. Oh! I don't want to listen to your protests, you are queer and interesting even if you don't know it and you like queer and interesting people even if you think you don't." Yet such uses of the term were apparently rare. In Farmer and Henley's 1909 "Dictionary of Slang . . . Past and Present," "queer" continued to have many negative definitions, but not one of them referred to homosexuality. As late as 1927, a novel by

Fredrick Niven was entitled "Queer Fellows," but the eponymous characters were hoboes, not gay men.

5   By the time I came on the gay and lesbian scene in the 1950s, the term was interchangeable with other homophobic words such as "fairy" and "bulldyke." It even had a variety of forms, all expressing hostility: "eerquay" in Pig Latin, "queervert" in place of "invert," "Timesqueer" to mean a "queer of Times Square," etc. The word was certainly "queered" for us homosexuals. Linguistics researcher Julia Penelope, in a 1970 article for American Speech, said that the gays and lesbians she interviewed all knew the term but felt it was only used by heterosexuals to express their disdain for homosexuals. However, pejoratives were beginning by then to be put to interesting use. African-Americans had already adopted the term "black," perhaps because it had once been the worst thing that could be said about a person of color in America to insult him or her. They knew that to coin slogans such as "Black is Beautiful" would defuse that word, take all its power to hurt and turn it around to make it heal.

6   Lesbians understood the same thing to be true about the word "dyke" by the early 1970s, when young lesbians began to prefer calling themselves "dyke" to any other label. "Dyke" became synonymous for them with a brave, beautiful, powerful modern "Amazon." Harry Hay, the founder in the 1950s of the first national gay organization in America, the Mattachine Society, began using the term "fairy" publicly in 1970 to say that he and his friends were not only different from heterosexuals but more spiritual, more artistic and much nicer. He formed another organization, which he called Radical Faeries in 1978. But "queer" remained a politically incorrect term in the gay and lesbian subculture.

7   For some gays and lesbians, it remains politically incorrect today. When the rather conservative national gay and lesbian news magazine, The Advocate, first used the term in a positive manner in late 1990, the Letters to the Editor section was filled with protests and many threatened to cancel their subscriptions. My middle-aged lesbian friends tell me, "It will always be an insult to me," and "It's a put-down: Queer as a three-dollar bill. False currency. Like you don't ring true." But many younger gays and lesbians have embraced the term "queer" in self-description that not only valorizes it but also says to straights who might still want to use that word derogatorily, "In your face!"

8   Young gay and lesbian culture has become suffused with it in the last year or two. The crossover lesbian rock group 2 NICE GIRLS flash the term in many of their lyrics. . . .

9   In April 1990, a New York group of young gays and lesbians who felt that homosexual rights were not advancing quickly enough designed some radical militant tactics that hark back to the 1960s and 1970s and began to call themselves Queer Nation. The idea caught on quickly. There are now enclaves of Queer Nation all over the country. Yoav Shernock of Los Angeles Queer Nation explains that "queer" is an ideal term because it includes "faggots," "fairies," "lezzies," "dykes." It's an umbrella term for both men and women (as the term "gay" once was but ceased to be in the 1970s when many lesbian-feminists wanted to break away from

all men, including homosexual men, and form their own women's culture). But it does more than bring gay men and lesbians together, Shernock observes. "Gay" used to be an empowering term 20 years ago. But now it means middle-class white men who want to assimilate. It hasn't included blacks or poor people or women. The word "queer" helps set up a new community that "gay" has excluded.

10   It is a fighting word, a rallying cry to battle and a warning to heterosexuals of the new homosexual militancy. Shernock, explains of the term "queer": "It's a word of pride. It tells people that we're opposed to assimilating. Those who believe that they're just like anyone else except for who they sleep with aren't queer. They're gay. Being queer is more than who you sleep with. We don't want to fit into the straight world like gays do. We just want to make our own safe space. Sure, the dictionary says that 'queer' means deviating from the normal. We do—we're exceptional. We're fabulous—we're queer."

THINKING CRITICALLY

1. Why, according to the author, was *queer* a particularly hateful word to gays and lesbians? How do any gays or lesbians you know feel about this term?

2. Why won't some conservative gays and lesbians accept the word *queer*?

3. Do you still hear the word *queer* used? If so, is it used pejoratively against gay men? against lesbians? Have you heard it used with pride by gays and lesbians? Do you think that the word is, in fact, becoming defused? Do you suppose gays and lesbians who speak with pride of being queer hope that straight society will accept the term as being neutral as it has accepted *gay*?

4. Faderman draws a parallel between blacks reclaiming *black* and gays and lesbians reclaiming *queer*—that is, taking a harmful word and turning "it around to make it heal." Do you think the parallel is legitimate? That is, do you think that the one-time slur, *black*, was equivalent to *queer* in its power to hurt? Do you think that *queer* will be as successful in its turnaround?

5. Why does Faderman say that *queer* is preferred to *gay* as an umbrella term for homosexual men and women? Do you agree with the explanation? Do you agree that *gay* excludes some people? Explain your answer in terms of your own observations.

6. As shown throughout this text, language is a powerful political tool for raising consciousness. Did Faderman's discussion here in any way raise your consciousness regarding lesbians and gays? Explain your answer.

7. In paragraphs 2 and 3, Faderman briefly discusses the etymology of the word *queer*. How does that historical glimpse add to her discussion and to the credibility of her argument?

8. Although this is not strictly a personal essay, Faderman does occasionally measure the history of homophobic terms according to her own past experience. How do these personal accounts add to the discussion?

9. Can you tell from the writing that the author is a professor of English? Comment on the style of the writing, the vocabulary, allusions, secondary sources, references, and so forth.

10. Discuss the impact of the final Shernock quotation. Did it succinctly summarize the author's points? Did the tone of the passage help convey the message of the words?

Discrimination at Large

Jennifer A. Coleman

In 2002, the U.S. Surgeon General announced that America was facing an obesity "epidemic." But unlike other threatening medical conditions that are treated with sensitive language, obesity seems to incite ridicule. Socially, many people feel it is acceptable to make fun of fat people. In the next piece, Jennifer Coleman explains that "fat is the last preserve of bigotry." Although we socially try to be sensitive to issues of race, gender, sexual orientation, religion, and disability, we harbor no such linguistic sympathy for the obese. Coleman asks, why do we feel it is OK to mock fat people?

Jennifer A. Coleman is a lawyer in Buffalo, New York. This article first appeared in *Newsweek*.

1 Fat is the last preserve for unexamined bigotry. Fat people are lampooned without remorse or apology on television, by newspaper columnists, in cartoons, you name it. The overweight are viewed as suffering from moral turpitude and villainy, and since we are at fault for our condition, no tolerance is due. All fat people are "outed" by their appearance.

2 Weight-motivated assaults occur daily and are committed by people who would die before uttering anti-gay slogans or racial epithets. Yet these same people don't hesitate to scream "move your fat ass" when we cross in front of them.

3 Since the time I first ventured out to play with the neighborhood kids, I was told over and over that I was lazy and disgusting. Strangers, adults, classmates offered gratuitous comments with such frequency and urgency that I started to believe them. Much later I needed to prove that it wasn't so. I began a regimen of swimming, cycling and jogging that put all but the most compulsive to shame. I ate only cottage cheese, brown rice, fake butter and steamed everything. I really believed I could infiltrate the ranks of the nonfat and thereby establish my worth.

4 I would prove that I was not just a slob, a blimp, a pig. I would finally escape the unsolicited remarks of strangers ranging from the "polite"—"You would really be pretty if you lost weight"—to the hostile ("Lose weight, you fat slob"). Of course, sometimes more subtle commentary sufficed: oinking, mooing, staring, laughing and pointing. Simulating a foghorn was also popular.

5 My acute exercise phase had many positive points. I was mingling with my obsessively athletic peers. My pulse was as low as anyone's, my cholesterol levels in the basement, my respiration barely detectable. I could swap stats from my last physical with anyone. Except for weight. No matter how hard I tried to run, swim

or cycle away from it, my weight found me. Oh sure, I lost weight (never enough) and it inevitably tracked me down and adhered to me more tenaciously than ever. I lived and breathed "Eat to win." "Feel the burn." But in the end I was fit and still fat.

6   I learned that by societal, moral, ethical, soap-operatical, vegetable, political definition, it was impossible to be both fit and fat. Along the way to that knowledge, what I got for my trouble was to be hit with objects from moving cars because I dared to ride my bike in public, and to be mocked by diners at outdoor cafés who trumpeted like a herd of elephants as I jogged by. Incredibly, it was not uncommon for one of them to shout: "Lose some weight, you pig." Go figure.

7   It was confusing for awhile. How was it I was still lazy, weak, despised, a slug and a cow if I exercised every waking minute? This confusion persisted until I finally realized: it didn't matter what I did. I was and always would be the object of sport, derision, antipathy and hostility so long as I stayed in my body. I immediately signed up for a body transplant. I am still waiting for a donor.

8   Until then, I am more settled because I have learned the hard way what thin people have known for years. There simply are some things that fat people must never do. Like: riding a bike ("Hey, lady, where's the seat?"), eating in a public place ("No dessert for me, I don't want to look like her"). And the most unforgivable crime: wearing a bathing suit in public ("Whale on the beach!").

9   Things are less confusing now that I know that the nonfat are superior to me, regardless of their personal habits, health, personalities, cholesterol levels or the time they log on the couch. And, as obviously superior to me as they are, it is their destiny to remark on my inferiority regardless of who I'm with, whether they know me, whether it hurts my feelings. I finally understand that the thin have a divine mandate to steal self-esteem from fat people, who have no right to it in the first place.

10   Fat people aren't really jolly. Sometimes we act that way so you will leave us alone. We pay a price for this. But at least we get to hang on to what self-respect we smuggled out of grade school and adolescence.

11   Hating fat people is not inborn; it has to be nurtured and developed. Fortunately, it's taught from the moment most of us are able to walk and speak. We learn it through Saturday-morning cartoons, prime-time TV and movies. Have you ever seen a fat person in a movie who wasn't evil, disgusting, pathetic or lampooned? Santa Claus doesn't count.

12   Kids catch on early to be sensitive to the feelings of gay, black, disabled, elderly and speech-impaired people. At the same time, they learn that fat people are fair game. That we are always available for their personal amusement.

13   The media, legal system, parents, teachers and peers respond to most types of intolerance with outrage and protest. Kids hear that employers can be sued for discriminating, that political careers can be destroyed and baseball owners can lose their teams as a consequence of racism, sexism or almost any other "ism."

14   But the fat kid is taught that she deserves to be mocked. She is not OK. Only if she loses weight will she be OK. Other kids see the response and incorporate the

message. Small wonder some (usually girls) get it into their heads that they can never be thin again.

15   I know a lot about prejudice, even though I am a white, middle-class, professional woman. The worst discrimination I have suffered because of my gender is nothing compared to what I experience daily because of my weight. I am sick of it. The jokes and attitudes are as wrong and damaging as any racial or ethnic slur. The passive acceptance of this inexcusable behavior is sometimes worse than the initial assault. Some offensive remarks can be excused as the shortcomings of jackasses, but the tacit acceptance of their conduct by mainstream America tells the fat person that the intolerance is understandable and acceptable. Well it isn't.

THINKING CRITICALLY

1. What does Coleman mean when she says that "fat is the last preserve for unexamined bigotry"? How does Coleman compare the treatment of fat people to the treatment of other groups?

2. How do people learn prejudice against fat people in the first place? What does Coleman say about this issue? What are your own opinions on prejudice against fat people?

3. How can words be used to hurt people who are obese? Why does insulting the obese seem more acceptable (Coleman says many think it is even funny) than ridiculing other groups of people? Explain.

4. What words does Coleman identify that hurt her? Why are these words so painful? Explain.

5. What is the tone of Coleman's essay? Identify parts of her essay that you consider particularly effective in making her argument. How does her tone contribute to the effectiveness of her piece? Explain.

Where Heaven and Earth Touch: A National "Speak No Evil" Day
Joseph Telushkin

The articles in this case study have focused on words that hurt—words that cause pain and distress to others because they ridicule ethnic, mental, racial, sexual, or physical differences. In the next piece, Joseph Telushkin makes an interesting proposal. He recommends a national "Speak No Evil Day." As you read his proposal, consider the implications of his idea. What would such a day be like?

Joseph Telushkin is the author of *Words That Hurt, Words That Heal* (1996), from which this essay is excerpted.

1 What if we could share our consciousness of the power of words with many others—even the whole nation?

2 Tens of millions of Americans annually observe "The Great American Smokeout" and "Earth Day," one concerned with eliminating pollution of our bodies, the other the pollution of our planet. A national "Speak No Evil Day" could work to eliminate the pollution of our emotional atmosphere, the realm in which we interact with others.

3 "Speak No Evil Day" would have both short- and long-term goals: to eliminate all vicious and unfair talk for twenty-four hours, and thus plant the seed of a more permanent shift in our consciousness.

4 On this day people will attempt to refrain from saying a single nasty comment about others, even if true. Only in the very rare instances when it's absolutely necessary to transmit negative information will they do so. Otherwise, like those who engage in periodic cleansing fasts to purify their bodies, people will go for an entire day without uttering unfair and hurtful talk.

5 On this day people also will monitor and regulate how they speak to others. Everyone will strive to keep his or her anger under control. If a person does express anger, he will do so fairly, and limit his comments to the incident that provoked his ire. People likewise will argue fairly, and not allow their disputes to degenerate into name-calling or other forms of verbal abuse. No one, not even a person offering deserved criticism, will humiliate another.

6 In short, on "Speak No Evil Day," people will strive to fulfill the Golden Rule, and will speak about others with the same kindness and fairness that they wish others to exercise when speaking about them.

7 I hope that journalists and other media professionals will be touched by the spirit of the day. While retaining the right to report *relevant* negative items about public figures, they will omit innuendos, sarcastic asides, rumors, and the publicizing of private scandals.

8 On "Speak No Evil Day," all of us will refrain from disseminating rumors, particularly negative ones.

9 On this day too, people will strive to avoid hurting and defaming groups as well as individuals. By avoiding bigoted sweeping comments—even for one day— we may finally come to view others as individuals, and realize that negative stereotypes of large ethnic, religious, racial and gender groups are unfair and untrue.

10 A rabbi once told me that his grandmother used to say, "It is not within everyone's power to be beautiful, but all of us can make sure that the words that come out of our mouths are."

11 "Speak No Evil Day" will be a twenty-four-hour period of verbal beauty:

—It will be a day when a young child frequently teased by his classmates, and called by an ugly nickname, can go to school confident no one will say a cruel word to him.

—It will be a day on which an employee with a sharp-tongued boss can go to work without fearing that he or she will be verbally abused.

—It will be a day on which that sharp-tongued boss, the type who says, "I don't get ulcers, I give them," might come to understand how vicious such a statement is, and will say nothing that will cause pain.

—It will be a day when a fat adolescent will not have to fear a biting comment about his weight from parents or peers.

—It will be a day when a man who once served a prison sentence but who has led an exemplary life since being released will not have to fear that a journalist will publicize his earlier behavior.

—It will be a day when a congressional candidate who suffered a nervous breakdown will not have to worry that his opponent will use this painful episode to publicly humiliate him.

—It will be a day when an African American or Hispanic American can be among other Americans without fearing that she will hear prejudicial comments or ugly words about herself or her racial group.

—It will be a day when a husband who usually only tells his wife his complaints will tell her instead that he loves her and why.

—It will be a day when people will use the words that heal others' emotional wounds, not those that inflict them.

12   In short, "Speak No Evil Day" will be a day when, through humankind's collective efforts, we will experience a taste of heaven on earth.

13   A Jewish proverb teaches: "If you will it, it is no fantasy." If we only want it enough, "Speak No Evil Day" is possible. Let us try.

THINKING CRITICALLY

1. Why does Telushkin propose that we have a national "Speak No Evil Day"? Could it work? Why or why not?

2. In a single day, note the number of unkind words you hear or read—from friends, television programs, magazine articles, etc. At the end of the day, tally them up and write an evaluation of your results.

3. Write a response to Telushkin in which you explain why you do, or do not, support his proposal.

■ MAKING CONNECTIONS

1. When did you first become aware of the word *nigger,* or of some other powerfully charged, negative label for a group of people? When did you first become aware of racism? Were your recognitions gradual, or can you trace your recognition to a specific time and place? What did you do to try to understand the word or the problem? Write up your answers in a paper.

2. With classmates, brainstorm as many derogatory terms for racial and ethnic minorities as you can think of. Select one of these terms and examine the following resources: an unabridged dictionary, a dictionary of American slang, an encyclopedia. What did you find out from each

about the term's primary meaning and its connotations? About its origins and history? Prepare a report on your findings for classmates.

3. Almost everyone has been exposed to some form of ethnic, sexist, or racial insults. Write an essay discussing how the media—movies, television, books, even music—contribute to the growth of prejudicial language.

4. Write an essay answering the question posed at the end of Berlitz's essay: "Will man ever be able to rise above using insults as a weapon?"

5. As best you can, try to trace the history of the word *gay*. When did it first connote sexual behavior? Was this connotation exclusively homosexual? Was it ever a "code" used by gays? About when did the term begin to lose its pejorative sense? Use etymological and slang dictionaries.

6. Several authors in this unit employ satire or irony as part of their rhetorical strategy (i.e., how they construct their argument). Write an essay that employs irony/satire to make a point about any stereotype that bothers you. Be sure to shape your essay so that a careful reader will pick up on your tone, but at the same time, try to avoid being "heavy handed" (i.e., hitting the reader over the head with scorn).

7. Faderman describes the effort of lesbians in the 1970s to defuse the term *dyke*. Using etymological and slang dictionaries, try to trace the word from its earliest usages to the present usage.

8. Several of the authors in this section examine the issue of epithets and how context affects their meaning. Charles F. Berlitz looks at definitions mainly in terms of their etymology, whereas Naylor and Faderman rely more on definitions from the community. Choose an epithet and research its denotation and connotation by employing both methods. First explore various source books—standard dictionaries, slang dictionaries, encyclopedias, and so forth. Then interview class members about how they define these words. Do you find a difference between how the books define the words versus how your classmates define them? Organize your findings and report them to the class.

9. All of the authors in this unit have strong opinions about the nature of prejudice and stereotypes, opinions that you may or may not agree with. For this assignment, play devil's advocate and write a critique of one of the authors using a letter format. Be sure to refer to the writer's text when drafting your essay so that you can be specific about where you disagree.

Language in the USA

9

■ What is the language of the American people? Is a common language necessary for social unity? Or, as a nation comprised of many peoples from all nations, should we embrace the idea of many languages as well?

Ours is a nation of immigrants—of people with different racial origins, ethnic identities, religions, and languages. Our national motto, *e pluribus unum* ("one out of many"), bespeaks the pride we feel in our multicultural heritage. Our unity is predicated on like-minded moral values, political and economic self-interest, and of course, a common language. What exactly is the language of the American people? Is it the rigid, rule-laden language of our grade-school grammar books? Is it the language we use at home, at work, or within our peer groups? Or is it even a form of English at all? This chapter focuses on issues concerning language and our nation—on how we define the language of the American people.

What Is "Standard" English?

John Simon, one of America's most famous and formidable language guardians, argues that good English is a serious social and personal issue in his essay, "Why Good English Is Good for You." Learning to express oneself properly, grammatically, is worth the effort because it not only improves memory and thinking but it also instills pride in expression that could profit careers and social affairs. Linguist John Esling explores the way accents influence our perceptions of others and ourselves in "Everyone Has an Accent but Me." We take a time-out for humor with Richard Liebmann-Smith's essay on who wrote the rules on how we label people of various nationalities and regions. The section concludes with an engaging discussion by Bill Bryson on just what is "good" and "bad" English.

Case Study: English Only or Bilingualism

It might come as a surprise to some people to learn that English is not the official language of the United States. Nowhere in the Constitution is there such a provision. The founders of our nation were apparently more concerned with establishing a common political philosophy than a common tongue. For the next 200 years, the new republic swelled with immigrants from every country on earth to become the "great melting pot" of cultures. However, this melting pot has overheated with controversy. A growing number of Americans feel that the English language should be declared the national language. At stake in the controversy are the competing American traditions of multicultural tolerance and national unity. Proponents of the "English-only" movement argue that bilingualism creates cultural division and hinders assimilation and successful integration. Opponents contend that such attitudes deny non-English-speaking Americans their cultural heritage, encourages xenophobic attitudes, violates civil rights, and inflames prejudice against immigrants. This case study examines the different sides to this still unsettled issue.

WHAT IS "STANDARD" ENGLISH?

Why Good English Is Good for You
John Simon

John Simon, who currently reviews theater for *New York Magazine*, is a renowned critic of the arts and of the shoddy language of Americans. For years he wrote a regular language column for *Esquire,* from which some essays were published in a collection about the decline of literacy, *Paradigms Lost* (1980). The essay below, taken from that collection, is not just a wry and incisive look at the way American English is being abused; it is a strong argument in favor of using good English—an effort that improves not only communication but also memory and thinking.

1   What's good English to you that . . . you should grieve for it? What good is correct speech and writing, you may ask, in an age in which hardly anyone seems to know, and no one seems to care? Why shouldn't you just fling bloopers riotously with the throng, and not stick out from the rest like a sore thumb by using the language correctly? Isn't grammar really a thing of the past, and isn't the new idea to communicate in *any* way as long as you can make yourself understood?

2   The usual, basic defense of good English (and here, again, let us not worry about nomenclature—for all I care, you may call it "Standard English," "correct American," or anything else) is that it helps communication, that it is perhaps even a *sine qua non* of mutual understanding. Although this is a crude truth of sorts, it strikes me as, in some ways, both more and less than the truth. Suppose you say, "Everyone in their right mind would cross on the green light" or "Hopefully, it won't rain tomorrow," chances are very good that the person you say this to will understand you, even though you are committing obvious solecisms or creating needless ambiguities. Similarly, if you write in a letter, "The baby has finally ceased its howling" (spelling *its* as *it's*), the recipient will be able to figure out what was meant. But "figuring out" is precisely what a listener or reader should not have to do. There is, of course, the fundamental matter of courtesy to the other person, but it goes beyond that: why waste time on unscrambling simple meaning when there are more complex questions that should receive our undivided attention? If the many cooks had to worry first about which out of a large number of pots had no leak in it, the broth, whether spoiled or not, would take forever to be ready.

3   It is, I repeat, only initially a matter of clarity. It is also a matter of concision. Space today is as limited as time. If you have only a thousand words in which to convey an important message it helps to know that "overcomplicated" is correct and "overly complicated" is incorrect. Never mind the grammatical explanations; the two extra characters and one space between words are reason enough. But what about the more advanced forms of wordmongering that hold sway nowadays? Take redundancy, like the "hopes and aspirations" of Jimmy Carter, quoted by Edwin

Newman as having "a deeply profound religious experience"; or elaborate jargon, as when Charles G. Walcutt, a graduate professor of English at CUNY, writes (again as quoted by Newman): "The colleges, trying to remediate increasing numbers of . . . illiterates up to college levels, are being highschoolized"; or just obfuscatory verbiage of the pretentious sort, such as this fragment from a letter I received: "It is my impression that effective in*ter* personal verbal communication depends on prior effective in*tra*-personal verbal communication." What this means is that if you think clearly, you can speak and write clearly—except if you are a "certified speech and language pathologist," like the writer of the letter I quote. (By the way, she adds the letters Ph.D. after her name, though she is not even from Germany, where *Herr* and *Frau Doktor* are in common, not to say vulgar, use.)

4   But except for her ghastly verbiage, our certified language pathologist (whatever that means) is perfectly right: there is a close connection between the ability to think and the ability to use English correctly. After all, we think in words, we conceptualize in words, we work out our problems inwardly with words, and using them correctly is comparable to a craftsman's treating his tools with care, keeping his materials in good shape. Would you trust a weaver who hangs her wet laundry on her loom, or lets her cats bed down in her yarn? The person who does not respect words and their proper relationships cannot have much respect for ideas—very possibly cannot have ideas at all. My quarrel is not so much with minor errors that we all fall into from time to time even if we know better as it is with basic sloppiness or ignorance or defiance of good English.

5   Training yourself to speak and write correctly—and I say "training yourself" because nowadays, unfortunately, you cannot depend on other people or on institutions to give you the proper training, for reasons I shall discuss later—training yourself, then, in language, means developing at the very least two extremely useful faculties: your sense of discipline and your memory. Discipline because language is with us always, as nothing else is: it follows us much as, in the old morality play, Good Deeds followed Everyman, all the way to the grave; and, if the language is written, even beyond. Let me explain: if you keep an orderly apartment, if you can see to it that your correspondence and bill-paying are attended to regularly, if your diet and wardrobe are maintained with the necessary care—good enough; you are a disciplined person.

6   But the preliminary discipline underlying all others is nevertheless your speech: the words that come out of you almost as frequently and—if you are tidy— as regularly as your breath. I would go so far as to say that, immediately after your bodily functions, language is first, unless you happen to be an ascetic, an anchorite, or a stylite; but unless you are a sty*lite,* you had better be a sty*list.*

7   Most of us—almost all—must take in and give out language as we do breath, and we had better consider the seriousness of language pollution as second only to air pollution. For the linguistically disciplined, to misuse or mispronounce a word is an unnecessary and unhealthy contribution to the surrounding smog. To have taught ourselves not to do this, or—being human and thus also imperfect—to do it

as little as possible, means deriving from every speaking moment the satisfaction we get from a cap that snaps on to a container perfectly, an elevator that stops flush with the landing, a roulette ball that comes to rest exactly on the number on which we have placed our bet. It gives us the pleasure of hearing or seeing our words—because they are abiding by the rules—snapping, sliding, falling precisely into place, expressing with perfect lucidity and symmetry just what we wanted them to express. This is comparable to the satisfaction of the athlete or ballet dancer or pianist finding his body or legs or fingers doing his bidding with unimpeachable accuracy.

8   And if someone now says that "in George Eliot's lesser novels, she is not completely in command" is perfectly comprehensible even if it is ungrammatical, the "she" having no antecedent in the nominative (*Eliot's* is a genitive), I say, "Comprehensible, perhaps, but lopsided," for the civilized and orderly mind does not feel comfortable with that "she"—does not hear that desired and satisfying click of correctness—unless the sentence is restructured as "George Eliot, in her lesser novels, is not . . ." or in some similar way. In fact, the fully literate ear can be thrown by this error in syntax; it may look for the antecedent of that "she" elsewhere than in the preceding possessive case. Be that as it may, playing without rules and winning—in this instance, managing to communicate without using good English—is no more satisfactory than winning in a sport or game by accident or by disregarding the rules: which is really cheating.

9   The second faculty good speech develops is, as I have mentioned before, our memory. Grammar and syntax are partly logical   and to that extent they are also good exercisers and developers of our logical faculty—but they are also partly arbitrary, conventional, irrational. For example, the correct "compared to" and "contrasted with" could, from the logical point of view, just as well be "contrasted to" and "compared with" ("compared with," of course, is correct, but in a different sense from the one that concerns us here, namely, the antithesis of "contrasted with"). And, apropos *different,* logic would have to strain desperately to explain the exclusive correctness of "different from," given the exclusive correctness of "other than," which would seem to justify "different than," jarring though that is to the cultivated ear.

10   But there it is: some things are so because tradition, usage, the best speakers and writers, the grammar books and dictionaries have made them so. There may even exist some hidden historical explanation: something, perhaps, in the Sanskrit, Greek, Latin, or other origins of a word or construction that you and I may very easily never know. We can, however, memorize; and memorization can be a wonderfully useful thing—surely the Greeks were right to consider Mnemosyne (memory) the mother of the Muses, for without her there would be no art and no science. And what better place to practice one's mnemonic skills than in the study of one's language?

11   There is something particularly useful about speaking correctly and precisely because language is always there as a foundation—or, if you prefer a more fluid image, an undercurrent—beneath what is going on. Now, it seems to me that the

558 ■ Chapter 9 / Language in the USA

great difficulty of life lies in the fact that we must almost always do two things at a time. If, for example, we are walking and conversing, we must keep our mouths as well as feet from stumbling. If we are driving while listening to music, we must not allow the siren song of the cassette to prevent us from watching the road and the speedometer (otherwise the less endearing siren of the police car or the ambulance will follow apace). Well, it is just this sort of bifurcation of attention that care for precise, clear expression fosters in us. By learning early in life to pay attention both to what we are saying and to how we are saying it, we develop the much-needed life skill of doing two things simultaneously.

12   Put another way, we foster our awareness of, and ability to deal with, form and content. If there is any verity that modern criticism has fought for, it is the recognition of the indissolubility of content and form. Criticism won the battle, won it so resoundingly that this oneness has become a contemporary commonplace. And shall the fact that form *is* content be a platitude in all the arts but go unrecognized in the art of self-expression, whether in conversation or correspondence, or whatever form of spoken or written utterance a human being resorts to? Accordingly, you are going to be judged, whether you like it or not, by the correctness of your English as much as by the correctness of your thinking; there are some people to whose bad English is as offensive as gibberish, or as your picking your nose in public would be to their eyes and stomachs. The fact that people of linguistic sensibilities may be a dying breed does not mean that they are wholly extinct, and it is best not to take any unnecessary chances.

13   To be sure, if you are a member of a currently favored minority, many of your linguistic failings may be forgiven you—whether rightly or wrongly is not my concern here. But if you cannot change your sex or color to the one that is getting preferential treatment—Bakke case or no Bakke case—you might as well learn good English and profit by it in your career, your social relations, perhaps even in your basic self-confidence. That, if you will, is the ultimate practical application of good English; but now let me tell you about the ultimate impractical one, which strikes me as being possibly even more important.

14   Somewhere in the prose writings of Charles Péguy, who was a very fine poet and prose writer—and, what is perhaps even more remarkable, as good a human being as he was an artist—somewhere in those writings is a passage about the decline of pride in workmanship among French artisans, which, as you can deduce, set in even before World War I, wherein Péguy was killed. In the passage I refer to, Péguy bemoans the fact that cabinet-makers no longer finish the backs of furniture—the sides that go against the wall—in the same way as they do the exposed sides. What is not seen was just as important to the old artisans as what is seen—it was a moral issue with them. And so, I think, it ought to be with language. Even if no one else notices the niceties, the precision, the impeccable sense of grammar and syntax you deploy in your utterances, you yourself should be aware of them and take pride in them as in pieces of work well done.

15   Now, I realize that there are two possible reactions among you to what I have said up to this point. Some of you will say to yourselves: what utter nonsense! Lan-

guage is a flexible, changing, living organism that belongs to the people who speak it. It has always been changed according to the ways in which people chose to speak it, and the dictionaries and books on grammar had to, and will have to, adjust themselves to the people and not the other way around. For isn't it the glory of language that it keeps throwing up new inventions as surf tosses our differently polished pebbles and bits of bottle glass onto the shore, and that in this inexhaustible variety, in this refusal to kowtow to dry-as-dust scholars, lies its vitality, its beauty?

16   Others among you, perhaps fewer in number, will say to yourselves: quite so, there is such a thing as Standard English, or purity of speech, or correctness of expression—something worth safeguarding and fostering; but how the devil is one to accomplish that under the prevailing conditions: in a democratic society full of minorities that have their own dialects or linguistic preferences, and in a world in which television, advertising, and other mass media manage daily to corrupt the language a little further? Let me try to answer the first group first, and then come back to the questions of the second.

17   Of course language is, and must be, a living organism to the extent that new inventions, discoveries, ideas enter the scene and clamor rightfully for designations. Political, social, and psychological changes may also affect our mode of expression, and new words or phrases may have to be found to reflect what we might call historical changes. It is also quite natural for slang terms to be invented, become popular, and in some cases, remain permanently in the language. It is perhaps equally inevitable (though here we are on more speculative ground) for certain words to become obsolescent and obsolete, and drop out of the language. But does that mean that grammar and syntax have to keep changing, that pronunciations and meanings of words must shift, that more complex or elegant forms are obliged to yield to simpler or cruder ones that often are not fully synonymous with them and not capable of expressing certain fine distinctions? Should, for instance, "terrestrial" disappear entirely in favor of "earthly," or are there shades of meaning involved that need to remain available to us? Must we sacrifice "notwithstanding" because we have "in spite of" or "despite"? Need we forfeit "jettison" just because we have "throw overboard"? And what about "disinterested," which is becoming a synonym for "uninterested," even though that means something else, and though we have no other word for "disinterested"?

18   "Language has *always* changed," say these people, and they might with equal justice say that there has always been war or sickness or insanity. But the truth is that some sicknesses that formerly killed millions have been eliminated, that some so-called insanity can today be treated, and that just because there have always been wars does not mean that someday a cure cannot be found even for that scourge. And if it cannot, it is only by striving to put an absolute end to war, by pretending that it can be licked, that we can at least partly control it. Without such assumptions and efforts, the evil would be so widespread that, given our current weaponry, we would no longer be here to worry about the future of language.

19   But we are here, and having evolved linguistically this far, and having the means—books of grammar, dictionaries, education for all—to arrest unnecessary

change, why not endeavor with might and mind to arrest it? Certain cataclysms cannot be prevented: earthquakes and droughts, for example, can scarcely, if at all, be controlled; but we can prevent floods, for which purpose we have invented dams. And dams are precisely what we can construct to prevent floods of ignorance from eroding our language, and, beyond that, to provide irrigation for areas that would otherwise remain linguistically arid.

20   For consider that what some people are pleased to call linguistic evolution was almost always a matter of ignorance prevailing over knowledge. There is no valid reason, for example, for the word *nice* to have changed its meanings so many times—except ignorance of its exact definition. Had the change never occurred, or had it been stopped at any intermediate stage, we would have had just as good a word as we have now and saved some people a heap of confusion along the way. But if *nice* means what it does today—and it has two principal meanings, one of them, as in "nice distinction," alas, obsolescent—let us, for heaven's sake, keep it where it is, now that we have the means with which to hold it there.

21   If, for instance, we lose the accusative case *whom*—and we are in great danger of losing it—our language will be the poorer for it. Obviously, "The man, whom I had never known, was a thief" means something other than "The man who I had never known was a thief." Now, you can object that it would be just as easy in the first instance to use some other construction; but what happens if *this* one is used incorrectly? Ambiguity and confusion. And why should we lose this useful distinction? Just because a million or ten million or a billion people less educated than we are cannot master the difference? Surely it behooves us to try to educate the ignorant up to our level rather than to stultify ourselves down to theirs. Yes, you say, but suppose they refuse to or are unable to learn? In that case, I say, there is a doubly good reason for not going along with them. Ah, you reply, but they are the majority, and we must accept their way or, if the revolution is merely linguistic, lose our "credibility" (as the current parlance, rather confusingly, has it) or, if the revolution is political, lose our heads. Well, I consider a sufficient number of people to be educable enough to be capable of using *who* and *whom* correctly, and to derive satisfaction from this capability—a sufficient number, I mean, to enable us to preserve *whom,* and not to have to ask "for who the bell tolls."

22   The main problem with education, actually, is not those who need it and cannot get it, but those who should impart it and, for various reasons, do not. In short, the enemies of education are the educators themselves: miseducated, underpaid, overburdened, and intimidated teachers (frightened because, though the pen is supposed to be mightier than the sword, the switchblade is surely more powerful than the ferrule), and professors who—because they are structural linguists, democratic respecters of alleged minority rights, or otherwise misguided folk—believe in the sacrosanct privilege of any culturally underprivileged minority or majority to dictate its ignorance to the rest of the world. For, I submit, an English improvised by slaves and other strangers to the culture—to whom my heart goes out in every human way—under dreadfully deprived conditions can nowise equal an English that the best literary and linguistic talents have, over the centuries, perceptively and painstakingly brought to a high level of excellence.

23   So my answer to the scoffers in this or any audience is, in simplest terms, the following: contrary to popular misconception, language does not belong to the people, or at least not in the sense in which *belong* is usually construed. For things can rightfully belong only to those who invent or earn them. But we do not know who invented language: is it the people who first made up the words for *father* and *mother,* for *I* and *thou,* for *hand* and *foot*; or is it the people who evolved the subtler shadings of language, its poetic variety and suggestiveness, but also its unambiguousness, its accurate and telling details? Those are two very different groups of people and two very different languages, and I, as you must have guessed by now, consider the latter group at least as important as the former. As for *earning* language, it has surely been earned by those who have striven to learn it properly, and here even economic and social circumstances are but an imperfect excuse for bad usage; history is full of examples of people rising from humble origins to learn, against all kinds of odds, to speak and write correctly—even brilliantly.

24   *Belong,* then, should be construed in the sense that parks, national forests, monuments, and public utilities are said to belong to the people: available for properly respectful use but not for defacement and destruction. And all that we propose to teach is how to use and enjoy the gardens of language to their utmost aesthetic and salubrious potential. Still, I must now address myself to the group that, while agreeing with my aims, despairs of finding practical methods for their implementation.

25   True enough, after a certain age speakers not aware of Standard English or not exceptionally gifted will find it hard or impossible to change their ways. Nevertheless, if there were available funds for advanced methods in teaching; if teachers themselves were better trained and paid, and had smaller classes and more assistants; if, furthermore, college entrance requirements were heightened and the motivation of students accordingly strengthened; if there were no structural linguists and National Councils of Teachers of English filling instructors' heads with notions about "Students' Rights to Their Own Language" (they have every right to it as a *second* language, but none as a *first*); if teachers in all disciplines, including the sciences and social sciences, graded on English usage as well as on specific proficiencies; if aptitude tests for various jobs stressed good English more than they do; and, above all, if parents were better educated and more aware of the need to set a good example to their children, and to encourage them to learn correct usage, the situation could improve enormously.

26   Clearly, to expect all this to come to pass is utopian; some of it, however, is well within the realm of possibility. For example, even if parents do not speak very good English, many of them at least can manage an English that is good enough to correct a very young child's mistakes; in other words, most adults can speak a good enough four-year-old's idiom. They would thus start kids out on the right path; the rest could be done by the schools.

27   But the problem is what to do in the most underprivileged homes: those of blacks, Hispanics, immigrants from various Asian and European countries. This is where day-care centers could come in. If the fathers and mothers could be gainfully employed, their small children would be looked after by day-care centers where— is this asking too much?—good English could be inculcated in them. The difficulty,

of course, is what to do about the discrepancy the little ones would note between the speech of the day-care people and that of their parents. Now, it seems to me that small children have a far greater ability to learn things, including languages, than some people give them credit for. Much of it is indeed rote learning, but, where languages are concerned, that is one of the basic learning methods even for adults. There is no reason for not teaching kids another language, to wit, Standard English, and turning this, if desirable, into a game: "At home you speak one way; here we have another language," at which point the instructor can make up names and explanations for Standard English that would appeal to pupils of that particular place, time, and background.

28   At this stage of the game, as well as later on in school, care should be exercised to avoid insulting the language spoken in the youngsters' homes. There must be ways to convey that both home and school languages have their validity and uses and that knowing both enables one to accomplish more in life. This would be hard to achieve if the children's parents were, say, militant blacks of the Geneva Smitherman sort, who execrate Standard English as a weapon of capitalist oppression against the poor of all races, colors, and religions. But, happily, there is evidence that most black, Hispanic, and other non-Standard English-speaking parents want their children to learn correct English so as to get ahead in the world.

29   Yet how do we defend ourselves against the charge that we are old fogeys who cannot emotionally adjust to the new directions an ever-living and changing language must inevitably take? Here I would want to redefine or, at any rate, clarify, what "living and changing" means, and also explain where we old fogeys stand. Misinformed attacks on Old Fogeydom, I have noticed, invariably represent us as people who shudder at a split infinitive and would sooner kill or be killed than tolerate a sentence that ends with a preposition. Actually, despite all my travels through Old Fogeydom, I have yet to meet one inhabitant who would not stick a preposition onto the tail of a sentence; as for splitting infinitives, most of us O.F.'s are perfectly willing to do that, too, but tactfully and sparingly, where it feels right. There is no earthly reason, for example, for saying "to dangerously live," when "to live dangerously" sounds so much better; but it does seem right to say (and write) "What a delight to sweetly breathe in your sleeping lover's breath"; that sounds smoother, indeed sweeter, than to "breathe in sweetly" or "sweetly to breathe in." But infinitives begging to be split are relatively rare; a sensitive ear, a good eye for shades of meaning will alert you whenever the need to split arises; without that ear and eye, you had better stick to the rules.

30   About the sense in which language is, and must be, alive, let me speak while donning another of my several hats—actually it is not a hat but a cap, for there exists in Greenwich Village an inscription on a factory that reads "CRITIC CAPS." So with my drama critic's cap on, let me present you with an analogy. The world theater today is full of directors who wreak havoc on classic plays to demonstrate their own ingenuity, their superiority, as it were, to the author. These directors— aborted playwrights, for the most part—will stage productions of *Hamlet* in which the prince is a woman, a flaming homosexual, or a one-eyed hunchback.

31   Well, it seems to me that the same spirit prevails in our approach to linguistics, with every newfangled, ill-informed, know-nothing construction, definition, pronunciation enshrined by the joint efforts of structural linguists, permissive dictionaries, and allegedly democratic but actually demagogic educators. What really makes a production of, say, *Hamlet* different, and therefore alive, is that the director, while trying to get as faithfully as possible at Shakespeare's meanings, nevertheless ends up stressing things in the play that strike him most forcefully; and the same individuality in production design and performances (the Hamlet of Gielgud versus the Hamlet of Olivier, for instance—what a world of difference!) further differentiates one production from another, and bestows on each its particular vitality. So, too, language remains alive because each speaker (or writer) can and must, *within the framework of accepted grammar, syntax, and pronunciation,* produce a style that is his very own, that is as personal as his posture, way of walking, mode of dress, and so on. It is such stylistic differences that make a person's—or a nation's—language flavorous, pungent, alive, and all this without having to play fast and loose with the existing rules.

32   But to have this, we need, among other things, good teachers and, beyond them, enlightened educators. I shudder when I read in the *Birmingham* (Alabama) *Post-Herald* of October 6, 1978, an account of a talk given to eight hundred English teachers by Dr. Alan C. Purves, vice-president of the National Council of Teachers of English. Dr. Purves is quoted as saying things like "We are in a situation with respect to reading where . . . ," and culminating in the following truly horrifying sentence: "I am going to suggest that when we go back to the basics, I think what we should be dealing with is our charge to help students to be more proficient in producing meaningful language—language that says what it means." Notice all the deadwood, the tautology, the anacoluthon in the first part of that sentence; but notice especially the absurdity of the latter part, in which the dubious word "meaningful"—a poor relation of "significant"—is thought to require explaining to an audience of English teachers.

33   Given such leadership from the N.C.T.E., the time must be at hand when we shall hear—not just "Don't ask for who the bell rings" (*as not* and *tolls* being, of course, archaic, elitist language), but also "It rings for you and I."

THINKING CRITICALLY

1. In your own words, why is good English good for you?

2. Consider the two examples Simon gives in paragraph 2: "Everyone in their right mind would cross on the green light" and "Hopefully, it won't rain tomorrow." If they communicate perfectly well, why haggle over the minor grammatical errors?

3. How does Simon justify so strong a statement as that in paragraph 7: "Language pollution . . . [is] second only to air pollution"? Do you agree? Can you think of circumstances in which bad language might be a threat to health—mental or otherwise?

4. Simon argues that good speech develops memory. How does he explain that? Can you substantiate that based on your own experience and practice?

5. One counter-response to Simon's call for upholding the standards of correct English is the assertion: "Language is a flexible, changing, living organism that belongs to the people who speak it." (This statement is nearly identical to Bill Bryson's claim in a following essay.) How does Simon answer that charge? Can the language have rigid standards and still allow natural changes to occur? If so, give examples.

6. Simon singles out the word *nice* as one of the many victims of too much change. What are some of the current meanings of *nice*? Can you think of other words that have suffered too much change? What about the words *awful, terrific, wonderful,* and *fantastic*? What changes have they undergone since their original meanings?

7. Simon claims that "the enemies of education are the educators themselves" (paragraph 22). How does he justify such an assertion? Do you agree, given your own educational experience?

8. According to Simon, who are linguistically "the most underprivileged" children? What suggestions does Simon make for dealing with them?

9. From the tone and attitude of this essay, what kind of man would you say Simon is? Does he sound cranky and pedantic or snobbish and elitist? Or does he sound reasonable and friendly? Cite passages to substantiate your answer.

WRITING ASSIGNMENTS

1. Simon says that "you are going to be judged, whether you like it or not, by the correctness of your English as much as by the correctness of your thinking." Write an essay about an occasion when you judged people on the basis of their English—or an occasion when you were judged on that basis. Describe how their language prejudiced you for or against them—or how such prejudices might have operated for or against you.

2. Simon criticizes parents strongly for not setting good language examples for their children. Write a paper describing the quality of language training in your own home. Did your parents encourage you to learn correct usage? Were they strict with you about it? Do you feel adequately trained in English usage, or handicapped because of your upbringing?

3. This essay by Simon was originally an address to a college audience. Imagine yourself addressing an audience on the same subject: "Why Good English Is Good for You." This time you are addressing not Simon's college students, but a group of people who speak nonstandard, "uneducated" English. Write a speech that they might benefit from in language that they would understand and not be repelled by.

Everyone Has an Accent but Me
John Esling

Everybody has an accent. Accent is the way we speak, pronounce our words, intone sounds, and inflect voice. From listening to others speak, we make judgements about their background, education, culture, nationality, and social status. In fact, we are far more likely to judge a person by his or her accent than by how they dress, carry themselves, or with whom they socialize. As John Esling explains in the next essay, we all have an accent, even if we think we don't.

John Esling is a professor of linguistics at the University of Victoria in British Columbia. He is also Secretary of the International Phonetic Association, and author of the University of Victoria Phonetic Database. This essay first appeared in the book, *Language Myths*, edited by Laurie Bauer and Peter Trudgill.

1 "I don't have an accent!" wails the friend indignantly. And we are all amused because the pronunciation of the utterance itself demonstrates to our ears that the claim is false. The speaker who voices this common refrain believes absolutely that his or her speech is devoid of any distinguishing characteristics that set it apart from the speech of those around them. We listeners who hear it are for our part equally convinced that the speaker's accent differs in some significant respect from our own. The key to understanding this difference of opinion is not so much in the differences in speech sounds that the speakers use but in the nature of "own-ness"— what does it mean to be "one of us" and to sound like it? It all comes down to a question of belonging. Accent defines and communicates who we are. Accent is the map which listeners perceive through their ears rather than through their eyes to "read" where the speaker was born and raised, what gender they are, how old they are, where they might have moved during their life, where they went to school, what occupation they have taken up, and even how short or tall they are, how much they might weigh, or whether they are feeling well or ill at the moment.

2 The fact is that everyone has an accent. It tells other people who we are because it reflects the places we have been and the things we have done. But the construct of accent, like so many other things, is relative. We may only realize that others think we have an accent when we leave the place we came from and find ourselves among people who share a different background from our own, or when a newcomer to our local area stands out as having a distinctly different pronunciation from most of those in our group—that is, relative to us. The closer we are to our native place and the more people that are there who grew up like us, the more likely we are to sound like those people when we talk. In other words, we share their local accent.

3 Some countries have one accent which is accepted as "standard" and which enjoys higher social prestige than any other. This is true of RP (Received Pronunciation) in the UK, of standard French in France and of many countries that have evolved a broadcast standard for radio and television. We may feel that this national standard is accentless and that non-standard speakers, by contrast, have accents. Nevertheless, it has to be recognized that standards that have evolved in the broadcast industry have their roots in language varieties that already exist in distinct social groups and their institutions. To use one particular group's accent in broadcasting is to give that accent a wider reach than perhaps it had before, but the accent itself is no "less" of an accent than any other, although it may represent

groups and institutions with more political and economic power than groups whose members use another accent.

4   Our perceptions and production of speech also change with time. If we were to leave our native place for an extended period, our perception that the new accents around us were strange would only be temporary. Gradually, depending on our age, what job we are doing and how many different sorts of folks with different types of accents surround us, we will lose the sense that others have an accent and we will begin to fit in—to accommodate our speech patterns to the new norm. Not all people do this to the same degree. Some remain intensely proud of their original accent and dialect words, phrases and gestures, while others accommodate rapidly to a new environment by changing, among other things, their speech habits, so that they no longer "stand out in the crowd". Whether they do this consciously or not is open to debate and may differ from individual to individual, but like most processes that have to do with language, the change probably happens before we are aware of it and probably couldn't happen if we were.

5   So when we say, "I don't have an accent," we really mean, "You wouldn't think I had an accent if you knew who I was and knew where I'd been." It has more to do with acceptance—agreeing to stop listening to the other as "other"—than with absolute differences in the vowels, consonants or intonation patterns that a speaker uses. At the most basic level, we acknowledge that every individual will always have some speech characteristics that distinguish him or her from everyone else, even in our local community. This is the essence of recognition—we can learn to pick a friend's voice out of the crowd even though we consider everyone in our local crowd to have the same "accent" compared to outsiders. So what we call accent is relative not only to experience but also to the number of speech features we wish to distinguish at a time.

6   Human perception is categorical. When it comes to placing an accent, we listen and categorize according to accents we have heard before. We have a hard time placing an accent that we have never heard before, at least until we find out what to associate that accent with. Our experience of perceiving the sounds of human speech is very much a question of "agreeing" with others to construct certain categories and then to place the sounds that we hear into them. In contemporary constructivist psychology, this process is called the "co-construction of reality", in which differences can be said not to exist until we construct them. One result of these principles is that we can become quite attuned to stereotypical accents that we have heard only occasionally and don't know very well, while we become "insensitive" to the common accents we hear all around us every day. The speech of our colleagues seems "normal" to our ears, while the speech of a stranger stands out as different from that norm. So we feel that we don't have an accent because of the weight of experience that tells us that we are the best possible example of the "norm".

7   Details of pronunciation conjure up stereotypes. A few consonants and vowels or the briefest of intonation melodies cause us to search our memories for a pattern that matches what we have just heard. This is how we place speakers according to

dialect or language group. It is also how we predict what the rest of their conso-nants and vowels and intonational phrasing will be like. Sometimes we are wrong, but usually we make good guesses based on limited evidence, especially if we've heard the accent before. Because we are used to the word order and common ex-pressions of our language, a stranger's exotic pronunciation of a word which we recognize and understand can be catalogued as foreign, and we may ascribe it to one familiar stereotype or another and predict what the speaker's pronunciation of other words will be like. In this way, we see others as having an accent—because we take ourselves as the norm or reference to compare and measure others' speech.

8   It is interesting for the student of phonetics to observe the various ways in which one person's accent can differ from another's. There are three "strands" of accent which Professor David Abercrombie of the Department of Linguistics of the University of Edinburgh for many years taught his students to distinguish: the very short consonant and vowel sounds which alternate in rapid succession; the longer waves of rhythmic and melodic groupings, which we call rhythm and intonation; and the longest-term, persistent features that change very little in a given individ-ual's voice, which we call voice quality.

9   Consonants and vowels are the building blocks of linguistic meaning, and slight changes in their quality inherently carry large differences in meaning, which we detect immediately. *Bought, but, bet, bait* is a four-way distinction for an Eng-lish speaker, but may only be a two-way distinction for a Spanish or Japanese speaker. Differences in vowels can make dialects of English incomprehensible even to each other at first. An American pronunciation of "John" can sound like "Jan" to a Scot; and a Scots pronunciation of "John" can sound like "Joan" to an American. Consonants are also critical in deciding the meaning of a word. The American who asked if she could clear away some "bottles" was understood by the pub owner in Scotland to have said "barrels", not only because of the vowel but also because the d-like pronunciation of the t-sound is almost exactly like the d-like pronunciation of the rolled r in Scots. Again, it is the speaker generating the utter-ance who thinks primarily in terms of meaning and not in terms of the sounds being used to transmit that meaning. It is the hearer who must translate the incoming speech sounds into new, meaningful units (which we usually call words) and who cannot help but notice that the signals coming in are patterned differently from the hearer's own system of speech sounds. Confusion over the meaning of a word can only highlight these differences, making the translation of meaning more difficult and making each participant in the conversation feel that the other has an accent. The impression is therefore mutual.

10   Another meaningful component of accent is intonation or the "melody" of speech. Differences in the rises and falls of intonation patterns, and the rhythmic beat that accompanies them, can be as significant as differences in the melodies of tunes that we recognize or in the beat of a waltz compared to a jig. One of the char-acteristics of the American comedian Richard Pryor's ability to switch from "white talk" to "black talk" is the control of the height and of the rising and falling of the pitch of the voice. Even more rapid timing of these rises and falls is an indication of

languages such as Swedish and languages such as Chinese which have different tones, that is, pitches that distinguish word meanings from each other. Pitch can have the greatest effect on our impression of an accent or on our ability to recognize a voice. Our mood—whether we are excited or angry or sad—can change the sound of our voice, as the tempo of our speech also speeds up or slows down, so that we may sound like a different person.

11   Voice quality is the ensemble of more or less permanent elements that appear to remain constant in a person's speech. This is how we recognize a friend's voice on the telephone even if they only utter a syllable. Some voices are nasal; others low and resonant; others breathy; and still others higher pitched and squeaky. Presumably, the better we know a person, the less we feel they have a noticeable accent. Naturally, however, if they didn't have a distinguishable ensemble of accent features, we couldn't tell their voice apart from other people's. Travelers to a foreign country often experience an inability to tell individual speakers of a foreign language apart. As it once did in our native language, this ability comes with practice, that is, with exposure. The reason is that we need time to distinguish, first, to which strand of accent each particular speech gesture belongs and, second, which speech details are common to most speakers of that language and which belong only to the individual. Unless the individual's speech stands out in some remarkable way, we are likely to perceive the collection of common, group traits first.

12   Much of our perception of accent could actually be visual. Hand and facial gestures which accompany speech could cue a listener that the speaker comes from a different place, so that we expect the person to sound different from our norm. If we expect to hear an accent, we probably will. Sooner or later, wherever they live, most people encounter someone from another place. A stranger from out of town, a foreigner, even a person who had moved away and returned. But even in the same community, people from different social groups or of different ages can be distinguished on the basis of their speech. One of the intriguing linguistic aspects of police work is to locate and identify suspects on the basis of their accent. Often, this technique comes down to the skill of being able to notice details of speech that other observers overlook. Sometimes, an academic approach such as broadcasting a voice to a large number of "judges" over the radio or on television is necessitated. In this case, an anonymous suspect can often be narrowed down as coming from a particular area or even identified outright. Computer programs are also having moderate success at verifying individual speakers on the basis of their accent. These techniques are sometimes called "voiceprints", implying that each individual is unique, but as with human listeners, success may depend on how much speech from the individual can be heard and in how many contexts.

13   One of the most popular characterizations of the notion of accent modification has been George Bernard Shaw's *Pygmalion,* revived on stage and screen as *My Fair Lady.* The phonetician, Professor Higgins, is renowned for tracing the course of people's lives from their accents, and Eliza Doolittle, at the opposite extreme, while probably aware of different accents and able to identify them to some degree, appears at first quite unable to produce speech in anything other than her local-

dialect accent. The transformation of Eliza, explained in sociolinguistic terms, is the apparent result of her accommodation to a new social milieu and her acceptance of a new role for herself. In terms of constructivist psychology, she co-constructed a new reality—a new story—for her life and left the old story behind. The transformation had its physical effect (she was no longer recognized in her former neighborhood) as well as its linguistic realization (her accent changed to suit her new surroundings). We all leave parts of the speaking style of our early years behind, while we adopt new patterns more suited to our later years. Whether we change a lot or a little depends on individual choices within a web of social circumstance.

THINKING CRITICALLY

1. What do we mean when we say that someone doesn't have an accent? Is there a type of English that we seem to recognize as "accentless"? Why, according to the author, is such a determination false?

2. Consider the title of Esling's essay. How does it connect to his essay's thesis? Why do so many people feel that they don't have an accent? Explain.

3. Before reading this essay, how would you have described your accent? Would you have said you had one? After responding to this question, ask a friend or classmate from a different part of the country if they would agree with your assessment.

4. What stereotypes are associated with accents? Try to identify as many accents as you can think of and what stereotypes we associate with them.

5. Have you ever made presumptions about a person based on his or her accent? How did the phonetic elements Esling describes, such as intonation, pronunciation of consonants and vowels, and voice quality influence your judgement? Why do we use these phonetic cues to form opinions about other people?

6. According to the author, what makes it possible for us to distinguish accents? Why can't we distinguish our own?

WRITING ASSIGNMENTS

1. In his opening paragraph, Esling comments that accent serves as a "map" that tells others many things about us, including where we come from, our age, gender, education, and background. Write an essay in which you explore the relationship between accent and how we judge others. Do you judge people by how they speak? Is it automatic? Have you ever been wrong? Why do we tend to judge people by their accents?

2. At the end of his essay, Esling refers to George Bernard Shaw's book, *Pygmalion*. Read the preface Shaw wrote regarding the subject matter and the social commentary behind his story at <http://www.bartleby.com/138/0.html> in which he notes, "it is impossible for an Englishman to open his mouth without making some other Englishman hate or despise him." What did Shaw mean by this statement? Does his observation hold any truth for Americans today? Why or why not? Explain.

Label Babel

Richard Liebmann-Smith

The method the English language uses to label people from various places is, to say the very least, erratic. In fact, it would seem that there is no infallible method at all. National and regional labels seem to be driven more by linguistic whimsy than by hard-and-fast language rules, as the author of the following humorous look at this aspect of the English language reveals.

Richard Liebmann-Smith is co-editor of *The Best of the Journal of Irreproducible Results* (1989) and author of *The Question of Aids* (1985). He is the co-author of many episodes of the Fox cartoon "The Tick" (with Ben Edlund). This article appeared as "The Last Page" feature in the December 2002 issue of *Smithsonian Magazine*.

1 Ever since George W. Bush set eyebrows rising when he mistakenly called the East Timorese by the name East Timorians, I've been lying awake nights trying to figure out the rules for the way we label people from various places.

2 Let's start with something ese-y, like the Chinese, the Japanese and those beleaguered East Timorese. At first blush it seems there's a simple rule in operation here: people from countries in Asia take the suffix "ese." Hence, in addition to the aforementioned, we have the Taiwanese, the Vietnamese and, naturally, the *West* Timorese. It all looks perfectly neat. Yet if the Asia rule held, wouldn't we also have the Cambodese, the Tibetese and the Indonesiaese? Conversely, how can we account for the non-Asian Congolese, Senegalese and Lebanese? And if you believe the answer lies in Eurocentrism, how do you explain the Portuguese?

3 Perhaps these designations derive not so much from geography as from spelling. Maybe the "or" at the end of Timor should have tipped Mr. Bush off to the appropriate "ese" suffix. Sounds plausible, but then why aren't people from Ecuador called Ecuadorese or those hardy souls up in Maine known as the Bangorese? (Speaking of Maine, if people from Spain are Spaniards, shouldn't Down Easters be Maniards?)

4 Once you start obsessing along these lines, you quickly realize there's precious little rhyme and not much reason to these quirky designations. Consider, for example, the ticklish "ish" situation: countries whose names end in "land" tend to produce "ish" people. England and Ireland are nicely behaved examples. But it turns out that a "land" country by no means guarantees an "ish" people. Iceland is home to the Icelanders, not the Icish. Likewise, the upstanding citizens of Newfoundland are not Newfoundish, but Newfoundlanders. And to totally muddy the linguistic waters, while the people of England are indeed English, New England is the land of New Englanders, not of the New English. Worse, if Thais come from Thailand and Finns come from Finland, why aren't people from Holland called Holls? (They're Dutch, of course. Go figure.)

5 Deeper mysteries abound: people from Canada and Florida somehow pick up an internal "i," becoming Canadians and Floridians, yet those from other "a" places

do not, or else we would have Americans, Alaskians and Arubians. So, you say, an "a" ending is not sufficient. After all, both Canada and Florida end in "da." Well, tell that to the Ugandans.

6   And how did people from Peru come to be called Peruvians? Who slipped in that silly "v"? It certainly wasn't dictated by the "u," or we would also have Honoluluvians and Timbuctuvians. Likewise, if the "o" at the end of Kosovo makes for Kosovars, where are the Congovars, the Ohiovars, the Pago Pagovars and the Tierra del Fuegovars? Come to think of it, are those folks more properly the Tierra del Fuegans or the Tierrans del Fuego?

7   If the denizens of Rome, Italy, are Romans, what are people from Nome, Alaska? Nomans? And if residents of Los Angeles are known as Angelenos, why aren't those who live in Las Vegas called Veganos? Norway gives us Norwegians and Galway supplies Galwegians; but are those suburbanites out on Long Island Far Rockawegians? Is Hunan Province in China populated by Hunaners, Hunanese or Hunanians? Or Hunan beings?

8   No doubt you now understand why these linguistic mysteries have disturbed my sleep for the past couple of years. Just last night, as I was about to drift off to the Land of Nod, I began to wonder: Who lives there? The Nodians? The Noddish? The Nodlanders? The Nodese? The Nodovars? The Noss?

9   As I'm sure George W. would agree, this is not an endeavor for the timorous. Not to mention the timorish.

THINKING CRITICALLY

1. Liebmann-Smith opens his essay with a reference to a mistake made by George W. Bush. What was people's reaction to this mistake? Do an Internet search of the phrase "East Timorese." Is this mistake understandable, or embarrassing? How does Liebmann-Smith defend the president's error? Explain.

2. Have you ever mislabeled another person's nationality or regional identity? Could you be making errors and not even know it? Try to give the correct regional label to the following areas.

Regions/Cities/States in the United States

Chicago	Florida	Midwest
Boston	Iowa	New England
Los Angeles	Texas	South
Atlanta	Oregon	
Manhattan	Wisconsin	

Countries

Algeria	Australia	Bolivia
Belize	Burundi	Chile
Costa Rica	Denmark	El Salvador
Fiji	Guyana	Hungary

Iceland	Jordan	Luxembourg
Mali	Monaco	Mozambique
Nepal	Niger	Norway
Peru	Poland	Rwanda
Scotland	Sweden	Tanzania
Turkey	United States	Venezuela
Yemen	Yugoslavia	Zimbabwe

WRITING ASSIGNMENTS

1. How do other languages label nationalities and regions? Select a foreign language and research it. What rules, if any, exist? How does the language you selected compare to the English "system" of labeling? Compare your results with other language studies conducted by your classmates. Is this a problem that encompasses many languages, or does it seem to be just an English language issue?

Good English and Bad

Bill Bryson

More than one billion people in the world speak English, and much of the rest of the world is attempting to. But as Paul Roberts explains in his essay (Chapter 1), the English language, with its various historical influences, is very complex. In fact, deceptively so. Even language authorities will stumble over its idiosyncrasies, as demonstrated below. And the reason is simple: In an effort to establish criteria for *good* English for generations to come, seventeenth-century grammarians wrote rules of English modeled on those of Latin, which, though dead, was considered the most admirable and purest tongue. But as Bill Bryson explains, imposing Latin rules on English is like asking people to play baseball according to the rules of football. They don't go together; likewise, ancient standards of usage don't always describe how the language works today. In this lively and engaging discussion, Bryson explains how the distinction of *good* English from *bad* English is mostly a matter of conditioning and prejudice.

Bill Bryson is an American journalist living in England. He has worked for the *Times* of London and the *Independent,* and has written articles for the *New York Times, Esquire, GQ,* and other journals. His books include *A Dictionary of Troublesome Words, The Lost Continent,* and the highly acclaimed *The Mother Tongue* (1990), from which this essay comes.

1 Consider the parts of speech. In Latin, the verb has up to 120 inflections. In English it never has more than five (e.g., *see, sees, saw, seeing, seen*) and often it gets by with just three (*hit, hits, hitting*). Instead of using loads of different verb forms, we use just a few forms but employ them in loads of ways. We need just five inflections to deal with the act of propelling a car—*drive, drives, drove, driving,* and

driven—yet with these we can express quite complex and subtle variations of tense: "I drive to work every day," "I have been driving since I was sixteen," "I will have driven 20,000 miles by the end of this year." This system, for all its ease of use, makes labeling difficult. According to any textbook, the present tense of the verb *drive* is *drive*. Every junior high school pupil knows that. Yet if we say, "I used to drive to work but now I don't," we are clearly using the present tense *drive* in a past tense sense. Equally if we say, "I will drive you to work tomorrow," we are using it in a future sense. And if we say, "I would drive if I could afford to," we are using it in a conditional sense. In fact, almost the only form of sentence in which we cannot use the present tense form of *drive* is, yes, the present tense. When we need to indicate an action going on right now, we must use the participial form *driving*. We don't say, "I drive the car now," but rather "I'm driving the car now." Not to put too fine a point on it, the labels are largely meaningless.

2   We seldom stop to think about it, but some of the most basic concepts in English are naggingly difficult to define. What, for instance, is a sentence? Most dictionaries define it broadly as a group of words constituting a full thought and containing, at a minimum, a subject (basically a noun) and predicate (basically a verb). Yet if I inform you that I have just crashed your car and you reply, "What!" or "Where?" or "How!" you have clearly expressed a complete thought, uttered a sentence. But where are the subject and predicate? Where are the noun and verb, not to mention the prepositions, conjunctions, articles, and other components that we normally expect to find in a sentence? To get around this problem, grammarians pretend that such sentences contain words that aren't there. "What!" they would say, really means "What are you telling me—you crashed my car?" while "Where?" is a shorthand rendering of "Where did you crash it?" and "How?" translates as "How on earth did you manage to do that, you old devil you?" or words to that effect. The process is called *ellipsis* and is certainly very nifty. Would that I could do the same with my bank account. Yet the inescapable fact is that it is possible to make such sentences conform to grammatical precepts only by bending the rules. When I was growing up we called that cheating.

3   In English, in short, we possess a language in which the parts of speech are almost entirely notional. A noun is a noun and a verb is a verb largely because the grammarians say they are. In the sentence "I am suffering terribly" *suffering* is a verb, but in "My suffering is terrible," it is a noun. Yet both sentences use precisely the same word to express precisely the same idea. *Quickly* and *sleepily* are adverbs but *sickly* and *deadly* are adjectives. *Breaking* is a present tense participle, but as often as not it is used in a past tense sense ("He was breaking the window when I saw him"). *Broken,* on the other hand, is a past tense participle but as often as not it is employed in a present tense sense ("I think I've just broken my toe") or even future tense sense ("If he wins the next race, he'll have broken the school record"). To deal with all the anomalies, the parts of speech must be so broadly defined as to be almost meaningless. A noun, for example, is generally said to be a word that denotes a person, place, thing, action, or quality. That would seem to cover almost everything, yet clearly most actions are verbs and many words that denote qualities—*brave, foolish, good*—are adjectives.

4   The complexities of English are such that the authorities themselves often stumble. Each of the following, penned by an expert, contains a usage that at least some of his colleagues would consider quite wrong.

> "Prestige is one of the few words that has had an experience opposite to that described in 'Worsened Words.'" (H. W. Fowler, *A Dictionary of Modern English Usage,* second edition) It should be "one of the few words that *have* had."
>
> "Each of the variants indicated in boldface type count as an entry." (*The Harper Dictionary of Contemporary Usage*) It should be "each . . . *counts.*"
>
> "It is of interest to speculate about the amount of dislocation to the spelling system that would occur if English dictionaries were either proscribed or (as when Malory or Sir Philip Sidney were writing) did not exist." (Robert Burchfield, *The English Language*) Make it "*was* writing."
>
> "A range of sentences forming statements, commands, questions and exclamations cause us to draw on a more sophisticated battery of orderings and arrangements." (Robert Burchfield, *The English Language*) It should be *causes.*
>
> "The prevalence of incorrect instances of the use of the apostrophe . . . together with the abandonment of it by many business firms . . . suggest that the time is close at hand when this moderately useful device should be abandoned." (Robert Burchfield, *The English Language*) The verb should be *suggests.*
>
> "If a lot of the available dialect data is obsolete or almost so, a lot more of it is far too sparse to support any sort of reliable conclusion." (Robert Claiborne, *Our Marvelous Native Tongue*) *Data* is a plural.
>
> "His system of citing examples of the best authorities, of indicating etymology, and pronunciation, are still followed by lexicographers." (Philip Howard, *The State of the Language*) His system *are*?
>
> "When his fellowship expired he was offered a rectorship at Boxworth . . . on condition that he married the deceased rector's daughter." (Robert McCrum, et al., *The Story of English*) A misuse of the subjunctive: It should be "on condition that he marry."

5   English grammar is so complex and confusing for the one very simple reason that its rules and terminology are based on Latin—a language with which it has precious little in common. In Latin, to take one example, it is not possible to split an infinitive. So in English, the early authorities decided, it should not be possible to split an infinitive either. But there is no reason why we shouldn't, any more than we should forsake instant coffee and air travel because they weren't available to the Romans. Making English grammar conform to Latin rules is like asking people to play baseball using the rules of football. It is a patent absurdity. But once this insane notion became established grammarians found themselves having to draw up ever more complicated and circular arguments to accommodate the inconsistencies. As Burchfield notes in *The English Language,* one authority. F. Th. Visser, found it necessary to devote 200 pages to discussing just one aspect of the present participle. That is as crazy as it is amazing.

6   The early authorities not only used Latin grammar as their model, but actually went to the almost farcical length of writing English grammars in that language, as

with Sir Thomas Smith's *De Recta et Emendata Linguae Anglicae Scriptione Dia-logus* (1568), Alexander Gil's *Logonomia Anglica* (1619), and John Wallis's *Grammatica Linguae Anglicanae* of 1653 (though even he accepted that the grammar of Latin was ill-suited to English). For the longest time it was taken entirely for granted that the classical languages *must* serve as models. Dryden spoke for an age when he boasted that he often translated his sentences into Latin to help him decide how best to express them in English.

7   In 1660, Dryden complained that English had "not so much as a tolerable dictionary or a grammar; so our language is in a manner barbarous." He believed there should be an academy to regulate English usage, and for the next two centuries many others would echo his view. In 1664, The Royal Society for the Advancement of Experimental Philosophy formed a committee "to improve the English tongue," though nothing lasting seems to have come of it. Thirty-three years later in his *Essay Upon Projects,* Daniel Defoe was calling for an academy to oversee the language. In 1712, Jonathan Swift joined the chorus with a *Proposal for Correcting, Improving and Ascertaining the English Tongue.* Some indication of the strength of feeling attached to these matters is given by the fact that in 1780, in the midst of the American Revolution, John Adams wrote to the president of Congress appealing to him to set up an academy for the purpose of "refining, correcting, improving and ascertaining the English language" (a title that closely echoes, not to say plagiarizes, Swift's pamphlet of sixty-eight years before). In 1806, the American Congress considered a bill to institute a national academy and in 1820 an American Academy of Language and Belles Lettres, presided over by John Quincy Adams, was formed, though again without any resounding perpetual benefits to users of the language. And there were many other such proposals and assemblies.

8   The model for all these was the Académie Française, founded by Cardinal Richelieu in 1635. In its youth, the academy was an ambitious motivator of change. In 1762, after many years of work, it published a dictionary that regularized the spellings of some 5,000 words—almost a quarter of the words then in common use. It took the *s* out of words like *estre* and *fenestre,* making them *[ace]tre* and *fen[ace]tre,* and it turned *roy* and *loy* into *roi* and *loi.* In recent decades, however, the academy has been associated with an almost ayatollah-like conservatism. When in December 1988 over 90 percent of French schoolteachers voted in favor of a proposal to introduce the sort of spelling reforms the academy itself had introduced 200 years earlier, the forty venerable members of the academy were, to quote the London Sunday *Times,* "up in apoplectic arms" at the thought of tampering with something as sacred as French spelling. Such is the way of the world. Among the changes the teachers wanted and the academicians did not were the removal of the circumflex on *[ace]tre, fen[ace]tre,* and other such words, and taking the *-x* off plurals such as *bureaux, chevaux,* and *chateaux* and replacing it with an *-s.*

9   Such actions underline the one almost inevitable shortcoming of national academies. However progressive and far-seeing they may be to begin with, they almost always exert over time a depressive effect on change. So it is probably fortunate that the English-speaking world never saddled itself such a body, largely because as many influential users of English were opposed to academies as favored them.

Samuel Johnson doubted the prospects of arresting change and Thomas Jefferson thought it in any case undesirable. In declining an offer to be the first honorary president of the Academy of Language and Belles Lettres, he noted that had such a body been formed in the days of the Anglo-Saxons English would now be unable to describe the modern world. Joseph Priestley, the English scientist, grammarian, and theologian, spoke perhaps most eloquently against the formation of an academy when he said in 1761 that it was "unsuitable to the genius of a free nation. . . . We need make no doubt but that the best forms of speech will, in time, establish themselves by their own superior excellence: and in all controversies, it is better to wait the decisions of time, which are slow and sure, than to take those of synods, which are often hasty and injudicious." [Quoted by Baugh and Cable, page 269]

10   English is often commended by outsiders for its lack of a stultifying authority. Otto Jespersen as long ago as 1905 was praising English for its lack of rigidity, its happy air of casualness. Likening French to the severe and formal gardens of Louis XIV, he contrasted it with English, which he said was "laid out seemingly without any definite plan, and in which you are allowed to walk everywhere according to your own fancy without having to fear a stern keeper enforcing rigorous regulations." [*Growth and Structure of the English Language*, page 16]

11   Without an official academy to guide us, the English-speaking world has long relied on self-appointed authorities such as the brothers H. W. and F. G. Fowler and Sir Ernest Gowers in Britain and Theodore Bernstein and William Safire in America, and of course countless others. These figures write books, give lectures, and otherwise do what they can (i.e., next to nothing) to try to stanch (not staunch) the perceived decline of the language. They point out that there is a useful distinction to be observed between *uninterested* and *disinterested*, between *imply* and *infer*, *flaunt* and *flout*, *fortunate* and *fortuitous*, *forgo* and *forego*, and *discomfort* and *discomfit* (not forgetting *stanch* and *staunch*). They point out that *fulsome*, properly used, is a term of abuse, not praise, that *peruse* actually means to read thoroughly, not glance through, that *data* and *media* are plurals. And from the highest offices in the land they are ignored.

12   In the late 1970s, President Jimmy Carter betrayed a flaw in his linguistic armory when he said: "The government of Iran must realize that it cannot flaunt, with impunity, the expressed will and law of the world community." *Flaunt* means to show off; he meant *flout*. The day after he was elected president in 1988, George Bush told a television reporter he couldn't believe the enormity of what had happened. Had President-elect Bush known that the primary meaning of *enormity* is wickedness or evilness, he would doubtless have selected a more apt term.

13   When this process of change can be seen happening in our lifetimes, it is almost always greeted with cries of despair and alarm. Yet such change is both continuous and inevitable. Few acts are more salutary than looking at the writings of language authorities from recent decades and seeing the usages that heightened their hackles. In 1931, H. W. Fowler was tutting over *racial*, which he called "an ugly word, the strangeness of which is due to our instinctive feeling that the termination -al has no business at the end of a word that is not obviously Latin." (For

similar reasons he disliked *television* and *speedometer*.) Other authorities have variously—and sometimes hotly—attacked *enthuse, commentate, emote, prestigious, contact* as a verb, *chair* as a verb, and scores of others. But of course these are nothing more than opinions, and, as is the way with other people's opinions, they are generally ignored.

14   So if there are no officially appointed guardians for the English language, who sets down all those rules that we all know about from childhood—the idea that we must never end a sentence with a preposition or begin one with a conjunction, that we must use *each other* for two things and *one another* for more than two, and that we must never use *hopefully* in an absolute sense, such as "Hopefully it will not rain tomorrow"? The answer, surprisingly often, is that no one does, that when you look into the background of these "rules" there is often little basis for them.

15   Consider the curiously persistent notion that sentences should not end with a preposition. The source of this stricture, and several other equally dubious ones, was one Robert Lowth, an eighteenth-century clergyman and amateur grammarian whose *A Short Introduction to English Grammar,* published in 1762, enjoyed a long and distressingly influential life both in his native England and abroad. It is to Lowth we can trace many a pedant's most treasured notions: the belief that you must say *different from* rather than than *different to* or *different than,* the idea that two negatives make a positive, the rule that you must not say "the heaviest of the two objects," but rather "the heavier," the distinction between *shall* and *will,* and the clearly nonsensical belief that *between* can apply only to two things and *among* to more than two. (By this reasoning, it would not be possible to say that St. Louis is between New York, Los Angeles, and Chicago, but rather that it is among them, which would impart a quite different sense.) Perhaps the most remarkable and curiously enduring of Lowth's many beliefs was the conviction that sentences ought not to end with a preposition. But even he was not didactic about it. He recognized that ending a sentence with a preposition was idiomatic and common in both speech and informal writing. He suggested only that he thought it generally better and more graceful, not crucial, to place the preposition before its relative "in solemn and elevated" writing. Within a hundred years this had been converted from a piece of questionable advice into an immutable rule. In a remarkable outburst of literal-mindedness, nineteenth-century academics took it as read that the very name *pre-position* meant it must come before something—anything.

16   But then this was a period of the most resplendent silliness, when grammarians and scholars seemed to be climbing over one another (or each other; it doesn't really matter) in a mad scramble to come up with fresh absurdities. This was the age when, it was gravely insisted, Shakespeare's *laughable* ought to be changed to *laugh-at-able* and *reliable* should be made into *relionable*. Dozens of seemingly unexceptional words—*lengthy, standpoint, international, colonial, brash*—were attacked with venom because of some supposed etymological deficiency or other. Thomas de Quincey, in between bouts of opium taking, found time to attack the expression *what on earth*. Some people wrote *mooned* for *lunatic* and *foresayer* for *prophet* on the grounds that the new words were Anglo-Saxon and thus somehow

more pure. They roundly castigated those ignoramuses who impurely combined Greek and Latin roots into new words like *petroleum* (Latin *petro* + Greek *oleum*). In doing so, they failed to note that the very word with which they described themselves, *grammarians,* is itself a hybrid made of Greek and Latin roots, as are many other words that have lived unexceptionably in English for centuries. They even attacked *handbook* as an ugly Germanic compound when it dared to show its face in the nineteenth century, failing to notice that it was a good Old English word that had simply fallen out of use. It is one of the felicities of English that we can take pieces of words from all over and fuse them into new constructions—like *trusteeship,* which consists of a Nordic stem (*trust*), combined with a French affix (*ee*), married to an Old English root (*ship*). Other languages cannot do this. We should be proud of ourselves for our ingenuity and yet even now authorities commonly attack almost any new construction as ugly or barbaric.

17   Today in England you can still find authorities attacking the construction *different than* as a regrettable Americanism, insisting that a sentence such as "How different things appear in Washington than in London" is ungrammatical and should be changed to "How different things appear in Washington from how they appear in London." Yet *different than* has been common in England for centuries and used by such exalted writers as Defoe, Addison, Steele, Dickens, Coleridge, and Thackeray, among others. Other authorities, in both Britain and America, continue to deride the absolute use of *hopefully. The New York Times Manual of Style and Usage* flatly forbids it. Its writers must not say, "Hopefully the sun will come out soon," but rather are instructed to resort to a clumsily passive and periphrastic construction such as "It is to be hoped that the sun will come out soon." The reason? The authorities maintain that *hopefully* in the first sentence is a misplaced modal auxiliary—that it doesn't belong to any other part of the sentence. Yet they raise no objection to dozens of other words being used in precisely the same unattached way—*admittedly, mercifully, happily, curiously,* and so on. The reason *hopefully* is not allowed is because, well, because somebody at the *New York Times* once had a boss who wouldn't allow it because his professor had forbidden it, because *his* father thought it was ugly and inelegant, because *he* had been told so by his uncle who was a man of great learning . . . and so on.

18   Considerations of what makes for good English or bad English are to an uncomfortably large extent matters of prejudice and conditioning. Until the eighteenth century it was correct to say "you was" if you were referring to one person. It sounds odd today, but the logic is impeccable. *Was* is a singular verb and *were* a plural one. Why should *you* take a plural verb when the sense is clearly singular? The answer—surprise, surprise—is that Robert Lowth didn't like it. "I'm hurrying, are I not?" is hopelessly ungrammatical, but "I'm hurrying, aren't I?"—merely a contraction of the same words—is perfect English. *Many* is almost always a plural (as in "Many people were there"), but not when it is followed by *a,* as in "Many a man was there." There's no inherent reason why these things should be so. They are not defensible in terms of grammar. They are because they are.

19   Nothing illustrates the scope of prejudice in English between than the issue of the split infinitive. Some people feel ridiculously strong about it. When the British

Conservative politician Jock Bruce-Gardyne was economic secretary to the Treasury in the early 1980s, he returned unread any departmental correspondence containing a split infinitive. (It should perhaps be pointed out that a split infinitive is one in which an adverb comes between *to* and a verb, as in *to quickly look.*) I can think of two very good reasons for not splitting an infinitive.

1. Because you feel that the rulers of English ought to conform to the grammatical precepts of a language that died a thousand years ago.
2. Because you wish to cling to a pointless affectation of usage that is without the support of any recognized authority of the last 200 years, even at the cost of composing sentences that are ambiguous, inelegant, and patently contorted.

20   It is exceedingly difficult to find any authority who condemns the split infinitive   Theodore Bernstein, H. W. Fowler, Ernest Gowers, Eric Partridge, Rudolph Flesch, Wilson Follett, Roy H. Copperud, and others too tedious to enumerate here all agree that there is no logical reason not to split an infinitive. Otto Jespersen even suggests that, strictly speaking, it isn't actually possible to split an infinitive. As he puts it: "'To' . . . is no more an essential part of an infinitive than the definite article is an essential part of a nominative, and no one would think of calling 'the good man' a split nominative." [*Growth and Structure of the English Language,* page 222]

21   Lacking an academy as we do, we might expect dictionaries to take up the banner of defenders of the language, but in recent years they have increasingly shied away from the role. A perennial argument with dictionary makers is whether they should be *prescriptive* (that is, whether they should prescribe how language should be used) or *descriptive* (that is, merely describe how it is used without taking a position). The most notorious example of the descriptive school was the 1961 *Webster's Third New International Dictionary* (popularly called *Webster's Unabridged),* whose editor, Philip Gove, believed that distinctions of usage were elitist and artificial. As a result, usages such as *imply* as a synonym for *infer* and *flout* being used in the sense of *flaunt* were included without comment. The dictionary provoked further antagonism, particularly among members of the U.S. Trademark Association, by refusing to capitalize trademarked words. But what really excited outrage was its remarkable contention that *ain't* was "used orally in most parts of the U.S. by many cultivated speakers."

22   So disgusted was the *New York Times* with the new dictionary that it announced it would not use it but would continue with the 1934 edition, prompting the language authority Bergen Evans to write: "Anyone who solemnly announces in the year 1962 that he will be guided in matters of English usage by a dictionary published in 1934 is talking ignorant and pretentious nonsense," and he pointed out that the issue of the *Times* announcing the decision contained nineteen words condemned by the *Second International.*

23   Since then, other dictionaries have been divided on the matter. *The American Heritage Dictionary,* first published in 1969, instituted a usage panel of distinguished commentators to rule on contentious points of usage, which are discussed, often at some length, in the text. But others have been more equivocal (or prudent

or spineless depending on how you view it). The revised *Random House Dictionary of the English Language,* published in 1987, accepts the looser meaning for most words, though often noting that the newer usage is frowned on "by many"—a curiously timid approach that at once acknowledges the existence of expert opinion and yet constantly places it at a distance. Among the looser meanings it accepts are *disinterested* to mean *uninterested* and *infer* to mean *imply.* It even accepts the existence of *kudo* as a singular—prompting a reviewer from *Time Magazine* to ask if one instance of pathos should now be a patho.

24   It's a fine issue. One of the undoubted virtues of English is that it is a fluid and democratic language in which meanings shift and change in response to the pressures of common usage rather than the dictates of committees. It is a natural process that has been going on for centuries. To interfere with that process is arguably both arrogant and futile, since clearly the weight of usage will push new meanings into currency no matter how many authorities hurl themselves into the path of change.

25   But at the same time, it seems to me, there is a case for resisting change—at least slapdash change. Even the most liberal descriptivist would accept that there must be *some* conventions of usage. WE must agree to spell *cat* c-a-t and not e-l-e-p-h-a-n-t, and we must agree that by that word we mean a small furry quadruped that goes *meow* and sits comfortably on one's lap and not a large lumbering beast that grows tusks and is exceedingly difficult to housebreak. In precisely the same way, clarity is generally better served if we agree to observe a distinction between *imply* and *infer, forego* and *forgo, fortuitous* and *fortunate, uninterested* and *disinterested,* and many others. As John Ciardi observed, resistance may in the end prove futile, but at least it tests the changes and makes them prove their worth.

26   Perhaps for our last words on the subject of usage we should turn to the last words of the venerable French grammarian Dominique Bonhours, who proved on his deathbed that a grammarian's work is never done when he turned to those gathered loyally around him and whispered: "I am about to—or I am going to—die; either expression is used."

THINKING CRITICALLY

1. How did early grammarians help shape the rules of current usage? According to Bryson, how did they contribute to some of the idiosyncrasies of English rules? Give some examples of rules that do not work.

2. Given all the anomalies in the English language, what is the author suggesting about standards of usage? How does his discussion make you feel about your own lapses in grammar?

3. What, according to Bryson, is the difference between "good English" and "bad English"? What is his basis of distinction? Do you agree with his views?

4. Bryson reports that for centuries grammarians called for the official regulation of English usage. What fundamental attitudes about language did these proposals underscore? What about the attitude of Thomas Jefferson and John Priestly? Where does Bryson stand on the issue of regulation?

5. What kind of personality does Bryson project in this essay? In other words, based on his tone, word choice, his style, the examples he chooses, his comments, and so on, how would you describe him?

6. What examples of Bryson's sense of humor can you point to? How does his humor contribute to the essay? Is this a strategy you might employ in your writing?

7. How would you evaluate Bryson's own use of English? How might Bryson respond to the criticism that while defending nonstandard usage, his own writing strictly obeys the rules of traditional usage?

WRITING ASSIGNMENTS

1. Do you think that dictionaries should be *prescriptive* instead of *descriptive*—that is, should they take a position on the traditional rules of proper grammar, usage, and spelling? Write a letter to Bill Bryson explaining how you feel about this and give three specific reasons.

2. Have you ever been bothered by someone's poor grammar or usage? If so, describe in a brief essay your experience and your feelings. Has this essay affected your attitude at all? Explain.

3. If you heard the president or some other official make grammatical and usage errors in an interview, would that affect your view of that person? Would it make him or her seem less deserving of your respect or seem more down-to-earth? Write out your thoughts in an essay, perhaps citing some examples of faulty presidential usage you've found on your own.

■ MAKING CONNECTIONS

1. As best you can, try to describe your own English usage. Do you think that you speak "good English"? How would the various authors from this section respond to your form of usage? Explain.

2. Now that you have read the different perspectives concerning "standard English," write an essay on where you stand on the issue. Do you think we need language guardians such as John Simon? Is English a changing and malleable medium to which we must adapt according to popular opinion? Do we have a right to use whatever form of English we choose? What is your opinion?

3. Consider the English language education you received in school. Was it prescriptive, or did it allow for more flexibility? Did you learn the rules of grammar and sentence structure? Has this instruction helped you in your daily life? Was your academic language useful to you as a writer and thinker, or has it proven largely unnecessary? Explain.

4. What is the difference between "good English" and "real English"? In your opinion, should one be used in certain cases and not in others? Explain.

5. Do you think you have an accent? Can you hear yourself speak it? Do you know anyone who claims not to have an accent? What do they mean? Are they accurate in their assessment of their speech? Write an essay in which you explore the concept of the accent in your local area and the way people react to speech. Is one way of speaking considered more educated or intelligent than another?

■ CASE STUDY: ENGLISH ONLY OR BILINGUALISM?

The question of whether America should have an official language is highly controversial. On one side is the fear that racism and xenophobia motivate the English-only movement. The English-only movement is particularly troubling for many Spanish-speaking areas of the country, such as California, the southwest, and Florida. Hispanic opponents to the movement fear that laws forbidding the use of Spanish on voting ballots, in marriage ceremonies, and in the classroom would only further violate their civil liberties. On the other side of the argument, English-only proponents insist that linguistic divisions prevent national unity, isolate ethnic groups, and reinforce the economic disparagement between the haves and the have-nots. They are quick to point out that bilingual programs in other countries such as Canada and Belgium have only led to unrest. Furthermore, they argue that laws providing bilingual education, such as the one in California, provide little inducement of non-English speakers to participate in mainstream American culture, preventing them from pursuing higher education and professional employment. As you read the articles in this Case Study, think about the issue of bilingual education—especially as it applies to Spanish-speaking groups—and the concept of a national language.

Bilingualism in America: English Should Be the Only Language
S. I. Hayakawa

> The late S. I. Hayakawa was a leading advocate of the English-only movement. A former U.S. senator from California and a professor of linguistics who published several books on language, Hayakaya was born in Vancouver, British Columbia, to Japanese parents. Hayakawa served as honorary chairman of U.S. English, a public-interest organization based in Washington, D.C., that is working to establish English as the nation's only official language.
>
> In the essay that follows, Hayakawa explains why he feels that English must be the only recognized official language of the United States. This article originally appeared in *USA Today* magazine in July of 1989, by which time English had been made the official language in 17 states.

1 During the dark days of World War II, Chinese immigrants in California wore badges proclaiming their original nationality so they would not be mistaken for Japanese. In fact, these two immigrant groups long had been at odds with each other. However, as new English-speaking generations came along, the Chinese and Japanese began to communicate with one another. They found they had much in common and began to socialize. Today, they get together and form Asian-American societies.

2   Such are the amicable results of sharing the English language. English unites us as Americans—immigrants and native-born alike. Communicating with each other in a single, common tongue encourages trust, while reducing racial hostility and bigotry.

3   My appreciation of English has led me to devote my retirement years to championing it. Several years ago, I helped to establish U.S. English, a Washington, D.C.-based public interest group that seeks an amendment to the U.S. Constitution declaring English our official language, regardless of what other languages we may use unofficially.

4   As an immigrant to this nation, I am keenly aware of the things that bind us as Americans and unite us as a single people. Foremost among these unifying forces is the common language we share. While it is certainly true that our love of freedom and devotion to democratic principles help to unite and give as a mutual purpose, it is English, our common language, that enables us to discuss our views and allows us to maintain a well-informed electorate, the cornerstone of democratic government.

5   Because we are a nation of immigrants, we do not share the characteristics of race, religion, ethnicity, or native language which form the common bonds of society in other countries. However, by agreeing to learn and use a single, universally spoken language, we have been able to forge a unified people from an incredibly diverse population.

6   Although our 200-year history should be enough to convince any skeptic of the powerful unifying effects of a common language, some still advocate the official recognition of other languages. They argue that a knowledge of English is not part of the formula for responsible citizenship in this country.

7   Some contemporary political leaders, like the former mayor of Miami, Maurice Ferre, maintain that "Language is not necessary to the system. Nowhere does our Constitution say that English is our language." He also told the *Tampa Tribune* that, "Within ten years there will not be a single word of English spoken [in Miami]—English is not Miami's official language—[and] one day residents will have to learn Spanish or leave."

8   The U.S. Department of Education also reported that countless speakers at a conference on bilingual education "expounded at length on the need for and eventually of, a multilingual, multicultural United States of America with a national language policy citing English and Spanish as the two 'legal languages.'"

9   As a former resident of California, I am completely familiar with a system that uses two official languages, and I would not advise any nation to move in such a direction unless forced to do so. While it is true that India functions with ten official languages, I haven't heard anyone suggest that it functions particularly well because of its multilingualism. In fact, most Indians will concede that the situation is a chaotic mess which has led to countless problems in the government's efforts to manage the nation's business. Out of necessity, English still is used extensively in India as a common language.

10   Belgium is another clear example of the diverse effects of two officially recognized languages in the same nation. Linguistic differences between Dutch- and French-speaking citizens have resulted in chronic political instability. Conse-

quently, in the aftermath of the most recent government collapse, legislators are working on a plan to turn over most of its powers and responsibilities to the various regions, a clear recognition of the diverse effects of linguistic separateness.

11   There are other problems. Bilingualism is a costly and confusing bureaucratic nightmare. The Canadian government has estimated its bilingual costs to be nearly $400,000,000 per year. It is almost certain that these expenses will increase as a result of a massive expansion of bilingual services approved by the Canadian Parliament in 1988. In the United States, which has ten times the population of Canada, the cost of similar bilingual services easily would be in the billions.

12   We first should consider how politically infeasible it is that our nation ever could recognize Spanish as a second official language without opening the floodgates for official recognition of the more than 100 languages spoken in this country. How long would it take, under such an arrangement, before the United States started to make India look like a model of efficiency?

13   Even if we can agree that multilingualism would be a mistake, some would suggest that official recognition of English is not needed. After all, our nation has existed for over 200 years without this, and English as our common language has continued to flourish.

14   I could agree with this sentiment had government continued to adhere to its time-honored practice of operating in English and encouraging newcomers to learn the language. However, this is not the case. Over the last few decades, government has been edging slowly towards policies that place other languages on a par with English.

15   In reaction to the cultural consciousness movement of the 1960s and 1970s, government has been increasingly reluctant to press immigrants to learn the English language, lest it be accused of "cultural imperialism." Rather than insisting that it is the immigrant's duty to learn the language of this country, the government has acted instead as if it has a duty to accommodate an immigrant in his native language.

16   A prime example of this can be found in the continuing debate over Federal and state policies relating to bilingual education. At times, these have come dangerously close to making the main goal of this program the maintenance of the immigrant child's native language, rather than the early acquisition of English.

17   As a former U.S. senator from California, where we spend more on bilingual education programs than any other state, I am very familiar with both the rhetoric and reality that lie behind the current debate on bilingual education. My experience has convinced me that many of these programs are shortchanging immigrant children in their quest to learn English.

18   To set the record straight from the start, I do not oppose bilingual education *if it is truly bilingual.* Employing a child's native language to teach him (or her) English is entirely appropriate. What is not appropriate is continuing to use the children of Hispanic and other immigrant groups as guinea pigs in an unproven program that fails to teach English efficiently and perpetuates their dependency on their native language.

19   Under the dominant method of bilingual education used throughout this country, non-English-speaking students are taught all academic subjects such as math,

science, and history exclusively in their native language. English is taught as a separate subject. The problem with this method is that there is no objective way to measure whether a child has learned enough English to be placed in classes where academic instruction is entirely in English. As a result, some children have been kept in native language classes for six years.

20 Some bilingual education advocates, who are more concerned with maintaining the child's use of their native language, may not see any problem with such a situation. However, those who feel that the most important goal of this program is to get children functioning quickly in English appropriately are alarmed.

21 In the Newhall School District in California, some Hispanic parents are raising their voices in criticism of its bilingual education program, which relies on native language instruction. Their children complain of systematically being segregated from their English-speaking peers. Now in high school, these students cite the failure of the program to teach them English first as the reason for being years behind their classmates.

22 Even more alarming is the Berkeley (Calif.) Unified School District, where educators have recognized that all-native-language instruction would be an inadequate response to the needs of their non-English-speaking pupils. Challenged by a student body that spoke more than four different languages and by budgetary constraints, teachers and administrators responded with innovative language programs that utilized many methods of teaching English. That school district is now in court answering charges that the education they provided was inadequate because it did not provide transitional bilingual education for every non-English speaker. What was introduced 20 years ago as an experimental project has become—despite inconclusive research evidence—the only acceptable method of teaching for bilingual education advocates.

23 When one considers the nearly 50 percent dropout rate among Hispanic students (the largest group receiving this type of instruction), one wonders about their ability to function in the English-speaking mainstream of this country. The school system may have succeeded wonderfully in maintaining their native language, but if it failed to help them to master the English language fully, what is the benefit?

Alternatives

24 If this method of bilingual education is not the answer, are we forced to return to the old, discredited, sink-or-swim approach? No, we are not, since, as shown in Berkeley and other school districts, there are a number of alternative methods that have been proven effective, while avoiding the problems of all-native-language instruction.

25 Sheltered English and English as a Second Language (ESL) are just two programs that have helped to get children quickly proficient in English. Yet, political recognition of the viability of alternate methods has been slow in coming. In 1988, we witnessed the first crack in the monolithic hold that native language instruction has had on bilingual education funds at the Federal level. In its reauthorization of Federal bilingual education, Congress voted to increase the percentage of funds available for alternate methods from four to 25 percent of the total. This is a great

breakthrough, but we should not be satisfied until 100 percent of the funds are available for any program that effectively and quickly can get children functioning in English, regardless of the amount of native language instruction it uses.

26   My goal as a student of language and a former educator is to see all students succeed academically, no matter what language is spoken in their homes. I want to see immigrant students finish their high school education and be able to compete for college scholarships. To help achieve this goal, instruction in English should start as early as possible. Students should be moved into English mainstream classes in one or, at the very most, two years. They should not continue to be segregated year after year from their English-speaking peers.

27   Another highly visible shift in Federal policy that I feel demonstrates quite clearly the eroding support of government for our common language is the requirement for bilingual voting ballots. Little evidence ever has been presented to show the need for ballots in other languages. Even prominent Hispanic organizations acknowledge that more than 90 percent of native-born Hispanics currently are fluent in English and more than half of that population is English monolingual.

28   Furthermore, if the proponents of bilingual ballots are correct when they claim that the absence of native language ballots prevents non-English-speaking citizens from exercising their right to vote, then current requirements are clearly unfair because they provide assistance to certain groups of voters while ignoring others. Under current Federal law, native language ballots are required only for certain groups: those speaking Spanish, Asian, or Native American languages. European or African immigrants are not provided ballots in their native language, even in jurisdictions covered by the Voting Rights Act.

29   As sensitive as Americans have been to racism, especially since the days of the Civil Rights Movement, no one seems to have noticed the profound racism expressed in the amendment that created the "bilingual ballot." Brown people, like Mexicans and Puerto Ricans; red people, like American Indians; and yellow people, like the Japanese and Chinese, are assumed not to be smart enough to learn English. No provision is made, however, for non-English-speaking French-Canadians in Maine or Vermont, or Yiddish-speaking Hassidic Jews in Brooklyn, who are white and thus presumed to be able to learn English without difficulty.

30   Voters in San Francisco encountered ballots in Spanish and Chinese for the first time in the elections of 1980, much to their surprise, since authorizing legislation had been passed by Congress with almost no debate, roll-call vote, or public discussion. Naturalized Americans, who had taken the trouble to learn English to become citizens, were especially angry and remain so. While native language ballots may be a convenience to some voters, the use of English ballots does not deprive citizens of their right to vote. Under current voting law, non-English-speaking voters are permitted to bring a friend or family member to the polls to assist them in casting their ballots. Absentee ballots could provide another method that would allow a voter to receive this help at home.

31   Congress should be looking for other methods to create greater access to the ballot box for the currently small number of citizens who cannot understand an

English ballot, without resorting to the expense of requiring ballots in foreign languages. We cannot continue to overlook the message we are sending to immigrants about the connection between English language ability and citizenship when we print ballots in other languages. The ballot is the primary symbol of civic duty. When we tell immigrants that they should learn English—yet offer them full voting participation in their native language—I fear our actions will speak louder than our words.

32   If we are to prevent the expansion of policies such as these, moving us further along the multilingual path, we need to make a strong statement that our political leaders will understand. We must let them know that we do not choose to reside in a "Tower of Babel." Making English our nation's official language *by law* will send the proper signal to newcomers about the importance of learning English and provide the necessary guidance to legislators to preserve our traditional policy of a common language.

THINKING CRITICALLY

1. Why does Hayakawa feel it is particularly important for a nation of immigrants to communicate in a single, common tongue? Does the fact that he is an immigrant himself lend credence to his argument? Do you agree with this viewpoint? Why or why not?

2. What is Hayakawa's assessment of countries that recognize two or more official languages? From what you know of multilingual countries, do you tend to agree or disagree with his assessment?

3. How does Hayakawa define bilingual education? What does he feel is its biggest flaw? Drawing from your own experience, do you agree with him? Explain your answer.

4. What alternative to current bilingual education does Hayakawa suggest? Do his alternatives seem like reasonable and feasible solutions?

Exploring the Language of V I S U A L S

"Please Do Not Feed Pigeons"

In countries that are officially bilingual or multilingual, it is not uncommon to see signs featuring more than one language. In many cities and regions of the United States, signs are written in both English and Spanish. Consider the impact of language both on the individual people who speak it and our society as a whole. How do we "read the signs" in our culture? The sign featured below is posted in the Chinatown section of San Francisco, California.

THINKING CRITICALLY

1. Besides the literal meaning of the words, what does this sign convey about the people who live in the neighborhood in which it is posted?

2. The sign featured here communicates a message in English and Chinese, for the convenience of the residents of the area who speak Chinese. In Quebec, many citizens want to bar all English words from signs entirely, in the name of preserving the integrity of the French language. In your opinion, is English "threatened" by this sign? Why or why not?

3. What difficulties might the United States face if an "English-only" policy for signs was adopted nationally? Or could such a measure create more problems than it would solve? Explain.

Let's Not Say Adiós to Bilingual Education

Lourdes Rovira

In June of 1998, California voters passed Proposition 227, terminating bilingual education in that state. Although supporters of bilingual education blamed politicians, educators, and the white power structure for this decision, opinion polls indicated that a significant number of Hispanics themselves had doubts about bilingual education. Since then, several other states followed suit. In 2002, Massachusetts Governor Mitt Romney made the debate over bilingual education a major issue of his election campaign. He promised to make "English only" a priority educational initiative.

In the next article, Lourdes Rovira, the executive director for bilingual education for the Miami-Dade County school system, criticizes the California vote. According to Rivera, denying students the option of bilingual education isn't simply a poor educational decision; it is an outright injustice.

1   A great travesty occurred in California on June 2, 1998. By passing Proposition 227, California's voters elected to terminate bilingual education in their state. It was a sad day for our country because we allowed ill-informed politicians and xenophobic voters to dictate educational policy.

2   The United States is a country of immigrants—immigrants who have come seeking freedom and the pursuit of the American dream. Throughout history, English has been the common language that has united these immigrants from all over the world. English is the language of this great country. None of us who support bilingual education question the validity or the importance of the English language, as some would like the public to believe. Quality bilingual programs emphasize the acquisition of English. English is taught to all immigrant students; it is required, and we aim to perfect it in the school setting.

3   Yet to learn English, students need not forget the language they bring to school with them—be it Spanish, Vietnamese, or Urdu. Bilingual education is not like an antibiotic that we give to children who are sick, their illness being lack of English. As soon as the children are well, that is, as soon as they know English, the antibiotic—bilingual education—is removed. Good bilingual programs are not remedial but enrichment programs.

4   One common misunderstanding is that bilingual education is the exclusive domain of immigrant students. No, studying a second language is a right that belongs to all students—recently arrived refugees, African Americans, and, yes, white Americans. Languages expand a child's cognitive development. Knowing more than one language is not an impediment to intellectual capacity. If it were, the rest

Lourdes Rovira, "Let's Not Say Adiós to Bilingual Education." Reprinted by permission of *U. S. Catholic* magazine (http://www.uscatholic.org). *U. S. Catholic* is published by The Claretians.

of the world's children outside of the United States would be intellectually inferior to ours. After all, the majority of them are bilingual.

5   Years ago, being bilingual was a privilege reserved for those who could afford to send their children to private tutors or to a finishing school in Europe. It was a privilege reserved for those who traveled and went to the opera. In today's global economy, being bilingual can no longer remain a privilege reserved for the elite. Today, being bilingual is a right that must transcend all socioeconomic strata. Denying all students that right is not only a mistake, it is an injustice.

6   Students are enabled—not disabled—by being bilingual; they are empowered by knowing more than one language. The American experience is strengthened, not weakened, by citizens who can cross languages and cultures. The United States can no longer afford to remain a monolingual country in a multilingual world. Being bilingual and biliterate not only gives people a political and economic advantage, it also allows them to be bridges between people of different cultures.

7   For immigrant students, being bilingual means having the best of two worlds—their home culture and language and our nation's culture and English language. For native speakers of English, knowing a second language means opening up their horizons to the richness of cultural diversity and becoming active participants in—and not merely spectators of—today's global society. In no way does it require supplanting one language and culture with another.

8   This may come as a surprise to many, but bilingual education is not a recent phenomenon in this country. Its history in the U.S. falls into two distinct periods: the first from 1840 to 1920 and the second beginning in the early 1960s.

9   In 1840 a form of bilingual education originated in Cincinnati with a state law designed to draw German children into the American schools. Several other similar initiatives, which provided instruction in Dutch, Italian, and Polish, among others, took place during the latter part of the 19th century and the beginning of the 20th. During World War I, strong anti-German sentiments increased, and by the end of the war bilingual programs were terminated and "Americanism" and English-only instruction were promoted. Some states went so far as to impose restrictions on the instruction of foreign languages.

10   Instruction in and through two languages disappeared in the U.S. from 1920 until 1963, when thousands of Cuban refugees poured into the Miami area, opening up a second phase of bilingual schooling in this country. In an effort to meet the needs of the Cuban refugee children, the Miami-Dade County Public Schools organized a dual-language instructional program at Coral Way Elementary with a student population evenly divided between Spanish speakers and English speakers. Both groups spent half of their day being instructed in English and the other half in Spanish, thus immersing themselves in two languages and cultures.

11   Since then, federal and state laws and court decisions have not only allowed but directed local school districts to create special programs to meet the academic needs of non-English-speaking students. But almost 30 years after the passing of the Bilingual Education Act, the debate over the benefits of bilingual education continues to be politically and emotionally charged. Also lingering after 30 years

seems to be a dreadful ignorance over the definition of bilingual education and its goals and practices. Those who make for themselves a political agenda over the issue attack bilingual education as a failure based on a very limited knowledge of one specific bilingual-education model while ignoring others that have been extremely successful, not only in this country but throughout the world.

12   Critics of bilingual education who regard it as a dismal failure claim that children enrolled in bilingual programs do not learn English and that the research regarding the benefits of bilingual programs is contradictory and inconsistent. They assert that immersion programs are superior to bilingual programs and believe that after one year of English immersion, non-English-speaking students will be ready to be mainstreamed into regular, English-speaking classes.

13   Much of educational policy, whether it is bilingual education or reading, stems from pendulum swings from one extreme to another. Unfortunately, immersion programs have failed to prove a successful track record. To wipe out bilingual programs in favor of a sink-or-swim curriculum is a simplistic political solution to a complex educational issue. Moreover, it hardly seems fair to blame bilingual education for all the ills of California's 1.4 million limited-English-proficient students when less than 30 percent of them are enrolled in bilingual programs.

14   Those of us who have dedicated our professional lives to the promotion of bilingual education can assert that properly organized and executed bilingual programs not only work, they work extremely well. This does not mean that some bilingual models cannot be improved. However, there is ample research that demonstrates without a doubt that good bilingual programs are successful—and none that could claim such success for one-year immersion programs.

15   The school district I work for, Miami-Dade County Public Schools, the fourth largest in the country, has been in the forefront of bilingual education since the establishment of Coral Way Elementary in 1963. Our programs are recognized nationally and internationally as programs that promote excellence in English and another language for all students who want to avail themselves of that opportunity.

16   Bilingual programs in our district provide instruction in English for Speakers of Other Languages (ESOL) to students with limited English proficiency as soon as they enroll in school. Students are provided instruction in their home language for approximately 20 percent of the instructional time, but the primary goal is the rapid acquisition of English. At the same time, Miami-Dade County Public Schools embrace diversity and offer all our students the opportunity to enroll in quality programs that promote literacy in a language other than English. We promote high standards for all of our students whether the instruction is in English, Spanish, Haitian-Creole, or French.

17   As the waves beat against the shore and drag everything in sight, it sometimes seems that whenever California voters make an earthshaking decision at the polls, the rest of the country wants to follow suit. How will California's decision affect bilingual education in the rest of the country? Thankfully, the Miami-Dade County Public Schools and districts in many other states (e.g., New York, New Jersey, and Connecticut) have no interest in eliminating bilingual education. Bilingual education is viewed as quintessential to living in this part of the country. In South

Florida, and much of the rest of the world for that matter, being bilingual and biliterate is not a liability but an asset.

18   Bilingualism not only prepares students for today's increasingly global economy and promotes cognitive development and creative thinking, it also instills pride. And, as a Catholic, I would also argue that bilingualism is rooted in gospel values and based on justice. What position should Catholics, and Christians in general, take in the continuing public debate of this issue? It seems to me that we are called to be more informed and passionate toward immigrants than the average California voter.

19   In 1963 Pope John XXIII addressed the treatment of minorities in his encyclical letter Pacem in terris (On Peace on Earth): "It is especially in keeping with the principles of justice that effective measures be taken by civil authorities to improve the lot of the citizens of an ethnic minority, particularly when that betterment concerns their language [and] . . . their ancestral customs." Language, notes a document of the Southeast Regional Office for Hispanic Ministry in Miami, "expresses the soul of the people."

20   The 1985 Vatican-sponsored World Congress on the Pastoral of Emigration observed in its final document: "Experience has shown that the inability of expression in the mother tongue and the elimination of religious traditions greatly damage the conscience, impoverish the cultural surroundings, provoke separation and even schism, and reduce the numbers of the faithful."

21   Those who question the need for bilingual education are often the same people who question why Masses have to be said in Spanish. Perhaps the words of Pope Paul VI in his 1975 apostolic exhortation Evangelii nuntiandi can do a better job of persuading them than those of us in bilingual education have been able to do: "Evangelization loses much of its force and effectiveness if it does not take into consideration the actual people to whom it is addressed, if it does not use their language, their signs and symbols, if it does not answer the questions they ask, and if it does not have an impact on their particular lives. . . . The split between the gospel and culture is without a doubt the drama of our time, just as it was of other times."

22   It is unfortunate that California's Proposition 227 passed. It is revolting that bilingual education has been killed at the hands of people who do not understand its virtues. It is offensive that bilingual education continues to be solely associated with immigration. And it is shameful that we have forgotten that when this nation was founded, English was not the exclusive language of the country.

23   Unlike the western waves, Florida's waves are of a different nature. They embrace the shores with the linguistic plurality needed to fortify the shores, not destroy them.

THINKING CRITICALLY

1. Do you think that the option of bilingual education should be a right? In light of the fact that Spanish is the second-most-spoken language in the United States, should it be a legally protected option for all children of Hispanic descent?

2. Rovira asserts that the vote was driven by xenophobic motives. What does she mean by this? Explain.

3. In the third paragraph, Rovira states that students shouldn't forget their native language whether it is "Spanish, Vietnamese, or Urdu." Do you think she is advocating that bilingual programs be established for languages other than Spanish?

4. Evaluate Rovira's comparison of the right to learn other languages in school to the principles of bilingual education. How do you think Hayakawa, Morales, and Kuntz would respond to her statement?

A Nation Divided by One Language
James Crawford

Over the last five years, many states have overturned bilingual education programs in favor of "English Only" programs. Many opponents of bilingual education express concerns that bilingual programs are ineffective, prevent mainstreaming children into the educational system, and put children at a disadvantage. In the next article, bilingual education specialist James Crawford explains that overturning bilingual education programs has less to do with helping children, and more to do with the political and cultural fears of its opponents.

James Crawford is a former editor of *Education Week* and a writer and lecturer on the politics of language. He is the author of several books on language and politics, most recently, *Bilingual Education: History, Politics, Theory, and Practice* (1999), and *At War with Diversity: U.S. Language Policy in an Age of Anxiety* (2000). This editorial first appeared in the British newspaper, *The Guardian*, on March 8, 2001.

1 "If you live in America, you need to speak English." According to a *Los Angeles Times* poll, that was how three out of four voters explained their support for Proposition 227, the 1998 ballot initiative that dismantled bilingual education in California. Many Arizonans cited the same reason for passing a similar measure (Proposition 203) last year.

2 Ambiguous as it is, this rationale offers some clues about the way Americans think about language. No doubt for some the statement has a patriotic subtext: one flag, one language. Rejecting bilingual education was a way to "send a message" that, in the United States, English and only English is appropriate for use in the public square.

3 Other voters merely seemed intent on restating the obvious. English is so dominant in the US that non-English speakers are at a huge disadvantage. Thus schools must not fail to teach English to children from minority language backgrounds. Students' life chances will depend to a large extent on the level of English literacy skills they achieve.

4 Immigrants have generally understood these truths more keenly than anyone, and behaved accordingly. As the linguist Elnar Haugen observes, "America's profusion of tongues has made her a modern Babel, but a Babel in reverse."

5 There is no reason to think the historic pattern has changed. Although the number of minority language speakers has grown dramatically in recent years, thanks to

a liberalisation of immigration laws in 1965, so has their rate of acculturation. Census figures confirm the paradox. While one in seven US residents now speaks a language other than English at home, bilingualism is also on the rise. A century ago the proportion of non-English speakers was nearly five times as large. As the population becomes increasingly diverse, newcomers seem to be acquiring the national language more rapidly than ever before.

6   The political problem is that many Americans have trouble believing all this. One conservative organisation claims: "Tragically, many immigrants these days refuse to learn English! They never become productive members of society. They remain stuck in a linguistic and economic ghetto, many living off welfare and costing working Americans millions of tax dollars every year."

7   Such perceptions are not uncommon. Perhaps this is because Americans who came of age before the 1970s had little experience of linguistic diversity. Growing up in a period of tight immigration quotas, they seldom encountered anyone speaking a language other than English, except foreign tourists.

8   So today, when Spanish and Vietnamese are heard routinely in public and when bilingual government services in Tagalog and Gujarati are not unknown, some Americans conclude that the hegemony of English is threatened, and perhaps their "way of life" as well. Suddenly they are endorsing coercive measures, as suggested by the US English lobby, to "defend our common language". An English Only movement based on these premises came to prominence in the 80s. Thus far it has succeeded in legislating English as the official language of 23 states, although such declarations have been primarily symbolic, with few legal effects as yet.

9   The campaign's ideological effects have been more significant. In particular English Only agitation has made bilingual schooling a lightning rod for political attacks from people concerned about immigration policy, cultural change and the expansion of minority rights. Debating the best way to teach English to children becomes a form of shadow-boxing that has less to do with pedagogical issues than with questions of social status and political power.

10   It does not help that the pedagogical issues are so poorly understood. Monolinguals tend to regard language learning as a zero-sum game. Any use of children's mother tongue for instruction, the assumption goes, is a diversion from English acquisition. Thus assigning English learners to bilingual classrooms would seem to delay their education.

11   Research has shown that precisely the opposite is true. Far from a waste of learning time, native-language lessons support the process of acquiring a second language while keeping students from falling behind in other subjects.

12   Stephen Krashen, of the University of Southern California, has documented the "transfer" of literacy skills and academic knowledge between various languages even when alphabets differ substantially. "We learn to read by reading, by making sense of what we see on the page," Krashen explains. Thus "it will be much easier to learn to read in a language we already understand." And literacy need not be relearned as additional languages are acquired. "Once you can read, you can read."

13   Other studies confirm that by the time children leave well-structured bilingual programs, typically after four to five years, they are outperforming their counter-

parts in non-bilingual programs, and in some cases students from native-English backgrounds as well. Yet such success stories remain poorly publicised. Until recently bilingual educators have done little to explain their methods and goals, while
14 the US media have become increasingly sceptical. "If all I knew about bilingual education was what I read in the newspapers," says Krashen, "I'd vote against it, too."

Mixed messages have compounded the public relations problem. Bilingual education, which began as an effort to guarantee equal educational opportunities, is increasingly promoted as a form of multicultural enrichment. To counter the English Only mentality, advocates have coined the slogan English Plus. They argue that the US remains an underdeveloped country where language skills are con-
15 cerned. In a global economy more multilingualism, not less, would clearly advance the national interest.

Some English-speaking parents have been receptive to the "bilingual is beautiful" pitch. Over the past decade a growing number have enrolled their children in "dual immersion" classrooms alongside minority children learning English. Yet despite excellent reports on this method of cultivating fluency in two languages, no more than 20,000 English-background students are participating. Compare that
16 with the 300,000 Canadian anglophones in French immersion programmes, in a country with one-tenth the population of the US.

By and large English Plus appeals primarily to language educators and ethnic leaders—that is, to those who already value bilingual skills. Other Americans remain suspicious of the "plus." Most harbour the false impression that bilingual education is primarily about maintaining Hispanic culture. Knowing a foreign language is wonderful, they say, but shouldn't English come first? The US language policy debate rarely seems to get past that question.

THINKING CRITICALLY

1. In paragraph 2, Crawford states that the argument that "if you live in America, you need to speak English," offers some clues about the way Americans think about language. What clues does he think this attitude reveals about language? Explain.

2. What is the author's position on the issue of bilingual education? At what point in his essay is his position clear?

3. Crawford observes that some Americans who are against bilingual education feel that "immigrants these days refuse to learn English." What is the author's position on this belief? Have you heard this argument made in educational, academic, and political discussion? Do you think it is a valid point? Why or why not?

4. According to the author, what are the real political issues behind opposition to bilingual education?

5. What is the relationship between bilingual education and multiculturalism? How has multiculturalism hurt the bilingual movement?

My Spanish Standoff
Gabriella Kuntz

Whereas much of the bilingual education controversy whirls around the language of the class-room, there is another side to the issue—the language spoken in the home. In the next essay, Gabriella Kuntz explains why she chose not to teach her children Spanish or to allow the language to be spoken in the home. In her opinion, English is the language of opportunity, power, and acceptance. Witnessing firsthand the differences between how English-speaking and Spanish-speaking people were treated, she decided to make English the only language spoken in her home, with some surprising reactions from her children. Kuntz, a retired elementary-school teacher, was born in Peru, but lived most of her life in America. This essay appeared in the "My Turn" column of the May 4, 1998, issue of *Newsweek*.

1 Once again my 17-year-old daughter comes home from a foreign-language fair at her high school and accusingly tells me about the pluses of being able to speak two languages. Speaker after speaker has extolled the virtues of becoming fluent in another language. My daughter is frustrated by the fact that I'm bilingual and have purposely declined to teach her to speak Spanish, my native tongue. She is not the only one who has wondered why my children don't speak Spanish. Over the years friends, acquaintances and family have asked me the same question. Teachers have asked my children. My family, of course, has been more judgmental.

2 I was born in Lima, Peru, and came to the United States for the first time in the early '50s, when I was 6 years old. At the parochial school my sister and I attended in Hollywood, Calif., there were only three Hispanic families at the time. I don't know when or how I learned English. I guess it was a matter of survival. My teacher spoke no Spanish. Neither did my classmates. All I can say is that at some point I no longer needed to translate. When I spoke in English I thought in English, and when I spoke in Spanish I thought in Spanish. I also learned about peanut-butter-and-jelly sandwiches, Halloween and Girl Scouts.

3 We went to a high school in Burbank. Again, there were few Hispanic students at the time. My sister and I spoke English without an "accent." This pleased my father no end. He would beam with pleasure when teachers, meeting him and my mother for the first time and hearing their labored English, would comment that they had no idea English was not our native tongue.

4 My brother was born in Los Angeles in 1959, and we would speak both English and Spanish to him. When he began to talk, he would point to an object and say its name in both languages. He was, in effect, a walking, talking English-Spanish dictionary. I have often wondered how his English would have turned out, but circumstances beyond our control prevented it.

5 Because of political changes in Peru in the early '60s (my father being a diplomat), we had to return to Peru. Although we had no formal schooling in Spanish, we were able to communicate in the language. I was thankful my parents had in-

sisted that we speak Spanish at home. At first our relatives said that we spoke Spanish with a slight accent. But over time the accent disappeared, and we became immersed in the culture, our culture. My brother began his schooling in Peru, and even though he attended a school in which English was taught, he speaks the language with an accent. I find that ironic because he was the one born in the United States, and my sister and I are the naturalized citizens.

6   In 1972 I fell in love and married an American who had been living in Peru for a number of years. Our first son was born there, but when he was 6 months old, we came back to the States. My husband was going to get his doctorate at a university in Texas.

7   It was in Texas that, for the first time, I lived in a community with many Hispanics in the United States. I encountered them at the grocery store, the laundry, the mall, church. I also began to see how the Anglos in the community treated them. Of course, I don't mean all, but enough to make me feel uncomfortable. Because I'm dark and have dark eyes and hair, I personally experienced that look, that unspoken and spoken word expressing prejudice. If I entered a department store, one of two things was likely to happen. Either I was ignored, or I was followed closely by the salesperson. The garments I took into the changing room were carefully counted. My check at the grocery store took more scrutiny than an Anglo's. My children were complimented on how "clean" they were instead of how cute. Somehow, all Hispanics seemed to be lumped into the category of illegal immigrants, notwithstanding that many Hispanic families have lived for generations in Texas and other Southwestern states.

8   To be fair, I also noticed that the Latinos lived in their own enclaves, attended their own churches, and many of them spoke English with an accent. And with their roots firmly established in the United States, their Spanish was not perfect either.

9   It was the fact that they spoke neither language well and the prejudice I experienced that prompted my husband and me to decide that English, and English only, would be spoken in our house. By this time my second dark-haired, dark-eyed son had been born, and we did not want to take a chance that if I spoke Spanish to them, somehow their English would be compromised. In other words, they would have an accent. I had learned to speak English without one, but I wasn't sure they would.

10   When our eldest daughter was born in 1980, we were living in southeast Missouri. Again, we decided on an English-only policy. If our children were going to live in the United States, then their English should be beyond reproach. Of course, by eliminating Spanish we have also eliminated part of their heritage. Am I sorry? About the culture, yes; about the language, no. In the Missouri Legislature, there are bills pending for some sort of English-only law. I recently read an article in a national magazine about the Ozarks where some of the townspeople are concerned about the number of Hispanics who have come to work in poultry plants there. It seemed to me that their "concerns" were actually prejudice. There is a definite creeping in of anti-Hispanic sentiment in this country. Even my daughter, yes, the one who is upset over not being bilingual, admits to hearing "Hispanic jokes" said in front of her at school. You see, many don't realize, despite her looks, that she's a minority. I want to believe that her flawless English is a contributing factor.

11   Last summer I took my 10-year-old daughter to visit my brother, who is work-ing in Mexico City. She picked up a few phrases and words with the facility that only the very young can. I just might teach her Spanish. You see, she is fair with light brown hair and blue eyes.

THINKING CRITICALLY

1. In what ways does Kuntz experience prejudice as it is connected to her ethnic background? Is this prejudice linked to her speaking Spanish? In light of the ways she experiences intolerance and suspicion based on her ethnic heritage, why is it ironic that she bans the Spanish language from her home?

2. Besides ethnic prejudice, what other reasons does Kuntz cite supporting her decision to speak only one language to her children?

3. What is the opinion of Kuntz's children regarding her "English-only" decision? Why does her 17-year-old daughter "accusingly" tell her mother of the benefits of speaking a second language? Why is Kuntz considering teaching her 10-year-old daughter Spanish? Explain.

■ MAKING CONNECTIONS

1. Write an essay supporting or opposing an amendment to the U.S. Constitution making English the official language.

2. A national language is the language of public discourse, control, and power. Do you think that English instruction for non-English-speaking children should be left to chance or be ap-proached by early, intensive instruction in school? Write a paper in which you explore your thoughts on this question. Consider in your discussion the effects of home language and cul-ture on personal pride.

3. One argument against bilingual education is that language-minority children cannot be sepa-rated from language-majority speakers if they are to enjoy the maximum benefits of public-school education. The argument further maintains that if children are taught separately, they will never properly integrate into blended classrooms and later the professional community. Write a paper in which you take a stand for or against this argument.

4. Lipka cites several articles appearing in *The Atlantic Monthly* on the issue of bilingual educa-tion. Read some of the articles she summarizes:

    Immigration, How It Is Affecting Us: <http://www.theatlantic.com/politics/immigrat/fallowf.htm>
    The Case Against Bilingual Education: <http://www.theatlantic.com/issues/98may/biling.htm>
    Should English Be the Law?: <http://www.theatlantic.com/issues/97apr/english.htm>

    Select one of the articles and respond to the argument it makes, citing information from the article, research gathered from other articles and essays in this section, and your personal experience.

5. An argument in favor of bilingual education is that mother-tongue instruction increases cul-tural and ethnic pride of the heritage of the mother country. Immigrant children are allowed to

take pride in their home culture, while learning in their native tongue. Write a paper in which you explore your feelings on this pro-bilingual perspective.

6. Contact some local schools and ask what bilingual programs they have. If possible, interview some teachers familiar with the programs and write a report evaluating the effectiveness of such programs.

7. Have you ever been in a place where you did not speak the language? What if you were a child entering a school in which you did not speak the local language? With your classmates, discuss what this experience might be like. If you have been in a similar situation, discuss how your experience influences your opinion about bilingual education.

8. Research the bilingual policy in your state. (If your state does not have a bilingual policy, find out if any legislation is currently under review.) What is the demographic profile of your state's immigrant population? How does your state provide for non-native speakers in terms of education and social policy?

9. *Education Week on the Web* is an online magazine addressing the issues facing education today and the pedagogical concerns of teachers. They have compiled a balanced fact sheet on bilingual education, including links to online articles that explore the issue <www .edweek.org/context/topics/ biling.htm>. Access their Web site and, based on your research, write an essay in which you support or condemn bilingual education. Support your perspective with facts and information from the Web site.

10. Interview a number of people who had to learn English as a second language. How did they do it? What difficulties did they encounter? What assistance were they given as they learned English? Encourage your interviewees to share stories of success as well as of failure.

11. Consider how information is articulated in your community. Do you live in a multilingual area? Do signs feature other languages in addition to English? If so, how does this multilingual environment affect your social and linguistic experience? Explain.

Credits

Image Credits

Page 25: Bettmann/CORBIS. Pages 57–60: "SignWriting, A Deaf Perspective" written by deaf author Lucinda O'Grady Batch. On-line at www.SignWriting.org, courtesy of the Deaf Action Committee for SignWriting and the non-profit Center for Sutton Movement Writing, directed by the system's inventor, Valerie Sutton, La Jolla, CA. Page 70: © Will Hart/Photo Edit. Page 91: Bettmann/CORBIS; Page 113: David Hanover/Getty Images. Page 154: © Tannen Maury/The Image Works. Page 238: © Leland Bobbé/CORBIS. Page 270: © 1997 The New Yorker Collection. Roz Chast from cartoonbank.com. All Rights Reserved. Page 307: © 2003 The New Yorker Collection from cartoonbank.com. All Rights Reserved. Page 348: Copyright © 2000. Permission granted by John Callahan/Levin Represents. Page 353: Mike Luckovich, Atlanta Journal Constitution, Creators Syndicate. Page 355: Tribune Media Services, Inc. All Rights Reserved. Reprinted with Permission. Page 356: Jeff Stahler reprinted by permission of Newspaper Enterprise Association, Inc. Page 357: Jeff Parker, *Florida Today*. Page 358: Corky Trinidad, *Honolulu Star,* September 16, 2001. Page 360: © Lee Snider/The Image Works; Page 435: Courtesy of the Arab American Institute. Page 438: Courtesy of Daimler Chrysler Corporation. Page 440: General Motors Corp. Used with permission, GM Media Archive. Page 443: © 2000 Rohan Van Twest/Stone/Getty Images. Page 458: Cover of *Adventures of Huckleberry Finn* by Mark Twain, edited by Walter Blair and Victor Fischer. A publication of the Mark Twain Project of the Bancroft Library. Published in cooperation with the University of Iowa by the University of California Press, Berkeley. © 1985 by The Regents of the University of California. Page 496: Max Whittaker/Liaison Agency/Getty Images. Page 553: © Royalty-free/CORBIS. Page 594: © 2000 John Elk/Getty Images.

Text Credits

John Leo, "The Selling of Rebellion." Copyright, February 1, 1999, *U.S. News & World Report.* Reprinted by permission.

Susanne K. Langer, "The Lord of Creation," *Fortune*, January 1944. Reprinted by permission.

Paul Roberts, "A Brief History of English," *Understanding English.* Copyrighted © 1958 by Paul Roberts. Copyright renewed. Reprinted by permission of Longman Publishers.

C. M. Millward, "The Story of Writing," from *A Biography of the English Language, 2nd Edition* by Millward. © 1996. Reprinted with permission of Heinle, a division of Thomson Learning: www.thomsonrights.com. Fax 800-730-2215.

Margalit Fox, "Another Language for the Deaf," Copyright © 2002 by The New York Times Co. Reprinted with permission.

Index of Authors and Titles